The Arborfield Apprentice

An illustrated history of the Arborfield Army Apprentices' School and Colleges

The Arborfield Apprentice
An illustrated history of the Arborfield Army Apprentices' School and Colleges

This book is dedicated to the thousands of apprentices who have passed through the 'hallowed gates of Arborfield', since its opening as the Army Technical School (Boys) in 1939; through its years as the Army Apprentices' School (1947 – 1966), Army Apprentices' College (1966 – 1981) and Princess Marina College (1981 – 2000); up until its present-day guise as the Army Technical Foundation College.

Peter Gripton, 2003.

"For life to be large and full, it must contain the care of the past and of the future in every passing moment of the present"

Joseph Conrad, 'Nostromo'

First Published 2003 by the Arborfield Old Boys Association
The REME Museum
Isaac Newton Road
Arborfield
RG2 9NY.

Author and Editor Peter Gripton 56B
Copyright © Arborfield Old Boys Association 2003

ISBN 0-9545142-0-3
ISBN 0-9545142-1-1

Typeset by Ken Anderson 58A
Printed in Great Britain by The Amadeus Press Ltd., Cleckheaton, West Yorkshire.

Contents

Acknowledgements

Numerous individuals have generously given their assistance in providing the author with primary source material, without which a subject as complex as this history would be difficult to comprehend. In no particular order, the publishers wish to offer them our thanks. An immeasurable debt of gratitude is owed to our friend Rodney Smith of 56B, now living in California, who funded most of the research in the preparation of the material for this book. Without his unsparing help and encouragement this book would not have been possible.

The publishers would also like to acknowledge the help given by the Director of the REME Museum, Lt Col (Ret'd) I W J Cleasby MBE, and to all the staff at the Museum, who provided tremendous support in making information buried in archives readily available.

Finally, from the 'author', a vote of thanks to Ken Anderson of 58A, who used his computer expertise to compile the original text and copied photographs into a 'printable' format.

Among the sources of material used in writing this history are the following publications and an acknowledgement is made to them for their contribution:

'A History of the Churches of Arborfield Garrison'   by Col Mike Dorward.
'Arborfield and the Army Remount Service, 1904-37'   by Col Bob Hume.
'Princess Marina College,   A Brief History' 1939 - 89'   by Bryn Richards
updated by Maj Mike Constanzo in 1992.
'The Story of the Army Apprentices' College, Chepstow 1923-1983' compiled by
Capt John Barnes RAEC & Maj David Thomas RAEC
'Army Apprentices Harrogate'   by Col Cliff Walters
Old Boys Association Newsletter: First series: Dec 1956 – Mar 1959
Second series: Spring 1992 to June 2003
The Arborfield Apprentice (incl. The Journal): Dec 1944 – June 1998
The Arborfield Informer: Feb 2001 to June 2003
REME Magazine / The Craftsman: 1946 to June 2003
10th edition of the REME Brochure 1998
Programme for 'J' Coy Parents' Day, December 1990

Abbreviations used in this history

AA — Anti-Aircraft (also referred to as 'ack-ack')
AAA — Amateur Athletics Association
AAC — Army Apprentices College
AAC — Army Air Corps
AAS — Army Apprentices School
ABA — Amateur Boxing Association
ACC — Army Catering Corps
ACE — Army Certificate of Education
ACI — Army Council Instruction
ACIT — Army Committee of Instructional Technology
ADC — Aide de Camp
ADP — Automatic Data Processing
AEC — Army Education Corps
AETW — Aircraft Engineering Training Wing
AFC — Army Foundation College
AFCENT — Allied Forces in Central Europe
AFV — Armoured Fighting Vehicle
AG — Adjutant General
AGC — Adjutant General's Corps
AGM — Annual General Meeting
Air — Aircraft
AITO — Army Individual Training Organisation
AKC — Army Kinema Corporation
ALC — Army Legal Corps
AO — Administrative Officer
AOBA — Arborfield Old Boys Association
AOC — Army Ordnance Corps
APC — Army Pay Corps
APC — Armoured Personnel Carrier
APTC — Army Physical Training Corps
AQMS — Artificer Quartermaster Sergeant
ARP — Air Raid Precautions
Art — Artificer
ARA — Army Rifle Association
ARV — Armoured Recovery Vehicle
ASB — Artificer Selection Board
ASC — Army Service Corps
ASH — Argyll & Sutherland Highlanders
ASM — Artificer Sergeant Major
A/T — Apprentice Tradesman
ATB — Armourers' Training Branch
ATFC — Army Technical Foundation College

ATR — Army Training Regiment
ATRA — Army Training and Recruiting Agency
ATS — Army Technical School
ATS — Auxiliary Territorial Service
AVA — Audio Visual Aids
AWOL — Absent without leave
A & E — Airframe & Engine
A & G — Armament & General
BA — Bachelor of Arts
BAOR — British Army of the Rhine
BATUS — British Army Training Unit, Suffield
BBC — British Broadcasting Corporation
BD — Battle Dress
BEC — Business Engineering Council
BEF — British Expeditionary Force
BEM — British Empire Medal
BER — Beyond Economic Repair
BFPO — British Forces Post Office
BFT — Battle Fitness Test
BIM — British Institute of Management
BMC — Basic Military Cadre
BMPA — British Modern Pentathlon Association
BOD — Base Ordnance Depot
BP — British Petroleum
Brig — Brigadier
BSc — Bachelor of Science
BSM — Band Sergeant Major
Bt — Baronet
BTEC — Business Technician Education Council
C & G — City & Guilds
CB — Companion of the Order of the Bath
CB — Confined to barracks
CBE — Commander of the Order of the British Empire
CCF — Combined Cadet Force
CCTA — Central Computer & Telecommunications Agency
CD — Compact Disc
CEG — Career Employment Group
CEO — Chief Executive Officer
CET — Control Equipment Technician
CET — Combat Engineer Tractor

Cfn — Craftsman
CF — Chaplain of the Faith
CF — Christian Fellowship
CFQ — Competing for Quality
CGLI — City & Guilds of London Institute
CGS — Chief of the General Staff
CI — Chief Instructor
CIGS — Chief of the Imperial General Staff
C-in-C — Commander-in-Chief / Colonel-in-Chief
CMG — Companion of St Michael & St George
CMH — Cambridge Military Hospital (Aldershot)
CML — Computer Managed Learning
CMS — Common Military Syllabus
CO — Commanding Officer
COD — Command Ordnance Depot
Col — Colonel
CoH — Corporal of Horse
COS — Chief of Staff
Coy — Company
Cpl — Corporal
CQMS — Company Quartermaster Sergeant
CREME — Commander REME
CSE — Certificate of Secondary Education
CSM — Company Sergeant Major
CSMI — Company Sergeant Major Instructor
CSV — Community Service Volunteers
DAE — Director of Army Education
DAR — Director of Army Recruiting
DAT — Director of Army Training
DCI — Deputy Chief Instructor
DEME — Director of Electrical & Mechanical Engineering
DERR — Duke of Edinburgh's Royal Regiment
DES(A) — Director of Equipment Support (Army)
DFC — Distinguished Flying Cross
DG — Dragoon Guards
DGAMS — Director General Army Medical Services
DGAT — Director General Army Training
DGATR — Director General Army Training and Recruiting

DGEME	Director General of Electrical & Mechanical Engineering	
DGES(A)	Director General of Equipment Support (Army)	
DGMT	Director General of Military Training	
DGOS	Director General of Ordnance Services	
Div	Division	
DLI	Durham Light Infantry	
DME	Director of Mechanical Engineering	
DMS	Directly Moulded Sole	
DS	Directing Staff	
DSc.	Doctor of Science	
DSC	Distinguished Service Cross	
DSM(A)	Director of Supply Management (Army)	
DSO	Distinguished Service Order	
DTP	Desk-top Publishing	
DYRMS	Duke of York's Royal Military School	
ECAB	Executive Committee of the Army Board	
EL	External Leadership	
EMERs	Electrical and Mechanical Engineering Regulations	
ENSA	Entertainment National Services Association	
EPC	Education Promotion Certificate	
EQC	Evaluation & Quality Control	
ES	Engineering Support	
E & E	Electrics & Electronics	
FARELF	Far East Land Forces	
FANY	First Aid Nursing Yeomanry	
FRCS	Fellow of the Royal College of Surgeons	
FRCP	Fellow of the Royal College of Physicians	
FRT	Forward Repair Team	
GCB	Grand Companion of the Order of the Bath	
GCE	General Certificate of Education	
GEC	General Engineering Certificate	
GEC	General Engineering Course	
GMC	General Motor Corporation	
GOC	General Officer Commanding-in-Chief	
GPMG	General-purpose Machine Gun	

GSC	General Service Corps	
HLI	Highland Light Infantry	
HM	Her / His Majesty	
HMS	Her / His Majesty's Ship	
HNC	Higher National Certificate	
HND	Higher National Diploma	
HQ	Headquarters	
HRH	Her / His Royal Highness	
IBA	Independent Broadcasting Authority	
IEE	Institute of Electrical Engineering	
IERE	Institute of Electronic and Radio Engineers	
IFTU	Intensive Flying Trials Unit	
IGT	Inspector General Training	
IMechE	Institute of Mechanical Engineers	
IMfgE	Institute of Manufacturing Engineers	
IMgt	Institute of Management	
IPMS	International Plastic Modellers Society	
IProdE	Institute of Production Engineers	
IRA	Irish Republican Army	
IS	Information Systems	
ISBA	Imperial Services Boxing Association	
IT	Information Technology	
ITG	Initial Training Group	
ITO	Individual Training Organisation	
ITV	Independent Television	
JAEC	Junior Army Education Certificate	
JLdr(s)	Junior Leader(s)	
JNCO	Junior NCO	
JRC	Junior Ranks Club	
JSATC	Joint Services Adventurous Training Centre	
JSMRU	Joint Services Medical Rehabilitation Unit	
JSPC	Joint Services Parachute Centre	
KCB	Knight Commander of the Order of the Bath	
KOBR	King's Own Border Regiment	
KOSB	King's Own Scottish Borderers	
KRRC	King's Royal Rifle Corps	
LAD	Light Aid Detachment	
LASS	Leading Artisan Staff Sergeant	
LCpl	Lance Corporal	
LCT	Landing Craft, Tank	
LE(A)	Logistics Executive (Army)	

LSGC	Long Service & Good Conduct (Medal)	
Lt	Lieutenant	
Lt Col	Lieutenant Colonel	
Lt Gen	Lieutenant General	
MA	Master Artificer	
MA	Modern Apprenticeship	
Maj	Major	
Maj Gen	Major General	
MBE	Member of the Order of the British Empire	
MBIM	Member of the British Institute of Management	
MC	Master of Ceremonies	
MC	Military Cross	
MELF	Middle East Land Forces	
MEW	Military Education Wing	
MLRS	Multi-Launch Rocket System	
MM	Military Medal	
MO	Medical Officer	
MoD	Ministry of Defence	
MP	Member of Parliament	
MP	Military Police (man)	
MPBW	Ministry of Public Building and Works	
MRS	Medical Reception Station	
MS	Multiple Sclerosis	
MSc	Master of Science	
MSC	Maths, Science and Computing	
MSM	Meritorious Service Medal	
MSRD	Mobile Servicing & Repair Department	
MT	Motor Transport	
MTO	Motor Transport Officer	
MTW	Military Training Wing	
MVO		
NAAFI	Navy, Army & Air Force Institutes	
NATO	North Atlantic Treaty Organisation	
NBC	Nuclear, Biological and Chemical	
NCC	National Craftsman's Certificate	
NCO	Non-Commissioned Officer	
NVQ	National Vocational Qualification	
NZ	New Zealand	
OBA	Old Boys Association	
OBAN	Old Boys Association News(letter)	
OBLI	Oxford & Buckinghamshire Light Infantry	
OC	Officer Commanding	
OIC	Officer-in-Charge	

OM	Order of Merit	RLC	Royal Logistics Corps	SNCO	Senior NCO
OME	Ordnance Mechanical Engineer	RMAS	Royal Military Academy, Sandhurst	SPEC	Student Performance Evaluation by Computer
ONC	Ordinary National Certificate				
PC	Politically correct	RMCS	Royal Military College of Science	SQMS	Squadron Quartermaster Sergeant
PFI	Private Finance Initiative	RMP	Royal Military Police	Sqn	Squadron
PLO	Project Liaison Officer	RMRO	REME Manning & Records Office	SSgt	Staff Sergeant
PMC	Princess Marina College	RN	Royal Navy	SSM	Squadron Sergeant Major
PoP	Passing-out Parade	RNF	Royal Northumberland Fusiliers	SWB	South Wales Borderers
PRE	Periodic REME Examination	RO	Retired Officer	TA	Territorial Army
PRI	President of the Regimental Institute	ROF	Royal Ordnance Factory	TEC	Technician Education Council
		ROPs	Restriction of Privileges	Tech Gp	Technical Group
PS	Permanent Staff	RP	Regimental Police	TQM	Total Quality Management
PT	Physical Training	RQMS	Regimental Quartermaster Sergeant	Trg Btn	Training Battalion
Pte	Private	RRF	Royal Regiment of Fusiliers	Trg Regt	Training Regiment
PTI	Physical Training Instructor	R Sigs	Royal Corps of Signals	TV	Television
QARANC	Queen Alexandra's Royal Nursing Corps	RSAF	Royal Small Arms Factory	UDR	Ulster Defence Regiment
		RSM	Regimental Sergeant Major	UHR	Unit Historical Record
QM	Quartermaster	RSR	Royal Scots Regiment	UK	United Kingdom
QMG	Quartermaster General	RTG	REME Training Group	UKLF	United Kingdom Land Forces
QMSI	Quartermaster Sergeant Instructor	Rt Hon	Right Honourable	UN	United Nations
RA	Royal Artillery	RTC	Royal Tank Corps	UNFICYP	United Nations Forces in Cyprus
RAC	Royal Armoured Corps	RTR	Royal Tank Regiment	US	United States
RAChD	Royal Army Chaplains Department	RWAAF	Royal West African Armed Forces	USA	United States of America
RADC	Royal Army Dental Corps	RWF	Royal Welch Fusiliers	VC	Victoria Cross
RAeS	Royal Aeronautical Society	R & D	Research and Development	VCP	Vehicle Checkpoint
RAE	Royal Aircraft Establishment	R & R	Rest and Recuperation	VE	Vehicle Electrician
RAEC	Royal Army Education Corps	SAE	School of Aeronautical Engineering	VE Day	Victory in Europe Day
RAF	Royal Air Force			Vehs	Vehicles
RAMC	Royal Army Medical Corps	SANDF	South African Naval Defence Force	VIP	Very Important Person
RAOC	Royal Army Ordnance Corps			VJ Day	Victory in Japan Day
RAPC	Royal Army Pay Corps	SAS	Special Air Service	VM	Vehicle Mechanic
RASC	Royal Army Service Corps	SAT	Systems Approach to Training	WD	War Department
RCB	Regular Commissions Board	SCLI	Somerset & Cornwall Light Infantry	Wksp	Workshop
RCEME	Royal Canadian Electrical and Mechanical Engineers			WO	Warrant Officer (Class I or II)
		SCM	Squadron Corporal Major	WOSB	War Office Selection Board
RCM	Regimental Corporal Major	SD	Service Dress	WPC	Woman Police Constable
RCMP	Royal Canadian Mounted Police	SE	South East	Wpns	Weapons
RCT	Royal Corps of Transport	SEAE	School of Electronic & Aeronautical Engineering	WRAC	Women's Royal Army Corps
RD	Regimental Duty			WRNS	Women's Royal Naval Service
RE	Royal Engineers	SEE	School of Electronic Engineering	WRVS	Women's Royal Voluntary Service
REME	Royal Electrical & Mechanical Engineers	SEL	School of Electric Lighting	WVS	Women's Voluntary Service
		SEME	School of Electrical & Mechanical Engineering	YHA	Youth Hostels Association
Rev	Reverend			2I/C	Second in Command
RFC	Royal Flying Corps	SEO	Senior Education Officer		
RGS	Royal Geographical Society	SES(A)	School of Equipment Support (Army)		
RHA	Royal Horse Artillery				
RHG	Royal Horse Guards	Sgt	Sergeant		
RI	Religious Instruction	SME	School of Mechanical Engineering		
RIF	Royal Irish Fusiliers	SMG	Sub Machine Gun		

Foreword

By the Honourable Viscount Alanbrooke of Brookeborough

Peter Gripton has firstly done a service to all Arborfield Apprentices and staff members; secondly he has done a service to clarity out of obscurity (*clario ex obscurio*). Of the latter, because of the diversity of sources, his seamless historical narrative is a singular success; of the former, he certainly deserves the accolades of the many Old Boys who will welcome this rendering of their story.

With relevance to both of these sentiments, Peter's light and readable style gives all the appearance that he enjoyed writing this history. But, bearing in mind the dictum, *'that which is written without pain will be read without pleasure'* – there is ample evidence that Peter took great pains to ensure that his readers will enjoy his book.

Many of his readers will have actually made the history that he has so faithfully recorded. The American writer, John Gardner, commented that, *'history never looks like history when you are living through it; it always looks messy and confusing and always feels uncomfortable'*. Most Old Boys may claim that they lived through the most messy, confusing and uncomfortable of times. The author has been punctilious in awarding an equal balance to each period of time.

In conclusion, a debt of gratitude is due to the Commandants who encouraged this undertaking, notably to Colonel Peter Gibson, and to lecturer Bryn Richards, who collected many of the facts in his earlier 'Brief History'. Enduring gratitude goes to 'Old Boy' Rodney Smith, who helped finance the writing of this book – without his interest in the project, it is likely that the labours of all would have been in vain.

The Army Apprentice system has been an outstanding success from its foundation. It is excellent that this chapter of a great tradition has now been recorded for posterity. This is an excellent volume.

June 2003

Prologue

Maintenance and repair

The maintenance and repair of the Army's equipment had always played a major part in ensuring its fighting efficiency. Right up until the late 19th-century, such equipment's very simplicity meant that a specialised repair system was not required, repairs being carried out instead by the soldier himself, ably assisted by artisans such as the regimental armourers, farriers and carpenters. This simple system of repair came to its inevitable conclusion, as equipment eventually became more complex, with the Army Ordnance Corps (AOC) coming into existence in 1896. The AOC was authorised to absorb those technical personnel from other corps, many of them ex-Royal Arsenal or ex-Royal Dockyard apprentices, as well as all regimental armourers.

The subsequent enlistment of technical boy apprentices into the Army Service Corps (ASC) commenced around 1913. Eleven years later, this practice ended when the junior intake at Aldershot was transferred to form the first group at the 'boys' school' at Chepstow.

First World War

The First World War provided the impetus for more technologically advanced military equipment but, even so, the repairs to such equipment were still an *ad hoc* affair. By the end of that four-year conflict, recognition of the AOC's excellent work, combined with the knowledge that a more rational system was required, led to it becoming the Royal Army Ordnance Corps (RAOC). The three other corps that used specialist equipment on a large scale were generally responsible for the repair and maintenance of such, being equipped with their own engineers and workshops.

The down side effect of that war, however, with its constant call upon the young men of Great Britain, was that there arose an acute shortage of skilled tradesmen throughout the country, as the normal apprenticeship training had been badly disrupted. Rather than wait for a steady return to normal levels, the Army decided that the time had come to look into the feasibility of training its own tradesmen. An Army Council Instruction (ACI) was issued to this effect during May 1919, stating that *"educational training is essential to the making of a soldier and an Army"*.

A War Office Committee was set up *"to examine the necessity for, and practicability of, establishing a School for training boys as tradesmen for the Army, in order to supply the deficiency consequent upon the impossibility of recruiting tradesmen in sufficient numbers from civil life"*. There were already in existence four Army boy-training establishments, but three of these each trained less than 250 boys at any one time. There was no intention of closing these schools, but the Committee wished to open a central School for training 1,000 boys. The original site chosen for this School was at Blandford in Dorset, where there was intended to be the 'Central Training School for Boys', due to open on September 1st 1923.

The establishment of Chepstow

However, insurmountable difficulties arose with this plan, a result of which was a visit by the Army Council, to an inn on the small Beachley peninsular in Gloucestershire, jutting out *"where Wye and Severn meet"*. From this meeting, the decision was made that a School would be established in an adjacent camp that had been used as a national shipyard during the First World War. It had lain idle for a number of years and been used to house prisoners of war. Following much trial and tribulation, on February 28th 1924 the 'Boys' Technical School, Chepstow' finally opened for the training of blacksmiths, carpenters, electricians and fitters. There were no workshops, no administrative offices, no gymnasium and not even any roads, but it was a start.

For many years, Artificers for the Royal Artillery (RA), Armourers for the RAOC, both specialist trades, and other tradesmen for the technical corps, were being trained at Woolwich (in London), Hilsea (near Portsmouth) and, of course, at Chepstow. Young boys were taken directly from school and taught a trade, in a manner similar to the then current industrial practice. The exception, of course, was that the military apprentices were also to be fully trained as soldiers, in order that they could subsequently take their proper place in those Regiments or Corps to which they would eventually be attached.

Three more Schools proposed

By the early Thirties, with mechanisation going full-speed ahead, it had become patently clear that the Army would be unable to obtain sufficient tradesmen to fulfil its needs merely from adult enlistment and the existing apprentice training units. Thus it came about that 200 Fitter Apprentices were recruited and enlisted on October 1st 1936, of whom half started their

Farmland to army garrison

UNTIL nearly 100 years ago the land now occupied by the sprawling garrison of the Royal Electrical and Mechanical Engineers at Arborfield was known as Bigg's Farm, reputed for its abundant corn crops and owned, like most of the land at the time, by the Walter family.

Then, in 1907, several farms were sold. The War Office bought one and, almost overnight, an army of workmen had moved in and transformed the great meadows into a vast camp of wooden huts and stables.

Within a short time hundreds of horses began to arrive and Arborfield Cross became a Remount Depot and one of the Army's main training centres for chargers, cavalry and gun-carriage horses, the forerunner of today's modern army base there.

training at Bramley, near Basingstoke, and the other half at Hilsea. There was still a shortage of specialist soldier-tradesmen however, and so it was decided that three new 'Army Technical Schools' (ATS) would be built, one at each of the following locations: Arborfield (near Reading, Berkshire), Fort Darland (at Chatham, Kent) and Aldershot (in Hampshire) – the *"home of the British Army"*.

This decision was announced in ACI 290 of August 1938. These schools were designated to produce tradesmen for the specialist needs of the RAOC, Royal Engineers (RE) and Royal Army Service Corps (RASC) respectively. The latter unit, with an initial intake of some forty boys, was soon moved to Jersey (in the Channel Islands) in October 1938, coinciding with a second intake of some 120 RASC boys and around ninety RAOC boys. The total strength of 240 RASC apprentices was made up by the arrival of the third RASC intake in August 1939. The RAOC contingent trained on Jersey until Arborfield was ready to receive them, after their summer leave of 1939.

Here then, more than sixty years ago, were planted the first seeds from which has grown the present-day 'Army Technical Foundation College' (ATFC) at Arborfield. The School, as it was then, was originally designed to house and train up to 1,000 Apprentice Tradesmen (A/Ts) at any one time.

During the Summer of 1939, around a dozen of the first Bramley apprentices moved to Woolwich, to be trained as Instrument Mechanics (Inst Mechs), whilst the remainder of the intake, plus a few from Hilsea, proceeded to Aldershot to complete their training. Some of the older apprentices, who had completed their training during 1939, went on to serve in France with the British Expeditionary Force (BEF), at various Field Workshops. The BEF at that time numbered some 158,000 troops and 25,000 vehicles, under the command of General Gamelin, the French Supreme Commander.

Back on Jersey the following year, some three weeks after the withdrawal from Dunkirk under 'Operation Dynamo', the island was declared a demilitarised zone, and hurried arrangements were made to evacuate the boys, staff and families to the mainland. The numbers of boys dwindled after a move to Aldershot in October 1940 and eventually the unit disbanded. On September 1st 1941, the remaining 105 boys were transferred to Chepstow to complete their training.

An excellent aerial view showing the barrack room 'spiders', Cookhouse and Workshop buildings.

Army Remount Depot

While the dark storm-clouds of war were gathering over Europe and the Far East, building work began here at Arborfield in 1938, on the original site of the old 'Army Remount Depot', which had been acquired by the War Office as long ago as March 1904. During that far distant time, three separate farms had worked the area of land, namely Bigg's Farm, Old Bigg's Farm and Ellis's Farm. The purpose of the Remount Depot had been to provide a home for those horses purchased by the Army for all sorts of different uses. At the Depot the horses received the equine equivalent of basic military training, before being sent on to their respective units. For over thirty years local rural rides must have echoed to the drumming of hooves and the jingle of bridles until, inevitably, the horses were forced into well-earned retirement by the arrival of mechanisation.

(A brief history of the Army Remount Depot, 1904-1937, was published by Colonel (Col) Bob Hume in the 1980 & 1981 REME Journals, and subsequently as a booklet in 1984. It is available from the REME Museum.)

Under construction

In September 1938, British Prime Minister Neville Chamberlain returned from Munich with his infamous 'Peace in our time' message, but it was only the following month that German military forces marched across the border into Czechoslovakia. Meanwhile, here at Arborfield, the Camp site quickly began taking shape with the construction of workshops, offices, barrack blocks, a gymnasium, sports fields, the Navy, Army & Air Forces Institute (NAAFI), both Officers' and Sergeants' Messes and a hospital.

The buildings, like many others of that period, were of timber-framed construction with a corrugated iron cladding, fitted with a coal-fired hot water central heating system. They were known as 'spider blocks', due to their central communal ablutions area and six barrack rooms arranged like 'spider's legs', and were destined to stay in use for the next forty-two years. Long before their completion, the selection of a suitable staff was being considered and some of the first incumbents were as shown below.

The civilian instructors were selected from retired Armament Artificers RAOC, Engine-room Artificers from the Royal Navy (RN), Senior Artificers RA and similar high-class practical men. Most had served in the Forces, knew the requirements of the job and, due to their long service, had the knowledge, experience and interests of the boys at heart. They could thus guide and advise the boys on the technical military career on which they were now taking their first tentative steps.

Commandant and Chief Instructor (CI):	Col F A Hilborn, MBE (late RAOC)
Deputy Chief Instructor (DCI):	Maj W Tanner, RAOC
Adjutant:	Captain (Capt) C Morgan, South Wales Borderers (SWB)
Company Officers:	Capts P Kaye, 5 Dragoon Guards (DG) and W Hughes, SWB
Workshop Officers:	Lieutenants (Lts) G Trevithick and C Zweigberg, RAOC
Chaplain:	The Reverend S J Squires, Chaplain of the Faith (CF)
Quartermaster (QM):	Lt Pryor, RAOC
Regimental Sergeant Major (RSM):	H E Cook, Grenadier Guards
Civilian Workshop Instructors:	Mr MacKereth, Mr Pugh, Mr Wheater and many more, of whom there appears to be no record.

The way ahead

The original Commandant combined his post with that of CI. He and his DCI were early and frequent visitors to the site from their base at Aldershot, advising on both the construction and fitting-out of the premises. It is to their keenness and drive in its early days that the School owes much of its later success. During the Camp's earliest construction period, Maj Tanner paid many exploratory visits to existing boys' training establishments such as the Military Repository at Woolwich, the other ATS at Chepstow and the RASC School on the Channel Island of Jersey. What he saw there helped in the drawing up of the first curriculum here at Arborfield.

The roads around and through the Camp were all named after famous men of an engineering background, names that should have a special significance to all aspiring technicians. In no special order, these names were Nuffield, Faraday, Whitworth, James Watt, Stephenson, Kelvin and Newton. All these men, despite their humble beginnings, had a profound effect upon their particular era and chosen area of expertise. It was later stated, in the first issue of 'The Arborfield Apprentice', published at the end of 1944:

> *"They served their apprenticeship and for us are the symbol of true greatness, as shown in their remarkable capacity for work, their pursuit of scientific knowledge, and their regard for their fellow men".*

Ben Cook – an Arborfield legend

H E 'Ben' Cook, whose legend still lives on today, remained as the RSM until April 1941, after which he was commissioned and took up post as the School's QM, reaching the rank of Captain. In this appointment he was instrumental in laying out the School's playing fields, gardens and hedgerows – no small task. Many who followed were able to obtain their sporting prowess as a result of his agricultural labours. In 1944, Mr Cook's work was duly recognised by his being made a 'Member of the Order of the British Empire' (MBE).

(Much of the above information is based upon an article first published in 'The Arborfield Apprentice', Volume II, Number 2, dated December 1951. It was written by Brigadier (Brig) W Tanner, MIMechE, Royal Electrical and Mechanical Engineers (REME), under the title 'The A.T.S. (Boys), Arborfield, 1939'. Brig Tanner had served as the Deputy Chief Instructor of the School, in the rank of Major (Maj) when it first opened. Another valuable source of information was 'The Story of the Army Apprentices' College, Chepstow, 1923 – 1983.)

Col Holborn and RSM Cook, along with the other permanent staff

1939 'D' Compnay

Chapter 1

1939 - 42

The first boys arrive

By May 1st of 1939, the almost completed 'Army Technical School (Boys)' was ready to receive its first intake of almost 400 young boys, who were all cap-badged to the RAOC. The first prospective apprentice, Jack Oakley, is reputed to have hired a taxi to bring him from the nearest railway station at Wokingham, for fear that he would be late in reporting for duty. Another tale is that he actually walked all the way here. Whichever version is the right one, he certainly was the first apprentice to arrive, well ahead of the expected main party.

Later that month 'the Square' was completed, but the Workshop accommodation was not made ready until June. Almost at once, the soon-to-be-familiar

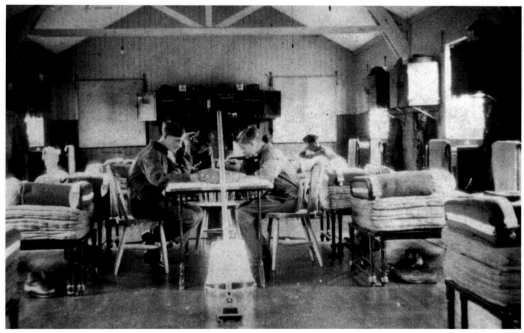

burly figure of RSM Ben Cook could be seen, leading around squads of small, trembling, newly-joined 'boy soldiers' and, even from a distance, his brusque voice could be heard, with remarks such as *"Now, who is that Officer over there? 'Aven't I already told yer?"* Despite an air of excitement and expectation, many boys' thoughts must have centred on the momentous

events that were taking place in Europe. German forces, having annexed Austria the previous year, had by now occupied the whole of Czechoslovakia, while Germany and Italy had signed their infamous 'Pact of Steel' soon after the School opened.

'Old Soldier' Ben Cook seemed to be always one step ahead of the boys in most of their schemes and tricks, especially any potential malingerers and dodgers, appearing in their midst when least expected. Furtive smokers appeared to be his special target and many of those who were caught were then forced to sickly 'enjoy' smoking his thick black twist (tobacco) for their pains, rather than suffer the usual 'CB' (which stands for 'confined to barracks' but was more commonly referred to as 'jankers'). According to legend, Ben Cook was not a man to make deals!

"In the beginning the floors were brown, the windows bare. The made-up beds were 4 foot long. On the floors were 96 bed feet, 32 boots, 32 gym shoes, 16 chair legs, 8 table feet and, of course, the utensils. Everything, or rather the lack of anything else, giving an impression of impoverished discipline."

Thus was the accommodation at Arborfield described at the time, although the above description was to be published in a newsletter almost twenty years later.

For the first twelve months, church services were held in the Chaplain's hut and one of the NAAFI games rooms. After that period, the main Sunday morning services were to take place in the Camp Hall,

A/T Pat Bowman - one of the first

where a permanent pulpit was constructed at one side of the stage, whilst a large altar, conveniently mounted on castors, could be wheeled to the appropriate central position as and when required. During the whole of their three-year apprenticeship, the boys' spiritual needs were catered for by an hour's Religious Instruction (RI) each week.

Arthur Crisp was one of the first members of staff upon the School's opening that May. He was a Private (Pte) in the RAOC at the time, stationed a few miles away at Aldershot. One of his roommates there was a bugler-boy by the name of Cook who, it later transpired, was the son of none other than the RSM at Arborfield. Prior to the School's opening, and along with a few others, Arthur used to make the journey between Aldershot and Arborfield on a daily basis. He also recalls making duty trips to Wokingham railway station, where he was detailed to pick up stores and rations.

As far as he can remember, the Sergeants' Mess was the first living accommodation to be brought into use, no doubt because the majority of incoming instructors would be from the senior ranks. As one of

only two 'junior ranks' here at the time, Arthur recalls that both of them were fortuitously allowed to dine in the Sergeants' Mess, a state of affairs that continued right up until the arrival of the first boys.

RAOC and RASC boys were transferred to Arborfield from such places as Jersey, Hilsea, Bramley and Didcot, just south of Oxford, arriving here during the summer months of 1939. Further intakes were to follow in October of that year, then again in the April and October of 1940, with yet more arrivals from Hilsea and Chepstow.

Early Recollections

Dudley Martin was one such boy who was transferred here, courtesy of the Luftwaffe (German Air Force) bombing raids aimed on Portsmouth dockyards, from Hilsea in 1940, having first joined up in July 1938. Many years later, at one of the annual Reunions, he was proud to display his '1938' identification, as he shared the 'top table' at dinner with 'Bomber' France, an old colleague from those far off days. Dudley well recalls being taken down to Hilsea from the *"backwoods of Sussex"* by his dear mother, while 'Bomber' still insists that she actually made Dudley's bed for him on that auspicious day!

Amongst that first batch of boys to arrive in early 1939 was Douglas 'Lofty' Howes, who had joined up at Jersey in October of the previous year. Having already been promoted to the dizzy heights of Lance Corporal (LCpl), Lofty soon found himself put in charge of some coal shovelling, or 'fatigues', and was more than happy to pick up a shovel himself and 'get stuck in'. But from a distance came the bellicose roar of RSM Cook – *"You're supposed to be watching 'em, not helping 'em"*. Despite this admonishment, Lofty still remembers Ben with the greatest of affection. Attending his very first 'Old Boys' Reunion', thirty-six years after leaving the old School, he was astonished to be told he could park his car on the Square. He recalls that in his day, Ben Cook wouldn't have even allowed him to *walk* across the sacrosanct Square, never mind park his car there!

Lofty also recalls a period when, to his great delight, some of the boys had a break from their normal working routine, being sent off by coach on a daily mission to the *Sunbeam Talbot* factory, situated *"somewhere along the Great West Road"*. Here, they were shown how to carry out modifications to Bren-gun Carrier steering mechanisms. This was at a time of increasing air raid warnings and alarms but, despite the impending danger, the boys actually looked forward to running off to the shelters, no doubt due to the fact that they shared these dark, secret places with some very pleasant young ladies from another factory nearby!

On Monday May 1st 1939 at 9.00 a.m., along with eleven other young boys, Les Wiffen turned up at Brighton railway station, on part of what was then the Southern Railway. Just three weeks short of his sixteenth birthday, Les was probably one of the oldest of the group, all bound for the ATS (Boys). Following their reception and stipulated visits to the doctor, dentist and barber, Les found himself installed in room 'A1', part of 'A' Company (Coy), and also the room nearest to the Guardroom. He hoped that this wasn't an ill omen! He remembers that his issued service trousers were very narrow at the bottom and that boys were permitted to have a 'V' of material inserted for 'ease of maintenance'! A few of them actually ended up looking like sailors in 'bell-bottoms'.

From then on, life became one hectic round of kit inspections and 'Square bashing', although he admits that the 'bashing' really wasn't too hard at first, as the *"tar had barely settled on the Square"*. With all the exercise and drilling in the warm sunshine, Les soon found that he was not only nicely sun-tanned, but also very fit. Les has long since retired to a happy life on the other side of the globe, at Dunedin in New Zealand (NZ), otherwise known as 'land of the long white cloud'.

Fred Ford also arrived here at Arborfield when it was *"so new that the buildings still smelled of fresh joinery and creosote"*. Like Les Wiffen, he recalls that workmen were still laying tarmac at the top end of the Parade Square. He remembers that the foundations for the Camp Hall were not even laid until well after his arrival. Once built of course, the building was also to serve as Gymnasium, Church, Cinema, Theatre and Dance Hall – what would be called today 'multifunctional'! Having himself experienced what he terms *"a fairly deprived childhood"*, Fred is probably one of a minority in fondly remembering the meals provided at the Cookhouse as *"wholesome"*.

Fred recalls one retired officer, a very large and learned gentleman, who, with the aid of an immense model railway layout, demonstrated the 'magical' effect of the infrared light, that invisible beam that he would use to start and stop the model trains. 'Magic'

then of course, but something we all take for granted today with our alarm systems and remote controls.

Some confusion with numbers and letters!

Due to the fact that Fred was in the first intake of 1939, he and those who joined at the same time are forever now known as intake '39A'. However, at first, intakes were generally allotted the titles of 'No.1 Intake', 'No.2 Intake', etc. *(Just peeping into the future slightly, John Dutton has always sworn to the title '1943 April, with intake '1943 October' following his. Ed.)* This had always been a source of confusion to the unwary, and was finally abolished around the end of 1944. After that, intakes became known as '45A', '45B', '46A' and so on, with retrospective re-grading of the intakes of previous years, and this numeric tradition, with some dissent from older 'old boys' of course, has remained in force ever since. *(Don't ask Peter Gibson for an explanation, whatever you do! Ed.)*

Fred goes on to recall the wonderful cinema shows that were given thrice weekly as entertainment. He especially liked the Hollywood-style musicals and reckons that most of the boys of his day were madly, though secretly, in love with the beautiful singing star, Deanna Durbin. However, Sergeant (Sgt) Arthur Leatherland of the Sherwood Foresters, a permanent staff (PS) member who lived in a bunk in one of the 'C' Coy spiders, had his bunk walls literally plastered with pictures of another favourite, Alice Faye. *('Pin-ups' have obviously been around for longer than one would think! Ed.)*

Many of Fred's intake were the sons of servicemen, who arrived at Arborfield with their in-built suntans from such far-away and exotic-sounding places as Gibraltar, India and Malta. He recalls that the Commandant had a *"deep booming voice"*, while cavalry-type breeches, with highly polished brown leather leggings and boots, always accompanied his mode of dress. Apart from gaining the boys' respect and admiration, it certainly didn't go unnoticed that Col Hilborn happened to have a rather charming young daughter!

On May 2nd 1939, James 'Dick' Wade was one of a group of sixteen young boys, just arrived from the Lawrence Military School in India. Coming from that sub-continent, Dick thought he was in for a treat when he was taken for his first meal in the Cookhouse, for there on the menu was 'curry and rice'. It turned out to be *"an absolute disaster"*! It was actually meat and vegetable stew, merely sprinkled with a dusting of curry powder and poured over some lumpy rice that would have been better used as wallpaper paste! Dick later overheard one member of staff say that the meal must have made the boys homesick – at least he agreed with the 'sick' part of it! One of the PS recalled by Dick is Cpl Freddie Fox. He says that RSM Cook would take great delight in bellowing across the Square for *"Corporal Cunning"*, at which Freddie would *"always respond at the double"*.

Dick is another entrant who recalls that May was such a hot month that year, that the melting tar on the half-finished Parade Square kept sticking to the boys' boots. This made it quite difficult for them to keep in step, despite the drill experiences already gained by many of the boys at their various military schools. Dick has less than fond memories of guard duty – two hours on, four hours off – with the inevitable urn of tea stewing away in the Guardroom all night until, by dawn, *"you could cut it with a knife and fork"*. *(Dick must have enjoyed it though, he came back to attend his very first Reunion in 1996. Ed.)*

Dick also states that leave periods were always a cause of some homesickness and concern for those boys who, like him, had parents who were still living abroad. He himself was fortunate enough to be invited to share one leave with another boy at Romford, Essex, and gratefully remembers being treated to a trip to the Tower of London. At Christmas 1939, those who had nowhere else to go were dispatched to spend their break at a home at St Leonard's-on-Sea, near Hastings.

Following his 'boys' service', Dick was fortunate enough to be posted to Crookham, not far from where his parents owned a house in Sandhurst. The corporal in charge of his Nissen hut was none other than Sidney Wooderson, one time holder of the world record for running the mile. Dick suffered a hearing disability during the war, but still says that his apprenticeship training enabled him to cope with all circumstances, for which he remains truly thankful. Also at Crookham at the same time was John Moir (39B), who actually ran in a relay race at Motspur Park, London, with the great

Instruction on an early Crypton Automatic Test Bench

athlete in his team, in September 1942. John proudly retains the medal he won that day, but says that most of the credit must be assigned to Cpl Wooderson.

Another of that 39A intake, Gerald Johnson, is now well settled in the United States (US), a long way from his 'roots' in the Midland town of Nottingham. Upon his arrival at the railway platform at Wokingham, Sgt 'Taffy' Evans of the SWB was there to relieve all boys of cigarettes, uttering dire threats against those later found to have 'fags' still on them. Gerald also recalls that the Square was still incomplete, with only that end nearest the Cookhouse available for the business of drilling. For the first few days, boys were even marched around in their 'civvies' (civilian clothes), until such time that the QM's stores were able to properly kit them out. Gerald swears that he used the same razor blade for eighteen months, as there wasn't much to come off anyway! *(I think it was called bum-fluff! Ed.)*

Gerald adds that in those days, boys were allowed out of barracks on Tuesday and Thursday evenings – but only having passed a thorough uniform inspection at the Guardroom. He was caught smoking on several occasions and, as well as *"serving time"* on jankers, his pay was reduced by sixpence a week. This still didn't discourage Gerald's taste for the illicit thrills of tobacco and, along with others of the same bent, he would hide his packets of *Woodbines* (five for tuppence) in secret holes in the rafters of his barrack room.

Ron 'Doc' Savage, again of intake 39A and nowadays living in Zimbabwe, recalls taking the *"oath of allegiance"* but wonders *"did I ever receive the (King's) shilling?"* But what he *can* well remember is the presence of three or four female ambulance drivers, members of the First Aid Nursing Yeomanry (FANY), who were then attached to the Camp. Initially billeted in the Camp Hospital, they were later moved to a house overlooking the School.

Ron recalls the young ladies once being presented with a rusty old motorbike. Because he had rather a heavy crush on the youngest, a gorgeously blonde apparition of about nineteen years of age, answering to the name 'Miss Poole', Ron wasn't backward in coming forward when a volunteer was sought to get the bike into running order! At a mere sixteen years of age himself, he confesses that he was still learning to be thrilled by the *"mystery of the female sex"*.

Of Dukes and Queens

Ron had arrived here at Arborfield from the Duke of York's Royal Military School (DYRMS) at Dover, as one of the 'Dukies', as they have always been popularly called. He recalls that his band of Dukies was housed in 'A' block, while lads from the Queen Victoria School (known as the 'Queen Vics'), at Dunblane in Scotland, were put into the neighbouring 'B' block. Raids and pillow-fights used to take place between the blocks, and sometimes degenerated into more serious affairs. But once this was out of their systems, both sets of boys picked themselves up, dusted themselves down, and finally settled down to some proper soldiering.

Ron's family had been stationed in Aldershot during 1935 and still maintained contact with some friends there. Thus, on a Sunday after the morning's church parade, Ron would often cycle over there and then back in the evening. He could never get the time below an hour and ten minutes, but considering he was in SD and had his gas-mask – or respirator in modern terminology - slung over his shoulder, he reckons that was pretty good going! But he says he did tend to perspire rather a lot during the summer months.

There is one dark secret that Ron feels he can now finally share with the world at large! Whilst doing a *"stretch of jankers"*, on one particular evening he and another chap were delegated to deliver a 'kettle' of soup to the Sergeants' Mess. Halfway across the Square, they paused for a quick breather, and to get some sense of feeling back into their numbed fingers. In a while, Ron asked his 'oppo' if he was ready to carry on. At the affirmative reply, Ron lifted the handle on his side of the container, but he was too fast, as the other side was still firmly on the ground. Thus about half of the soup ended up all over the Square. The two lads hurriedly carried the remainder to the Mess, topped it up with some gravy powder and hot water – and beat a hasty retreat!

Joe Griffiths was another who joined in the month of May 1939. He remembers standing alone on Stockport railway station, wearing his first pair of long trousers, holding the 'King's shilling', three days' ration money and three days' pay. Adding up to about fifteen shillings, it was an unbelievable sum of money for a schoolboy in pre-war England. Joe also remembers being drilled in his civvies – he says that his new long trousers were already shredded around the turn-ups after only a couple of weeks! He describes the

The roof of the Spider has always been an ideal place to sunbathe (and for water fights)!

transformation from *"skinny, pimply-faced youths from working class backgrounds into a group of fit, muscular young men, with gleaming teeth and short hair"*. RSM Ben Cook certainly made a strong impression on Joe, who later described him as *"rubicund and moustached, in his long purple greatcoat, towering over me, his face ruddy and grim"*

Look out for the smart guys!

Joe's first-day experience at Arborfield became memorable, when an ugly looking and powerfully built figure stood at his elbow outside the Dining Hall – or Cookhouse - and uttered the famous phrase, *"Can yer lend us a shilling, mate?"* Thinking that this fellow may wield some influence around the place, Joe meekly handed over the silver coin. *"I'll let yer 'ave it back termorrer"*, came the cheery response. But each time that Joe glanced anxiously in this chap's direction afterwards, he was completely ignored, and he slowly realised that he had been 'done' by one of the 'smart guys'. Experience is everything though, and Joe made

sure it was the last time he'd be caught out.

He found the dining activities somewhat primitive. Although the tables were neatly laid out with vases of flower arrangements, boxes of breakfast cereal, jugs of milk and bowls of sugar, it was the biggest and toughest boys who always got the most! Joe was another who found that *"the black asphalt burned hot under our inadequate civvie shoes"*.

One of the School's 'hallowed traditions' started almost immediately upon its opening, and Joe remembers it with reverence, if not downright fear! Whilst on parade and standing 'at ease' during a *"sweaty ten-minute break"*, the boys would find the RSM bearing down upon them and knew what was coming. *"Commandant's name? Adjutant's name? Company Commander's name?"* These questions about the School's hierarchy were to be answered by *"well behaved puppets, chanting in unison, not only their names, but their regiments, honours and awards"*. If they got it wrong then they would be doubled around the old oak tree, shimmering in the haze at the distant top end of the Square.

Joe's departure from Arborfield led him to his first posting, an Anti-Aircraft (AA) unit at Upton-on-Wirral, a small village on the opposite side of the Mersey to the Liverpool docks. *(Les Wiffen also ended up at the same unit. Ed.)* The unit had been formed mainly from ex-Territorial Army (TA) men, who seemed to resent the presence of this callow young regular soldier in their midst. Life was very exciting and dangerous during the bombing raids on the dockyards of both Liverpool and Birkenhead, but Joe still found time to attend afternoon tea dances and concerts. People had certainly not turned their backs on their amusements during the war. On the contrary, it became almost a patriotic duty to have as much fun as possible, just to spite Adolf!

Following the later formation of REME in 1942, Joe swapped his shiny RAOC cap badge, proudly displaying the three balls and cannons, for what he describes as *"a nondescript brown plastic thing"*. Joe went on to reach the rank of Captain by the end of his service and has now settled 'down under' in Australia. Around sixty years later, the first parts of what he hoped would become his life history appeared in the pages of *The Craftsman*, REME's own monthly magazine.

Another memory of that new cap-badge comes from Bill Tingey, who had started his Army life with intake 39A and would later go on to spend his last years in far off NZ. At the time of the badge's issue, Bill was serving in London at Park Royal. The men were lined up and reminded of the importance of the occasion, before being handed over their new *"dark brown plastic cap-badges"*. Bill added that these were not well received and that, when they were eventually replaced, the 'prancing horse' style of badge was deemed *"much more in line with the Corps image"*. Bill also recalls that, during what later became 'the blackout', he and his colleagues would march to the workshop whistling *"Hi Ho, Hi Ho, it's off to work we go"*, with the last man in the column actually carrying a lantern on a stick. Despite the hard times, Bill recalls *"courting during an air-raid"* and listening to the famous 'Mrs Mills' playing the piano at a local dance – he reckons that Gwladys was *"a big girl, even then"*!

California, here I come!

'Paddy' O'Brien of 39A has some slightly more salubrious memories to contend with! He and one of his colleagues, Arthur Sainsbury, had decided to go out for a stroll, to *"shake the camphor from their new uniforms"*. Paddy reckons that, at the time, he was *"built like a hockey stick with the wood scraped clean"*, while Arthur was taller than Paddy's four-foot nine, but would still have to *"jump twice to create a shadow"*! When they reached the Guardroom, they were confronted with a mirror and a notice that asked, *"Are you a credit to your unit?"* On reflection (oh, spare us the wit!) they decided that they were just about up for it.

Finding themselves only a short distance from Camp, the pair heard some merry music coming from the other side of a large hedge. Peeking through a narrow gap in the foliage, they were astonished to be confronted with the none-too-pretty sight of a party of dancing nudists! Arthur reckoned it must have been some sort of 'fertility rite', but in fact the boys had stumbled upon *'Little California in England'*, a sort of local holiday camp based around a large lake.

As an almost-as-large lady, *"with the complexion of a road mender"*, danced towards the pop-eyed duo, the boys were brought down to earth by the roaring voice of 'Chesty' Jackson, one of the School's Physical Training Instructors (PTIs). He rapidly doubled the lads back to Camp for their first personal encounter with RSM Ben Cook. After a period of interrogation, and with the RSM's mutterings about *"white slavers"* ringing in their ears, our heroic pair were 'politely invited' to participate in a session of Cookhouse fatigues – the inevitable 'spud bashing'! *(This story brings to mind the 'under the counter' magazine 'Health and Efficiency', where anything that remotely suggested 'short and curly' was carefully air-brushed out of the photographs! Ed.)*

Bertram 'Mike' Champken had hardly ever been outside his home town of Pershore in the Vale of Evesham, so arriving at Arborfield was like *"going to the moon"* for him in May 1939. He can also recall the Square being rolled out with wet tarmac, with the hot sunshine baking the boys' necks. Their pay of two shillings (ten pence) a week didn't go very far, what with black boot polish, *Blanco*, *Brasso* (or *Bluebell*), soap and toothpaste to buy, as well as the letter-writing equipment and stamps, necessary to write home to Mum!

Mike even took to 'bulling' other boys' boots and cleaning their webbing, in order to earn a 'few bob' on the side. But as far as he was concerned, the chance of learning a trade was far more preferable to his previously planned future, that of either being an errand-boy or working on the land. *(You couldn't have heard of Ben Cook's 'agricultural' endeavours then, Mike? This must have been brought about by Government plans to reclaim some 1.5 million acres of 'derelict land' for just that purpose. Ed.)*

Mike recalls that he was probably the only boy in the School's history ever to be put on jankers for kissing his sister! The young lady in question had joined one of the women's branches of the Army, and was serving at nearby Aldermaston. The two of them had met up in Reading town centre one Saturday afternoon and, returning to the station terminus to catch their respective buses in the evening, a familial kiss on the cheek seemed a harmless and polite way for Mike to say 'Goodbye'.

However, a sharp tap on his shoulder from a Military Policeman (MP) was quickly followed by an order that he had better report to his Company Commander, Capt Ingram, on the following Monday morning. Fortunately, the business was sorted out

when Mike's sister herself arrived in a staff car to back up Mike's explanation of his innocent 'transgression'. The incident ended with them both being given a cup of tea by the kindly Captain, along with sufficient money for them to enjoy a slap-up meal on their next free weekend.

Harry Shaw, who would eventually become one of the stalwarts of both Arborfield and its Old Boys some forty years later, was one of those boys who joined the ATS at Jersey, in the Channel Islands. Originally from Portsmouth, he remembers a rough crossing in a Force Eight gale from Southampton to St Helier, then ending up at St Peter's Barracks on the western side of the island. Most of the boys with him there, around 150 in number, were due to join the RASC, with the other fifty detailed to the RAOC.

He duly reported to Arborfield at the end of August 1939, thus answering to the label '39B'. It was the very next day, at 5.45 a.m. on September 1st, that German military forces marched across the border, launching their 'Blitzkrieg' in the invasion of Poland

Practical Trade Training training – can you tell a Heinkel from a Messerschmitt?

– although Harry swears to this day that the blame for this infamous action had nothing to do with him! However, he does admit to that event being *"the end of my childhood"*.

Harry recalls that, in those early days, boys were sent directly into one of five Companies, each based upon their trade designations. He was put into 'E' Coy, commanded by Maj Rigden of the RAOC. With his steel-rimmed glasses, Harry quickly decided that the Major must have been Himmler's brother! One thing that has stayed vividly in Harry's mind was the variety of different cap-badges worn by the PS; strange-sounding names such as the Seaforth Highlanders, East Yorkshires, East Surreys, West Sussexes, Coldstreams, you name it, they all seemed to serve at Arborfield.

Whilst here, Harry trained as a Fitter and could eventually turn his hand quite well to most things; his previous educational prowess stood him in great stead. He was later to come back to what would then be 'the College', serving as a lecturer for some twenty-five years from 1963 onwards.

Another story told by Harry would hardly be out of place in one of those epic prisoner-of-war films! A bunch of boys, feeling rather ravenous during those days of severe food rationing, picked the lock on the Ration Store and pinched a load of potatoes. But what to cook them in? Having clubbed together to buy an electric iron for uniform pressing, they turned this upside down, wedged it between two bedsteads, and used it to heat candle wax in a mess-tin. The potatoes were then thinly sliced into the hot wax and cooked to some state of perfection. As Harry puts it, *"Anyone who wants a new taste, try it!"* Well, try it they did, with no apparent ill effects, the only thing missing was the salt 'n' vinegar! *(And the name of the film? Perhaps "Who dares, eats!" Ed.)*

Harry's memories of the food situation are not nearly as pleasant as those of some of his contemporaries – he says he was forever hungry! Fortunately, he always seemed to have some spare cash of his own, so was able to take advantage of the cooked snacks available at the NAAFI Canteen. Harry also recalls that the cleanliness of the water supply was not what it should have been, which is probably what caused an outbreak of impetigo, a fairly serious skin complaint that seemed to be prevalent in those days.

For the duration of that terrible war that followed Harry's arrival, Germany did its best to starve Britain into submission, with the imports of fresh produce from abroad severely restricted by the menace of German submarines – or 'U-boats' – all around our shores. Rationing of such items as bacon and ham, butter and sugar, were restricted as early as January 1940, followed over the next two years by cooking fat, meat, tea, cheese, jam and eggs. Despite all this, many boys have since remarked that the food at 'boys' school' was always 'adequate', if not necessarily going under the title of *haute cuisine*! Rationing, in one form or another, was to continue well into the Fifties.

A fierce winter to contend with

Ianto Metcalfe is another who has long since settled in distant NZ, but is still able to vividly remember his early days as a member of intake 39B, particularly that very first winter (1939 - 40), which saw plenty of heavy snow and freezing temperatures throughout the land. In London, during January 1940, the Thames froze over for the first time since 1888, followed by the *"worst storm of the century"*, which swept across the country before the end of that month.

Closer to home, there was a succession of burst pipes all around the Camp. Ianto was to spend most of those winter days, not on normal training, but assisting the REs to lay new water pipes. Having been on the squad that repaired the pipes in Ben Cook's house, he recalls then enjoying a splendid hot lunch cooked by none other than the kindly Mrs Cook herself. When the RSM arrived home, to find that he himself had no hot food ready, it was surely no coincidence that Ianto spent the next day shovelling coal into the boiler house! However, it was Ben who later recommended Ianto for promotion to the highest obtainable rank in those days – LCpl! Poor Ianto managed to last a mere three days at that dizzy height, before a certain amount of *"hot water"*, which he contrived to get into, returned him to a mere A/T. More than fifty years later, despite his living so far away, Ianto proudly presented a Cup, 'The Ianto Metcalfe Trophy' to the College, to be awarded to the 'Rugby player of the season'.

Another boy who joined intake 39B was Andy Smallpage. With his father being a Recruiting Officer and the job situation in Leeds being a bit fraught, it seemed like a good idea (well, to his Dad!) that Andy should join the Army, rather than ending up *"sweeping the floor at Burtons"*. Originally designated as a Vehicle Mechanic (VM), Andy soon found out that the required skills of filing and drilling were a bit too subtle

Some apprentices, such as these Instrument Mechanics, had to grow into the job

for him. Fortunately, a noticeable shortage of boys in the trade of Blacksmith at that time presented him a whole new opportunity, which he gratefully seized with both hands.

One memorable period Andy remembers from his Arborfield days must have coincided with the formation of the Army Catering Corps (ACC). It would appear that a party of cooks arrived here at Arborfield from Aldershot, as part of their trade test. Allocated a table of sixteen hungry boys each, these cooks then proceeded to vie with each other in their efforts to see who could produce the best results, from the rather sparse rations available. This went on for around a fortnight and Andy recalls that even 'Army grub' tasted halfway decent for a while!

Due to the uncertain conditions prevailing at the time, Andy's qualifications and education tended to suffer, no doubt along with many other boys of that era. He recalls that it wasn't until around 1950 that the education system got back into a semblance of working order and, on a personal basis, he reckons that he didn't himself become properly 'qualified' until 1952. It was very difficult to devote the requisite time to studying,

as Andy says, because there was *"still a job of work to be done"*.

Sense of humour - definitely required!

Allan 'Tuck' Tucker was another boy from intake 39B. He recalls some of the humourous sayings of those days, which obviously stuck in his memory bank for numerous years afterwards. One day he had been found 'leaning' against the Company Office verandah, by Paddy Corr, PS member of the Royal Ulster Rifles (RUR). Now, if it's one thing that boys didn't do in those days, it was *'lean'*. Wanting young Tucker to stand up straight, Paddy scornfully told him *"I've shot better things than you"*! Then, on the weekly pay parade, Paddy would take great delight in looking out for anyone named Phillips, and telling them to *"Get down there in the effing effs"*!

Amongst the other so-called staff 'comedians' of those days was Corporal (Cpl) Bates, who played clarinet with the School Band, but was still required to do his stint as 'duty wallah'. He would stride into a barrack room full of sleeping apprentices, rousing them with such phrases as, *"Come on Jack, get off yer back"* or *"Come on Fred, get off yer bed"*. *(These characters could have been appearing on 'ITMA', the popular wartime wireless (radio) series! Ed.)*

Another of the PS that Tuck remembers was Cpl McCarthy of the Lancashire Fusiliers, who had spent many long years in India and was a particularly good hockey player. McCarthy found out that Tuck had become 'rather keen' on one of the NAAFI girls, and was *"getting a few things on tick"*. Tuck rolled into the Canteen one Wednesday morning, deplete of cash with pay parade still a couple of hours away, and asked for his usual bottle of pop and a sticky bun. He was told that his bill was way over the top, so it was a case of 'no deal' until he'd settled up. He subsequently found out that McCarthy had been putting his NAAFI breaks on Tuck's bill. Not only that, but he later married the very same NAAFI girl! Tuck later heard that McCarthy had been killed during the landing at Anzio and, not being one to bear a grudge, added that *"he wasn't really a bad chap"*.

The same Cpl McCarthy was spotted relieving himself against a tree, whilst taking the boys out on a route march in the snow – yes, snow! - around the Easter of 1940. Several boys took advantage of this 'natural break', gathering up snowballs and hurling them at the corporal. Some even hit the target area, which was still on view, causing great mirth amongst the throwers. But McCarthy's revenge was soon taken. He shouted out the warning, *"Gas! Gas!"* thus making the boys swiftly don their gas-masks, before marching them off to complete the route – breathing rather heavily!

One of Tuck's roommates was the recipient of *"much cash and many parcels from a doting mother"*. However, he was so reluctant to share in this good fortune that he locked the goodies in his locker and procured the very latest in padlocks in order to secure it. Imagine how perplexed he was, on opening the locker one afternoon, only to find that the remainder of his favourite apple pie had disappeared, with only a few crumbs left in its memory! One of the ex-Dukie boys in the room had made a special pin-punch with which to remove the pins from the locker's door hinges.

A favourite game of the time was used to relieve the boredom of Sunday afternoons. The bed biscuits would be piled up in the centre of the room and, using the bottom end of one of the folding beds as a springboard, the boys would have a contest to see who

could fly over the most biscuits. This caused no end of fun, until one boy nearly took off the top of his head when he hit one of the crossbeams! Good old days!

John Moir of 39B struck up a close friendship with John Foreman, who had arrived at Arborfield from Didcot, along with a number of other boys. They had a common interest in the sport of boxing and John recalls his namesake visiting the family home over at Church Crookham on occasions. On leaving the School, John Foreman was stationed in Essex, where he was later wounded during an air raid. Upon being discharged from hospital, he returned to Church Crookham to collect his old motorcycle, and that was the last John Moir ever saw of him. John's sister used to correspond with him however, but after his being posted to North Africa, the Moir family sadly learned that 'the other John' had died.

Fifty years later, John heard that there was now a set of medals, including the North Africa Star, held in trust at the REME Museum, which had belonged to his old friend. Upon enquiries into this by Judy Booth, the Corps Archivist, it was confirmed that the medals in question had indeed been donated to the Museum, by the sister of John Neville Foreman, in 1985. His boxing prowess had obviously continued, culminating in his winning the Palestine middleweight championship, for which he had received a silver cup. It transpired that young Foreman had been tragically killed in a motor accident on a test track in 1943, at the tender age of only twenty-one years.

Outbreak of World War II

At around five minutes before eleven a.m. on that fateful Sunday, September 3rd 1939, all boys in the School were marched smartly down to the Games Room, adjacent to the NAAFI, where Col Hilborn sat hunched at the controls of a huge old-fashioned Bakelite wireless set. They were told to be quiet and, after the chimes of Big Ben had heralded the hour of 11 o'clock, the boys sat in total and stunned silence as they heard the Prime Minister, Mr Neville Chamberlain, announcing that *"This country is now at war with Germany. We are ready"*. Little could anyone then have realised that the conflict was to last for almost a full six years, be on a world-wide stage across all oceans and continents, and that it would cause the death of millions of people, both fierce combatants and innocent bystanders.

Doc Savage recalls that the Commandant added a

A thorough apprenticeship in all skills

from fitting......

...... to blacksmithing

few words of his own, no doubt in an effort to 'stiffen the sinews', but his final ringing phrase, *"Courage mes enfants"*, seems to have gone well over the heads of most of the assembled boys. There obviously weren't too many fluent French speakers amongst the audience! Dick Wade says that there were quite a few tears from some of the older ladies present, no doubt caused by those unpleasant memories gained during the previous war. It is probable that many boys also listened to King George's broadcast to the Commonwealth later that evening, when he told his millions of subjects, *"We can only do the right as we see the right, and reverently commit our cause to God"*.

Following that morning's famous broadcast, the boys were told to return to their barrack rooms and gather up their tin hats and gas-masks, which (initially) they were ordered to carry wherever they went. RSM Ben Cook then took charge of the filling of sandbags, used to protect the MRS (standing for Medical Reception Station and not *"More Ruddy Sick"*, as some would have us believe!) and Administration blocks from the effects of any future bomb blast. The 'spiders' themselves were not protected, as, during any raids, the boys were meant to use the air-raid shelters, which had been specially constructed at the top of the Parade Square. However, an increase in 'furniture' was provided in the barrack rooms by the addition of plywood blackout shutters, one per window, which remained in place for many years, until the cessation of hostilities.

Peter Styles, who had joined in the previous May, recalls that it wasn't long after that when the School had its first air-raid warning, which turned out to be a false alarm, no doubt the first of many during that period which came to be called 'the phoney war'. In fact, the first German bombs dropped on British soil eventually landed on the Shetland Isles on November 13th, although zealous members of the Irish Republican Army (IRA) were making bomb attacks on main-line railway stations in London that same month. Throughout the country, people lived in dread of being attacked from the air, having been warned by former Prime Minister, Stanley Baldwin, that *"the bomber will always get through"*.

Life must go on

War or no war, found that *"the interminable activities of the School (still) went on"*. He recollects Padre Squire's choir practice sessions on Saturday mornings, and sitting among the *"grizzled older boys from Bramley or Didcot, their bare-faced intent to dodge drill parade never in question"*. That *"indulgent and popular Padre"* even took his charges out on a 'choirboys' outing' to Wokingham, plying them with tea and buns at one of the town's teashops. Joe was later to recall that outing as the *"fount of democracy, where the 'rough serge' sat down at the same table as 'fine barathea' to eat"*. He also says that the boys never took advantage of that kindly gentleman, they were just happy to enjoy their break from the normal routine.

One highlight of the motorbike repair element of Joe's training was a trip to a scrap-yard, located somewhere on the outskirts of Reading. With a great deal of enthusiasm and armed with their trusty spanners, the boys rummaged among the filth and oil, in order to rescue assemblies and spare parts. On the way back, they sat in the back of the truck, singing loudly, grinning their grimy smiles and waving to the astonished passers-by. What must they have thought of that singing band of oily grease monkeys? Returning to Camp, the boys noisily unloaded their haul of trophies onto the workshop floor, as envious eyes looked on.

Just prior to the year's summer recess Les Wiffen had fallen sick and, instead of going home on his allotted three week's leave, had been sent to the military hospital at Aldershot, not returning until the end of August. He was then sent on delayed leave and was actually in Hove when he heard news of the outbreak of hostilities, closely followed by the shrill wailing of an air-raid siren. He felt very conspicuous in his SD and white belt, as all around him, military personnel were hastening to report in at their nearest call-up centres.

Upon his return to the School, Les was transferred to 'C' Coy and moved to room 'E3', the one nearest the Sergeants' Mess. He can still see, through the Mess windows of his mind's eye, the *"senior ranks at play"*, relaxing with the odd pint or two, after a day's work. One game played by them was 'bull fighting', which entailed using the RSM's purple greatcoat as a matador's cape and his pace-stick as a sword!*(Boys will be boys, as the saying goes, but they should have included the permanent staff too! Ed.)*

Les recalls a couple of amusing occasions from his own experiences at the School. With only pushbikes as their means of transport, he and some pals had been over to Wokingham one late summer evening, when they stopped to 'scrump' some apples from a nearby orchard. Just about to tuck in to their illegal booty, they spotted a local bobby (policeman) approaching them at a fast pace on *his* bike – and made it back to Camp in record time!

On a similar trip into the larger town of Reading, he and his group of mates had hired a rowing boat and moored up alongside a small island along the river. With a blazing sun overhead, the absence of swimming trunks was quickly overlooked and an impromptu session of 'skinny-dipping' took place. It was only as the boys rowed back towards the boat station that a party of giggling land-girls appeared from their hidden viewpoint! Before riding back to Arborfield, the boys slipped into a local hostelry for their first taste of beer – or at least a 'beer and lemonade shandy'!

The Monday after war was declared, September 4th, as Winston Churchill was recalled to the Cabinet as First Lord of the Admiralty, saw the arrival of a new member of staff, in the shape of civilian typist, Miss Eileen Golding. She recalls being the only civilian girl in the Headquarters (HQ) office for quite some time, and thoroughly enjoying the 'service' style of life, with regular dances and cinema shows taking place in the Camp Hall. Eileen also remembers that, at Christmas parties held during those war years, she and her mother used to scrounge scraps of material, in order to make soft toys for children of the School staff. Some years later, Eileen met and married Jim Huber, himself an ex-apprentice from the School at Chepstow (1933 - 36), who later served here as a Supervising Instructor at the subsequent College during his last years of service until 1982.

Kenneth Green had actually arrived at the ATS (Boys) on September 3rd, soon learning that it was the very day on which the war had been declared. On the personal side, he happily found Arborfield to be a bit of a 'culture shock'! *"Large, spacious and well appointed barrack rooms, central heating, spring beds and good quality mattresses"* – these were a far cry from the conditions he had found during his previous two years' service at Bramley. Even the food was edible, he says, and the tea tasted like nectar!

It must have come as a nasty surprise to 'our Ken' when he returned after the Christmas leave period, to find that all of the heating radiators in the Camp had cracked open. For some unknown reason, they had not been shut down and drained off prior to the holiday and the subsequent harsh frosts had soon frozen the water in them. There thus followed a hectic period of activity as, under the supervision of some of the civilian instructors, many boys soon found out how to repair central-heating radiators.

Ken admits that he found his apprenticeship *"basically flawed"*, with far too much *"regimental running around"* and not sufficient time spent dedicated to trade training. He eventually found himself qualified as a Fitter (Motor Vehicle), without ever understanding, in his own words, *"the working of a Constant Voltage Control"*. However, the theory of the 'Steam Engine' was one thing he became very proficient at, and he was later to put this knowledge to good use when asked to get an old steam tug back into working order during the Suez crisis of 1956. Ken eventually returned to Arborfield as a Master Artificer, serving on the PS of the School for two years between 1961 and 1963.

'Put that light out!'

As well as within the confines of the Camp, all civilian properties, be they houses or business premises, were under strict instructions to put up their blackout shutters and curtains, as it was envisaged that the showing of lights would help guide enemy aircraft to their targets. Whether or not this was ever proven, the ruling was strictly enforced by a civilian army of Air Raid Precautions (ARP) wardens. However, when the expected air raids at first failed to materialise, these wardens, who obviously took their job seriously, suffered from a mood of resentment from certain mean-spirited members of the public.

Meanwhile here at the School, the military regime ensured that the ruling was properly enforced at all times. With the ensuing petrol restrictions and the need to mask vehicle headlamps for any nighttime journeys, the roads around Arborfield must have seemed very quiet indeed during those many months that followed. Therefore, it is an amazing fact that, during those first few weeks of 'the blackout', some 4,000 unfortunate people were to die as a result of road accidents. The first 'real' civilian casualties of the war were to be two innocent members of the public, killed when a German bomber crashed down onto Clacton, Essex, on May 3rd 1940.

Paddy O'Brien had just celebrated his fifteenth birthday when war broke out. He well recalls the installation of the blackout shutters, humourously adding that it was only a problem for the more deeply

The Military Band in its early days

tanned, who tended to *"vanish from sight at sundown"*. Of more concern to Paddy were the changes on the culinary front – eggs suddenly shed their shells and became of the tinned and powdered variety, whilst the accompanying ham had turned into that well-known imposter, *'Spam'*. Paddy also tells the story of one boy in his barrack room who they were amazed to find *"slept with his eyes open"*. After one such example, the Orderly Sergeant one morning actually pronounced him dead! He was miraculously resurrected of course, between the *"auctioning of his kit and the funeral arrangements"*, thus depriving Paddy of a spare pair of boots!

One of the ex-RAOC boys, who later had be transferred here to Arborfield, was Alec Day, this time from Didcot, where he had been ever since joining up in 1937. Arriving at the Camp gates, he and his mates were busily unpacking their bulging kit bags from their transport, when they were almost paralysed by the sound of a stentorian voice that bellowed at them from the darkened innards of the Guardroom.

It wasn't long before they became even more personally acquainted with the RSM, the legendary Ben Cook! Alec recalls sneaking off to the Workshop toilet at break time for a nifty fag, only to hear Ben's dulcet tones from outside – *"I know who you are!"* The fact that Ben couldn't possibly see through the dirty windows to identify an individual smoker didn't prevent a whole load of cigarettes being quickly extinguished, and the 'fag ends' flushed down the nearest toilet bowl.

The first Army meal of his life for Bill Sullivan was upon his arrival at the ATS (Boys) on October 23rd 1939. It obviously left a lasting impression on him, as he was able to describe it in almost grisly detail almost sixty years later. *"The menu – stew. Large lumps of lamb complete with fat and gristle, potatoes, carrots, onions and dumplings. The former floating merrily but the dumplings, having either committed suicide or been scuttled, lay firmly on the bottom of the cook's cauldron. But, fair play, he dug deeply with his ladle and landed one each for most of us. For sweet, a much better offering, chocolate pudding with chocolate sauce – great!"* It's not surprising that, to this day, Bill is still not too keen on stew, but retains a great penchant for chocolate pud! The start of meat rationing, which came about on March 11th 1940, probably provided some welcome relief to Bill.

At some time during those first few months of the War, it was perhaps inevitable that the School would be hit by an epidemic of that most unpatriotic of diseases - **German** measles! One of the boys' accommodation blocks had to be set aside as a designated isolation unit. Those who succumbed to the infection were isolated, fed on the 'fat of the land' for a week, then dispatched to their own homes for twenty-eight days sick leave. Needless to say, the unlaundered bed-sheets and pillows of the infected boys were much in demand by the other lads, who also hoped to catch the disease and partake of this preferential treatment!

Doug Phillips of 39B tried vainly for the same effect, by first borrowing, then sucking on and blowing into an infected mouth organ! Those boys who were fortunate enough to be sent to the 'School Hospital', at the far end of the playing fields, all seemed to 'have a crush' on the very lovely nursing Sister – *"a vision of loveliness, with Officer status in a red cape, much admired at a respectable distance"*.

Arborfield under attack

Both Doug (or 'Phil', as most of his era would remember him) and Fred Ford call to mind a bombing raid which was aimed at Arborfield Camp during their time at the School. *"One fine sunny Sunday morning"* around 9.50 a.m., most boys were 'bulling up' their kit ready for church parade, when the ominous sound of an approaching airplane brought them rushing from their barrack rooms and out onto the Parade Square to see what was happening. Some of the more foolhardy individuals actually climbed up onto the verandah roofs for a closer view, with Lofty Howes swearing that he, along with many other boys, was hanging out of his room's window yelling *"Bomb the Workshops!"* Young Phillips seems to remember that an AA site somewhere began to open up with Bren guns and that he *"stood in awe"* as a couple of bombs appeared, dropping from the German raider.

Molly Cook, the RSM's daughter, has her own clear impression of that incident, recalling that the family had not long finished eating their breakfast. Her brother Clifford was very young at the time, just about able to talk. He was leaning out of the window, shouting what appeared to be the words *"pretty airplane"*. The rest of the family looked out to see what was afoot and saw the German bomber, its machine-guns firing rapidly with red tracer – hence young Clifford's description of 'pretty'. Her father had been shaving at the time of the commotion and rushed out of the house with soap still clinging to his chin and his braces hanging down.

Coming back indoors, he said that the plane had flown so low that, if he had been armed with his trusty rifle, he could have shot it down. After all, Ben had been the Battalion sniper with the Grenadier Guards. Making sure that his family was all safe and sound, his next priority was in the safety of the boys under his command just down the road.

Joe Griffiths also has a vivid memory of that dramatic raid, saying that the plane was a *Junkers 88*.

He had never seen an aircraft so near and so low, its smoky exhaust trail floating behind it as though in slow motion - even the pilot's face was clearly visible. Time seemed to stand still and Joe says he was *"frozen – not in fear, but in utter amazement"*. At first, complete apprehension was slow to dawn, until the boys noticed the large black crosses painted on the plane's fuselage and wings.

Joe recalls hearing the warning shouts, as the boys finally realised the danger, then scattered and hurried for cover like a *"herd of startled sheep"*. Air-raid drills had still not been practiced at that stage, so many boys quickly burrowed beneath the most obvious protection, the barrack-room floors and verandahs. RSM Ben Cook had arrived quickly on the scene, dashing the mere hundred yards or so from his home and, in his eagerness to get the boys into a safe place, fell ungracefully over on the Square. Much to the amusement of the boys of course, but this inadvertent piece of comedy probably helped to relieve the tension of the moment. Dick Wade was convinced that it was a Lewis-gun mounted in a sandpit in the middle of a field that fired at the raider, but Doc Savage says he is sure there were a couple of RA training camps nearby, from where any retaliatory fire would have come from.

Les Wiffen had also been waiting to go on church parade on that fateful Sunday morning and recollects that, if the attack had been just a little while later, the assembled boys in their white blancoed belts would have stood out as tempting targets. He swears that he could see *"the front gunner in his cupola"*. Front mounted guns on the plane spat out flashes of light and bullets as it swooped gracefully over the parade ground, tracking the line of the road from the main gate down towards the rear 'hospital' gate. This was followed by the dropping of the bombs, which caused the ground to shake and instantly had everyone dashing for a safe haven in case the plane came back. Many boys expected to see a chasing RAF fighter in hot pursuit, but this never materialised and the German raider flew off at high speed, low over the horizon. *(Fred Ford reckons that the plane was a 'Heinkel', while Doc Savage thought it was a 'Messerschmitt' – but at least ALL who saw it agreed that it was German! Ed.)*

Fortunately, not a single boy was hurt in that cowardly attack and the only casualty was later found to be an unfortunate cow that had been standing alone, grazing in a field near the hospital. However, the Padre was later to stand up in his pulpit, holding up a piece of shrapnel from the bomb, which brought the inherent seriousness of the situation firmly to the boys' minds. Ronald Le Rendu of 39B recalls that, as a result of this dangerous incident, the boys were later made to 'double' up and down the slopes of the air-raid shelters several times, so that they would be in no doubt as to where they were located next time!

A uniform to be proud of

M J 'John' Wintle arrived here from Newport, South Wales, on the same day as Bill Sullivan, thus becoming firmly established as another member of 39C. Having not long graduated from the wearing of short trousers, the appearance of another boy arriving in 'plus fours' didn't exactly boost John's initial confidence. On his first visit back home that Christmas, whilst proudly wearing his uniform on a shopping trip to Cardiff, he was approached by an elderly gentleman who warned him that it was a punishable offence to wear the King's uniform unless in the Forces. John quickly produced his AB64 to prove his legitimacy and was promptly given a ten-bob (50p) note for good luck! Weighing a mere seventy-five pounds and standing only four feet nine inches tall on enlistment, John reckons it is no wonder that he did not look *"the full ticket"*.

John joined the other boys of room 'B6' in 'A' Coy and it wasn't long before the room as a whole was offered the chance of owning its own wireless receiver for the sum of only 'a tanner' (sixpence) each. The money was duly collected, but the recipient of the cash, who hailed from Barnstaple but who shall remain nameless, never did come up with the goods, and the boys later learned that he had been picked up by the local police on a charge of breaking and entering. This miscreant was never seen again, but sadly nor was their money!

With a regime of regular exercise, accompanied by substantial intakes of food, John's frame soon filled out, and he reckons that he was always *"well looked after"* whilst at the School. He does recall, however, one occasion when there must have been some sort of health hazard as, for a while at least, all boys had to wash and disinfect their 'eating irons' in some sort of potassium permanganate solution. This story no doubt confirms Harry Shaw's earlier tale, about an outbreak of impetigo. During his time here, John did his fair

The long and the short and the tall!

share of 'spud bashing' and coke shovelling and has ghastly memories of boys being marched at the double over the air-raid shelters at the top of the square, whilst wearing gas-masks. However, as with the majority of ex-boys, most of John's recollections remain happy ones.

John recalls that, on leaving boys' school, he was posted back to South Wales and was so happy to be finally receiving a decent amount on payday! One drawback though, was that in order to bathe, the soldiers there (at Castleton, just outside Cardiff) had to travel twelve miles each way to partake of the baths at a pit-head. A later posting was as an advance party to start up a new workshop, situated in a garage at Petersfield, Hampshire. As this was directly across the road to the *'Red Lion'* public house, he found it quite handy! John is another who shared the pleasure of watching Sidney Wooderson run at Crookham.

One of those 'adults' who arrived at the School during 1940 was Stan Swalwell, who joined from the RA as a PS PTI. It was to be over fifty years later that he responded to a request for 'historical information' about the early days here at Arborfield by sending in, from his home in distant Victoria, Australia, a variety of nostalgic photographs, mainly showing the members of the training staff. At that time, this consisted of three Senior Non-commissioned Officers (SNCOs) of the Army Physical Training Corps (APTC) and ten others who, like Stan, had arrived here from various other regiments.

Stan recalls taking small parties of boys on swimming trips to the lake at nearby 'Little California' and also that time when some boys climbed onto the roof of their 'spiders' to get a better glimpse of the German bomber previously mentioned. He names one of his colleagues at the time as Arthur Cunliffe, who had played soccer for Aston Villa and England in pre-war days. He recalls that the 9 a.m. start to their instructional day changed to a more rigid 8 a.m. when RSM McNally later arrived as the replacement for Ben Cook – not a universally popular decision! However, Stan was proud to stay here as a PTI throughout the war years until 1945, wearing the familiar red and black hooped pullover. Who can ever forget those famous phrases uttered by PTIs the world over? *"Up on the wallbars, go!"* and *"Round the stripes on my jersey, move!"* seem to echo through every gymnasium ever used by the Army.

Dark days – and Dunkirk

Despite what must have seemed like an 'end of the world' scenario during early 1940, with Hitler's troops having invaded both Denmark and Norway, there was still a school to be run here at Arborfield. On the 19th of April, a fifty-six-page booklet was issued, which stated the 'Standing Orders' for the guidance of all ranks serving at the School. Issued under Paragraph 1651 of King's Regulations, 1935, the Commandant advised that *"they should be interpreted reasonably and with due regard to the benefit of all concerned"*. No attempt had been made to legislate for exceptional circumstances, except that these were to be dealt with *"intelligently, on their merits, as they arise"*. The Commandant also decreed that the orders be strictly observed by all ranks, and that all PS members should be in personal possession of a copy at all times.

The School at that time came directly under the control of the War Office for all matters pertaining to the intake and training of apprentices, as well as the provision of staff. Responsibility for all matters relating to discipline and local administration was put into the hands of the General Officer Commanding-in-Chief (GOC), Aldershot Command. The stated function of the School was to train, *"to a high standard, specially selected boys who are enlisted into the RAOC as apprentice tradesmen, in the trades of Blacksmiths, Coppersmiths, Electricians, Fitters and Turners"*. For normal administrative purposes, the School was divided up into five separate Companies, each corresponding to one of the five trade disciplines.

Ronald Holland had joined the School as a member of intake 39B. He recollects those *"dark days"* that followed the fall of the lowland countries of Belgium and Holland and the eventual evacuation of an estimated 325,000 men from the French beaches of Dunkirk, which began on May 30th 1940. They were mainly the remnants of the BEF, with possibly around 100,000 French and Belgian soldiers also brought to safety. The whole rescue effort, under the codename 'Operation Dynamo', had been undertaken by a flotilla of Royal Navy vessels, reinforced by a myriad of barges, dinghies, fishing smacks, motor cruisers, pleasure launches and yachts.

Controversy surrounded the operation, with many of those rescued from the beaches bemoaning the lack of air cover from the RAF. But in fact, it was very much down to the RAF that the whole evacuation was able to take place. Most of the aerial battles actually took place inland, not above the coast itself and, even if those dog-fights had been directly above the besieged troops, they would have been invisible through the thick black smoke that filled the air. On the other side of the coin, the 'boys in blue' were most impressed by the incredible fortitude of the men below, as they waited patiently for rescue, amidst scenes of tremendous carnage and destruction.

One brave pilot later described the beach scene as *"a shambles, littered with the smoking wreckage of engines and equipment. The sands erupted into huge geysers from exploding bombs and shells, while a backdrop . . . was provided by the palls of oily black smoke, rising from the burning harbour and houses. Yet there stood the orderly lines of our troops, chaos and Armageddon at their backs, waiting their turn to wade into the sea"*.

Armed to the teeth

The 'phoney war' had ended and each morning, as Ron puts it, *"a fearsome force of half-awake Arborfield apprentices, armed to the teeth with pickaxe helves, would be 'stood to', with the simple task of hitting any German paratrooper on the head, should they land on our green fields"*. Ron enjoyed all of his further service, with postings to India, Egypt, Cyprus and Germany, including eight years with Airborne Forces, but will always say that it was those years spent at the School between 1939 and 1942 that *"taught him how"*!

Left -
Monty with Capt Ben Cook

With Col Hilborn and RSM McNally

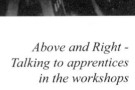

Above and Right -
Talking to apprentices
in the workshops

Monty's visit in 1942

Ex-Bramley boy Ken Green also remembers being sent out 'fully armed', in his case with an old-fashioned rifle, but says that there was no ammunition in it. However, on one occasion when the Commandant was about to send the boys out on patrol, he attempted to boost their morale with the following stirring words, *"If German parachutists land in the fields over yonder, how many of you will follow me?"* To which the smallest boy on parade is reputed to have replied, *"It all depends on which way you're going, Sir!"* Ken adds that the RSM was almost on the point of collapse at this retort, whether from anger or suppressed laughter is not mentioned! As they say, 'boys will be boys'.

In the early hours of Thursday 20th June 1940, Joe Gutteridge was one of 240 apprentice tradesmen suddenly deposited here in the barracks at Arborfield. Their RASC apprentices' school had been hurriedly evacuated from Jersey the previous day and it was a weary bunch of lads that gratefully sank onto their straw-filled palliasses in the Camp Hall. Joe still thinks with much gratitude of those RAOC boys who must have worked overtime to fill that bedding as a rush job. The boys' move to the mainland was only just in time, as it was only the following month that German forces took occupation of the Channel Islands, where they would remain for the next five years.

Joe's stay here at Arborfield, which qualified him as one our old boys, lasted all of two days! During that brief time, many of the senior boys were able to renew acquaintance with those RAOC boys who had been previously moved here from Jersey in July 1939. But, all too quickly, Joe was off to Dettingen Barracks at Blackdown and then, some ten weeks later, he moved on once again, to Buller Barracks at Aldershot – that was on October 1st. After the next summer leave (1941), that RASC School was disbanded, with the last 105 of the youngest boys going on to Chepstow to complete their training. So Joe can justly lay claim to being an Arborfield Old Boy – but it was a close run thing! Joe later became Treasurer/Secretary for the 'RASC Jersey Boys' and still fondly keeps a close eye on the contents of the Arborfield *Old Boys' Association Newsletter (OBAN)*.

The Battle of Britain

Following that never-to-be-forgotten retreat across the Channel from Dunkirk, the 'Battle of France' was over and the 'Battle of Britain' about to begin. At the beginning of July 1940, German bombers made their first daylight raids on shipping targets in the English

Channel. It was to be the start of many such raids, with the 'boys in blue' of the Royal Air Force (RAF) 'scrambling' their trusty *Hurricanes* and *Spitfires* over the months ahead. These derring-do exploits became known as *"their finest hour"*, with Fighter Command as a body bearing the collective title *"The Few"*, following the stirring wartime speeches of the now Prime Minister, Winston Churchill. There are few indeed of that generation who will ever forget his words:

> *"We shall defend our island whatever the cost may be. We shall fight on the beaches, we shall fight on the landing grounds, we shall fight in the fields and in the streets, we shall fight in the hills, we shall never surrender".*

During one tragic afternoon, shortly after the last 'little ship' had completed its heroic journey back to Dunkirk, the relative peace at the School here in Arborfield was shattered by the sound of a single rifle shot. As recalled by Les Wiffen, a young apprentice from 'D' Coy, whilst sitting on his bed and playing the accordion, quietly slumped to the floor with a fatal bullet wound in his neck. One story goes that another apprentice, having brought some live ammunition across with him from the island of Jersey, and now being seventeen years of age, had been issued with a rifle, believed to be an American-made 'P14', in order to assist in warding off an expected invasion. Somehow the rifle and bullets had been brought fatefully together in the same place and at the same time, and this unfortunate incident then occurred.

It proved a sad day indeed for the School, and was followed by the burial service at nearby Finchampstead Church. Afterwards, the barracks were subjected to a full and thorough search, and one of the 'C' Coy rooms apparently yielded a blanket full of unused ammunition. The result of this and any follow-up action are not recorded. One must remember that this was a wartime situation, fraught with danger to all inhabitants of the country, which no doubt caused many frayed nerves countrywide, never mind at a military establishment.

Despite that incident, and the retreat of our Forces from Europe, daily life at the School seemed to go on pretty much as normal. There were a few scares, as some hapless character would be found wandering about the cross-country routes or near the swimming lake at California. All such 'sinister' sightings by the ever-vigilant boys were dutifully reported back to Maj

Hughes, who carried the nickname 'Captain Reely Foul'! The gallant major, holder of the Military Cross (MC) and bar, would thoughtfully stroke his luxurious moustache with feigned gravity, before interrogating the boys in his upper-crust drawl. Despite the boys' sense of great importance at their alertness and eagle-eyed sightings, nothing appears to have ever come from any of these incidents.

Sgt Joe Pettit had served at the School since 1939, a member of the Army Education Corps (AEC) and an excellent instructor in mathematics. They were dangerous days indeed for the country, so Joe decided that he'd like to *"do something about it"*. He asked for an interview with the Commandant and told him of his desire, but was told that everyone at the School was already 'doing something'. A further interview, this time with the local Brigadier, was then requested and, following that, Joe found himself posted as Education Officer to a unit in East Anglia, as part of an organisation that became known as the 'Air Defence of Great Britain'.

After falling out with the authorities on what he thought was the menial form of some of his duties, Joe was told in no uncertain terms that he could, if he so wished, transfer to the local Field Regiment (Regt) of the RA. But this would also mean him reverting to the lowest possible rank, that of Gunner. Joe stoically accepted this, but was quickly promoted back up to Lance Bombardier and, after some exciting service in Italy as an Artillery observer, eventually saw the war come to an end. Having been compulsorily transferred back to the AEC in the rank of Warrant Officer Class 1 (WO1), Joe later returned to the Apprentices' School here at Arborfield, where he subsequently became a civilian lecturer. A silver model of a '25-pounder' still adorns his sideboard, as a vivid and permanent reminder that, during the war, he certainly *"did something"*.

On July 19th 1940, General Sir Alan Brooke became Commander-in-Chief (C-in-C) of the British Home Forces. He remained in this vital post throughout the long war and was instrumental in both Britain's survival and its eventual victory against all odds. Some fifty-odd years later, it was the General's son, Victor Brooke, by then the inheritor of his father's title, 'Viscount Alanbrooke', who took up the challenge of making the first real attempt to put together this comprehensive history. Victor was then serving here at Arborfield as a Burnham Lecturer, following service in a previous military post.

The famous 'One Hundred'

March / April of 1941 saw the School's only intake of that year, exactly 100 potential Armourer apprentices who, apart from those who fell by the wayside, became the last boys to be cap-badged to the RAOC. Peter Langley was one of that unique 'one hundred' and remembers the momentous day that he climbed aboard a train at Chesterfield, in rural Derbyshire, *en route* to Reading. Full of apprehension, he was grateful to find another boy, Bill Hunter from Glasgow, also engaged on 'the great adventure'. Almost inevitably, he and Bill became *"close pals"* during their three Arborfield years, but have never seen each other since those

Gleaming porcelain and polished chrome.

distant days.

Peter recalls disembarking from the old steam train *"on the station forecourt, in blacked out wartime gloom"*. A number of other boys got off the same train, all similarly *"bemused, dishevelled and apprehensive"*, and Peter wondered why it hadn't been arranged for them all to travel in the same carriage, where their spirits may have been boosted by each other's company. Herded onto a waiting bus, the boys were driven to Wokingham station, where another group of boys joined them, this time, according to Peter, *"depressingly large, noisy and confident"*. On top of that, they were all dressed in khaki uniforms and wore shorts! Peter's heart sank, as he had only recently moved into long trousers and thought that now he would have to revert to shorts for the next three years. It turned out, however, that this group was from the DYRMS, the shorts being part of their customary mode of dress.

Upon arrival at the ATS, the boys were first led to *"a dimly lit, noisome cavern"*, which turned out to be the Cookhouse! Only the stodgy 'duff' and watery custard remain in Peter's memory, as his next port of call gave a further shock to the system. The boys had entered their barrack room, only to find that their so-called beds were only three feet long! It took a little while for it to sink in that the beds were adjustable, where the bottom half pulled out to extend to a six foot length, or less, as required. The 'mattress' was made up from separate parts, for some reason unknown to Peter at the time, being referred to as 'biscuits'. One fact that he *does* remember is that, after all the nervous excitement of that first day, he crawled gratefully under the blankets and slept like the proverbial top!

One of Peter's drill sergeants, who went by the name of 'Turkey' Cooper, probably due to his long neck, which would turn red when he was annoyed, once told his squad that they were *"the pick of the bunch"*, in the fact that they were training to be Armourers. *"You,"* said the sergeant, a member of the King's Own Yorkshire Light Infantry (KOYLI), *"will learn a proper trade. Vehicle mechanics? All they do is assemble engines and then run them in"*, or words to that effect. Peter says there must have been a *"smidgen of truth in it"*, as they, the Armourers, made all their own tools, without recourse to a lathe and, even today, Peter can put his hands on an odd-shaped punch that he thought had been confined to the *"Lee-Enfield scrapbook"* of memories!

As part of the School's general 'health-care' facilities, Peter had occasion to pay an unforgettable visit to the dentist's chair, an unhappy experience he had no desire to repeat afterwards. The dental equipment *"came out of the Ark"* and Peter had to endure several painful fillings. Better days were ahead however, as he began regularly attending the Baptist Church in nearby Wokingham, along with fellow apprentices 'Polly' Packman and 'Kitch' Kitchener. Rather than religious fervour however, perhaps it was the appearance of two pretty girls, named Betty and Joyce, which encouraged the three boys to pursue this church-going pastime!

The subject of education figures strongly in Peter's memories, particularly in the shape of a couple of his military instructors. Sgt French was one of a family who ran the pub, in the very village in which Peter had grown up, while the sergeant's brother had actually married Peter's English teacher. One thing that has always stuck in Peter's mind is Sgt French's remark, upon America's eventual entry into the war after the Japanese surprise and infamous raid on Pearl Harbour in December of 1941 – *"Good, now we shall win"* – prophetic words indeed.

Another of Peter's educators was WO2 'Lofty' Armstrong, who he reckoned had a physique that would make even a split-pin look voluptuous! Lofty had a saying that would always make the boys laugh, *"I've got a brother at home, he's taller than me but not so well built"*. This gentleman must have been the same 'Lofty the Schoolie', as recalled by Fred Ford, being almost seven feet high. Fred recalls that both Joe Pettit and 'Lofty' were *"very patient, excellent teachers and a credit to their calling"*.

The McNally years

May 1941 brought the arrival of a new RSM, R L McNally of the Scots Guards, who was destined to serve the School so memorably for the next fifteen years. It was also in 1941 that the 'Drum and Fife Band' was formed, composed entirely of twenty ex-Dukie boys from Dover. They supported those *"unfit for war"* members of the Band of the 4th/7th Royal Dragoon Guards, who had been temporarily stationed here at the School whilst their own Regiment was away on active service. These 'musical maestros' became very popular over the next couple of years and were much in demand to play at local concerts and other such events.

They were to grow in strength by 1943 to some

fifty members, but the enforced 'dispersal' of the following year saw numbers fall away drastically, until the School was once again able to settle back into its normal routine. The Band played and marched under the leadership of its proud Bandmaster, WO1 Cyril Nel, who was the arranger of the first official Corps March 'Lillibulero – Heigh Ho'. Fred Ford recalls him as *"a smart, dapper, not very tall gentleman"*. Apparently he was saluted in error by all and sundry, by virtue of the fact that he was the only Warrant Officer, at that time, permitted to wear collar and tie with his uniform. *(This seems to have been a common error amongst boys of many following eras! Based no doubt on the premise – if it moves, salute it! And if it doesn't move, well salute it anyway! Ed.)*

Many boys will call to mind the Bandmaster as 'Bandy', while Art Cockerill, who was to join up with 43B remembers him by the nickname 'Shiner' Nel. Yet another old boy, 42A's Brian Conway, called him 'Shiny-O', in reference to his *"ever-immaculate turnout, shining like a new pin, from his highly polished shoes and Sam Browne belt to his slicked-down shiny black hair"*.

Whatever name may have been given to Mr Nel by the boys at the time, Peter Langley remembers meeting up with the same gentleman some years later, during a period of service in Palestine in 1948. Trevor O'Callaghan, who was at the School between 1942 and 1945, reports that when he later met up with the 4th/7th DG Band in Tripoli in 1949, most of the original 'Arborfield' members had by then either moved on or left the Army.

(A short history on the Bandmaster, along with some 'Band Notes' by the man himself, are attached as separate annexes to this chapter.)

Many years later, Roger Millard of 46A submitted an article to the *OBAN*, which included an account of life at Arborfield, written by a George White, a member of the 4th/7th military band at the time. In his own words, George described his experience:

"My own service with the regiment started at the AAS Arborfield. The 4th/7th Band, very much depleted at the time, formed the nucleus of the School Band, supplemented by about fifty apprentices. They played at most of the usual functions, providing the

dance band, pit orchestra for shows, marching band for parades and drills. Then, on Sunday's church parade, a band for three successive church services of the main denominations, followed by a march-past."

George had transferred to the Band after serving for about eighteen months as an apprentice electrician. When he became a band boy, he recalls that 'Boy' was an actual rank. George later went on to study at the Royal Military School of Music, Kneller Hall, and was subsequently appointed Bandmaster of the King's African Rifles in Dar-es-Salam, Tanganyika, East Africa. Following that country's subsequent independence from British colonial rule, there was a mutiny, and George and his family eventually had to be rescued by troops from the British Army stationed in neighbouring Kenya.

As previously mentioned, there were many boys who had already benefited from a military-style upbringing at one of those schools dedicated to the teaching of servicemen's sons. The Duke of York's was one such school – resplendent in their forage caps, tunics and khaki shorts; another was the Queen Victoria School, whose boys wore glengarries, tunics and short trews; while a third was the Gordon Boys' School, based not too far away at Woking, in Surrey. Fred Ford also recalls several boys from Dr Barnados' Homes, with *"their little red jackets and huge white starched collars"*.

Harold Price had joined up with 42A from a purely civilian background, but affectionately remembers both the Dukies and the Queen Vics, with whom he shared room 'K1', as a *"great bunch of lads"*. One of that 'great bunch' was Harry Budd. With his father already a Major with the Gloucestershire Regiment, Harry had joined his brother as a Dukie at the tender age of nine years and six months. On the outbreak of war, with Dover deemed an unsuitable place for young boys, several boys, including Brian Conway, were moved up to join the Queen Vics at their school at Dunblane in Scotland. It is likely that Dukie boys were moved around quite a lot during those days, as Brian also recalls being at Cheltenham for a time.

Anyway, after a period of indefinite leave, Harry Budd and the other boys with him later found themselves ensconced at a *"magnificent hotel"* at a place called Saunton Sands, on the north coast of Devon near Barnstaple. Brian Conway was also to end up there and the Dukie boys' educational studies were able to continue in a more peaceful atmosphere. Then, in January 1942, dressed in his khaki uniform, with short trousers, Harry arrived at the ATS (Boys).

In that very same month, approximately 250 other 42A apprentices arrived here at Arborfield, the first to be badged into the General Service Corps (GSC). Harry's choice of trade was decided by the toss of a coin – 'heads', mechanical, or 'tails', electrical. He thus became one of the first Radio Mechanics, still bearing the scars on his thumb, left from chipping away at steel with hammer and chisel. Harry soon became a LCpl in 'C' Coy, and recalls that he always looks back on those days as *"life in the fast lane"*.

Remember old 'Wotsisname'?

John Shaw also joined as one of those 42A boys. It is not an uncommon name, but John shouldn't be confused with the 46B boy as mentioned later in 1994! This John recalls *"very few names of the permanent staff"*, but goes on to say that one name that has always stuck in his memory is that of Sgt Taffy Evans of the SWB. John couldn't quite remember just why he had carried Taffy's name with him through all those years that followed, he hadn't been particularly 'hard' on him, or anything like that, but must just have come across as *"a good soldier, someone to imitate"*.

Harold Price recalls one of the PTIs, a Cpl Peacock, who certainly lived up to his name as he had a magnificent tattoo of that famously multi-coloured bird covering the whole of his back! One of Cpl Peacock's favourite 'games' was Bingo. But hardly the one we know today! In the Gym, the windows were very high up, operated by long strings pulled from below at floor level. At the ends of the strings were attached wooden 'acorns'. Cpl Peacock would line up any boys deemed to have misbehaved against the wall-bars, hit them on the head with one of these 'acorns' and yell, *"Bingo"*!

Harold also seems to remember that it was a certain Sgt Hotchkiss who cut down the tree at the top of the Square (where the later accommodation block was built around 1957). Robert Powell, who joined in October '39 also remembers the same tree! He has a photograph of 'No.3' Wing, 'C' Coy, taken under that very tree. Robert recalls the time he was called up before Col Davies, who commanded the School for around a year, for a misdemeanour. Having been given fourteen days leave, Robert calculated that as he

had left on a Tuesday, he was due back on a Tuesday too – wrong! Fortunately, the Commandant lent a sympathetic ear to Robert's tale of woe and let him off with *"a strong admonition"*. Robert was medically discharged in 1945, following an accident.

Those early years of the Second World War had already brought about the realisation that the Army's existing repair system, as efficient as it may have previously seemed, was not now able to support the massive scale of equipment being deployed in every far-flung theatre of war. Thus it was that, during 1941, the War Cabinet directed Sir William Beveridge to conduct an enquiry, which would look closely into the employment of technical manpower in the Services.

January of 1942 brought further bad news from the Far Eastern warfront, with Japanese troops landing in Borneo, then later laying siege to the island of Singapore, the British Empire's great bastion in south-east Asia. Another of the ex-Dukies who joined Arborfield that month was Bert Austin, who also recalls that the DYRMS had by then been moved to Saunton Sands. Bert remembers going to the pictures in the nearby town of Barnstaple the night before arriving here at Arborfield but, to his eternal shame, cannot now recall a single name of those boys who accompanied him at the time. *(It's a long time ago Bert! Maybe one was Harry Budd? Ed.)*

Bert's memory did manage to recall that, after he arrived at the AAS, he took a trip out to Aldershot with some mates. This was in order to see the local football side, packed with League-class players in those wartime days, take on the mighty Arsenal. They saw the game all right, but then an oily fog came down and all buses were cancelled for the night. Fortunately for the boys, the Military Police took pity on them and gave them a lift as far as Camberley, but from there on it was still a long walk back to Camp.

Formation of REME

As a result of the 1942 recommendations made by the *'Beveridge Inquiry'*, the Corps of the 'Royal Electrical and Mechanical Engineers' was formed on 1st October of that very same year, its very existence based upon the necessity to concentrate the Army's equipment repair resources into one specific organisation. As described in the words of then General Montgomery himself, *"REME exists to keep the punch in the Army's fist"*.

From its inception, the new Corps was deemed to be 'combatant', with detachments serving with front line troops in every major theatre of operations. Its very motto reinforces that fact – 'Arte et Marte' is the Latin for 'by skill and by fighting'. REME inherited many establishments and projects that, for some time, had involved its principal predecessor, the RAOC Engineering Branch, which had formed only one and a half per cent of the Army. Significantly, from the formation of the REME, all of the current RAOC boys here at the AAS were immediately re-badged into REME, the remainder keeping their GSC badges. Arborfield was thus, to all intents and purposes, the first school with a direct affiliation to the newly formed Corps.

Early cap badges

In January earlier that year, at the tender age of fifteen, young Eric Corscadden had never travelled away from home on his own before. So, rather than inflict the terrors of the London Underground upon him, his parents sent him from his home in Crewe, Cheshire, first by one train to Birmingham and then on another to Reading. But instead of then getting a bus directly to Arborfield, Eric inadvertently managed to take yet another train, this one to Wokingham, before he eventually made his entrance at the School. Although this was only a single week behind other members of 42A, Eric was really concerned that he would be at a disadvantage.

Met at the Camp gates by the Provost Sergeant, Eric was duly asked for his name. Upon hearing his response, with mention of his rather unusual surname, Sgt Hotchkiss quickly asked another question, *"Is your father in the Army?"* When Eric replied in the affirmative, yet another question rapidly followed – *"What regiment is he with?"* Having noticed the sergeant's shoulder flashes, Eric's reply was *"The*

same one as you, Sergeant". *"I thought so,"* said the sergeant, *"he was my RSM at the Depot"*. Eric tended to steer clear of Sgt Hotchkiss from then on! Oh, and his travelling skills must have improved somewhat, as he later found his way to NZ, where he is now happily settled on its North Island at Auckland.

Personal tragedy had unfortunately preceded Ronald Callaghan's entry into intake 42A. Back on one fateful day in September 1938, a full year before the outbreak of the Second World War, a RAF plane had tragically crashed out of the skies, demolishing not only his home, but a large part of the surrounding area. Fourteen people had died in that dreadful accident, amongst them his mother, his sister and two of his brothers. Another brother, as well as his father, was badly burned at the same time.

Bravely putting this all behind him, in January 1942 a rather bedraggled Ron arrived here at Arborfield in the *"hissing rain"*, in company with another young lad called Murray. They were welcomed into the Guardroom with a couple of mugs of steaming hot cocoa, then marched down the road to 'D' Coy Office, where they met up with the Company Commander, Capt Johnson, and Squadron Sergeant Major (SSM) Towler. The SSM was affectionately known by the name 'Trumpy', being one of the members of the 4th/7th DGs and an accomplished French horn player in the School's Military Band.

Roy (Dusty) Ashman and John (Swiper) Saxton, April '42

What *did* they put in our tea?

To this very day, Ron retains less than fond memories of the infamous 'Cookhouse tea', with its insidious 'chemical' taste, which all the boys *knew* to be caused by the addition of bromide. This 'rumour' has persisted throughout the ages, that a daily dose of bromide was added to the tea-urn in order to stifle the 'natural urges' of the adolescent boys. *(The rumour was still rife in the late Fifties, but the tactic hardly seems to have worked! Ed.)* Whether true or not, Ron became an avid coffee drinker during those days and has remained so ever since! *(Was it real coffee then Ron, or 'ersatz'? Ed.)*

Harold Price, also of intake 42A, remembers a well-worn footpath that led across to the Auxiliary Territorial Service (ATS) girls' quarters on the other side of Ben Cook's ploughed field. Apparently, one nasty boy from 'B' Coy had taken to frightening the girls on this path early in the morning. Fortunately, he was caught when one girl managed to knock off his glasses, from which he was later identified. Harold reckons this caused almost as much excitement as when one of those same ATS girls, while cleaning the hot-plate from where meals were served, got a little too close and got burned in two rather tender but prominent spots, well off limits to all boys!

One of those ATS girls who joined the School in August 1942 was Pte Marjorie Clarke, now Mrs Baker and living in peaceful West Sussex. Marjorie and her civilian counterpart, Eileen Golding, were later able to boast that they typed up the very first issue of *The Arborfield Apprentice*, the School magazine, although this didn't happen until 1948. Marjorie recalls that, in her day, the ATS girls were encouraged to take part in many of the School leisure activities, she herself being part of the Choral Society, which was formed in 1943, as well as a member of the Dramatic Society. Perhaps a bit of a shock to the system was that the girls were also regularly taken out onto the Parade Square for drill practice under the beady eye of RSM McNally!

A visit by 'Monty'

As recalled by John Kidney (42A), it was also during 1942 that General Montgomery, or 'Monty' as he was universally known to the troops under his command, visited the School for the very first time. Monty had been made GOC Southern District in December the previous year, taking over from General Claude Auchinleck, the recently appointed Commander of British Forces in the Middle East, and was later to take command of the Eighth Army in the North African desert sands of Libya and Egypt. John had joined boys' service in April of that year, following five and a half years of incarceration with the Queen Vics.

Eric Cook, also of 42A, is another who recalls the visit from Monty that year, prior to his eventual taking up of the Middle East post. Here at the School, the General exhorted all of the assembled boys to *"aim high"*. Eric adds that those words really sank into his consciousness, but that the same advice was obviously not heeded by Monty's tank crews and gunners in the desert – which is just as well! Harry Budd's recollection is that, just before that parade, it was discovered that the General did not like 'highly bulled' boots, so that a hasty application of dubbin became the order of the day.

That visit from Monty also figures large in the memory of Mike Champken, who had joined in May 1939. He recalls that, on the big day, he was to be found lying on a stretcher, having injured his leg whilst going over an obstacle course the day before. Despite his injury, or rather due to the fact he hadn't realised how serious it was, he had gallantly continued to complete the course. When Monty was told this story by School Commandant, Col Frank Hilborn, he then told Mike that he (Monty) was soon to take up a new command and hoped that his men would show even half of Mike's courage in the battles to come. It is now history that his Eighth Army – including the famous 'Desert Rats' of 7th Armoured Brigade - certainly did all that was asked of them.

Unauthorised modifications

Lawrence Nixon joined Arborfield as an apprentice Inst Mech in April 1942. Reflecting upon his 'boy's service', he brings to mind the efforts that boys made in those days to make their uniforms rather less uniform! High on the list of priorities was 'slashing' the peak of the Service Dress (SD) cap and then 'propping' the front, usually with a piece of a toothbrush handle, trying to emulate a Guard's hat. Another dodge was wearing REME coloured fringe caps and replacing the ATS flashes with the REME badge as soon as they got away from Camp. All of these embellishments would certainly give the boys a hugely improved potential with any young ladies they may be fortunate enough to meet - or at least they hoped that would be the case!

Lawrence also mentions the seating arrangements in the Cookhouse, with senior boys 'at the top' and juniors 'at the bottom' – it is needless to say where the largest part of the food ended up! One of the exceptions was the occasional canister of 'chocolate rice', a concoction of rice pudding mixed with cocoa powder that, hardly surprisingly, was universally unpopular. Because of this, Lawrence forced himself to become the world's best 'chocolate rice' consumer, tucking away vast quantities of the stuff – at least *he* didn't go hungry!

Intake 42A also included Charles – or Charlie – Ashdown, who went on to complete more than fifty years of service with the Armies of various countries. Even almost sixty years later, and now living in Charlotte, North Carolina, USA, he recalls Arborfield as his *"defining experience"*. Writing in the *OBAN* of autumn 1999, he went on to say:

> *"When we joined the School, we were very young and extremely malleable. We learned (sometimes willingly) the elements of soldiering, physical fitness, personal hygiene, trade and educational subjects, team dynamics and tradecraft skills. To some, a few of these experiences were considered of little value and have been discarded. To many others, myself included, these experiences have remained throughout our lives, shaping our careers, whether within the service or without."*

Charlie was also reminded of a certain musical incident, of which he had retained no memory, until reading a letter from Bryan Norman to the *OBAN* many years later. As a member of the 'Corps of Drums', formed in early 1942, Charlie was subsequently appointed as bass drummer. The drum at the time was rather a small nondescript affair and Col Hilborn had decided that a much larger one was required, to provide a more adequate output of 'pomp and circumstance'. The main drawback was that, in order for Charles to beat both sides with sufficient gusto, the drum had to be hoisted so far up onto his chest that his forward vision was seriously impaired. This led to the incident in mind, when poor Charlie, during the counter-march, managed to clout the neighbouring cymbal player violently on the nose, causing a rather unfortunate loss of blood from his nasal passages!

There is another 'Charlie and his Bass Drum' story that has him being carefully guided, by the rest of the Corp of Drums, onto a post in the middle of the entrance to Cintra Park in Reading. This is disputed by Brian Conway who says that, as Drum Major,

he wouldn't have allowed such a thing to happen; certainly not when one considers the damage it could have done to the bass drum!

Young Ashdown's talents were obviously wide-ranging! As well as being a talented Band member, he also found that he had inherited, from various members of senior intakes, the skill and dexterity that was required of being able to modify the peaked hats that went with the '1908 pattern' SD cap. This he would convert into a more fashionable style, as mentioned earlier by Lawrence Nixon, where the peak pointed straight down at one's nose, Guardsman-style, rather than at right angles to it. Charlie's great skill was in achieving all this 'by natural means', without recourse to either a 'prop' or 'slashing'. Still highly illegal of course, this modification was frowned upon by the powers-that-be as 'destruction of Government property' – but then the School was always a hotbed of the current fashion!

Thus, Charlie was often asked by his comrades to perform this sleight-of-hand operation on their own caps, and eventually built up a collection of such in the top compartment of his locker. It was his ill luck that Sgt Taffy Evans spotted this array of headgear and Charlie found himself 'on orders'. However, since no actual 'damage' could be attributed to Charlie, he was instead charged with that good old Army stand-by offence, of *"conduct to the prejudice of good order and military discipline"*. Funnily enough, the worst part of his punishment was not the actual ten days CB, but the tongue-lashing he received from Mr McNally, delivered at a distance of about one inch from Charlie's face, which remains imprinted on his brain-cells to this very day!

Get those arms up!

Bryan Norman had also joined in April 1942. He remembers one particular parade, sometime during that year or the following one, when the RSM was standing beside the saluting base, exhorting the marching boys to *"Get those arms up"*. To his severe and lasting embarrassment, his set of false teeth suddenly flew out of his mouth, right into the path of and under the crunching boots of the advancing 'B' Coy platoon. Unfortunately for the RSM, none of the boys was in a position to stop and avoid them! *(Suppose that was a right kick in the teeth then? Ed.)*

John Kidney's recollections of those far off days

are, as he is the first to admit, a little hazy and he is always amazed at the ability of others to remember their past so vividly. He had arrived at Arborfield after more than five years at the Queen Victoria School, which he had hated, and he was less than enamoured by his subsequent time at the ATS (Boys) too! But it had been a choice of *"join the Army or go home to Daddy"*, so John had chosen what he thought would be the lesser of two evils. Looking back, he reckons that all the stories written about the School are basically variations on the same scheme, equally plausible whether labelled 1942, 1952, or 1962! *(Each to his own, or so the saying goes. Ed.)*

By mid-1946, John was on board a troopship on his way to the Middle East, spending most of the voyage trying to get a sun tan, as he didn't think that white knobbly knees, poking from beneath starched khaki shorts, quite looked the part. Disembarking at Port Said, he soon found that the locals were quite good at selling things. Because, when he got onto the train, he found that he now owned a leather cosh, two dirty books and a watch that didn't work! Having served briefly – but not briefly enough - at Tel-el-Kebir, known to one and all as 'TEK', John later found himself in Palestine at 3 Base Wksp. Here, the military staff was looking for ex-boys willing to become Regimental Training Instructors. John quite fancied that, quickly became a sergeant and actually started to like the Army a little more.

Back at Arborfield, another member of that 42A contingent, Ken Burren, was most impressed by his first six months in the Fitting and Machine Shops. First lesson – how to reduce a three-inch block of metal down to the size of an *'Oxo cube'*! (Dick Wade remembers this test-piece well, but says that all his needed was a set of dots, from one to six, on its sides and it could have been used as a dice!) Having got through that meaningful task, Ken then found his true passion in life – operating the lathe and other such turning machines. He learned all he could under the patient instruction of 'Baldy' Boylett, who he believes was an ex-Woolwich Arsenal man, becoming highly skilled at all aspects of the fitting trade. After leaving the Army, Ken went on to run his own small machine shop down in Whitstable, Kent, giving thanks to the painstaking assistance he had received, both here at Arborfield and later during his adult service in REME and the world at large.

Many years later, Ken was lying in a lonely hospital bed and was pleasantly surprised to get a visit from Paul 'Tug' Wilson, from his old intake. They went on to meet up for a chat on a regular basis – their wives would say that they could *"talk the hind leg off a donkey"*. Up to that visit from Tug, Ken hadn't even known of any Arborfield organisation for old boys. He, being a 'man of Kent' thought that anyone between the ages of six and sixty was an 'old boy' – either *"this old boy"* or *"that old boy"*. *(It's the way he tells it! Ed.)*

The life of Brian

Brian 'Titch' Conway's father, a regular soldier in the RE, had always wanted his son to concentrate on learning a trade, rather than taking up a musical career. Brian also believes his father had visions of him going to 'the other School' at Chepstow, with perhaps a career in the same Corps to follow. When Brian eventually arrived here at Arborfield to join intake 42A however, fate had decreed that both trade *and* music would figure large in the rest of 'The Life of Brian'.

One of the first persons that Brian met was the previously mentioned 'Bandy' – sorry, 'Shiny-O' - Nel. Having just spent five years as a member of the band at the Dukies, Brian was instantly able to recognise the harp badge on the Bandmaster's sleeve. This gave him a 'slight edge', and it wasn't too long before Brian was told that he was to join the School Corps of Drums – *"music to my ears"*, as he later put it! Largely due to his previous experience at the DYRMS, Brian was later to be appointed as the first boy Drum Major of Arborfield's Corps of Drums.

Brian recalls a particular morning drill session, during which one unfortunate boy just couldn't get it right. Unknown to the squad, RSM McNally had come riding up behind them on his bicycle. Pointing his pace-stick at the hapless apprentice, he yelled, *"Get a hold of it, lad!"* The poor lad obviously didn't appreciate the meaning of this term in its 'drill' sense. He actually grabbed hold of the shiny pace-stick and pulled it from the astonished RSM's grasp! *(He no doubt got the message after that! Ed.)*

On his first visit to the NAAFI canteen, shortly after arriving in January 1942, good-natured Bernard Gilbert fell for one of the oldest tricks in the book. A senior A/T asked him if he could *"change a two-bob piece"*, and of course he could. It was only later that Gilbert found the coin to be a copper penny, tightly wrapped in silver foil! You had to learn quickly in those days. Bernie also recalls that, on parade one fine morning,

RSM McNally reported a shortage of toilet paper, as far too much was being used. To the eternal amusement of the assembled lads, they were sharply told that *"one wipe upwards, followed by one wipe downwards"* should be sufficient. Well, it was wartime, after all!

A newly arrived member of the PS during 1942 was Cpl Herbert J Valentine, RAOC, operating as the Company Clerk to 'A' Coy, but also 'doubling up' as a trumpeter in the School Band. He recalls that the Band was always in demand at 'Wings for Victory' parades and such like at Wokingham while, on one occasion, they provided the orchestra for an evening of 'old-time dancing' at the dignified venue of Reading Town Hall. A sizeable dance band could often be produced in those days and Herbert can remember playing one engagement at the Officers' Club in Aldershot. During his later days here, Herbert was one of those soldiers involved in the dispersal of 1944, going first to Gopsall Hall and then on to Bury, in south Lancashire.

Many boys of the era still reminisce about Cpl Alf Danahar, here on the PS at the time, and also the Amateur Boxing Association (ABA) welterweight champion, who had made full use of his speciality, a notorious and devastating left-hook to the body. Alf's brother Arthur, here at the same time, was a contender for the professional title at the same weight. Peter Langley recalls the pair of them putting on an 'exhibition bout' for the benefit of the boys, but reckons it was a fairly tame affair.

More dark days

In the early days of 1942, Japanese forces were rampaging through the Philippines, New Guinea, the Solomon Islands and Borneo. By February 15th, the great British naval base of Singapore, seemingly impregnable, had fallen. June 1942 brought the dark news that Tobruk, with its deep-water harbour, had fallen to Rommel's forces in Libya. Some 25,000 Allied troops, mainly British, Australian and Indian, are believed to have been captured. However, with the German advance on Cairo and the Suez Canal brought to a halt at El Alamein in July, a great turning point was finally about to be reached in the fortunes of war. Command of the Eighth Army was given to Lt Gen Montgomery the following month, while around the same time, General Sir Harold Alexander took over the post of C-in-C, Middle East.

Joe Griffiths's boys' service is recalled, like hundreds of others of the time, against a backdrop of menacing wartime news. The British Army had been chased out of France and was being overrun in mainland Greece and on the island of Crete. That desert battle against Rommel's Afrika Corps see-sawed back and forth – Tobruk, Benghazi, Buk Buk, these were the places much in the news. One of Joe's friends told him that his father had been wounded in the desert – *"a bullet in the back"* was how he described it.

When Joe heard that the Royal Navy's two mighty battleships, His Majesty's Ships *'Prince of Wales'* and *'Renown'* had been sunk, attempting to defend Singapore against the Japanese, he *"felt sick to his stomach for days"*. Closer to home, the Luftwaffe bombing campaign was laying waste to the major industrial cities, but from the comparative safety of rural Arborfield, the boys could only fearfully hear and read about such events. Behind it all though, lay the quiet confidence that the British Army would win through. Joe's father had told him so – and what further authority did he need?

Edward Tanner joined the School on October 6th 1942, which qualified him to remain forever afterwards, part of intake 42B. He remembers just how tall and menacing the RSM looked, towering over this miniscule boy of only fourteen years. He also called to mind the inter-room competitions held each month, to find out which room would benefit by having access to the wireless for the next four weeks – usually won by the 'old sweats' by fair means or foul.

Another vivid memory he has is of the number of boys whose faces were painted with 'gentian violet' by the Medical Officer (MO), as borne out by tales of impetigo by other boys of the time. With the milk ration having just been reduced to only two and a half pints per person per week, it is no wonder that many boys were 'out of sorts'. Edward's one over-riding recollection of his three-year stint however, as he puts it himself, is – *"What a wonderful basis for life in general the School provided"*.

Frank Penfold would certainly echo that thought. He was a 42C apprentice, who went on to achieve the rank of Lt Col, be awarded the MBE and serve a total of thirty-nine years. His father had held a commission in the Royal Army Medical Corps (RAMC) during 1942, but was away on active service, so joining up to learn a trade seemed the natural thing for young Frank to do.

He recalls that one of his intake was *"rather*

sweet" on one of the Army girls who worked in the Cookhouse. The strictness of the regime at the School made *"courting"* rather difficult, but Frank's pal soon found a way around this. He became very adept at getting himself *"put on jankers"*, which would inevitably lead to a period of scrubbing pots and pans in the Cookhouse. As no one else really fancied the task, the young man in question would always volunteer to take it on. Thus, he was able to carry out his romantic encounters in the Army's time and even walk the young lady back to her quarters in the evening, without ever being suspected. As Frank was later to put it, *"That's enterprise!"*

Frank, who later in 1944 was one of those boys dispersed to Ashford in Kent, can also recall the day when a 0.303" rifle was fired in one barrack room, with the bullet crossing the whole width of the Square and passing through two wooden walls. Finally, it lodged itself deeply in the leg of a rather surprised boy named Judson. Frank fails to name who fired the weapon, or whether the incident was accidental or not, which is probably just as well!

A musical interlude

One of the 42A intake was Alex 'Sandy' Cunningham, who fondly recalls a notorious film show in the Camp Hall, one which caused some rather riotous behaviour. Those of us who can remember the 'Busby Berkeley' musical extravaganzas will be able to picture this well, even though the film was shot in the old 'black and white'. A large troupe of long legged, lavishly – though scantily - dressed dancing girls descending around a revolving fountain, each one carrying a rather large man-sized banana, with the fountain's output gushing out all around them.

Peter Langley says that, in the particular scene that caused a near riot, the girls were lying on their backs amongst these fountain jets, arms and legs moving in the fashion of today's 'synchronized swimming'. This gave the appearance that the girls were actually peeing into the air! Needless to say, this brought forth a lascivious cacophony of sound from the assembled audience of apprentices, and RSM McNally had to roar, implore and threaten at the top of his voice, generally causing even more bedlam, before he was able to bring things back into some semblance of order.

The next morning, the whole School population of boys was marched into a 'hollow square' formation on the Square, while the RSM 'got tore in' to the bunch of 'orrible 'ooligans that paraded in front of him. He reminded the boys that there had been ladies present at the film-show, including not only the Commandant's wife, but also the Adjutant's daughters and an assortment of ATS girls from the Cookhouse and typing pool. He admonished the boys, telling them that their behaviour had not been up to the required standard. They were *"a shame to the School and a disgrace to the Army"*. Anyway, this right old rollicking went on for some twenty minutes or so before the RSM eventually ran out of steam, sternly warning of the dire consequences for any future repeat of such excessive antics.

'Sandy' Cunningham also tells of a certain Reg Stipling, who must have been in one of the senior intakes. On the day that Sandy arrived at the School, Reg and a bunch from his intake decided that these new boys – the usual motley crew of 'Jeeps' (the long-used derogatory term for any junior person) - should undergo some form of 'initiation ceremony'. The younger lads were then 'stood to their beds' in various states of dress – or undress – while this terrifying gentleman, mimicking the authoritative voice of Provost Sergeant Hotchkiss, examined them in detail, prodding each one of them in turn with his stick. Sandy goes on to say that Reg became a very popular figure with the Arborfield boys during his time, so they obviously didn't hold that impromptu inspection against him.

Ron Jones arrived at the School in October 1942. His one abiding memory is of an incident when the boys in his barrack room 'A2' were standing in their gym shorts and plimsolls, awaiting the start of a hygiene inspection. Just before this, 'Bluey' Preston had discovered that the elastic in his Army shorts had broken. He had pulled it from the waistband and tied it around the outside of his shorts. Room NCO Ron Soanes called the boys to attention as the MO led his inspection party into the room. To his dismay, as he stamped his foot down, Bluey's knot was none too tight and a length of elastic *"catapulted lazily onto the middle of the deck"*. His voluminous shorts sank slowly to the ground and the embarrassed Bluey stood trembling, with his tackle on display to the world at large!

Another of that 42C intake was Alan Pritchard, who recalls two of the PS members of his day. Sgt Taffy Evans – yes, him again! - hailed from Swansea and his 'cheesecutter' cap hid a mop of *"flaming red hair"*. Taffy's speciality was the polishing of chinstraps and Alan remembers making such a hash of his own that Taffy took over the task, transforming what had been a scruffy-looking piece of leather into a highly polished strap. Taffy was also a maestro on the Drill Square. If the squad had performed badly, he would make them go around at the slow march until it hurt. As Alan puts it, *"Our calves suffered more than those in the veal trade!"* Alan also recalls Sgt 'Jock' Hunter of the King's Own Scottish Borderers (KOSB) – he of the cut-away tunic and trews, while a certain Corporal in the RAOC had a saying that went *"My name's Joe King – and I ain't joking!"*

Robert 'Bob' Dann well remembers his own days with 42C. Although he had never been very religious, he did find that going along with the biblical train of thought held certain advantages! Having first had the *"temerity, or maybe even bravery"* to become confirmed, he then began attending at morning communion, which meant missing the early morning muster parade. This would then be followed by a late breakfast, which would more often than not be a much larger helping than the normal one – so a good start to the day all round.

A victory to celebrate

November 1942 and, at last, some encouraging news came in from the different fronts of the war. General Montgomery's Eighth Army had broken through Rommel's Afrika Korps to win a famous victory at El Alamein, in the sand dunes and minefields of Egypt, during November and the Russian Army was now routing the Germans at Stalingrad. It has been said that up until that memorable battle, British forces had never tasted victory, but that afterwards they were not to taste defeat again throughout the remainder of the war.

Here at home, on November 15th, church bells were allowed to ring out in celebration across the land, for the first time since the threat of German invasion in 1940. Winston Churchill, having been Prime Minister since the early days of the long war, was moved to make his famous statement in the House of Commons: *"It is not the end. It is not even the beginning of the end. But it is perhaps the end of the beginning."*

For Michael Allcock of 42C, that Christmas was his first leave period. He remembers packing up every piece of kit to take home and show to his family. What a homecoming it turned out to be, with his family highly relieved to find out that their young

son and heir had settled down so well to the 'Army life'. However, upon returning to Arborfield, a serious bout of homesickness inevitably set in. But, thankfully, supportive letters from his family cheered him up and he was able to settle down once more.

Looking back to 1942, one must sympathise with the apprentices – all young boys - of the day in their aversion to wearing the brass 'ATS' insignia on their epaulettes, being thus often confused with the then familiar female element of the war-time Army, also named 'ATS' of course. This ATS had been formed in 1938, but was later to become the Women's Royal Army Corps (WRAC) in 1949.

However, behind every cloud is the fabled 'silver lining'. Bob Dann recalls that, on his first home leave at Christmas 1942, on a bus to Bishop's Waltham, down in deepest Hampshire, a lady passenger asked him what the letters 'ATS' stood for. Quick as a flash, Bob replied that it meant 'African Tank Service', at which the lady promptly paid his bus fare! With recent newspaper headlines heralding the great victory at El Alamein, it is no wonder that Bob was considered a hero! After the 1943 intake, the powers-that-be finally got the message. Cloth shoulder flashes, showing the words 'Army Technical School' in gold lettering on a black background, gave the boys a more dignified title, which they were able to proudly display from then on.

Another variation on the ATS theme is recalled by Doc Savage, who says that he heard it stood for the 'Academy of Technical Science'! Ron also makes an observation on the 'drainpipe' style of trousers during his era, as he says, they were *"a relic of the days of puttees"*. Even when they had that 'V' insert let in, they still didn't look right, while the variety of different shades of khaki never lent itself to the uniformity that was required. Perhaps there was another way of looking at it, as remarked by Brian Conway, many years later, *"Gad! How we apprentices must have fooled those dastardly German spies who lurked around the Bramshill Hunt, by wearing our ATS shoulder titles"*.

John Peters can also recall having some 'altercations and confrontations' (fights to the rest of us!) over his ATS shoulder brasses. He was another boy who had joined in 1942, at the age of fifteen. He says it took him hours to get here by train from Birmingham, but then there **was** a war on! John seems to think that only one boy was ever discharged during his (John's) three-year stay and that because of losing his leg after a tank had crushed it. *(This must have been Eric Clarke, as*

The Instrument Mechanic Workshops in later years. The roads are looking a little tired and to park a car there would have been unheard of in RSM McNally's days. There were a number of static water tanks scattered around the Camp - being repositories for all manner of objects over the years!

mentioned by Mike Dickinson, during the dispersal of 1944. Ed.) John goes on to say, referring to his apprenticeship, that *"they put you in a mould, closed the lid, applied steam and pressure – and at the end you emerged a far better person"*.

John fondly remembers his early days. He later ended up back here, towards the end of his career, as a civilian lecturer. It had been a hard life, but at least there was no confusion, everyone knew where he was going. There was no Ministry of Defence (MoD) then, only the War Office, and it was everyone's duty to destroy the King's enemies. John says that all kit could be left on one's bed, even personal valuables, it was guaranteed that they would still be there on return. He hadn't found anything difficult since the day he left, the training had been thorough and enabled him to spend the next fifty-four years either in, or working for, the Army.

Apart from a break that lasted for twelve months (from November 1939 to November 1940), during which time Col P G Davies, CMG, CBE, RAOC was in post, the first Commandant was to 'hold the chair' until September 1943. His regime thus saw not only the opening of the School, but also the formation of REME, forged in the heat of battle in the deserts of North Africa. Col Frank Hilborn was the only Commandant ever to serve a 'double tour', and this event was later commemorated by the re-naming of the then Stephenson Road (after the famous engineer) into Hilborn Road in his honour. It was during the 'first half' of his tour that Col Hilborn presented 'The Commandant's Cup' to the School, which was to be awarded each term to the apprentice judged to be 'Best Soldier and Leader'.

—§—

The art of Blacksmithing was an important piece of learning in the Craftsman's toolbox for over 50 years

Annex to Chapter 1

Bandmaster (WO1) Cyril Nel

Extract from a letter written by his son, Mike Nel, courtesy of Roy 'Slash' Gunby (42A):

Mike and his wife were on holiday in Madrid, when they found themselves in the company of Roy and Sally Gunby. Mike and Roy then found out that they had both served at Ford, had both been in the Army at Aqaba. Prior to that, Roy had been in Palestine, as had Mike's father. Mike then mentioned that his father's regiment had been the 4th/7th Dragoon Guards and that his father, Cyril, had been the regiment's Bandmaster. Imagine the surprise when Roy responded that he had known the Bandmaster at Arborfield, during his 'boys school' days here during the war years. Mike was indeed startled to find that his father should be so well remembered after a gap of some sixty years. Roy suggested that Mike should write some details of his father's life, as he was sure that members of the Old Boys' Association would find them of interest. Those details follow:

> *"We had lived in Farnborough (Hants) since 1939 and stayed there for many years. Dad remained with the 4th/7th, with postings to Palestine, Barnard Castle, Tripoli, Crookham and Germany, until 1955, when he retired from the Army. He then went, with my mother, to Baghdad on a three-year contract with the Iraqi Army (pre-Saddam of course) to set up and train two Army bands. Fortunately, he had a bit of Arabic from his earlier days in Egypt, but did not need to use it much.*
>
> *In 1958, they returned to Farnborough and, in 1960, moved to East Preston, in Sussex. He took up a job with the West Sussex Education Department and taught band instruments at a number of schools, as well as giving private tuition. There was a brief moment of fame, when one of the school bands was featured on television.*
>
> *In 1970, when he was 65, he stopped teach-*

> *ing in schools, but continued with the private tuition for another six years. Although he was in reasonable health and spent a lot of time in his vegetable garden, he eventually died in late 1982, after a short illness."*

Mike goes on to say that he remembers, when he was about seven or eight years old, being given either Christmas or birthday presents, toys that he felt sure had been made by Arborfield apprentices. One such toy was a wheelbarrow, while the other was a ship that 'exploded' upon the release of a button on its side. He says a belated *"thank you"* to whosoever made these toys, as toys were generally hard to come by in those days.

(The above article is based upon that published in the OBAN issue Number 23 of autumn/winter 2001.)

Band Notes (Drum and Fife)

This band is composed entirely of A/Ts and was formed in 1941. Like the Military Band, it started with a modest twenty. All the boys were from the Duke of York's School. This band grew until, last year, it numbered fifty performers. Unfortunately, over half have recently left the School and now, after a five-month break, they are starting (again) from scratch. They now number twenty-two but there are many volunteers who, as soon as they are trained, will take their place in the band.

From 1941 until April 1943, the Drum and Fife Band was in constant demand for outside engagements. Nearly every Saturday and Sunday they would be playing in some town or another. They were always very popular, wherever they played. Each week there was invariably a letter of congratulations from the various Boroughs; these were published in School Orders. Apart from the letters, one only had to mention the name of the 'Drums' of the ATS (Boys) in Reading, Henley, Wokingham, Basingstoke and countless other towns, to invoke a universal reply like the following: *"I think they are a splendid lot of boys, so smart and so keen"*. It is such remarks that gladden the hearts of the boys, as well as the Staff of the School. From the boys' point of view, they are happy in the knowledge that they are helping to put the School on the map and, for the Staff, it is good to know their training has borne fruit.

A/T Conway, the original Drum Major, has left us now, along with A/T Connell, the leading tipper, and many others. We wish them all the best of luck. At the time of writing, A/T Parsons, a very capable and smart boy, is acting as Drum Major for both the Military Band and the Drum and Fife.

Upon the outbreak of war, the 4th/7th Royal Dragoon Guards were immediately drafted overseas, leaving the Bandmaster, his boys, and a few members of the Band at Aldershot. After a month of inactivity, we were sent to this School for musical duties. We were not sufficiently strong in numbers to form a properly balanced band but, fortunately, there were two or three of the Staff who were ex-bandsmen, plus a few A/Ts who had previously played in school bands. So, after a fortnight's concentrated practice, we were able to turn out a band of twenty-nine for our first parade; this was voted a huge success. Previously, a loudspeaker at the bottom of the Square gave out the only available music. As regards volume, this was very good; the drawback was the necessity of changing records during the march-past, causing the boys to lose their step!

Since its first appearance, the band has grown larger and larger until, last year, it reached its peak with a complement of eighty-six. This was composed of twenty-three Staff and the remainder A/Ts. These boys have all had a grounding in music from either the 'Duke of York's', 'Queen Victoria's' or 'St Mary's' and, with the small amount of practice they receive, some very good results have been obtained. Last year, fourteen A/Ts, all Armourers, left the School. These had all played in the band since their arrival. Consequently, they had become very proficient upon their instruments and, naturally, their departure was a great loss to the band.

During the last three years, the band has had numerous engagements. Every year they have played for the Savings Campaign, and great was the praise for both their marching and playing. Out of the large band, a combination numbering some twenty-six to thirty is chosen, to play Military Band programmes. This band has played twice at Basingstoke, three times at Cintra Park, Reading, besides at several garden parties. The majority of these have been paid engagements.

We have had many changes since 1939, too many

to mention in detail. We regret to say that three of the 4th/7th band-boys, who attained the age of eighteen and re-joined the Regiment for active service, have since been killed in action, following D-Day. Their names are Troopers Cox, Edmed and Moffatt. To the others who have left, we wish the best of luck; to those who have recently arrived, we extend a hearty welcome, especially to Cpl Coombes, who was originally the solo cornet of the 4th/7th RDG's Band. He was unfortunately shot in France and taken prisoner. After three-and-a-half years at German hospitals and Stalags, he has now been re-patriated.

Due to the five-month lapse while the School was temporarily disbanded, the band itself ceased to function. During that time, a number of A/Ts 'came of age' and left the band. We wish them luck in their new venture, as well as speedy promotion. A number of new boys who are instrumentalists have arrived and we hope that, by the time that this appears in print, they will have settled down to become seasoned players.

We are very sorry to lose Squadron Quartermaster Sergeant (SQMS) McCarthy, who was recently discharged from the service on medical grounds. He had served twenty-three years in the 4th/7th and had done yeoman service for the School during his four-year stay. We wish him a speedy recovery and may good fortune attend him wherever he goes!

And now to finish with a touch of humour. Every year, it is the custom for the Director of Music of the Royal Military School of Music to inspect each band of the British Army. The Bandmaster, Band Sergeant and band are tested upon everything in the curriculum of band work. One of the tests for the band is on 'the elements of music'; everyone is supposed to know these. One boy was asked, *"What is an interval?"* - to which the correct answer should have been, *"The difference in pitch between two musical sounds"*. The boy's reply, much to the amusement of all present, was given as, *"An interval, Sir, is a break for a tea and a wad"*!

(The above article is based upon that published in the first ever edition of The Arborfield Apprentice, dated December 1944. It was initialled 'C.N.' and was obviously written by the Bandmaster himself, Cyril Nel.)

Visit of the Secretary of State for War circa 1941/42

Chapter 2

1943 - 44

The tide begins to turn

The early months of 1943 saw the fortunes of war gradually being turned in favour of 'the Allies' in most parts of the globe. With the threat of a cross-Channel invasion of Britain now long since removed, it was announced that church bells could once again be rung out on Sundays and other special days. However, even with victory at last in sight, there was still no time to relax, with the famous *'Dig for Victory'* posters displayed everywhere. Back gardens and public parks had been conscripted for the war effort, and these posters with their national slogan no doubt brought a wry smile to Ben Cook's face! With Arborfield's position in a mainly rural area, road names and signposts would soon start to re-appear, with a relaxation of the previous legislation that had seen all such displays removed in the interests of national security.

April of 1943 saw the arrival of young Archie Smith, about to start his three-year apprenticeship as a General Fitter, which eventually evolved into him becoming a Gun Fitter. He 'fondly' remembers groups of boys being marched briskly down the road from morning parade to the Workshops, dressed in their greatcoats and steel helmets, carrying 1914-style gas masks, and led by the School's Pipe Band. He hastens to add that the Band was excused from dressing in the same manner as the rest of the boys!

Other memories he has are the quotations, such as the one attributed to Sgt Herbie Payne. When he was on duty as Orderly Sergeant, Herbie would stride purposely into the barrack rooms at the 06.30 hours *Reveille* each morning, with the stirring shout of *"Come on Fred, get out of bed, you know I have a liver complaint"*. Another member of staff, Cpl Hall of the RAOC, would harangue the boys during their drill sessions, with those immortal lines, *"Don't bend your arms at the elbows. I've told you once, I've told you twice – and I won't tell you a second time!"*

Whilst on the subject of 'quotations', the well known name of Sgt Taffy Evans again comes to mind, dear to the memory of Brian Atkins of 43A. He recalls Taffy most vividly in that, when he was Orderly

Sergeant, he used to come around, again at *Reveille*, beating a dustbin lid with a stick and reciting the following odd ode:

"Wakey, wakey, rise and shine,
Hands off -----, feet in socks,
Get out of bed you English -----."

Anyone of a poetic talent will be able to fill in the gaps themselves! Tony Guy of 43A was another 'Taffy' fan, recalling that he later met *"the man himself"* on a London bus in 1948, by which time Taffy was collecting fares as the conductor! He must have progressed rapidly after that, as Herbert Valentine, a one-time PS colleague, bumped into him, again on a bus, in Hornsey, London, in about 1950. By then, Taffy was in plain clothes as an investigator of fare dodgers. He'd obviously used his previous experience of 'dodgers', gained here at Arborfield, to further his career!

Also starting his career that April was Ian McIlraith Miller, as an apprentice Electrician. During the morning break one fine day, he was just leaving the smoke-filled Workshop toilet when he fell foul of Staff Sergeant (SSgt) Frank Gillians, who was about to charge *"anyone under the age of seventeen"* with illegal smoking. Ian protested his innocence, as he was a non-smoker, but his very presence, plus the blue haze emanating from the toilets, persuaded the SNCO to charge him anyway. Thus started Ian's 'criminal career', with a sentence of seven days CB.

Ironically, Ian's first posting after boys' school was to Middle East Land Forces (MELF) where, even though still a non-smoker, he was presented with a tin of fifty free 'ciggies' every week, courtesy of the philanthropic Lord Nuffield! *(Ian did start on the tobacco habit at that stage, and by a remarkable coincidence, both Frank Gillians and Ian Miller, along with myself – much younger of course! – all ended up as civilian instructors at Bordon many years later. And yes, Ian was by then a heavy smoker! Ed.)* Norman Donnithorne was another of those April '43 arrivals. He went into 'E' Coy, recalling that the

Company Commander was a Capt Shaw, ably assisted by CSM Prior of the King's Royal Rifle Corps (KRRC). This is well remembered, as the CSM wore coveted black buttons – no endless polishing for him! Norman says that promotion for boy-NCOs in those days was only up to the rank of Sergeant, although there was one boy in 'E' Coy at the rank of Staff Sergeant by the name of McPhee, an RAOC 'left-over' from Hilsea.

K G 'Mitch' Mitchell was one of that band of 43B boys. His first barrack room was 'D5', as he was put into 'B' Coy. Mitch retains fond memories of the outings to California for swimming lessons, though he says that the dancing lessons were less memorable – his 'quick, quick, slows' became the *"death throes of a demented octopus"*! One of the Danahar bothers, he cannot recall which one but describes him as *"the slobbery one"*, used to take delight in punching the boys in the stomach, whilst muttering, *"Keep your guard up, son"*. Then there was *"good old Herbie Payne"*, who had a saying, *"Fred, name in book, not a hook ... ... Dig!"* And you did, adds Mitch! *(Sounds like everyone was 'Fred' to our Herbie! Ed.)*

Boxing Clever!

Another boy who joined 43B was Charles E Pepper, who recalls that, somehow or other, he was persuaded to take up *"the noble art"* of boxing. His incompetence at that sport was soon noticed by one of the Danahar brothers, who decided to hand out some *"personal tuition"*. Sparring away, he told Charles, *"Hit me as hard as you can"*, which actually proved quite impossible to Charles's flailing fists. Until, that is, another PTI caught his colleague's attention by shouting to him from outside of the ring. And as he turned his head away, Charles saw his chance and actually carried out instructions to the letter! There was no real power in the punch, a bit of a powder-puff offering really, but it didn't stop Cpl Danahar from casting doubts on Charles's parentage, followed by a menacing glare.

At that stage, Charles sensibly decided that sparring was over for the day and beat a hasty retreat. Much to his relief, the School boxing team thereafter decided that they could dispense with his services and Charles took an early retirement. The other 'sporting' pastime that Charles remembers was 'bunker running', something that was still in vogue some thirty years later. The 'bunkers' were, in fact, the air-raid shelters, by then in 1943 having become redundant of their prime use. Charles was often run up and down those bunkers, by another celebrity, the one and only Denis Compton. A narrow 'swinging bridge' was later added as part of an obstacle course, and woe betide any boy

An early pciture of the Pipes and Drums

who misjudged it and caught a nasty blow to a delicate area!

Charles recalls that the Adjutant of his day was a gentleman who had served with an Indian Regiment, he thinks it went by the strange title of 'Skinner's Horse'. He wore a rather strange green-coloured uniform and sported one of those wonderful military-style moustaches that were so popular at the time. Charles goes on to say that a German fighter happened to buzz over the Camp one day, causing the same Adjutant to dash out of his office and noisily fire his pistol into the air. No damage ensued to the fighter, but the sharp sound scattered a squad of boys marching up the main Camp road!

Harry Hughes had joined the ATS (Boys) at Chepstow in 1935, to train as a RAOC Fitter. Amazingly, by September of 1943, some rapid promotion meant that he arrived here at Arborfield as a WO2 in charge of the Instruments Workshop, a post he then went on to hold for the next three years, including the short-term move to Bury during 1944. He recalls that he and his wife rented a bungalow at nearby Winnersh, as his wife had started working as a clerk, in the 'B' Coy office, for Capt Gardiner. They both used to cycle backwards and forwards to work in all sorts of weather, *"come rain or shine"*.

Harry was once asked to engrave a silver-gilt cigarette case, as a retirement present for the Bandmaster, 'Bandy' Nel, and diligently set about the task with great skill and concentration. A young subaltern, with obviously not a lot to occupy him, wandered into the Workshop whilst Harry was concentrating on the engraving and, after hanging around for a while, looked nosily over Harry's shoulder to see what was going on. Harry politely asked the officer to leave and, to ensure his departure, began to carefully wind away the table from the cutting tool. Unfortunately, this caused a 'technical hitch' in the operation and Harry began to berate the officer with words somewhat unfitting to his rank! Peace eventually prevailed, with the arrival of Capt Dalby, who calmly settled the ruffled feathers, and Harry was then able to correct the error and complete the delicate task.

Harold Price (42A) remembers that one of the highlights of 1943 was when the *British Broadcasting Corporation (BBC)* came to the School to broadcast a church service from the Camp Hall. This may well have been that year's Remembrance Service, when wonderful versions of both *Reveille* and *The Last*

Post were played by buglers of the Corps of Drums, including Brian Conway, standing rigidly to attention outside that same Camp Hall.

Colonel Hilborn moves on

As Col Hilborn moved on to take over the Gordon Boys' School at Woking in Surrey, Col J D White, DSO, MC (late RAOC) took over as Commandant at the School in October 1943, quickly being nicknamed affectionately by the boys with the appropriate moniker of 'Chalky'. Two events of particular note, which were to occur during his tour, were firstly the so-called 'Dispersal' of 1944 and, secondly, the initiation of the 'Woolwich Arsenal Engineering Apprenticeship' (later Cadetship) scheme. The latter was evolved in order to enable certain apprentices to proceed to Woolwich Polytechnic and the Royal Arsenal, with the object of taking a course which would culminate in the attainment of an engineering degree or diploma, thereby qualifying the successful student for an engineering commission.

Prior to his departure, the previous Commandant made a personal presentation to Ben Cook, the ex-RSM who had been commissioned and was now serving as the School's QM. The item presented was a *"lovely clock with an engraved plaque"*, which remains a treasured possession of Ben's daughter Molly's family almost sixty years later. The plaque reads:

> LIEUT. H.E. COOK.
> A SLIGHT TOKEN OF REGARD FOR
> 4 YEARS OF LOYAL FRIENDSHIP,
> 1939 - 1943.
> F.A. HILBORN, COLONEL.

Walter Jobber also joined the School that October. He had sworn his *"allegiance to the King"* at Holloway, north London – the Recruiting Office and not the (women's) prison, he hastens to add! Upon arrival at the train platform in Wokingham, he was told to *"join those others over there"*, which was quite a common introduction to boys' service from all the tales that have been told! Walter confirms the story told by Gerald Johnson (39A) of Sgt Taffy Evans confiscating any fags that the boys had about their person! Getting to the School, he then found out that, like it or not, he now belonged to the Church of England – he was an instant 'C of E'. *(As far as can be recollected, the only other religions 'allowed' in those days were 'RC' (Roman Catholic) and 'OD' (Other Denominations). Ed.)*

Walter's memory is that Arborfield tended to be rather 'cut off' from civilisation in those days, with buses to the local 'fleshpots' of Wokingham and Reading being all too infrequent and far too expensive for his limited funds. Instead, the prime entertainment was provided by regular film shows in the Camp Hall, where there seemed to be a relaxation regarding the usual anti-smoking regulations. He recalls viewing most films through a thickening smoke haze, sent up by those older boys at the back who were privy to a cigarette ration. Then there was the NAAFI snooker hall, containing only four tables, which had to be shared by the whole School population. Needless to say, intense competition for even getting near one of those tables caused no end of problems.

Highlight of the film shows was the 'serial' that ran each term, split into weekly episodes, each one ending in the inevitable 'cliff-hanger' situation for the hero. Not to worry though, the start of the next episode would always see our hero, 'with one swift bound', escape the clutches of whatever villain or situation last week had left him with! One such hero was *'Flash Gordon'*, played by Larry 'Buster' Crabbe. Who can forget that cigar-shaped spacecraft soaring across the silver screen with sparks and smoke spluttering from its tail? As for the 'other' type of smoking, older boys who didn't actually partake of the evil weed still drew their ration, selling them on to younger boys at some exorbitant price, one at a time!

Walter recalls that he was a keen sportsman in his youth, partaking in most of the sports that were available. He thinks that the School always lived up to the old saying, *"a healthy mind in a healthy body"*. Football and boxing were his favourites, with the latter just having the edge. After winning their bouts and being presented with NAAFI vouchers after one competition, the boys were dismayed to have them immediately taken away again. It had been discovered that the award of vouchers was considered 'payment' and thus infringed their amateur status. Walter never did find out who put 'the bubble' in!

As long as the war lasted, the older Arborfield boys were designated as being *"on active service"*, although the privileges gained by this designation were hard to find! Washing and shaving – if one could find something to shave off – were generally carried out in three grades of water - tepid, cold and

freezing! Food was reasonably plentiful, considering the rationing situation, but it did tend to be rather monotonous. Curries would occasionally be served, whether for jaded palettes or to ward off the cold, who knows? They tended to be *"green in colour and mostly edible"*.

Chaucer Harvey was another who arrived at the School in October 1943. His memories of those film shows are more based on what happened both before and afterwards – the dreaded 'Chairs'. The 'Duty Company' was responsible for converting the Camp Hall/Gymnasium into a fully seated Cinema some time before each show opened. That, perhaps, wasn't too bad – but there were not many that wanted to hang around after the evening performance, stacking the empty fold-up chairs away in the old Nissen hut at the back. Once the National Anthem had signalled the show was over, there would be an almighty stampede of boys through the six exit doors, trying to avoid this onerous duty. Supervision of this became slightly easier once Company shoulder-tags of a particular colour were issued, making Duty Company more recognisable.

Art Cockerill joined 43B directly from the DYRMS, where he had played a musical instrument, and was thus one of several other musical types immediately 'dragooned' – if you'll pardon the term - into the Arborfield Band. He doesn't recall having a lot of affection for 'Shiner' Nel, who once reduced poor Art to *"a quivering mass of pulp"* with a scathing rebuke, calling him *"a loud mouth and a big head"*. This followed Art's attempt at busking a march, possibly 'Colonel Bogey' or one of the other favourites of the day. By 'busking', Art meant 'playing without music' and, as this was done at *double fortissimo*, the outcome was probably quite ghastly to someone with an ear for military music!

That 'someone' happened to be the Bandmaster, who had been sitting quietly in his cubbyhole in the corner of the Band-room, until he heard the cacophony! As Art was to remark in much later times, the Bandmaster was undoubtedly correct with his rebuke, though Art wouldn't have agreed with the description at the time! One point about 'Shiner' is that he was in fact a consummate musician and taught all his boys with great skill and discipline. This had its obvious effect on Art, who later went on to play in a dance band during service in the Middle East. He followed that with positions in *"a variety of police and military style bands"* over the years, now recalling old Shiner with *"grudging affection"*.

Early in 1944, Brian Conway, by then in his final term at the School, recalls being driven by truck to Woking, along with two other boys, by Mr Giddings, one of their technical instructors. The purpose of the trip was to deliver some items to Brig Hilborn, previously the Commandant at Arborfield, but now filling the same appointment at the Gordon Boys' School. With the Arborfield School's closure pending, Peter Langley found the last weeks of his training and trade tests somewhat 'squashed together', but his intake was duly passed out as *"proper soldiers"* and he found himself heading for the delights of Aldershot.

The 'Dispersal' – and attacks by flying bombs

The aptly named dispersal took place during that period when the Allied invasion forces were being

'Ross' an ATS Driver

secretly assembled in preparation for the Normandy landings, which eventually got under way on June 6th 1944 (D-Day). A few months earlier, American General Dwight Eisenhower – or 'Ike', as he became popularly known – arrived in this country to take over as Supreme Commander of these forces. In March of that year, Prime Minister Winston Churchill announced that *"The hour of our greatest effort is approaching"*. Great events were obviously imminent and, on April 1st, a government ban was placed on visitors going within a ten-mile distance of any coastline, along the whole length of England that lay between the Wash (Norfolk) and Land's End (Cornwall). At the end of the month, another ban – this time on all travel abroad – was evidently not meant to apply to the gathered troops!

The School's population, including both apprentices and members of the PS, was consequently evacuated, as Arborfield became a temporary transit camp for certain elements of REME and RAF personnel. Exactly what went on at Arborfield during the next few months has long been a subject of much speculation, but is probably destined to remain a mystery. Many years later, in 1994 to be exact, Bryan Adams of 42B remembered that the Camp might have been used for 'waterproofing'. He went on, *"Were the spider-blocks occupied by strangers? Were the Workshops used? On our return I did not notice any evidence of a temporary takeover and the School magazine never published the story. Did any staff remain there over the period? Does any photograph exist of its temporary function?"*

The previous year, in an edition of *The Craftsman* magazine (July '93), Ken Jenner of 44A had read an article by Maj Ray Job, who in 1944 had been a member of 231 Infantry Brigade Workshop (Wksp) REME. An extract of his article read:

> *"... ... ... then, about the middle of June (1944), we drove north to the Army Apprentices' School at Arborfield, where we did our own maintenance, stores re-stocking and initial waterproofing etc. Much of the time was also spent fighting heath fires ... ..."*

Whatever the answers may be, it is a fact that, beginning on April 17th 1944, Col White's command was posted away into separate far-flung detachments around the country at large, at such diverse places as Aldershot, Ashford, Ashton-under-Lyne, Bury,

Chilwell, Donnington, Greenford, Gopsall Hall, Old Dalby, Sevenoaks and Woolwich. This, then, was the famous dispersal, long since remembered, mostly with humour and fondness, by those boys, men – and girls - who were to take part.

The ATS contingent

Upon arriving back after their Easter leave, the Platoon of ATS girls was most upset to find that, as part of the general dispersal, they were to be temporarily sent to Gopsall Hall, at Twycross, near Nuneaton, Warwickshire.

The majority of the girls had been together here at Arborfield in happy fashion for at least two years and didn't relish the thought of being split up from the rest of the School population. Upon their move north, the girls found themselves billeted in a large mansion, situated in the heart of the country. However, they appear to have stayed there for only a short period, having just about settled in, before being sent even further north to join the detachment of boys at Bury, not far from the centre of Manchester.

Their arrival at Lowercroft Camp was hardly momentous; it was raining hard and there was a strong wind blowing. Still dripping wet, the girls were first taken to be interviewed, only to then find that there were no beds or blankets available! This was duly corrected and the party began to settle in for their four-month sojourn, in accommodation very similar to that at Arborfield. Marjorie Clarke recalls that during that time spent at Bury, the School's Pipe Band led many local processions and became very popular with the civilian population. *(Hands up all those who remembered it as 'Lowestoft'! Ed.)*

Ashford

One young boy, who was amongst the 140 sent down to 14 Command Wksp, Ashford, was Paul 'Tug' Wilson of intake 42A. Paul has it on official record that some 2,400 'V1 doodlebugs' (flying bombs) fell on the county of Kent during those summer months of 1944, with Ashford being located directly under their flight path. The V1 was a pilot-less jet-propelled aircraft, capable of a speed of around 400 miles per hour and carrying a payload of nearly a ton of high explosive. They made a distinctive droning noise, before falling in an unpredictable way when the engine ran out of fuel.

A delay of around fifteen seconds occurred between the engine noise ceasing and the subsequent explosion. Also known as 'buzz-bombs', at first they were dubbed 'Bob Hopes', because it was said that all one could do, once the engine's noise ceased, was to 'bob' down and 'hope' that they had passed over you! The first of these deadly 'secret weapons', almost certainly one of Adolf Hitler's last desperate throws of the dice, killed three people when it fell in south London on June 13th 1944.

In the early hours of June 24th that same year, another flying bomb was actually shot down, but fell onto the men's living accommodation at 6 Guards Tank Brigade Wksp at Charing Heath, not far from Ashford. Paul reports that none of his party of apprentices came to harm, but that tragically some forty-six young soldiers, almost all of them REME chaps, were blown to pieces by the subsequent explosion. Another eighty men were seriously injured in the same incident, of whom six later died from their injuries. At the time, they had all been awaiting embarkation to Normandy. Paul still finds time to occasionally visit the cemetery at Lenham, in order to pay a sad salute to the orderly ranks of white crosses laid there.

Edward Tanner, of 42B, was also amongst that Ashford group and one thing that always stuck in his mind was the wonderful reception the boys got when they arrived there, still vividly remembered some fifty years later. Trevor O'Callaghan (42C) recalls the *"relaxed working environment"*, as compared to that they had endured at the School, plus the extensive variety of veteran vehicles and equipment that kept pouring in for priority repair. He has always said that it *"taught him a lot about REME"*.

The accommodation at Ashford was very basic when the boys first arrived, with cement-floored Nissen huts and the familiar lack of hot water for morning ablutions. Some extra comforts were provided as time went by, with coir mats on the floor and sheets on the beds, while some budding artists were allowed to decorate the hut walls with murals of 'Popeye' and other contemporary cartoon characters. No doubt these would have included the gorgeous 'Jane' from the *Daily Mirror*, as pin-ups were eventually added to the décor. Jane could always be depended upon to lose most, if not all, of her clothing ration during her many exciting escapades!

Weekly cinema shows and dances added to the boys' pleasure, while the glorious summer weather of 1944 allowed for cricket, bathing and the like to become an essential part of their sporting activities. Letter writing lost a lot of its joys however, due to the 'blue pencil' amendments and crossings out of the wartime censors, but it is no secret that a lot of boys used this as a good reason for *not* writing! During this period, stalwart Band member SQMS McCarthy had to be removed to hospital, to be greatly missed by his fellow Mess members of the Workshop.

Aldershot

The Aldershot detachment, which consisted of 115 apprentices and eight staff, continued with its trade training at 13 Command Wksp. Only sixty-seven of these boys eventually returned to Arborfield, while of the remainder, twenty-nine had already passed their trade tests and were awaiting adult postings. The boys settled down quickly in their new surroundings, finding the life quite congenial. Some sporting activities were included in their training programme, although the working hours proved very demanding as the production and preparation for the D-Day assault on Europe reached its peak.

One boy who was sent to Aldershot was Brian Conway of 42A, but this was directly to the Motor Fitters' School for a trade test and not as part of the dispersal procedure. Following a driving instruction course up at Ashton-under-Lyne, he was then posted to the Infantry Training Centre at Colchester. Brian was not to see Arborfield again until returning here as a military instructor in January 1954.

Mick Dickinson had joined in January 1942, later being another of those boys sent to 'the home of the British Army' at Aldershot, where he remembers working long and hard in the Workshop Tank Section. He recalls the sad occasion when one of the boys, Eric Clarke, was working at a grinding machine, when he was unlucky enough to be hit by an American *Sherman* tank, which was being reversed back into one of the repair bays. Poor Eric's leg was severed in the accident, *"like a hot knife through butter"*, after which he is quoted as showing *"great fortitude and courage"*, but Mick never did find out what happened to the lad afterwards.

Mick had reached the age of eighteen by November of 1944, so he is another who didn't return here to the School, being posted directly to REME at that stage. He was a member of 'C' Coy during his time here and, fifty-odd years later, can still recall most of the names

A/T Jim Hutchinson

of those boys with whom he shared Room 'G6'. Mick eventually left the Corps in the Sixties and finished his working life as a lecturer at the School of Electrical and Mechanical Engineering (SEME) at Bordon, Hampshire. His main source of outdoor leisure, fitness training and entertainment nowadays is provided by the local golf courses.

Bryan Adams, of October 1942 intake, was another of those boys who arrived at Aldershot in 1944, again at 13 Command Wksp, and given accommodation at Parsons Barracks. Just prior to (or perhaps just after!) the dispersal, Bryan recalls that one of the most famous sportsmen of all time made a brief appearance here at Arborfield. This was Joe Louis – the so-called 'Brown Bomber' – heavyweight boxing champion of the world, performing a demonstration bout for the benefit of the assembled boys in the Camp Hall. Bryan still proudly holds the event programme for a ceremony at which a completed American Air Force station was handed over to the flyers – with Joe's autograph adorning its front.

Bryan recalls that Aldershot had somewhat cramped conditions and unfamiliar multi-tier timber and wire bunk beds, but also fondly remembers the kindness and generosity shown by the adult troops. This was particularly true of the Canadians, who would unofficially hand over many items of clothing just for the asking. He also remembers breakfast as a vast improvement on what he was used to, with the novelty of a newspaper seller at the door allowing a scan of 'what was happening' in the world.

At the same time, the emplacement of a *Bofors* gun just outside the workplace, plus the arrival of much battle-damaged back-loaded equipment from Normandy, must have proved a sobering sight for all. Bryan also recalls that accident to A/T Clarke, setting the date as September 5th. The strained urgency and purpose of the Workshop was an eye-opener to the boys, used as they were to the well-ordered discipline and more leisurely training programme that they had now left behind at Arborfield.

Jim 'Paddy' Hutchinson remembers that period 1942 - 44 as being the *"most exciting, enjoyable and challenging"* years of his life. He had joined up in Belfast in January 1942 – and immediately given his first command! On the dock, waiting to board the steamer, Jim was told, *"You are in charge of the other seven boys, take them to Reading. Here is your warrant"*. To this day, Jim swears that he was chosen because he was the only one wearing a hat! The rough journey across the Irish Sea to Heysham caused him to be violently seasick, but somehow he and the other boys found their way to the correct platform to catch the train for London's Euston Station.

Upon arrival at Arborfield, the eight boys were split up, two per Company – just in case there was the chance of a take-over by the 'Irish Mafia', according to Jim! He was 'thrown in at the deep end' as far as sports were concerned, being made to partake in both boxing and rugby. By late 1943, Jim was an A/T Sergeant and, when going home on leave, again across 'the pond', he was put in charge of one of the lifeboats! This was at the time that all shipping was subject to attack by the dreaded U-boats of the German Navy, so he must have heaved a huge sigh of relief when the safety of Belfast Lough was finally reached.

Jim was later also one of that group of boys dispersed to Aldershot. He recalls that one task on which he was subsequently employed involved the shaping of large pieces of metal, which were later welded as a modification to the sides of *Sherman* tanks, in order to cover up what had been found to be a weak spot in their construction.

Jim was later one of those chosen to participate in the Woolwich Cadetship Scheme, mentioned earlier. After a year, however, he had met a young lady who distracted him from his studies and decided instead to apply for an infantry commission, rather than an engineering one. He later went on to serve with the Royal Irish Fusiliers (RIF), with periods spent in India, Palestine and Egypt, before retiring to civilian life in 1949.

Greenford

The party dispatched to the Central Wksp at Greenford, Middlesex, in April of 1944, was composed almost entirely of Telecommunications (Tels) and Inst Mechanics, many of whom were already at an advanced stage of their training. The first Arborfield trained 'Tels Mechs' were trade-tested there, obtaining a magnificent 100 per-cent pass rate, much to the delight of their instructors. Accommodation at Greenford was not quite up to Arborfield standards, but the messing was beyond criticism. Not only were the usual meals served in appetising fashion, and in good quantity, but also tea and milk were served to the boys during both their morning and afternoon breaks.

Donald Smith had joined in January 1942 and was one of this *"small particular group"*, under the supervision of two sergeants from the staff, namely Taffy Evans and Jock Hunter. He recalls that, despite being still serving only as 'boy soldiers', they were soon pitched into the technicalities of repairs to radio sets. They were very grateful to find that they were not alone in this task, being supported by a large contingent of ATS (the real thing!) and civilian young ladies. Their education took a large leap forward of course – and Donald recalls that they even managed to learn a bit about the intricacies of telecommunications during the same period!

Donald recalls one occasion in the summer of 1944, when a group of boys had assembled outside a Nissen hut at the '*Aladdin*' works. Suddenly one boy, believed to be Peter Baldwin, spotted a doodlebug making its menacing way across the skies, seemingly just a few feet above their heads. Its engine had already cut out and Donald can still vividly call to mind the rivets on its wings and stencilled writing on the bodywork, as the weapon continued its deadly flight. It just about skimmed over the embankment of the nearby Grand Union Canal, crossed a meadow, broke through a line of poplar trees, and finally exploded, sending a shower of debris into the air. Sadly, the explosion also killed a number of ATS girls who were marching on their way towards the Workshop.

Great efforts were obviously made to intercept those V1 weapons, the main area for such attempts being based at Ashford. Large silver-coloured barrage balloons – or 'Blimps' - were hung every few hundred yards, while much AA fire was directed into the sky and the fastest fighter aircraft were sent up to shoot them down. Many tales are even told of attempts by certain pilots to fly under the rockets, in order to 'tip over' their wings to divert them back from whence they came, although any success rate must have remained minimal.

Some also found time to make new friends!

Prior to the dispersal, Donald says that, because his group was the first to be trained as Tels Mechs, there had seemed to be no established curriculum for them to follow. They had spent an inordinate amount of time learning how to file, chip and drill, as well as on battery charging! Later, when based at Greenford, he and fellow 'wobbly head' Tony Wheatley found themselves seconded to two separate and secret sections of the workshop. Donald was first given a severe lecture on security and had to sign the *'Official Secrets Act'* – a daunting task for a mere seventeen-year-old. He later learned that he had been involved in the design and construction of certain *"deception equipment"*, which was intended to mislead the German wireless intelligence services.

Peter Baldwin had joined the ranks of 42A at the tender age of 'almost fifteen'. His arrival at Wokingham railway station caused him some consternation when he saw that his three fellow travellers on the truck to Arborfield all wore short trousers! Standing himself at a height of five feet eleven inches, Peter thought that he would be humiliated if he was forced to follow suit. Luckily, the trio was all from the Dukies, hence their attire. Train journeys figure a lot in Peter's recollections – especially when going home on leave,

when everyone would be dashing into the nearest railway station toilet to don various insignia – anything but the ATS titles they wore at the School!

Peter's trade designation at the time was that of 'Radio Mechanic', a forerunner of the 'Tels' tag that was to be used later. Peter well remembers his first day at Greenford, for having spent an hour trying to impress the young ladies with his indisputable charm and wit, he was dismayed to hear a voice over the Tannoy announcing, *"Will boy soldiers assemble at the entrance to receive their morning milk and cake"*. Bit of a turn-off eh, Peter? The good news is that Peter later went on all the way to become a Major General, one of only two ex-boys to attain that rank.

(A brief description of Peter's career is included as a separate annex to this chapter.)

Eric Corscadden, of the same 42A intake, also went to Greenford during that period of dispersal and regrets later having to miss out on what he terms *"every boy's dream"*, that of 'passing out' on a proper parade from the School here at Arborfield. For Eric and many more of his ilk, there was to be none of the thrill and privilege of marching out through its famous gates for the last time, gaily throwing their hats high into the air as off they went into adult service.

Having recovered from his earlier bout of homesickness, Mike Allcock of 42C soon found

Greenford to be *"a plum posting"*. With its location in the western outer suburbs of London, Greenford provided an excellent variety of foods, while dance bands played all the most modern jazz and swing in the large entertainment hall every lunchtime and weekends in the local Nuffield Centre. Mike adds that, during his few months there, he even managed to mend a few instruments! Added to this was the daily bliss of an ogle at ATS girl Peggy Prentice, which made him quickly put even the doodlebug threat to one side!

Harry Budd (42A) had already had a *"period of indefinite leave"* as a former Dukie, so it was probably no surprise when he found his training interrupted once again by his move to Greenford. He was another who was delighted to find that, as well as 'ATS Boys', there were others in the world that were 'ATS Girls'! However, he also recalls that his stay at Greenford terminated in a six-week spell of military training at an Infantry Depot at Chichester – the dream was over and it was back to reality.

Ashton-under-Lyne

The seventy-two boys in the Ashton-under-Lyne detachment had initially started off at Aldershot in the Motor Fitter's School. They then went on to Ashton, near Manchester, to the 14th Technical Training Centre, in order to complete the driving part of the course. This began with sessions on motorcycles and graduated on through various 'light' vehicles onto Bren-gun Carriers, with many of the allotted routes passing through the wonderful scenery across the Pennines. Twenty-five boys from this group later returned to Aldershot to await their 'coming of age' prior to posting.

Bury

The Bury group, numbering around 200 boys, found some initial difficulties, both in their accommodation and training facilities. But they soon settled down into a happy, compact unit, sharing facilities at Lowercroft Camp with the School of Electric Lighting (SEL). Fred Wells, who had recently joined up with 44A, can remember that when they got to Bury, the boys' first task was when they were set to collecting *"hay and straw to fill the striped mattress covers"*.

At the completion of their stay, the boys returned to Arborfield with many happy memories, especially the weekly 'music hall' shows, provided by the Entertainment National Services Association (ENSA). Then there was the indefatigable staff of the Women's Voluntary Service (WVS) Canteen, who somehow came up with a seemingly inexhaustible supply of hot chocolate. There was genuine regret on both sides upon their eventual departure, due both to the kindness and hospitality of the local folk as well as the generally good impression left by the Arborfield boys.

Tom 'Honker' Pearce, who had joined the School from the Dukies in February of 1944, passed out three years later as an Armourer and accomplished euphonium player, which is where he no doubt gained his nickname. He was another of those boys sent off for an *"historic summer"*, to that mill town in Lancashire, located on the outskirts of Manchester. He remembers the Camp as one of two halves, surrounding a reservoir. The boys slept in two-tier bunks and made acquaintance with the 'dry scrubber' – a device that replaced the 'bumper and wax polish' of Arborfield. No account was taken of their previous Companies, all boys being re-shuffled into 'X' and 'Y' Companies.

Tom recalls that, for some unfathomable reason, his group managed to take with them the most prominent members of the disciplinary side of the PS. Included amongst these were the RSM, Mr McNally, and the Provost Sergeant, Sgt Hotchkiss, who served in that post from 1944 - 45. According to one boy who was there at the time, Sgt Hotchkiss was *"easily disliked, without too much effort"*. As far as Fred Ford can remember, Sgt Hotchkiss had arrived at the School as a mere 'Lance Jack', but was rapidly promoted to fill the Provost post – the first of that particular appointment. Pete Langley (1941 intake) recalls that Sgt Hotchkiss was known to one and all as 'Grockle', apparently named after some cartoon character, and that he was a member of the Cheshire Regiment.

Provost Sergeants are hardly likely to ever be popular and Grockle was certainly no exception, often boasting that he *"Got me own brother seven days when I was in China"*! He used to make the janker wallahs parade for a full kit layout at 10.00 p.m. – and woe betide anyone who was late. Boys used to be waiting behind the Guardroom with their kit loaded onto a wheelbarrow, ready to dash out at the required deadline. Another of his dastardly 'tricks' was to make boys do press-ups on the grit-strewn tarmac whilst wearing respirators! Pete always said that Grockle could have given lessons on mental torture to the Marquis de Sade!

As a final footnote on Sgt Hotchkiss, Brian Conway originally and mistakenly thought his surname was 'Hospice', due to the ribald banter that generally went on between the Provost Sergeant and his *bete noir*, RSM Ben Cook. Ben's raucous voice could be heard at most places around the School, as he called for Sgt *Hospice* to report to the Guardroom – but Brian eventually realised that Ben was actually calling for Sgt *'Hoss Piss'*!

Quite a few PTIs and Education instructors also accompanied the Bury contingent; thus it was that most of their working days seemed to contain lots of PT and brain bashing! The Camp itself was located on hilly countryside and a lot of the nearby roads were still of the traditional cobbled variety, so that walking around in studded boots became something of a slippery ordeal. Tom also recalls that, as well as the members of School staff who had accompanied them to Bury, they also inherited some locals. Notable amongst these was the medical orderly, a short grey-haired and grizzled Lance Corporal from the Lancashire Fusiliers, who bullied and shouted at all those who had the temerity to report sick. Not surprisingly perhaps, he became known to one and all as 'Adolf'!

Walter Jobber, of the October 1943 intake, was another boy who later found himself sent to Bury. He has fond memories of the fact that not only was the town centre within easy walking distance from the Camp, but that there was a remarkable number of friendly public houses and local hostelries readily available! Not that funds ran to riotous living of course, but even half a pint, sipped at leisure, could be made to last an inordinate long time.

Bury also boasted an indoor swimming pool that contained many members of the opposite sex, showing off their physiques in far less than their normal clothing allowance, so the boys' eventual return to Arborfield was not looked forward to with a great deal of enthusiasm! On August 24th 1944, history was made when the School held its first 'Swimming Gala' at the Municipal Baths in Bury, whilst on the same day, all boys took part in a quickly-arranged athletics meeting. *(Many will remember the bathing costumes of those days, made from 'parachute silk'. The material would become transparent when wet - a great eye-opener! Ed.)*

Another of that group at Bury was Norman Donnithorne, of the April 1943 intake. His recollection of those days is that it was the Jeeps who had been

sent there, while the 'old sweats', with much of their training already behind them, were posted to the various fully operative Workshops. He recalls that the boys' training continued much as before at Bury, with an old building, originally a cotton mill, being used for classrooms, while the sleeping arrangements consisted of bunk beds in an overcrowded accommodation. Norman was destined to become a Tels Mech, while his main sporting interest of hockey remained with him for all of his playing life.

'Jesse' Pye of October '43 also remembers those happy days at Bury. He recalls that one of the staff members posted alongside him was Sgt 'Jock' Thornton, who almost *"spat haggis as he spoke"*. Jesse can still picture that partly derelict old mill, newly painted in a brilliant white in order to lighten the classrooms. Just prior to the dispersal, Jesse well remembers one particular sports day at the ATS (Boys), participating in a 'Staff versus Boys' cricket match, when A/T Tony Basham, in his first over, bowled out none other than cricketing legend, Denis Compton. Denis was then a PS member, but will perhaps be better remembered in a later role, as the first famous 'Brylcreem Boy' of the advertising world. Along with his brother Leslie, Denis played football with 'the Arsenal', and also represented his country, England, at both cricket and football.

George Head is another 43C boy who recalls those 'away days' at Bury, but nowadays finds himself a little confused on memories of 'Company colours'. He seems to think that these identification tags began to be used shortly after the return from Bury but, many years later, had to confess that he couldn't recall that his own 'B' Coy colour was red! George did however have a strong memory that the first 'boy RSM' was a lad by the name of Dave Ratter, thus joining in a discussion that was to rumble on through many issues of the *OBAN* some fifty years later.

George went on to serve with the RE, but envying those who had carried on into REME. He recalls his first post-School job taking place at Malvern during the 1946 / 47 winter – *"a bit cold to be square bashing and throwing Bailey bridges together"*. As if to counteract the memory of those bitterly cold days, George has now retired to sunnier climes in Spain.

Len Horton had joined up as a member of 44A, but having caught a helping of 'scarlet fever' after about three weeks at the School, he found himself incarcerated at the Aldershot Military Isolation Hospital for the next seven weeks. Imagine his surprise when, on leaving the sickbay, he found himself sent directly up to the 'wilds of Lancashire', just after the Easter break.

Having missed an awful lot of the standard drill instruction, Len got himself into all sorts of scrapes, such as often throwing up a smart salute – but this usually on the command 'about turn' or something else! Fortunately, as a North Yorkshire lad himself, he found he had landed in the sympathetic hands of a drill instructor from the KOYLI, who treated him rather gently, giving him a lot of leeway and assistance.

Harry Peers of 44A reckons he has got *"a memory like a sieve"*, but was still able to come up with the following rhyme, which he says became the 'Bury School Song' in those halcyon days:

> *"We are some of the boys,*
> *We are some of the Bury boys.*
> *We spend all our tanners, we mend all our manners,*
> *We are detested (?) wherever we go.*
>
> *When we go marching down the avenue,*
> *Doors and windows open wide.*
> *All the lads and lassies cry,*
> *'The Bury boys are passing by,*
> *Bring all your cats (?) inside!"*

A humourous postscript to that whole Bury adventure, later to be printed in what became the second School magazine, read as follows:

A certain Bandmaster was adjudicating at a Dance Band concert up in Lancashire. The first test was for the leader in rehearsing his Band. After stopping the Band several times, he said in a broad Lancashire dialect, *"Now lads, we will play the chorus ensemble and the ninth and tenth bars will be a trumpet break"*. Off they went and, at the ninth and tenth bars, the whole Band stopped, with the exception of the trumpet player and the drummer. The latter, who was slightly deaf, proceeded to crash at everything he could lay his hands on. The leader stopped the Band and shouted to the drummer, *"Ee, lad, what the eck are you doing? I said 'trumpet break'."* The drummer replied, *"Ee, I'm reet sorry, I thought you said 'Thump it, mate'!"*

Donnington

Donnington, located deep in rural Shropshire, also appears to have been a happy posting for those boys fortunate enough to find themselves there. Ken Burren of 42A recalls that there were only about fifteen of them and that their unit was 3 Base Ordnance Depot (BOD). As Ken was a Turner by trade, he was set to work with a civilian tradesman on a large facing and boring lathe, finish-turning muzzle brakes for 17-pounder and 25-pounder guns.

After feeling rather strange and out of place for about a week, the small squad of boys soon began to 'turn heads', due to their smart turnout and bearing. There were no complaints about the food or training, while the accommodation had been well prepared for their arrival. This was situated alongside that of some American troops, so the boys picked up many tips on baseball, as well as a smattering of the 'Yankee drawl'. *(Got any gum, chum? Ed.)* Those boys at Donnington gained much experience on such equipment as Searchlights, AA Guns, Predictors and Field Instruments and there was no doubt that these boys left behind them an excellent impression of their ATS background. Tucked away in one part of a huge shed at Donnington was an 'off limits' area – because it was staffed by some twenty pretty civilian girls!

Ken Burren, who maintains that he cannot talk too much about Arborfield, having only served here for two years, recalls that there was one particular American soldier who would occasionally drive the boys over to RAF Cosford in his truck, so that they could partake in a swim. This 'Yank', named Bill, would say to the boys, *"Ten miles ain't it?"* Then he would stick a long 'ceegar' in his mouth and say, *"Twelve minutes!"* Most times he would make it too. The American 'mess' was like Aladdin's Cave to those Arborfield boys – as many eggs as you wanted, *Spam*, tinned fruit, chips and ice cream. Unfortunately it was, just like the girls' area, out of bounds!

Lawrence Nixon also ended up at Donnington, recalling that the workforce was tasked with the job of converting *Ford* vehicles from automatic to manual control, as well as preparing 150mm searchlights for use in Russia. Sadly, he adds, this was a too frequent task, due to the heavy losses sustained by the supply convoys that sailed the dangerous waters to Murmansk. Oh, and he does recall that the *"civilian girls were something else"*!

Old Dalby

Old Dalby, not far from Loughborough, provided a rather different story. Despite the workshop's modern appearance and its ideal situation for optical work, arriving there on May 18th, the apprentices found they would have to sleep on straw-filled palliasses, without the luxury of sheets. But the war diary records that, like the good soldiers they were later to become, the boys adapted well and indeed rather enjoyed 'roughing it'. As some reward for their tolerant attitude, the Camp Adjutant kindly issued the boys with permanent free passes for attendance at the local cinema and other shows, while a good number were also able to participate in sporting activities, with a few of them representing outside local teams.

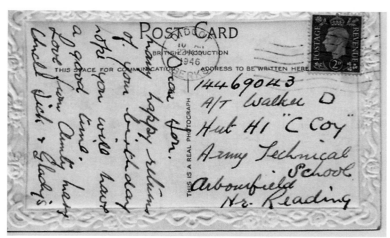

A birthday greeting from home in 1946

Chilwell

The Chilwell detachment, situated only a short distance from Nottingham, found considerable interest in attending Workshops, due to the wide-ranging variety of materiel being turned out during the run up to the invasion of Europe. This ranged from heavily armoured tanks down to the latest airborne equipment, including motorcycles and even bicycles.

Bert Austin of 42A found himself as one of those boys at Chilwell, 8 Central Wksp to be exact. With D-Day only a matter of weeks away, little or no time could be spared for training, and Bert found himself either working on motor-cycle magnetos or trying to remove and replace the massive six-volt batteries, located deep in the turrets of American *Sherman* amphibious tanks. Fortunately, as compensation for all the hard work involved, Bert and his colleagues were provided with a good and plentiful supply of food. Much of the credit for this went to Capt Wilson, the Messing Officer.

Sevenoaks

At 17 Command Wksp, Sevenoaks, Kent, the staff was most appreciative of the help that the newly arrived apprentices were able to provide with the pre D-Day activities. But the record states that, owing to the wartime non-availability of certain equipments, trade instruction tended to be a lot more theoretical than practical. These boys were accommodated in Nissen huts, separated from the rest of the Camp, and located in *"a fine old English park"*.

Education was carried out in one particular Nissen hut, which the boys themselves had converted into a classroom. Several sporting fixtures were arranged, mostly against Army Cadet Forces based in the locality. The Sevenoaks contingent also went through the experience and horrors of flying bomb attacks during their stay but, after the initial buzz of excitement, 'familiarity bred contempt'.

Woolwich

The Woolwich detachment consisted of twenty apprentice Armourers employed in the Arsenal and another twenty Inst Mechs in the Dockyard. They were all attached to 7 Central Wksp and billeted in some old converted married quarters at Brookhill Barracks. Here, life proved it could be decidedly unpleasant, as the boys found themselves more or less in the 'front line', due to the ever-present threat of the dreaded flying bombs. They soon had to get used to sleeping in their normal working clothes for much of the time. Broken windowpanes and falling plaster became a regular feature, until one morning, during education classes, a bomb exploded just outside the building they were in. Fortunately, apart from shock and superficial injuries, only one boy, A/T Meek, was admitted to hospital.

After this incident, it was quickly decided that it would be prudent to send the boys across London to the relatively safe environment of 6 Central Wksp at

Greenford, and this party, less those boys who had already passed their trade tests, eventually returned to Arborfield on September 18th 1944. During their time away, there had been little time for social activities, apart from games and swimming, with the occasional concert or picture show.

D-Day, the sixth of June

During the few months of the School's enforced closure, events on the warfront had moved on dramatically. The liberation of Europe had begun with the cross-Channel invasion of the Normandy beaches on June 6th. As well as the build-up of troop formations for that epic event, the Army had been confronted with a massive technical and logistical workload. Upon its formation in 1942, REME had been presented with a large number of these tasks and, as well as the familiar ones of repair and recovery, was much involved in some *"experimental engineering"*. But perhaps its greatest contribution was the expertise that was built up in the art of waterproofing, without which the whole D-Day endeavour would probably have come to naught.

Shortly after the landings, Allied troops seized two of the V1 launching sites on the Cherbourg peninsular, though the threat still continued from other sites. The first of these weapons had fallen on England on September 8th and over 2,500 AA guns were quickly moved to the south coast in an attempt to shoot them down before they could reach London. However, a deadly toll was still extracted, with over 6,000 killed and half a million homes destroyed. One such device fell on the Guards' Chapel at Wellington Barracks during a Sunday service, sadly killing a total of 119 people.

Ron Savage of 39A was at Mill Hill during that period, recalling the occasion when one of those dreadful instruments of death went overhead, until its engine cut out just above him. He was in the bottom of a set of bunk beds at the time, so quickly rolled over to get under cover. He swears that the guy in the top bunk hit the deck before him! Ron explains that there were two very important targets in the vicinity, the *'Adam and Eve'* public house and the Women's Royal Naval Service (WRNS – or 'Wrens') Depot! On the subject of those Wrens, he was sat in the local *'Toc H'* club one day when the door opened and a husky voice exclaimed, *"Look girls, MEN!"* Ron made a fast exit to the little boys' room upstairs

until the coast was clear – he was still a bit green in those days!

Between 100 and 150 doodlebugs were still being launched against southern England every day and around 2,750 people had been killed by their devastating explosions. In London, some 41,000 children and mothers were being quickly evacuated from the city, out of the weapon's range. In Europe, with American and Commonwealth soldiers advancing from the west and the Soviet Army making large inroads from the east, the infamous 'Thousand-year Reich' was at last beginning to crumble.

Arborfield's 'Secret Weapon'

Norman Dalhousie of 43A had an interesting article from the pages of the *Daily Express* sent to him by his mother, sometime during 1944. It told the story of a 'secret weapon' that had apparently been produced at Arborfield in readiness for a forthcoming military operation. It reported as follows:

"BOYS MADE SECRET WEAPON FOR INVASION"

"At a crucial period in the War, the Army wanted a new type of fitting for an Anti-aircraft gun. It had to be produced secretly in great numbers, and fast. Part of the order went to a special class of boy technicians in the Army. They knew they were making something in the 'Top Secret' class. Not until long afterwards did they know that their work was in preparation for the North African landings. The boys are members of the Army Technical School at Arborfield, near Wokingham, Berkshire."

Over fifty years later, Norman, referring to the present day television (TV) pictures of soldiers, flying off on sleek modern airliners, recalled the troopships of his day, such as the *'Asturias'*, *'Devonshire'*, *'Dilwara'* and *'Dunera'*, plus those with *'Empire'* in front of their name – the *'Fowey'*, *'Ken'* and *'Windrush'*. He thought that the latter may have later caught fire and Brian Hornsey, the OBAN editor of a later age, was able to confirm this. Brian reported that the old ship had indeed caught fire, returning from the Far East on

March 28th 1954. Those on board had been forced to abandon ship and a survivor told the story of a dramatic rescue at sea in the *REME Magazine* of May later that year.

Another 43A apprentice was Peter Coleman, who went on to join the RE and, in 1979, was proud to be posted, in the rank of Major, as the Senior Instructor at Chepstow. He remembers, whilst here as a boy at Arborfield, being a member of the Fitters Shop, actually working on *"a toothed quadrant in mild steel, to very tight specifications."* As recalled by Peter, the work was quite difficult but probably very good training. The boys knew that there was an urgent requirement for their product, but had no idea of what it was to be used for and were also heartily fed up with it by the time they were allowed to finish working on the project.

Hoping not to contravene the *'Official Secrets Act'*, Eric Cook of 42A believes that the said 'secret weapon' was a precision-made bracket that was to be fitted, as stated, to an AA Gun. The purpose of this was to allow the sights to be easily adjusted, which would then let the Gun be used in an anti-tank role. Eric's mind leaped to the thought of a 'high-flying' enemy Panzer commander finding himself gazing down the barrel of an AA gun! In hindsight, he wonders if there was any truth in the rumour that Ben Cook later requisitioned the device, in order to determine the correct planting distance between his parallel ranks of finest broad beans!

Colin Williams of 44A had his memory bank jogged in no uncertain manner more than fifty years later. Having recently suffered a broken leg and with extra leisure time on his hands, he decided on a long-overdue sort of dust-gathering old papers and magazines. Amongst them was the very first copy of *The Arborfield Apprentice*, the School magazine.

Colin then recalled some of his more painful days spent here at Arborfield, reckoning that he must have clocked up something like one hundred days on jankers. He remembers Sgt Hotchkiss very well – *"Get yer bucket, scrubber and cloth and get dahn to the Cook'ouse"*. He also seems to think that, on one occasion, Col White had 'awarded him' fourteen days for losing his own, as opposed to the War Department (WD) issue, spectacles! *(And we did say **spectacles**! Ed.)*

What about the musicians?

Peter Simmonds, also of 44A, came originally from Portsmouth, but is now resident in County Cork, in the south of Ireland. His heartfelt plea is, *"It was always soldiers first, tradesmen second, but what about the musicians?"* As can be gathered from this, Peter had always been interested in music and was fascinated during his first few weeks at Arborfield, listening to the Band, under the command of 'Bandy' Nel. He was determined to get into that Band, even though he could only knock out a few tunes on a tin whistle.

Peter was one of those boys dispersed to Bury, where he taught himself to play the fife and, because there were few musicians at Bury, he was soon allowed to join the Band. After return here to the School, Peter then took up lessons on the saxophone. After a temporary promotion to A/T LCpl, Peter gained the luxury of living in his own bunk, at the top end of his barrack room. From here, he would belt out the bars of *'American Patrol'*, the old Glenn Miller classic, which would encourage those boys who were engaged on the time honoured tradition of 'bumping' the barrack room floor to 'put their backs into it' – which they would then do 'with a swing'.

Peter was once awarded seven days jankers for a *"dirty rifle barrel"*, despite his explanation that there wasn't any dirt, the barrel was just 'pitted'. On his first night, having scrubbed the Guardroom floor and then sat down for a tea break, the Provost Sergeant overheard Peter saying that he could play the sax. He was sent to pick it up and spent the rest of his sentence entertaining the Provost staff and sharing their suppers!

A further member of that 44A intake was Pete Crowson, who was also one of the boys who had been sent off to Bury. He remembers that, on arriving back at Arborfield, he found a Canadian battle-dress in his old company lines, a treasure indeed when there were girls to impress! Pete unfortunately went down with an attack of lice on one occasion, causing him to be caught 'scratching his backside' on parade. This of course was classed as an offence, 'moving in the ranks', for which he was awarded '3 days'. As Pete recalls, once you were on jankers, it inevitably led to even more, as the offences one could be caught for were now more easily spotted.

Names that are well remembered by Pete include 'the usual suspects', Sgt Hotchkiss and his successor, Sgt Dransfield, but he also thinks there may have been

Sporting heroes of yesteryear

another Provost Sergeant around his time here, 'Jock' Ellesmore. 'Jock' may well have been just one of the Company SNCOs, but it would appear that he had false teeth which occasionally popped out when loud orders were being shouted!

Going back to Sgt Dransfield, Pete says that he was on jankers the day Dransfield took over. When the sergeant discovered that Pete wasn't wearing braces, he was accused of, *"Standing there looking like bloody Pontius Pilate, with no bloody braces"*. He was given another three days for this 'offence', but to this day, the reference to the biblical character has puzzled Pete. His favourite sergeant was Herbie Payne – he never once put Pete on a charge! Bill Thomas, also of 44A, remembers Herbie as *"a man of strong character, who put many of us (boys) on the right path"*.

The School starts to reform

After the School's dispersal and then the reformation that followed, many of the returning boys were sent to Companies that differed from the one they had originally joined. This only added to the confusion as to how they would identify themselves in the future, a subject of much banter and leg pulling in the years to come. For a boy who joined in April 1943 in 'A' Coy, then returned in 1944 to 'C' Coy, was he 'April 43/A', or perhaps '43A/A', maybe he should now be '43A/A/C' or even, heaven forbid, changed completely to '44/C'! The arguments rage on!

John Maddox was fourteen years old when he heard those never to be forgotten words, *"There you are lad, you've taken the King's shilling and you are now a soldier"*. His father was already a soldier and an Officer to boot. He was over six feet tall and looked smart and debonair in his uniform, always kept immaculate by his personal batman. John was around five foot six inches – and he hadn't yet seen the uniform he'd be wearing!

John was in intake 44B, and remembers with vivid clarity that his first day at Arborfield was Thursday, September 7th. Having arrived at Reading railway station, he found that the rain was coming down like the proverbial *"stair-rods"*. Along with a few others, he was ordered to jump into the back of a 3-ton lorry, being reminded that, in the interests of safety, he was not to sit on the tailboard.

His first meal in the Cookhouse, served up by an ATS girl dressed in khaki overalls and clogs, appears to have been some type of 'rissole', soon followed by 'duff', although he wouldn't swear to the contents of either! John also shows an amazing ability to name every single roommate who was bedded down beside him in Room 'A1', along with where each individual came from – not bad after fifty years!

John's feelings about those times are that there were both good times and bad but, on reflection, says that he wouldn't have missed the experience, comradeship or training here at Arborfield. He learned how to live with other people, to make the best of a difficult situation – and, just as importantly, how to keep his head down when the fur was flying! He recalls many happy occasions, such as walking all the way back from Reading, following a football match, stony broke, but laughing and joking in the company of good – and equally broke, no doubt! - mates. And mates they certainly were in those days, according to John – where else would you find someone to lend you his only pair of civvy shoes for the Thursday dance? As John recalls, there weren't all that many boys who could even afford a pair of their own shoes!

One thing that John learned during his time here was that he was far happier firing rifles and machine guns than he was at repairing them. In fact his one main achievement was to be made captain of the shooting team and be awarded his School colours for that sport. He quite *"fancied the life of a rifleman, all black buttons, black cap-badge and none of that eternal work with a button-stick"*. Thus it was that, the day before his Passing-out Parade ('PoP'), John happily found out that his application to be transferred to the KRRC had been accepted.

It was during his first posting, at Hollywood, County Down, that John realised what a fortunate position he was now in. His new unit, naturally but incorrectly, assumed that he was a new recruit, with no previous training, and therefore treated him as such. The advantages of remaining silent on the matter soon became apparent, as John started to earn himself a few bob by showing his new colleagues the intricacies of 'beezing' (boot 'spit and polishing'), sewing and

ironing. All the things he had cursed in boys' service were now proving useful. Mind you, he always ensured that his own uniform was just that bit smarter than anyone else's was!

He almost gave the game away one day during a lesson on stripping and assembling the Bren Gun, performed by a rather ham-fisted Corporal instructor. John had just about fallen asleep when, noticing John's rather bored expression, the Corporal thrust the weapon at him and told him to show what he had learned, fully expecting the embarrassment of a sad display. If John couldn't prove that he'd been paying attention, then he would spend the weekend peeling potatoes.

John couldn't resist the temptation to diligently strip down the gun to its very last component at high speed, then put the whole thing back together again in working order just as quickly. He was fortunate not to get caught out and, at the end of his twelve weeks 'initial training', was awarded the enviable, if somewhat ill-deserved, title of 'best all-round recruit'. Some *recruit*, eh John?

John's Arborfield experience paid off in other directions too and he blessed RSM McNally and his staff, who had insisted on a smart turnout and clean rifle barrel at all times. Whenever called up for guard duty, John's efforts would inevitably earn him the title of 'Stick Man', which excused him from the duty. He didn't know the origin of this custom, but took full advantage of it and enjoyed many a night out in Belfast as a result of his 'bulled' appearance.

Getting back to normal

Bob Ward also joined the School in September 1944, his first memory of Arborfield being of his *"five feet nothing frame, struggling under the weight of a ten blanket roll"*, collected from their storage place in building 'MT1', where they had been during the dispersal period. Bob adds that the whole place was just about empty when he arrived, with the dispersed elements returning in *"dribs and drabs"*. His was the first intake to be issued with Battle Dress (BD) as the second-best uniform, with two-inch rather than three-inch belts. Great amusement was gained from the issue of 'drawers, long', which were popularly known to the boys as 'Wilsons', due to their similarity to the running-gear worn by the eternal athlete of that name in the popular boys' comic, *The Wizard*.

It was shortly after Bob's arrival that the wartime

'blackout' restrictions were finally lifted. The plywood shutters came in very handy, he recalls, for pressing trousers in a sandwich arrangement between the mattress and bed-frame! Another use came when they were converted into some 'castle walls' for the Changing of the Guard display during a 1945 Parents' Day.

Bob recalls that he joined the Army to get away from farm work, so was horrified to find that 'agriculture' was one of Ben Cook's notorious fatigues! Fortunately, Bob's small stature meant that he was usually by-passed for that particular torture. His favourite duty was reporting to the Sergeants' Mess before breakfast, where he could scrounge a tasty portion of something or other. Bob remembers that the anteroom always had to be made spick-and-span well in time for lunch, as thereafter Bandmaster Nel would be stretched out on a settee for his afternoon siesta!

During Bob's time at the School, he can remember that boys were freely allowed to visit nearby Wokingham, but that the larger towns of Reading and Aldershot were still off limits, unless a special pass had been obtained. Wokingham had few attractions at the time, apart from the one cinema and a *Woolworth's*. Aldershot's main port of call seemed to be the tattoo parlour, despite the fact that having such an adornment on one's body was looked upon as a 'self-inflicted injury'. Reading had a good choice of cinemas and was an excellent shopping centre. A Forces Canteen was situated in an underpass at the railway station, but the best canteen was provided by *'Toc H'* in Friar Street. Here, 'Bangers and Mash' was a popular meal with all boys, not only tasty, but well within their impoverished means!

The Woolwich Boys

'Family Messing' is the phrase used to describe the boys' eating arrangements in 1944. Tables were allocated to parties of twelve apprentices, with two boys of the senior intake in charge of each table. It was their job to collect all food for the boys allotted to their table. If a couple of 'hard cases' were in charge, they made sure that they got the lions' share! Later, a cafeteria style of food issue was used, but of course this didn't stop the older boys from 'gypping' (jumping) the queue to still end up with the best servings. It was every junior boy's dream to be in the senior intake, with the 'privileges', such as gypping, that this brought.

Whilst still of any junior intake, of course it made good sense to steer clear of one's seniors' accommodation. A certain amount of bullying must have gone on, as in all walks of life, but any punishment meted out to junior boys probably meant no more than being made to stand on a table and either recite a poem or sing a song. 'Fagging' also occurred, when a senior boy's kit would be handed out for cleaning, but if one made a right good botch of this, you probably wouldn't be asked again!

According to Bryan Norman of the April 1942 intake, the first 'Very Important Person' (VIP) to take the salute at a Sunday march-past, on October 1st 1944, after the School had re-assembled, was none other than Major General (Maj Gen) E B Rowcroft CB, CBE, MIMechE, MIEE. The General has long since been regarded as 'the father of REME', and was, at that time, Director of Mechanical Engineering (DME). Many years later (1978), when the then-to-be Depot REME left its home in Poperinghe Barracks, it moved to new accommodation on the site of the boys' school. It is believed that this was when the term 'Rowcroft Barracks' was first applied to the site.

(A brief description of the General's career is given in a separate annex to this chapter.)

The Woolwich Scheme

In November of 1944, eight apprentices from Arborfield were selected for the previously mentioned Woolwich course, with another two kept in reserve, from those candidates put forward by both schools at Arborfield and Chepstow. The Selection Board commented very favourably upon their high standard of intelligence and soldierly bearing. D J Hutchings was one of those boys who became a 'Woolwich Cadet' and was moved to write the following report:

"At the moment we are attending classes at Woolwich Polytechnic five mornings a week, Monday to Friday, and the balance of our time is spent in the Arsenal, where we have been posted to various (work) shops. We are not finding the work as easy as we might wish, as our standard of education was considerably below that required. We have had to cover a lot of ground in a relatively short space of time. However, I honestly believe that we have all held the pace pretty well. The factory is rather uninteresting on the whole, as most of our work is only application of that knowledge gained at Arborfield, and we have leaned little in addition to that."

At one stage, Bob Ward must have become one of the Woolwich nominees and recalls that a room in 'F' Block was set aside for their use, probably to ensure that the rest of the apprentices *"didn't realise what we bomb-heads were getting away with"*. Not that it did Bob much good, as he was weeded out at the half-way point and returned to normal trade training, where he then had to work hard to make up for the five months he had lost.

'The Arborfield Apprentice'

In December of 1944 a School magazine, entitled *The Arborfield Apprentice*, was published for the very first time. Col White proudly described it as *"a very good first number"* and paid tribute to an *"energetic and capable editor"*, in the shape of Sgt J H Pinder, who was a member of the AEC, serving at the School on the PS. Sgt Pinder, in his first editorial comment, welcomed the magazine as *"the School's very latest recruit"*. Thanks were expressed to Maj Johnson for his advice and ready help, as well as to the two gallant typists, Miss M E Golding and Pte M A Clarke, of whom we have previously heard.

The Commandant also referred to the *"great events of the year (that) had gone rumbling by in the world outside"*, comparing them with Arborfield's own memorable events of the dispersal and the Woolwich scheme. In that same edition, RSM McNally saw fit to write an article of his own, exhorting all apprentices

to take pride in being an Arborfield boy and, on continuing on into adult service, carry with them the traditions and good name they had gained during their apprenticeship.

(The full text of the above article can be found in a separate annex to this chapter.)

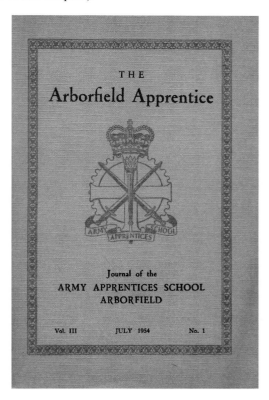

Extra-mural activities

That first magazine also gave reports from the many societies and clubs that were being run in the School at the time, providing a fascinating snapshot of 'the way it was'. The list is as follows:

Arborfield Union Society
Aero-modelling Club
Angling Society
Appreciation of Music Society
Choral Society
Dramatic Society
Photography Club
Scouting and Rambling Club
Sketching Club
Shooting Club
Swing Club (for enthusiasts of 'swing' music).

Great pleasure was taken in the fact that the Aero-modelling Club had re-opened only two weeks after the School's return from the dispersal. The Club Room had been moved from its original home in the Library to Barrack Room 'F6', where there was more privacy. Club membership had already been filled to its upper limit of sixty apprentices and was available every weekday between 17.30 and 20.30 hours, with an extension of 12.30 to 20.30 hours at the weekends. An end of term exhibition had been arranged, with Col White having offered three prizes of thirty shillings; a pound; and ten shillings (£1:50p, £1 and 50p) for the three best models.

The 'Swing Club' was still in its infancy towards the end of 1944, but was fast gaining an enthusiastic audience, as the Club attempted to build up a library of 'swing' classics by both American and British bandsmen and musicians. At one 'concert', a crowd of an estimated 350 fans crowded into a room normally capable of holding only thirty-five. President of the Club, Capt Gardiner, addressed these stirring words to the uninitiated: *"Get hep to jive, dig that trench and cut a rug!"*

Also included in the first magazine was an article by A/T LCpl Middleton, who reported on how the School was settling back to normal, after the upheaval caused by the dispersal:

> *"The School began to re-form in the late days of August and, as the month of September progressed, the different detachments began to return to Arborfield. Normal routine was the order and minds were turned to Workshops and Education, not forgetting regimental training. Under the RSM, the members of the School started to reach the high standard of efficiency that it had possessed before it was broken up."*

Regarding the naming of the Camp roads after famous men, an unknown author using the initials 'N.G.' was quoted with the following message, which seemed to foot the bill quite aptly:

> *"Lives of great men all remind us*
> *We can make our lives sublime*
> *And, departing, leave behind us*
> *Footsteps in the sands of time."*

Another famous man was making his own headlines during 1944. On August 31st, His Majesty King George VI was pleased to announce that 'Monty' had been promoted to the highest rank of Field Marshall. During the following month, evacuations from London were suspended. This may have seemed a premature decision as, only two days after this announcement, a terrible new weapon, the long-range 'V2 rocket' and forerunner of the subsequent 'Space Age', fell on the western fringe of the capital at Chiswick and killed three more unsuspecting people.

Closer to home, it was proudly announced in the first School magazine that Capt H E Cook had been awarded the MBE, whilst the British Empire Medal (BEM) had been awarded to Mr E A Burgess, an instructor in charge of the Machine Shop.

(An affectionate look at Ben Cook's life and exploits is given as a separate annex to this chapter. Thanks go to his daughter Molly for providing a personal view of her famous father.)

Following the *'Dig for Victory'* national campaign that had been pursued during the war, it is perhaps no surprise that, upon their return to the School, boys were encouraged to set up individual 'Company Gardens', where flowers and vegetables could be grown. Prizes were awarded as an incentive to this productive pastime. Keen competition was also taking place between individual barrack rooms, for possession of 'the Company wireless' and table tennis equipment.

A sporting future

Towards the end of 1944, it was proposed that, in future years, there would be regular sporting competitions between the apprentice schools at Arborfield and Chepstow. The first 'away' fixture was dated December 8th 1944, with the return match here at Arborfield pencilled in for March 17th 1945. These fixtures were to include Boxing, Cross-country, Hockey, Rugby and Soccer, with a Shooting competition also likely. These initial meetings became the fore-runners of the famous Triangular and Quadrangular Games that were to take place between apprentices and boys of all three services, over the following decades.

Whilst on the subject of sport, the first School magazine contained three articles from famous sporting personalities of the day, who were actually

Oil storage tanks between the Technical Stores and Fitting & Turning Workshop off the East Square

serving here as members of the PS. Cpl Alf Danahar gave an appreciation of the boxing skills of his brother, Arthur, who was then the number one contender for the welterweight title of Great Britain. Stan Clayton of the AEC, and inside right for Notts County, provided some tips on *"How to become a good footballer"*. Last, but not least, Arthur Cunliffe of the APTC, who had played for Blackburn Rovers and Aston Villa, as well as representing England at one time, presented his own 'best eleven' football team of the day.

Great play was made at the time about the *"unquenchable thirst and insatiable appetite"* of the boys using the NAAFI. In a week, the boys would down 3,000 cups of tea, 2,000 glasses of lemonade, six hundred bottles of minerals and around three hundred and fifty cups of coffee. More than seven hundred cakes were consumed, again on a daily basis, with the favourite being apple tart. The boys were very fond of chipped potatoes, but rather less so of cheese! Fruit was very popular; the boys ate every piece that the NAAFI could obtain, adding up to one hundredweight a week. The 'NAAFI girls' worked exceptionally hard, being both courteous and cheerful, with only a small

proportion of their working day spent serving from behind the counter.

On the PS in those days, one of the AEC instructors was a Scotsman, teaching English, with the Italian name of Sgt Fattori. His chief claim to fame is that he actually rewarded the boys' efforts with ready cash – although at a penny a time, it was reckoned more as a sign of his nationality than his largesse! Padre Beer was another well-known figure, having been wounded during the fighting in northwest Europe. He was a heavy smoker, a real 'Woodbine Willy', but his religious lessons were well attended, as they also promised a certain amount of sex education.

During November of that year, ominous events were taking place in the Middle East that were to eventually take the life of one of the School's 42B intake just a few short years later. Zionist terrorists of the 'Stern Gang' murdered the British Minister Resident, Lord Moyne, in Cairo and here at home the Prime Minister announced that all such terrorist groups in Palestine should be eradicated. Sadly, this did not become the case, and an ex-apprentice was to die as a result.

—§—

Annex to Chapter 2

Ben Cook and Gilbert

RSM, and then later Captain, H E Cook was familiarly known to all Arborfield boys as 'Ben', but to his family he had always been known as 'Harry'. He came from a farm-labouring family who lived in the low-lying Fenlands of Cambridgeshire and his lifelong love of carthorses came along naturally with this agricultural upbringing. At the age of nine, he was given the job of leading one such large horse, laden with hundredweight sacks of beans, to the local windmill. On the way, one sack fell to the ground and young Harry had to await a passer-by to help lift the sack up onto the horse's back, being too small to manage the task by himself.

Gilbert

When the First World War was declared in 1914, the Army sent men around lots of farms to requisition horses for working at the front. It should be remembered that this was quite a sacrifice to the farms, where these horses were the main source of power for so many everyday tasks. Harry almost cried when some of the farm-horses were led away, knowing that he would never see them again. From these facts, it is not surprising that Ben, as we shall subsequently call him, ended up in the Army himself, and that he always maintained his love and admiration for those large 'beasts of burden'.

Ben himself must have generated similar feelings, a mixture of awe, affection and respect, in the hearts and minds of those young apprentices who came to Arborfield in those early days of the School's existence. Walter Jobber, of intake 43B, reminds us that tales about both Ben and 'Gilbert', his famous grey Clydesdale Shire horse, are legion. Gilbert was a relic from the days of the Army Remount Depot and one of the last such Army horses to be stationed in Arborfield, although there was still a number of draught horses on the Garrison establishment as late as 1966.

Walter recalls the occasion when he and his party of 'fatigue wallahs' were caught out by Ben, throwing potatoes at Gilbert. The proscribed punishment for this was a turn in the shafts for the boys themselves, as they took Gilbert's place at pulling the plough. Ben justified this by saying that they were *"sabotaging the war effort"*, but it was probably more because of possible injury to his beloved horse. Along with Norman Donnithorne (April 1943), Walter recalled one occasion, when on gardening fatigues (or 'agriculture,

digging for victory') with the duo and the tea and NAAFI 'slab' (cake) arrived, Ben gave it all to Gilbert, reckoning that he had worked harder than all the boys!

Ben's daughter Molly, now living on the Isle of Wight with husband John Pewsey (45A), was only a young girl of nine when the 'Boys' School' first opened. She remembers that her father had been brought up to always respect his animals, and that he would always ensure that both the horses and chickens were fed before he sat down to his own breakfast. She therefore admits that the boys' impression that the *"horses came first"*, before their needs, has the ring of truth about it. She adds that there was nothing malicious about this, it was merely a testament to Ben's natural upbringing.

The story of the 'slab cake' is apocryphal, no doubt handed down with extra embroidery from one intake to another, as it also appears in the memoirs, along with those of many others, of Guy Cordeaux of 47A! He recalls that one day, he and a few other boys were supposed to be 'weeding' the onion patch, but couldn't tell weeds from onions – in their eyes, a Ben Cook ploy to make a little mischief and amusement at their expense.

Ben would no doubt have seen this in a completely different light. With seed still as scarce as it was, and with memories of an agricultural heritage, it was essential to a farmer that weeds were destroyed and food crops maintained. Anyway, the 10 o'clock 'NAAFI break' arrived, with its big slice of slab and a bucket of cocoa, and along with it Ben and his horse. Ben took one look at the onion patch and decided that the boys hadn't done any work at all. Needless to say, the boys got the cocoa, while Gilbert got the slab!

David Ferns was a 44B boy, also with memories of the famous duo of Ben and Gilbert. As he said in a letter to the OBAN many years later, *"Who will ever forget the morning that Ben led Gilbert along the top of the square during muster parade, stopping right in the middle to allow the horse to urinate, caused by Ben using a 'cavalryman's trick' to start the horse off"*. Now this conflicts with the story told by Charles Pepper, who says that it was another soldier, called 'Bomber', who carried out this daring episode, in an attempt to extract some sort of revenge on Ben! *(Perhaps it happened twice – just as it says on the label! Ed.)*

Don Walker of 45A recalls that fateful day that has long lingered in the mind of many ex-boys. Ben Cook was by then the Captain QM, while Peggy Crowe was leader of the 'Cookhouse girls'. It was suddenly discovered that Gilbert 'had decided to go for a swim' in one of the static water tanks that served the Camp. Daughter Molly recalls that Ben had been enjoying his usual after-tea pastime, having a quick snooze in his armchair, with a newspaper draped over his face. He may have had a premonition of trouble, as he unexpectedly jumped to his feet, saying that he was worried about the horses. It was only later, as Molly enjoyed a performance at a Camp Hall film show, that someone dashed onstage to announce, to loud cheers all round, that Gilbert had been rescued.

Initially, Ben did all he could to hold Gilbert's head above water. The poor animal had injured itself, thrashing about in the tank and cutting his legs on the metal crossbars. George Ulyet (43A) was one of a party of 'D' Coy boys then tasked with assisting in Gilbert's rescue. They had to support the unfortunate horse with a tarpaulin under its belly, held by about forty boys on ropes, until the tank's water was gradually pumped out and the tank itself cut open by oxy-acetylene torches. Norman Donnithorne is another boy who can confirm the above story of Gilbert's 'swim', and seems to remember that the unfortunate horse was retired from active duty after that event. K G 'Mitch' Mitchell of 43A wonders if Ben ever keep his promise of a new BD for everyone who jumped in to assist in the rescue?

Not all boys agreed on the 'universally popular' version of Ben and Gilbert however! Mervyn 'Taff' Bowen of 39C certainly has some reservations and, as he explains, certain recalcitrants, when having to haul Ben's plough over rough stony ground, were much irritated by the sight of arrogant Gilbert, in his appointed role as spectator, sneering down his *"long ugly nose at their puny efforts"*. While Ben himself may have been beyond the reach of any revenge, rumours abounded that Gilbert's foray into the static water tank may not have been totally accidental!

This claim was probably just 'schoolboy' mischief and it rather saddened Ben and his family at the time. If Gilbert had indeed been 'pushed', then Ben had a more reliable version of what may have happened. His second horse, Bob, was a difficult animal, unpredictable at the best of times, and liable to lash out with his back legs. It is quite likely that both horses were at the top of the slope, drinking at the water tank, when Bob nudged into Gilbert, causing him to topple into the water. Poor Gilbert was never the same animal after that escapade and eventually had to be 'put down'.

Molly Pewsey, as she is now, has another sad tale concerning that second horse, the naughty Bob. During June 1948, Ben was forced to spend some time in the Cambridge Military Hospital (CMH) at Aldershot. Whilst he was in there, recovering from a major road accident, some unknown personnel took it upon themselves to administer poison to the unfortunate Bob. Whether deliberate or simply accidental, no one ever found out, but Bob later died from the effects. As Molly comments, *"What would today's Animal Rights people have to say about that?"*

Brian Conway (42A) recalls that he also did his *"fair share of 'agriculture'"* under the tender tutelage of Ben, adding that, *"nobody was exempt from digging for victory"*. But Brian certainly preferred to do that type of useful endeavor than having to do jankers under the dreaded Sgt Hotchkiss, and reckons that most boys would have thought that way too.

Dick Wade of 39A describes Ben as *"that wonderful man"*. He recalls that Ben once got him to drive a 'slave carrier', a sort of half-track vehicle, behind which was pulled a large harrow, in order to plough a field. Dick was quite happy in his task, *"merrily jogging along, pulling the steering levers left and right"*, until Ben ran up alongside, red faced and arms waving, telling him that he had missed a bit! Dick also tells the story of another boy, who thought of a possible way to get into Ben's good books. Having just harvested a load of potatoes, the boy sat himself down and carefully rinsed each one clean before putting them in his sack. When Ben spotted what was happening, he made the lad fetch a bucket of soil and mix it with water into sludge. Each separate potato had to be then carefully dipped into the sludge and put out to dry again. *"You'd never make a good farmer"*, said Ben.

Gordon Bonner has good reason to remember Ben too, at a much later date. Gordon was of intake 49B, so estimates that his session of 'agriculture' must have taken place around 1950. He had already embarked upon his career of becoming the *"School's champion defaulter"* before reporting to Ben, who instructed him to plant out hundreds of cabbage plants. Working at this onerous task all day long, he was astonished when Ben turned up to inform him that every single plant had been put in upside down. Gordon draws a veil over the immediate consequences, but says that it was *"worth twenty-eight days"* just to see the amazed look on Ben's face!

Gerald Johnson joined up in May 1939 and was forever being caught out at the smoking habit. He and another two 'janker wallahs' were sent *"up the hill"* to cut the grass outside Ben's house, each armed only with a pair of scissors. Whilst there, they decided to *"lighten the load"* on one of Ben's apple trees, stuffing the ripe fruit down the fronts of their denim blouses. Unfortunately for the three miscreants, Ben caught them at it! Having requested that they leave their 'loot', and having thanked the boys for saving him a job, Ben promptly 'doubled' them down to the Cookhouse and reassigned them to the pleasure of cleaning up all the greasy pans.

Fred Ford (39A) recalls his RSM as *"a very smart man of fine physique"*. Even more than fifty years later, whenever he saw an RSM in person, or perhaps on TV, he would always make a mental comparison with *"our beloved Ben"*. Despite Ben's normally gruff exterior, Fred found him a *"big softie"* at heart, with a great sense of humour. He was often heard ordering defaulters to *"Go lock yourself in the Guardroom and bring me back the key"*. Fred remembers one occasion when Ben shouted to one of his Drill Sergeants, *"Sergeant Oldfield, what sort of tree is that at the top of the Square?"* Sgt Oldfield pondered for a minute and then replied, *"It's a wooden tree, Sir"*. Whereupon, Ben stomped off in feigned disgust, muttering to himself, *"Wooden tree, wooden tree, hrmph!"*

Fred tells another little tale, passed on to him from Nick Ozanne, Company Sergeant Major (CSM) of 'A' Coy. Ben once caught a boy at the dreaded smoking, and instructed him to go out and collect 100 spent matchsticks, tie them up into neat bundles of ten and deliver them to the Orderly Room. Nick was present

Lt Ben Cook

when the dishevelled boy finally came to deliver, having scraped around for ages to find those 'vestas'. Ben, eyes glinting wickedly, pointed to a fire bucket full of water and said, *"Now sink 'em!"*

Another incident that has stayed vividly in Fred's mind was when Ben ordered one boy to blow his runny nose. The lad replied that he didn't have a handkerchief, at which Ben ordered him to report to his married quarter that evening. The lad duly returned from Ben's house clutching six crisp, white hankies in one hand and a bright shiny half-crown in the other, which in those days was a lot of money. As Fred now puts it, *"Good for Ben, what a character he was"*.

Doug Phillips of 39B says that Ben must have looked *"a fearsome sight to most fourteen-year olds"*, but that once they had got to know him better, they found out that *"there was always a chuckle lurking around inside him"*. Doug was waiting outside the QM's Stores one day for an issue of kit when Ben suddenly appeared, towering over him. *"Where're you from, boy?"* growled Ben. *"Oxford, Sir"* came Doug's timorous reply. *"Well I'm from Cambridge and they will win again next year"*, said Ben with a mischievous grin, before striding off to go about his business.

Peter Langley, who joined in 1941, says that Ben was *"the epitome of what a Regimental Sergeant Major, and a Guardsman to boot, should look like"*. Alongside Scots mate Harry Warburton, Peter had spent the morning 'weeding' a particularly large potato patch. Ben turned up to see how they were getting on, with the question *"Where's your weeds?"* After a shuffling pause, Harry replied, *"They're in the bur-r-urn, Sir"*. *"In the what?"* yelled Ben, to which Peter gave the translation, *"In the stream, Sir"*. Not to be outfoxed, Ben responded *"Then you'd better go and get 'em then!"* Thankfully, the few handfuls of bedraggled greenery the boys eventually produced seemed to satisfy Ben.

Apparently Ben didn't always look as smart as Peter's description! One party of boys had been marched directly from their morning parade to join in their agricultural duties. Thus, their turnout had already been checked. But, of course, Ben had to check them himself – being immaculately turned out in his standard uniform of no hat, no jacket, a collar-less shirt, belt and braces for all to see – and a pair of gum-boots!

Tom Pearce, who joined in February 1944, also comments on Ben's unusual mode of dress, especially as he was a Captain QM, ex-RSM and ex-Grenadier Guards. One fine day, the local Brigadier was paying a visit to the Commandant and his driver, a lance-jack, was sat in the staff car, dressed in SD and peaked cap. He later told this tale: *"I was sitting there, when this figure comes along on an old Army bike, wearing Wellington boots, denim trousers with braces, an old khaki shirt and no hat. He asked me 'what I was doing there' and I asked him 'who the hell are you?' He replied that he was 'Captain Cook' and so I told him that 'if you're Captain Cook, then I'm Christopher ruddy Columbus!' At which, said figure laughed and rode off on his bike!"*

Ben always wore some sort of headgear when out and about; a trilby when in civvies; Army caps and hats of various sorts when he was on agricultural duties; sometimes a straw hat. Moving about, working on the land or dealing with his beloved horses, he always wore clothes suitable to the task. As Molly tells it, picking hayseeds from the creases of a woollen Army battle-dress jacket is not something you wish to do too often – no need to ask who got that job! The family has an old photograph of Ben on a tractor, cutting the hay and wearing his regulation Captain's peaked cap. After his near-fatal accident in 1948, when he suffered severe head injuries and two broken legs, Ben hardly ever wore a hat again, except maybe an old beret when it was raining.

Along with the boys, Ben had a particular dislike of Sgt 'Grockle' Hotchkiss, the Provost Sergeant. He would stand at the end of Nuffield Road and call for him. *(Brian Conway has thoughts on just what Ben would call him! Ed.)* Given Ben's loud authoritative voice, perhaps 'call' is too gentle a term, but call him he did, adding the famous term *"At the double!"* When the puffing and panting Grockle arrived, Ben would say to him, *"Just wanted to see how long it would take you!"* The story of Grockle being told to build a greenhouse, which he did from the inside, then forgetting to put in a doorway, seems too tall a tale even for the pages of this history!

Les Wiffen was one of those boys who decided to improve his SD cap. The usual piece of hacksaw blade or toothbrush handle would make the front stand up straight like a Guardsman's hat, but of course Ben had the answer to this! He would bring his pace-stick down firmly on the offending cap, causing the 'stiffener' to come through its top, in which case the wearer would either have to replace or repair his cap. But Les and his mates tried another method – stiffening the material with either soap or starch. When Ben 'tested' one boy's hat, it bounced right back without damage. *"How did you do that?"* asked Ben, to which he got the prompt response, *"Will power, Sir!"* Les adds that Ben was not impressed.

As recalled by Eddie Broomfield of 45A, having been sent off in a group of six on 'agricultural duties', they would be greeted by the burly figure of Capt Ben Cook, who would then bellow out the word 'Bomber' in his loudest voice. This would bring forth, at the gallop, the arrival of the said Bomber, actually a Bombardier from the RA, who would then lead the lads off to their day's toil. Charles Pepper of 43B remembers that Bomber was, to use the RA term, the 'driver' of Gilbert and the agricultural wagon. He would turn up for his daily work, wearing his SD, and displaying a whole row of pre-1939 medal ribbons. There was a rumour going round that Bomber had two SD jackets, one with

Ben - hay making wearing his regulation cap!

a single stripe, the other with two. He would apparently wear the one that best suited what Ben thought about him at the particular time!

If Ben wasn't present himself in the fields, working his horses, he would appear occasionally during the day – inevitably just as the boys were about to have what they thought would be a well-earned break. Eddie Broomfield says that outwardly Ben was a hard task-master, but that he always had the welfare of his horses and boys very much at heart – and definitely in that order!

Those agricultural fatigues included a lot of potato picking. As recalled by Molly Pewsey many years later, the boys were not alone! She and her younger sister, Pamela, were often roped in for this backbreaking task. In fact, during the war, schoolchildren across the country were allowed time off school to assist in such essential work. But Molly remembers that they wasn't allowed to take time off during the term at nearby Farley Hill, their stint was always during the summer holidays.

She recalls that one day when her Dad was out on his tractor, he saw one young apprentice sitting on an upturned bucket, right in the middle of the potato field and directly in the tractor's path. Jumping down from the machine, Ben grabbed the unfortunate boy's nose

between his large finger and thumb, hauling him to his feet and administering a sound telling off. Then Ben's sharp eye detected a movement beneath the boy's denim jacket, which turned out to be a field mouse. Ben immediately threw it to Betty, his dog, who killed it in a flash. The lad was then given a lecture about taking vermin into the barracks, where it could cause an infestation.

Molly wonders if any boys remember Betty? She was Ben's faithful black Labrador – a one-man dog, always to be seen running alongside Ben as he rode his trusty bicycle around the Camp. Ben had inherited Betty in a rather mangy condition, but eventually brought her coat back to glossy perfection by the administration of engine-oil! Ben's horses were kept in stables in the School coal-yard, and it was there that, on one occasion, Betty produced a litter of pups.

The faithful dog followed Ben everywhere. Even when Ben was a Captain, he would still occasionally pop into the Sergeant's Mess 'for a quick one', leaving Betty out on the verandah. Should Ben leave the Mess by the back door, as was often the case, sometimes Betty would be left there outside the front entrance, waiting for her master. Nobody could tempt her to leave her station – so Ben occasionally had to be called back to the Mess to pick up his devoted companion!

Walter Jobber recalls many occasions when Ben wanted a 'day out', joining his numerous contacts within the surrounding area. One such a day turned out to be a pheasant shoot, with Walter and others of his intake 'volunteering' to act as beaters, without having any real idea of what this entailed. Still, on finding out that it meant spending a sunny afternoon beating the devil out of grass and undergrowth, the task was borne with some humour. What really made it memorable was that, at the end of their efforts, a local high-ranking

Ben - enjoying the outdoor life to the full

civilian gentleman lined up the boys and presented each of them with five bob! That's only 25p in today's money, but was a small fortune to the boys at the time.

Bob Ward also recalls those pheasant shooting expeditions, in particular that Ben always delivered the boys' morning break rations in person, no doubt to keep them out of sight of the gentry! They would stand around in a huddled group, drinking cocoa and consuming their 'wads', whilst 'the guns' would be knocking back their whiskeys and brandies and tucking in to their more refined diet of smoked salmon and cucumber sandwiches.

Molly adds a few thoughts of her own on this subject. She recalls that her Dad often organised 'beating' expeditions around the local farmland, most usually on the Bramshill estate. Ben had been, in his day, a crack shot and, in fact, held the Sniper's Medal from his service with the 3rd Battalion, Grenadier Guards. She adds that it wasn't only 'the boys' who got paid for their endeavours, as local farm workers would supplement their meagre wages in similar fashion, often turning out to 'beat' in the most ghastly of weather.

Ben's eventual son-in-law, John Pewsey, who joined Arborfield just as the war was coming to an end, recalls that Ben was always strict about any tendency to waste food, whether at home with the family or on duty in his capacity as Catering Officer. He would berate the Cookhouse staff, when they inevitably turned his perfectly grown green cabbages into a yellow, watery and almost inedible mush, which neither he nor the boys saw as suitable fodder for *"growing lads"*.

Joe Griffiths of 39A tells a tale of what he calls *"The Great NAAFI Robbery"*. On two consecutive nights, the canteen had been well and truly raided, with all sorts of delectable items 'going missing' – such as chocolate, shoe polish and *Brilliantine* and other marketable goods. But by now, 'Sherriff Ben' was on the case and had set a trap! On the third night, the raiders attempted to strike again, opening the door with their skilfully made skeleton key and gently prising up the counter shutters. The lights came on and there was Ben, quietly but menacingly approaching in his carpet slippers – the game was up. *"Gotcha!"* he roared, as his band of Regimental Police (RP) blocked all exits. The perpetrators of this heinous crime were brought before Col Davies, who waxed fiercely on the fact they were not 'heroes', as maybe they had assumed and, whatever punishment was meted out that day, the

incident was never repeated.

Another NAAFI tale concerning Ben comes from Doc Savage of the 39A intake. One late night, Ben is said to have caught one of the NAAFI girls in 'fragrant delicious' with a Bandsman of the 4th/7th DG on the smooth green baize of one of the billiard tables! Whether Ben was outraged at the pair's lack of decorum, or simply by the incorrect use of the billiard table, is not known. However, as they say in the trade, *"a marriage was arranged"*.

Joe Griffiths has another story, of the day he was on parade one freezing day, with snow all around. Suddenly a snowball hit him on the back of the head and, without thinking, Joe picked up and threw one back in retaliation. *"Come out the boy who threw that snowball"*, came the RSM's rasping voice. With dumb determination, Joe took that first fatal step out of the ranks and marched towards Ben. *"Pick up a snowball"*, came the order. Joe scraped together a lump that was probably more gravel than snow and held it tentatively towards the RSM. Ben's quick brown eyes twinkled with wicked humour. *"Now eat it"*, he said. Without hesitation, Joe did as he was told, much relieved that he was not to be escorted to the Guardroom!

Ben is also remembered, with much fondness, by Gerry Preston (44A). He and three of his mates, James, Johnson and Hall, had nipped out (against the rules, of course!) to a friendly pub at nearby Farley Hill one night. On opening the pub door and finding nobody they recognised, they went up to the bar and timidly ordered 'four halves please', when a loud voice boomed out from behind them – *"Give 'em pints!"* The barman duly obliged, their pockets were entirely depleted, and the four whole pints had to be downed fairly rapidly. It was Ben Cook's voice of course, and once the drinks were drunk, four rather sickly boys were double-marched back to camp. At the Sergeants' Mess gate, Ben told them to get back in the same way that they had got out, then rode off on his bike, chuckling away loudly to himself.

Peter Styles was one of the earliest arrivals at the School gates, joining up in May 1939. His memories of Ben match those of many other boys, that he was *"a strict disciplinarian when on parade, but soft hearted when not"*. He remembers the time when Ben somehow learned that the duty bugler had played 'Reveille' whilst cycling slowly around the Parade Square – the 'holy of holies'. Needless to say, Ben soon put a stop to this, by getting up early enough one morning to catch the unfortunate cycling bugler and, no doubt, put *"a spoke in his wheel"*!

Another ex-boy with a 'Ben Cook tale' to tell is Don Driscoll. He had originally joined up at Bramley in 1938, but was then 'claimed' by his elder brother at Hilsea. When things got 'too hot' down there, due to the bombing raids on neighbouring Portsmouth dockyards, the boys were moved up to Arborfield and came under the tender care of Ben. Don remembers many afternoons spent 'gardening', on jankers of course, under Ben's watchful eye. His final memory of Ben was when he (Don) eventually arrived at the Depot REME for his 'demob'. He was amused when a tractor came flying through the gate with the familiar figure of Ben at its wheel, singing away happily for all he was worth.

Daughter Molly explains that there was a good reason for all Ben's whistling and singing – which he would always carry out whilst out on his bike or tractor. It was to act as a warning to any boys that, if they were causing either mischief or mayhem, then it would be best for them to scarper before Ben's arrival! For those not 'in the know', Molly says that Ben's favourite tune – or hymn – was *'The Old Rugged Cross'*.

Bill Tingey of 39A, another ex-boy who went off to live in NZ, remembered Ben as a man of both *"humour and compassion"*, quoting an example of each as follows. Ben had caught around six lads 'out of bounds' - and out of their depth - in a flooded quarry not far from Camp. He barked at them *"Stand to attention"*, which they patently couldn't do of course, then proceeded to tick them off, saying that non-compliance with an order was the first step on the slippery road to mutiny!

Another time, on a cold day during the winter of 1940 - 41, some boys were mournfully attending the military funeral of another boy who had recently died. Ben was visibly upset, along with the party of pall bearers, but was then kind enough to share his cigarettes with the boys, adding the warning that *"boys who smoked could get into big trouble"*.

Molly has memories of her Dad having to attend a fair number of apprentices' funerals, which certainly took far more out of him than perhaps he ever let on. At one time, she remembers an outbreak of meningitis, which brought Ben the unhappy duty of attending some funerals up in the industrial north. Young as she was at the time, Molly recollects her father's tales of the poverty and deprivation he had found, during these enforced trips.

She also says that she once cycled with her Dad over to Finchampstead churchyard, to look at the graves of some boys who had been laid to rest there. The graves were smothered in grass and weeds, causing Ben a lot of pain and resentment. The two of them quickly set off home, with Ben returning to the church alone with some shears to cut down the offending vegetation. Molly certainly remembers her Dad as a compassionate man.

Looking back on the many tales about Ben, he must have had the livelihood of the boys as a top priority. Bill Baker of 44B certainly thought so. He and a mate, Dick Eyrie, had been out on 'agricultural' duties one cold, drizzly autumn day in 1945, working all afternoon, unsupervised. At 16.45 hours, they decided it was time to *"call it a day"*, reasoning that the Captain (Ben) must have forgotten all about them. As is usually the outcome in such events, Sgt Thornton of the Black Watch caught them, in 'D' Coy washrooms, and immediately 'put them on orders' for being in Company lines before the stated time of 17.00 hours. No sneaking back to your pit during working hours in those days!

The following morning, the luckless pair of boys was sentenced to three days CB by their Company Commander, Capt Shaw. Bill wasn't too pleased at what he saw as a complete injustice and so, dashing to the QM's office, he asked Ben whether he could remember dismissing his two charges at 16.45 on the previous afternoon. Ben gruffly acknowledging that this had, indeed, been the case, turned smartly on his heel and marched into Capt Shaw's office. The boys never heard any more, apart from the fact that the charges were dropped and removed from their records.

Tony Blackwell, who also joined as a young lad in early 1944, remembers Ben as *"basically a hard man, feared by the apprentices, which his obviously deep voice enforced, and to be avoided at all costs"*. But of course the softer side of Ben's nature occasionally saw the light of day. Feeling quite ill one morning, Tony was sat in the MRS, awaiting the arrival of the MO, when in walked Ben. All the other boys shot off their seats and stood to attention, but Tony just wasn't up to it, remaining rooted to his seat. Realising that Tony was in some distress, Ben ensured that he was first patient to see the MO on arrival.

Tony recalls meeting up with Ben in a local hostelry some years later and, over the odd glass of beer or three, engaging him in chatting about 'the good old times' with Gilbert. He mentioned to Ben that he must have loved that horse, to which Ben replied, much to Tony's surprise, *"He (Gilbert) couldn't do the work I wanted, so I sent him to the knacker's yard"*. Ben's daughter Molly reckons that this gruff and seemingly unfeeling retort would have been Ben's own way of dealing with the obviously deep sorrow caused by the loss of his 'gentle giant'.

Even legends eventually come to the end of their line, and this Ben did early in 1978. He lies in the churchyard at Arborfield, close to the countryside that was always *"his fondest love"*, in the words of his daughter. Molly's brother-in-law, by the name of Leo Kemp and once RSM of the Trg Btn and Depot REME at Poperinghe Barracks (1973-75), has his ashes lying next to Ben's grave and, as Molly explains, this allows them to *"discuss regimental topics at the dead of night"*. Molly and John Pewsey's own daughter, Briony, has two stepdaughters, Gemma and Rachael, who for a time ran *'The Bull'* at Barkham, having had no connection with the area in the past.

Even so, in their mind's eye they could see this *"ghost from the past"*, riding up on his bike to meet old farming chums for a pint or two. He could be in officer's uniform or civvies, depending on his mood, but always happy in the knowledge that he had brought his family to enjoy life in the tranquil countryside at Arborfield, rather than the spartan married quarters in such places as Aldershot, Windsor and Caterham. *"Arrived 1938, left 1978"*, that's Ben's Arborfield legacy, still vivid in the memories of so many 'boy soldiers'.

(The above account of 'the life and times' of Ben Cook was concocted from some of the countless stories sent in to the OBAN by many old boys of the time, plus a response to those stories given by Ben's daughter Molly early in 2002.)

'Our School' by RSM R L McNally, MBE (Scots Guards), Arborfield, 1944

'Tradition dies hard' is an expression that is widely quoted in this country, especially during these war years. Sometimes, when it refers to the saving of a difficult situation, it is uttered with a note of pride. At other times, on those occasions when restraining Age has applied the rein to impetuous Youth, it is said with annoyance. Tradition dies hard: there is nothing so

difficult to create as Tradition.

We who are at this school – our School, Arborfield – have had but a few years in which to build Tradition. It has not been easy, and only *you* can enlarge upon it and make it stronger. Only *you* can undo what has been done or retard its progress. Have you 'the School feeling' in the right way, the way that will be most beneficial to yourself, to us, to the Army, to the country?

The years you spend in this School are some of the most important in your life; they represent the transition from 'boy' to 'man'. How are you succeeding? Are you giving of your best? Would you have acted differently, had you your time over again? So many of us would act differently given another chance, but time is one of those precious things that we can never reclaim.

You have all had the meaning of *'esprit de corps'* explained to you. It is something that starts in a very small way and grows into a feeling that will affect your whole life for good, both during your service and afterwards. The essence of *'esprit de corps'* is loyalty and, within a very short time of joining us, you should have developed a feeling of pride in your School, a feeling of loyalty, respect and affection for it. This feeling, if fostered in the right manner, will not only influence your own character and conduct, but also of the School to which you belong.

How can you build up this feeling in the School? Firstly, by your own conduct – by trying to be a decent, clean-thinking, clean-speaking and clean-living lad - by trying to use all the knowledge that is available in the School, to improve your trade skill and education, by taking a pride in your personal appearance and turn-out, wherever you are, both inside and outside the School. Secondly, by helping to promote the feeling in weaker or more wayward members of the School.

When you leave here and anyone asks you where were you trained, you can say with a note of pride and without any apologies, 'Arborfield'. Some schools and establishments turn out products with a distinct stamp upon their life, the 'hallmarks' we find on gold and silver. Eton, Oxford, Sandhurst, Dartmouth and Cranwell are all accepted names that mean something. We want Arborfield to also mean something. This is the aim of everybody responsible for your training here; the country's acknowledgement of the School, as a place fitted for your training, is their reward.

Too many of us think that the expression *'playing the game'* only applies to our activities on the sports field. I we could only live up to this saying in all our actions, we would build our character along the right lines. Discipline yourself now to obey, so that you may fit yourself later to command. Obedience does not only mean doing something when ordered and under supervision, but doing it because you know it is right and, the greatest test of all, when you are alone.

Be alive and enthusiastic in everything that you do. The fellow who says *'That will do'* to a bad job of work is a failure to himself and to his comrades. Live cleanly and let your standards be high, and everything should be within your grasp.

Whilst this great Empire, to which you have the honour to belong, is engaged in the greatest struggle within its history, you are laying the foundations for the future. It is to the youth of today that the world will look for the reconstruction of tomorrow, see that you make yourself worthy of that responsibility.

If this article has helped you in any way to understand our aims here, the answer will be found in the manner in which you speak of *'Our School'*.

(The preceeding article was published in the very first edition of The Arborfield Apprentice magazine in 1944 and reproduced, courtesy of Bryan Adams (42C), in Issue 3 of the OBAN in spring 1993.)

Major General Sir Bertram Rowcroft KBE CB

The new home of the Training Battalion and Depot REME was named after the first Director of Mechanical Engineering, the late Major General Sir Bertram Rowcroft, KBE, CB, MIMechE, MIEE, whose tenure as Director General spanned the years 1942 to 1946. He continued his association with the Corps as Colonel Commandant until 1956.

General Rowcroft was born in 1891 and first served with the Royal Engineers, Territorial Army; he passed into (what was then) the Royal Military College, Sandhurst, in 1909 and was gazetted into the ASC in 1911. He had a distinguished career, with the emphasis on the technical aspects of the ASC, later the RASC. He was commanding the RASC Training Battalion on the outbreak of war in 1939, but was quickly called to the S and T Directorate at the War Office, where, for outstanding work, he was made a Commander of the Order of the British Empire (CBE) in 1941.

Early in 1942, the formation of a new technical Corps was approved. Undoubtedly, a major problem of the time was the choice of a man of outstanding organisational and technical ability, to put this great project into effect in time of war. General Rowcroft was the man selected and subsequent events proved the wisdom of this decision. The Corps of the Royal and Mechanical Engineers was born.

After the conclusion of hostilities, in 1946 the General was made a Companion of the Order of the Bath (CB). From then, until he retired at the end of 1946, he devoted his energies to the re-shaping of REME's post-war form. Combatant status of the Corps was recognised, the REME Association was formed, the REME magazine was launched, the Corps Band was raised, the Benevolent fund was started, as was the Officers' Club and REME Rifle Association. Upon his retirement, the General's services were recognised by his being awarded his Knighthood. He died on December 27th 1963.

(The above is based upon a short history, published as an annex to those briefing notes produced at the time of a visit to Rowcroft Barracks by His Royal Highness the Duke of Edinburgh, in April 1978.)

Major General Peter Baldwin CBE

On January 20th 1942, Peter Baldwin left the King Edward VI Grammar School in Chelmsford, Essex and enlisted at the Army Recruiting Office at Romford. He was just a few weeks short of his fifteenth birthday as he travelled to the ATS (Boys) at Arborfield, where he began his training as a Radio Mechanic.

In 1944, when the School became required for D-Day troop concentrations, the whole School population, staff and boys, was dispersed to various sites to continue their training. Peter was amongst those sent to a Central Workshop in Greenford, Middlesex. From there he was sent directly to the field army, forming part of a Z-Lorry inspection team that toured those parachute forces preparing for operations in Europe.

In December 1945, he and another ex-apprentice (P G Harrison) were dispatched to Khartoum, where they became the only two Radio Mechs with the Sudan Defence Force. Peter completed a War Office Selection Board (WOSB) in Cairo at the end of 1946 and, after returning to this country to train at Aldershot and Catterick, he was commissioned into the Royal Signals in the rank of Lieutenant.

The following years included a tour as Radio

Officer in Berlin, both before and during the famous airlift of 1948. In 1950, whilst in Hong Kong, Peter was sent to Korea with 27 Commonwealth Brigade at the outbreak of that war. Another spell in Germany (at Munster) was followed by service at the War Office and, in 1960, attendance at the Staff College at Camberley. He returned there in 1969 as a member of the Directing Staff (DS).

After yet another German tour, Peter attended the Joint Services Staff College at Latimer, Buckinghamshire and was posted to 5 Infantry Brigade as Brigade Signals Officer. This included a year in Borneo, where he was mentioned in dispatches, towards the end of that particular confrontation. He then commanded 13 Signal Regiment at Birgelen, Germany, having served there as Adjutant some fifteen years previously.

From there he was posted again, this time as Colonel, to be Secretary for Studies at the NATO Defence College in Rome. This was followed by promotion to take command of 2 Signal Brigade in England. A NATO appointment recurred when Peter was appointed Assistant Chief of Staff (COS) at HQ Allied Forces in Central Europe (AFCENT) in Holland, from where he was promoted to be Chief Signal Officer in British Army of the Rhine (BAOR).

Peter left the Army in November 1979 and immediately became deputy director (later director) of radio at the Independent Broadcasting Authority (IBA) in London. He created the Radio Authority and became its first Chief Executive. In 1994, he was appointed CBE for his services to broadcasting. Retiring in 1996, Peter soon found himself 'helping out' at the Television Corporation as its company secretary!

Major General Peter Baldwin CBE

Peter is married to Gail and lives in Buckinghamshire. He is a trustee of both the D'Oyly Carte Opera Company and the Community Service Volunteers (CSV). He is chairman of The Eyeless Trust, a charity that supports children born without eyes and also belongs to many ex-Service organisations.
(The above brief biography was supplied by Peter himself, following the 2002 Old Boys' Reunion.)

How we were in 1945

Chapter 3

1945 - 49

The War draws to a close

During January 1945, despite severe snowstorms and four-foot high drifts, the previously victorious Panzer Battalions of the German Army had finally been beaten at the Ardennes Forest in what became renowned as the 'Battle of the Bulge'. The way now seemed clear for Allied Forces to fight their way into the heartland of Germany itself. At the end of that same month, Russian troops broke across the German border from Poland and, in early February, American units finally crossed the 'Siegfried Line'. The end of the war was finally becoming a realistic accomplishment to the war-weary nation. Even then, however, deadly V2 rockets were still falling as late as March. By the time it all ended, over 1,000 of these weapons had landed on British soil, over half of them on London, with the final death toll reaching 2,700.

On March 25th, the Allied armies fought their way across the Rhine and, by late April, the Russian 'Red Army' was plunging into the very heart of the Reich itself. This still didn't stop the final act of aggression towards English territory, when the Germans launched its last V2 on March 27th, followed by three V1 doodlebugs aimed at us on March 29th. The V2 killed one unfortunate person at Orpington, while of the three V1s, one plopped harmlessly into a sewage farm at Hatfield, Hertfordshire; the second failed to find a target at Sittingbourne in Kent; while the third was shot down by AA fire off the Suffolk coast.

April 29th saw the last day of war in Italy, as Fascist forces from both Italy and Germany surrendered to Field Marshall Alexander. On April 30th, Russian troops finally overran the last German defences in their capital city of Berlin. With Hitler taking his own life in the infamous Reichstag 'bunker' and German soldiers surrendering on all fronts, peace finally came to a battered Europe at 2.41 a.m. on May 7th, in a small red schoolhouse in Rheims, when General Jodl signed the instrument of unconditional surrender. The final capitulation by Field Marshall Keitel came about in Berlin on May 8th.

The Great Escape

That most popular prisoner-of-war film, 'The Great Escape', seems to be broadcast on our TV sets almost every Christmas nowadays, but Tony 'Ginger' Guy (43A) has vivid memories of the School's very own version, the great escape from 'Stalag Arborfield' on the night of 7th / 8th May 1945. VE (Victory in Europe) Day had just been announced as May 8th. Despite Winston Churchill's announcement that *"We may allow ourselves a brief period of rejoicing"*, no special leave period was to be allowed for the School at that time. This inevitably proved such a challenge – *"like a red rag to a bull"* - to many of the lads that every effort was made to 'be there' in London for such an historic event.

Tony recalls making a 6 a.m. getaway via the ATS lines and then on to Smokey Joe's café. Here, he and his gang was lucky enough to be given a lift to Wokingham on a low-loader lorry, hanging on for dear life as the driver drove *"like a bat out of hell"*. They eventually arrived at Waterloo by train, then walked across Hungerford Bridge to Charing Cross and into Trafalgar Square. They joined the swirling throng, singing and dancing its way up and down the Mall; via side streets to Leicester Square, and around the hub of Piccadilly; they were just carried along by the delirious crowd. Pubs were packed to bursting, so the only way to be sure of getting a drink was to order about six rounds at a time!

The strange thing is that Tony cannot even remember anything after midnight, whether he slept, ate, washed or shaved – it is still *"all a blank"*! He does recall that he eventually returned to Camp around 10 p.m. on May 11th, climbing over the fence from Ben Cook's potato field, tearing his BD blouse on the fence as he did so.

A great time was obviously had by all those who had made it, with many abiding memories of the crowded Mall, and Churchill's own appearance, complete with his famous cigar and 'V for Victory' hand salute, on the balcony of Buckingham Palace alongside smiling members of the Royal Family. Even the fact that, on arrival back at Camp, all the boys were immediately charged with being 'absent without leave' (AWOL), did not dampen their high spirits.

Tom Pearce (44A) believes that, after the early morning 'escape' mentioned above, the 'powers that be' must have relented, because he can remember subsequently being allowed out, on the firm understanding that he returned by the normal 'return to Camp' time of 21.30 hours. Needless to say, a large number of boys inevitably failed to meet this deadline, with the result that over 300 of them appeared on Company Orders the following morning. Justice appears to have been based and dispensed on the degree of lateness, with the maximum sentence probably set at some four days of jankers. However, David Ferns (44B) says that he was away for only two days, yet was awarded ten days! *(Must have been the 'cut of your jib' David. Ed.)*

The Commandant eventually decided that it would be sensible to parade the whole School for a 'pep talk' and remitted the remaining sentences – hard luck on those who had already served their time! Jesse Pye was one of those who remembers 'serving his time', although it was only for three days, due to his having been a whole two-and-a-half minutes late back! He had just completed his sentence when the remission was announced.

Walter Jobber (43B) certainly doesn't recall having **his** sentence curtailed! As far as he can remember, it was *"five days CB"* and he did them all. He also describes one of the ways that was used to help the boys *"pass the time"* during that confinement. They were told to take small granite chippings, one at a time, from two piles that had been deposited outside the Cookhouse after the Square had been re-surfaced. They then had to 'double' to the air-raid shelters at the top of the Square and hurl the chipping as far as possible in the direction of the perimeter fence. Rather ironic in Walter's case, as that was at the very point of his exit and re-entry in his own great escape!

Tom Pearce tells an amusing tale about one of

the PS Junior Non-Commissioned Officers (JNCOs), a Cpl Walker, who he believes was from the Royal Tank Regt (RTR). Walker had a rather elaborate, indeed almost Shakespearean mode of speech. At roll call one evening, he strode into Tom's barrack room and announced that, *"My tenure as Orderly Sergeant is drawing to a close"*. Quick as a flash, one of the barrack wits – yes, there were a few! - responded with the comment, *"Come off it Corporal, you haven't been on for ten year, you've only been on for a week!"*

More thoughts upon the VE Day episode come from Charles Pepper of 43B. Charles had an elderly uncle living in Walthamstow at the time. This uncle had been one of the original members of the Royal Flying Corps (RFC) during the first World War, but had missed the 'peace' celebrations then, and certainly didn't want to miss out on this particular party! Along with another pal from his barrack room, and in company with the said uncle, Charles enjoyed wandering among the massed crowds, soaking up the wonderful convivial atmosphere. It was hard work pushing through the celebrating crowds on the way back to Waterloo. He and his pal eventually arrived back at Camp about half an hour later than they should and, like many others, were charged with being AWOL and given a sentence of 'seven days CB'.

There were so many 'offenders' at the time that the first morning jankers call must have taken on the form of a full Company parade. Col White detected the unrest and addressed the assembled boys. Recalling an incident from his dim and distant past, he told them that, during the First World War, his Company had *"committed a misdemeanour and been awarded extra days in the front line"*. The message was basically this – hard luck lads, your punishment pales by comparison, so take it like men. But after a few days of parades and fatigues, the Provost staff seemed to lose interest and Charles then recalls being left under the command of a rather unimpressive-looking Lance Corporal. He saw the chance of a 'skive' and duly took it. But unfortunately for Charles, the Lance Jack wasn't as dozy as he looked, and Charles was consequently awarded another seven days!

For one reason or another, usually associated with the forbidden pleasures of smoking, it wasn't long before he totted up an extended sentence of more than thirty days of the dreaded fatigues. However, towards the end of his 'time', Charles tended to get the cushier jobs and became so well known to the ATS girls in the Cookhouse, that he was soon able to enjoy all the benefits of extra helpings of the meagre wartime rations.

Although Lawrence Nixon had left the School just a few weeks before that great escape, he found himself in a similar predicament at his unit in Chichester. He was also denied any celebratory day off, but did a *"mirror image"* of those boys still at Arborfield, by heading off to London to celebrate, then finishing with seven days jankers for being AWOL. Having never even been placed on a charge at the School, Lawrence now felt that he was *a soldier at last"*!

Bob Dann (42C) doesn't know if he should be considered as one of the genuine escapees, because he never got as far as London! He and another lad (he thinks his name was 'Waters', from Gosport) instead made their way to Blackwater railway station by bus, and then by train to Portsmouth. Having no tickets, it was fortunate that the ticket collector seemed to have made an escape of his own! For two *"smashing days"*, the pair of them enjoyed celebrating in the pub opposite the entrance to the Maritime Museum.

Writing in the School magazine, under the heading *'VE Day'*, A/T T J Hoyes of 'B' Coy (44C) remembered the sun going down *"on a tired but happy little island"*. He described the merry streets, with their red, white and blue bunting and bonfires, a pleasant contrast to the depressing gloom of six weary battle-scarred years. But there was a tinge of sadness in his words too,

as he thought of all the fathers and sons who would never return to share the happiness for which they had bravely laid down their lives. Even the sweetness of victory could not erase all the bitterness of those years of struggle and sacrifice.

On July 15th 1945, after more than 2,000 nights of blackout and dim-out, Britain was ablaze with light once more. In London, thousands flocked to the West End to see the great 'switch-on', to see Piccadilly Circus return to its pre-war brilliance. The event was timed to coincide with the end of 'double summer-time', and brought a carnival-like atmosphere to many parts of the country. No doubt the most relieved people of all were the Channel Islanders, who had borne a whole five years of German occupation. Those islands had been the only part of the British Isles to suffer that fate.

Peace – at long last

However, the war in the Far East was still going on and it took the dropping of the first two atomic bombs, on the Japanese cities of Hiroshima and Nagasaki in early August, to bring the end of hostilities on that far-eastern side of the globe. Some 120,000 people are believed to have died directly in those bombings, with many more left dreadfully injured and suffering from the effects of radiation. But it no doubt saved the lives of many thousands, even millions, more who would have been involved in the defence and taking of the main Japanese islands of Honshu and Kyushu.

Frank Fendick (45A – and whose surname was Hill in those days) remembers the feeling of missing out on the celebrations being set up for the subsequent Victory in Japan (VJ) Day on August 14th, barely a hundred days after VE day. He informed his father that he was definitely going to be up in London this time, whether leave was given or not. As his father was an ex-RSM, his reply is remembered word for word after all these years. *"Do you think that after thirty years in His Majesty's Army, I would harbour a deserter?"* Somehow, one has the impression that Frank didn't make it up to 'The Smoke' after all! If he didn't, he missed out on a momentous sight as bonfires blazed along the southern bank of the Thames, from Orpington to Ramsgate. Finally, and at long last, the dark shadow of war, with its *"blood, sweat and tears"*, had been lifted. Hopefully, the country as a whole, including the apprentices' home here at Arborfield, could now return to a settled way of life.

Frank was another of that band of men, the Dukies, who came directly from there to Arborfield, swapping one famous School for another. When he had turned up at Wokingham, he had had his pocket tapped as part of the 'grilling' over cigarettes. When he replied that he didn't smoke, he was asked, *"Are they glasses in there?"* Poor Frank, who was pretty ashamed at the fact that he needed glasses, responded negatively, even though it was his spectacle case that had indeed been tapped!

Don Walker arrived at the gates of the ATS (Boys) on 21st February 1945 as a young lad, fourteen years of age and weighing a mere five stone, 'soaking wet'. As he says himself, *"Not everyone's idea of a fearless fighting soldier"*! Don's father had tried to get him an apprenticeship at the local Workshops, but Don himself was more impressed by what Arborfield had to offer. Passing the entrance examination at Reading, he then attended his medical exam. As Don had always been considered *"delicate"*, following several childhood illnesses, Don's parents were rather dismayed when he triumphantly returned, waving a piece of paper that declared him 'A1' – and thus fit to serve.

Having gone through the familiar induction process, Don was kitted out in *"clothes you will grow into"* and soon found himself involved in all the normal activities of those distant days. He retains many fond memories of Arborfield, amongst them those evenings when RSM McNally and his dear wife would attempt to teach the boys the intricacies of ballroom dancing. Other names recalled are Sgt Dransfield, Sgt Herbie Payne, Peggy Crowe and her 'Cookhouse girls', as well of course as the eternal Ben Cook. Don's brother Arthur also served here at Arborfield, having originally signed on at Chepstow in 1946. Don proudly recalls that, as a REME sergeant, Arthur was later awarded the BEM for his work in the Gulf State of Oman.

Don himself left the School in 1948, one of those *"marched up the road to complete a regular REME craftsman's course"*. Following one short posting to Brackley, he was then sent on his way to East Africa on the troopship *'Empire Ken'*, accompanied by several other old boys. He has always regarded the next three years with the King's African Rifles, first in Zomba (Nyasaland) and then Lusaka (then Northern Rhodesia), as the *"highlight of my service life"*. After many years shuttling across the world, from Egypt to BAOR, back to England, then to Kuala Lumpur, Don

found himself instructing at Bordon, Hampshire, for four years, before spending his last two years with the RAOC in Dorset, and leaving the service in 1970.

Another lad from that 45A intake, George Oliver, admits that the memories of his time at the ATS (Boys) tend to come only in *"little snippets"*. These include being picked up at Reading railway station; ATS girls cadging clothing coupons during those days of rationing; his first meal being simply bread & butter, a lump of cheese, a tomato and mug of tea, due to the Cookhouse being closed when he arrived. Later on he recalls that parties of apprentices would be taken on visits to civilian factories, such as *AEC* at Southall, *Ford* at Dagenham and *Modern Wheel Drives* at Slough.

George can also recall being taken for a river trip on the Thames in a 'DUKW', a type of amphibious craft, which involved negotiating the narrow railway bridge at Pangbourne, between Reading and Oxford. In the event, the 'Keep Left' sign was brought down, apparently not an unusual occurrence in those days. Another highlight of the trade curriculum was motorcycle training, which seemed to involve riding around in circles and diagonals, across the length and breadth of the square, somehow dodging the squads of boys out there at the same time on drill exercises! One of George's educational teachers, he can only remember him as *"a Scots WO2 schoolie"*, gave his class a spelling test, with the winner to be awarded a *"handsome plaque"*. It turned out to be no more than a penny piece!

(The 'DUKW' – or 'Duck' as it was more commonly referred to – was an amphibious wheeled vehicle, American built, based upon the General Motor Corporation (GMC) two-and-a-half ton truck. It had widely used in the D-Day landings at Normandy, ferrying supplies and men to shore, then transferring casualties back to off-shore ships. Ed.)

The time of his life

Eddie Broomfield was also part of intake 45A and still retains vivid memories of his daily routines, from *Reveille* at 06.30 hours until *Lights Out* at 22.15 hours, all regulated by the shrill sounds from the duty bugler. As Eddie recalls it, there were not many boys in those days who could afford the luxury of a watch so, apart from those daily bugle calls, time was more or less governed by the large clocks that ticked away on the walls of the Cookhouse and Guardroom.

Eddie remembers that 'flagpole fatigues' was a routine used to sort out which 'dirty job' was to be allotted for the day. Parading by the flagpole on the Square, the boys would be ordered off – two for the Officers' Mess, two for the Sergeants' Mess, another four for the Cookhouse, for example. These were of course the 'good jobs', which most boys didn't mind doing, but there was also the dreaded service of 'agriculture', as administered by the famous Ben Cook in the green fields that surrounded the Camp.

Morning break was generally taken in the trade training area, consisting of a mug of cocoa, dispensed from a huge steaming urn, and a lump of what the cooks laughingly called cake! Eddie remembers that the enamel mugs in question were kept in one's toolbox, along with the assorted files and chisels or whatever, inevitably leading to lots of chipped enamel. Not the most satisfactory of hygiene arrangements, but Eddie cannot remember anyone dying as a direct result!

Lunchtime meant a march down the road to the Cookhouse, where Eddie reckons the staff did a *"grand job in feeding nearly a thousand hungry growing lads"*. Still vivid in his memory is the sight of two ATS Sergeants, they were definitely sisters and maybe even twins, standing behind the hotplate, resplendent in their clean white smocks, with sets of three gold stripes on a background of red. The food in those days was prepared in 'Dixie' cans, one per table, with twelve boys at each table. Dished out by the senior boys, the amount you got depended upon your seniority!

Eddie recalls that the barrack-rooms held *"little comfort"*, but at least there was plenty to keep the boys fully occupied, with the interminable demand for kit presentations, tidiness and cleanliness. But even with a full complement of serviceable light bulbs, which was rare indeed, the rooms remained rather dull and the 'central heating' system, when working flat out, only managed to bring a modicum of warmth with it. *(Eddie went on to reach the rank of Captain before terminating his service, but his days as a Warrant Officer, serving in BAOR during the early Sixties, will long be remembered by those many ex-boys who followed him there. Eddie, or 'Q' as he was known, of course, never had an unkind word for any of them and always a word of almost fatherly advice. I know, because 'I was that soldier' – well, one of them anyway! Ed.)*

Derek Williams joined the School on February 21st 1945 and was eventually commissioned in 1954,

gaining the rank of Captain by 1962. Amazingly, he then changed tack, being accepted into the RAF, where he continued to serve until 1987, right up to the rank of Squadron Leader. One of his never-to-be-forgotten memories of boys' school concerns the issue of light bulbs, which were inevitably in extremely short supply at the end of the war. Replacement for a 'dud' was usually gained by removing the bulb from a less alert comrade, or – even better – a surreptitious raid on another room. A recent entry to the ranks of the Jeeps was heard to remark, *"If it's not there when I get back, I'll know it has gone"*!

Another member of that 45A intake was John Pewsey, who later went on to become the husband of Molly Cook, daughter of the famous Ben Cook. John had started work as a *"junior acting under-clerk"* in a well-known bank in Worthing, on the Sussex coast, thanks to the good offices of his father, a Colonel in the Pay Corps. 'Junior' he certainly was, as the rest of the staff was still in a time warp of goose-quilled nibs, hardly able to master the newfangled fountain pens! His lowly employment lasted for all of the glorious month of June 1944 but, by the time the Allied troops had begun to reinforce their first foothold on Normandy shores, John's own foothold at the bank had been terminated! So it was that he later found himself at the gates of Arborfield on February 21st 1945.

John soon took his place in 'D' Coy, which he recalls included one boy from Dr Barnados'. Along with the rest of his intake, John soon sorted out his *"hay foot"* from his *"straw foot"*, but he never did come across the oft promised 'Field Marshall's baton' in his knap-sack! He did, however, become quite a proficient member of the School cross-country team. This led to him becoming what he terms a *"fag runner"* for some of the senior boys. This illicit night-time activity rarely ran further than the shop in the 'Robinson Crusoe' club, not too far away, but occasionally John found himself down the Nine-Mile Ride in his quest for the precious *Woodbines*.

An explosive tale!

One *"fine but boring Sunday afternoon"*, along with close pal Billy Fagen, John took a walk down the nearby Nine-Mile Ride. Located at regular intervals along the roadside were a collection of small corrugated iron shelters, which in later years were probably used as residences for pigs. Rumour had it that, at the time, these shelters were being used for storage purposes. Boringly, John and Billy now found them empty. However, behind a barbed wire fence, in a wooded area towards Crowthorne, the two boys found a large Nissen hut with its doors left unlocked and inside was an 'Aladdin's Cave' of ammunition. These ranged from shells and flares to grenades, with lots of bullets too. Carefully retreating, the boys made their way back to Camp to hatch a cunning plan!

The following week, John returned to the hut, now with another mate, R A L Harris, both boys fully kitted out with small-packs. It wasn't long before these were hauled back to barracks, bulging with explosives. Needless to say, there were a few impromptu 'fireworks' displays over the following few nights!

Disaster was to follow however, when John attempted to convert a 20mm shell into a fashionable table lighter. The detonator exploded, and John ended up minus part of one finger and one thumb from his left hand. His mates rushed him to the 'ablutions' to run his hand under cold water, and then quick-thinkingly wrapped it in a clean towel. An ambulance took him to CMH Aldershot, where certain modifications were carried out on the aforesaid digits! John then spent some time at the hospital, while the surgeons looked for, then removed, several *"bits of brass"* from his left eye.

Meanwhile, *"back at the ranch"*, RSM McNally was leading a search for any more explosives – all of which had been carefully stored by the other boys behind John's bed-space! The only other 'loot' found was an electric doorbell that Billy Fagen – purely for scientific research, you understand – had liberated from one of the trade classrooms and then hidden under his greatcoat. Billy got fourteen days for his efforts. When eventually John was 'brought to book' before the Commandant, Col White decided that he had already suffered enough punishment, telling him that it mustn't happen again! Well, it didn't, and John finally passed out of Arborfield at the same rank as that at which he entered – Apprentice Tradesman.

John recalls that Capt Ben Cook took the appointment of Catering Officer at one time. He particularly coincides that time with Sunday lunch, as the pudding always seemed to be trifle, made up from time-expired cake supplied by Miss Ames, who was the NAAFI manageress in those days. The trifle would be served with a dollop of custard, dished up in a square tin, one per table, in the Cookhouse. John says

that he used to stagger back up the square to his room afterwards, fully replete with SD jacket unbuttoned and his white belt hanging around his neck! *(No doubt the same fare is still dished up at home each Sunday by Molly, eh John? Ed.)*

Keith Evans, who was still serving (just!) at the boys' school some fifty years later, recalls the ordeal of sitting at his table in the Cookhouse, waiting to be served by one of his seniors. The table sat twelve young apprentices, with two senior boys at 'the top', in charge of rationing out the lovely grub. Steamed pudding would arrive in a twelve-inch square tin, and then be *"cut in two"* by those same senior boys. The two portions would then be divvied out, one between the two seniors and the other half between the ten Jeeps! The custard, or *"yellow water"* as described by Keith, stood in a large aluminium jug. If it arrived at your position with some liquid still in it, you could count yourself lucky!

Living at peace

Young Gerald Thompson of 45B wondered if he was *"doing the right thing"* as he joined the train at Norwich, bound for Liverpool Street station in 'Lunnon'. At Ipswich, a battle-hardened sergeant from the Royal Armoured Corps (RAC) entered his compartment and enjoined him in conversation. Despite the fact that he (the sergeant) was on his way to Aldershot to be 'demobbed', he applauded Gerald's wish to join the Army and told him to *"make a good soldier"*.

This Gerald always tried to do, of course, eventually becoming an A/T Corporal. On one particular parade, the inspecting General asked him if he got paid for his stripes, to which Gerald innocently answered *"No, Sir"*. His Coy Commander, Maj Senior, quickly interjected, *"Oh, but he does Sir, one penny a day Sir!"* Poor Gerald genuinely hadn't realised there was a payment for being an NCO, as those pennies were absorbed into 'credits' and only drawn upon at leave periods.

The term 'demob', the shortened version of demobilisation, was on many lips during that period, as a total of some four million men were returned from active wartime service to 'Civvy Street'. Once the euphoria of victory had faded away, it became clear just how much it had cost the country as a whole. For several years, the so called 'austerity years', the regime of rationing was to become even more severe than it

Apprentices on morning parade (note the Cookhouse and Water-tower to the right of the parade)

had been during the war. The people overcame their sentimental feelings towards wartime leader, Winston Churchill, and voted in a Labour government.

Churchill's wartime leadership had been exceptional, especially when England stood virtually alone against the Nazi tyranny in the early days of the war. But his relationships with his generals had been tempestuous to say the least, as he had almost attempted to do their jobs for them at times, and was always intolerant of any delays in battle plans. To him, it was always *"Action this day"*. His C-in-C, Alan Brooke, was moved to say afterwards that, *"I shall always look back on the years I worked with him as some of the most difficult and trying ones of my life. For all that, I thank God that I was given the opportunity of working alongside such a man"*.

The battered country now looked ahead to a rebuilding phase to overcome the acres of bomb-damaged sites that served the country as a reminder of the dark days just behind it. Perhaps it was with this 'rebuilding' effort in mind that, during 1945, a curious thing happened to 'D' block. As an experiment, the occupants – the boys themselves - were given the task of painting out their own rooms. That no other block continued with this dubious experiment perhaps speaks for itself! The room floors subsequently had to be scraped and scrubbed, before being re-stained and brought up to their polished perfection once more. And so 'D' block started off once again with brown floors, although slightly speckled with the remains of *eau de nil,* some of which probably remained there until the

Camp was eventually demolished around thirty-five years later!

David Tilt is one who joined the School soon after the cessation of hostilities, as a member of intake 45B. Over fifty years later, wherever he goes, and whatever he does, he has never forgotten his three years at Arborfield. As he says, *"It taught me so much, it moulded my life, it educated me, guided me and taught me many skills"*. David was to go on to write a book, *'Hey you, Boy'*, tracing his steps from his early childhood, through to his becoming a boy soldier, and then finally becoming established as a professional 'toastmaster', operating at the highest levels. *(You didn't know Michael Bentine did you David? Ed.)*

Resettlement and reconstruction

On Tuesday October 16th 1945, the April 1943 intake had their 'PoP', with the inspecting officer being Lieutenant General (Lt Gen) Sir John T Crocker CB, DSO, MC, the GOC of Southern Command. In his address to the boys, the General announced:

> *"You have joined the Army at a momentous time. The war is over, but the Army still has a very great part to play in this time of resettlement and reconstruction"*. He went on to add, *"The boys who have been trained at this School are going to form an important element in the post-war Army"*.

December of 1945 saw the second edition of *The Arborfield Apprentice*. In it, Sgt Pinder the editor was pleased to report a greater preponderance of articles written by the boys themselves. He went on to describe the type of material that was wanted for future magazines, such as views on important world events; interesting occurrences in the School or at home; School visits; technical articles and humourous sketches.

The Commandant, in his foreword to that magazine, said that *"During the year, the tide of aggression has, after threatening to engulf the world, been forced back to its very source and has overwhelmed its originators"*. It is interesting to note that many pages of that School magazine were filled with poems, including this one by A/T Hoyes of 'B' Coy, dedicated to *'The Jeep'*:

"The New Boy – Jeep, as he is known,
Fresh and foolish, straight from home;
In his rookish civvy ways he
Drives the Sergeants nearly crazy!

The queues he left in Civvy Street
He finds in no way can compete
With pushes, scrums and methods crude
To be the first to get his food.

The bugle heads his list of woe,
He groans whene'er he hears it blow;
The only tunes he thinks well played
Are 'Cookhouse', 'Lights out' and 'No Parade'.

When on fatigues (QM's of course)
He's made to imitate a horse,
He sighs 'Oi be a varmer's boy,
But Gilbert gets the praise, not Oi!'

Our Jeep, of course, is taught a trade
And swears he's grossly underpaid!
Of trucks and tanks he glibly speaks,
But all he does is file for weeks!

E'en while our Jeep bemoans his fate,
Another intake's at the gate;
Those early days he'll soon forget,
Our Jeep – excuse me – our 'Old Sweat'!"

A/T J Barrows of 'A' Coy was moved to write, in another contribution to the same magazine, the following eulogy:

"For a long time I regarded poetry as 'cissy' stuff. I pictured a poet as a lazy, useless sort of creature with a pale face, long hair and dreamy eyes – a Sergeant Major's nightmare! Since then I have learned that Rupert Brooke was killed in action; that both Lawrence of Arabia and Orde Wingate of the Chindits were classical scholars and great readers of poetry; that Field Marshall Wavell recently compiled an anthology of his favourite poems. There is nothing 'cissy' about these names, and what is good enough for them seems good enough for me."

Two 'roving reporters', in the form of A/Ts M Axford and R Burton of 'B' Coy, gave a fascinating report of a tour of the Camp Cinema. They described the two projectors, *"both very up-to-date machines"*, where the light was produced by a carbon arc. They explained how the operator had to be aware that, as one reel on one machine was running out, the second machine had to have its carbon arc *"burnt in"* ready for a quick changeover, before the second reel started running. The whole procedure would be repeated every seventeen minutes during a normal feature film.

Sport was once again beginning to take its place in the normal life of the School. The soccer team was now entered in the Reading District Minor League, as well as the Berkshire and Buckinghamshire Cup. Attractive fixtures had been arranged against the boys of Winchester, Charterhouse and Bradfield, all first-class public schools. One of the PS staff 'coaches' to the team was a Corporal Allenby Chilton, who had played for Manchester United. A fine 1944 – 45 playing season provided a record of only nine defeats in fifty-nine games.

Hockey was fast becoming another popular sport within the School, thanks largely to the introduction of indoor hockey on a pitch laid out within the confines of the Gymnasium. The players had not been too impressed with the state of the outdoor pitch, it was very bumpy and uneven, thus unsuitable for the high skill level required to control the ball. The petrol requirements of the heavy roller meant that it had to be used sparingly and, even when fuel was available, the roller always seemed to be out of action.

In that same December 1945 edition of *The*

Arborfield Apprentice, Cyril 'Bandy' Nel gave his report on the progress of both the School Band and the School Choir. However, things were moving to a close for some long-serving Band members. As a postscript to the Bandmaster's notes, the Editor gave the following note: *"Our best wishes for their future success and happiness go to Bandmaster Nel and members of the 4th/7th Royal Dragoon Guards, who are going to the 61st Training Regt RAC, prior to rejoining their own unit."*

Changing of the Guard

Some photographs, which were published many years later in the OBAN, certainly gave a jog to the memory of Doug Boucher of intake 43A. He thought that they had all been taken on a particular sports day in September 1945, on the field between the Camp Hall and Sergeants' Mess. One photo showed an enactment of the 'Changing of the Guard', as would have been carried out at Buckingham Palace. A 'mock up' of

the Palace walls was constructed in front of the Mess and Doug remembers that a lot of time was spent on rehearsals, the parade being the brainchild of RSM McNally, who was always on hand to give lots of usually very loud *"verbal encouragement"*.

On January 16th 1946, REME published its very first magazine under the title of *"REME"*, having shared its gestation period prior to this with the excellent RAOC Gazette. Maj Gen Rowcroft said it was *"the last brick in building the edifice of the Corps"*. He regretted its late arrival, some three years or more after the formation of the Corps, but put it down to the shortage of paper, which had been under the control of the Ministry of Supply. This REME Magazine was to continue under that format until October of 1959, when its title was changed to the now familiar one of *The Craftsman*.

On February 8th that same year, a dinner was held at London's *Café Royal*, at which the toast was *"Maj Gen Rowcroft"*. The General had taken over the direction and organisation of REME in 1942 and, due to his *"zest and ability"*, the Corps had been moulded into

'Changing of the Guard' in front of a fine looking castle!

Marching onto the parade, ground the conquering hero....

Field Marshall Viscount Bernard 'Monty' Montgomery, GCB, DSO,
re-visits the Army Apprentice School to review and address the November 1946 'PoP'.

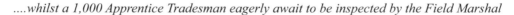

....whilst a 1,000 Apprentice Tradesman eagerly await to be inspected by the Field Marshal

A veritable honour for these Apprentices to be inspected by such an important historical figure

and after the parade time to talk with Col White

Of the parade itself, Monty said "I would go anywhere to be able to see what I have seen this morning."

A/T CSM O'Callaghan receives his award from 'Monty'

a fit and fighting instrument of war. In response, the General told of how indebted he had been to the RAOC in *"the weaning of the new baby"*. The 'baby' had then 'teethed' in the battle of Alamein, and proved itself in the chase towards Tripoli, followed by the landings in Sicily and the 'soft underbelly' of Europe.

The spring of 1946 brought a *"famous day"* for Norman Donnithorne and his fellow members of 43A, when they were all posted, some 150 in all, to Maidstone in Kent for *"infantry training"*. A good time was had by all, apparently, except for the long-suffering men of the Royal West Kent instructional staff! Following that, vehicle driving tuition was arranged for some. The Tels Mechs were sent to Gopsall Hall, Rutland, for a short stay, after which they were informed that they were all to be converted to Radar Mechs and be sent for further training – back at dear old Arborfield.

The conquering hero returns

One of the great days in the annals of the School was when the then Chief of the Imperial General Staff (CIGS), and one of the best-known heroes of World War II, Field Marshall Viscount Bernard 'Monty' Montgomery, GCB, DSO, re-visited the School to review and address the November 1946 'PoP'. The 'PoP' was, and still remains, an important milestone in the young soldier's career, providing an opportunity for both the staff and remaining apprentices of the School to wish 'God Speed' to those boys now about to enter adult service.

Walter Jobber of 43B recalls the occasion well, ready to pass on to his first posting. But, going on parade at 11.00 hours, he reckons that someone must have forgotten to tell the Field Marshall, as he didn't arrive until about an hour later. This wait, plus the fact that it was spent in *"continuous drizzle"* on a cold November day, did not raise the spirits that high. On parade that day were 973 boys, of whom 120 were actually passing out. The Field Marshall eventually took the salute and, after the parade, everybody – distinguished visitors, old boys, parents, staff and boys – filled the Camp Hall to overflowing. 'Monty' presented the prizes, then had these words to say to the proud visiting parents:

> *"The aim here is to turn your boy into the very best type of soldier tradesman. We aim that he shall reach the highest ranks of sol-*

dier tradesmen in the Army, or the best type of specialised commissioned officer. His training is continued, so that he reaches the highest grade of educational standards."

Of the parade itself, Monty continued: *"I would go anywhere to be able to see what I have seen this morning."* High praise indeed from the famous man, who also presented a signed photograph of himself to the School's 'head boy', A/T Sergeant Major P M O'Callaghan.

(A full report on Monty's speech is included as a separate annex to this chapter.)

That parade is also well remembered by Peter Simmonds of 45B intake, not to be confused with his 44A namesake. Peter was one of those junior boys required to line up along the main road, prior to Monty's arrival. It was a very hot day and, combined with tightened belts and close-fitting tunics, the two hours of waiting in the sunshine took its inevitable toll on many of the assembled apprentices. Peter recalls that Platoon Sergeant Herbie Payne had told his young men to change their weight backwards and forwards, as well as wriggling their toes inside their boots, and this simple advice paid off, with most of 45B surviving to 'swing another lamp'. *(Walter Jobber mentions the drizzle, while Peter remembers the sunshine. Perhaps it was a bit of both! Ed.)*

Another ex-boy, who remembers that 'PoP' very well, but for a vastly different reason, is Brian Atkins of 43A. He recalls that, on being marched off the square, and before being allowed to leave the Camp, the boys had to turn out all their kit, because someone had stolen the model of the proposed new School badge! Without naming names, he says that a certain member of his posting eventually owned up to the offence, joining them at Maidstone some fourteen days later than he should have – if you get his drift! Brian was later to describe 'Monty' as *"a very small man and quite pale in colour"*.

James MacDonald, of the same intake, tells of the anger and consternation amongst the boys, when they learned that their kit bags would be searched. Just imagine the 'mementos and souvenirs' that would come to light! James admits to a varied younger life, having been both a Dukie and a Queen Vic, prior to his joining the ATS. The '44A' Peter Simmonds says that the badge in question was actually found in a kit bag at Wokingham Station. He was then on his way to do six weeks regimental training with the Oxford and Buckinghamshire Light Infantry (OBLI), where he and his mates learned to march faster than the Guards did!

Great play was made by the national newspapers of the day during 1946, regarding what came to be called 'Monty's New Army'. This referred to the Field Marshall's enthusiastic and well-intentioned drive towards the provision of better living conditions for those soldiers under his command. *'Bedside Lamps for Squaddies'* could well have been one of the headlines. Probably the first evidence of this new order of things, at Arborfield anyway, came with an issue of 'pyjamas, cotton, striped, bedtime, for the wearing of'. This was closely followed by bed-sheets, which even had a set of thin stripes down the middle – a great assistance when folding the sheets accurately into bed-blocks. And then, as the final height of luxury, sets of curtains were issued for the windows!

During that same year, three Infantry Officers, part of the PS of the School, decided to make a permanent gesture in recognition of the pleasure they had in serving here. Maj Herbert, Capt Hollingshead and Capt Wadham presented 'The Infantry Officers' Challenge Cup', which from now on would be awarded to that apprentice achieving the position of 'Best Rifle Shot'.

Charles Pepper (43B) was nearing the end of his three years' apprenticeship at the School when he was selected to drive the 'milk float' as it delivered break-time drinks to the various Workshops. The machine was a fairly simple device, but had a tendency to jack-knife if not diligently steered. Charles had delivered his fare to most buildings, switching off the engine during delivery at each one as ordered. Having just dropped off the drinks at the Armourers Shop, he clambered 'on board' once again, but the engine decided not to re-start.

Charles commandeered the assistance of a very small and innocent looking apprentice, who was told to stand on the front of the float, holding the clutch disengaged, while Charles pushed from behind. Unfortunately, when the engine fired, the younger boy panicked and tried to jump off, causing the steering to take on a life of its own. The float eventually demolished the wooden steps leading into a hut, while the remaining milk churn slid off the float and deposited its contents all over the small boy, who ran off in a trail of milk and steam. Charles formed the impression that

the boy must have been one of the Polish contingent, he certainly didn't seem to have understood a word of Charles's instructions.

'Here, Here, the Reds are here'

Many questions have been asked about the origin of the unofficial School song – or *'The Reds'*, as it is more popularly known. Chaucer Harvey of 43B asserts that it had originated in 'B' Coy, whose members wore red shoulder flashes, and was in fact originally intended to be a 'rugby song'. Certainly, as the School rugby team also wore red shirts, they naturally adopted the song as their own, singing it merrily as they travelled to away matches.

The line *"We don't care what ... ... says"* was originally completed by the term 'anybody' until the winter season of 1945 - 46. Arborfield were then playing a well-remembered match against Chepstow apprentices at rugby and, due to the preponderance of Welsh boys in the Chepstow team, they had never been beaten. *(How things have sadly changed for Welsh rugby, almost sixty years on. Ed.)* At half time, it was no surprise that the opposition were ahead, despite the fact that the Arborfield boys seemed to be gaining the upper hand.

In the second half, in a surge of enthusiastic support, the whole population of the School seemed to line the pitch and burst into *'The Reds'*, but this time with the name 'Chepstow' inserted instead of 'anybody'. Needless to say, this was inspiring stuff and Arborfield went on to win a famous victory, so the words of the song have included the name of Chepstow ever since. *(Has anyone got a better story than this? Ed.)* As a postscript to the above tale, Wally Footner of October 1939 era confirms the 'B' Coy heritage, but then adds his own recollection, that the song was actually brought to Arborfield by those boys who arrived here in 1939, following the closure of the RAOC Boys School at Didcot.

Bob Ward of 44B thinks the song may have originated from a Dublin football team, using music from an original piece written by Gilbert and Sullivan. He remembers that when Bandmaster Newman joined the School, he composed a 'School March', which not only included the boys' version of *'The Reds'*, but also the School's own bugle call. Sadly, it could not be officially recognised, due to its musical rights being held by the D'Oyly Carte Company.

Intake 46A saw the arrival at Arborfield of Steve Johnson, who came directly from the Dukies at Dover. There, he had been able to wear his Dad's Scots Guards badge on Sunday church parades but, on finding that RSM McNally was from that same regiment, decided to give him a wide berth just in case his Dad had ever locked up the now-RSM as a young recruit! Steve did get to do a bit of 'gardening' for the RSM at one stage, but that was for being caught smoking during a film-show in the Camp Hall!

Steve later served in Tripoli, in some old Italian barracks. The workshops had housed the old works of *Alfa Romeo* and *Lancia*. Another time, whilst travelling through the Formosa Straits, he found himself dropped off in Japan, only twelve miles from Hiroshima, which was still, as Steve puts it, *"a little worse for wear"*. Later still, following one of the H-bomb tests on Christmas Island during 1958, Steve had just had his kippers for breakfast when a film was shown, showing the effects of sitting in the open during such a test, with no protective clothing. It rather put him off kippers for the rest of his life!

Getting up to mischief

David Panter, also of 46A, believes he holds *"the dubious honour of being the first apprentice at Arborfield to be caned"*. David had set himself up as one of the 'cigarette barons', who would buy these illicit items at the normal price, then sell them, one at a time, at a vastly inflated price. He had broken out of Camp one night, climbing over the fence by the cricket pavilion, and had just bought his supply of the 'evil weed' at a local pub. Suddenly his mate, acting as lookout, warned him that Ben Cook was coming.

Despite attempting to hide in a nearby garage, the two boys were caught red-handed and marched off to the Guardroom, closely followed by Ben, riding on his trusty bicycle. David and his partner in crime were awarded the inevitable fourteen days CB but, as this was found to coincide with the next leave period, they both accepted the alternative sentence of only 'seven days', but with the addition of six strokes of the cane from the RSM. Following their punishment, David recalls that they were later medically inspected at the MRS for any sign of permanent damage.

David often wonders how the Camp didn't burn down, considering some of the methods of cigarette lighting employed at the time! Two pencils, sharpened

to a fine point at both ends, would be inserted into the nearest power point, with a piece of *'Duraglit'* (brass-polishing abrasive wire wool) wedged across the two outer ends. Upon closing the switch, the wire wool would quickly become hot enough to glow, thus providing the 'lighting-up' source.

Another ingenious – or downright foolhardy! – electrical device was the 'instant' method of brewing up a mug of tea. 'Spindle' Mailes, another of 46A, would filch a couple of carbon rods from the Cinema projection room, dip them into a mug of water and wire them up to the mains. This would instantly cause the water to boil furiously – all that was required now was a supply of tealeaves, sugar and condensed milk, stolen (or borrowed?) earlier from the Cookhouse!

David himself didn't tell the next tale, leaving this to another of his intake, Thomas 'Len' Edgecock. David had somehow constructed a gun barrel from a length of metal tubing, using some ball bearings as ammunition. With an explosive mixture made up by resident chemist 'Appy' Appleyard, no doubt another 46A boy, the stage was set for the experiment! With a heavy chair and the six-foot barrack-room ironing table set up in front of this 'cannon' as protection, the device was strapped to a bedstead, loaded up as necessary, and a hot needle inserted into the touch hole.

Needless to say, the ensuing explosion brought retribution, in the shape of Sgt Roberts, who instantly put three boys 'in the nick' – one of whom was the 'designer', another was David Panter, while the third was an innocent bystander. Len later investigated the aftermath of the event, finding holes in the chair, the table – and the barrack room wall! It was even later when a boy from the other side of the Square reported a hole in his room wall and duly returned a ball bearing to its original owners. The legend goes that Col White later had it mounted and displayed on his desk.

Sgt Herbie Payne was a popular member of staff, indeed many saw him as *"the best liked sergeant in the School"*. Herbie was also a keen gardener and would use this pastime to dole out his own punishments, rather than the standard jankers. This would inevitably include a session of 'gardening', but hardly of the Percy Thrower (the Alan Titchmarsh of his day!) kind! Digging with an eating fork and cutting the grass with nail scissors – those were just a couple of ideas that would keep the 'criminals' busy – and quiet – on a Saturday afternoon!

Denis Marshall was one of the next intake, 46B.

As he now says, *"Much water has passed under the bridge since we were chased around by 'Bing' Lakes in 'J2' Barrack Room at the end of 1946"*. Denis reckons that by the end of that year he and his mates all thought that they were on a 'starvation diet', taking into consideration the fact that they were all 'growing lads'.

However, one way of getting a good breakfast was to go to Communion service in the School church each Wednesday morning. Denis did this, missing the muster parade and helping himself to as much bread, butter and marmalade as he could eat after the service. His latter-day Confirmation by the Bishop of Oxford was gained on the back of this hearty weekly beanfeast! It obviously paid off in other ways too, as Denis's wife Jean was later ordained as a Vicar down in Cornwall!

Swimming lessons and ferry trips

Harvey Liddell, also of 46B, remembers the wonderful 'sporting' practice that generally took place on a Saturday afternoon, when fewer than usual 'nosey types' were about. He and his mates would block the waste-water outlets in the ablutions shower area, which was surrounded by a low concrete dividing wall. They could thus flood the said area to a depth of about two and a half feet – and then use the area as a temporary 'swimming pool'! Whether or not they actually learned to swim in those shallow waters is doubtful, but it must have given a lot of fun at the time.

Many years after joining as another member of 46B, Jim Baker was enjoying reading his latest copy of *OBAN* and not too surprised to find that there was such a disproportionate amount of material written by ex-boys who had been here in the Forties. As Jim puts it, that decade was, to use the modern parlance, like a *"game of two halves"* – the first half spent under the constant shadow of war and the second basking in the afterglow of the peace celebrations. He remembers that, after the cessation of hostilities, when the Luftwaffe could no longer be relied upon to amuse the apprentices by dropping the odd bomb or two, the boys then had to fall back upon their own wits, if they were to have some amusement and entertainment.

Jim adds that it was also unrealistic to expect the owner of the local 'Rainbow' fireworks factory to continue blowing it up, in order to keep the boys on their toes – this was apparently a regular occurrence during the wartime years. *(It certainly carried on again*

in the Fifties – as will be seen in later stories! Ed.) After the war, self-help became the thing and, when not fantasising about the young ladies who attended church on Sunday, the boys came up with many promising schemes. One of these was a 'ferry trip' across one of the Camp's static water-tanks, the 'ferry' consisting of a toilet door, crewed by one terrified Jeep! *(The term Jeep has long been used at Arborfield, as a derisory term for anyone of an intake junior to one's own. Peter Langley of 1941 intake cannot recall the term being used for his particular bunch and thinks it may have first been coined for 42A, the first of the GS boys. Ed.)*

Jim fondly recalls the two Camp barbers. Jack was an ex-Navy type and not a bad sort, while Cyril, on the other hand, knew *"the precise specification of an AAS haircut"*, so that was that, off it all came, right down to the bone! This was a fact of life, one took a place in the queue and just hoped it was Jack's chair that was the next available. *(Strange how today's youths all sport the same 'short-back-and-sides' that we all hated. I must confess to now having a regular Grade IV myself! Ed.)*

John Shaw was also part of that 46B intake and well remembers the regular Sunday ritual, where all apprentices would become compulsory (but temporary?) Christians. Hymns, *'Onward Christian Soldiers'* in particular, would be sung lustily, if not tunefully, whilst the boys would have pointed out to them the error of their ways and be exhorted to improve. Church Parade over, off would march the boys, led by Peter Green at the front of the Band. Passing through the School gates, Peter, taking his cue from his predecessor D'Arcy Davidson, would hurl the mace up over the gate entrance arch and – hopefully - catch it as it came down on the other side. This custom was no doubt brought about by the strictly given instruction that it was **not** to be attempted!

John remembers listening to the radio – or wireless, as it was termed in those days – and laughing at the antics of the two 'spivs', or 'wide-boys', on the Charlie Chester programme *'Stand Easy'*. The pair were known as *'Tish and Tosh'* and John goes on to say that there were quite a number of their like serving here at Arborfield at the time! These were usually senior boys, who could always supply the needs, at a small price of course, of those Jeeps still making their way in the world. Such items as a well-worn web belt, a spare set of 'eating irons', a half tin of *Brasso*, or even a signed photograph of Diana Dors, would be surreptitiously handed over for a few coppers. These would then either supplement the senior lad's own supply of cigarettes or be used to get another supply of unwanted kit and other worthless items!

Many years later, as part of the initial project to put this history together, John was able to supply a whole folder full of written memories and drawings of his time here at Arborfield. There are far too many to all be included here, but who knows – perhaps John will one day put together a history of his own, it's never too late. John, now settled in Ormskirk, Lancashire, also made a most generous contribution of kit and equipment to the REME Museum, of which more is mentioned in a later chapter.

Fred 'Lofty' Cotsford also joined intake 46B. Now living in Hamburg, that famous seaport on the north German coast, Fred has always thought of his three-year apprenticeship at Arborfield as *"character forming"* – the food certainly made him aware of what he was missing at home! One of Fred's major memories is having to attend 'dress calls' every fifteen minutes, during a fourteen-day dollop of jankers, having been caught out at the deadly sin of smoking – a common enough offence those days.

Lofty casts his mind back to the days of the 'button-stick'. By the time had arrived for him to be discharged from the Army in 1971, he had somehow managed to lose this cleaning utensil – and no amount of pleading could prevent the QM staff at Bordon not to make him pay for it! This despite the fact that 'stay-brite' buttons and badges had then been 'in' for years. Mind you, Lofty also managed to *"lose"* his *"jersey, heavy wool"* – he still wears it when gardening and reckons it was the best couple of quid he ever spent.

Yet another member of that 46B intake was John Smithson. He had arrived at Reading railway station, where he was then ordered to join some other boys in the 'underground' Forces Canteen, to await transport onwards to Arborfield. After sipping several mugs of tea, John eventually found himself packed with the other boys into the back of a 3-ton truck, but the first destination turned out to be Wokingham – another station, even more boys! Before leaving for the School, the boys were sent into the town's Public Library to pick up what appeared to be 'the usual' supply of out-of-date books donated by the library to the School, which at the time had very few facilities of its own.

Arriving at last at Arborfield, John remembers being issued with a knife, fork and spoon set, his 'eating irons', all tightly wrapped in a shiny green greaseproof paper, with the utensils themselves immersed in a yellowish preservative grease. The hot water supply being what it was in those days – lukewarm at best and not much of it – John cannot confirm how much of the grease went down with the first meal! In those days, the boys were issued with both SD and BD, but allowed to wear only the *"awful old service dress, buttoned up to the neck"*, when setting off home on leave. The trick was to ensure that your BD was safely in the local dry cleaners just before leave, where it could then be picked up on the way home. According to John, this seemed to prove a *"little more eye-catching for the ladies"*.

John's recollections of his time at Arborfield are many and varied, in fact he could probably fill up a whole chapter of this history himself, though modesty forbids it. *(There are many more ex-boys in a similar position! Ed.)* Thus it is no surprise to find that, some fifty-odd years later, John was instrumental in the production of a videocassette, which gave a glimpse of 'how it was in the good old days'. No doubt his interest in films and such like was initiated by working in the projection room in the Camp Hall on 'cinema nights' – a hobby which he has enthusiastically pursued at his home town of High Wycombe in later years.

In the third edition of *The Arborfield Apprentice*, issued in December 1946, one representative of the Boy NCO's Club bemoaned that the Club equipment was suffering from the general shortage of commodities. But, apart from uncurtained windows, a billiard table short of balls and a dartless dartboard, everything else seemed to be going quite well! A special mention was made of 'Taffy', the boys' pride and joy, who valiantly accepted the fun and jokes provided by some of the lighter-hearted Club members. *(Unfortunately, there is no explanation of who Taffy was, military or civilian, or of his role in life. Ed.)*

'Music of the Gods'

The same magazine saw an article by the RSM, in which he gave tribute to the way that the Band had survived, after the 'established' members of the 4th/7th DGs had been posted. Mr Newman had now taken over as the new Bandmaster, and had found *"a great fund of enthusiasm"* among the remaining boy members. So much so that the RSM was also able to greet the recent establishment of a 'Pipe Band'. When this had been first mooted, the retort from a number of people had been, *"Yes, so long as you keep it a long way from the School"*! Mr McNally now made the statement, *"Hail, Caledonia! In spite of yourselves, you Sassenachs shall hear the music of the Gods"*. At the time, however, boys who aspired to be members of this Pipe Band had to be able to play the bagpipes before arrival at the School, as there was nobody sufficiently able to instruct on the required skills.

One of the School's 'roving reporters' gave an account of a visit to the School Hospital. For one reason or another, most boys tended to pay at least one visit to the hospital during their tour of duty. Some appeared many times, particularly during the winter months – the pleasant transition from *"the bleak, foggy outside world to the warmth and brightness of the wards"* seemingly a good reason for this! Our reporter went on to describe the duties of the medical orderlies, which included the administration of *"unpleasant tasting concoctions"* - that usually brought a grimace to the face and an involuntary shudder down the back!

December 1946 brought the final copy of the *REME Magazine* for its inaugural year. An article appeared telling about the meeting, on a bus back from Reading, between the author (presumably the magazine's editor) and *"a very severe man, wearing an extraordinary colourful cap"*. This latter gentleman turned out to be RSM McNally, and the meeting gave rise to the article that followed, which gave a vivid description of life at the boys' school in those days just after the war.

(The article appears as a separate annex at the end of this chapter.)

The same magazine announced the retirement from the Army of Maj Gen Rowcroft, who was relinquishing his post of DME at the War Office at the end of that year. His record during the First World War had made it abundantly clear that he was exceptionally qualified to deal with all the technical and mechanical concerns in which the Army was involved. With the Second World War under way, on May 10th 1942, he was appointed as DME and promoted acting Major General. In May 1945, when REME's *"fully combatant status"* was agreed in principle, the General was awarded the CBE and, on conclusion of the war, he devoted all his energies to organising the run-down of those who had been called up, and to shaping the future of the Corps.

Another severe winter

The winter of 1946 - 47 had brought severe weather conditions across the whole length and breadth of the country, with deep drifts of snow making many roads disappear from sight. It had started on Friday, January 24th, when the inhabitants of rural Berkshire awoke to find a thick peace-inducing blanket of snow had covered their gardens and fields. However, this was to presage a long spell of ferociously cold weather, the worst of the century. Ten-foot snowdrifts covered the countryside, turning it into one huge white maze. Icicles hung from the eaves of most houses, in some cases so long that they reached down to the ground, like prison bars. The treacherous conditions engendered a fuel crisis, as hardly any coal supplies were able to get through to power stations, factories and homes. In the towns, people with wheelbarrows and prams queued up outside the gasworks for free supplies of coke. Three hundred major roads became impassable and the RAF was called in to drop food supplies to many isolated communities.

Arborfield obviously suffered along with everywhere else, with both Lofty Cotsford and Peter Daykin (46B) recalling that the so-called heating system failed to deliver much in the way of either warmth or comfort. Rumour had it that the remainder of Arborfield Garrison had been sent home so that the School could have all of the coal supply! Lofty remembers that, in an effort to keep the boys warm, they would spend the mornings on route marches and afternoons in the Gymnasium. As a result of these enforced exercises, he caught rheumatic fever, which forced him to be 'sick on leave' for six months.

Peter recalls that Ben Cook refused to take his horses out on the frosty roads, and so the wagon that delivered coke to the MRS had ten A/Ts on each shaft, with another ten pushing from behind! Lofty – well named, as we shall see - tells the story of when Ben told him off for not bringing a squad of apprentices to attention as he approached. When Lofty tried to explain that he was only an apprentice himself, Ben told him that as he was tallest, it should have been him!

That dreadful winter also left a lasting impression on Don Walker (45A). He recalls being ensconced in his 'spider', where *"anything freezable froze"*. *"Was it really as bad as I remember, or has there been another winter as bad since?"* he asks. *(That of 1962 / 63 springs to mind. I was at Fallingbostel – the dreaded*

The RSM with Sgt 'Blossom' Dransfield and Provost Staff

'effing B'- and the snow was still on the ground in May! Ed.) For a very long period, there was neither training in the Workshops, nor education in the classrooms. Route marches and runs became the order of the day, with the roads around Arborfield packed with squads of soldiers being sent out to keep both exercised and warm. Don remarks that *"without doubt it was bloody cold"*, but he has no recollection of the actual recorded temperatures.

The conditions obviously affected the health of many boys; it was no surprise that some succumbed to another of those flu epidemics that seemed to visit the School on an annual basis. Don managed to catch that bug just as the majority of boys were getting over it, also suffering severe chest pains. After a few days in the MRS, he was sent to the military hospital at Aldershot, where it was found that he actually had pneumonia. He stayed there for two weeks, enjoying the welcome sight of the nurses, dashing about keeping everything neat and tidy. Sheets were turned down to a regulation width and, when the Matron made her rounds, patients lay to attention not daring to cough or sneeze! Another pleasure for Don was that he was then sent down to the Royal Victoria Hospital at Southampton for an extensive period of convalescence, where he met up with quite a number of other boys from the School.

Meanwhile back here at Arborfield, at least the Cookhouse remained in full working order, doling out a plentiful supply of hot steaming tea, cocoa and soup to the still fit boys, made even more ravenous than usual by their enforced physical exercise. According to John Smithson, the NAAFI was probably the warmest

place to be at the time. Boys would attempt to stay on there as long as possible, making their suppers last for ages. Eventually of course, they would have to return to their 'spiders', with their frozen ablutions and equally cold barrack rooms. They would pile up their beds with greatcoats and such, anything to try to keep out the terrible cold. This, despite the issue of an extra two blankets for each A/T, up from the usual four to a mountainous six! Fortunately, there were no reports of any cases of frostbite.

Donald Hall of 45B recalls that the Christmas carol, *'Good King Wenceslas'*, using the words about the snow being *"deep and crisp and even"* had never been more true than it was that winter. Some boys developed an intense hatred of the daily routine of route marches, the burning question being *"how can we get out of it?"* Don and a couple of mates decided to chance their arm one day, when lined up in the rear rank outside the Guardroom. As the duty NCO had moved to the main gate to check that the road was clear, on his command of *"Quick march"*, they noticed that he couldn't actually see them. So they did a smart turn along the side of the Guardroom and went back to their beds!

The next morning, they thought they would try the same trick but, as they marched gaily around the back of the Guardroom, another sharp command, this time of *"About turn"*, wiped the smiles off their faces. Unknown to them, their footprints in the snow had been spotted by the then Provost Sergeant, Sgt Dransfield, RAC, who no doubt went on to wreak a terrible revenge.

David Ferns (44B) still shivers at the thought of that winter. As previously detailed, warm-up games and runs were organised for the more energetic apprentices, but David wasn't one of them! He was one of those boys who hung around the cold radiators, stamping their feet, beating their arms and singing, over and over again, their entire repertoire of ribald songs – it seemed to go on for weeks, rather than the days it probably was.

Keith Evans of 45A is another for whom that winter stays etched on his memory. The main priority for the boys was to stay as warm as possible, and if this meant raiding the coal-yard for an extra bucket of coal, then so be it. Although the surface of the coal heap had been whitewashed to deter any would-be thieves, the boys had a trick or two up their sleeves. They would gently remove the top layer, remove the required supply of fuel from the heap, and then carefully replace the whitewashed coal back over the top of what was now a black hole. *(So that's where the term came from! Ed.)* Then there would be a furtive dash back to the barrack-room to top up the one and only stove.

Nearing the end of his stint here, Bob Ward remembers that the boiler house had to make use of old tent duckboards for fuel. His thought on the rest of the Garrison being sent home, whilst apprentices were kept behind, was that it was to keep the boys' parents happy. The RSM's command *"Put your kit down"* would then be followed by another – *"Hand and foot, quick mark time"*. This was to get the boys marching on the spot and clapping their hands together, which certainly brought the blood to one's extremities. One educational instructor told some boys that a sure fire way of keeping one's feet warm was to make sure their socks were clean every morning – some hope!

A thaw point!

When the spring of 1947 finally did make an appearance, the thaw quickly turned ice and snow into torrents and a great storm, on March 16th, spread floodwaters far and wide. It was during this period, on completion of their training as Motor Transport (MT) Fitters, that four fully-fledged apprentices from Arborfield, plus another four from Chepstow, volunteered to fill vacancies in the RA. Len Horton was one of the Arborfield four, having joined as a member of intake 44A. As he would admit many years later, *"this was not a very clever career move"*, but then, he was very young at the time. Eventually the boys were sent off to various RA regiments around the country, but not before completing their initiative training at the then MT School at Bordon.

Here, they were quartered at some distance from the workshop, revelling in the unaccustomed freedom compared to that at their respective Schools. No regular visits to the barber, no checks on the cleanliness of their barrack room, in fact nobody seemed to realise that they were even there! It couldn't last of course, as one morning, arriving at work in their now usual dishevelled state, they bumped into the Artificer Sergeant Major (ASM), himself an ex-Chepstow boy, who quickly put this motley crew in their place. It was countless years later, in the October 2001 edition of *The Craftsman* magazine, that Len finally put this story into writing. Having originally been brought up

A/T Peter Daykin

in North Yorkshire, he now lives in Nottingham, where he had recently joined the local branch of the REME Association.

On March 15th, the London Association of Engineers had held a celebratory dinner, at which the CIGS, Field Marshall Montgomery, gave an after-dinner speech. In it, he paid tribute to the efforts of REME personnel during the war, encouraging the Corps to greater achievements in the future. His speech included the following statements:

> *"The Corps of REME was formed in 1942, with the object of concentrating our electrical and mechanical maintenance services and introducing new and improved methods. It exists, in fact, to keep the punch in the Army's fist. Amongst the REME's greatest achievements during the last war were their contribution to the defeat of the mine men-*

ace in the Middle East, their preparation for amphibious operations in the Mediterranean and NW Europe, and their maintenance of the AA defences of Great Britain. The REME is a new Corps, which was born in the late war. The Corps has done magnificently and has won its spurs in battle".

John Northam joined the School as a member of 47A, where he came up against his *bete noir* in the shape of a particular 'Guards Sergeant' who was known as 'Curly' Hooper. He describes Curly as *"a nasty piece of work, with a face like an unsuccessful prizefighter and a temperament to match".* John recalls having to attend at Sgt Hooper's bunk, known to the boys as *"the piggery"*, in order to collect a parcel from home. Curly insisted that the parcel be opened there and then and boldly helped himself to some of the goodies contained therein, before sending John back to his barrack room.

On another occasion, John was awaiting the issue of his new *"prescription glasses"* and was thus excused from his normal session of fitting. Glancing out of the Drawing Office window, he watched in amazement as Curly dashed amongst a squad of marching apprentices and thumped one unfortunate lad from behind, then proceeded to shout all kinds of abuse at the youngster. But retribution was to hand. Master Artificer Hogg had also seen this incident. Now he was a short grey-haired and very quiet character, *"seldom seen and almost never heard".* However, he called Sgt Hooper over and gave him what John can only suppose was the *"quietest, yet severest, rollicking"* – and to the boys' delight, the sergeant disappeared from the scene within twenty-four hours!

A unique new cap-badge

The apprentices' cap badge, which was subsequently worn with pride by thousands of A/Ts, from both Chepstow and Arborfield, was first seen on parade on August 19th 1947. It was designed by Sgt Jack Bolden, REME, made up from various ideas and suggestions put forward by the School Commandant. It was composed of four main symbols – the 'Cross of Christ', the 'Torch of Learning', the 'Crossed Swords of the Soldier' and the 'Gear Wheel of Technical Skill'. The final design had to be passed by the Inspector of Regimental Colours. Now that it is no longer in use, it

is fitting to recall some of the words previously written about it, in The Arborfield Apprentice of December 1946, by Col White himself:

"I cannot do better than invite attention to the new Badge on the outer cover (of the magazine) and to what it represents. Prominent and most important among its symbols are the Cross and Crown. These stand respectively for Character and Loyalty; character based upon the principles of Christianity and loyalty to the School, to the Army, to the nation and to the King. The next symbol I wish to draw attention to is the Torch, which stands for Learning and for Training, of both the mind and body, on good sound health lines. Next are the Crossed Swords, which stand for the military virtues of Discipline, Steadfastness and Devotion to Duty. Finally, but by no means least, is the Gear Wheel, which forms the basis and background of the whole design, and stands for Technical Knowledge and Skill".

Larry Le Var, who later went on to become the Honorary Secretary (Hon Sec) of the Arborfield Old Boys' Association (AOBA), or just Old Boys' Association (OBA) to many, was a member of 47A. His was the first intake to go into the newly formed 'HQ' Coy, under the command of Maj N D Charrington, 10th Royal Hussars, on February 22nd of that year. Larry recalls that on one memorable occasion, when he nervously complained that his uniform didn't seem to fit him properly, he was reminded what a lucky boy he was, because if it **had** have fitted him properly, then he would have been deformed! *(That does have a certain amount of logic behind it, Larry! Ed.)*

Bill Tate of intake 44B also recalls Maj Charrington, and with heartfelt gratitude. It was the Major who had recommended Bill for a regular commission, and was thus responsible for Bill's subsequent attendance at the Royal Military Academy Sandhurst (RMAS), where he was accompanied by two other ex-Arborfield boys, Gordon 'Bing' Lakes and Tony Tracey. Bing later went on to serve with that famous regiment, The Gloucesters, in Korea, where he won the MC and, following completion of his Army service, went on to reach a high position in the Prison Service. Like Bill, Tony Tracey was another commissioned into the RASC, and later went on to become Commandant of the Army School of Motor Transport. Bill goes on to say that he never did rise to such dizzy heights himself, retiring as a Captain in 1966 – but he did make it to A/T Sgt in 'HQ' Coy!

A change of title

The year 1947 saw not only the new School badge on parade for the first time, but also a change of title. From February 1st of that year, the powers-that-be dictated that the School would now become the 'Army Apprentices' School (AAS), Arborfield'. Before departing at the end of his tenure here at the School, Col White made a presentation of a fine new trophy, 'The Chief Instructor's Cup', which would in future be awarded each term to the apprentice judged to be 'The Best Tradesman'. On May 10th of that same year, Col C E M Grenville-Grey, CBE, late KRRC, succeeded Col White as Commandant.

He used his first foreword, in the School magazine in December of that year, to pay tribute to his predecessor, who had retired after a meritous thirty-five years service. It was Col Grenville-Grey who, during his time here at the School, instituted the 'Champion Company' competition and the award of the 'Medal of Honour', as well as founding the AOBA which, happily, continues to prosper right up until the present time.

As Col White left the School upon his retirement, he was presented with a scale model of a *Cromwell* tank. He asked permission for it to be kept at the

School, so that he could *"come back and look at it sometimes"*. He was also presented with a manuscript copy of the unofficial School song, 'The Reds', by Bandmaster Newman. The Colonel said that the song had been "forwarded to official quarters", and that he hoped that the incoming Commandant would try to get it officially adopted as 'the School song'. *(This may never have happened on an official basis, as explained earlier by Bob Ward, but the song's popularity is displayed by the lusty version of it that is sung every year at the Old Boys' Reunion. Ed.)*

Col White had due tribute paid to him in the July issue of the *REME Magazine*, which gave a brief account of his Army career, which had lasted since the beginning of the *"great war"* of 1914 – 18. He had later been selected to be one of the Deputy Directors at the War Office during the phase of evolution of the electrical and mechanical engineers of the RAOC into the REME. The strain had told upon his health and retirement was imminent, but 'JD' was fortunately able to take over as Commandant at the boys' school. He had finished his service in a *"glow of friendship and the respect of a very wide range of friends, both old and young"*.

1947 was also the year when the PS welcomed the proud recipient of a Victoria Cross (VC) to its ranks. It is thought that Sgt Eardley VC, of the Worcestershire Regt, who was also awarded the French *Croix de Guerre* and Military Medal, must be the only member of the School's staff ever to have been presented with that famous medal. In April, the school-leaving age was raised to fifteen, but this caused no discernible fall in entries to the School here at Arborfield.

The Toy Soldiers

Bill Pusey (46A) is still a staunch Arborfield supporter to this day and, at the time of writing, is the OBA representative on the College Trust Fund Committee. 1947 proved to be a memorable year for Bill, as he was chosen to be one of the party from the School to participate in the very first post-war Royal Tournament, held at Olympia, in West London. Many difficulties had to be overcome during the preparatory time of rehearsals, not least of all the question of 'uniforms'.

Harvey Liddell (46B) recalls the backdrop scenery of 'barrack room' walls made out of hessian, lining the entrance for Queen Mary, as well as *"the smell of the greasepaint and the thrill of going on stage"*. David

Rehearsals on the Camp Hall sports field for the Toy Soldiers

Ferns of 44B didn't actually take part in that effort but later heard many tales of *"glamourous nights out in London"* by those who did! Pretending not to believe the tales, he does admit that he was still *"green with envy"*.

Rehearsals for the grand occasion were twofold. Most were carried out on the School's football pitch, so that the boys would presumably get used to the tree bark that covered Olympia's floor. But a select group was taken to the Temperance Hall in Reading, which provided a taste of how it would be to parade in a restricted area. Bill recalls giving a 'full dress rehearsal' display on the car park of a local town, he thinks it was West Wycombe. Bill also admits that he spent a lot of his spare time, whilst up in London, playing chess with one of the managers from the local 'Joe Lyons' teashops.

As described by RSM McNally himself, those rehearsals were carried out during days of *"shortages, coupons and dockets"*. The selected boys had to train

Left - The short and the tall of it!

Right - and at the show there were girls!

extremely hard for the task, but despite all the snags and setbacks they encountered along the way, their 'Toy Soldier' display was eventually regarded as a great success. No less an 'interested party' than His Majesty King George VI showed a great attention in the display and was later pleased to comment favourably on the boys' excellent turnout and bearing.

After that memorable performance, his first sight of members of the Royal Family enlightens Bill's memories. He was particularly smitten by the beauty of Princess Margaret, who must have been about sixteen years old at the time. In his own words, *"She had a flawless complexion, lovely hair, a beautiful face and a perfect figure. I think she took the breath away of every member of the Guard of Honour – she certainly took mine"*.

(The page from the Royal Tournament programme appears as a separate annex to this chapter.)

The *Punch* magazine of June 18th gave a report on the Tournament, under the heading *'Through the Hoop at Olympia'*. One part of that report read as follows:

"One amusing affair was a Toy Soldier display by fifteen-year-olds of the Army Appren-

tice (sic) School. The lads had fine chests on them for their age, and I imagine they may have been rebellious about wearing make-up (one scarlet blob per cheekbone), but their precise evolutions suggested that they would grow up to be real soldiers in no time.

The illusion of being impelled by clockwork was bravely maintained, even to their collapse in rotation when the whole company was mown down by a single round from a small golden cannon . . . so that even the sad spectacle of their red coats, prone and symmetrical in the dust, brought a burst of applause. They got another special burst as they marched off, from some fellow red-coats – the party of Chelsea Pensioners, spruce and scrubbed in the stalls opposite the Royal Box."

RSM McNally was subsequently to recall some memorable highlights of the whole episode, such as taking a representative number of boys to the Alexandra Palace – or 'Ally Pally' as it was nicknamed - then the home of broadcasting, to appear on 'live' TV. He remembered that on the third day of the show, the

Sporting activities of all varieties....

....have always played an important part of life.....

....even sword dancing!

Toy Soldier officer found himself completely without a voice, and had to be fed pastilles and gargles at all hours of the day. One boy officer, who dropped his sword, recovered it magnificently and fooled the crowd into thinking he had fainted and that it was all part of the act!

One night the boys were late in lining up outside the arena, and had to be 'doubled' all round Olympia just in time to march boldly on parade. On another occasion, one young lad, just three minutes before due to march on, found that he 'needed to be excused' and made it just in time! The RSM went on to say that the three weeks were extremely hard work for one and all, boys and staff alike, but that the very experience gained by the participants would recompense them for their efforts.

Striving for one's 'colours'

Guy Cordeaux had spent all of his formative years at a boarding school in India, until he managed to pass an entrance exam in 1946, which gave him the opportunity to both come to England, as well as to learn a trade. Before he was allowed to leave India however, it was the required custom that he had to first be a member of a British Army unit, and so it was that he found himself temporarily seconded to the Somerset Light Infantry.

This state of affairs continued until his arrival at Arborfield, via the delights of disembarkation at Liverpool Docks, an overnight stop at Lichfield in Staffordshire, and a long detour via Chepstow, Monmouthshire, to drop off some other boys. Arriving here at the late hour of 11 p.m. at night, to a cold and frosty Army camp, with not even a water supply, thanks to the severe conditions, it is amazing that Guy survived to become a member of 47A. As recalled by Guy, the organisation of the School at that time meant spending the first six months in 'HQ' Coy, before being sent on to one of four other companies for the final two and a half years. Depending upon promotion and a suitable personality, some apprentices would later find themselves posted back to 'HQ' Coy as A/T NCOs, being placed in charge of barrack roomfuls of newly arrived youngsters – the infamous Jeeps!

Guy himself was later placed into 'B' Coy to train as a VM, under the command of Maj Ironside, and recalls an occasion when RSM McNally told the assembled parade that he was going to hold what he termed a 'gaiter inspection'. Ordering all boys to remove their left gaiter, the clatter of lead weights and hoops of bicycle chains hitting the square must have been heard as far away as Wokingham! This didn't prevent the boys from continuing the age-old custom of 'weighting' their denim trousers, which custom and practice had decided made them look a lot smarter, but it made them very much aware that the RSM was well up to all their little dodges.

During his time with 'B' Coy, Guy became quite proficient at the game of hockey, going on to play for both the School team and the staff side. He recalls being awarded his 'colours' for that particular sport, which consisted of a small shield with the School badge mounted upon it, along with number, name and rank, plus the sport one played. As an added privilege, the normal beret could now be discarded in favour of a forage-cap, blue in colour, with gold-braid piping and the sort of badge which required no polishing! Guy certainly wore his with pride.

It was possibly not too well known at the time, but when the 'colours' scheme was first introduced, the Commandant stipulated four conditions upon which they may be awarded. The recipient must: be outstanding in his game or sport; be worthy of representing any major unit; have taken part in sixty-percent of the season's events; have behaved in a sportsmanlike manner on all occasions. To strive for one's colours was itself considered a worthy aim, but the main consideration, after all, was to actively participate in sport at some level or other.

'No smoking' - please!

Tony Blackwell of 44A later came back to serve as a Company Commander at what would then be 'the College', between 1972 and 1977. He recalled that, during the last few days of his own apprenticeship, excitement mounted amongst those boys preparing to say goodbye. He was one of a bunch of lads who purchased a number of smoke cartridges from a local hardware store, they knew that Ben Cook used these for smoking out rabbits. But in this case, they were to be used for a more nefarious reason!

On the evening of their end-of-term dance, they managed to throw these smoking cartridges into the bunks of some PS NCOs, holding the doors tightly shut on the unfortunate occupants, before making a rapid withdrawal under cover of the smokescreen. It wasn't until later that they realised just how dangerous this prank could have been – and there was a price to pay. RSM McNally insisted that a bill for barrack damages be raised, and the whole intake had to share this cost before being released onto the unsuspecting outside world!

The summer months of 1947 brought the threat of an outbreak of infantile paralysis, or 'polio', as it was more commonly known. Large gatherings were frowned upon as a possible source of cross-infection, so the School's church services were moved out of the Camp Hall, and onto the sports field alongside. Although these outdoor services were deemed successful, many people found great difficulty in keeping up with the songs and prayers, due to the way the sound echoed from the surrounding barrack blocks.

That 'hardy annual', the Company Allotment, was back in fashion, no doubt a leftover from the 'Dig for Victory' campaign. A field of irregular shape had been set aside and, with some difficulty, been divided into four more-or-less equal parts, one per Company. It appeared to have been liberally sown with every type of local weed, before having several cartloads of stones scattered all over it! The autumn was thus to be devoted to the arduous task of clearing, digging and manuring, before leaving 'Jack Frost' to do the rest. However, no laurels were to be gained from a nice crisp lettuce, nor one's colours awarded for carrots!

Following a request from the War Office, a party of five of His Majesty's Inspectors, from the Ministry of Education, carried out a searching inspection during June 1947, of the Apprentices' Schools at both Arborfield and Chepstow. Their final report recommended the necessity for integration between technical and general education, with co-ordination of the various curricula and syllabi under the control of a single body. This conclusion resulted in the setting up, in December that same year, of a working party that included the Chief Instructors of both Schools. This working party was tasked to investigate the possible educational targets, as well as the general facilities that then existed at both Schools. The eventual outcome of their enquiries was the publication of the 'Cuddon Report' in October of the following year.

The REME Magazine published in July 1947 announced that the present REME badge had been abolished and a new one designed. King George VI had subsequently approved this design. The horse and chain of the badge were symbolic of "power under control", while the lightning flash was a reminder of electrical engineering. The globe upon which the horse was balanced indicated the impact of engineering upon the world in general. As well as the cap-badge, the new design was also incorporated into collar-badges, but minus the REME scroll that adorned the cap-badge.

Clifford Martin

A sad episode must be injected into the story here, one which occurred during the 'troubles' that led up to the establishment of the independent State of Israel in May of the following year. *(This was referred to earlier, towards the end of 1944. Ed.)* On Thursday 31st July 1947, the bodies of two British Army sergeants were found hanging from a tree in a eucalyptus grove near Nathanya, in what was then the British Mandate of Palestine. The two soldiers had first been held hostage by one of the Jewish terrorist organisations, possibly *"Irgun Zwei Leumi"* according to Peter Langley, before meeting their fate, apparently in retaliation for the previous execution of some of those terrorists.

One of those soldiers was Sgt Clifford Martin, who had enlisted at the ATS (Boys) Arborfield in April 1942. Clifford had spent his early years in Egypt, spoke Arabic extremely well, and must have been a great asset to the Intelligence Corps, which he had subsequently joined in the summer of 1946. He and his fellow sergeant, M Paice, had been kidnapped, held prisoner, and subsequently executed, whilst going about their official military duties.

Peter Langley was serving in Palestine with the 3rd Hussars at the time and had briefly met Clifford there, but could not confirm any previous acquaintance at Arborfield, despite their boys' service coinciding for a while. Peter still has some press cuttings of the sad incident, but adds that a lot of what they report just *"doesn't add up"*. He also retains a rather macabre press photo taken of the hanging bodies and, in later years, happened to show it to a fellow villager, a man who, it turned out, had been *"something big in Intelligence"* during those dangerous days. The gentleman was surprised to see the photo, saying, *"I thought we had suppressed or confiscated them all"*.

Ernie Cummings of 39A intake remembers returning from Italy in August 1945, then serving with the same Clifford Martin, having been posted to 23 Corps Troops Wksp in Palestine later that same year. Clifford was then a Craftsman at that unit, popularly known to everyone by the nickname 'Pincher' Martin. At that time he was a general fitter – and a very good one too, according to Ernie - in the Armament & General (A & G) Platoon. Ernie became quite a good friend and, recalling that Clifford's father had been a Superintendent in the Egyptian Police force, reckons that was the main reason why Clifford had volunteered for 'intelligence' duties.

Ernie presumes that the two dead soldiers had been on an 'eavesdropping' mission and recalls that when the two bodies were discovered, they had suffered the further indignity of being 'booby-trapped' by their executioners. This so incensed the local Brigadier that he immediately sent out a fully armed Airborne Brigade to patrol and search the area, but, unsurprisingly, not one civilian was to be seen out on the streets.

(Further details of this notorious incident can be found in a separate annex to this chapter.)

Joe Adey of 42A was another ex-boy serving in the same theatre of operations during those turbulent times, as a member of the Light Aid Detachment (LAD) with the 1st Regiment Royal Horse Artillery (RHA). He well remembers that the Jewish and Arab forces were marshalling their forces and drawing up battle lines for the day when 'partition' would become a reality in 1948. Jewish 'freedom fighters' of the Irgun and Stern Gang were stepping up their attacks on British troops and installations, while most Jewish settlements now had roadblocks manned by the 'Haggannah', their unofficial 'army'. It was part of Joe's job to try to remove these, made up as they were from forty-gallon oil drums filled with rocks and lashed together with timber. They certainly hadn't taught that at boys' school!

Also on 'overseas service' during 1947 was Charles Ashdown, ex-42A. Having already served in India for twelve months, Charles now found himself posted to take charge of a Workshop detachment in Malaya, at a small place called Batu-Pahat. Given the fact that most of the vehicles encountered were of either US or Canadian origin, coupled with the detachment's position at the end of a very extended supply chain, a somewhat 'improvised' system of repair had been found necessary. But Charles is happy to report that the 'team dynamics' expounded here at Arborfield had prepared him well for such a situation, where a certain amount of 'elasticity', rather than a slavish obedience

to orders and routine, was called for. Perhaps it was Charles' experience with the Canadian vehicles that led him to later serve with that country's Armed Forces, and to settle down there, after joining them in 1953.

Recruiting drives

Meanwhile back at Arborfield some time during the Summer of 1947, a War Office Photographic Unit visited the School and took a picture of A/Ts Alan Barrett and David Hitchcock, both of intake 45A, showing them posing alongside – sorry, re-assembling - an engine in the Vehicle Workshop. This picture was then literally cut in half, with only one portion being used as an advertising poster in two separate boys' weekly comics, the *Adventure* and *Rover*. Alan was the lucky one to survive 'in print', and he later went on to serve up to the rank of Major, before finally ending his civilian career as a Head of Department in the Engineering Science Department at SEME, Bordon. The advertisement itself exhorted boys, aged fourteen to sixteen, to join the Army *"for a grand life and a fine career"*. Alan reckons that just about summed up his own situation, while the advertisement went on in the following vein:

> *"You can be accepted for training at the Army Apprentice (sic) Schools, from which the Regular Army picks its best (and most highly paid) Technicians and Tradesmen. For three years you will enjoy all the amenities of a fine Public School. You will be well boarded, fed, clothed and cared for, entirely without cost to you or your parents, and you will actually be paid while you learn to handle modern tools and equipment with skill and precision. Your training over, you will be ready to join one of the Army's Technical Corps, with every chance of quick promotion to Warrant Officer and opportunities of reaching commissioned rank."*

As of September 16th 1947, Maj Charrington assumed the duties of Unit Recruiting Officer. A concerted drive was then taking place to encourage new recruits at all Apprentices' Schools, and Arborfield was helping out in many ways. 'Window displays' of various School activities and products had been shown in various towns; several boys from the northern

Left - A/T/Cpl Fox 1949

*Right - 2282124 A/T Worland
testing the sight on a 25 pdr
using a field clinometer*

Below - 1946 Passing Out Parade

Left - 1943 Intake ready for their Passing Out Parade in 1946

Below -
Centre Lathe Turning exercise

Bottom - 1946 'B' Coy

CSM Brady, Irish Guards, 'HQ' Coy, middle CSM 'Bull' Weston, Grenadier Guards, A Coy. There is a story of a revenge action taken by his A/Ts involving his dog 'a bitch' and its arranged introduction, to a 'male dog' overnight whilst in its kennel area surrounded by the former barrack 'spider', alongside the ablutions. The drill period parade, next morning, was of the utmost severity for 'A' Coy. The other CSM was from 'D' Coy, believed to be Durham Light Infantry.

reaches of Cumberland and Westmorland had written essays about their lives at Arborfield, forwarding them to the Recruiting Office at Carlisle, with a view to publication in the local press. Recruiting posters had been also been displayed here in the Library, where School visitors were received.

'Curly' Hoare had joined the School as a member of 47B at the tender age of fourteen and a half, recalling that by the time he left he was on a weekly wage of ten shillings and sixpence (fifty-two pence in present day terms). He describes the pay rise he then received as pretty incredible, having reached 'man service' and trade pay at the same time. Curly also has some not-so-fond memories of 'dress calls'. These consisted of having to report on parade in one particular form of dress, then being told to 'double away' and report back in completely different attire some fifteen minutes later. *(Were these the norm, just to keep boys 'on their toes', or were they only used for punishment? Ed.)*

Curly remembers one such call, which meant the lads reporting on parade dressed in PT kit, plimsolls and greatcoat, and carrying freshly blancoed webbing. When they were asked, in a not unkind fashion, *"Is anyone cold?"* there would always be some 'Herbert' who would unwittingly reply in the affirmative, which would inevitably result in some physical exertions to warm them up! As Curly says, *"It teaches you something"*.

His other preoccupation, high on the list of pastimes for many boys in those days, was smoking. The very fact that it was not allowed added to the thrill of lighting up, but of course one also had to have some ciggies to smoke! For Curly, this involved breaking out of Camp at night, buying packets of cigarettes at the nearby *'Robinson Crusoe'* bar, then returning to sell half the quantity at double their value to those boys less inclined to take the risk of going 'over the wire'.

This must have been reinforced on one occasion when Curly saw five boys enter the bar one evening, but none came out again. A quick glance through the window showed that they had fallen foul of Sgt Dransfield. Curly's worst memory is standing throughout a room inspection, in tears and sporting a black eye. This had come as retribution for not having partaken in one of the senior boys' weekly 'raffle', the prizes for which consisted of 'a coat-hanger' *(a nail!)*, 'a cigarette case' *(an empty packet!)* and 'a cigarette lighter' *(one Bryant & May red-tipped special!)*.

Curly recalls being one of twelve right-hand markers on morning parade, standing at ease waiting for things to get started. As RSM McNally marched out in front of them, he first glanced at his pocket-watch, then looked across at the Cookhouse clock, yet still asked, *"What's the time?"* Immediately, twelve right feet crashed to attention and an equal number of eager hands shot into the air, as the markers shouted out the correct time. Curly adds that this was the custom each morning – it was the way that the RSM concealed his failing eyesight!

A short apprenticeship

Another boy who can still lay claim to the title '47B' is Cliff Charlesworth, despite a late arrival and an early termination! Having been full time at Technical College for two years previously, he was allowed to start his apprenticeship about a month behind the rest of the intake. Being sixteen-and-a-half years of age at the time, he believes he may have been the oldest A/T to ever enlist into Arborfield. He recalls that one of the boy-RSMs during his time was named 'Olley' and that he was 'sweet' on one of the glamour-pusses working in the NAAFI. It is reputed that this young lady had a tattoo of a violin on one thigh and one of the violin's bow on the other thigh, in order that she could make sweet music! *(The phrase 'Pull the other one' springs to mind! Ed.)*

Cliff also recalls the legendary Pete Green, he of 'the hurled mace' fame, and another apprentice, Mick Kelly, who 'stopped a bullet' on Ash ranges. Unfortunately for Cliff, he never quite finished his apprenticeship, being 'invalided out' after two short years. By November of 1949, he had progressed to A/T Sgt in 'B' Coy, but collapsed in the 'MT2' Workshop one day and rushed into hospital. It was found that he was suffering from *"pneumonia, pleural effusion and TB"* (tuberculosis) so, after nine months in a sanatorium, his Army career was over. Cliff never had anything to do with Arborfield after that until, over fifty years later, he one day logged on to the Old Boys' Website.

Having left the Army, he took up with the nursing profession and can now boast the letters *"RGN, RMN, RNMH"* after his name. Incredibly, Cliff is still nursing, spending some 40 – 50 hours per week in *"old peoples' nursing homes"* – at the age of seventy-two! He puts his own youthfulness down to the fact that, after his first marriage failed, he then met and married a 'young lady' some twenty-three years his junior.

Imagine his delight – or shock? - when she told him that he was going to be a father again, at the age of fifty-seven! Cliff had lost his first son in a motorcycle accident, but now has two other 'new' boys, aged fourteen and fifteen, who are now as big as he is and whom he swears *"eat him out of house and home"*. *(It's no wonder that you're still working Cliff! Ed.)*

Stan Horne also joined as a member of 47B on September 3rd, starting his training as a Radio Mech. On leaving the School, he then went on to Lydd, in Kent, where he was converted into a Radar Mech. Late in 1952 he was posted to Japan for a year, before he was 'claimed' by his elder brother in Benghazi. However, there being no Radar sets in Benghazi, Stan asked for a transfer to Egypt in 1954. In quick succession he enjoyed postings to Hong Kong and Singapore, before finally returning to Blighty in late 1955, at the REME Wksp in Donnington. Stan later travelled to Australia, in October 1957, as part of the team carrying out service trials on the *Thunderbird* guided weapon. He finally left the Army on Christmas Day 1959, losing contact with all his Army pals. *(Around 1994, Stan eventually made contact with Rob Loader of his intake, who then put him back into touch with the OBA. Ed.)*

In September of that year, the first apprentices began arriving at a new AAS at Penny Pot Camp in Harrogate, Yorkshire. The boys of that first intake (47B) commenced their training in HQ Coy, and were assigned to become clerks, electricians, fitters, VMs and welders. They were soon joined by small detachments from the other schools at Chepstow and Arborfield. The first Royal Signals (R Sigs) boys didn't start arriving at Harrogate until September of the following year, from the Boys' Squadron (Sqn) at Catterick. The inception of Harrogate now brought the number of Army Apprentices' Schools to three and, in the years that were to follow, great rivalry and friendships, particularly on the sporting fields of play, were built up amongst these famous establishments.

It was during 1947 that, after much consideration and debate, the Drum and Fife Band had marched along the Camberley road and through the Sergeants' Mess gates for the last time. It was appreciated at the time that the School would miss the Band's tunes (both of them, as someone unkindly remarked!). As if in compensation for the demise of those 'spit and dribble' flautists, calls upon the recently formed Pipe Band now greatly increased. One of their best displays had been

at the Gordon Boys' School, in front of Field Marshall the Viscount Wavell. Also that year, Bandmaster Newman had left to take up a prestigious appointment as Director of Music in Adelaide, capital city of South Australia.

December of 1947 brought the fourth edition of *The Arborfield Apprentice*, by now an established and well-received magazine, despite the fact that, unlike the previous issues, this one had to be paid for, due to its rising production costs. However, the editor admitted that having only an annual issue was *"scarcely a suitable medium for a commentary which is expected to cover every aspect of the School's affairs"*. He suggested the possibility of having an issue each term, following the rule of 'little and often' as the best way forward. This advice was accepted and a double issue, in June and December, duly took place the following year.

First impressions

That magazine published a *'composite essay by Number One Intake'*, under the heading *'First impressions of Arborfield'*, which contained the following paragraph, very indicative of the prevailing times and conditions:

> *"The next morning I woke up while it was still dark and heard a sweet tune being played on a trumpet. I thought it was very funny at such an hour, until a harsh voice shouted 'Come on, get out of it!' It was very cold and the taps were frozen in the wash-room. We were told to fall in for breakfast and, after standing for about ten minutes in a draughty corridor, we were marched off to the Cookhouse.*
>
> *I was not very impressed by the way the meal went on. For one thing, we were expected to queue longer for the food than we had time to eat it! I thought the tea tasted very funny and wished I could have put more sugar in it. On the whole, I don't think it was worth queuing for. After the meal, I still believed the old music-hall jokes about Army food. After a few days, however, I agreed that 'the Army marches on its stomach' – and ate all I could get!"*

During the winter of 1947, much-needed repairs were carried out to the boys' Dining Hall and Cookhouse, in an effort to reduce the lengthy queueing – and gypping? - at the hot plate. On the negative side, it was also announced that rations had once again been cut. Surely on a humourous note, this is reported to have caused great distress to the Provost Sergeant's cat! This monstrous beast was now restricted to only six meals a day, excluding snacks and perquisites. That particular Provost Sergeant was Sgt Dransfield, who is later recalled as working for the local council as a road-mender, much to the delight of boys out running, who would jeer and hurl cat-calls *(How apt! Ed.)* at him in his now virtually powerless position.

The School Padre was able to look back upon a year that had contained two Confirmation Services, during which exactly one hundred boys had made their vows. During the previous December, the Lord Bishop of Oxford had made an eventful journey through fog and ice, while the Bishop of Reading took a very impressive Service in August, during warmer and sunnier hours. The year, however, had also been tinged with sadness, following the death of George Eades, following a short illness. George had kept the School Chapel spotlessly clean, his constant cheerfulness and devotion to duty had been an inspiration to all. With no resident caretaker, George's duties were now being shared amongst various boys and members of staff.

Just prior to Christmas 1947, the Band of the 7th Queen's Own Hussars combined with the School Band to give a concert of light and dance music in the Camp Hall. It was in the way of a farewell performance for the Hussars Band, who must have enjoyed temporary residence at Arborfield, as they went off to re-join their unit a few days later.

As an example of how the School depended heavily upon Officers and staff members from all arms of the Forces, the *'School Notes'* at the end of 1947 reported that, in the previous twelve months, all four Companies were under new command. 'A' Coy was led by Maj P S Morris-Keating, of the Rifle Brigade; 'B' Coy by Maj P W A Ironside, 3rd Carabiniers; 'C' Coy by Maj F W Senior, of the Bedfordshire and Hertfordshire Regt; and 'D' Coy by Maj H D Follett, from the East Yorkshires. As has already been mentioned, Maj Charrington of the 10th Hussars commanded the newly formed 'HQ' Coy.

Overheard in the Instrument Shop during 1947, a rather long-in-the-tooth military instructor reputedly threatened one 'teenage delinquent', *"You've got an* **incurable** *streak of laziness in you, son, and I'm going to* **cure** *it"*! *(Surely a case of what would be called today 'a contradiction in terms'? Ed.)* Another snippet of well-known School humour is illustrated by the tale that, during one of the Company dances, one blushing apprentice came up with the following classic chat-up line to his dancing partner: *"I'm afraid I'm a little stiff from Rugby"*. *(Please supply your own interpretation to that one! Ed.)*

A time to look back

Some research into REME records had been undertaken that same year, in order to obtain details for the setting-up of a 'Roll of Achievement'. It was hardly a surprise, though still a great pleasure, when it was found that over sixty-per-cent of all the boys who had left the School since 1939 had already reached non-commissioned rank. Apart from those who went directly to Sandhurst or Woolwich, no less than fourteen of those ex-boys had now gained commissioned rank, serving in REME. It was the intention that the 'Roll of Achievement' be inscribed on an honours-board, to be hung in the Library as a source of encouragement to all serving boys at the School.

At the same time, despite the relevant 'youth' of the School, now just eight years of age, thoughts were turning to the setting up of an 'Old Boys' Association', made up from boys who had already served their time here at the School. After all, it was these 'boys', now in their own right as soldier/tradesmen, who could pass on the traditions and *"way of doing things"* to their successors. The School as a whole had already made a name for itself, a name that had been carried to the four corners of the earth by its sons. Thus it was that, in the fourth edition of *The Arborfield Apprentice*, the School advertised its intention of an inaugural meeting of old boys later in that year.

The January issue of the *REME Magazine* carried the same message, feeling that it was *"a long overdue innovation"*. It reported the proposal for a reunion, at which office bearers would be elected and hoped that the whole affair could take place over a weekend, and include *"a dinner, dance and football match"*. The magazine also announced the intention of a 'memorial tablet' to be constructed in the School Chapel, bearing the names of old boys who had lost their lives in the war.

Another important visitor to the School, on

A smiling RSM McNally with his wife and children

February 26th 1948, was the Secretary of State for War, the Right Honourable (Rt Hon) Emanuel 'Manny' Shinwell, Member of Parliament (MP). Arriving at 11 a.m., Mr Shinwell made a comprehensive tour of the School, which included the Workshops, Education and Trade classrooms, Library, NAAFI and Camp Hall. The normal daily training programme was strictly adhered to, just as the Secretary of State had requested, so he was able to appreciate a typical day in the life of the apprentices. Mr Shinwell commented upon the inadequate equipment and accommodation, promising in the time-honoured way that politicians do, that *"something will be done"*.

It is interesting to note that the February intake (48A) of that year included five boys from the central European country of Poland. This was at a time before the dreaded 'Iron Curtain' was drawn tightly across

many borders of Central Europe by the Union of Socialist Soviet Republics (USSR). Life at the School would no doubt have been very strange for Polish boys at first, and they must have found it difficult to settle down. But they were heartily welcomed to the School with these immortal words from CSM 'Big Bill' Swinfield, *"Serdecznie witamy Polskich chlopcow my spodziewamy sie ze bedziecie z nami szczesliwi"*. It was later reported that the boys were doing well and were very popular with the other members of 'HQ' Coy. It was also expected that further parties of such boys would join later intakes.

Frank Conroy also arrived here as part of that 48A intake and says that he always felt hungry going to bed. Frank became very keen on 'Padre's Hour' whilst serving here, going on to become a committed Christian for the rest of his life. And yet despite this,

Frank always seemed to be in trouble! No matter how hard he tried to avoid it, Frank could easily fall foul of the system somehow, spending lots of time on CB. He was once awarded 'six of the best' – the dreaded cane - by Col Grenville-Grey for a fighting offence. The punishment was duly meted out by the RSM, whilst Frank was being held down by the Provost Sergeant. Frank later went on to be commissioned but perhaps understandably, never had a lot of time for either RSMs or Provost staff after that incident!

On Palm Sunday of that year, March 21st, a service was held in the School Chapel to commemorate those ex-boys of the School who had given their lives in the service and defence of their country during World War II. Among the guests that day were former Commandant Col White and his wife. Maj Gen Sir E Bertram Rowcroft KBE, CB, by then the retired and 'knighted' Director of Electrical and Mechanical Engineering (DEME), unveiled a memorial tablet, which was then dedicated by the Chaplain-General to the Forces, the Reverend (Rev) Canon F L Hughes. This fine tablet later adorned the wall of the Garrison Church, where the following names were inscribed:

Bateman G, Brewster J, Cale R H, Edwards P B, Estall C, Ford E A F, Halleybone J, Hammond T P, Hodge L E, Hughes H T, Martin C J V, Mear R W, Myers D M, Perrins T H, Ralph K, Tarrant R and Walker R A.

All the comforts of home!

A most welcome addition to the boys' comforts arrived during 1948, with the replacement of the original and ancient 'biscuits' by a modern style of mattress on which they could rest their weary bodies. Shortly afterwards, beds were 'made down', chopping around five feet from the space down the room centre. It was noted that this loss, of both 'biscuits' and space, must have curbed the activities of certain gymnastics enthusiasts, probably confining their activities to work 'on the beams', no doubt a more natural habitat, as some would say!

In *The Arborfield Apprentice* of June 1948, the first of the 'two per year' editions, the Commandant thanked the previous editor, Capt Eric Morrison, who had been posted off to East Africa. He congratulated 'B' Coy, who had the honour of becoming the School's very first Champion Company, and added that the award *"was by no means easily won"*. Later that same year, on the

'PoP' of August 17th, the Champion Company banner was paraded for the first time. The banner bore the School badge and the inscriptions *"Arborfield"* and, of course, *"Champion Company"*. It had been presented to the School by Mrs Ironside, so it was appropriate that her son, Maj P W A Ironside, was Officer Commanding (OC) of 'B' Coy at that time.

That same School magazine contained another article from the erudite pen of RSM McNally. Entitled *'Red Coat and Green Jacket'*, it gave a vivid insight into the regimental dress and traditions that had stood the British Army in such good stead over the centuries.

(The full text of the article can be found in a separate annex to this chapter.)

During that same year, the School proudly gained two Army Boxing Champions, A/T Sgt O'Brien at featherweight and A/T Smith at mosquito weight. Col Grenville-Grey was also proud to announce that the 'L-Z' team from 'A' Coy had become Arborfield's first soccer team to win the Army (Enlisted Boys) Football Cup, feeling confident that this would be the first in a succession of such victories. He added that he would like to encourage all A/Ts to continue to participate in some form of sport whilst in the Regular Army, thereby setting the standard for the conscripted National Service man to copy.

Having worked as a laboratory assistant with *Imperial Chemical Industries* – the famous 'ICI' – at one of their plants near his home in Bracknell, Berkshire, Ray Jenkinson was advised to *"try and obtain an engineering apprenticeship"*. An old school friend was already down at Chepstow and Ray was very tempted by the *"long summer holiday"* that his friend was enjoying. Thus it came about that Ray made the pilgrimage to the Army Recruiting Office at The Butts in Reading and later found himself on the inevitable truck-ride to Arborfield, where he joined intake 48B.

Ray was always of the opinion that he had joined the Army to *"learn a trade"*, but he soon found that there were some in authority who had other plans that involved him also becoming a soldier! End-of-term reports on Trade and Education showed 'excellent', whilst those on Physical and Military Training read only 'fair'. The eventual closure of the AAS Taunton in 1949 came to Ray's rescue, when he was selected to make up the course numbers for the 'new' trade of

Draughtsman. This was a wonderful opportunity for the *"mechanically minded"* youngster and from that point he never looked back.

Ray remembers many interesting visits, outside of the daily routine of the School, which helped to reinforce his interest in all things mechanical – an interest to which he still puts time to today, more than fifty years later. He recalls going to *Stuart-Turners* of Henley; the *Great Western Railway* works at Swindon; and the *"brilliant"* Science Museum at South Kensington – all places of wonder to Ray.

The religious side of life also played its part, under the guidance of School Padre, the Rev Dacre, and Ray attended confirmation classes alongside RSM McNally's daughter. He went on to serve with the Sappers until 1972 and then joined SEME Bordon as a Burnham Lecturer from 1974 until his retirement in 1991. Ray also has a musical bent, having become an accomplished piano teacher, and often plays the organ at his local church, where his wife Hugette is the lay preacher.

Saluting problems

Michael Addison, now happily settled in Australia, remembers his first few weeks as a member of intake 48B. He, like Larry Le Var the previous year, recalls that Maj Charrington was OC 'HQ' Coy and that his drill sergeant was one Sgt Buckley of the Grenadier Guards. Mike gave great credit to the sergeant, who had most of the squad marching in step in quite a short time. It was slightly different, however, when it came to saluting! Sgt Buckley had previously sustained a war wound during the Italian campaign, to either his right hand or arm, as a consequence of which he had been given special dispensation to salute with the left hand. Michael recalls the utter confusion this used to cause in his squad, with Sgt Buckley continually having to explain that it was only *he,* and not the boys, who had been awarded this unique privilege!

Another of that 48B intake was David Wright, who ended his apprenticeship as a Tels Mech. He has a memory that one of his trade instructors had been a Mr Stagg, who was later tragically killed, at the Farnborough Air Show of 1952. He thinks that a *Gloster Meteor*, possibly the first jet-propelled airplane to enter service, and being flown by test pilot John Derry, lost an engine, which then landed amongst some spectators, including the unfortunate Mr Stagg.

A happier memory from those days concerns the whitewashing of a pigsty during jankers, where the inhabitants of said sty – no, they weren't apprentices, contrary to rumour! - ended up whiter than the walls of their home! One of David's favourite characters was Sgt Paddy Laverty, of The Loyals. Paddy was well known for wandering into a barrack room in the evening, then keeping the boys enthralled with what were probably 'tall stories'. Paddy could also recite most of the verses of several poems by Kipling.

Like many boys both before and after him, David found his three years at the School of great value, giving him a great sense of humour and a feeling of belonging, as part of a team. Some of the things he could have done without, such as pushing a tin of boot polish along centre floor with his nose, and the endless inspections, when 'dirty' kit would be flung out of the window by an irate 'boy' NCO. As this only made the kit even dirtier, there didn't seem a lot of sense in it! *(Were these incidents mere schoolboy pranks, an essential form of discipline or just puerile bullying? Everyone has his own thoughts about these matters! Ed.)*

It was during 1948 that the decision was taken, at War Office level, to terminate the Woolwich Arsenal Cadetship scheme, as the success rate with the first students had proved to be something of a disappointment. The apprentices had been faced with a difficult task, under circumstances not exactly under their control. They suffered a fate of gradual withdrawal, as it became obvious that they would not complete the three-year course. Despite that, much additional and useful knowledge had been gained and two candidates, A/Ts Evans and Norman, were successful in gaining degrees.

With the proverbial hindsight, the termination of the scheme seems to have been a premature and unfortunate decision, as all seven of the apprentices selected for the last course, five of whom were from Arborfield, graduated with either a degree or diploma in engineering. One of those students, A/T Barrie Keast (45A), who gained a Higher National Diploma (HND) in Electrical Engineering, was destined to later become the first ex-boy Commandant of what would then be the 'Army Apprentices' College' (AAC) in 1976.

The School Band reported a busy year in 1948, with many varied presentations. The most outstanding of these was at Bradfield College in July. Field Marshall Montgomery was present, first inspecting the parading cadets but, to the Band's great pride and pleasure, then inspecting the Band too! In the Band's own humble opinion, it was they themselves who rather *"stole the show"*. At the same time, the 'dance band' section of the Band was also going from strength to strength. The number of enquiries and requests for it to perform, received from outside sources, indicated the current popularity of these so-called 'jive merchants'.

Unfortunately that same year, there had been a quite remarkable turnover in Bandmasters! In a short space of time, Mr Goddard was replaced by Mr Underwood, followed by Mr Pooke of the South Lancashire Regt. It was written that *"after such a bewildering succession of conductors, we (the Band) should be able to play under any baton, from John Barbirolli to Spike Jones, without batting an eyelid!"* The situation was finally summed up by the following anonymously written ode:

"Goddard's going was quite a blow
But his tour was ended; he had to go.
What wasn't so easily understood
Was the lightning visit of Underwood.
And that's not all – for already, look,
Pooke is come and going is Pooke."

Although by now the Pipe Band had become one of the accepted fixtures of the School, the RSM was at pains to point out all the hard work that was required to keep things going. He paid tribute to A/T Dowie, who had manfully filled the post of Pipe Major, in the absence of an experienced staff member. He thanked all members of the Pipe Band for their devotion to the cause and reminded them that, when things did go wrong, they had more chance than most to *"blow the clouds away"*. The boys were also indebted to Brig Hilborn, now Commandant at the Gordon Boys' School, who had kindly provided a supply of kilts in the past and had promised to do so again in the future.

Getting out and about

External visits by apprentices of all Divisions (Divs) were undertaken, which provided an instructive and productive addition to the normal training routine. During a period that covered around five months, more than four hundred boys were able to visit either a civilian firm or Regular Army unit, where they were able to add to their trade education. One notable visit was made by a party of Fitters to the School of Artillery, Larkhill. A worse day could not have been

chosen, as Salisbury Plain decided to greet the boys with a miserably wet, cold setting. They were able, however, to see a self-propelled twenty-five pounder in action, which livened up their day. Amongst the other places visited that year were:

Great Western Railway Locomotion Works, Swindon;
The Science Museum; The Royal Arsenal, Woolwich;
EMI Factories, Hayes, Middlesex;
Sperry's Gyroscope Works;
CAV, Acton;
Ford Motor Company;
13 Command Workshop, Aldershot;
AEC Limited, Southall, Middlesex;
School of Artillery, Larkhill
and the Royal Small Arms Factory (RSAF), Enfield.

1948 saw the twenty-fifth anniversary of the founding of Arborfield's 'sister school' at Chepstow. To celebrate this momentous occasion, a special parade was held there on August 16th, at which that great man 'Monty' took the salute and presented the prizes. Their annual reunion of old boys was to take place the following month, so it was good that Arborfield was about to start on this long and honourable tradition too.

The Shooting Team was very pleased that 1948 had seen the completion of two shooting ranges, one a 30-yard .303" outdoors and the other a 25-yard indoors miniature range. Brig J A Barlow officially opened the latter on October 8th. At the time, he was a 'big name' in the shooting world, who came along and kindly lectured the whole School on the general principles of this sporting pastime. After tea, the Brigadier gave a demonstration of match shooting, before joining in a shooting match between two invited teams. In the apprentices' shooting world, a good result had been achieved against the old enemy from Chepstow, followed by a close-run victory over RAF Halton, based just outside of Aylesbury in Buckinghamshire.

The year proved a memorable one for those boys who participated in Athletics. Captain Boyenval had prepared a training programme that had the lads *"hard at it"* each morning, but this paid off in the end with probably the best team that the School had produced so far. Also, the team now had the benefits of a properly laid-out track and first-class long jump pit. Not only that, but 1948 saw the first post-war Olympic Games, held here in London. The presence of the cream of World Athletics in Britain that year must have given an incentive to many a budding sportsman. It certainly seems to have rubbed off on the Arborfield boys.

Having entertained two representatives of the Reading branch of the Youth Hostels Association (YHA), all members of the Cycling Club were so impressed that they enthusiastically joined the YHA *en masse*. During subsequent weekend bike runs, to Canterbury in Kent and to the Isle of Wight, the boys were able to make good use of the hostel accommodation on offer. During one mid-term break, the Club also ventured out on a cycling marathon down to Chepstow, leaving Arborfield at 8 a.m. and not reaching their destination until around 9 p.m. that same evening. With legs still aching, the boys left Chepstow around noon the following day and gratefully arrived back at Camp just after 10 p.m. *(No motorways or Severn Bridge crossing in those days! Ed.)*

The Stamp Club resumed its activities in April of 1948, although with a membership of only four, but this was soon increased to a far healthier twenty-two ardent philatelists. No doubt their interest had been boosted that year by the issue of the 'Royal Silver Wedding' stamps on April 26th. *(If any of you guys has a spare copy of the £1 stamp, please could you send it to the editor!)* The only other 'special' issue that year was to commemorate the Olympic Games, mentioned earlier. It had been the RSM, Mr McNally, who had originally sown the seed that led to the Stamp Club's establishment.

Towards the end of the previous year, a School Film Unit had been set up, with the assistance of funding from the PRI. Shooting had subsequently begun in January 1948, with the progress since then deemed *"steady, if slow"*. The film in production during 1948 was called *"The Target"* and it was intended to serve as an introductory film, to be shown to each new intake. It portrayed new boys arriving at the School and traced their careers, bringing in most of the aspects of their varied lives. Finally, it showed those same boys walking out of the Camp gates, fit in their knowledge and training for their future success in the Regular Army, having achieved their 'target'.

Despite being handicapped by a lack of proper facilities, the Swimming Club had endeavoured to somehow set up a 'life-saving' class. What little practice they were able to get was in a small tank at Poperinghe Barracks and in the lake at nearby *California*. It was thus a great achievement when, at Reading Grammar School in September, all candidates

Two boys of intake 47A, dressed to kill

successfully passed their tests for Bronze Medallions.

Birth of the Old Boys' Association

The inaugural Old Boys' Reunion Dinner was successfully held at the School on August 28th 1948, when about seventy ex-boys were in attendance, most of these being graduates from the previous two years. The dinner was followed by 'a dance', attended by a good number of local girls, to whom the old boys – still relatively young of course - were able to show their paces on the dance floor. This, along with the odd pint or three, obviously had a detrimental effect, because at the sports meeting against the School teams the following day, the old boys were soundly beaten in all events – shooting, hockey, cricket and football.

(A copy of the first ever 'Club Rules' is included as an annex to this chapter.)

Young Gerald 'Gerry' Berragan.....

correct! They certainly did have a 'right one', for Gerry was to have a long and illustrious career, which ended with the rank of Major General! But that was well into the unforeseeable future – Gerry was still at the learning stage in 1948. He was none too happy in his early days and even managed to get his gaiters on upside down on one particular occasion. Sgt O'Brien, his drill sergeant, invited him to stand on a small table, while the other members of his Platoon were invited to comment on Gerry's dress sense – it took him a while to live that one down. Even his own room NCO described him as *"the doom boy"* of the Platoon and, if Gerry had owned the requisite twenty pounds at that moment, he'd have happily bought his own discharge.

Fortunately for everybody, Gerry persisted and did his best to please. When the Orderly Sergeant walked in one day, begging the question *"Can anyone here ride a bike?"* it was Gerry's hand that shot into the air, with a certain amount of pride. He was then selected to 'cycle' to the Cookhouse and report to the Cook Sergeant. As he left the room, he was told that there

In that same summer of 1948, young Gerald 'Gerry' Berragan enlisted at the Army Recruiting Office in Fishergate, in the historic city of York. He was following in the footsteps of both his brother, Clifford, and cousin, Derek Kirkpatrick, who had joined the ATS in September 1944 and were now serving as adult tradesmen. Arriving at Wokingham station, clutching a small suitcase full of all his worldly possessions, Gerry joined the usual transport for the few short miles to Arborfield. Given a piece of paper, on which was written the full postal address (for use when writing home), he noticed the regimental number *'12345678'* followed by the name *'A N Other'*. Well, that's an easy number to remember, thought Gerry, with much gratitude, but then told one of the staff that his name was *'Berragan'*, and not *'Other'*. The exact wording of the reply is not remembered, but went along the lines of *"We've got a right one 'ere!"*

Little did they – or Gerry – know that they were

....and then ready for mans service.

was no bike and that he'd have to walk. Not only that, but he spent the rest of the evening feeding potatoes into the peeling machine and then having to remove the 'black eyes' from the forlorn looking vegetables! *(Never volunteer! Ed.)*

Gerry's chosen trade was VM and he was to spend many happy hours *"filing and chiseling blocks of metal"*. He could never understand how the Polish boys managed to know what was expected of them. Indeed, he was most envious of the fact that they would finish before everyone else, gaining the highest marks for the finish and excellence of their work. Not only were these boys skilled fitters, but they were also outstanding sportsmen. As a VM, Gerry would normally have gone to 'B' Coy, but with a surfeit of VMs at the time, he was sent to 'A' Coy instead, where he developed his great love for the game of cricket.

It was also during 1948 that Bryan Adams (Oct '42) found himself posted as the Unit Armourer to the then 3 Central Wksp at Havannah Barracks in Bordon. This was his first 'independent command' where, in a fully equipped and purpose-built workshop, he was able to *"duplicate the exacting standards of the ATS (Boys)"*. He was never again to come across such a *"fine little facility"*. The workload was negligible and he found the company congenial, the Sergeants' Mess even took him as a guest to the Epsom Derby that year.

A new pamphlet, entitled *'A Proud Career'*, was issued by the War Office during that year. The foreword was written by the CIGS himself, Field Marshall Montgomery of Alamein, in which he stated:

> *"I commend this career to all boys who wish for a life of comradeship, interest and achievement. At the Army Apprentices' School you will become fitted, both in character and technical ability, to play an important part in the work of this great team, the Army. The opportunities you will have afterwards, to become both leaders and skilled craftsmen, will be of the greatest value to you throughout your life".*

The Cuddon Report

October of 1948 finally saw the publication of the *'Report of a Working Party set up by the Director of Military Training'*. Instantly abbreviated to the title *'Cuddon Report'*, in respect of Col P B Cuddon CBE MC, The Loyal Regiment, Commandant of the AAS Chepstow, who had chaired the working party, it had taken the best part of a year to be finalised. The School here at Arborfield had been represented by Lt Col A W Sturgess, the CI, and Maj P H Redford, a staff member from the Royal Army Education Corps (RAEC).

The study leading up to the eventual Report had been a wide-ranging one, covering all aspects of the recruitment, education and training of Army Apprentices. It made recommendations upon the joining age; syllabi and curricula; the technology content of courses; and the preparation for City and Guilds (C & G) examinations in respect of craft courses. The Schools were in future to be run as 'schools' in the fullest meaning of the word, and not merely as military establishments for the training of technicians.

As well as the acquisition of recognised civil qualifications, the Report recommended that these qualifications should lead to increases in pay, as both an incentive, and in recognition of endeavour and ability. The Report concluded that *"improvements in educational organisation and provision at the Schools"* were necessary. One outstanding observation was that *"all Warrant Officers and NCOs of technical Corps are required to be leaders, in addition to being technicians"*. Thus was set the standard that was to be adhered to during many years ahead.

There was much concern around December that year about the level of punishment that could be meted out to apprentice tradesmen. Letters were flying about between the authorities, laying down what could or could not be done, particularly under the legalities of the civil system. The general consensus had always been that any corporal punishment, in the form of caning, should be only what could be regarded as 'reasonable', and then only carried out with the given consent of the boys' parents. Although a directive was not issued, the War Office felt that Commandants should at least have some guidance, as an update to documents issued as long ago as 1933 and 1936. This guidance stated that the legal position was that caning was not provided for under the Army Act, as a punishment for enlisted boys, and that any amendment to the Army Act was *"not considered desirable"*.

In the December 1948 edition of *The Arborfield Apprentice,* the Commandant announced that the School had recently been visited by no less than four members of the Army Council, proving that the School's needs were not being overlooked. The

Marching through Reading

magazine also reported, *"with great regret"*, on Ben Cook's serious accident, but failed to give any details of this sad event.

Rumour has it that he was on his way home from either the local *'Bramshill Hunt'* or British Legion with Sgt Dransfield, when Ben was hit by a car. *(Whether it was Ben or the car that was 'wandering' was not mentioned! Ed.)* Happily, the magazine also gave the news that Ben was now *"well on the road to recovery"*, wishing him God speed along that road. Ben's successor as QM was Capt A T Hatchard, who forsook the agricultural gyrations of his predecessor for the rather smoother technique of ballroom dancing.

Get on parade!

'PoPs' had always tended to be seen from a purely parochial viewpoint, but the one that took place during February 1949 was reported upon by the editor of none other than *The Army Quarterly*. It will have come as no surprise to find the glowing report that followed:

> *"Early in February, the Editor was privi-leged to witness the Passing-out Parade of the Army Apprentices' School at Arborfield, near Reading. The turnout and drill of these youths, whose ages run from 15 to 17 and a half, was excellent and they did credit to their Guards Sergeant Major and young drill instructors. The RMA Sandhurst, the 'ne plus ultra' in educational establishments, could hardly have staged a smarter parade or a more moving spectacle.*
>
> *But the Editor was equally impressed by the general bearing and behaviour of the Apprentices off parade. They showed such obvious pride in themselves and, one felt, also in their calling. Admittedly they had had the benefit, according to age, of one, two or three years' careful training, under a first-class Commandant and staff of instruc-tors. They had clearly benefited by it"*

Ian Hume has long since settled in NZ, but is still able to recall his early days at the School. He originally enlisted at the AAS at Norton Manor Camp, down at Taunton in Somerset, in February 1949. However, upon the closure of that School the following August, Ian was one of only a few boys who were sent on to Arborfield, the majority being split between Chepstow and Harrogate. At the end of his three-year apprenticeship, Ian joined the RE rather than REME, having qualified as a Draughtsman (Mechanical).

Despite having joined at Taunton, Ian was still eligible to be classified as 49A, and it was his intake whose 'PoP' was later to be saddened by the death of the King, in February 1952. He recalls that the parade was completed in its entirety but, as a sign of respect, the dance that would normally have been held in the evening was cancelled. Ian had tried desperately hard to learn the rudiments of ballroom dancing whilst at Arborfield, there was certainly plenty of opportunity. Like Keith Evans (45A) before him, he enjoyed the tutorship of both RSM and Mrs McNally. But he never quite mastered the required skills, he still uses the same steps for waltzes, foxtrots and quicksteps, though, as he hastens to add, he does manage them at different speeds!

A long-delayed reorganisation of the School Library had finally been completed by that same February. Re-cataloguing had been achieved, and all books were now re-bound with linen paper. Every apprentice and member of staff had been issued with a personal membership card, which had greatly speeded up the issue and return of books. The Library could now boast around 1,400 books of general fiction and some 1,000 non-fiction or technical books. In May, the Library started issuing a regular broadsheet, giving news of those new books and periodicals that had just become available.

The School Football Team reached quite a high standard of skill during the 1948 / 49 season. The boys reached the semi-finals of both the Reading Minor Cup and the Berks & Bucks Minor Cup. Unfortunately, they found themselves pitched against the same side in both competitions and, on both occasions, the opposition from *Huntley & Palmers* proved the stronger. In the inter-school games, they were beaten only the once, by what was agreed *"an exceptionally good side"* from RAF Halton. The following season was eagerly anticipated, with many vows of revenge against the so-called *"biscuit wallahs"*.(Huntley & Palmers was an old-established firm in Reading, having opened its first shop in London Street back in 1841. Their slogan went along the lines of "the first name you thought of in biscuits, second to none in cakes". Ed.)

The 'PoP' held in July 1949 took place in what was termed *"a blaze of near tropical sunshine"*. Despite the discomfort this must have caused to many among the Junior Divisions, it certainly enhanced the spectacle of the parade, causing brasses to gleam and boots to shine. It was Col Grenville-Grey's last parade at the School after some two-and-a-half years as Commandant, so it was fitting that the inspecting officer for the occasion was a General with whom the Colonel had shared a long regimental association in the KRRC. The gentleman in question was Sir H Evelyn Barker, KBE, CB, DSO, MC, ADC, who was the GOC Eastern Command at the time.

An outstanding feature of the prize-giving ceremony that year was the presentation to A/T Sgt Kitchen, who had taken both the Award of Honour and the Commandant's Cup – a really fine achievement on his part. Following the `prize giving the General made a special point of meeting and talking with all ranks of the KRRC who were presently serving on the School's PS.

In the July 1949 issue of *The Arborfield Apprentice*, an appreciation was published regarding the Commandant's tour of duty. Col Grenville-Grey had previously served at the School of Infantry and commanded the Small Arms School at Netheravon, so had brought a great deal of military training experience to his appointment here at Arborfield. Upon his departure, the Colonel left behind him three lasting memorials. These were (i) the vast improvement in the sports grounds and facilities, to which he himself gave thanks to his able assistant, Maj H W Tyler; (ii) the inauguration of the Champion Company competition; (iii) the founding of the Old Boys' Club – or Association, as it was now being regarded.

Changes were afoot in the educational world that year, according to Maj R J W Durant, BSc, the School's Senior Education Officer (SEO). In the School magazine, he described the contents of a recent ACI. In future, in order to be eligible for promotion to SSgt, a soldier must now be in possession of the Army Certificate of Education (ACE) Second-class, and to continue on to Warrant rank, a First Class Certificate was now required. He exhorted the boys on what to do about it. *"The answer is, of course, quite simple"*, he explained, *"get your First Class while you are here!"*

At the beginning of that year, at School level,

Apprentices with an early Cossor osscilloscope, BFO and AVO meters

Ah yes, I remember it well

David Matyear was a member of that 49B intake and finds it a *"bit of a slog"* trying to remember all that went on so long ago. But the RSM's wife, Mrs McNally, is recalled with great affection, for her generosity for those apprentices who found themselves on jankers at the McNally's family home. David also recalls the long fistfights that went on between A/Ts Devine and Phayer in the 'B' Coy washrooms – fights that seemed to go on forever, with never an outright winner. Another incident that sticks in David's mind is the stabbing of Sgt Silvers (the Provost Sergeant) by one of his 'colleagues', causing him to be away from his duties for a considerable time. David's brother was also an apprentice here at the time and the two of them would walk into Reading on their one 'free Sunday' per month, to catch the train home for the day.

David's memory obviously continued to 'warm up' as he remembered, as a Band member, the hours he used to spend in the old stable block, practicing his drumbeats until *"almost perfect"*. Several hours each week were spent on adjusting the ropes on the drum, thus maintaining the drum skin as tight as possible, very necessary if a parade had been held in the rain. He goes on to recall the sweet smell of syrup, as the pipers poured this 'liquid gold' into their bagpipes to keep them supple and pliable.

The OBA had been pleased to welcome an influx of new members during 1949, with around two hundred attending the second Reunion held on September 3rd. Looking back in retrospect on those days, with the country still under a regime of severe rationing, and a lack of life's little luxuries, it isn't surprising that, going out alongside invitations to the Reunion was a notice which read: *"All ranks below Sergeant are reminded to bring along their knife, fork, spoon and a drinking utensil"*.

Owing to the large number present for dinner, one of the Cookhouse dining-halls was brought into use. But, of course, there was no queueing or gypping, as the old boys were waited upon by some forty 'new boys'. A short announcement, to the effect that charabancs of ladies had arrived at the Camp Hall, brought dinner to

another major change had seen education training organised according to trades, a system which had by now been seen as *"fully justified"*. It meant that the time boys spent in the 'schoolroom' was not so frequently interrupted and that educational endeavour would now be more closely related to workshop training.

The technical home of Senior Div VMs, 'Workshop MT1', under the control of Workshop Foreman, 'ex-Desert Rat' SSgt Howard, was striving to maintain an interesting final stage of practical instruction. The CI, Lt Col A W Sturgess, OBE, had introduced a new syllabus, consisting mainly of the removal and replacement of major assemblies. The work was augmented by a short specialist course, covering such subjects as recovery, dynamometer, brakes, chassis alignment and fault finding, all with the objective of teaching engineering methods and to prove the apprentices' ability to carry out 'real' work.

The 140 Jeeps of intake 49B had hardly had time to settle into their new way of life when, still 'wet behind the ears', they took part in the dreaded GOC's annual inspection. The staff, of course, were all in a dither over this and *"grey hair grew overnight on some heads"*. Thankfully, all the worry proved in vain, as the Deputy Commander declared himself very pleased with the efforts of the Juniors, after only two weeks' service.

an abrupt end, indeed, it was said that shouting *'Fire!'* could not have achieved more spectacular results! *(What about arranging some 'charabancs of ladies' to arrive at future Reunions – are there enough nursing homes in the area to provide a supply? Ed.)* The dancing that followed was said to be the *"best ever"* and the whole evening was later summarised as one of *"wine, women and song"*.

The cricket season that year had been rather spoilt by – wait for it – the lack of rain! This does appear to be a contradiction, but in fact the groundsmen found it very difficult to prepare a nice flat strip, as the ground was too hard and bumpy. Even net practice was becoming almost impossible, due to the iron-hard and uneven surface giving the bowlers a most unfair advantage. With these problems, it was no surprise that the season ran on into September, where it then clashed with the so-called 'winter' sports of hockey, rugger and soccer.

Great things were expected for the following season – and in particular of 'old colour' A/T LCpl Berragan, now back with 'HQ' Coy, in charge of the Jeeps. Gerry did in fact do very well at cricket, going on to captain the School team and gain his 'colours' during the 1951 season, prior to his leaving the School. It didn't do him any harm either, as he took his first step up the promotion ladder to the very top. He proudly recalls that in one game at Harrogate, when his mother came across from York to see him play, he and his opening partner, a lad by the name of Lyons, put on over 100 runs for the first wicket.

The standard of rugger in the School was thought to have greatly improved, though a glance at the results tended to disprove this! There were few sides in the area of comparable youth and inexperience, so it really was a case of 'men against boys'. Previous seasons had seen the team sprinkled with more mature members of staff, but that season was different, picked solely from apprentices. They were definitely in a 'school of hard knocks' and getting their experience in an extreme way.

Hard knocks must have also definitely figured in the sport of boxing. The season had opened with an unprecedented number of 112 entries for the 'Novices Competition',

including no less than forty-four youngsters from 'HQ' Coy. Astonishingly, this selection of boys in only their first term actually produced four eventual winners. As stated afterwards, in the School magazine, *"where experience was lacking, courage was well evident"*. A party from the boxing team had a great evening out watching the Army team defeat Wales and a future match against Sweden was eagerly anticipated.

Some changes in trade training

In September 1949, the School welcomed Col E L Percival DSO, late Highland Light Infantry (HLI), as its next Commandant. His predecessor, Col Grenville-Grey had issued the following *'Special Order of the Day'*, before handing over his responsibility:

> *"On relinquishing my command tomorrow, I should like to wish you all the best of luck in the future. The next few years are likely to be full of difficulties and the Regular Army will have a big share of them. I am confident that, on leaving this School, you will all realise your responsibilities and keep up the tradition of Arborfield. I have been very proud to have commanded you. Goodbye and God speed."*

Due to that year's closure of the AAS Taunton, accompanied by a redistribution of trade training

Workshop practice - fitting and filing

Fire Station and Sentry Box opposite the Guardroom

reminding readers that, in order to make effective use of such materiel, a high standard of training was required, which was only to be achieved by much effort. The Colonel remembered that, when he himself was a boy, the late Lord Northcliffe had written the following statement in his (the Colonel's) autograph book: *"Work makes life sweet"*. There is no doubt that the new Commandant believed in the work ethic, as borne out by his following words:

"My earnest wish is that the good reputation of the School shall continue to prosper and, to ensure this, I would like to impress upon you the one factor that is essential, not only to all of us at this School, but to the whole country today – HARD WORK. This factor, I believe, people are at last beginning to realise is an absolute necessity if our country is to be put back on its feet again."

across the remaining three Schools, a new commitment was placed upon Arborfield. In addition to Armourers, Electricians (Control Equipment), Fitters, Inst Mechs, Millwrights, Tels Mechs, Turners and VMs, the School here was now asked to train Draughtsmen (Mechanical). On passing out, these tradesmen were intended to go to RA, RAC, RAOC, RASC, RE and REME but, in 1950, the War Office deemed that future postings from the School would be to either RE or REME only. Capt L J Durkin, of the Royal Fusiliers, had been the Adjutant at Taunton, but now moved to Arborfield to take command of Champion Company, in this case 'A' Coy, who had won the title for the very first time.

On 13th November 1948, our colleagues down at the other Apprentices' School at Chepstow held a dedication ceremony on behalf of those old boys of the School who had paid the *"supreme sacrifice for King and Country"*. A Book of Remembrance, which had been inaugurated over two years previously, was officially 'opened' in the School Chapel. Generous subscriptions had been received from many parts, including the REME Association.

Col Percival wrote his first *'Foreword'* in the December 1949 issue *of The Arborfield Apprentice*. He recorded, with pleasure, that the School buildings were at last being painted, both inside and out. He asked all boys to join him in making a New Year's resolution to keep the barracks *"bright and clean"*. He reported that *"the Army of today is supplied with a multitude of new weapons, vehicles and equipment"*,

At the time, the recently inaugurated Apprentice Sergeants' Mess, described by one member as *"the baby of the School"*, was doing its very best to grow up. One idea that became reality was the playing of a soccer match against the RAEC element of the School. The game ended in a 3-3 draw after a tough struggle and the boy NCOs hoped that, *"in spite of the heavily-limping figures that populated Stephenson Road"* afterwards, that many more such games would be played in the future.

A successful pantomine

As reported in a local newspaper during 1949, the School's Cinema and Dramatic Club proudly presented a pantomime in December of that year, based loosely on the tale of *Dick Whittington, Lord Mayor of London*. The newspaper cutting later reappeared in *OBAN 9* during 1996, courtesy of Michael Addison (48B). The familiar old story had a topical slant, showing Dick leaving his village to join the Army Apprentices' School. The production was *"a remarkable success"* and was given by a number of boys, together with members of staff, their wives and families. The standard of chorus work was reported to be of a high standard, the first presented by some child dancers, while the second, a mock ballet by members of the Sergeants' Mess, *"brought the house down"* with their frolics.

Having read that report in *OBAN 9*, it certainly brought some happy memories flooding back for Ted Brigham of intake 49A. Ted recalls that prior to the inception of a panto, the Camp Hall had only a stage, with one set of curtains and a roll-up cinema screen. A 'behind-the-scenes' gang, including the intrepid Ted, was recruited, under the supervision of Capt McAuliffe REME, to put together a suitable set of stage lighting. Most of the equipment had to be begged, borrowed or 'acquired', with improvisation the order of the day. Many evenings of hard work led to quite professional skills that would never have otherwise been learned by those boys seconded onto the scheme. Ted himself, training as a Tels Mech, tried his hand at welding – not all that successfully by the sounds of it, as 'Capt Mac' had many blowholes to fill later! It is not surprising that Ted afterwards left those welding skills to others, opting instead for joining the Pipe Band as a trainee Drum Major.

Bedside lockers, one per bedspace, were issued during 1949, putting to an end the squabbles over the mere four chairs that were issued per room. At the same time, and on into 1950, boys were allowed to keep their own suitcases in their rooms. It is assumed that, with the end of post-war clothes rationing, boys would now have more civilian clothing to store away. This no doubt gave rise to a certain increase in 'individualism' and a relaxation of the 'uniform only' culture.

Gordon Bonner enlisted at Arborfield on September 9th that year. He well remembers one occasion when he had been detailed for *"RSM's fatigues"*. He marched up the road to Mr McNally's quarter and knocked on the back door. A well-known voice bellowed, *"Who's there?"* to which Gordon replied, *"Defaulter, Sir!"* Gordon was then handed over a set of kit – boots, belt, gaiters, Sam Browne and pace-stick and told to *"blanco that lot"*. So he did! Even the Sam Browne got scrubbed (with half a house-brick) and blancoed! Gordon finally left his offering on the back step and fled. There was one thing he always admired about Mr McNally – next morning he appeared on parade as immaculate as ever. Gordon later, of course, received just retribution!

As the Forties, the first full decade of the School's existence, finally 'bowed out', it is interesting to note the wide variety of extra-mural activities that were available to the apprentices of those years. Apart from the obvious sporting outlets of boxing, cricket, football and rugby, *The Arborfield Apprentice* is full of potted notes that cover the participation of many boys in such creditable pastimes as the Film Society, Music Club, Stamp Club, Beagling Club, Angling Club, Camera Club and Model Makers Club, as well as the previously mentioned Cycling Club and Cinema & Dramatic Club.

—§—

Some '49ers attending the 2003 Old Boys Reunion

Annex to Chapter 3

Pro Patria

On Thursday 31st July 1947, the bodies of two British Sergeants were found hanging in a eucalyptus grove near Nathanya, Palestine. The ground round the tree had been heavily mined. They had been held by the Jewish Terrorist Organisation for over two weeks, as hostages against the execution of three terrorists who had been sentenced to death by a British Military Court. One of these men, Sergeant Clifford Martin, will, we are sure, be well remembered by members of the Corps, especially ex-boys from Arborfield.

Clifford Martin joined the Army Technical School on April 14th 1942 and completed nearly two years' training there before the School was temporarily disbanded in March 1944. About 200 boys were then moved to 14 Command Workshop, Ashford, Kent, to complete their training. In September 1944 he passed his trade test and was posted to Colchester. *"The next time"*, to quote a friend, *"we saw him was in September 1945, at 21 Command Workshop, Burscough, Lancashire, on a 'Block Training Course"*.

When he left Burscough, many of his numerous friends said goodbye to him for the last time, as he joined 23 Corps Troops Workshop in October 1945. Then in November he went out to Palestine where, to quote from a letter from Cpl P Langley, *"He was a pillar of strength and the only fitter we could trust to do a good job"*.

Clifford had spent his early years in Egypt, spoke Arabic well, and must have been a great asset to the Intelligence Corps, which he joined in the Summer of 1946. It was while performing the arduous duties of policing the Holy Land in those difficult and dangerous times that, together with fellow Sergeant M Paice, he was kidnapped and held prisoner by the terrorists and finally hanged.

Regrets, however profuse and genuine, are of little comfort to the families and friends of these men, but we know that all members of the Corps will join with us in expressing our most profound sympathy to their relatives.

(The above article was first published in the REME Magazine, Volume 2, Number 10, for October 1947, and then, following research by the Corps Documentary Archivist, Maj

(Ret'd) Derek Gilliam, an ex-Chepstow boy of July 1939 vintage, re-published in OBAN 19, spring 2000. Harold Price (42A) reports that many years after the event, around 1998, the above incident was recalled in 'Yours' magazine, under the title 'The way you were')

Red Coat and Green Jacket
Regimental Dress and Tradition

> *"There is far more in tradition than mere sentiment, as the men of every British regiment, battalion and battery well know."*
>
> *Field Marshall Viscount Montgomery of Alamein, GCB, DSO*

During a war, a nation's armed services have to adapt themselves to the most efficient and up-to-date methods available in dress, tactics, arms and equipment. Thus, as the scientific and mechanical side of warfare develops and mobility increases, so the old order of things becomes swiftly outmoded and changes. This naturally gives rise to a school of thought which would make the Army like a collection of robots at all times, in peace as well as in war – a collection all of a drab sameness, with as much individuality as the inhabitants of an ant colony. They seek in fact to sink all national, county or local identity and association in a service of mere numbers, such as '112th Regiment of Infantry' or '16th Regiment of Artillery'. If this ever came to pass, I feel that the gain in index-filling efficiency and simplicity would be far outweighed by the loss of all that has been built up in a wealth of varied circumstance, through glorious years of victories and reverses, in monumental struggles through joy and anxiety.

Through the long history of the British Army, a man who wanted to be a soldier didn't just say that he wanted to join 'the infantry', 'the cavalry' or 'the artillery'. He named his choice of regiment or corps and, if asked for his reasons, invariably replied 'because my father was in the regiment' or 'because I have heard and read so much about the regiment that I want to belong to it'.

I do not question that, possessing the qualities of a good soldier, a man could soon acquire a love for the

RSM McNally and General Whitworth
Director oif Military Training

regiment to which he was sent, and take a pride in it. It would grow on him and he would become so steeped in its traditions and glory that the fact, that he had been drafted into it, would never occur to him, and he would probably resent the suggestion that it had.

But I have not found anyone who will dispute the fact that a man will be a better soldier in the regiment or corps of his choice, than in one for which he was just detailed. For, after a soldier's loyalty to his King and country, and complementary to it, he needs a more local and tangible loyalty – something he can talk about, some immediate thing he can get his teeth into, something which makes him feel that he personally is turning the smaller cog in the larger machine. Here then, is the function of his prided of regiment, his turnout, sport, drill, smartness, regimental efficiency and skill at arms, all wrapped up in the greater issue of preparing for war, should it arise. To get the maximum benefit from all these activities, he must be able to sport a favour, in the form of his regimental crest or badge, together with any special distinctions in the way of dress that the nation has bestowed upon his regiment, for gallant conduct or honourable service.

Many recruits joining their units today find some distinction peculiar to that regiment or corps alone – a distinction of which they have never heard, which may have had its origins in the past, sometimes the dim and distant past (if the history of soldiering can ever be called dim). Examples leap rapidly to mind – the two cap-badges of the Gloucestershire Regiment, worn front and back; the black silk ribbon attached to the back of the Royal Welch Fusiliers' collars; the red sash worn on the left shoulder by the warrant officers and sergeants of the Somerset Light Infantry; the black buttons of the Rifle Regiments; the different number of buttons and differently coloured plumes worn by the various regiments of the Brigade of Guards; the tartans of the Scottish regiments, the kilts of the Highland regiments and the trews of the Lowland regiments.

Yes, this young recruit, this British boy, will so imbue himself with such an honour or tradition, that it will remain a living thing to be proud of, to live up to – something he can hold high in days of peace, something that will sustain him in days of battle. For these are not only honours and traditions that have been lightly granted, they have taken years to come into being, and have their origins in deeds and happenings from the four corners of the world. What numbers could ever replace such illustrious names as 'The Greys', 'The Black Watch', 'The Foresters', 'The Green Howards', 'The Inniskillings' and dozens more?

I appreciate that soldiers can no longer fight in red coats and white buff, that brass buttons could now ruin the best tactical scheme or battle-plan. But, during these days of worried peace, great efforts are being made to restore our nation to its proper place among the elite, to maintain and improve our standard of life. A little colour, a little pomp and ceremony, would do a lot to brighten the heart and lift the spirit. Nowhere in the world can such traditional pomp and ceremony be laid on as here in Britain. No Hollywood director, with all his dollars and superlatives, could put on a show that could compare with what is only part and parcel of the British way of life – a Coronation, a Royal Wedding, a levee of investiture in London, a trooping of the colour on His Majesty's birthday, a Lord Mayor's Show, or any one of the many other ceremonies where those taking part are not mere actors, but inseparable parts of the nation doing its job.

His Majesty's Household Cavalry, The Life Guards and The Blues, all turned out in full ceremonial dress for the wedding of Princess Elizabeth. What a brave sight they made. Splendid too will be the appearance of the troops of the Brigade of Guards, when they are once more dressed in their traditional peacetime uniform with bearskin, red tunic, blue trousers and white equipment.

I may have laboured examples to drive home my point, but I am firmly convinced that if you take away regimental colours, badges, distinctions and local associations, grouping regiments and corps into large formations under obscure and drab numbers, then you have lost a great and important factor that has helped mould our Army to its greatness.

Although the major tactical factors of modern warfare, financial cost, scarcity of labour and materials, all stand in the way of the Army returning to full peacetime dress, let us retain all we can in the way of names, badges, crests and mottoes. Let soldiers keep their national, county and local identities; let them retain their hard-won distinctions, so that the glory built up through the ages may never fade. This can only augment and never detract from the teamwork and fighting efficiency of our regiments and corps.

R L McNally, RSM, MBE.

(The preceeding article is based upon that published in The Arborfield Apprentice, Volume I, Number 5, in June 1948.)

The Good Soldier

During Army life, one occasionally hears the words *"He's a good soldier"*. Sometimes it is said cheerfully and willingly, but now and then grudgingly. But however said, have you ever thought what a wonderful compliment it is? Have you ever wondered if anyone has said it of you? Have you gone into it, to find out just what it means? Or, better still, do you deserve that compliment?

After reading many books on the subject, I have tried, not once but many times, to write down in some order all the attributes required of a good soldier. Each time, I have found myself writing on and on, using word after word, each looking different yet, in some ultimate meaning, being alike. I have erased them, only to find still others begging to be put down on paper.

It can be said of a man that he is a good driver, or painter, or horseman, oh! A hundred and one things, but in all other aspects of life he could be a failure, a liar, a cheat or thief. No, I cannot think of anything harder in life to earn, and even harder to live up to, in its true meaning, than the reputation of being a *'Good Soldier'*.

So many attributes go towards the making of such a man that it is almost impossible to select any as being more important than the others. It is not just smartness and cleanliness. There's loyalty and obedience, aptitude and fortitude, fitness and stamina, intelligence and initiative; clear, quick thinking and an orderly mind; a brave yet humble spirit, imbued with the lofty ideals of a wonderful career; with the approach of a crusader, believing in what is right.

I could go on in this strain for hours but I can hear you say *"Stop! This is surely too much to expect of any man. Such a superman is not possible. Man is only human and you are asking too much"*. To this I must reply that history has proved that, from the ranks of the people that were only human, 'the common clay', there have been many who, by their courage and devotion, their loyalty and sacrifice, and by an intangible, intransient something, have been lifted to rank with the immortals.

A well-cut polished diamond is a thing of beauty and fire, a live thing, but let one facet contain a flaw and its value is considerably reduced. So it is with the soldier. Everything is so closely interwoven in his character that the *'Good Soldier'* cannot have one weak side in his make-up.

There are no short cuts on the way to becoming such a soldier, there can be no letting up; no time when one can say *"Well, that's that, I can lie back now, I am the finished article"*. Many famous soldiers, having spent almost a lifetime in the Army, have admitted that they still had many things to learn, new problems to be tackled and new conditions to be faced. It is an ever-present fight to keep bodily and mentally fit, in the struggle to follow what is right, against every type of opposition.

As a youngster, I disagreed with Henley's lines *"I am the master of my fate, the captain of my soul"*. But here, in this School, these lines are very real. Many of you do grasp, with both hands, the opportunities given you and so get everything possible from the School. What is even more important is that you also put a great deal of good back into the School. Unfortunately there are a few (thank God they are only a few) who ignore or throw away all that matters, until it is too late.

It is while you are at this School that you have a really fine chance of building the foundation necessary for you to become a *'Good Soldier'*. So that, one day should the nation have need of you, in either peace or war, you will be ready and fit to play your part. If, at the end of your time, you can say and believe in your heart that you have been a 'Good Soldier', you will have fulfilled the promise contained in the words of the hymn so well known to us all:

"I will not cease from mental fight,Nor shall my sword sleep in my hand till we have built Jerusalem in England's green and pleasant land."

R L McNally, RSM.

(The above article is based upon that published in The Arborfield Apprentice, Volume I, Number 3, in December 1946.)

Col J D White, DSO, MC

Since the last issue of *The Arborfield Apprentice*, we bade farewell to Colonel White, who had been the School's Commandant and Chief Instructor for nearly four years. Colonel White started in the engineering profession by serving an apprenticeship. He joined the Army and served throughout the 1914 / 18 war with the Royal Engineers, Royal Tank Corps and Infantry.

He was transferred to the RAOC as an Ordnance Mechanical Engineer (OME) in 1926 and, at the outbreak of the 1939 / 45 war, he was the COME of Aldershot Command. In 1939, Col White went to France as POME of the British Expeditionary Force. After the evacuation (Dunkirk), he went to the War Office as a Deputy Director and was eventually posted to be the Commandant and CI on October 1st 1943, when he retired as a Brigadier and was re-employed from the retired list as a Colonel.

During his period of command at the School, Col White had to guide it through some difficult times. When the invasion forces were concentrating for the Normandy landings, the School was evacuated and the Camp given over as a concentration area for troops. This meant that Col White's command was distributed in detachments throughout the country for several months.

Col White was indefatigable and his personal knowledge of every apprentice was a mark of his zeal and interest. He took the greatest interest in all their work and sports, and every kind of School activity. To the Staff he was known as an approachable and friendly commander. He was always accessible and willing to

Col White DSO MC, 1943-47

discuss any problem, whether it was in the nature of duty or a personal affair.

When the School was re-organised on February 1st 1947, and became the Army Apprentices School, Col White was largely concerned in that re-organisation. He completed his three years' tour of duty in October 1946, but was retained to see through the new set-up of the School. On May 10th 1947, he finally handed over command to Col C E M Grenville-Grey and was obliged to go to a hospital and convalescent home for a complete rest and overhaul, after his strenuous duties.

We understand that he has now recovered however, and we all wish him and Mrs White health and happiness in which to enjoy their retirement.

(The above appreciation was first published in The Arborfield Apprentice, Volume I, Number 4, issued in December 1947.)

Arborfield Daze (an odd ode)

Reveille blows: *'Get out of bed!'*
The A/T lifts his weary head
Then, springing out, dons trousers, boots
And out into the washhouse scoots.
He washes, tidies up his sheets
And bumps the floor with regular beats.
Breakfast call; he joins the queue;
Then gives his number, *'One-oh-two'*.

Bolts his food with such a rush
To get back to his button-brush.
He makes his cap-badge shine like new
And polishes his buttons too.

'Sweep up the floor and make that bed',
The Sergeant shouts, his face quite red.
Now, *'On Parade'*, out on the square
He's standing to attention there,
Then marches off to do PT,
'Up with your arms, now, just like me'.
And next he sits in Education,
Head in hands, in meditation.

The bell! He dashes off to dinner,
'This food', he says, *'it makes me thinner!'*
When all are served, why, then you'll see
Him always first up for buckshee!

Parade again, his face shines clean,
And on his boots, a glossy sheen,
A soldier smart from head to toes.
In 'shops we find him in the throes
Of making circuits, wireless sets,
Though work is hard, a rest he gets
When break bell goes and he can sit
And slyly – maybe – smoke – a bit!

But when the day's work's nearly done,
The last bell rings. As from a gun,
You see him shoot away for tea,
It really is a sight to see.

He always grumbles at the food –
Why, every British soldier should!
But every last crumb soon goes down;
'What, no buckshee?' – just see him frown.
Back in his room, he blancoes kit,
The day's last task, now he can sit
Down on his bed and read a book,
Or think of when he'll be a 'rook'.

Or more, perhaps, an NCO.
Then new 'jeeps' he will have to show
How making beds look nice and neat
Is not an easily mastered feat.
And, boy, will he spin them a line
'Bout how it was, back in forty-nine!'

*(The above poetic effort, by A/T J Collins, was first published in
The Arborfield Apprentice, Volume I, Number 4, issued in December 1947.)*

Club Rules

The following rules were proposed and passed at the first General Meeting of the Arborfield Old Boys' Club.

1. That the Club be known as the "Arborfield Old Boys' Club".

2. That any ex-A/T who has passed through the School be eligible for membership, providing he has not been ejected for gross misconduct.

3. That any member who, in the opinion of the Committee, has disgraced himself and the Club, be debarred from future membership on a majority vote of the Committee.

4. That a Committee be formed, consisting of:
A President
Two Vice-Presidents
A Secretary (resident in the School)
(All to be elected at the Annual Reunion)
A Treasurer – Office I/C PRI Accounts, by appointment)

5. (a) That subscriptions be levied as follows:
Annual – 5 shillings
Life   - 2 guineas (£2 and 2 shillings)
(b) That for these subscriptions, members are entitled to:
(i) The two half-yearly journals, post free
(ii)   Free dinner at the Annual Reunion

6. That the President takes the Chair at the Annual Reunion Dinner or, in his absence, the Senior Vice-President.

7. That Honorary Members would be:
Commandant, 2I/C, CI, RSM, MA (Master Artificer), Padre
Any such other members who are proposed, seconded and accepted by a majority vote of the Annual Meeting.
Capt H E Cook has been elected as an Honorary Member.

(Copies of the Old Boys' Reunion photograph in this issue may be obtained from the Officer I/C Photographs, Army Apprentices School, Arborfield. Prices are subject to fluctuation, but will be approximately three shillings per copy unmounted and five shillings mounted.)

(The above Club Rules were first published in The Arborfield Apprentice, Volume I, Number 6, issued in December 1948.)

Toy Soldier Display

A copy of Page 42 of the programme issued for the Royal Tournament, held at Olympia between June 12th and 28th, 1947 is shown below.

TOY SOLDIER DISPLAY

BY

Boys of the Army Apprentices School

ARBORFIELD

ENTRY

The Band leads the Toy Soldiers, preceded by the "officer" mounted on a large toy horse, into the arena in ordinary quick time, in fours, to the music of the School Quick March, "The Reds."

EVOLUTIONS

as follow are then carried out: Halt—Right turn and form two ranks—General Salute—"Present Arms" while the Salute is played. Inspection by the "officer" to the music of "Pageantry."

COMMENCEMENT OF TOY SOLDIERS' DRILL

while the band plays "Parade of the Tin Soldiers":—

Form two Stars and wheel once.
Form two Circles and Stars and wheel once.
Re-form into two ranks.
Form eights and march up and down.
Form fours, left wheel, form two ranks. Ground arms. (During this movement a large model gun is drawn into the arena.)

Gun fires, Toy Soldiers fall down stiffly in succession, and the drill ends.

The Toy Soldiers are brought to attention form two ranks and dress by the right.

FINALE

March past the Royal Box in slow time to the Slow March.
Break into quick time. Quick march to the music of "The Reds." Form fours on the march and, headed by the Band, march out.

BOVRIL PROMOTES ENERGY

42

A Great Day for the School

We were highly honoured and greatly delighted when Field Marshall Viscount Montgomery visited the School for the November Passing-Out Parade. The CIGS took the salute at the march past, presented prizes won during the term and did us the honour of having lunch in the Officers' Mess.

On parade were 973 boys, 120 of which were passing out that week to join their new units. After inspecting the parade and taking the salute, the CIGS talked with many members of the School staff. Everybody – distinguished visitors, old boys, parents, staff and boys – filled the Camp Hall to overflowing in order to see the presentation of prizes and to hear the Field Marshall's address.

After presenting the prizes, the Field Marshall said that he wanted to give to the head boy of the School a special prize to mark the occasion. He thought the most suitable thing would be a signed photograph of himself, and this he gave to Apprentice Sergeant Major P M O'Callaghan.

The Field Marshall meets some of the Permanent Staff and shame some can't keep their eyes to the front!

Then, stating that he woulds speak to the parents and boys separately, he told the parents:

"This is a great privilege and an opportunity for me to get over some points to you parents. I feel that I would like to tell you what is my conception of the Army into which your boys go. The man or boy who comes into it is firstly a citizen of Britain, like you or I. He comes into the Army and becomes a soldier. But he is only a soldier because, while he is in the Army, we impose upon him certain fixed patterns of behaviour and graft onto the civilian core, military discipline. He remains primarily a British citizen and, when he is finished soldiering, goes back into civilian life with the ordinary citizens of this country. That being the case, it is obviously very necessary that when he leaves the Army, he will not find himself at a disadvantage with those fellow citizens. He must be able to compete with them, without having suffered by having been in the Army.

Our aim is that a young man, who has begun to learn a certain trade in civil life, continues to learn it in the Army, and is returned to civil life in that trade. We want in the Army a good resettlement scheme, which will put him back into civil life without disadvantage, that is what we aim at. Those who serve the nation in the Armed Forces must not suffer thereby; that is how I see the Army and I shall always maintain that the Army is part of the nation, it is not anyone's private affair.

During the last war, and even today, we have compulsory National Service. Some 200,000 young chaps come into the Armed Forces to do their service. We have a great responsibility to look after them properly; not only to teach them soldiering but to put them back into civil life, better able to play their part and compete in civil industry when they return.

With that background, what about this technical school? The aim here is to turn your boy into the very best type of soldier/ tradesman. We aim that he shall reach the highest ranks of soldier/tradesman in the Army, or the best type of commissioned officer. While that is going on, his training is continued, so that he reaches the highest grade of educational standards. This batch passing out today has the opportunity of competing for vacancies at the Military Academy at Sandhurst; the best boys can get a commission in the Army through it.

I would say that this school is a most valuable place and we aim at having three more like it in Britain. If I were a boy, I would be into this school before you could say 'knife'. If I were a parent, with a boy of suitable age, I would get my boy into it as quickly as I could. But getting in is not easy, you have to pass an examination to do so. A boy from here has a very fine commercial value when he goes back to civil life."

To the boys, the Field Marshall continued:

"While you have been here in this school you may think, and have good reason to do so, that you have been taught only the technical side of the trade you have learned. But by far the most important part of your training here has been the forming of your character. You have been taught tolerance and given a balanced outlook; this view of life is very necessary these days. Having had this training here, and been given a well-rounded character, you now have great opportunities in front of you. You have security; you have confidence in a secure future, knowing that you are of great commercial value; you have had good training for the life ahead. What you make of that is up to you.

I don't know whether you boys ever read Longfellow. I often do and was reading the other day a poem about Hiawatha. Much of that poem is applicable to what is going on in the world today. The Big Chief, Creator of Nations, saw all the tribes fighting on earth and said he could not go on with that. He called them all together to a great conference and spoke to them. He used these words – 'All your strength is in your union; all your danger is in discord'. Very applicable, that. What if the President of the United Nations stood up and said those words? That is what I would say to the world today and the same thing applies to a school like this".*

The Field Marshall then referred to that morning's parade and said that he would go anywhere to be able to see what he had seen that morning.

"The parade", he went on, *"was a very good cross-section of the youth of Britain. When you think that the future of our race is in the hands of youths such as these, and as long as we continue to produce chaps like we have here, we need fear nothing".*

(The above is based upon an item issued in The Arborfield Apprentice, Volume 5, Number 9, in winter 1965, and itself copied from one that followed the Passing-Out Parade of November 1946.)

Soldiers in the Making

'Returning from the usual Saturday night jaunt in Reading, we discovered to our chagrin that the only available seat on the top deck of the smoke-laden, noisy bus was next to a very severe man, wearing an extraordinary colourful cap. He reminded us of recruiting posters of a bygone age when, as a small boy, the same features attracted us, as now older and wiser, filled us with distaste and misgiving.

We are not usually particular as to where we sit – Australian neighbourliness combined with a year in crowded Britain has destroyed what little reserve was possessed – yet there was something about this character that made us hesitate, although we knew the only unoccupied seat was next to him. Not taking it meant walking home and the road to Arborfield is long and tortuous, so we took what we believed to be the easy way. As you can see, it has lead to all this and, even if nothing else, this article will surely convince you that the least line of resistance is not always the shortest. But more of that later…

We knew his type only too well, or so we thought,

and therefore hardly expected conversation to begin, leastwise without us provoking it. So, after *The Merry Maidens* had been passed, without so much as a murmur from this military zombie, we took the bull by the horns and suggested that the weather was running true to English form. *"The youngsters with me never seem to complain of the weather. We usually have to detail them to wear greatcoats"*, he replied, eyeing our sheep-lined Irving jacket with obvious contempt.

It was on the tip of our tongue to retort about the blistering heat of Cyrenaica on half-a-gallon of water a day, and the effect it has on the viscosity of your blood. But we didn't and instead mumbled a platitude about the best years of our life having been spent at school, or something equally futile. A pause ensued, but rather than spend the rest of the journey in silence, we broached the subject that was obviously so dear to him, asking tamely, *"How many boys are you in charge of?"*

"Nine hundred and fifty-nine – one went sick this morning", was the prompt response. We were appalled at the number of infants apparently condemned to a life of blanco and 'bull' and, as if reading our thoughts, he went on, *"I suppose you're thinking that Army Technical Schools for boys are run on strictly military lines. I also suppose you'd send your son to any other school, bar Borstal, rather than one of ours"*. His voice was filled with contempt, it was obvious that he considered us one of the many people he had met, whose views he despised.

> *"Perhaps sometime"*, he continued, *"we'll be as well-known as some of the non-military schools. One of the things I hold against the Army is that it won't advertise itself. Everybody knows the sort of thing that goes on at those so-called public schools; everybody seems to know what goes on at Borstal even; but when it comes to the Army's boys' schools, everyone is like yourself – they've no idea what they're talking about"*.

We were very tempted to tell him who we were and what our job was, but somehow we guessed that, if we did, we would provoke as much scorn on our Magazine as we had on ourselves – and we'd had enough for one day. So we just grunted an approval of what he had said and sat back and confined our thought to ourselves.

We hadn't long returned from Otley *(Holding and*

Col Grenville-Grey CBE 1947-49

Drafting Centre. Ed.) and we'd been racking our brains to think of somewhere we could go to produce the second installment of this feature *"Report on REME"*. Here, it suddenly struck us, was the answer on our own editorial doorstep. Moreover, if we did agree, after seeing for ourselves, that the strong feelings of the check-hatted person we had just talked with were based on fact, and not just on illogical enthusiasm, we could probably do him a good turn by telling at least our own Corps all about this school for tomorrow's military engineer soldiers.

It is with this thought in our minds that we said goodbye to our friend as we got off the bus; and it was also with this thought in our minds that we phoned the Commandant of the Army Technical School at Arborfield and suggested to him that we come over sometime, with our photographer, have a look around his school, then write an article about it for our readers. The idea, Colonel White thought, was a good one. He'd help us as much as he could and we were perfectly at liberty to wander over the School to our heart's content.

When parents have decided to send their son away to boarding school, they naturally like to convince themselves that the place they have chosen is suitable for him. So, having read in the national press that there are to be held, in the near future, entrance examinations for the Boys' Schools at Arborfield and Chepstow, the parents first arrange an interview with the headmaster – only in this case the headmaster is called the Commandant. Arriving, perhaps with, perhaps without, their son, mother and father would first contact the Commandant's Adjutant. He takes them in to see the Commandant, who at Arborfield is Colonel J D White.

After the original introductions, and they've had time to glance around his office, they'll probably remark, as we did, on the large number of beautifully executed charts that adorn the walls. From these charts, anyone can see what a boy covers in his stay at the school, and at what stage he studies each particular item. Soon, no doubt, the parents will be introduced to the man that perhaps has most to do with the moulding of each boy's character. In RSM McNally, the boys' school at Arborfield is blessed with more than the usual type of Sergeant Major.

The particular parents that we have followed so far will probably, if they take the trouble that all parents should take, discover that Mr McNally holds an insight into the ways of dealing with young men, at least the equal of that held by the equivalent in any school, anywhere. *"Man management"*, Mr McNally calls it; *"Child psychology"*, the modern educationalist prefers it to be called.

Next, mother and father will be shown around the buildings. They are not very impressive, these buildings, for they were originally planned to last for three years only -–and are to be replaced as soon as possible. They are built of wood, not brick, but if they're not impressive, they are, notwithstanding, perfectly healthy, and a coat of paint would make a great improvement.

If it were term time when mother and father were on their tour, they could be shown boys on each particular stage of their schooling. If they were lucky, they might be shown, as it were, a new intake completing a period or two of matrix tests, designed to give Col White and his staff an idea as to which particular branch of technique each boy is suited.

Obviously, these tests form no more than a guide, and the authorities are fully aware of the fact that few boys have developed sufficiently at the tender age of fourteen or fifteen to be able to show just for what exact job they are cut out. This can be better explained if we pause for a moment and watch the newest intake being shown over the place that is to be their home for the next three years. As the boys come to the tanks standing outside the Workshops, they swarm on top and tell their friends that they were definitely born to be tank drivers. Then they are shown into the Armament shop and, with eyes agog with enthusiasm, each vies with the next in trying to persuade the others that their fathers have been Armourers for generations and that they too were cut out to carry on the heritage. And so it goes on – from the guns to the welding department, from welding to 'B' vehicles to instruments. At each shop, the same thing occurs.

From four weeks on the Square, the boys now start the technical side of their training and go indoors into the shops for five solid months of chipping and filing. Most of our readers have, we feel, at one time or another, cursed their lot when they've had to stand at a bench for a mere hour, filing some job or another. We sympathise with these boys and admire the spirit that, so soon after these monotonous weeks, restores the fervid enthusiasm of most of them!

For, when we pass on with mother and father, if they are lucky enough to still be with us to watch the next stage of instruction, we see in the Armourers' shop the enthusiasm that we found when we first arrived. At this stage the boys have been sub-divided into different specialist sections. So, in each part of the school where this intake is working, we found boys who are starting to learn to do the job they want to do. Perhaps 'Mr and Mrs Prospective Student' might pause, as we did, to talk to one of these schoolboys.

Budd was typical of the students in this shop. He was keen and alert and he liked his work, but he had hated those first few weeks. He had apparently been used to a considerable amount of freedom of movement before coming to the school and, naturally enough, found the discipline, to say the least, irksome. The boys were allowed out two evenings a week, but child psychologist or man manager McNally saw to it that no boy went out only to wander around the streets of Wokingham or somewhere. A dance is arranged on one of the evenings, to which girls come from local youth clubs and organisations; whilst a cinema show is a contrary attraction on the other evening. No effort is spared to ensure that the dances are a success; lemonade and other soft drinks are provided at a penny a glass for the boys and girls.

The story of how this exorbitant price was arrived at gives an interesting insight into the methods used, not only to look after the welfare of the boys, but also to increase the sense of importance of each and every one, an aspect of education invariably overlooked in the more well-known schools. When the dances were started. The authorities provided refreshments free of charge but, to their consternation, found that no one wanted to drink anything. Inquiries were made and brains were racked, and the conclusion was arrived at that perhaps a young man would be more tempted to bring his 'girlfriend' up to have a drink, if he had the personal satisfaction of delving into his pocket and producing some money. Now the lemonade is drunk, thirsts are quenched, and everyone is satisfied.

Our conversation with Budd was rather cut short by his having to go to attend a PT parade. We thought it would be a good idea if we went with him, watched for a bit and perhaps spoke to his instructor. We were glad we did, for we found CSMI Forward to be a mine of information; furthermore, from now on, he was to be a great assistance to us in our wanderings around the school. Each boy, we were informed, took exercise in the form of PT or organised games on at least five days per week throughout the whole of his time at the school. As he knew he was going to have each boy under his control for a whole three years, it was comparatively simple to arrange a long and comprehensive course, starting with simple exercises and getting more complex as the age and ability of the boy increased.

In summer, as much as possible was done outside, a fact that was typical of the policy of the whole school; although the grimaces of the Adjutant who had joined us, and the fact that we had already found out that Sgt Maj Forward was an international boxer of considerable repute, made us feel that perhaps he was just a little biased. In the summer, cricket, tennis, running and many other games were extremely popular; whilst in the winter, both rugger and soccer were played with great gusto. But there was no doubt that not only their instructors, but also the boys, were very proud of the school's boxing record and, from the accounts we heard, we got the impression that the threat of overseas boxing champions completely swamping ours was only a temporary one.

We said previously that every boy did PT five days per week during his stay at the school. But, naturally, if he were unwell for some reason or other, he would be excused. For the health side of the boys' welfare is looked after at least as well as any other side. He receives three good large meals every day; when he enters the dining room to get his food, he is checked-in on a list that is scrutinised by Company Commanders. If any boy misses a meal, then the Company Commander wants to know why and, if he is unwell, the boy is put to bed in the hospital, a place that looks after each patient as well as any school's sanatorium.

We talked for some time with Sister Halliwell, the Matron. She informed us that boys were brought under her care into this hospital for every little ailment. Anything very complicated or serious was immediately sent to the Cambridge Hospital at Aldershot. *"Are your wards very often full up?"* we asked, eyeing the rows of empty beds. *"We seem to have more in towards the middle of the week"*, Matron replied with a twinkle in her eye, *"and it's surprising how well everyone gets towards leave time"*. We made no comment and smiled as we passed on to talk to a patient who was very obviously enjoying his enforced rest. Yes, he'd been excellently treated whilst in hospital and felt that even influenza was almost worthwhile.

Walking back from the hospital, we began to feel that a cup of tea in the NAAFI would go down well. We walked along with a young man who boasted a stripe on his arm and our conversation with him gave us a considerable insight into the 'prefectorial' system within the school. A boy becomes a 'prefect' if he is proficient at all sides of his training. That is to say, no particular sphere, be it educational, technical or physical, is given preference of importance, the one over the other. This particular boy claimed that he was about the youngest ever to be an NCO and he was justly proud of his record.

We found the NAAFI to be similar to those the world over and, having swallowed our tea, we were immediately whisked off to be shown the library, where books of every different type could be taken out, or read on the spot. The general education side of each boy, it will be seen, is as well catered for as the technical, although as he grows older, he gets less and less general education. By the time they leave, between the ages of seventeen and eighteen, about five per cent of the boys have in their possession a certificate at least equivalent to the normal School

Certificate. About seventy per cent have a First Class certificate of education, which is slightly below that of the School, Certificate.

And, as the general educational side is well catered for, so the spiritual side of the boy's life is looked after. For the whole of his three years, each student receives one hour a week of religious instruction, whilst every Sunday a Church Parade is held and services conducted in the school's churches. So, no matter if the boy were Church of England, Roman Catholic or Free Church, his religious leanings are well cultivated. It's worth a special visit to the school just to be shown the C of E and RC chapels. Each contains ornaments and decorations constructed by the boys themselves, each beautiful to look at. Both Padres are proud of their churches and both have every reason to be so.

We've mentioned and described, inadequately no doubt, both the technical and the educational side but, as yet, except at the beginning of this article, haven't touched on a side that the parents who began this tour with us would have been bound to have noticed. For, it must be remembered, the title of this article is *"Soldiers in the Making"* and nearly all these boys are destined for the REME, a Corps that houses a combined technician and fighting man. Consequently, as much stress is laid on the production of a good fighting unit as a good technician and citizen.

After the original first four weeks of regimental training, at least seven hours per week are set aside for drill, weapon training and other activities that, combined, produce the English 'Tommy'. Just as the other sides of the boy's education produce results in the form of certificates, so the effect of this military training manifests itself on the parade ground every Sunday and, especially, at each passing-out parade that heralds the end of each boy's schooling.

These parades rival in smartness and efficiency anything any unit in the British Army can produce.

Secretary of State for War, the Rt Hon Emanuel 'Manny' Shinwell MP, inspects the Apprentices in 1948.

The different distinguished officers who take the salute at each parade invariably and sincerely comment upon the fact. It seems peculiarly fitting to us that Field Marshall Viscount Montgomery GCB, DSO – the CIGS, should have come down again to take the salute at the most recent of parades. For he was one of the instigators of this, our 'new army', and is, without doubt, the idol to which most of these boys look for inspiration.

And so there leaves the Army Technical School the finished product; what the School sends out into the Army proper is a combination of fine soldier and citizen, a fact of which we were ignorant just a few weeks ago. So, as we passed out of the gates of the school, we were wiser men, a fact upon which we remarked to our friend in the multi-coloured cap, to whom we had talked to on the bus.

"Glad to have been of service", he replied, *"and remember to write this in your article. That it is most important for mothers and fathers, anxious to send their sons to these schools, to spend as much time as they can on educating their children before they arrive at the age at which they can enter. At each entrance examination held, many more boys sit than we can possibly absorb. Therefore, although the exam is not a difficult one, nevertheless it is imperative that, for a boy to be sure of getting in, he must do more than just pass".*

We remembered.'

(The above is a virtually verbatim presentation of an article in the REME Magazine issued in December 1946, under the banner 'Report on REME'.)

Cover Photograph

The photograph on the cover of this book which is also reproduced at the start of this chapter was taken late 1945 according to Doug Boucher. Doug who had been surprised to see the photograph, on a proof for the cover of the book, displayed at the 2003 reunion sent the following note.

"I don't know where in the School this photograph was taken or why. We were all from barrack room E2 and I was the Boy Corporal (I was a Boy Sgt a few weeks earlier but that's another story)! Why the rest of the room weren't in the photo I don't know.

Of the ten in the photo I know the whereabouts of six (two of us regularly attend the reunion) and two more were found recently. We are continuing our search for the 210 of the intake and have been quite successful.

We are planning to hold a reunion at Coventry in August 2003 to include wives/ sweethearts and I think that there are about 60 coming.'"

Doug also mentions that Syd Smy can be seen wearing gym shoes and suggests that he was obviously on an 'excused boots' skive! The names of those in the photograph are:

Rear Row left to right:

I G Frost	Inst Mech
Maurice Darton	Vehicle Mech
Doug Boucher	Armourer
Chunky Bax	Fitter General
Taffy Holmes	Electrician
Taffy Rice	Fitter General

Front Row left to right

Jim McDonald	Fitter General
Syd Smy	Electrician
Jim MacDonald	Vehicle Mech
Fred McCarthy	Armourer

1949 School Rifle Team with Colonel Grenville-Grey and Captain Dawson RE.

Chapter 4

1950 - 55

War and Peace – or Peace and War?

The Fifties would eventually become regarded by many as a time of peaceful change. In fact, by the end of that decade, most people were prepared to believe that, to quote the words of Prime Minister Harold MacMillan, they had *"never had it so good"*. However, the start of the Fifties saw a mainly weary Britain, still exhausted by the effort and sacrifice of the long war, with many of its largest towns and cities pock-marked by bombsites. These were being filled, as quickly as possible, by the construction of pre-fabricated homes, to accommodate the thousands of people whose houses had been destroyed. Austerity was still severe, especially when applied to food rationing, but at least the end of petrol rationing in May 1950 seemed to herald a new, slowly unfolding sense of freedom. A popular radio show of the day, 'ITMA' ('It's that man again', starring Tommy Handley), could even raise a laugh with the rhyme:

"Down in the jungle, looking for a tent,
Better than a pre-fab – no rent!"

The first issue of that year's *REME Magazine*, in January, was of a new format, consisting of a larger page size but with a corresponding decrease in the number of pages. Consideration was also being given at the time to the production of a *'REME Journal'*. The *REME Magazine* would continue with topical articles and Corps domestic news, while the proposed *Journal* would contain matter of a high-grade military and technical content, written mainly by members of the Corps. Meanwhile, HM the King had approved the appointment of Maj Gen Rowcroft as representative Colonel Commandant REME for the year of 1950.

It was during 1950, here at Arborfield, that wooden wardrobes, although of only modest proportions, were issued at a rate of one per apprentice. This brought with it the problem of where to stand them. Naturally enough, boys were loathe to place their beds directly under the windows, especially during the cold wintry months, whilst the placement of these new wardrobes in front of the same windows was hardly practical from

the point of view of allowing some daylight into the room. Some overlapping of beds, bedside lockers, wardrobes and window thus became inevitable, while room NCOs strove to arrange things so that they were able to observe every individual bedspace – no hiding away lads!

The intake that 'passed out' on February 7th that year had started off as 210 strong early in 1947 but, as a result of the re-organisation of trades across the Apprentices' Schools, only 138 now remained. Of these, the vast majority was going into the REME, with only a handful to the RE, RA and RASC, and just one each to the RAC and RAOC. At some time previously, the War Office had already intimated that, in future, postings from the School would be only to either RE or REME. At the 'PoP', the Reviewing Officer was General Sir Ouvry L Roberts, KBE, CB, DSO, and GOC Southern Command. He stressed *"the importance of the School as a nursery for REME, providing a valuable regular element in a corps which, though young, had done much during the war, and since, to recommend it to the Army"*. The General also commented upon the three qualities that he had noticed on the parade – *"good turn-out, alertness and steadiness"*.

As reported in the *REME Magazine*, under the banner that *"Valuable Manpower comes to REME"*, that February 'PoP' had brought the spotlight, once again, on the Corps of REME. Draughtsmen, Fitters, VMs and allied trades too numerous to mention were among the successful apprentices and it had been pleasing that their educational standards were judged *"more than satisfactory"*.

Korea – the forgotten conflict?

June of that year brought about another dangerous situation in the Far East, one which could so easily have ended in another World War and did, in fact, cause no end of problems for quite a number of ex-Arborfield boys in the following months. The situation that arose in Korea was a legacy of that country's domination by the Japanese, ever since its annexation

A/T Hennessy, Intake 50B

be bought for the Chapel floor. It was hoped that grants could be obtained for all this work but, in the meantime, special collections would be taken once a term.

The end of the soccer season brought the conclusion that things had not gone too badly. One memorable fixture had been when both the First XI and the Second XI were entertained at Eton College. Both games were cleanly and keenly fought, with a draw the fair result on each occasion. What really stuck in the boys' minds however, was the 'high tea' that had been served afterwards, when the buns and ice cream consumed must have created a record! Another fixture, away at RAF Yatesbury, Wiltshire, ended with the School team almost stranded in the thickest fog seen in many a long day. The boys didn't arrive back at Camp until 8 p.m. that evening.

The School was very pleased that year to be able to lay its hands on the Inter-Services Boxing Trophy. This had been held tightly in the grip of the Royal Navy since 1932, but at this year's Championships, the Army had fought its way to a tie. The RN sportingly allowed the Army to hold it for the first six months, which meant that the Trophy would be held firstly by Arborfield and then by Harrogate, who had a wonderful boxing record that season. The School here had produced two individual winners, A/T Danby at middleweight and A/T Moreshead at midgeweight, while A/T Keating was the runner-up at bantamweight.

July 1950 brought a new edition of *The Arborfield Apprentice*. With summer leave only a matter of days away, cricket, athletics and leisurely outings were uppermost in the thoughts of the boys – well, that was the view of the Commandant in his usual *'Foreword'*. A most successful Sports Day had recently been held, in which the introduction of a steeplechase course was only just edged out as 'top highlight' by the 'Officers v. Sergeants' race – always very entertaining for the boys!

Due to the efforts of the cross-country athletes in track events, added to the prowess of the Polish boys at field events, the School had been able to more than hold its own in several good athletics meetings, of which Col Percival was justifiably proud. He was also happy to report the opening of a new, suitably furnished 'reading and writing room' in part of the NAAFI, reminding the boys that they no longer had an excuse for not writing home! At the same time, the cinema equipment had been thoroughly overhauled and Padre Dacre had made a great effort to provide the boys with some excellent

in 1910. The end of World War II saw the country split, with the Japanese surrendering to the forces of the Soviet Union, north of the 38th parallel, while south of that demarcation line, it was the Americans who took command. South Korea's independence, as recognised by the United Nations (UN) in 1948, was never accepted by North Korea, whose forces illegally invaded their southern neighbours in June 1950. The following month the first American contingents, on behalf of the UN, landed in the south. By September the same year, men of 11 Infantry Workshop provided the first major REME unit at Pusan.

The School Chaplain, the Rev R A Dacre, had plans for the Chapel, which for some time he had thought *"quite unworthy of the School"*. New altar rails, in oak, were being made, to replace the ugly and cheap-looking rails already there. It was intended that the lower part of the Sanctuary walls should be curtained; the woodwork of the Altar and Credence be darkened; the Cross and candlesticks be silver-plated; new carpets films.

Col Percival welcomed the arrival at the School of Maj John Biddulph, Gloucestershire Regiment, as its Assistant Commandant. The indefatigible Major had been Army Athletics champion as long ago as 1927 and, indeed, had represented the Army on many occasions during the years that followed. The Commandant obviously hoped and expected that Maj Biddulph's vast experience would 'rub off' on the School Athletics Team, particularly in time for the forthcoming 'Quadrangular Games', due to take place at the School of Technical Training, RAF Halton.

The School's Cross-country team had enjoyed a most successful season by the summer of that year. A hard core of some twenty running enthusiasts had trained hard throughout, and this dedication paid off with victories at every meeting except the very first. That initial defeat could be put down to the fact that the boys were competing against the much older and more experienced runners from local club Reading, but they certainly learned a lot from that first race. Against High Wycombe Grammar School, revenge was gained for the previous season's defeat. That was followed by a narrow win over the Royal Aircraft Establishment (RAE) Farnborough and then a memorable victory against the previously invincible RAF Halton. At the end of the season, in a competition held between the best fifty teams in all England, Arborfield was able to record a creditable twelfth place.

In response to many requests, 1950 brought the proposal that a Musical Society be formed in the School, for the benefit of all apprentices, members of staff and their families. It was hoped that the Society would be made up of three separate sections, an orchestra, a choir and an 'appreciation' group. A successful male voice choir had given some concerts the previous year, before being largely absorbed by the School Pantomime. Also on the musical front, as an incentive to recruit more members to the Pipe Band, an annual piping competition had been instituted, to find the 'best piper' and 'best learner piper'. Pipe Maj Coffield, along with three of his enthusiastic followers, were due to soon play at the GOC's garden party.

At the 'PoP' in July of 1950, for the first time the Inspecting Officer was the Quarter Master General (QMG) to the Forces, Lt Gen Sir Ivor Thomas, KCB, KBE, DSO, MC. In his address, the General paid tribute to REME. He admired its high standard of efficiency and said that, although it was still a young

Corps, its traditions were already second to none. He told the boys of the intricacies of modern equipment, such as the fact that a tank could now contain some sixteen miles of electrical wiring. He asked the boys to follow the motto, *"You want the best service; we will give it to you"*.

Welcome recruiting figures

The intake of 150 boys that arrived in 'HQ' Coy during September 1950 was the highest number for three years. A recent pay increase may well have been partly responsible and the Commandant was hopeful that the numbers would be further increased the following term. Recruiting efforts were now being assisted by two extremely long 'Travelling Vans', a blue one from here at Arborfield and a red one based at Harrogate. Again with recruiting in mind, it had also now become the custom for a party of boys from the Duke of York's School to pay us an annual visit.

That same month saw the inauguration of yet another Society here at the School, the Christian Fellowship (CF). Its main intention was for boys to meet regularly, in order to discuss portions of the Bible. Despite it being *"the world's best seller"*, many were, and are perhaps still, quite unaware of its contents.

The *REME Magazine* for September contained a follow-up article to that which had been written in its April edition, where it had announced the arrival of 'valuable manpower' from the School into REME. After that article had been publicised, the Commandant, Col Percival, had given permission for the magazine's reporter to produce a *"commentary on the training and activities of the School"*.

(The article is published as a separate annex at the end of this chapter.)

Memories and Misunderstandings

Maj Charrington, OC 'HQ' Coy – or 'Chinny', as the boys used to affectionately call him – must have made a lasting impression. This is borne out by an article that was published in an edition of the *OBAN* almost fifty years later. Written by Nick Webber of intake 50B, it is entitled *'Memories of a Gentleman Officer'*. Although Chinny suffered from an unfortunate stutter, he had long accepted this impediment without any recriminations. He was always kind and considerate

What's this boy doing out on his own then?

to the young boys under his charge, both inside and outside of the School's entrance gates.

Nick, who hailed from Dorchester, capital of Dorset, knew that Chinny hailed from nearby Sturminster Newton, but only finally visited him there some nineteen years after finishing his boy's service. He found that Chinny lived in a house which dated back to around 1640, a real 'English-garden picture postcard' style place, so it was with some apprehension that Nick awaited an answer to his tentative knock on the front door. It was opened by an elderly chap in a woollen cardigan, who diligently looked Nick up and down as if on parade and said, *"A/T CSM Webber, how nice to see you. Is your father still serving?"* What a phenomenal memory!

Inviting 'young' Nick into his house, Chinny then proceeded to dig out some old photograph albums, full of pictures that had been taken at the School and including some of Nick's own intake. Chinny was able to describe the history of many of them, knowing which

ones had sadly died, those who had been commissioned – he even knew where some of them were stationed. All of them, Chinny proudly referred to as *"my boys"*.

Looking back on his own days at Arborfield, Nick recalls that Chinny had once asked him and some other A/T NCOs if they would kindly punt him and a party of friends along the Thames. They agreed of course and soon found themselves at nearby Henley, where Chinny and his entourage disembarked at a riverside pub. Turning to the boys with a twinkle in his eye, Chinny said, *"I know some of you boys drink"*, at which he pulled back a tarpaulin sheet to reveal a crate of aptly-named *Charrington Ale*! The Major then asked the boys not to go ashore, and not to drop the empties into the river, before leaving them to their own recuperation.

Nick remembers another occasion in 1951 when, as an A/T LCpl, he was detailed to accompany a then ex-boy around the workshops. The 'old boy', who couldn't have really been that old, was using a walking stick and

Nick could hardly imagine that he himself would end up in similar fashion, indeed he later attended the 1995 Reunion in his wheelchair. Delving back into past experiences, Nick recalled serving with an Australian Captain at Inchon, Korea, who told him, *"You know Sergeant, one of the hardest jobs here is having a squad of mostly you Brit ex-boys – you are all so sure of yourselves and are bloody good engineers"*. Nick hoped that reputation was maintained in subsequent years.

Ron Hague was another member of 50B and, like many other ex-boys of his era, retains only the fondest memories of RSM McNally. He recalls one of his mates, who shall remain nameless, once walking directly past the splendidly kilted figure of Col Percival, after which he snapped up a smart salute – not at the Commandant, but at the RSM! He was taken quickly to one side to find himself 're-educated' in no uncertain manner.

On another occasion, that of a rehearsal for a 'PoP', Ron remembers an A/T LCpl who took a wrong turning and ended up standing lost and forlorn on a large area of otherwise deserted Parade Square. *"Where did you come from, boy?"* yelled the RSM, to which the gallant - but unfortunate - lad could only reply, *"From Wolverhampton, Sir"*! *(Just what response this gained from the RSM is unknown, but no doubt our reader can imagine it for himself/herself – or at least something like it! Ed.)*

A further member of that 50B intake was Mike Webb-Morris, who returned and attended his first Old Boys' Reunion almost fifty years later. During the evening, he became amazed at the memories that were brought back to him and joined in the laughter with old comrades, at stories from so long ago. But he also realised that they probably hadn't seen the funny side of things at the time!

One individual that he well remembered was his old drill sergeant, 'HQ' Coy's own Bill Buckley of the Grenadier Guards. Mike says that Sgt Buckley was one of the fairest NCOs he ever served under, not the type to indulge in public humiliation like some he could name. The boys would have done anything for Bill – or else! Mike recalls one particular drill exercise, when Bill became so upset at his squad's inability to perform to his satisfaction, that he gave the boys an impromptu performance of 'pace-stick abuse'. The said instrument ended up in being stamped into several pieces in the middle of the Square! Bill then told the squad that it was their fault and that they would have to

pay for it – unless, of course, they won the forthcoming drill competition. Needless to say, they did just that.

Also able to recall those drill sessions is Charlie Ayre, again of 50B. At the end of the first six weeks of basic training, or 'square bashing', his squad's drill sergeant, Sgt Roberts of the East Lancashire Regt, turned the squad over to Charlie for the inter-squad drill competition. Much to his surprise and delight, his squad not only turned in a first class performance, but also won the competition. As reward for his efforts, Charlie was presented with a military-style book which gave the breakdown of all the regiments and corps of the British Army.

Weston 'West' Robertson was another of that 50B intake, with the title *'Misunderstandings'* at the top of his list of memorable events. One such episode took place in the Cookhouse, where West was probably on 'fatigues' and had been told to prepare a case of tinned tomatoes for the oven. Being a careful and 'safety-first' type, West duly unpacked the tins from their cardboard case, thinking that it would be dangerous to put such inflammable material into a hot oven. What he failed to do however, was to open or even pierce the lids of the said tins. They subsequently exploded within the confines of the oven, much to the detriment of said oven – and to the chagrin of the kitchen staff, once they had managed to raise themselves from the floor and stand up from 'the prone position'!

Another tale involves the six-foot high hedge that ran along the outside road, from the Guardroom all the way along the sports field and up to the Sergeants' Mess. Having been banned from the Cookhouse kitchen, for reasons explained above, West's next punishment was doled out by Sgt Fred Silvers, newly appointed leader of the Provost staff – *"Cut off 'a foot' from the top of that hedge"*. Having started on this monumental task, West was then joined by two other miscreants, Bill Orme and Brian Balman, who told West that they had been given the same instruction.

What the Provost Sergeant had failed to communicate to the three boys - or could it be that the boys deliberately failed to understand? *(Perish the thought! Ed.)* - was that 'the foot' applied collectively, not individually. As their work progressed, one hedge-trimmer following the other, from the safe side of the hedge, the inevitable result of their labours relentlessly turned into a dense tangle of hedge trimmings all across the road outside. Now, in those days it was the main Reading road, and the boys had soon caused what was probably Arborfield's first ever traffic jam!

Before long, this led to the sound of a police car, its bell ringing, arriving on the scene, with two 'boys in blue' having been sent to investigate. Our three hedge-trimmers had already been working for a couple of hours, knowing that the RP staff was probably sat in the Guardroom, listening to the Saturday afternoon's football on the radio. To the civilian policemen, they explained that they were not allowed to leave Camp, thus the road would have to remain in its current state. Eventually the RP staff came out to see what all the fuss was about, and there soon developed a slanging match between the military and civilian forces of the law! It ended with the three 'innocent bystanders' – *"We only did what we was told, Sir!"* - being dismissed by the Orderly Officer, while the RPs cleared the road, directing the traffic as they did so.

On another occasion, West was detailed for Officers' Mess fatigues, certainly a step up for him! He spent the evening washing pots and pans whilst furtively eyeing a leg of lamb that had been left so temptingly in its roasting tin. West bided his time and, at an opportune moment, smuggled the meat outside to a hiding place. He then concocted a tale about a *"black Labrador"* that he had seen lurking about the kitchen and subsequently chased off – taking care not to actually mention the roast lamb. He was praised for his diligence and actually requested a loaf of bread as a reward. West and the fellow members of his barrack room eventually scoffed both the bread and the lamb!

'Clem' Clements must have joined in early 1950, admitting the fact that he knew nothing about either life or work, having been very much influenced by those old 'apron strings' that belonged to his dear mother. Clem was later to suffer an unfortunate infection of the hands and arms, no doubt dermatitis, and after spending some time in the MRS, was 'back-squadded' (or relegated) to join the next intake 50B. He had been 'Army barmy'

ever since his youth, his father having been an RSM in the Northamptonshire Regt, serving in India. Clem is happy to report that the illness didn't interfere with his career and he is ever grateful to a certain ASM at the School, who swiftly spotted his potential to become a Tels Mech, rather than his originally chosen trade of Inst Mech.

Clem looks back on his Arborfield days with affection. Possibly two years would have been better than three for him, but he was made aware of *"comradeship and teamwork"*, both of which were to serve him well in later life. He thinks that today's boys still have the *"quality, bearing and good manners"* of their predecessors, and thanks the three men who influenced his early days. First his father, for his insistence that his son learned a trade; then the workshop instructor who recommended that he be relegated; and, last but not least, that forward-looking ASM who had fortunately spotted his potential.

Ex-boys make progress

The School magazine that came out at the end of 1950 was the first one to give some news about the progress of some of its ex-apprentices. The three chosen for the article were SSgts Wheatley and Norman, plus 2/Lt Owen, all of whom had been proud holders of the Commandant's Cup, between 1943 and 1947. They had followed this by being cadets together at Woolwich and were now working in close co-operation at Bailleul Camp, back here in Arborfield. All three agreed on one principle that had been essential to their success in the Army – hard work whenever this was required, plus plenty of useful interests when relaxing outside of their normal round of duties.

The same publication gave news of *"a miniature invasion of the School"* that had taken place during the first weekend of September, when 160 old boys

The Military Band steps out in tune

had gathered to celebrate the third annual reunion of their Association. Heavy rain meant that the series of games against the boys had to be cancelled and, instead a cinema-show was put on in the Camp Hall, which was very well attended. Dinner was followed by an amusing speech from the Commandant, after which the gathering repaired to the Camp Hall once more for an enjoyable dance session, to music from the School Dance Band. Again that year, the ladies turned up in strength, being spirited away, Cinderella-like, on the stroke of midnight to their homes in Reading and Wokingham.

The successful pantomime of Christmas 1949 obviously provided the incentive for another attempt on December 14th and 15th 1950. As a contrast to the previous rendering of 'Dick Whittington', this show was instead a straightforward pantomime, rather than a locally written topical one. Rehearsals were plagued with problems, however, from winter coughs and colds to the frequent power-cuts that took place right up to the final 'dress rehearsal'. From comments made afterwards, the audience had obviously not found this show so amusing as the last one, but it was still hoped that a start had now been well made on producing an annual event.

December's edition of the REME Magazine brought an article from the Depot REME, a unit that will be etched on the memories of thousands of ex-boys. The unit had started life as the 'Holding and Mobilisation Centre' at Nottingham, then later moved to Otley, near Leeds, where it became the 'Holding and Drafting Centre'. Its move to Arborfield took place in November 1948, into Poperinghe Barracks, where it was to remain into the far and distant future.

In the middle of December 1950, things were going disastrously wrong for the UN troops in Korea, with the 29th Independent Brigade Group being forced to withdraw over 200 miles in the space of just over a week. However, REME elements were praised for their efforts during this most difficult phase of operations. As quoted by Brig T Brodie CBE, *"They have done a wonderful job, working all hours, under the most frightful conditions of extreme cold, biting winds and an overall pall of dust. Improvisation and long hours have earned for our REME Units a reputation never previously excelled."*

In January 1951, the School supplied a stand at the Schoolboys' Exhibition. In order to attract the public's attention, two young apprentices, one from the telecommunications trade and the other a mechanical draughtsman, were to be seen working at their respective trade disciplines. Also on display was the School-produced working model of the famous locomotive and its tender *The Royal Scot*. This fine piece of craftsmanship had been constructed by a number of apprentices who had already completed their School syllabus and had carried out the demanding task, under the guidance of instructional staff.

Much activity had been taking place on the carpentry line, where the new altar rails for the Chapel were now about half-completed. The boards showing School records in the Camp Hall had been re-arranged and transferred to the side-walls. A large vote of thanks went to the Commandant at Harrogate, who had allowed his School to make an imposing board listing all of Arborfield's Commandants to date – with enough estimated space to reach to the year 2000!

The March edition of the REME Magazine gave details of the 'REME, Phase II' scheme, which introduced the transfer to REME of direct responsibility for Unit Repairs in the Household Cavalry, Foot Guards and Infantry, RAC, RA, R Sigs, RASC and RAOC, and for Field Repairs in the RASC. Thus, various trades, which had previously been part of the regimental system, would now be wholly taken over by REME alone – the old 'squadron fitters' were to disappear.

In May of 1951, Michael Addison (48B) found himself *"lucky to be chosen"* to go on a recruiting mission around the southeast, accompanied by Sam Weller, a motorcycle escort and RASC driver. The vehicle used was a sixty-foot trailer, known as a *'Queen Mary'*. Mike found the whole experience *"interesting and enjoyable"*, with big crowds gathering at wherever they stopped. He has no idea what effect his effort actually had on recruiting, but hoped that it was a positive one! Mike eventually completed his Artificer course on December 18th 1968, nine days after his thirty-sixth birthday; he thus stakes his claim to be one of the oldest 'tiffies' on record!

The Festival of Britain

1951 heralded the 'Festival of Britain', held exactly 100 years after the 'Great Exhibition' of 1851. This had been presented at the Crystal Palace during the reign of Queen Victoria and largely organised by her husband, Prince Albert. Charlie Ayre (50B) is one of a number of boys who remembers going up to London,

Ray Jenkinson and two other '48 intake boys marvel at some of the sights seen at the Festival

construction, held in position by guy-ropes". What left the most lasting impression on him, however, was the transport section. One part showed the latest underground train unit, fully sectioned to expose the motor unit and driving wheels, the braking system, plus the door and cab controls – all accompanied by "realistic running noises". There was also a brand new steam locomotive, painted in a vivid 'British Rail' green.

resplendent in uniform of course, to visit the Festival site on the South Bank. These educational visits were under the guidance of Maj Durant, with twelve parties of forty-five apprentices a time covering almost the whole School.

The site of the Festival had been reclaimed from twenty-seven derelict acres of bomb-scarred land. Above it now soared the concrete curve of the Festival Hall, the 300-foot high 'Skylon', looking like a giant silver cigar, and the 'Dome of Discovery', the forerunner of the controversial 'Millennium Dome' almost fifty years later. The Festival marked the centenary mentioned above, but also served to remind the battle-scarred people of the country that perhaps it was now time to shake off any remaining negative thoughts and look to the future with some degree of confidence.

Ray Jenkinson still retains a photograph of himself, along with two other lads, taken during their attendance at the Festival, with the *Dome* providing a fitting background. This would have been taken during his intake's last term at the School. One of the lads was Pete Brunnen, but Ray cannot recall the other's name. Ray can remember the *Skylon*, as "*a tall pointed*

Although he cannot remember any details, Gerry Berragan of 48B also attended the Festival. As a VM, he also recalls trips out to the *Morris* car factory at Oxford and *Vauxhall* at Luton. Now in his last term, he had succumbed to the illicit thrill of acquiring an old motorcycle, which he jointly owned with a colleague called Routledge. This was a 1936 *Zenith* and was kept hidden away in a farmer's barn just up the road towards the *Bramshill Hunt*. Despite the lads' mechanical skills (or perhaps because of them!), the bike was continually breaking down and Gerry has a vivid memory of pushing it all the way back from Reading. Even when the bike was running, Gerry often found himself soaked to the skin, probably leading to his catching rheumatic fever soon after going home on leave from Arborfield after his 'PoP' that summer.

Having consequently been hospitalised in York for four months, Gerry almost found himself medically discharged, as he was downgraded to a health rating of 'P7 HO' (Home Only). Amazingly, he then found himself posted back to the School, in late 1951, for convalescence reasons, as a Craftsman VM on the

PS! At least he was now able to obtain a more modern motorcycle and be allowed to keep it – legally! – in the Fire Station opposite the Guardroom.

Extended responsibilities

Following the end of the Second World War, demobilisation of Service personnel, plus the need to return expert technical manpower to a depleted industry, brought about the last major adjustments to REME's core organisation. In 1951, the Corps assumed responsibility as the technical agency for almost all of the Army's mechanical and electrical equipment, while the engineering manpower that had remained in other units was now transferred, to come directly under REME's control.

The Arborfield Apprentice of July 1951 reported on a film that was being made at that time, one which was to last a whole twenty minutes and illustrate the Army Apprentices' scheme. Commissioned by the War Office, the film was to be circulated amongst serving regular soldiers and their families, in order that they would be encouraged to send their own sons and brothers to one of the Apprentices' Schools. In the interests of economy, most of the film was to be shot here at Arborfield, with a visit to Harrogate to cover the RE and R Sigs trades. Maj Charrington had been appointed as Military Supervisor to the film's makers.

In the same magazine, the Commandant remarked upon the posting, at very short notice, of Capt Denison of 'D' Coy, who had left to re-join his regiment in far-off Korea. The Captain was a member of the famous Gloucesters, who had recently been engaged in some fierce fighting on behalf of the UN forces. Col Percival also commented upon the recent re-structure of the Champion Company competition, which was now to run on an annual basis and have its scope broadened to include all aspects of training and School life.

Since it was 'A' Coy that had retained the 'Champion' banner in the most recent competition, they were entitled to hold it now for the whole of 1951. Obviously proud of this fact, they announced in the School magazine some of the factors that went with the achievement of the accolade. The cleanliness and tidiness of both barrack rooms and Company gardens, together with each individual's Workshops result, would in future be taken into account, so that no individual apprentice would feel that he had not contributed something towards the final result.

With the School's Companies still organised by trade, an article on behalf of 'B' Coy gave the following tongue-in-cheek details about itself:

"To the aliens not 'in the know', 'B' Company is a place where people sit on their big-ends, twiddling their differentials in their spare time. Spare lockers are brimming over with king-pins, crown-wheels, silent blocks and universal joints – every other person grooms his hair with axle-grease. This is not strictly true – there are more important things to think about, like the NAAFI and Saturdays at Reading, to mention them both! Throughout our barrack rooms, the pin-ups are a mixture of automobiles and bathing beauties, a little strange at first sight, but see the subtle connection – flashy chassis and streamlined bodywork!"

By the time that edition of *The Arborfield Apprentice* came out in July 1951, the athletics season was in full swing. Earlier in the year, bad weather had delayed the marking out of the training track; in fact it wasn't until the beginning of May that training was able to start in deadly earnest. On the 19th of that month, about fifteen young apprentices entered for the Reading Athletic Club Handicap meeting. Unfortunately, the occasion was spoiled by heavy rain, with some events held in very unfavourable conditions. The only event won by one of our boys that day was the discus. A visit to Wellington College, just a week later, was again attacked by the elements, as a triangular tournament was held between the hosts, the School and London Athletic Club.

Despite a close victory over Chepstow and a decisive one against RAF Halton, the Boxing Team was still happy to welcome the arrival of Sergeant Instructor (S/I) Trayner, APTC. He had recently won the British Army featherweight title and it was the hope that he would be able to bring a wealth of experience and skills to the School team for future events.

The Music Society had become firmly established by mid-1951. The Musical Appreciation group meetings were now dedicated to gramophone recitals, while the Choir had recently sung to an assembled audience of almost six hundred enchanted spectators at a garden-party in the town of Basingstoke. The Society as a whole was actively considering a School Concert, at which all members would have the opportunity of seeing and listening to the results of some of the funnier noises that had been heard emanating from the Band Room!

'Food, glorious food'

Alan 'Algy' Morton was one of a group of almost 150 boys who formed intake 51B, but it wasn't until many years later (forty-five in fact) that he came across some of his own letters that he had sent home during his boys' school days. Like many other boys of that time, early memories seem to home in on the subject of *"food, glorious food"*! In his first letter, for instance, he had written, *"Yesterday dinnertime we had corned beef, mashed potatoes and runner beans. For sweet we had bread and butter pudding. For tea yesterday we had lovely fried bread with an egg on top, also a mug of tea and some bread and jam"*. One wonders what the nutritional experts of today, with their calorific content, vitamin levels and such, would make of it all! Mind you, that diet didn't hold Alan back, for he went on to become A/T CSM of 'B' Coy.

Alan was Portsmouth born-and-bred, and came from a family of a long-standing Army background. His great-grandfather had served a total of nineteen years in India, his grandfather had been gassed in the trenches of World War I, while his father, having served with the RAOC, later obtained an emergency commission into the REME on D-Day. Alan has always thought that, mixed in with his remote tartan blood, there must have been a thin streak of khaki! Living in Portsmouth, with its huge Naval dockyard, during the war brought *"the chorus of air-raid sirens, the drones of Nazi bombers, the whistling of incendiary bombs and the 'chug-chug' of doodlebugs"*, but somehow Alan managed to survive the lot.

During 1948, Alan gave up the delights of *'Spam'*, powdered egg and rationing when, along with his family, he set off on the long sea-voyage to Melbourne, on the far-off continent of Australia. He hadn't taken too much persuading, as Alan *"didn't know what a real egg looked like, had only seen pictures of bananas and once got a Canadian apple as a prize for best turned-out Cub in his pack"*.

Returning from Australia's sunny climes after three years and arriving back in 'Pompey' during 1951, to find a Great Britain still suffering from the deprivations of wartime-style economies, it's no wonder that Alan opted for a stint in the armed services himself. *(Note that the 'Spam' referred to by Alan was slightly different to that delivered through the mail and Internet nowadays! It was always best fried, in my humble opinion! Ed.)*

And so it was that Alan walked through the Arborfield gates on a *"fine crisp September morn"*, his father's final words ringing in his ears. *"It's going to be a bit tough, son, so if you've any complaints, don't tell your Mum, tell me."* Alan watched his father's 1939 *Ford Prefect*, DCG 359, as it drove off up the hill and away. From now on, it would be 'The Life of Alan' – not Brian!

Alan is happy that the life lasted a little longer than he first expected. During his first week in Room 'F1', he watched in horror as two 'ruffy-tuffy' London 'Teddy boys' threw their flick-knives with unerring accuracy at the fire door at the end of the room. He wondered if, after 'lights out' each evening, his own lights would be put out, by cold steel being drawn across his delicate throat! Alan is now able to give a 'vote of thanks' to those two Londoners, Graham Goodwin and George Fleck, for putting him firmly onto the rapidly rising 'learning curve' of life.

Of course it fits!

Another of that 51B intake was Manchester lad Jack King, one of whose memories concerns the issue of uniforms to his Mancunian mate, Ken Abram. It was blatantly obvious that his (Ken's) two SD jackets were of two different sizes. But, on his complaining about the tight one, he was told that, of course the jacket had to be tight, to make him look smart. Upon asking the what now seemed ridiculous question, *"Why is the other one so loose then?"* he was told, in no uncertain manner, that if it was too tight, he wouldn't be able to swing his arms whilst marching! *(There's no reasoning that can sort that one; the QM's staff has always lived in their own world, on a far higher plane than the rest of us mere mortals. Ed.)*

Jack is another who has fond memories of Sgt Buckley, and recalls visiting him at home whilst on leave, after Bill had gone on to become a member of the recruiting staff at Piccadilly in Manchester. Another character who stands out in Jack's memory is CSM Weston of 'A' Coy, who was known to all the boys as 'The Bull'. Though woe betide anyone who was overheard using this nickname. It is said that the whole spider block shook when The Bull entered, he really was a massive man. One of the CSM's favourite tricks was to whisper in the ear of a newly arrived Company member, *"What do the lads call me, son? I know they have a name for me, what is it?"* But foolish was the young man who answered this one truthfully!

CSM Weston is also remembered for his rather dubious cycling skills. He was usually accompanied on his rides around Camp by his pet bull terrier, which ran behind him, tied by a lead to the rear of the cycle. As told by David Wright of 48B, the CSM would place his heels upon the pedals, his feet being so large that they would stick out at ninety degrees on each side. Being such a large man, The Bull seemed to be in a precarious position, balanced on what must have looked such a tiny bike. But, despite the inevitable comedy situation that this presented, there weren't too many boys who volunteered to laugh until the CSM was well on his way to being out of sight!

Brian Fielding, also of 51B and writing from Dubai during 1999, has always been proud to mention that he is an old boy of the School. He asserts that people duly recognised this and understood that someone from that background would not only *"know his way about"*, but also be both *"trade-wise and worldly-wise"* into the bargain. The Dubai repair yard in the United Arab Emirates, where Brian currently worked, probably then dealt with around half of the world's repair business. Having been part of the North Sea oilfield boom during the early Seventies, Brian is still able to work well, even within the stressful environment of being a welding engineer. He likes to think that the groundwork for this was laid down at Arborfield in those first three years of his long career, which is undoubtedly the truth.

That intake of 51B spent their first four weeks on 'square bashing', as was the custom, followed by a week in workshops, no doubt on the dreaded 'fitting and filing'. During this short period, they had been introduced to many other common Arborfield pastimes, such as queuing for their meals, making up their beds and making their appearances on muster parades. Inevitably slightly awed by these new customs, it must have been a great relief to be sent home on leave, where they could revel in being the centrepiece of family attention for a short time. The harsh reality of returning to Camp was brought home to one and all when, during their first fortnight back, they experienced both the Commandant's and GOC's Annual Inspections.

Brian is yet another boy who can remember having his *"packet of ten Greys"* confiscated at Wokingham station - that 'custom' must have lasted a few years! On free weekends, Brain would join with mate Dave Paul to catch the last train back from Camberley to Wokingham. Here, they would *"hitch a lift"* on the van that collected and delivered the movie reels for the Camp cinema shows. They did this so many times that, in the end, the driver would wait for them at the level-crossing gates!

Although the Athletics team had not had a distinguished record during the 1951 season, some personal performances were worthy of note. At Aldershot in June, at the Army Individual Championships, A/T Rogers won the 100 yards – metres were yet to be invented! – while A/T Penn won the high jump, with a height that not only broke the School record, but also the Army record for boys under eighteen. Gen Sir Gerald Templer KCB, KBE, CMG and DSO presented the trophies. At the Quadrangular Games, held at Chepstow, the efforts of Kalmykow and Marciniak won the shot and the discus events. Although not recorded as such, it would appear that these boys were obviously from our Polish contingent. At the final event of the season, the School competed against the Athletic Clubs of Reading, Newbury and Eton, running out as winners by a single point at Reading's home track of Palmer Park.

First glimmers of a history

The School magazine of December 1951 was of special interest, in that it contained an article recording, possibly for the first time, how the School had come about, back in 1939. The School had by then been established for over twelve years, all that time building up the proud traditions which had already made it what it was. The Commandant remarked upon the debt owed to the article's author, Brig Tanner, who had served as the School's first DCI in those early years. When at the School in 1939, it had been as a Major in the RAOC, but he was now quoted as Brig W Tanner, MIMechE, REME. It was the Brigadier who had donated the 'Tanner Cup', which was now competed for annually during the cricket season.

A further link with the past, at that year's Old Boys' Reunion, had been the very first march-past by a contingent of old boys at the Sunday morning Church Parade, where the President of the OBA, Col White, proudly took the salute. Some atrocious weather over

Some proud young jeeps of 52A

the weekend had led to an attendance of around one hundred, certainly less than had been anticipated. The introduction of a '72', rather than a '48', meaning that ex-apprentices could now arrive at the School on the Friday evening, had been welcomed by those who had to travel the furthest. Despite the rain on the Saturday, a full programme of games was again followed. Against the current boys, the ex-boys again came off second best at rugby, hockey and shooting, but trounced the School staff team at soccer to the tune of 6 - 2.

Meanwhile, the film *'Soldier Apprentice'*, lasting some twenty-five minutes, had been completed and shown at the School, following its London review. Made by *Verity Films*, on behalf of the Army Kinema Corporation (AKC), the film had been approved by the Adjutant General (AG) for release in early 1952. It had been well received and it was hoped that it would show, to the rest of the Army, the merits of the Apprentices' Schools, thereby attracting more eager recruits. *(Whether or not the film can be blamed, the opposite effect occurred! Ed.)*

(The official resumé issued with the film can be found as an annex to this chapter.)

Recruiting figures on the wane

That same School magazine gave less happy news regarding those waning recruiting figures, which seemed to be general at military units across the country. As a temporary measure, to have effect until numbers reached a higher percentage of their allotted establishments; the War Office ordered a discontinuation of the fourth training company in each of the Apprentices' Schools. On September 15th 1951, it was 'D' Coy that felt the full measure of this order and ceased to be - a sad day indeed. Particularly poignant was the fact that the boys had been leading in the Champion Company competition at the time. To balance this, each of the other Companies reported that ex-'D' Coy boys were now contributing well alongside their new companions.

By the end of 1951, the social activity known as 'modern ballroom dancing' had been under instruction here at the School for around eighteen months. No doubt there had been a few sniggers about the benefits of this pastime, begging the question, *"Are we turning out soldiers or dance-hall gigolos?"* However, it had been decided that dancing could be classified either as a sport or a hobby and, certainly, the participants found it useful. The more proficient dancers were entitled to enter competitions that turned out to be just as exacting and strenuous as the more generally acknowledged 'team sports'.

Since the foundation of the Radio Club, *'G3HOS'* had become the Club call sign, already well known over the air, through which medium contact had been made with many countries. Work was well under way for the construction of a grand network of aerials, designed to contact the entire surface of the globe, only the dark winter nights curtailing the project. Various Club members were now constructing their own one- or two-valve receivers (the term 'superhet' still comes to mind!) and, on Club nights, it was not uncommon for shouts of joy to be heard, as individuals heard their first message emanate from their own headphones or speakers.

Despite serving for a somewhat shorter tour than the normal three-year stint of those days, John 'Jock' Simon still brings to mind a fondness for the time he spent here at the School. John had joined as a member of 52A, but a mere seven months into his service he contracted that skin condition known as 'dermatitis'.

Following several unsuccessful attempts by the MO to cure it, he was eventually sent to the CMH at Aldershot but, some five months later, the staff there also admitted defeat and John was granted a full discharge on medical grounds. *"Pensioned off at the age of seventeen years, with a demob suit and pension of 10/6 per week"*, that's how John described it! Thankfully, John was cured at Edinburgh Royal Infirmary in around three weeks, but by then he was already a 'civvie' and too old to start an apprenticeship at seventeen.

John joined the Arborfield Scout Group during his short stay here. He and a pal were sent to the Cookhouse to collect some rations one weekend. This was only for two, but the cook sergeant must have thought it was for twenty-two by the amount of boxes he gave them! Hardly daring to believe their good fortune, the delighted boys took the surplus back to their room and sold it off to those lads who lived close enough to take it home, making just enough to pay for their own 'beer and ciggies' on the weekend hike. *(Drinking and smoking – and in the Scouts? Tut, tut! Ed.)*

Charles 'Eddie' Cooper was another member of 52A, having left Chesterfield Grammar School to 'sign on' at Derby. Eddie wanted to be a VM, but an 'intelligence test' put him on the way to a career in electronics. This proved *"the best decision anyone ever made"* as far as Eddie is concerned, as he later went on to be the director of an electronics business. Eddie fondly remembers the previously mentioned Maj John Biddulph. Apparently, he was quite deaf and wore a luxuriant moustache large enough to qualify him for the nationally recognised 'Handlebar Club', of which 'Professor' Jimmy Edwards, the comedian, was a well-known member. On sports days, the Major would trot around the sports arena, wearing a rather jaded tracksuit, with 'LONDON' emblazoned across its back.

Death of the King

Intake 49A had enjoyed a bright but rather cold day for their 'Pop' in February of 1952. Joseph 'Stevie' Chalmers of 50A was excited that day, not so much by the parade alone but by the fact that, as soon as it was over, he would be on his way to Chepstow to take part in the Army Junior Boxing Championships. That parade, under the eagle eye of RSM McNally, and commanded by A/T CSM T R Tuckwell, went off as smoothly as ever but afterwards the boys were ordered

to re-form on the Square, then quickly marched off to the Camp Hall. As soon as they were all assembled the Commandant, still resplendent in his highland attire, but with a most melancholy air about him, came onto centre stage and announced to the boys, *"It is with the deepest regret that I have to inform you that His Majesty King George VI died this morning"*.

The Reviewing Officer that same day was Maj Gen Sir Bertram Rowcroft, who paid a 'Soldier's Tribute' to the late King, the titular head of the Services. He said that King George's life had been that supreme example of unselfish service, which it would be well for all Arborfield boys to have constantly in mind. *(Still in my first year at Grammar School, I recall the day well, sitting in my school classroom, lying in the shadow of the gothic might of the Liverpool Anglican Cathedral, listening to its great bells chiming out their mournful message for hour after hour. Ed.)*

The trip to Chepstow still went ahead, though it was a dispirited group of boys who made the long journey. It was well after the hoped-for tea meal when they finally arrived, only to be told that the boxing match had been cancelled, they would be given a sandwich and a cup of cocoa, sent to bed and then returned to Arborfield next morning. Stevie and a handful of pals decided to go into Chepstow town-centre for the evening, surely a pie and a pint would cheer them up? But as they trudged their way round the town, it became evident that the King's death was being mourned nationwide – every pub and café was shut down for the night. By the time the Championships were eventually re-organised and then held, the disappointed Stevie had passed the age limit.

The following month, the *REME Magazine* published the following paragraph:

> *"All readers will be interested to learn that at the Lying-in-State of His Late Majesty King George VI in Westminster Hall, ex-RSM Cook MBE was accorded the honour of being selected to attend the first tour of Guard Duty at the Catafalque, in his capacity as a member of the Queen's Bodyguard".*

The School's athletes were again feeling rather depressed at the beginning of yet another season spoiled by the weather, it appeared to be an annual disaster of 'monsoon' proportions! Practically no training was possible, right up to the Individual Championships, held in mid-May. Three new events were introduced at that meeting, namely the hammer, pole vault and the 'hop, step and jump' – or triple jump, as it later became better known. Nine apprentices later entered the Berkshire County Championships, but none of them managed to gain any distinctions or certificates. It was mooted that *"our runners were rather worn out"*!

Our boxers had mixed fortunes in the season that ended in 1952. The first inter-School match was lost against Harrogate, but there then followed two excellent triumphs over RAF Halton and Chepstow. In the District Individual Championships that followed, no less than eleven of the twenty-three weight categories were won by boys from the School. At the Inter-Services Boxing Association (ISBA) Championships, held at the Camp Hall, the School's only representative, A/T Phayer, delighted the audience by winning at his weight.

A letter published in April's *REME Magazine* looked ahead to the probable formation of another OBA – this one for ex-apprentices of the School at Harrogate. Col R N Thickness hoped that there would be many members of REME who had entered the Corps by way of Harrogate and hoped that they would now assist in the formation of this new Association. He later wrote back to the magazine to say how pleased he had been to receive so many responses and that the formation of the Harrogate OBA would now definitely go ahead. In fact, the inaugural meeting was to be held at Uniacke Barracks, at 8 p.m. on the 20th February the following year.

But that's what Old Boys do!

An article in the School magazine reproduced that which had been published by the *Kentish Independent*, under the title *'Arborfield Old Boy Keeps Wheels Turning in Korea'*. It gave news of REME SSgt Albert Tanner, who had joined the School in January 1942 and trained as a Fitter. Albert was now serving in No.1 Infantry Troop Recovery Section. He had been posted to Korea in November 1951, having previously served in Greece, Egypt, Palestine and Germany. Albert's unit had the task of collecting all types of vehicles, ranging from American *Jeeps* to *Centurion* tanks, which were too badly damaged to be repaired locally, then recovering them to a Base Workshop. It was in no small way due to the hard work of Albert and his workshop section that the unit was able to function so efficiently.

At the Aldershot District Small Arms Meeting in May 1952, ten apprentices were entered in the Boys and Cadets individual 0.303" Rifle Shooting competition. Well trained by Maj C W Beardall, MBE, Officer-in-Charge (OIC) of the Armourers' Shop, the boys performed admirably. With a fine score of seventy-two points (against a possible seventy-five), A/T Davis of 'B' Coy won the competition, thus retaining the shield that had been won for the School in the two previous years; by A/T Anieco in 1950 and A/T Bowden in 1951.

Here in Arborfield, Col F A M 'Bobby' Magee (late of the East Surrey Regt) took command of the School in June 1952, at a time of no little difficulty. As previously reported, the War Office had found it necessary to order the disbandment of 'D' Coy the previous year. This meant that the total strength of the School had been brought down to a disappointing figure of only 643 apprentice tradesmen. In *The Arborfield Apprentice* of July that year, it was left to Col Percival to write the customary foreword. His one regret was that he had not seen the present Senior Div (49B) pass out, as he and they had arrived as 'new boys' at the School at the same time.

At the summer 'PoP', held on July 25th, commenting upon the population of the School, Col Magee said that we were running at only around two-thirds of the total capacity of one thousand. The School badly needed the right kind of recruit to make up the numbers and he believed that a lot of the problems could be solved with the help of parents. If they felt, as the School did, that Arborfield offered something of real value, and that the Army still offered a fine career, then they could assist by encouraging other parents to send their own boys along too. The Parade's Reviewing Officer reinforced this thought, adding that the parents of the boys passing out that day should be proud, not only of their sons' achievements, but also of their own. He encouraged them to pass on this vital message to other parents, declaring that REME had already built up a magnificent tradition during its first ten years of existence.

By that time of the year, plans were already being made for the next Annual Old Boys' Reunion, to be held in September. Rising costs had led to the necessity of a charge of four shillings (twenty pence!) for the proposed dinner, while all other entertainments, board and lodgings were to be free. In those days, of course, there was still a 'dance' held on the Friday evening, no doubt some of the old boys who attended such events were not really that old!

B A 'Eggy' Egleton joined the School on September 9th 1952 and, immediately following his arrival, was sent off to get some dinner. Returning to barrack room 'F1', it was to find a large pile of suitcases stacked up on the floor in the centre of the bed-spaces. When the owners of these cases duly appeared, they turned out to be a party of Burmese boys, already wearing extremely shiny 'bulled' boots. These five boys had already served some time in uniform in their own country. The first batch of apprentices from Burma had arrived in February that year and, for a number of subsequent years, each intake would include four or five of these "happy, industrious young visitors".

An abundance of cap-badges

Eggy recalls that 'HQ' Coy at that time was commanded by Maj 'Pete' Stocker, of the Rifle Brigade, who wrote regular entries in The Arborfield Apprentice in reference to bird watching – of the feathered variety, he hastens to add! The 'HQ' CSM was named Brady and the Company Quartermaster Sergeant (CQMS) was named Drury. Both of these gentlemen came from the Irish Guards and would answer to their fellow senior ranks to the name of 'Paddy'. The pair had each served for about twenty years and been awarded their Long Service and Good Conduct (LSGC) Medals at a presentation parade, held on March 16th 1952. Another of Eggy's recollections is that the PS of that time was served by no less than thirty different cap-badges, all of which were proudly displayed in a glass case at the Guardroom.

Upon the subject of cap-badges, Eggy has another fond memory, which concerns his own personal collection of such items. Lt Col I Jarman, SWB, was the QM at the time, and keenly followed his own interest in military memorabilia. One day, spotting a prize item in Eggy's collection, he remarked that if Eggy would part with his badge of the Palestine Regt, he could have five different badges in return. This was an offer that could hardly be refused and Eggy was given a choice of badges to select from. Six months later he was summoned to see the QM, who informed young Egleton that another copy of the Palestine badge had since come to light and that he (Eggy) could now have his own one back. The QM never did ask for his other five badges to be returned, so Eggy always

considered the Colonel a true gentleman from that day onwards.

Eggy had initially wanted to be a VM, but after about six months of chipping and filing, he found himself in the "top education class", and was deemed by the powers-that-be, much to his chagrin, that he was of suitable 'telecommunications' material – so that's what they made him! Having been forced into this change, Eggy became what he termed "demob happy" – even CSM Brady advised him to "go regimental" when he left the School. Despite never being the most enthusiastic of soldiers, Eggy was a lot happier later in his career when he managed to convert to Recy Mech and rues the day when he turned down the chance of transferring to the Military Police.

Another regret on Eggy's part was when he had to cut-off the two 'G-flogs' from his sleeve when his substantive rank came through – he had been rather proud of them. (Most old boys of that era will remember the 'G-flog', an upside down 'good conduct' stripe worn on the lower sleeve – most people suspecting that it was a reward for many years of 'not being found out'. Am I right Eggy? Ed.)

Despite his reticence about trade matters, Eggy had a sense of 'righteousness' about him. As a 'boy NCO' back in 'HQ' Coy, he was on Cookhouse duty one day, controlling the queue, when he noticed the usual gypping by senior boys taking place. Eggy called the whole queue to attention, marched them onto the Square and did a couple of 'right wheels' to bring the rear of the queue to the front as they re-entered the dining hall! On another occasion, the room's six-foot table disappeared. Eggy detailed four of his young lads to form a squad, then marched them smartly and swiftly through the Cookhouse doors. There, to the astonishment of the bemused duty cooks, his squad lifted one of the six-foot tabletops from its trestles and marched just as swiftly out again!

Another member of 52B was David Barrett, who has since gained a certain amount of fame amongst present-day old boys as a splendid cartoonist. Indeed, his pictorial description of those first days, back in the early Fifties, graced the pages of OBAN 17 almost fifty years later. David says that his own memories are nothing new, but did recall a certain 'old soldier' from the Gordon Highlanders, known to one and all as 'G-flog Jock'. The boys would inevitably find Jock, untidily draped over a tea-urn in the Cookhouse, hurling his foul unpleasantries at all and sundry! He guarded that tea-urn with his life, telling the boys, *"Ye'll get nay tea with twa mugs"*!

David recounts that he left the AAS *"relatively unscarred and definitely overfilled with confidence"*. He arrived at his first posting at Burscough, Lancashire, as a *"multi-starred General, posing as a lowly Craftsman"*! Service in Libya and Benghazi was followed by a course at Middle Wallop that failed to turn him into an Aircraft Technician (Air Tech). He then did a tour in Cyprus, before an enjoyable 'home posting' at Ashford. His next posting to Kuala Lumpur began what he calls his *"life-long love affair with Asia"*. David did *"the grand tour"*, including Singapore, Brunei and Hong Kong, before eventually becoming a civilian in 1979. *(Last heard of, David was living on the tropical island of Bali. Ed.)*

Tragedy at Farnborough

On September 6th 1952, tragedy struck at the Farnborough Air Show. On that very day, Gerry Berragan, now an ex-boy of 48B, was riding his motorcycle through Farnborough, on his way between Ashford and Arborfield – it may even have been to attend the OBA Reunion, though he cannot be too sure. He was discussing with his pillion passenger whether or not to go and see the Air Show, but in the event, their decision not to turned out to be a most fortunate one.

As well as Mr Stagg, as previously mentioned, twenty-six other spectators lost their lives when an aircraft engine fell into the spectators. Although David Wright named the plane as a *Gloster Meteor*, Gerry thinks that it was a *de Havilland 110*. By an amazing coincidence, Gerry found himself at the Paris Air Show many years later (1973), when a *Tupolev 144*, the Russian copy of the famous *Concorde* (and christened *'Konkordski'* in the West), crashed and killed eleven spectators.

In September 1952, attendance at the Old Boys' Reunion proved to be most disappointing. Only about fifty members attended the Friday evening dance, despite a good turnout by the invited ladies. Col Magee put this down to the difficulties for soldiers in obtaining three-day passes, from units engaged on manouvres. For this reason alone, it was later decided that a two-day programme would be reverted to for the following year. The Commandant went on to hope that *"as many members of the Association as possible will endeavour to visit their old School, which is so eager to welcome them"*.

Col Magee's first foreword, in the December 1952 edition of *The Arborfield Apprentice*, came shortly after the Winter Games fixture, which had been held at Harrogate. He remarked upon the *"fine spirit in which each hard fought contest was carried out"*. As a newcomer to the School, he had rarely seen a more admirable display of sportsmanship, from both sides, or enjoyed more thrilling entertainment. He gave thanks to the generous hospitality of our hosts and hoped that, when our colleagues from Chepstow visited the following month, they would leave with a similar impression of Arborfield.

That same School magazine reported on some of the more notable events that had occurred during the late summer and autumn, especially that athletics meeting at Harrogate. Through the good offices of Maj Stocker, a magnificent open-air display of 'trick motorcycling' had been laid on here at the School, presented by the Army Mechanical Transport display team from Bordon. Despite wet conditions, a most convincing display of perfect machine management and control was presented. No details were given about Guy Fawkes Day, however, when the School was apparently *"all but set on fire"*!

More recently, as told in the magazine, a group of highly technically minded VMs had paid a visit to the Motor Show, held at Earl's Court in London. The car attracting the most attention at that time was the *Jaguar XK120*, fresh from its record-breaking run at a track in France. Written contributions to the magazine were in abundance, and it was noted that Burmese boy, A/T Ohn Thwin, had won five shillings, as second prize. On a sadder note, School Chaplain, the Rev S Hilton, CF, asked for prayers to be said for those unfortunate enough to be held as prisoners-of-war in Korea.

The Pipe Band had had its usual summer season of hectic activity and was proud to have been selected to appear on the regimental Christmas card later that year. Members looked forward to another high profile year, especially with the Coronation of a young Queen looming large on the horizon, when a bigger than usual demand upon their services may well assist in the Band's ongoing recruiting drive.

Another article in that magazine of December 1952 came from the pen of Craftsman (Cfn) F A Gleed, REME, who had visited the School on his way to the Military College of Science, having recently returned from the war-zone of Korea. An ex-boy from the School, he had been most apprehensive when he had learned of his posting. Cfn Gleed's first sight of Korea was on the 4th November 1950, when he saw the grey hills bounding Pusan harbour. The following day, he was treated to an unexpected fireworks display – well, it was November 5th! – when a truck full of ammunition caught fire during unloading at its berth. As a Tels Mech, Cfn Gleed was away from the surroundings of his workshop for long periods, whilst his overall impression of the country was of how mountainous it seemed.

Although not reported upon until the following summer, 1952 ended in a memorable evening, when the School's four remaining Companies competed in the field of comedy and drama - the rival revelry certainly entertained everyone who saw it. The joy of such entertainments is often in the mistakes that are made, so the disappearance over the footlights by one A/T Hughes, balanced precariously on a scooter, certainly deserved its howls of laughter and prolonged applause. 'A' Coy presented a *'Batman and Robin'* sketch with speed, originality and humour, while the performance by 'B' Coy sadly lacked the martial air that should have been present in *'Soldiers of the Queen'*.

The pranks from 'C' Coy tended to fall a little flat, mainly because they couldn't be seen by anyone further than four rows from the front! The offering from 'HQ' Coy depended more upon individual performances than a team effort, but some of these were very well received. Remembering the best and forgetting – though not ignoring – the faults, the evening stood out as most enjoyable in the minds of most of the audience.

Apprentice gunfitters recharging the recuperating gear on a 3.7" HAA gun

Coronation Year

Intake 50A passed out through the School gates for the last time on February 3rd 1953. Recruiting had lately picked up slightly, with an increase of some thirty boys now resident at the School. The new intake of 53A would be 138 strong, compared to the previous year's 109, although the Commandant stressed that there was still a long way to go. Sporting achievements were still good, while the standard of education was deemed satisfactory. All but two boys of those passing out had gained their ACE Second-class, while twenty-four of these had already attained their First-class certificate. Eighty-two boys were now leaving to start their career in REME, with another eight designated to join the RE.

During their last term at the School, the Senior Div was taken to No.5 Training Battalion (Trg Btn) to see an exercise called *'REME in the Field'*. This dealt with those military tactics used by the LADs and their methods of recovery, in circumstances typical of the current methods of warfare. After a tour of all the different types of truck on display, the group watched the 'recovery' of an abandoned tank, by another tank, a *Cromwell*, which had been specially modified by REME personnel for the task.

Next on the agenda was a mock tank battle, with a track-blowing exercise, while the concluding part of the agenda was the complete re-assembly of a *Jeep* (vehicular type!), which had previously been dismantled into its component parts. The re-assembly team of six men completed this task in one minute and twenty-two seconds! The apprentices returned to Camp with some idea of what lay in wait for them, proud that they would soon be part of their adult Corps.

Anyone attending the cinema early in 1953 may have seen a *Pathé News* program entitled *'Front Line Workshop in Korea'*. Ron Jones, ex-boy of 1942 vintage, had already been privileged to see *"its Asian premiere"* at 16 Infantry Wksp in Korea itself. During the film, the camera pans across the workshop area, coming to rest on its latest acquisition, namely the Armourers Shop, still to be erected and put to use. Ron adds that this had come none too soon! The original shop was just an unpainted, galvanized, windowless, corrugated iron hut.

Inside, the Armourers worked under the light of a couple of lamps and in the glow of a drip-fed American heater, all rather primitive. All the workers were *"dark adapted"*, according to Ron, meaning that they had learned to find their way around and pick up the correct tools in the dim interior. But when the cameraman tried to film what was going on inside the shop, nothing could be seen. In the event, he decided to shoot the rest of the film on the outside!

March 18th 1953 saw the end of his *"eight years with the Colours"* for Charlie Ashdown, ex-stalwart of 42A. During his service, Charlie had been permanently attached to the Indian Army, with time spent in that country, Malaya and Singapore. In 1950/51 he attended an artificer course and completed his service as a Staff Sergeant. But that didn't seem enough for Charlie because, in April 1953, he enlisted in the Canadian Army (RCEME), where he was eventually commissioned in 1970. Most of Charlie's subsequent service was spent in Canada, but at one time he served as an Observation Post Officer for the UN on the Golan Heights, bang smack between the Syrian and Israeli forces!

1953 proved to be a memorable year in many ways, despite the fact that in Kenya, white settlers were panicking as the 'Mau Mau' uprising took hold. In the FA Cup Final at Wembley, ever-popular Stan Matthews at last won a Cup winners medal with Blackpool, while Gordon Richards, the veteran jockey, finally won 'The Derby' on Pinza, in the autumn of his career. Both of these popular and enduring sportsmen were later rewarded with a Knighthood from the Queen, as tribute to the years of entertainment they gave to an adoring public.

1953 had also certainly proved memorable on June 1st, for those thirty-odd proud boy soldiers from Arborfield, who formed the 'Guard of Honour' in St George's Chapel, Windsor Castle, on the occasion of a dedication service to the Commonwealth Youth Movement. The boys were inspected by Maj Gen E Hakewill Smith, CB, CBE, MC, the Governor of the Military Knights. In a letter subsequently received by Col Magee, the General referred to the turnout and bearing of the Guard as *"outstanding"*.

(A report on the service at Windsor Castle is attached as an annex to this chapter.)

Amongst their number that day was Ron Hague of 50B, who recalls that the squad was made up from *"the tallest and best looking boys in 6 Div"* – he's always been that modest! Given an hour's 'breather' before the ceremony, Ron and his mates were allowed to have a look around the town before reporting back for duty. Needless to say, an open pub door proved irresistible and Ron was *"volunteered"* to enter first. The toe of a well-polished boot caught his eye, quickly followed by a pace-stick, then a well-pressed uniform and – finally – the steely eye of RSM McNally!

Ron was out of there like a shot, explaining his reasons to the squad of boys hot on his heels. They made it back to the Castle on time, where Ron was told by A/T CSM Nick Webber to report to the RSM. Ron, expecting the worst of retribution, then got a right old scolding – not for going into the pub, but for leaving just because Mr McNally had been in there! Ron recalls the RSM's words as, *"Never do that again boy, I was very embarrassed"*. Ron only met Mr McNally once more after that episode. By then he looked much older, but still retained his guardsman's bearing, and Ron says he will *"always remember him with the greatest respect and fondness"*.

A Queen is crowned

The main event that year was, of course, the Coronation of Queen Elizabeth II at Westminster Abbey on June 2nd, with a fitting complement to the day's celebrations being the news that the world's highest mountain, Mount Everest, had finally been vanquished by a British-led expedition on May 29th. The team leader was Col John Hunt, while the two climbers who conquered the summit were New Zealander Sir Edmund Hilary and Sherpa Norgay 'Tiger' Tensing. Back in London, thirty-three young apprentices from the School had the privilege and pleasure of witnessing the Coronation Procession, with the Queen riding in her Golden Coach, from their vantagepoint on The Mall.

A/T CSM Nick Webber was in charge of that group and has the most pleasant memories of a momentous occasion, despite the fact that it rained ceaselessly during a long, grey day. He still retains the photographs he took on the day, showing such personnel as the Yeomen Warders of the Tower of London, the Royal Canadian Mounted Police (RCMP) and a squad of Gurkha soldiers, with whom Nick was later to serve during the Malaysian troubles of 1959. The boys had left Arborfield early that morning and their vehicle parked at the barracks of the Household Cavalry, near Buckingham Palace. They eventually ended up on the Victoria Monument, which afforded the most wonderful view, straight down the Mall.

With TV still in its infancy, it was left to the filmmakers to make an historic record of that Coronation. The full-colour film, *"A Queen is crowned"*, was watched by millions of cinemagoers in the months that followed. It was in July that the war in distant Korea came to an official end, as the country's partition into North and South Korea was recognised by the signing of a peace treaty.

In his foreword to *The Arborfield Apprentice* in that same month, the Commandant wrote the following:

"The Coronation of our beloved and gracious young Queen has been, for millions throughout the Commonwealth, the outstanding event of the year. The memory of this day will remain imperishable, not only with the fortunate few who were privileged to attend as spectators, but also with all of us who were able to follow the ceremony on the television screen; and in some measure to share the homage and jubilation of her subjects."

The School Chaplain was also moved by the occasion and made his own contribution to the School magazine with the paragraph below:

"We have a young Queen on the throne – a Queen who has pledged herself to her God and her peoples. Upon her shoulders a great responsibility has been placed and there it will remain throughout her life. The path of duty is never easy and that of royal duty is even more difficult. But somehow we feel confident that another Elizabethan age is beginning, and the devotion to duty, the joy of work well done, the spirit of adventure and the limitless horizons that characterised the first Elizabethans, will be seen again in their descendants."

Following that historic event, which placed her upon the throne at the age of twenty-seven, Her Majesty had this to say to her subjects:

"Many thousands of you came, from all parts of the Commonwealth, to join in the ceremony, but I have been conscious too of the millions who have shared in it by means of television in their homes. I know my abiding memory of it will be not only the solemnity and beauty of the ceremony, but the inspiration of your loyalty and affection. I thank you all from a full heart."

The Commandant was most pleased with the successes gained by the Shooting team. Describing himself as a *"dyed-in-the-wool musketry enthusiast"*, he said that he was constantly reminding all boys, as future leaders, of the importance of skill at arms, whether in war or at peace. Thanks to the inspiration of Capt V H Viney, the School's assistant CI, successes at Aldershot District, the Army Boys Challenge Cup (the Salisbury Cup) and the Army Rifle Association Small-bore meeting had proved most gratifying to all competitors.

On Sunday 12th July that year, following the traditional morning church service, Brig Howard-Jones, Garrison Commander, presented the LSGC Medal to CSM E T Weston. A member of the Grenadier Guards, and now responsible for the welfare of boys in 'A' Coy, the CSM had notched up almost a full twenty-one years in the Army.

John Lister (53A) has rather mixed memories of his three years spent here at the School, but is still proud to have passed through its 'portals' – we've always called them gates, John! He still reminisces about such things as walking back along the country road to Camp from Wokingham Station; greasy fry-up breakfasts at nearby *'Smokey Joe's'* café on Langley Common Road; the panties hanging from the flagpole just before one Sunday church parade *(whose were they then, John?)* – and, of course, 'Rodeo'.

This infamous pastime must bring a certain amount of terror back into the memories of those who had been sentenced to it. Those boys who had broken one of the rules, and were now on 'CB', had the extra benefit of an hour's 'Rodeo' on Saturday afternoon. This entailed being 'drilled' out on the Square, at an exceptionally rapid rate, left turn, right turn, about turn, on and on until exhaustion set in – none who endured it will ever forget it!

The Quadrangular Cricket Competition was the highlight of what had been a short season in 1953. Bowlers were in charge against Halton and Harrogate, both matches ending in victory for our boys. The final game against Chepstow was as keenly fought as ever, the opposition being all out for 89, having been 72 for 3 wickets. But the Arborfield eleven finally capitulated to a jubilant Chepstow side, by the narrow margin of six runs.

Basketball had until then always been considered a 'Cinderella' game at the School. But now, with the introduction of two open-air pitches of a mixture of tar and gravel, the game was at last beginning to blossom. The fact that these two pitches had been constructed upon the *"holy of holies"*, at the far end of the Barrack Square, was to the delight of some and the consternation of others! *(There is no report of what the RSM thought*

about this arrangement. Ed.) However, this would certainly ease the strain on the Camp Hall, which had always proved difficult to use, with its infamous sloping court! A recently held course for basketball referees had resulted in a number of both boys and staff being now qualified to officiate in future.

Progress and change

Within the School, steady progress had been made on upgrading the boys' amenities. New classrooms were in the process of being built and the NAAFI restaurant had been freshly decorated, while there were now improvements being made to the seating arrangements in the dining halls. The 'PoP' of July 23rd had been held in brilliant sunshine, under the command of A/T CSM N T Webber. A record number of friends, relatives and parents attended that parade, at which Col Magee was able to report, with much pleasure, on improved recruiting figures and to pay tribute to the parents, who had obviously taken his previous words to heart.

The Commandant also announced some much-needed changes on the educational side of the boys' training. In future, apprentices would study for special 'equivalent' examinations, designed to suit their particular needs. These would be the 'Apprentices' Certificate' at Senior, Intermediate and Junior levels, which would be of the same standard and conducted along the same lines as the ACE 1st, 2nd and 3rd Class examinations.

Denis Elshaw had joined the School as a member of intake 53B on September 10th, along with a group of other lads from the north. He recalls that, within only a couple of days of his arrival, most of his civilian identity had *"all but vanished"*, together with a large amount of his 'civvy' clothes! These had been returned to the north of England, wrapped in the standard Army-issue brown paper and tied with the standard Army-issue string!

He and the other boys quickly learned how to 'box' their denims and 'box' their bedding – in fact he was pretty amazed at the amount of boxing that went on – and none of it sport related! Under the watchful eye of the drill sergeant, Sgt 'Ginger' Roberts (East Lancs Regt), Denis recalls the *"crash of ammo boots being driven into tarmac"* and feels that things were never quite the same after leather and studs were later replaced by the issue of 'Boots, Directly Moulded Sole' (DMS).

That intake 53B descended on 'HQ' Coy with a formidable strength of 182, of whom four new arrivals came from far-off Burma. To their great and obvious delight, their joining of the School coincided with the issue of a new wireless set, one to each barrack-room. If you now took a leisurely stroll around Company lines at the appropriate time, the use of elbow grease, *Blanco*, *Bluebell* and *Cherry Blossom* would be accompanied by the strains of such programmes as *'Music while you work'*! *(Apparently, there were lots of boys who rather enjoyed the alternative 'Music while you shirk'! Ed.)*

By now, 'HQ' Coy had been taken under the wing of Maj Stoddard who, like Maj Charrington before him, suffered the affliction of a stutter. There was one unfortunate occasion when a boy by the name of Ravell, himself a stutterer, was brought before Maj Stoddard on a charge. When asked if he had anything to say, young Ravell thought it best to just say *"No, Sir"*, rather than appear to be taking the mickey! He still ended up with five days CB for his trouble.

Denis Elshaw recalls the day when his room was *"on inspection"* and one apprentice panicked when he found that his bar of soap had been reduced to a mere sliver. Quick as a flash, another lad in an adjoining bedspace produced a piece of cheese from a food parcel, which had been received from his mother that very morning. The 'finest mature' cheddar was soon fashioned into the shape of a bar of *'Coal Tar'* and proudly laid out on the bed with all the other *"ablutions paraphernalia"*. The inspection party then arrived – the Commandant, his Adjutant, OC, RSM, CSM, old Uncle Tom Cobley and all! It must have come as a great shock to all when the Adjutant's large dog ran off with the 'bar of soap'!

Denis is another who remembers 'G-flog Jock'. Finding himself on 'cookhouse fatigues' one day, Denis had been assigned to shovel several tons (well, it seemed like that!) of coke from A to B, for reasons better known to the authorities. Noticing Denis's tremendous work rate, Jock had a quiet word in his ear. *"That's a grand job ye're daein' laddie. When ye come in fer yer tea, report tae me and I'll gi' ye something special"*. Full of anticipation, Denis duly did as requested – and received an extra slice of bread! That 'generosity' was never forgotten.

Days of hope and glory

That same intake (53B) included Greg Peck, who

Some of 53B on manoeuvres in Brighton!

travelled down from Luton accompanied by *"another potential victim"*! On Waterloo Station, they managed to convince a rather gullible canteen lady that they had been called up to do their National Service, and were thus eligible to swill back a *Whitbread's Pale Ale* each. Still glowing from this triumph over adversity, they duly arrived at Wokingham to find another half-dozen apprehensive lads climbing down off the same train.

That evening, ensconced in Room F4, Greg and his companions were told to stand up for a visit from the A/T RSM – not that it made any sense at the time! They were soon being inspected by this upright young soldier and Greg thought he had got off to a great start when it turned out that this 'RSM' and he shared a background of having lived for a while in Australia. Passing on to the next bed-space, the A/T RSM asked the young occupant for his name. The reply came out as *"Lander"*. To which our 'boy RSM' quickly responded, *"Lander, what?"* Of course, he was hoping to hear the term *"Sir"*, but it was our young Greg who, in a fit of inspiration - or madness - yelled out *"Lander hope and glory"*! He quickly became acquainted with the inside of the blanco-room, as he spent most of the evening scrubbing it out.

Greg goes on to remember the Saturday evening cinema shows, a welcome break from the 'spit and polish' during the week. Most popular of all were the cartoons, especially *'Tom and Jerry'*. Whenever these started, the producer's name coming up on screen – 'Fred Quimby' – evoked roars of raucous laughter! An incident also lodged in Greg's memory concerns the new soft-drinks dispenser in the NAAFI. It was soon discovered that it had no bottom to it and so it wasn't long before it was found lying on its side with the cash drawer missing!

The whole School was paraded in the Camp Hall, with warnings of everyone being finger-printed by the Berkshire Constabulary, but in the event, three boys confessed to the dastardly deed. Their twenty-eight days of detention was followed by their being dismissed from the service. When the local police eventually did find some fingerprints, it turned out that two boys who had 'confessed' were entirely innocent! They had used the incident to make their escape from Arborfield – and they never did come back.

Greg is another who remembers the Burmese boys – especially as he had to face one of them in the boxing ring! After hammering away at the boy's head for two rounds, Greg found himself knocked flying across to his corner just before the bell. Some quick advice from his corner told him to *"go downstairs"* – in other words, attack the midriff. This Greg did, much to the Burmese boy's consternation, and the fight was stopped in Greg's favour halfway through the third and final round.

Young Peck was quite keen on his boxing. One of his best mates, *"a little nugget of a Scotsman called Bob Malcolm"*, was the same – and of an equivalent weight, so the two were destined to meet in the ring on five occasions in all. Things were pretty even between them and, on one occasion, they put on an exhibition bout at Wokingham Drill Hall, when their respective opponents failed to turn up! At the end of the bout, just edged by Greg, the crowd showered them with silver coins. For the main prize, Greg was presented with fourteen bars of scented soap, while *"wee Bobby"*, the loser, picked up a three-tier cream sponge cake. *(Such was the price of fame in the Fifties! Ed.)* In the event, they decided to share the spoils.

When Greg eventually reached 5 Div, he fell victim to one of those afflictions that nobody really likes to talk about, but affects the rear end in a rather nasty way! For his treatment, Greg spent about seven weeks in hospital, and found himself in the company of several soldiers who had returned wounded from Korea and, having had operations, were still awaiting discharge when they were deemed suitably fit. All of them were allowed a bottle of stout every day and, when they realised that Greg wasn't going to get his ration, being a mere 'boy soldier', they raised such a fuss that the nurses relented and allowed Greg the same daily bottle.

'The life of Brian' - continued

1953 also saw the return/arrival of Brian Conway, now as a member of the military PS, Brian having himself joined here as a boy back in the wartime days of 1942. Brian was soon able to pursue the advantages of both his technical training and his favourite hobbies – music and boxing – the sporting type! He stayed on here until 1957, helping to establish the Corps of Drums as one of the essential pastimes of those boys with a musical bent, and earning for himself the sobriquet of *"the oldest teenager in the British Army"*.

Many years later, Brian was to recall that during his three years as an instructor, all WOs (except the RSM), SNCOs and JNCOs of the PS wore BD and various types of beret during their normal everyday duties. The exceptions for headdress were the three Brigade of Guards CSMs, who wore plain khaki SD caps. On Wednesday mornings, these three gentlemen took it in turn each week, while all apprentices were at morning assembly in the Camp Hall (out of sight, out of mind), to parade all other non-technical PS members. They would be inspected by the Admin Officer and then 'chased' around the Square for half-an-hour of drill. It would have been deemed inappropriate for the boys to see their beloved – or hated, take your pick – PS men being put through the hoop themselves for a change!

At some time during the year, a magazine was received from the Army Apprentices' School at Balcombe, in Australia. The editor of our own School magazine congratulated the 'Aussies' upon the excellence of their publication. It was especially good to know that there were apprentices 'down under' and it was to be hoped that this link, now established, could be maintained.

Also during that year, ex-boy Steve Johnson from 46A had been posted out to the British Commonwealth Base Wksp at Kure, in Japan. Both the Commanding Officer (CO) and RSM were 'fair dinkum' Australians, the Second-in-Command (2I/C) and CSM were from the UK, the Workshop Officer was a 'Kiwi' (New Zealander), while there was also a small group of Canadians. Steve found it hard work, seven days a week, but enjoyed good evening entertainment as well as Rest and Recuperation (R & R) breaks in Tokyo. Being only twelve miles from Hiroshima, the troops were well able to see the effects of the atomic bombs dropped in 1945. Little did Steve know that he was to get an even closer view of those effects some five years later.

Pipe Maj R J Batt was now looking after the talents of the Pipe Band and, despite the continuing loss of senior members, he was still able to report on the Band's success. He had read, with interest, some statistics on the number of pipers who had passed through Edinburgh Castle at the Army School of Piping, and wondered just how many such pipers had passed through our School here, since the Band had been formed by RSM McNally. He thought that perhaps REME could adopt, as one of its regimental tunes, *"We're a thousand pipers, an a', an a'"*! Pipe Maj Batt was also pleased to note the progress of some folk dancing classes, where 'The Highland Fling' had been mastered and 'The Foursome Reel' was now being taught by A/T J Gordon, who had himself been instructed at the Queen Vics at Dunblane.

During the first weekend in September, the School again played host to the Reunion of the OBA, the sixth such annual occasion. That year, it was good to see that more than one hundred members sat down for the Friday evening dinner, at five bob a time, which was followed by the customary dance in the Camp Hall. The AGM was set for mid-day on the Sunday, followed by sports fixtures against the School teams in cricket, hockey, rugby, shooting and soccer. It was noted, with much satisfaction, that there was a large number of the 'original' boys present that weekend, those from the 1939 - 40 vintage. The old boys truly were now becoming *old boys*!

A tale of two Maces

On October 24th 1953, at a ceremony held on the village green of Badshot Lea, on the outskirts of Aldershot, Hampshire, two handsome Drum Major's maces were presented to the School Bands. The first was given by local residents, in appreciation of *"services rendered during the previous three years"*. It was presented to A/T Cpl I Grounsell, who was the apprentice Drum Major of the Pipe Band.

The other came as a gift from *Messrs George Potter & Company*, the well-known Aldershot musical instrument makers, being presented to A/T R H Nixey, apprentice Drum Major of the Military Band. After the presentations and a speech of thanks by the Commandant, the two Bands carried out the 'Beating of Retreat', which was greeted with prolonged applause by the large number of appreciative spectators.

A few days later, Senior Div VMs again made the pilgrimage to that year's Motor Show. Prior to their departure from Arborfield, they had been given their haversack rations and an allowance of one shilling (5p) each for refreshments. With bottles of 'pop' on display at around a shilling and eight-pence each, and lunches priced at an extortionate ten shillings and sixpence, it didn't take a First Class ACE to work out just how many purchased lunches were eaten by the forty-two apprentices at the Show!

Another edition of *The Arborfield Apprentice* was published in December 1953; already the sixteenth School magazine in what was now a well-established tradition. All past and present members of the School were delighted that RSM McNally had recently been awarded the Meritorious Service Medal (MSM). The Commandant announced that *"no decoration could have been more richly deserved, nor given more universal satisfaction"*. He eagerly looked forward to the ceremony of presentation, which would be held on the School parade ground, which throughout the years had come to be regarded as the RSM's *"own special province"*.

In order to qualify even for consideration of recommendation for the MSM, a soldier must have completed twenty-seven years reckonable service with the colours and attained at the rank of at least substantive sergeant. He must have previously been awarded the LSGC medal and performed good, faithful, valuable and meritous service, with conduct adjudged to have been irreproachable throughout this service.

Over a period of time, some of the apprentices had formed the 1st Arborfield Senior Scouts Troop, with a regular attendance of around fifty members. A high standard had been built up, with the award of many proficiency badges; the most notable being the award of two 'Queen's Scout' badges. During the recent summer break, three young Scouts had spent camping holidays abroad, two in Denmark and one in Finland. A party of boys attended a rally at Windsor, when not only was the Chief Scout present, but the campsite was also paid a visit by Her Majesty the Queen. 'County weekends' had been spent at nearby Crowthorne and Bearwood, where the Troop had established a well-deserved reputation as campfire builders.

As Christmas approached at the end of 1953, thoughts turned once more to the Christmas Concert, which catered for everyone's taste that year. The slapstick, the mysterious and the musical – all had their

Apprentice Vehicle Mechanics of Intake 54A

part to play in the fare on offer. Members of 'A' Coy presented a comedy called *'Merrie England'*, set in the time of *'King Henry the Last'*, while 'C' Coy enacted a farce, depicting what was generally imagined to be 'the typical all-American hero'. *'Thread o' Scarlet'* was on offer from 'B' Coy - a one-act play set in a village inn. Without doubt, 'HQ' Coy were judged to have provided the most polished performance of the evening, with a finely balanced mixture of piano playing, singing and highland dancing.

(The programme for that Christmas Concert is attached as a seperate annex at the end this chapter.)

Numbers rise once again

The population of the School had happily begun to increase again during the previous year, so that on February 7th 1954, the Commandant was delighted to report that 'D' Coy had now been re-instated, from the 'suspended animation' in which it had lain since September 1951. The newly formed Company was to be commanded by Maj A J H Martin of the East Surrey Regt, *"reborn like the Phoenix of old to full strength*

and vigour". The total School population numbers had risen quickly to around 800, with the prospect of these reaching 900 by September of the same year. Just a few days prior to that announcement, at the 'PoP' held for intake 51A, RSM McNally was presented with his well-merited MSM.

On March 3rd 1954, 5 Div VMs had the pleasure of visiting the *AEC* factory in Southall, Middlesex. Their first port of call was the works canteen, for some welcome light refreshments of coffee and biscuits. The apprentices then went on to see how their civilian counterparts were being instructed, before a tour of the factory itself gave them some experience of how production was actually carried out. The assembly bays showed how engines and gearboxes were constructed and, finally, they saw the finished product, with completed trucks going out of the factory doors for their road tests.

A surprising increase of one

It is surprising that the increase in numbers during 1954 wasn't one less than that published! Brian

Hornsey, later to become the sole editor and publisher of the *OBAN*, is recorded as arriving here as a member of 54A. But prior to joining, and no doubt unknown to his fellow apprentices, Brian's father had brought him to Arborfield on what must have been a reconnaissance visit, during which the weather blew up into a proverbial blizzard. Whatever Arborfield could offer to Brian was to be explained by Maj Stocker, Rifle Brigade, and OC of 'HQ' Coy.

Peering through a misted office window, Brian watched parties of soldiers in PT kit, shuffling through the snow, on what he later found to be a 'road run'. Then he spotted three other unfortunate bedraggled beings, laboriously shovelling snow-covered coke into the depths of a boiler-house. Poor Brian - he failed to identify all these roadrunners and coke-shovellers as apprentices, thinking of them as mere servants to the cosseted boys – and we know the rest!

"Spuds? Gravy? Get your tea from the urn over by the door. You didn't know to bring your eating irons and mug with you? And you're supposed to be our hopes for the future! Bleedin' hell!" These words, or something very close to them, greeted Brian and his fellow Jeeps when they arrived at the Cookhouse. Mercifully, it was to be the only occasion when they didn't also have some evil A/T NCO yelling *"Plates!"* at them – and we all know what that meant! Brian soon learned to by-pass that little duty – in fact he learned quite a lot in pretty quick fashion.

Brian initially started training as a Tels Mech, but eventually volunteered to change his trade to that of Radar Mech, following its introduction in 1955. One 'electrical' instructor who stands out in his memory is Bill Riddiford, an excitable sort of chap who used to get into quite a dither at times. Pete Gripton (56B) shares this memory, later finding out that poor Bill suffered from diabetes, which no doubt caused him problems when his sugar level went off balance. Bill had eventually published a great little book, *'Radio Reference Riddiford'*, a cartoon-style introduction to electronics, which proved very popular at the time.

Promotion obviously didn't figure too largely in Brian's three-year apprenticeship curriculum, he had started as an A/T – and he would finish as an A/T! Perhaps that was due to rather a lot of *'woulds'* being present in his Company reports, as he quoted in the *OBAN* of many years later. His Company Commander peppered Brian's reports with the words, *"Would like to see him on the sports field more often"*, *"Would like to see him become more interested in Company activities"* and *"Would like to see him interested in games"*. *(Perhaps you couldn't see the 'woulds' for the trees, Brian! Ed.)*

Still, things couldn't have been all bad for Brian; at least he knew that 'Ma Beasley' would provide a good healthy fry-up on Saturday afternoons! *(Better than the cold fried bread at break-times, Brian? Ed.)* Many boys of that era will remember the delights of Ma Beasley's café in Reading. Located just around the corner from St Mary's Butts, (wasn't it in Sun Street?) the place was really a home-from-home for the many numbers of boys who used to frequent it.

Ma herself was a large homely woman, dressed in a large apron, rather like the actress who later starred as the café owner in the TV series, *'Last of the summer wine'*. She was quite proud of the fact that her daughter had married an American serviceman, and displayed their photograph on the wall. There was always a friendly smile and, probably for something like two shillings and sixpence (half-a-crown), one could stuff one's face with steaming plates of egg, chips, sausage and beans, some generous slices of bread and butter, all washed down with a fresh pot of tea (without the bromide!). You could, of course, opt for something similar in the Camp Cookhouse, but nobody cooked it quite like Ma!

Old Boys to the rescue

Fred Wells had originally been a R Sigs boy at the Boys' Sqn, Catterick, but had been transferred to Arborfield in March 1944 and taken under the wing of his brother, who had enlisted in 42B. Whether or not this was a wise move on Fred's part is debatable, as it gave him the rather enviable – or unenviable, take your pick! – record of a four-year spell as a boy soldier. In 1952, Fred had undergone a nine-month course on studying the intricacies of medical equipment at Woolwich, followed by a spell of service maintaining and repairing such equipment at the hospital at Mill Hill. During 1954, whilst serving at the Command Wksp in Kenya as a Staff Sergeant, Fred and two other fellow ex-boys, WO2 L W Merrick and G A Bourne, were involved with the treatment of an outbreak of 'polio' amongst the troops posted there.

The three soldiers were able to make the necessary improvements to some mechanical respirators (commonly termed 'Iron Lungs') at a hospital in

Nairobi, an action that greatly improved the treatment available to their patients. Out of seventeen patients, sixteen were evacuated back to the UK by air, assisted by the use of portable respirators, which had been sent out from Oxford. The fact that the three NCOs also had to isolate themselves within the environment of an epidemic brought them to the notice of the authorities. Thus it was that these three ex-boys each received a 'Certificate of Commendation' from General Erskine, the C-in-C, East Africa, plus a mention in the Queen's New Year Honours List for 1955.

Joining the School's PS during June 1954 was Cpl Joe Kinson REME. He got his third stripe after a probationary period, with his promotion subsequently backdated to the time of his arrival here. Joe went on to serve three years at the School, firstly in the Fitting Shop, then later in the Armaments Section. Many years later, upon his retirement from the Army, Joe returned to what would then be 'Princess Marina College' (PMC), again in the Armaments Section, but now as a civilian Instructional Officer, between 1982 and 1987. Joe retains many fond memories and can just about name every one of the PS members who were here in the mid-Fifties.

The editorial printed in that summer's edition of *The Arborfield Apprentice* poked some gentle fun at the miserable weather that had bedevilled the School a few weeks earlier. It would appear that the powers-that-be might have been considering the planting of rice on the 'paddy fields' that were supposed to be playing fields! Perhaps they would have been able to take advice

Cfn Dick Glister (54B) driving a 'Ferret' Scout Car in Muscat, March 1960

from the Burmese boys then present at the School – particularly A/T Kyaw Ohn, who actually wrote an article on that very subject in the same magazine. Fortunately, the sun had at last appeared and it was noted that the surrounding fields had now been planted with cabbages.

Another article in that School magazine came from Cpl C Markley, an ex-apprentice then serving with the LAD of an Armoured Regt in BAOR. He explained how each armoured regiment contained a number of Squadrons, which themselves were sub-divided into Troops. Although the term 'Troop' did not appear in the REME vocabulary, it aptly described the small number of REME Craftsmen attached to a parent Squadron. Cpl Markley went on to give a description of the type of work he and his colleagues carried out in a typical working day. In conclusion, he explained to the current apprentices that a REME tradesman attached to the RAC must be able not only to replace a spark plug, but also be able to *"twiddle the controls of a wireless-set"*!

The Military Band was still *"going strong"* with a total membership of about forty, allowing a typical playing strength of thirty. They had enjoyed only two recent outside engagements, most of their calls being at School parades. Meanwhile, the Pipe Band had been kept very busy and were looking forward to playing at the forthcoming 'Sandhurst Day' at the Academy, where the massed bands of the Brigade of Guards were also due to perform – something all the boys were naturally thrilled about.

At the 'PoP' on July 22nd, the School was delighted by a visit from the then Secretary of State for War, the Rt Hon Antony H Head, CBE, MC, MP. With so many demands on his time, it was a signal honour for the School to have this 'old soldier' taking the salute on parade, which saw the entry into adult service of boys from 51B. Over one hundred new Craftsmen would soon be joining their parent Corps of REME, with just seven apprentices posted to units of the RE. Two of the intake had successfully passed a WOSB and had been accepted for entry to the Eaton Hall Officer Cadet training unit, situated a few miles south of the fair city of Chester. The day was blessed with sunshine and the parade commanded by A/T CSM A J 'Algy' Morton, of 'B' Coy.

In his foreword to the School magazine, Col Magee reported upon the award of the BEM to CSM Brady in the recent Queen's Birthday Honours List. This well merited decoration gave special pleasure to all those young apprentices who, as juniors – or Jeeps! – in 'HQ' Coy, had passed under his vigilant and sympathetic eye.

The boys of 'C' Coy were celebrating their third successive winning of the Champion Company banner, though they bemoaned the fact that the re-formation of 'D' Coy had depleted their ranks of some talented sportsmen. 'A' Coy mourned the passing out of 51A, as it had taken with it three of their most outstanding sportsmen, all of them School captains in their individual sports no less. Meanwhile, 'B' Coy looked ahead to the forthcoming Drill Competition where, under the expert tuition of Corporal of Horse (CoH) Wilcox, they had great expectations of finishing in first place. 'D' Coy had been strongly placed in the Champion Company competition prior to their break-up, and was now looking ahead to the time when it could once again achieve the title that had once seemed within its grasp.

The Pipe Band had quickly welcomed the arrival of new Adjutant to the School, Capt I B MacHorton, of the Cameronians. He had now personally taken over the instruction of the Scottish Dancing classes every Thursday evening and performances had improved a hundred per cent. Another welcome change had been the new Pipe Band Room, kindly given by the Commandant, and close to the home of the Military Band. A very busy summer had seen the boys playing an engagement every single weekend.

The formative years

Clive Soord was, in his own words, an *"innocent fifteen-year-old"* when he first walked through the famous gates as a member of 54B. He had signed on in Egypt, where his father was then serving with the RAOC, but actually flew into England from Malta on a *York* aircraft, the civil version of the famous war-time *Lancaster* bomber. That journey took ten hours in those days. Clive had diligently made his way to Arborfield from the airport at Stansted, but then inadvertently reported to the Depot REME, where he was almost recruited as a member of the REME Boys' Band! *"All rather confusing"*, as Clive was later to put it.

Eventually things got sorted out, of course, and

Clive started his training at the School about a week after other members of the intake. He found a great mate in Mick Owen, who always had his own kit *"spick and span"* in no time at all and who helped Clive make up for his lost time. Clive's memories of the next three years – which he correctly names as *"the formative years"*, follow much the same pattern as hundreds of others, with plenty of mixed feelings! High on his list come the count-downs to summer leave; the lie-ins on free Sundays; the 'big fight' between the Memmot brothers, Bob and Dave; compulsory cross-country runs, with Brian Kitchener seemingly always at the front; listening to the 'Top Twenty' on *Radio Luxembourg*. He could go on and on - and usually does when prompted! Three long years at the *"school of hard knocks"*, is how Clive finally describes it, and who are we to argue?

Clive, and no doubt the rest of his intake, probably thought that the hardest times were behind them when they finished their first six months as Jeeps in 'HQ' Coy. But it wasn't as simple as that. Being in 2 Div, and now separated into individual Companies, they soon realised that they had been *"shielded to a large extent"*, but that they were now *"bottom of the pecking order"*. They found themselves at the back of the queue for meals, being 'persuaded' to clean kit for the senior boys and being generally *"put upon"* in numerous other ways.

Training to be an Inst Mech, Clive did wonder at the time why he spent so much time on *"filing, tin bashing, blacksmithing"* and the like, but it all eventually stood him in good stead in later years. He remembers the food as *"mainly awful"*, and he was always in the rush to grab the leftovers from the bread-slicing machines. Despite the meagre wages, it was occasionally great to blow some of it on a plateful of egg, chips and beans down at the NAAFI. Clive also recalls those occasions when he went on 'fire crew', failing to connect the hoses correctly and getting a drenching for his sins – plus the usual rollicking from the dreaded Fred Silvers, of course!

That's an awful lot of apprentices!

By September 1954, Col Magee was able to announce to the old boys, at their annual Reunion, that the number of apprentices who had now passed through the School had reached the grand total of 3,700. However, the number of fully paid-up members of the OBA was just 233, which represented only a small percentage of those eligible to join. Many apprentices, having 'almost automatically' joined the Association upon leaving Arborfield, failed to renew their subscriptions the following year. At least the Reunion had been better attended that year, with 176 members present, as opposed to one disappointing previous total of only forty-five.

Early in November, a party of Senior Div Armourers were able to visit the RSAF at Enfield Lock in London. Here they were able to see how the 'proofing' of Bren-gun barrels was carried out. For this operation, where a chamber pressure of 25 tons per square inch is built up, all guns were encased in a steel jacket, not to protect the guns, but the testers themselves, in case of a burst barrel. The boys also visited what amounted to a museum, where a most varied and interesting collection of weapons had been collected, from the latest Russian medium machine-gun to a homemade 'Mau Mau' Rifle.

In previous years, the School soccer team had played their games in the Reading Minor League, which had age limit restrictions, meaning that Arborfield was never able to field a full team. Having taken the decision to withdraw from that League, and concentrate upon friendly fixtures, this had led to a far greater success rate in the season up to December. Having played nine games, eight of these had been won, with a scoring record of forty-eight goals 'for' and only twenty 'against'. Meanwhile, the Staff side were enjoying rather leaner times, having to rely on some 'old faithfuls' such as Artificer Quartermaster Sergeant (AQMS) Pete Whitehorn, a reliable 'stopper-style' centre-half, to stem the tide of opposition attacks.

At the same time, members of the Basketball team were overjoyed to find that official recognition had finally been given for the inclusion of their game as a *bona fide* inter-school winter sport. They had now been asked to produce a team to play against RAF Halton, and looked forward to similar matches against other opposition in the future. A series of trial games was currently being planned.

The AAS Cycling Club had a membership of around thirty boys and had recently, with the Commandant's permission, become affiliated to the National Cyclists' Union. Club runs had been made to Windsor, Haslemere and Oxford, as well as places further afield. Under a keen committee, the Club was hoping that their sport would also soon become a recognised sport in the School for the first time.

On November 30th 1954, a Presentation Parade was held at the School, on the day of the Annual Administrative Inspection, at which the MSM was awarded to WO2 D R Hobbs, REME. He had enlisted as an apprentice himself, way back in 1929, as an Armourer with the RASC. Captured at Tobruk in Libya, during the desert campaign of the early war years, he had later escaped and eventually made his way to join the 8th Army in Italy. He had since served in South Wales, Washington D.C., BAOR and the Gold Coast, before joining Arborfield earlier that year.

By general opinion, *"one of the best (Christmas) concerts of recent years"* took place on Wednesday 15th December. 'A' Coy kicked off proceedings with a *'Guide to Modern Music'*, presented by a small band and chorus. Then it was 'D' Coy's turn, with three sketches that were collectively titled *'Tour of London'* – orators on a Sunday morning at Hyde Park; buskers entertaining the crowd outside the Old Vic; and finally, a meeting of the committee of a Football Supporters Club. 'C' Coy weighed in with a *'Palace of Varieties'* show, while 'D' Coy ended the whole concert with a preview of commercial TV – where an advertiser gave a splendid performance, well lubricated by *'Guzzler's Gin'*, the sponsor's product!

History never stops growing

A letter, dated 17th December, from the Commandant to the Under-Secretary of War, gave what must have been the second set of details of a history of the AAS up to that date, no doubt leaning heavily on Brig Tanner's original work of 1951. Certainly, the opening paragraphs of this particular history you are reading, itself based upon research carried on over many years, reflect much of what was written on Col Magee's behalf at that time.

The War Office must have been gathering data for a survey, as other letters of a similar nature and from around the same date, were sent from the other two Apprentices' Schools at Chepstow and Harrogate. The advance party for Chepstow had arrived at Beachley on February 14th 1924, whilst the opening of Harrogate did not take place until February 1st 1947, on the same day as the short-lived School down at Taunton, in Somerset.

During that same year, 1954, the War Office had given approval for the unofficial affiliation of the

School with the Royal Scots (The Royal Regt). Her Royal Highness (HRH) the Princess Royal, Colonel-in-Chief of the Regiment, gave consent to the wearing of the 'Hunting Stuart' tartan by members of the School's Pipe Band. Strangely, there is no written evidence of this in regimental records, or that it was ever worn, nor do the archives reveal how or why the Band came by the Fusilier's hackle. However, the news was definitely part of Col Magee's foreword in December's version of *The Arborfield Apprentice*. The Commandant added that he was sure that this would give a lot of pleasure to all members of the School, both past and present.

The Commandant was also able to report on successful visits by parties of Headmasters and Youth Employment Officers, which had become a regular feature of School life. From the remarks passed and letters received, Col Magee was in no doubt as to the favourable impression the young apprentices had made upon our visitors, a matter of real importance if the School was to continue its growth, *"both in quality and quantity"*. On a more parochial theme, congratulations were given to Miss Marie McNally, daughter of our famous RSM, on her wedding to Sgt B Mawson, RAEC, early in December.

The February edition of the *REME Magazine* contained an article that reviewed a War Office publication called *"The Boy Soldier"*, and was accompanied by a photograph, showing a new boy recruit being welcomed at the Arborfield gates by the Provost Sergeant. There are many who would argue against the apparent warmth in that welcome!

(The article is produced as a separate annex to this chapter.)

New trades

At the 'PoP' in February 1955, the Commandant announced that new trades were to be introduced and taught at the School later that year. Radar Mechs, Electricians REME and Fitters Gun were to be additional, but the accompanying loss of Turners and Draughtsmen (Mechanical) would sever a long-standing link with the 'Sappers' (RE). Col Magee reminded parents of the importance of the Fitter's trade, which was still of great importance to the modern Army, with its own vast variety of equipment.

The Commandant was also pleased to announce that steady progress was being maintained by the Works Services people. New classrooms were already in use, work had commenced on five new Company sitting rooms and the War Office had approved plans for the building of a new workshop, six new classrooms and a lecture hall. Reporting on the 52A Senior Div that was passing out, Col Magee was proud to announce that it contained, for the first time, a number of Burmese apprentices who had completed their training. One of them, Ohn Thwin, had achieved the highest aggregate in Technical Training and Education, and also been honoured by the award of the Chief Instructor's Cup. Another 'first' was the posting of twenty-one REME personnel directly to BAOR, something that would become a regular occurrence in the future.

That parade was reviewed by Maj Gen W A Lord CB, CBE, who was DME at the time. He praised the senior boys for their progress and looked back some five years, to when he had been Commandant at the REME Training Centre at Arborfield. He said that he *"was pleased to see that the apprentices not only maintained their high standard of drill and training, but that today's educational standards are so much higher"*. He gave the newly qualified Craftsmen the following advice:

> *"Aim high in the new life before them; be determined to improve in skill and knowledge; maintain a high standard of turnout and discipline".*

'Look Lad, this is the entrance to the start of the rest of your life'

Despite the strongest protestations from his mother, early one morning in 1955, fifteen-year old Chris Fussell was ordered out of his parents' married quarter by his father, who was Orderly Sergeant that day, standing there in his *"best BD and red sash"*. Chris was off to join 55A at Arborfield. At the time, he was the proud owner of an 'O' level in Maths from an Army children's school in Egypt and intended to become trained as a Tels Mech.

Chris got through his 'square bashing' under the watchful eyes of Sgt Philips of the Royal Welch Fusiliers (RWF) but, to the despair of AQMS Pete Whitehorn, Chris turned out to be rather ham-fisted at his attempts at practical work. However, this didn't stop him from taking home lop-sided brass cannons and disfigured models of the Eiffel Tower, with which to decorate his Mum's mantelpiece!

Eventually, it was decided that young Chris wasn't going to make the grade in electronics, and after a stay of only 336 days at the School, he was 'kicked upstairs' to Welbeck College. He thoroughly enjoyed his final

Apprentice Fitters with Sgt Boynton in March 1955

parting from the School, as he cycled out through the gates, past 'Fred's Hotel', shouting *"Cheerio, Sarge, I've got my ticket"*. Fred managed to shout a few words back, but Chris never did hear what they were – he can only guess! He went on to spend many happy days afterwards with the RAOC, but still reckons that those days spent here at Arborfield were amongst his happiest.

AQMS P F Whitehorn, REME, then looking after events in the Tels Shop, had joined as a boy soldier at the Military College of Science, Woolwich, in 1937. He saw wartime service in Egypt, Palestine, Iraq, Trans-Jordan and Persia (now Iran). He later took part in the invasion of Sicily and Italy with the American 5th Army and served in the post-war Far Eastern Land Forces (FARELF), being *"Mentioned in Dispatches"* for gallant and distinguished conduct against the local terrorists. At the School on May 22nd 1955, he was proudly presented with his LSGC Medal.

Another boy of intake 55A was Andy Rackstraw, one of the many who later chose NZ as his permanent home. But 1955 remains vivid in his memory as the time he *"lost his teenage years"*! Andy never understood the discipline that determined an extremely short haircut, yet clothed him in a 'hairy' shirt that played havoc with his fair skin. He later went on to learn the 'noble art' of boxing, in an attempt to dissuade the bullying from senior boys.

Also learned in those days was how to drink and survive 'scrumpy' (rough cider for those who have never tried it!) and how to hold a *Woodbine* down to the last drag with the aid of a pin! Another of Andy's memories is that some members of the IRA raided the Armoury 'just up the road', which brought about a great increase in security and vigilance for a long time afterwards. All in all, Andy's recollections of his time at Arborfield are of many gloomy moments – but interspersed with enough good memories of sports and music, plus old friends, to make up for it.

An administrative review

April of 1955 saw the production of another 'Report', this one by the *'Committee on the Organization (yes – that's with a "z") and Administration of Boys' Units in the Army'*.

The Committee had been set up in December 1954 to investigate such matters, both of the Apprentices' Schools at Arborfield, Chepstow, Harrogate, as well as Regimental Boys' Units in certain other Arms and Services. Generally known under the heading of the 'Miller Report', the Committee *"widely accepted that the Apprentices' Schools are fulfilling their purpose"*. The fact that both of the schools, at Arborfield and Chepstow, had been kept going throughout the wartime years indicated their great value. The Army Council, having studied the Report, was in no doubt that there was a continuing requirement, accepting in principle that both *"should be conducted more as schools than as military establishments"*.

The following list may already be familiar to older readers, but shows the great variety of 'Boys' Units' that were available to the less technically minded boys during the Fifties:

Boys' Sqn, RAC, Bovington, Dorset
Boys' Regt, RA, Hereford
Boys' Sqn, RE, Aldershot
Boys' Training Regt, R Sigs, Beverley, Yorks.
Boys' Infantry Btn, Plymouth
Boys' Company, RASC, Aldershot
Boys' Company, RAOC, Blackdown, Hants.
Apprentices' Chef School, Aldershot

The Report went on to admit that there had been some rather telling misconceptions in the early days of the Apprentices' Schools. The daily routine had been *"that of the soldier"* and thus unsuitable for adolescents, while the quarters had also been designed for soldiers, unlikely at best to be ideal for boys and, in some cases, totally unacceptable. On that second point, not until a special visit was paid to the DYRMS at Dover, did Committee members see *"a range of buildings planned and built for the purpose"*. Many conclusions were drawn, and recommendations made, in the final Report, under a variety of headings. These included: Selection of Boys, the life of the Boy, the Curriculum, Staff, Location, Accommodation and Amenities.

June 25th 1955 proved a very proud day for the School Athletics Team. Competing in the Inter-Schools Quadrangular Tournament, held 'oop north' at Harrogate, as far as records show, the Arborfield boys claimed victory for the very first time. This was after a *"breath-takingly close finish, with all four teams so close in scoring that the issue hung in the balance right*

up to the end". At the death, the final result depended upon two events – the Senior 4 x 440-yard Relay and the Junior Pole Vault.

In the Relay, on the third lap, A/T Cpl Brian Kitchener took up the baton fully ten yards behind his Chepstow opponent. An impressive turn of pace saw him overtake and hand over some five yards in front, for A/T Cpl Stanley to finish a magnificent effort. One of our Burmese boys, Than Soe, then had to clear nine foot six inches in the Pole Vault, to maintain our aggregate lead. This he did, but then it was found that we were only level with Chepstow, could this be trouble? Well, maybe, but now it was down to technicalities – our lads had made the fewest faults and Arborfield were declared the winners. Close run indeed, but a glorious result.

For the first time ever, at the 'PoP' of July 21st 1955, the Reviewing Officer and his retinue arrived at the School by helicopter. The Officer in case could not have been more well known, in the splendid form of Field Marshall Sir John Harding, GCB, CBE, DSO, MC, in his appointment as CIGS. Apprentices were already drawn up on the Square as the helicopter came into sight, circled the School, and then came in to land on the sports field behind the Gymnasium. After the Parade, the CIGS announced his pride and pleasure in being invited to participate. Congratulating all who took part, he said that he had been particularly pleased during the march-past that every young man had *"looked him straight in the eye"*.

A standard to fight for

Col Magee was about to bid a fond farewell to the School when he wrote his final foreword to *The Arborfield Apprentice* of July 1955. He had been *"proud and honoured"* at the start of his tour, and the three years that had since passed had added a *"sense of achievement and of gratitude"* that would follow him into a well-earned retirement. He had been pleased to see numbers rising term by term and especially as this had culminated in the restoration of 'D' Coy. He announced that he would be handing over the torch of command to Col R G Pine-Coffin, DSO, MC, but in fact this move never came about.

The Commandant hoped to keep in touch with the School and reminded all apprentices of the School Charter, to produce for the Regular Army the Soldier – Craftsman – Leader. He concluded with a brief verse that he thought apt for the future:

"Unless you've a standard to fight for,
Unless you've a banner unfurled,
It's better by far that you stay where you are
And never go out in the world".

The School Chaplain, Rev J P Morgan, BA, was pleased to report that Church life was progressing on a steady basis, despite the fact that he had succumbed to mumps just prior to the Easter break! He went on to add a vote of thanks to RSM McNally and Sgt Silvers, the Provost Sergeant, who had regularly supplied the flowers for the Chapel and Camp Hall on Sundays. *(He didn't mention that these two probably provided a great number of the congregation too! Ed.)*

The Armoury raid, recalled by Andy Rackstraw, took place at No.5 Trg Btn REME in the early hours of Saturday August 13th. Even a guard of some eighteen men was quickly subdued by the armed raiders, who are believed to have got away with around 80,000 rounds of ammunition and a collection of rifles and machine-guns. Happily, the gang, consisting of just three men, was quickly apprehended, after a police patrol spotted a suspiciously 'overloaded van' in the Ascot area. The two Irish occupants were taken into custody and police later arrested a third man in London. All three were charged with *"stealing a quantity of arms"* at Wokingham Police Station. The raid obviously stirred up a 'hornets' nest' of activity throughout the Armed Forces, as guards were quickly armed, doubled and even trebled, in an attempt to prevent a reoccurrence.

On August 28th 1955, the OBA held its eighth Annual General Meeting (AGM), chaired by Col Magee and under the presidency of Col White, the School's first Commandant. The Chairman reported that the total number of A/Ts who had passed through the School now exceeded 3,900 and that, with the newly arrived intake, the School's strength stood at a healthy 800. As for the Association, membership now stood at 308, of which sixty-six were 'Life Members'. The really big event of the year had been at that summer's 'PoP', when the School had once again been honoured by a visit from Field Marshall Montgomery, CIGS.

Unfortunately, regarding the Reunion itself, numbers were again down and disappointing, with only sixty-one at the Saturday dinner. Even 'the girls' were scarce that year, but the evening's dance was still considered a success, despite the shortage of partners. Perhaps it was a case of *"After you, Claude. No, after you, Cecil"*! At the sports meetings, held on the Sunday afternoon, the old boys managed to win at basketball, no doubt due to lowdown cunning, but were well beaten at soccer, hockey and shooting.

'A merry old soul'

In October of that year, Col J R Cole (late The Loyal Regt) succeeded as the School's Commandant, having recently served at HQ Aldershot District. Col Cole had been born in 1907 and joined up in 1927. He had served during 'the troubles' in Palestine during 1936, before being posted to Shanghai, then Malaya. In 1942, he was one of the many unfortunate soldiers captured by the Japanese Army, and was held as a prisoner-of-war, under the severest of conditions, in Singapore for the next three years.

No prizes are awarded for guessing that, when he arrived at the School, the boys immediately nicknamed him 'Old King' Cole. It had, in fact, been intended that a chap by the name of Pine-Coffin would be the next Commandant *(what would the boys have made of a name like that we wonder? Ed.)*, but the fact that Col Cole was a married man swung the vote his way. The School's Adjutant at the time was Maj Ezra Rhodes of the King's Own Border Regt (KOBR). The boys reckoned he should have been a traffic sign, denoting 'Major Road(s) Ahead'!

Colonel Cole remembers that, upon his arrival, the School's Military Band was in some difficulty, due to there being no real leader and having recently suffered the loss of ten members. Indeed, the Padre is supposed to have visited him one day to ask if the Band could ***not*** play at Church any longer, as they were ruining the services! Fortunately, a new Bandmaster, Sgt F Backley, was recruited from the Inniskillings, and it was he who managed to pull the Band into shape once more. The Band Room had been given a face-lift in 'green and cream', thanks to the efforts of the boys themselves, who bore the 'scars of battle' i.e. paint daubs, on their faces for several days afterwards!

Many years later, Col Cole, reflecting upon his time spent at the School, remembered coming under increasing pressure from his Company Commanders to re-arrange the Companies back into 'trades'. The Commandant, however, thought that it was best to continue with the 'spread' of boys of differing trades across the Companies, as the possibility of having all the 'brightest' boys in the same Company could prove detrimental to the others.

Peter Gibby of 55B recalls what he later termed 'Wally's Disastrous Pay Parade', the 'Wally' in question being A/T O'Grady of the same intake. Most old boys will remember the pay parade, marching up to the six-foot pay table by alphabetical order, coming to a halt, snapping up a smart salute and uttering those famous words 'Pay and Paybook correct, Sir', before turning about and marching off, clutching a small handful of loose silver. *(Something less than ten bob in those days, eh, Pete? Ed.)*

Poor Wally, who, despite the 'Oirishness' of his name hailed from the Swansea area, was another boy who suffered from a slight stutter. This became more pronounced whenever he became slightly flustered, usually in the presence of a higher authority. On the day in question, he just couldn't get the words out, standing in front of the desk in a state of confusion. The paying officer, Maj Williams, was ready to put on a sympathetic smile, but from behind came the roar of CSM Brady, *"Alright O'Grady, GET FELL IN!"* Wally had no option but to obey the last order, and marched away having been underpaid by a shilling. He never did get it back, nor did the pay clerk's account of 'the extra bob (shilling)' ever come to notice.

Another of those 55B boys was Colin 'Dras' Drasutis, who went on to become the A/T RSM of his intake. Colin had already enjoyed some previous 'military' experience with the Combined Cadet Force (CCF) at his old school, the Liverpool Institute High School for Boys. Apart from the pride he took in leading the 'PoP' at the end of his three years, his most memorable moment came during a cricket match. Not any old cricket match of course, but the 1958 Champion Company final between 'B' Coy, of which Colin was skipper, and 'C' Coy, led by A/T CSM Eddie Wilson.

'C' Coy's last wicket pair were making a superb attempt at overhauling the 'B' Coy total, with some devastating hitting against what was becoming a slightly ragged bowling attack. Just as it seemed that 'C' Coy would win the game, depriving 'B' Coy of the Champion Company banner, Colin caught a hard hit ball on the long-off boundary. As he led his team off the pitch, applauded every step of the way, Colin heard the Commandant asking him, *"Do you need medical attention?"* Apparently, the heroic effort of catching that ball had turned Colin as white as a sheet!

It was probably during 1955 that the badly worn floorboards in the spider blocks were replaced with hardwood strip flooring. The picture regarding the barrack-room floors thus became one of a central patch of brown, edged by the original boards, quite black, due to the many years of *Zebo* (black-lead) application and ingrained dirt. The numerous knots in those old boards now stood proud of the surface, above the level of the softer grain surrounding them.

The 'Big Bang'

At some time during mid-December of 1955, with darkness already having fallen, groups of boys settled down to their evening's activities, their tea meal a recent memory, with perhaps a late supper to look forward to. 'Janker wallahs' had departed for their various types of entertainment and the gossip alternated between food, sport and sex – and how much each was getting of each! Charles Elsey of intake 53A seems to think that there was a concert in the offing, either that night or the following one, probably in time for the Christmas season. But suddenly a loud explosion rent the air, sending 'top kit' flying from locker tops and falling onto recumbent A/Ts, and causing loose panels to fall from the wooden walls of those spiders closest to the incident.

The cause of the commotion quickly became evident, when flames rose up and a mushroom cloud of smoke was seen hovering over the local *'Rainbow'* firework factory in Hogwood Lane, just across the track that ran along the perimeter fence at the top end of the Square. The force of the explosion was felt as far as three miles away and Greg Peck described the cloud as of *"magnificent proportion and colour"*. A large number of other fires were started by burning debris, which became scattered over a wide area. As reported later in the *Daily Mirror*, *"soldiers, including boy apprentices, raced to the factory from a nearby Army training school"*. Despite the obvious dangers, they pulled people from burning buildings while rockets and bangers continued to explode all around them.

Sadly, there were a couple of fatalities and several injuries amongst the workers, most of whom were young girls, with a few well known to their apprentice boy-friends. However, the two killed outright were both men, while a third person, a middle-aged woman, died later from the severity of injuries received. Rumours abounded of course, with one story telling that one young girl worker, wearing forbidden nylon knickers, had inadvertently caused an electrostatic spark, thus setting off the 'big bang'. Certainly, nothing remained of the mixing shed where the 'flash' was said to have originated. The truth was probably never properly established and never made the local papers, so perhaps we'll have to settle for the rumour!

Here within the confines of the barracks, the collapsing wall panels caused little physical damage, but brought rather a large amount of contraband and spare kit into the light of day! Charles Elsey recalls that this was particularly so amongst the Burmese boys, who maintained a large collection of forbidden ornamental knives and daggers in those dark recesses. These would provide a source of extra income when sold on as souvenirs and mementos to the English lads. Another hidden treasure was a supply of smuggled Burmese cigars – which Charles reckons were *"far more dangerous that any of the weapons"*!

In order to play together as a team as often as possible, the Soccer XI had entered the Arborfield Garrison League that season. Considering the age and experience of the opposition, they had managed a satisfactory level so far, having won four of their seven games. Where this experience had benefited the side was in the first inter-School game, where RAF Locking had been well beaten by two goals to nil. Basketball continued to gain popularity and was now recognised as an event at the winter competitions against other Apprentices' Schools. At each of these inter-School meetings, there were now seven separate events, meaning that no longer could a competition end in a draw.

Had the bangers - now for the mash!

Ted Blowers was a member of the PS during the period 1953 – 1956. From the Royal Regiment of Fusiliers (RRF), he worked in the kitchen of the Cookhouse under the command of Sgt Viger and Cpl Jack Snow. As he recalls, all the food that came in for preparation was excellent, but that it *"took major work to turn it into what was dished up"*! *(He must mean that it deteriorated somewhat during the cooking! Ed.)* Ted adds that, as the cooks ate from the same rations, they somehow contrived to get the best for themselves, hiding it away under the hotplates until the boys had left the Cookhouse. Ted remembers *"the nectar"* that was brewed up as 'tea' for the staff, a far cry to that served to the boys – which was apparently boiled up in the same pans that had recently been used for stewing the cabbage! The 'cooks' tea' was made with *"lashings of sugar, a couple of tins of Carnation milk, and enough tea to give it that creamy brown look"*.

Ted recalls once being given the job of making the mashed potatoes and, as he loved mashed spud himself, he put in plenty of extra milk and butter and worked away until every last lump had been smoothed away. Imagine his horror when large numbers of boys refused this delicious delight, saying that they were fed up with pom! However, those that did take a chance on Ted's culinary extravagance soon came back for seconds – and in some cases, thirds! One of the kitchen assistants, old Tom Warren, who *"rolled his own"* (cigarettes, that is!), was usually called upon to *"mix the duff"* when this was on the menu, and it wasn't unknown for the duff to have a certain amount of extra fibre!

Ted and his wife have now been married for almost fifty years, have two sons of their own, and have lived in Canada since 1970. Most of his memories of boys' school are pleasant ones and he remarks that, as a staff member, *"Our lives were remote from most of the apprentices, though I was good friends with some. I admired the way that most put up with the same indignities that we had heaped upon us"*.

On October 5th 1955, the REME Regimental Boys' Company was formed at Blackdown, Hampshire, under the command of Maj C Kemp, REME. The boys were 'badged' to REME, but at that time formed part of the RAOC boys' school and utilised the same basic military training syllabus. The unit was later to move to Arborfield, a move that caused a certain amount of friction between the two sets of boys who became close neighbours!

1955 had certainly proved a difficult one for those countries and peoples that liked to live in peace. In May of that year, eight eastern European countries had signed the 'Warsaw Pact', and the so-called 'Cold War' between those countries of the east and the North Atlantic Treaty Organisation (NATO) in the west was perpetuated for many years to come. Later the same year, a state of emergency was declared in Cyprus, when two British soldiers were killed and public order crumbled, as those Cypriots of Greek descent made their bid for 'Enosis' (union with mainland Greece).

Internal Memos - Circa 1951/52

To: **Chief Instructor**
From: **Commandant**
On Thursday evening at approx 1800hrs, Halley's Comet will be visible in this area, an event which only occurs every 76 years. Please have the soldiers assemble in the area outside this building and I will explain this rare phenomenon to them. In case of rain we will not be able to see anything, so assemble the soldiers in the canteen and I will show them a film of it.

To: **Adjutant**
From: **Chief Instructor**
By order of the Commandant, on Thursday at 1800hrs Halley's Comet will appear above the area outside this building. It it rains, please assemble the soldiers and proceed to the canteen where this rare phenomenon will take place, something which occurs only every 76 years.

To: **Coy Commanders**
From: **Adjutant**
By order of the Commandant, at 1800hrs on Thursday the phenomenal Halley's Comet will appear in the canteen. In case of rain in the area outside the building, the Commandant will give another order, something which occurs only once every 76 years.

To: **Coy CSMs**
From: **Coy Commanders**
On Thursday at 1800hrs, the Commandant will appear in the canteen with Halley's Comet, something which happens every 76 years but only if it rains. The Commandant will order the Comet into the area outside the building.

To: **Platoon Sergeants**
From: **Coy CSMs**
When it rains on Thursday at 1800hrs, the phenomenal 76 years old Bill Haley, accompanied by the Commandant, will drive his Comet through the area outside the building and into the canteen.

—§—

The Permanent Staff 1955

Annex to Chapter 4

Soldier Apprentice

Success in war depends largely upon the ability to maintain and repair all the complicated equipment and machinery that is an essential part of the modern army.

To achieve this, the Army needs skilled craftsmen of nearly every known trade. But technical skill is not enough; the Army needs craftsmen who are also leaders.

Such men are found today among the Officers, Warrant Officers and NCOs of the Technical Arms; Manny of whom, only a few short years ago, were youngsters of fifteen starting a new life at one of the Army Apprentice Schools.

There are three of these Schools – at Arborfield in Berkshire, Chepstow in Monmouthshire, and at Harrogate – and their aim is to train the Army's technical leaders of the future.

Here, for three years, a boy lives and grows, works and plays. In a brief twenty minutes, this film tries to show some of the advantages of a career begun in one of these Schools – the value of environment and discipline for character training; the importance of a boy's physical, mental and moral development; the care of his religious and general education; and the wide range of trades open to him.

There are so many trades in which a modern Army needs craftsmen, that it is impossible, in the time, to show them all – but we do see that the training is extremely thorough and that it not only fits the Apprentice for his Army career, but will also enable him to follow his trade in civil life, when he leaves the Army.

By the time they leave the Schools, these boys have received an excellent education; moreover, the Army has taught them to become skilled craftsmen, good soldiers and responsible men.

(The above article, issued as a resumé with the film 'Soldier Apprentice' in 1952, first appeared in The Arborfield Apprentice, Volume II, No.2, issued in December 1951.)

Col E L Percival, DSO - an appreciation

Colonel E L Percival, DSO, became Commandant of this School in August 1949, having joined from the Army MT School. Prior to this appointment, he was GSO1 in General Headquarters MELF. During the War he commanded a battalion of 'The Buffs' in North Africa and Paiforce, and later a battalion of the HLI in Europe. He was awarded the DSO whilst serving in Eritrea, and a bar to his DSO for service in Europe. He was also mentioned in dispatches.

Colonel Percival took a keen interest in all branches of the School's activities, both military and recreational. He was himself an Army tennis player and also played hockey and football. His performances as left back for the Officers' football team have perhaps left their mark on some members of the Sergeants' Mess! As a Scotsman he was, of course, particularly concerned with the Pipe Band and, shortly before he left, he authorised the purchase of kilts for the pipers.

He always maintained that fine balance between the technical and the regimental sides of School life and never allowed undue emphasis to be given to one, to the detriment of the other.

He always sought to help Apprentices to make a success of their career in the Army and it was with the greatest reluctance that he ever recommended that a boy should be discharged. He took great pains to find out why an Apprentice was not making progress at his trade and gave a last chance to many who had been given up as hopeless by their instructors.

It was a great disappointment to him to have to leave the School before the Passing-out Parade on 25th July, as he had always wished to see the 49B intake right through the School.

He leaves on promotion to Brigadier and appointment as Deputy Commander of Highland District, and the good wishes of the School go with him.

(The above appreciation was first published in The Arborfield Apprentice, Volume II, Number 3, issued in July 1952.)

Guard of Honour, Windsor Castle

Monday 1st June 1953 proved an eventful day for the thirty Apprentices selected to form a Guard of Honour at Windsor Castle, on the occasion of a Dedication Service of the Commonwealth Youth Movement, in St George's Chapel. The Guard consisted of ten Senior

Apprentices from each of 'A', 'B' and 'C' Companies, with A/T CSM Webber as Guard Commander, and was to be inspected by Major-General E Hakewill Smith, CB, CBE, MC, Governor of the Military Knights of Windsor. A large and comfortable coach provided the transport and, under the care of RSM R L McNally, MBE, we left the Camp.

After a pleasant journey, our coach entered King Henry VIII Gate at Windsor Castle and stopped outside the Guard Room, where our rifles and equipment were deposited for the morning period. The Guard was due to form up at 14.30 hours so, with all the morning to spare, we were conducted around the State Apartments of the Castle, together with a large party of the Commonwealth Youth Movement. These were mostly Canadians but with some Australians, Pakistanis and other Commonwealth Youth, over for the Coronation.

In a matter of seconds, it seemed, we were in another world – a world of beautiful rooms, full of lovely furniture, pictures, carpets and tapestries. There was one room, adorned with exquisite furniture and large mirrors, with frames of solid silver, which we were told was the Queen's Drawing Room. The walls were decked with classical paintings and tapestries, which added to the serene beauty of the place. The closet, or private room, of the Queen proved equally interesting and seemed to match the drawing room. Her again, tapestries decked the walls, but the main feature was the paintings, many of them by Masters such as Rubens and Van Dyke.

Following on from this, we entered what to us was the most interesting feature of the castle. It was the guardroom, now converted into a museum, containing all manner of shining armour and guns. Much to our disappointment, there was not enough time to see everything, and the guide led us on to the Throne Room and Waterloo Chamber. Here, he pointed out the immense banqueting table, which was fully a hundred feet in length. Indeed, the whole castle seemed to take us back into the historic Age of Chivalry in Britain. We could visualise the Lords and Barons at a large and colourful banquet.

So absorbed were we with our surroundings that the time just flew past and it became apparent that lunch was near. Having satisfied our hunger and rested our legs, it was now time to prepare for the Guard. Now that 'zero hour' approached, we were soon engaged in a last minute clean up. Buttons, rifles, bayonets and boots formed the main topic of conversation in the final

few minutes. Nevertheless, at the pre-arranged time, we marched proudly out and took up our positions, outside the entrance to St George's Chapel.

The waiting seemed endless, but the sharp word of the Guard Commander, heralding the General's arrival, brought us to the alert. After the inspection and congratulations from the General, a short service was held. It ended with a wonderful surprise – a conducted visit to the Chapel of the Knights of the Garter. It was a terrific thrill to see and have explained this lovely and sacred place, where every inch is so richly steeped in the history of our land.

(The above report, by A/T Sgt B Richardson, was first published in The Arborfield Apprentice, Volume II, Number 5, issued in July 1953.)

Col F A H Magee - an appreciation

Colonel F A H Magee assumed command of the School in June 1952, upon his return from Kenya, where he had commanded Nairobi Sub-area.

During the War, Col Magee was taken prisoner by the Japanese when Singapore Fortress fell on February 15th 1942. At that time he was DAAG, Malaya. He remained a prisoner of war in Changi Jail until his release in September 1945. During his incarceration, he was three times 'mentioned in dispatches'. In November 1946 he was appointed to command the 1st Battalion, The East Surrey Regiment, in Greece, where he remained until 1949.

Col Magee identified himself with every School activity. He encouraged the School teams on pitch, track and at the wicket. He maintained that delicate balance between technical and regimental training and he took an intense interest in the progress of every boy in the School. His memory for faces and names was unerring and his intimate knowledge of individual histories quite incredible. It was always with great reluctance that Col Magee recommended the discharge of an apprentice, and only after every effort to retain him had been made.

It was through his unflagging interest that the School bands have achieved such a high standard of performance. Col Magee has been anxious that he should see a Division the whole way through the School and this he will achieve when 52B Intake passes out on July 21st 1955. He will be the first Commandant since the War to have succeeded in this aim.

Col Magee leaves the School to retire from the Service after thirty-four years. The best wishes of all ranks go with him, together with the hope that he will return to visit us frequently.

(The above appreciation was first published in The Arborfield Apprentice, Volume III, Number 3, issued in July 1955.)

The Advantages of an Army Apprenticeship

The Army tradesman says that a civilian apprenticeship is easier than an Army one, for the following reasons: in the first place, the civilian apprentice is nearly always at home and not away from his family during his off-work hours; secondly, he is able to go out any night he likes, because he is not confined to camp and liable for extra duties; lastly, neither has he kit to clean and parades to attend.

This is where the Army tradesman is being rather shortsighted because, in some civilian apprenticeships, the new apprentice is treated like an 'odd-job' boy. Usually for the first six months, his time is spent in picking up his trade through his own efforts. He may be in a firm that is keen on having good and expert tradesmen, so that he will have to attend evening classes several times a week to further his education.

While the civilian apprentice is serving his time for three and sometimes five years, working all day and having to attend classes at night, it is not going to be very pleasant for him. In an Army apprenticeship, he is taught his trade during the day, but then has the night free from educational duties, to use as he pleases. He may go to the NAAFI and the recreation room, where it is easy to relax and forget about work until the morrow.

An apprentice in civilian life does not have many holidays a year, whereas an Army tradesman has nearly nine weeks holiday each year. In this respect, an Army apprenticeship offers decided advantages.

Then comes the matter of pay. The Army tradesman once again has the advantage, because he is unable to go out during the week and so does not have to spend much money. Films are shown in the Camp cinema on Saturday and Sunday evenings for his entertainment. A small charge is made to pay for the films, but this is taken from the apprentice's 'credits' and he does not miss it.

In most cases, the Army apprenticeship is much more advantageous. The Army tradesmen are kept under constant supervision and are well looked after by physical training instructors. The best all-round tradesmen are promoted to be Apprentice NCOs. Some are able to go before a War Office Selection Board. If successful, they go to an Officer Cadet School and are commissioned.

The Army apprenticeship certainly offers chance upon chance of rising up through the ranks, with increases of pay all the time. Added to this is the knowledge of a trade, which will hold a soldier in good stead on his return to civilian life.

(The above article was attributed to a 3 Div apprentice in September 1954 and forty years later found its way into The Arborfield Apprentice of summer 1994.)

Army Apprentices' School Arborfield

The Readers will recall that, in the April Magazine of this year, we made a brief reference to the Army Apprentices' School Arborfield, which appeared under the heading 'Valuable Manpower comes to REME'. Since this date, the Commandant of the School, Colonel E L Percival DSO has kindly given permission for the REME Magazine to publish a commentary on the Training and Activities of the School.

This commentary, together with photographs of the boys taken during training, will, we feel sure, be of utmost interest to all, especially so to parents who have their son or sons actually at the school and to those parents who may be contemplating sending their boy to Arborfield.

Object of the School.

To produce the potential Warrant Officer and Senior NCO Tradesmen and Officer Technician.

Boys are admitted at school-leaving age and compete at entrance examinations held in July or December. The School term commences in February and September. Particulars of entry and terms of service may be obtained from Recruiting Offices, or from the Director of Military Training, MT3, War Office, or (from) AG10, War Office.

Trades taught at the Arborfield School are those of Fitter, Turner, Vehicle Mechanic, Armourer, Instrument Mechanic and Draughtsman (Mechanical). These are all first grade trades and receive the same period of training (three years). Other Schools are situated at

This aerial photograph shows the MRS and cricket pavilion and squares on the Sports fields

Harrogate and Chepstow, at which a variety of other trades are taught.

All first-term boys are kept together in HQ Company and, for the first four weeks, receive Military Training, which improves their bearing, appetite and physical fitness. Games and Physical Training form a large proportion of this initial training and continue throughout School life.

At the end of the initial four weeks' training period, the young apprentices are received and addressed by the Chief Instructor and taken into workshops to commence their Technical Training. First-term work consists of practice in the use of hand-tools, filing, chipping, drilling and fitting, with a short course of elementary carpentry interposed, the object of which is to give the young muscles and limbs respite from the continuous motion encountered in filing.

At the end of the first term, apprentices are again addressed by the Chief Instructor and given advice in their choice of trade. The apprentice's choice is scrutinised to ensure that the trade he has chosen is one

in which he may reasonably be expected to succeed. Apprentices who appear to have made an unsuitable choice are immediately interviewed and advised.

At the commencement of the second term, apprentices are moved to their appropriate trade departments and continue their basic engineering practice. They do not enter upon the theoretical commitments of their trades until the third term, by which time they have received the benefit of further education in the School and, being more matured, are able to absorb the theoretical training and appreciate its importance.

The Syllabus of each trade is progressive term by term. In addition to the main trades taught, courses are given in certain allied trades; e.g. apprentices engaged in the mechanical trades are given courses in Blacksmithing. Sheet metal Work, Welding and Machine Tools. Throughout his training, the apprentice is given instruction in Machine Drawing, Geometrical Projection and Workshop Practice. The selection of training as Draughtsmen is made from apprentices of

The Technical Drawing Department

the mechanical trades after the first year. Turners are selected after two years.

Education continues throughout the training period and is organised to correspond with the various trades e.g. the Motor Vehicle Mechanic receives educational training in the following main topics: Electricity and Magnetism, Mechanics, Mathematics; with additional instruction in History, Geography, English and General Knowledge. The Instrument Mechanic receives educational training in Heat, Sound, Mechanics, Mathematics, History, Geography, General Knowledge and English.

The apprentices in the various trades receive instruction in the particular Science subjects applicable to their trades, as well as up-to-date instruction in the more general subjects. Boys are therefore able to take City & Guilds of London examinations, followed by Forces Preliminary examinations.

All types of games are organised and encouraged in the School, inter-Company, inter-School and inter-Service competitions and meetings are arranged. School Colours are awarded to School representatives at sporting events. In addition to the time available for sport during weekends, each Company has a sports period during the week.

A canteen provides for the additional requirements of the apprentice, billiards and games rooms being incorporated in it. An extensive Library, containing a wide range of Fiction, Fact and Engineering books, is available to apprentices. A Hobbies Centre, containing tools and materials for the Model enthusiast is provided. Stamp, Photography, Cycling and Music Clubs provide relaxation and healthy exercise.

Two voluntary Bands, formed by apprentices, perform at parades and other functions. A Brass Band, fifty strong, is under the direction of a Band Master from Kneller Hall. A Pipe Band is under the direction of a Pipe Major.

The School is organised into a Headquarters Company and 'A', 'B', 'C', and 'D' Companies, one of which is known as Champion Company. Each Company is organised to administer itself, having its own Commander, Quartermaster Stores, Pay Office etc. Dining arrangements are communal, two large Dining Halls supplied by one Cookhouse catering for the needs of the School.

Each half-year, in July and February, the Senior Division apprentices pass out to join their Corps and the occasion is marked by a very impressive ceremony, presided over by a distinguished personage. Prizes are awarded for distinction in the various activities and training.

The School has an Old Boys' Association, which is growing stronger each year. A dinner is being held this year at the School, followed by a dance and a weekend of sporting fixtures.

In order that the apprentice and his parents can watch the progress made, term tests are held and a consolidated report is forwarded to parents. Two weeks' leave is given at Christmas and Easter and four weeks leave is given in the summer. During the term, apprentices are allowed out of the Camp, for periods according to the length and time they have been at the School. Arrangements are made for those apprentices who, for any reason, are unable to spend their leave with their parents or friends.

Successful apprentices leave the School to join their Corps, either REME or RE, as Class III Tradesmen and are already in possession of the Educational Certificates that enable them to qualify for promotion. It must then be the objective of the apprentice to qualify as soon as possible for Class II and Class I Tradesmen, after which he is eligible to apply for an Armament Artificer's Course. Successful completion of this course ensures immediate promotion to Staff Sergeant and it is quite possible for an apprentice to accomplish this within three years after leaving the School. The demand for Armament Artificers is great and, furthermore, trades taught at this School are recognised by Trade Unions.

(The above article was published in the September issue of the REME Magazine during 1950.)

One might be forgiven for thinking that the Ablutions with their showers, wash hand basins and toilet stalls were far better than those to be found in todays barrack room accommodation.

Army Apprentices School, Arborfield

'Christmas Concert'

Wednesday 16th December 1953 at 7.45 pm

'A' Coy presents:
'MERRIE ENGLAND'

Mrs Archer --- A/T Lewis
Dan Archer --- A/T Till
Richard (their Chief Serf) ------------------------ A/T Loftus
Other Serfs -- A/Ts Paton, Plant, Peacock, Pugh & Tidey
A Royal messenger -------------------------------- A/T Jackman
Merlin Monroe (A Wizard) ---------------------- A/Sgt Fleetwood
Charles Filth (His assistant) --------------------- A/T Sambrook
Members of Strodling Players ------------------- A/Ts Thompson, Pratt, Butler, Webb & Gibson
Sir Edmond Hilary --------------------------------- A/T Russell
Tensing (The Sherpa) ----------------------------- A/T Tha-Win
Kiwi-Dark-Tan ------------------------------------ A/T Tin Ohn.
(written & produced by S/SI Fincham & S/SI Havicon)

'C' Coy ENTERTAINMENT
The scene is set at a US Base on a South Pacific Island.

Announcer --- A/T Bennett
Top Sgt. Schiaparelli ----------------------------- A/Cpl Barnes
Medical Combat Team ----------------------------- A/Ts Holmes & Newton
The Skeleton --------------------------------------- A/T Deputron
Colonel - US Army --------------------------------- A/Cpl Giles
2nd Lt - British Army ----------------------------- A/T Jackson
L/Cpl - British Army ------------------------------ A/T Royle
Harmonica Players -------------------------------- A/Ts Morey, Oates & Henry
Cpl - US Army ------------------------------------- A/T Brown
G.Is - US Army ------------------------------------ A/Ts Wilson, Bennett, Eales, Smith, McLeod & Sinclair
Bathing Belles ------------------------------------- A/Cpl Clucas, A/Ts Goldie, Neil, Lagden, Deighton,
                                                       A/Ts Potter, Kidd & Barwick
Stage Manager ------------------------------------- A/T Bennett
Stage Hands --------------------------------------- A/Ts Smith & Stewart

'B' Company
Presents
'THREAD O' SCARLETT'
A Play in One Act
By J. J. Bell

Migsworth -- Vitel
Smith -- Harding
Butters-- Mills
Landlord of the Inn ------------------------------ Mills
Breen, an odd job man -------------------------- Hayhurst
A Traveller --------------------------------------- Johnson
Produced by ------------------------------------- D Bagley & J B Smith
Stage Manager ---------------------------------- D Furlong
Lighting -- Hawes & Adams
Make-up -- Hyde
Sound Effects ----------------------------------- Clark & McClachlan

Scene: Smoke room of a small village inn. An evening in February, about 20 minutes from closing time. The villagers are discussing the fate of one Jacob Forge, their neighbour, who has been hanged for the brutal murder of Farmer Jukes.
Time: When hangings were a public spectacle.

'THE HQ COMPANY SHOW'

1. "ZING ZING" -------------------------------- Chorus
2. "WHEN DAY IS DONE" -------------------- A/Sgt Lenihan & A/Cpl Stubberfield
3. "SWING NUMBERS" ----------------------- A/T Lane at the piano
4. "TWO FRONT TEETH" ------------------- A/T Berriman with A/T O'Dell on piano
5. "HIGHLAND DANCE" -------------------- A/T Davies
6. "ANSWER ME" AND "I BELIEVE" ----- A/T Johnson with A/T O'Dell on piano
7. "COCONUTS" ----------------------------- Full Chorus

(The above programme was contributed by Alan Morton (51B) and this is his note which accompanied it.

Whilst sorting through some old papers I came across a tattered old sheet of paper with almost obliterated typing on both sides. Thinking it was part of the Dead Sea Scrolls, I examined it further and guess what? it was the programme for the Christmas Concert held in the Camp Hall in December 1953. It was such poor quality that I painstakingly reproduced it and here it is. I have copied it as it is, warts and all. Some old names leapt at me from the sheet ---Till, Loftus, Jackman, Tidey, Fleetwood, Burmese boys, Barnes, Deputron, Brown(must be PFC!), Clucas, Barwick, Mills, Hayhurst, Lenihan, Stubberfield and Lane. I remember being App/CSM of HQ Coy and C/H "Donkey" Wilcox telling me to search the Coy for talent and get some acts together. This we did and it was fantastic!! One guy who stands out in my memory was "Jazz" Lane, a terrific piano player. I didn't meet him again until 1992 and Bernie Lane was the key man in the PRI Office in Arborfield. On passing out from AAS he went into the Sappers and came out a Major.)

—§—

.......and yet another batch of apprehensive newcomers pass through the hallowed gates.

Chapter 5

1956 - 59

The Miller Report

The 'PoP' that took place on January 31ˢᵗ 1956 was notable for its 'wet weather' routine – and amazingly, this was the very first time on which it had been utilised since the opening of the School. The early morning's intermittent rain gradually turned to sleet and snow, necessitating a smart manouvre indoors for the inspection of Senior Div and the presentation of awards. It is ironic that the camera crews of both the *BBC* and the fairly new *Independent Television (ITV)* had chosen that day to record the occasion for their millions of viewers.

In his post-parade address, the Commandant made reference to the long-awaited publication of the *'White Paper on Boys' Units'*, otherwise known as the *'Miller Report'*. The document had led to the appointment of a Director of Boys' Training and the setting-up of a Standing Committee at the War Office. The Committee's deliberations were still awaited, but some of the proposed recommendations were already being implemented – such as the welcome arrival of the School's first ever resident WVS lady, the inestimable Miss Josephine Gunning. Many happy hours were to follow for her boys, spent in the warmth and comfort of the WVS lounge, reading newspapers and magazines, or listening to gramophone records over a cup of hot, sweet tea.

Longer tenures at the School were now expected for members of the military staff, providing the benefits of continuity and a more settled outlook, while larger *per capita* grants were now available for the provision of sports equipment and other amenities. Col Cole also welcomed the arrival at the School of a number of boys from the Royal West African Armed Forces (RWAAF), the first ever to do so from their country. Boys from Burma had already been attending the School for a long period, with great success. School Chaplain the Rev J P Morgan was pleased to announce that the rite of 'Confirmation' had been carried out for twenty-nine boys on January 27ᵗʰ.

By that year, large steel locker-wardrobes had almost entirely replaced the old wooden types, as well as any remaining wall-lockers. Some rooms had them placed along the walls, usually at the expense of the windows; others placed them between bed-spaces, thus providing the occupants with a little privacy – depending upon the whim of the Room NCOs no doubt! *(What are you doing behind there, Scroggins?)* Both literally and figuratively, these larger lockers presented a larger problem – they took up a prodigious amount of floor-space and gave the rooms a much more cluttered appearance, as well as making them that much darker, due to the lack of daylight coming in. Another old 'barrack-room institution' – the 'White Cupboard' – had also disappeared by this time, mainly due to the application of a coat of paint of one colour or another. These cupboards could now be recognised by the description of 'utensil cabinet' or 'broom cupboard'.

A lesson in survivial

One of the first intake of that year (56A) was Bob 'Wally' Walters. He 'thinks' he was in 'A' Coy – though he may be mistaken! Wally reports that if he said he enjoyed his time here, it would mean that he was wearing *"rose coloured spectacles of the thickest kind"*. He recalls his Arborfield experience as *"a lesson in survival, which stood me in good stead in later life"*. Thankfully, he didn't find everything as bad as he first indicated, finding the opportunities for sport to be *"unrivalled for that time"*. Technical education he found to be *"first class"*, with perhaps the exception of one particular RAEC instructor who was *"heartily detested"*. *(That couldn't possible be dear Stan Cocking, could it? Ed.)*

Wally recollects that the biggest cause of misery was being kept within the confines of the barracks for such long periods at a time. From a personal point of view, he found it very restrictive. He recalls spending many a day on the football pitch behind the Camp Hall, wistfully gazing at the cars passing by in complete freedom. However, what really gladdened his heart was the end-of-term parade to collect his 'credits', saved on his behalf from his weekly wage. *(Remember those big white £5 notes? – now that was **real** money!*

Ed.) Wally recalls visiting the barber shop at Reading Station, where a close 'cut-throat' shave, followed by the luxury of a steaming-hot napkin and a splash of some sweet-smelling lotion, could be all his – or yours - for the sum of half-a-crown (twelve and a half pence). That's when he felt truly free – on his way home on leave.

Perhaps some of the 'hardship' endured by Wally paid off in the end because, in 1961, he reported to 22 Special Air Service (SAS) for a selection course! He served with the SAS for a few years before being transferred to the Parachute Brigade, then rejoined the SAS permanent cadre until retiring in 1986.

Presentation Parades were *de rigeur* during the spring term of 1956. On March 4th, two LSGC Medals were presented to members of the PS, one to AQMS F T Wood, REME and the second to the CSM of 'C' Coy, WO2 D J 'Duggie' Huxley MM of the Grenadier

A/T Ian Walker 56B 'D' Coy - a smart soldier!

Guards. Both of these School stalwarts had started off their Army service as 'boy soldiers'. AQMS Wood had joined the RAOC as an apprentice Fitter in 1937 and was one of those boys later evacuated from Hilsea to Arborfield in 1940, in order to complete his training. He had been posted back to the School as an instructor in 1952, following service in the Middle East, Sicily and Italy, where he had been attached to a tank troops workshop with the Polish Armoured Brigade.

CSM 'Duggie' Huxley also joined the Army in 1937, as a 'Drummer Boy' with the Grenadiers. Upon the formation of the Guards Armoured Division in 1942, he fought with them all across Europe, being awarded his Military Medal (MM) for 'bravery in action' at Munster in 1945. After further service in Palestine, Germany and North Africa, he was medically downgraded and selected for extra regimental employment with the Army Apprentices' Schools, coming to Arborfield in 1955. He became a great favourite with the boys under his command and it is believed that he later served on the staff of Black Rod, as an administrator at the House of Commons.

A second Parade, on May 13th, saw MSMs presented to another two of Arborfield's staff. The first went to AQMS E J R Burlison REME, who had joined the Army as an A/T at Chepstow as far back as 1929, passing into the RAOC in 1932. He later served with 7 Armoured Division, the famous 'Desert Rats', and showed devotion to duty beyond the normal whilst repairing tanks during the historic battle at El Alamein. The second recipient was WO2 A Brady, Irish Guards, CSM of 'HQ' Coy. He had joined up in 1932 and was engaged in the evacuation of Her Majesty (HM) the Queen of the Netherlands from Belgium in June 1940. He had joined the School here in 1948 and had previously been awarded the BEM in 1954.

Only five months after the fatal incident at the nearby *Rainbow Firework Factory*, which had eventually left three people dead and fourteen injured, a second explosion took place in May of 1956. Apart from the demolition of the one shed where the event took place and severe burning to the arm of one unfortunate male worker, there was no damage to the rest of the site.

The injured man was rushed into the MRS within the boys' school and, after some initial treatment, was taken on to Battle Hospital in Reading. Once again, both boys and staff from the School rushed to offer assistance, along with fire-fighting equipment,

1957 Cross Country Team with Col Cole and Major Campbell M.C.
Rear & Centre SSgt H Evans who served in the Vehicle Wing for many years and front right Jim Fox.

but thankfully the incident was nowhere as serious as the preceding one in December 1955. Following that almighty blast, certain safety procedures had been carried out, thus limiting the amount of damage that could occur. However, the fact that a second explosion took place so soon after the first must have caused no small amount of concern amongst the next-door neighbours in the AAS! *(It also galvanised the Home Office to carry out an investigation into safety procedures. Ed.)*

End of the McNally era

An outstanding figure in the history of the School finally departed its gates in July 1956, when RSM R L McNally, MBE, Scots Guards, retired after a full, and never to be repeated, fifteen years as its Regimental Sergeant Major. Altogether, the RSM had served a full thirty-two years. To quote *The Arborfield Apprentice - the School magazine -* of that time, *"No member of staff had played such an important role in the life of the School over such a long period".* The Commandant

added a few words of his own regarding the outgoing RSM, saying that he had *"identified himself with every phase of School activities".* Indeed, Mr McNally's son had himself passed through the School as an apprentice. The RSM's ramrod military bearing had always been his trademark and most boys stood in both awe and respect of him. In tribute to him, he became the very first Honorary Life Member of the OBA.

(Further details regarding RSM McNally can be found in separate annexes to this chapter.)

His replacement was RCM (Regimental Corporal Major) J T Sallis, of the Royal Horse Guards (RHG). His Regiment had been amongst those troops who had gone ashore in Normandy some three weeks after D-Day, and pushed on right through to the heart of Germany itself, where Mr Sallis then remained until 1952. He took up his post here after a short tour on the sunny Mediterranean island of Cyprus. Col Cole wished him *"as long and fruitful a stay as his predecessor"*, but of course history will show that

A/T Bilcliffe passing the finishing line

nobody served as long as RSM McNally did! Later that same year, an establishment change here at the School permitted a much-needed improvement to officer manning, in the form of an Assistant Adjutant and Company 2I/Cs.

(Further details regarding RCM Sallis can also be found in a separate annex to this chapter.)

Brian Conway (42A) was back at the School as an instructor at the time and had the pleasure of attending RSM McNally's Farewell Dinner, where he formally handed over to RCM Sallis. Handing over a pace-stick to the incoming RCM, he good-humouredly asked him, *"Would a donkey walloper know what to do with it?"* Brian adds that he never did see Mr Sallis carry the pace-stick, as a riding crop, plus riding breeches and boots, was far more his style. Often mistaken for an officer, the RCM would draw many a smart salute – some of which earned him a few extra pints at the Mess bar!

Joe Kinson, also a PS member in those days, and now a keen honorary Old Boy, is proud to have served here under the regimes of both RSM McNally and RCM Sallis. It had been Mr McNally who introduced Joe into the Sergeants' Mess on his promotion, and then kept a *"fatherly eye"* on him afterwards. Joe remembers that he met up with John Sallis on a couple of further occasions, the last one being when serving at Catterick, Yorkshire, a few years later. By this time, John had gained his commission, served out his time and retired from his last posting as a Major. He was then working as a Range Warden on the range at Warcop.

Middle Eastern mishaps

Although the next story apparently only came to light many years after the event, it brings to mind that in 1956 there was an altercation in the Middle East which could have caused another major war, this being the Suez Canal debacle of that year. Following a British interest in Egypt ever since 1882, it had finally been agreed that British forces would be withdrawn entirely from Egyptian soil by June 17th. But the Egyptian President, Colonel Gamal Nasser, had nationalised the Suez Canal in July of that year, and Anglo-French forces were sent to gain control of this vital waterway as 'a matter of life and death'. REME Airborne Forces were to find November 5th a true 'Guy Fawkes' occasion as they jumped into action, but the whole affair later fizzled out when American backing was not forthcoming and our troops had to face an ignominious withdrawal.

Peter Langley, one of the *'1941 one hundred'* was, by the time of his tale, a WO2 in REME, *en route* to the Suez war-zone by way of Cyprus. He recalls that, whilst on the island, he was driving an Austin *Champ* vehicle, Britain's disastrous attempt to emulate the American *Jeep*. He says that he probably shouldn't have been driving, as per current regulations, but that as they had just been *"placed on a war footing"*, perhaps it didn't matter.

However, what ***did*** matter was that he and his passengers were involved in an accidental collision with a much heavier vehicle. Peter himself suffered a nasty knock on the head, recovering to find himself pinned beneath the vehicle by the locating clips of the folded-down windscreen. Following some assistance from other soldiers who quickly arrived upon the scene,

Peter was somehow extricated from the overturned *Champ*, still bleeding profusely from his wounded arm. One of his helpers, a Battery Sergeant Major named Ernie Lambert, obviously having been trained in First Aid and remembering the cardinal rule of 'reassure your patient', did just that with the well remembered phrase, *"Effing 'ell, Pete!"* – which manual had Ernie been reading, we wonder?

A surgeon at a nearby Field Ambulance station eventually sewed up Peter's arm in deft manner, though he tended to be a bit short on sympathy. Standing back in admiration of his own needlework, he admonished Peter with the words, *"I suppose you were driving too fast"*. Any attempt at argument was cut short by the fact that, as an Army officer, the surgeon outranked him. Anyway, Peter obviously survived his ordeal and was able to eventually write his story on the pages of *OBAN Issue 21*, in 2000.

In July 1956, the School magazine paid tribute to Maj John Biddulph for his unstinting and loyal support for the School Athletics team over many previous years. In the scribe's words at the time, *"It must indeed be hard for many past athletes to visualise a meeting at Arborfield less the familiar figure, the moustache, the 'hat' and the famous stage whisper – not to mention the stentorian Biddulph bellow of encouragement, which has wafted so many past the finishing line"*.

Maj Biddulph's departure for the sunnier climes of Jamaica in the West Indies must have provided a welcome and deserved reward for his much-appreciated efforts here at Arborfield. In athletic terms, he 'handed over the baton' to Maj H N Yarde-Martin of the Royal Lincolnshire Regt, who had just taken up his appointment as Military Training Officer.

The editorial comment in that magazine was the last to be written by that particular editor. As he sat, pen in hand, the rain was pouring down as usual outside his window, on a tented but deserted School sports-field. Had it been fine, that field would have been thronged with competitors at the annual Champion Company sports day but, alas, it was not to be. The School had been most unfortunate that year, in that some continuous shocking weather had played havoc with its sporting fixtures.

The game of golf had been introduced into the School a few months previously and, by July, the Golf Club had seen much development. The most significant factor had been the introduction of a visiting professional from Calcot Golf Club in Reading, his fees being paid by the Golf Foundation. This had meant some proper coaching for all members and the provision of both new and second-hand clubs at reduced prices. It was intended that the practice ground would be converted into a nine-hole course in the near future and that eventually golf should join the list of inter-School sports.

By 1956, the School's Cycling Club was able to boast *"a full membership"*, although a large number of those members were still classed as *"inactive"*. A representative team had competed at the Southern Command Championship, at which A/T Beaumont had carried off the Novices' Prize, while friendly matches had taken place against teams from the neighbouring No's 3 and 5 Trg Btns. Now that the sport had been included in the Quadrangular Tournament, the 'wheelers' looked forward to pitting themselves against the other Apprentices' Schools.

Band Sergeant Tony Domoney

*Pete 'Scouse' Gripton, our erstwhile author
and editor, climbing the ladder to success*

The Band - at work and play

Many changes had been taking place within the membership of the Military Band, but members hastened to tell all old boys that they were *"on the upward path to great success"*. Sgt Wells of the 10th Hussars had left a large gap in January, leaving after two-and-a-half years in charge, his post being temporarily filled by Sgt Connors of the RASC. But the arrival in May of a new Band Sergeant had greatly encouraged the Band. Sgt Backley of the Inniskillings, and late of the RE Staff Band at Chatham, had great experience and enthusiasm, which were now having the desired effect. 'Number 1 Dress' had now been issued to the Band and was worn for the first time on

the Queen's Birthday Parade on May 31st. And, at long last, the Military and Pipe Bands had succeeded in playing a combined march, which it was hoped would form the *finale* of subsequent 'Retreats'.

August provided a hectic period for the Bands as they raced against time to prepare for two television broadcasts scheduled to take place within two days of each other. Rehearsals were held at almost every available moment, taking place under conditions as near to the real thing as possible. The first BBC programme was from Earl's Court, as part of an exhibition on Youth Organisations. Despite some technical problems – such as mixing up entrances and exits – the eventual performance was *"near perfect"* and the boys all returned to Camp very tired, but in high spirits.

Two days later, August 25th, saw the Bands entertaining the crowds at Chessington Zoo, as part of an outside broadcast by ITV. During both of these appearances, the Bands were most grateful for the services of some *"very new old boys"*, who had only passed out in July. Many thanks went to Capt I D MacHorton of the Cameronians, who had done an impressive amount of fieldwork in his post as Bands President.

Pete 'Scouse' Gripton finally arrived at the Arborfield Gates in August 1956. He uses the term 'finally' because he had actually reported to the Recruiting Office in Ranleagh Square, Liverpool, the previous day, having said his family farewells and fully expecting to travel that day. However, when he was given his train warrant, it turned out to be for the following day, and he had to catch the bus back home. His Mum burst into tears when he arrived back, thinking he'd been rejected!

When he at last walked through the Gates, suitcase in hand and mackintosh over his arm, he was glared at by a menacing figure who was 'digging weeds' outside the Guardroom. This turned out to be a lad on CB, who went by the name of John 'Dinger' Bell. Dinger then asked Pete where he was from, and at the mention of *"Liverpool"*, the menacing glare became a welcoming smile. It turned out that they were almost neighbours in their home city and leave periods after that saw the two of them strutting about their district in leather jackets and blue jeans. This was very much in the mode of the day, after all they **had** been to see *'The Tommy Steele Story'* – but not quite what the Commandant would have recommended!

Saved - by the Band

Also arriving as a 'new boy' at that time was Tony Domoney, who initially struggled to come to terms with his new way of life. The endless round of parades, inspections, fatigues and general 'bullshine' left him less than impressed and, after his first six months, *"going home to Mum"* seemed very much on the cards. But the prospect of somehow joining 'the Band' was to become both an inspiration and eventual salvation for him. He had already *"suffered"* about six months of tutelage on the piano at home, not very successfully if the truth be known, but at least having learned to read music, he thought that a musical future would be of benefit.

He went along to volunteer and soon found himself attempting to blow the trumpet - apparently his lips weren't quite right for the saxophone! It wasn't long before his skills were being sharpened under the tutelage of Sgt Backley and life became more settled and serene. Indeed, Tony even began now to enjoy the parades, happy to be playing the music that encouraged the other boys to step out proudly in step and swing their arms to the sound of the Band.

Lawrence 'Larry' Jarvis had travelled by himself from his home in Peterborough that August, a journey which seemed endless to him. He arrived at Wokingham railway station to be met by a sergeant and then driven to Arborfield in the back of an old *Morris* truck. Entering the Guardroom at around 18.00 hours, Larry was told to get himself down to the Cookhouse for a 'late meal'. He dragged all his worldly possessions behind him in a battered old suitcase and approached the hotplate. His meal was put in front of him, a couple of slices of greasy fried bread and a helping of what seemed like at least three tins of baked beans! *"There's no way I can eat all that"*, he thought, but he was wrong!

Having been brought up at boarding school, life in the barrack-room held no real terror for Larry. But, later that evening, having been taught how to 'stand by your bed', he and hid room-mates were asked the inevitable question, *"Who smokes?"* A few of the lads answered in the affirmative and were invited to throw their cigarettes onto their beds, Larry's contained in a splendid case, a leaving present from his mother. All the cigarettes were then confiscated in the usual manner, as the boys were told that they were too young to smoke.

Larry's stay at AAS came to an abrupt halt in 1958,

for reasons he prefers to keep to himself, and he was transferred to Blandford as a non-qualified tradesman. Here he completed his basic training, before moving on to Barton Stacey on a driving course. More training, at Bordon, completed Larry's education and he was now qualified at his chosen trade of Recovery Mechanic (Recy Mech). He eventually reached the rank of Sergeant, the *"top dog"* in that trade at the time, before finally deciding to transfer to the RD roll in order to gain further promotion. Serving a further nine years, he ended up as a WO2 (RQMS), which he reckons *"not bad for an AAS failure"*! Larry now lives at Wisbech, where he dabbles in digital photography, supports his local REME Association – and has recently joined the OBA after an absence of many years.

The ninth annual Reunion of the OBA was held in late August that year, with rising costs having forced up the price of the Saturday evening dinner to a princely seven shillings and sixpence! With dinner timed for 19.30 hours and a 'Dance and Smoker' due to start at 20.30 hours, the meal was obviously a bit of a 'rush job', when compared to the grand occasions that take place in the present day.

The *REME Magazine* published in October 1956 contained a story under the title of *"The oldest Soldier in the Corps"*. It was the fictional account of a REME soldier, having served for thirty-nine years, being seen off from his last unit by no less than the Commanding Officer, Adjutant, RSM and, indeed, most of the unit! The author was Sgt R O Holles, and this may well have been his first venture into the world of authorship, as his name was to crop up quite often in the years to come.

'Scouse' Gripton taking up his trade of Radar Mech seen here on top of a 3Mk7 Radar set

A/T Stephen Sam (Gold Coast) adjusting the hat of A/T Sunday Abasi (Nigeria)

New format for School magazine

In the newly enlarged format Christmas 1956 edition of *The Arborfield Apprentice*, another tribute was paid, this time to two former members of staff who had retired earlier that year. Mr F E Luff had been employed with Her Majesty's Forces and the War Department for a total of forty-seven years, and was awarded the Imperial Service Medal. His career had culminated in almost fifteen years at the School. Colleague Mr G A Erskine had been a long-time Armourer, since joining the Army as a boy in 1906 and serving for thirty years. He had found employment at the Armourers Training Branch RAOC, down at Hilsea, near Portsmouth, before eventually moving up here to Arborfield.

Another article in that issue gave a brief history of the long-established trade of 'Armourer'. Those individuals with a 'knowledge of arms' had been first sought for employment, at regimental level, as long ago as the beginning of 1802. A War Office circular had asked commanding officers to *"state names of such men in the regiment as from the knowledge in the construction of arms, may in your opinion be qualified for the situation of regimental armourer"*.

In order to ensure their better competence, in 1843 these individuals were commanded to undergo a type of 'trade test' at the Manufactory of Small Arms. By 1858, a 'Royal Warrant' from Queen Victoria had authorised the setting up of the 'Corps of Armourer Sergeants', which was based upon the Small Arms Factory at Millbank (London), and which was subsequently transferred up to Birmingham in 1889. This Corps finally came to an end when it was absorbed into the Army Ordnance Corps around 1894 - 95.

The training of enlisted boys as apprentice Armourers commenced at Birmingham in 1904, then returned to London, at Enfield Lock, two years later. Here the training remained for the best part of twenty years. Finally, in 1923, it was moved down to Hilsea and became the 'Armourers Training Branch' of the RAOC School of Instruction. When this unit itself became dispersed, following the outbreak of World War II, Armourer Apprentices finally ended up here at the newly set up ATS (Boys), Arborfield, in 1940.

The 'Fitters, Turners and Ancillaries' Department reported that the boys under instruction were *"settling down well to chipping and filing, despite heavy demands on the first aid box"*. The lads of 55A had been occupying themselves with pneumatic equipment and the greatest wonder was that this equipment was still functioning! The powers-that-be had decided to introduce the new trade of 'Fitter Gun', with the intention of providing quicker promotion prospects for apprentices. Two newly installed instructors, SSgts Loftus and Crowther, were ex-boys of the School and thus well equipped for the task.

The OBA under threat

In that same 1956 School magazine, Col John Cole expressed some mounting concern about the waning strength and viability of the OBA. He felt that, for a School which had been in existence then for over sixteen years, its OBA was *"not as flourishing as it should be"* and that a *"really keen OBA could be a tremendous asset"*. He would be pleased no doubt to know that, more than forty years later, despite some fairly lean times along the way, his concerns had been allayed and that the Association continued to flourish well into the following Millennium.

No doubt the Commandant's concerns regarding the OBA were keenly felt 'close to home', and taken to heart, because December 1956 saw the issue of the very first *'OBAN'* – the *'Old Boys' Association Newsletter'*. Ex-Commandant Col J D White, DSO, MC, was the serving President of the OBA, and he included the following words in his opening message to that first *OBAN*:

"Its primary object is to enable you to keep in touch, not only with your Old School, but with those who were your contemporaries there. As boys together, you got to know each other as you will know few other men. From among them you have made friends who will remain your friends for life. Such friendships are made because each party sees in the other qualities that he admires and respects. So it comes about that each one influences the other for good."

Such sentiments obviously still hold true today and the pages of the regular newsletter bear testament to the camaraderie built up amongst the boys (and now girls) at the School – and later College, of course - during their period of time spent here.

That first issue also paid a respectful tribute to RSM McNally, who had finally retired from the Army in July 1956 after thirty-two years of loyal service. It was also able to report that the OBA accounts at the time were 'in the black' to the tune of some £120! Amongst the announcements in the magazine's editorial was the fact that W E 'Bill' Pusey (46A and he of the 1947 'Toy Soldiers' fame) had become the proud father of a 'son and heir' the previous August. An amazing coincidence was that both Bill and his son had been born in the very same hospital on the island of Malta, with Bill's date of birth having been in 1930.

The same magazine put forward some forthright questions, which are still relevant at the time of writing (2001!), under the heading of ***"Who Remembers . . ."***

"When the Commandant's trousers were found behind 'F2' mirror?"

"General Montgomery's visit, before making his name in North Africa?"

"The 1943 Gymkhana, memorable for the blackout shutter 'castle'?"

"'Bandy' Nel, in all his finery and 'Gilbert', standing quite still whilst the clowns went through their antics?"

"The RSM's teeth dropping out on parade?"

"A lecture on the functions of a fountain, explained to the School in a 'hollow square', the day following a certain film show?"

"The tree at the top of the square?"

"The interest which 'Reveille' (a magazine of the day) took in the School, following an article by a would-be aspirant to civvy street?"

"'Agriculture', with 'Gilbert' taking the lion's share of cake and boys pulling the plough?"

"When 'Gilbert' fell into the water-tank?"

"'Hotchkiss' being chaired from a football match and finishing up in a ditch?"

"Matchsticks being collected in bundles of ten and then whitewashed?""

"The bugles which disappeared and turned up in the static water-tank, resulting in no 'defaulters' being played that night?"

(Answers on a postcard if you please, share them with your mates, but do not forward them to the editor of this history! Ed.)

A little prairie flower

Sgt Budd A, REME – and boasting a regimental number of 14469751 – contributed what he called *"a true story"*. From the gist of his article, he was obviously an ex-apprentice, as he referred to himself as *"a Jeep"*. While a search through the pages of that very same *OBAN* reveals a *"List of Life Members"*, of whom 'Budd A' is shown to be an ex-member of 46A. During his initial training period, now dating back some ten years, he had been called to the *"High Temple"*, by which he meant one of the 6 Div barrack rooms! A piece of paper was thrust into his sweaty little hand and he was told to *"Sing this!"* It was hardly an invitation he could refuse so, to the delight of the assembled 'giants', young Budd sang the following:

"I was a little prairie flower
Growing wilder by the hour,
No one cared a jot for me
But I was as happy as could be!"

Hardly the stuff of Byron, Keats or Shakespeare of course, but it certainly amused the senior boys. Our hero was then sent on an errand to another Company, to see a certain Corporal. He would present the Corporal with a chit, which was now handed over to him, whereby he would receive, from the Corporal, a *"Bolorometer"*. Young Budd then 'did the rounds' of the Camp, being set from one far place to another, in his search for the mythical Bolorometer! He eventually arrived at one of the PS Sergeant's bunk, where the penny finally dropped! He had been sent on a wild goose chase! Fortunately, the Sergeant was a friendly chap, who told our hero just what a Bolorometer was – *"a gadget for measuring the cheekiness of Jeeps like you!"* He never got the fabled instrument – but he did get a mug of tea and a selection of cakes for his pains!

Another article in that *OBAN* was submitted by a Cfn W Gibson, whom we shall have to assume was another of our ex-boys. He reported on his attachment to the 50th Gurkha Field Engineering Regt, stationed in Kuala Lumpur – the famous 'KL' – and busily building a road *"through dense and terrorist infected jungle"*. Despite the obvious dangers, he reflected upon the *"advantages that Army service has over civilian life ... ... the multiplicities of jobs that one is called upon to perform"*. Cfn Gibson was quick to add that the majority of his fellow workers were young men who had been called up for their National Service.

It was intake 54A that passed out of the School at the end of January 1957, under the admiring eyes of the Inspecting Officer, Lt Gen Sir James Cassells KBE, CB, DSO, who was the Director General of Military Training (DGMT), and led by A/T RSM Endersby. A surprisingly large audience watched the parade, especially when the miserable weather and petrol shortages were taken into account. However, the rain did little to dampen the spirits of the boys who were taking their place in the adult Army.

February's *REME Magazine* gave news that the REME Boys at Blackdown were making good progress. Trade training was now being given in the three trades of Clerk, Storeman and Regimental Instructor. As these same trades were being taught to the RAOC Boys, there was no conflict of interest. By the beginning of the previous term, grouping of the REME Boys into two Companies had also begun.

On Saturday 16th February, the Southern Counties Cross-country Association held an extremely large meeting for its annual championships, at Youths, Junior and Senior levels. The races all took place at the racecourse at Epsom Downs, with the School entering a team of eight young runners in the Youths race, against what looked like a fearsome list of other entries from all across the south-eastern area of the country.

Boys then passing through the Armourers' Shop had made some *"interesting and instructive visits"*. In March, members of 2 & 3 Divs were taken to the RSAF at Enfield Lock, where, at one time, **all** Army armourers had served their apprenticeship. In addition to seeing the proofing and testing of a variety of weapons, the boys were given an insight into the history and development of small arms and machine guns over the years. The following month took boys from the Senior Div to the School of Infantry at Warminster, where they attended a live firing demonstration. A recent visitor to the Shop had been ex-apprentice Bob Holles, who had returned to the School during research in his new career as an author.

A letter received early in 1957 came from Sgt N Toyer, an ex-boy then serving with the King's African Rifles out at the Command Workshop in Nairobi, Kenya. He had seen his name published in the first *OBAN*, referring to him as '46B' and was hastening to correct this to the correct intake of '45A'. He went on to give some details of his life out in Africa, before reminding anyone who remembered him that, whilst at the School, he had answered to the nickname 'Carlos'. He added that Sgt Dransfield had referred to him instead as 'Notorious', due to the fact that during a period of some sixteen months, he had spent a full 257 days on jankers! *(Surely no one will want to brag about breaking that particular record – or would they? Ed.)*

A well-kept secret!

George Vince arrived at Arborfield as a member of 57A, seemingly 'on the horns of a dilemma'. The RCM at the School, John Sallis, was none other than the same gentleman that he had come to know as 'Uncle John' over a number of previous years! George's father was himself a Staff Sergeant in the REME, attached to the RHG, who over a period of years had become an almost permanent member of that unit. This was due to the very salient fact that he had kept all the Guards officers' cars in good shape and at a very reasonable cost! Thus 'Staff Vince' and John Sallis had known each other for some time, both in Germany and in Cyprus.

George meanwhile had gone to school with the RCM's two daughters, Ann and Valerie, and at one time had committed the ultimate sin of destroying Mr Sallis's crop of prize rhubarb! Having now joined the Army himself, George thought that he may be in for a hard time and, when he was ordered to report to the RCM's office, shortly after arriving here at the Apprentices' School, he just 'knew' that his number was up. It turned out however that Mr Sallis wanted it to be known that George would be treated just like any other A/T, as long as he never let on about the established relationship. Another reason, of course, was that if the other boys had known that George was a 'surrogate nephew' of the RCM, then a certain amount of unwarranted retribution might well have been extracted!

When the Orderly Sergeant one evening told George to report to the RCM's house for 'special fatigues', it became the first of many such visits, when the actual purpose of the visit was for a slap-up meal in family surroundings. Of course this was never revealed to anyone else, in fact George's mates always thought that George's 'special fatigues' were something that they were grateful enough to give a miss! When George later moved to 'D' Coy, he found that the 'CSM' was actually Squadron Corporal Major (SCM) Jack Cosgrove, another Guardsman from the RHG.

Thus it was that George spent his three years here at Arborfield under the watchful eyes of not one, but two, 'guardian angels'. Some may say that he was a lucky so-and-so, but in fact George reckons that he always had to be just that little bit smarter and shinier than was the norm, and that in not always achieving this, he spent more hours on 'Rodeo' than he cares to remember!

Another arrival for intake 57A was Jim Cliff, who had flown in from Hong Kong. He has now returned even further than that and lives in the land of 'Aussie Rules' – or no rules! - Football. By his own admission, Jim was one of those who maintained a very low profile at boys' school – most of it *"hiding in the Band-room, particularly avoiding all sporting activities like the plague"*. As he was to remark many years later, perhaps he should have *"dropped (his) trade and transferred to music, as one or two did"*. Jim reckons that he was *"totally boring"* during his teenage years at Arborfield – he never tried to book out in 'drains' or draped jacket, outlandish colours or 'brothel creepers'. He was almost always on time and hardly ever went to *'Smokey Joe's'*; he didn't possess an illicit motorcycle in somebody's shed in Wokingham and, although he *"smoked like a trooper"*, he never took to the delights of alcohol. In fact it was years before he could actually have a drink and remain upright and coherent!

Jim goes on to recall that the only 'sport' he ever excelled at was skiving off them, so much so that he became an expert. As soon as the footballers, boxers and athletes were dismissed to kick, assault and pursue each other, he would *"slide as inconspicuously as possible from view and disappear"*! Not for nothing did our Jim gain his nickname of *"The Tweed"*. Still, it is refreshing to know that there is someone who will admit to not being your usual apprentice – but there will no doubt be many in 'A' Coy who will now say, *"Jim Who?"*

The Yorktown Gates

It was during 1957, following a request from Maj Gen Urquhart, the Commandant of the RMAS, that a set of new gates for the Academy's Yorktown entrance was manufactured, over a number of months, by members of staff and apprentices under instruction in the Blacksmith's Shop here at the School. Originally, Col Cole had harboured some grave doubts as to whether this task was a suitable one to be taken on by the School, but a chat with the Chief Instructor, Lt Col Harold Woolley, subsequently changed his mind and the prestigious project was given the go-ahead. As reported in the second issue of the *OBAN*, it had been *"a mammoth task, on something diverse from the usual run of events ... ... a fitting tribute to the skill and ingenuity of its makers"*.

Special mention was made at the time of civilian instructor, Mr E C 'Busty' Lay, whose vast knowledge and experience with forge and anvil had proved invaluable. Peter Brunnen was the CI's draughtsman at the time and had the honour and pleasure of doing a lot of the design work and drawings for the project.

Peter had himself been an apprentice of the 48B intake. When the trade of Draughtsman was moved from Taunton in 1949, he had converted to that trade from his previous one of Fitter and, on passing out in 1951, joined the RE.

Peter then served for some time at the NATO HQ in Naples, Italy, before attending an 'upgrading' course at the School of Mechanical Engineering (SME) at Chatham. He was pleasantly surprised when, after completing that course, he was posted back here to Arborfield. All those who had participated in the gates' manufacture proudly lined up either side of the approach, as Her Majesty the Queen drove through those very gates on June 27th of that year, when she presented new colours to the Academy.

Advances in Leadership Training were being made, following a series of Company Weekend Camps held on Thursley Common, not far from Guildford, in the county of Surrey. The School also keenly entered into the 'pilot scheme' for the Duke of Edinburgh's Award, with a great deal of effort being expended by those boys taking part. Meanwhile, the Commandant looked ahead to the forthcoming cessation of the country's 'National Service' system, when he predicted that the role of the Army's future young apprentices would be of more value than ever before.

Pete Gripton of 56B (and now keen collator of this history) fondly remembers one of those 'weekend camps' that he later attended in 1958. The first night under canvas turned out – almost! – to be also 'under water'! He and fellow 'A' Coy camper, Bob Lennon, had pitched their two-man 'bivvy' (bivouac) on the side of a hill and spent that night watching the rainwater pour gently through their canvas mobile home. The days that followed were better, however, as they were sent out on 'initiative tests'. He and Bob were challenged to find out some facts regarding Guildford Cathedral and set about hitching a lift along the nearby A3 trunk road.

Although none of those facts now spring to mind, Pete can still remember, whilst being transported to the city in the back of a large luxurious car, having pointed out to him the spot where Mike Hawthorn had met his unfortunate end in a car-crash on the Guildford bypass. This tragic accident had taken place only shortly after Mike had won the World Racing Championship from the legendary Juan Fangio. Later, whilst having breakfast in a café in Guildford, over their tea and toast the boys read the newspaper headlines, reporting that

Swedish fighter Ingemar Johansson had beaten the American Floyd Patterson for the world heavyweight boxing title.

The next day being allotted as being 'free', as well as sunny and warm, the two of them hitchhiked as far as Southsea, down on the south Hampshire coast, dressed in only their pullovers (woollen) and trousers (denim). Here they spent a pleasant hour or two walking along the sea-front promenade, mesmerised by the sight of so many girls (pretty) sun-bathing on the beach (pebbly). With hardly a penny between them, they were eventually pleased to grab a lift from a Naval Officer, who kindly treated them to a 'pie and a pint' at a pub in Petersfield on their return journey to the campsite.

Pete also remembers the mad dash down to the NAAFI during the morning break from work, steel-studded soles of boots skidding on the hard surface of the approach roads. This hadn't always been the case, as tea and cake was provided within the workshop itself. But having sampled that strange brown liquid and its accompanying slab of mysterious 'fruit cake' over a period, the NAAFI seemed to come into favour quite naturally.

It was a matter of 'first come, first served', as the morning break was of very short duration. The favourite 'scoff' of the day was either a meat or cheese and onion patty, shoved inside a bread roll. This would then be smothered in brown sauce and a bag of Smiths crisps crushed inside, then all washed down by a bottle of *'Fling'*, a type of fizzy orangeade, served in a bottle shaped like a space ship. How the digestive system coped with that, heaven alone knows!

The Rock and Roll years

The late Fifties saw quite a culture shock for the country at large, with the introduction of 'rock'n'roll' music from the States. With the hair-styles of those days including 'DAs' *(Don't Ask! Ed.)*, 'Bostons' and the famous 'Tony Curtis', and clothing of the drape-suit and drainpipe-trousers mode, it was hard for the apprentices of the day to appreciate their School mufti, blazer, flannels and haircut of the 'short back'n'sides' variety. This was hardly the stuff to 'pull the girls', so it isn't surprising that the buses to Reading and Wokingham were full of boys carrying large holdalls, ready for a quick-change act at the first public convenience in town! Then it would be a fast trip to

The Massed Bands march off to the skirl of the pipes playing 'Scotland the Brave'

the railway station to leave the bag in the left-luggage lockers until later. *(It was amazing just how many bags could be crammed into one locker - anything to save a few coppers towards the evening's liquid refreshments! Ed.)*

After that, it was time to do the rounds of the local public houses, before ending up at one of the many dance halls, such as the *Majestic* (or 'Magic Stick' in boy-speak), the Olympia or *Oxford Ballroom* in Reading, or the *Jazz Club*, situated down an alley in Wokingham. Those who couldn't manage 'real' dances, like the foxtrot, quickstep or waltz, rocked their luminous socks off in the darkened dingy venue of '*The Foresters*', a small club off London Street, Reading, where Elvis, Eddie Cochran, Little Richard, Gene Vincent and company were belting out their hits over the loudspeakers.

George 'Fleet' Fleetwood of 56B didn't need to use the bus. He was one of those boys who illegally, as far as the School was concerned, kept a motorbike stashed away down behind the local garage in neighbouring Eversley. Courting a Reading girl at the time, the bike obviously paid off in the romantic stakes, as he eventually married the same young lady. He also recalls the gypping that took place in the Cookhouse queue, but cannot quite count the number of times his one-pint white china mug was left as just a handle in his grasp, implemented by the deftly placed downward

tap of a finest Sheffield-steel 'eating iron'!

Fleet still asks many rhetorical questions about his three-year sojourn here at Arborfield. Such as, *"Did I really make up my bed each day, to look like a liquorice allsort? 'Box' clothes in my locker into simulated paving slabs? Line up articles on rows of beds with a string line? Turn brown gym shoes black and bumpy boots smooth?"* Well, sure you did, Fleet, just like all the other boys in the intake, from the hardest to the softest.

Another of those 56B boys was Gerry Hincks, who well remembers the subterfuge of those days – the illegally bought motorbikes and cars, the 'pegged' trousers, and trying to avoid the clothes check when booking out of Camp. 'Pegging' one's trousers meant some nimble-fingered sewing, desperately narrowing down the width of the trouser bottoms to a more fashionable 16", or even an ankle-hugging 14", which created one hell of a struggle to get into – or out of - them!

Against all the known rules, Gerry had originally bought a 1932 *Sunbeam* drop-head coupe from a local guy who kept a number of old cars in his barn. As the car probably used more oil than petrol, he eventually left it at his home in Leicestershire, where his father then sold it for the princely sum of ten shillings and sixpence (55p). After this, Gerry then picked up a 1938 *Morris 8* from one of his military instructors – he was

A typical Army Apprentices' School Colour Party

that should culminate in the award of an ONC in Electrical Engineering. Five 'ex-boy' JNCOs had recently passed their exam at Reading and were now qualified as Class II tradesmen, with the appropriate rank. It was hoped that many more boys from the School would follow in these footsteps during the forthcoming years.

Showing their medals - and their age!

By 1957, the School's first eligible ex-apprentices had become qualified to receive their LSGC Medals, with no less than ten senior ranks from REME assembling at the School to collect their medals at the 'PoP' held on July 18th of that year. General Sir Robert Mansergh GCB, KBE, MC presented the honours, amongst whose recipients were Warrant Officers C J Haslam, H J Cuss, H W Kelly and M R Pepper. It was around the same time that serious consideration began to be given to the establishment of a REME Museum. The purpose of this would be *"to acquire, house, preserve and exhibit equipment, trophies and mementos that illustrate the history and tradition of REME"*. There were many jokes of course, that there were enough old museum pieces around already, though hopefully this did not include the ten medal recipients!

WO2 H W 'Bert' Kelly was then a member of the School's PS (1954 – 59), having been an apprentice here himself in intake 39A. He remains a staunch Old Boy more than forty years later, attending Reunions and making his voice and opinions heard at the AGMs. In fact, *OBAN No. 2*, issued in July 1957, paid tribute to those ex-boys of the School who were serving on the staff at that time. As well as WO2 Kelly, we also had

'seeing' the instructor's daughter at the time! – and would leave it parked up at '*Smokey Joe's*' café, out on the Wokingham road, ready for one of those fast weekend getaways.

In June 1957, the latest edition of the *REME Magazine* reported on the career progression being made by ex-apprentice Electronic Tradesmen. Upon completion of their three-year stint at the School, they would probably go on to either 3 (Tels) or 5 (Radar) Trg Btn, and so remain here in Arborfield. If qualified, they would commence an eighteen-month course

WO2s Janes, Loftus and Nixon; SSgts Crowther and Keen; Sgts Brunnen, Buck, Downs, Robbins and Shaw, plus Corporal Hook. *(Did he ever make it to Captain, we wonder? Have to ask Tinkerbell! Ed.)*

That second edition of *OBAN* also contained an article headed *'Retrospect'*. In it, the author was remarking upon the 'welcome' that seemed to greet many ex-apprentices upon their arrival at a new unit. *"Ex-boy, eh? I can spot them a mile away. Just watch your step while you're here."* This feeling must have been prevalent then, and it certainly continued for many years afterwards. Perhaps, as the author explained, ex-boys themselves were in some way to blame, with their nonchalant 'seen it all' air and apparent displays of 'cockiness'. It may also be possible that we looked upon anyone who was *not* an ex-boy with a certain amount of contempt, tinged with pity. No doubt a somewhat similar problem arises in all walks of life.

A sad note must be introduced here, when one of the School's most popular boys met an untimely end. Apprentice Pipe Major Andrew 'Jock' Grieve had joined the School in September 1954. Right from his first day he became an enthusiastic supporter of both the Band and classes in Scottish Country Dancing. He led by example and was always on hand to pass on the benefits of his experience to new members. This all came to a sudden end when Jock met his death in a motorcycling accident on April 17th 1957, whilst on leave at his home in Scotland.

Meanwhile, the Armourers' Shop mourned the sad passing of Messrs Beardall and Craddock, both of whom had been respected civilian instructors. Maj C W Beardall MBE (Ret'd) had not long retired from his post as OIC of the Armourers' Shop. Another well-known gentleman to die that year was 'Puddler' Stagg, recently of the Drawing Office, but perhaps best remembered as a one-time exponent of Workshop Practice – hence the nickname. John Johnson of 56B recalls Mr Stagg as having a *"bushy beard"*. The tale was that he suffered from leukemia and that any cuts occurring during shaving would prove dangerous.

'Schoolboys at the double'

On June 29th 1957, the School was the subject of a most welcome complimentary article, *'Schoolboys at the double'*, presented in the pages of the *John Bull* magazine, and written by ex-Armourer Sgt Robert 'Bob' Holles, REME, himself an old boy of the School.

This no doubt followed his earlier 'research' trip to the School. *John Bull* was a weekly issue, coming out every Wednesday, at the sum of fourpence a copy. It usually contained a mixture of news photographs, short stories and articles of interest in its typical thirty-six pages. Along with the Arborfield story that particular week was an article about the annual musical *'Eisteddfod'* at Llangollen, Wales, and another about Britain's embryonic space programme. A third, by accomplished athlete Christopher Chataway, who had participated in the first 'four-minute mile' behind Roger Bannister, told of his recent visit to Moscow, then situated well behind the formidable 'Iron Curtain'.

The article referring to the School was well written and not the usual stiffly regimental description. It gave some humourous tales of the radical changes in dress, once boys had 'escaped' the School's confines, as described by RCM Sallis, who obviously knew a lot more about the boys and their outside activities than he was prepared to let on! Another soldier mentioned was the School's Master Artificer, WO1 ASM (but always referred to as 'Mister') Lilley, whose son, Ian, was also serving here at the time, as an apprentice of intake 56B. Mr Lilley had recently given up much of his leisure time, whilst making leather belts with silver buckles to go with the new blue tunics of the Pipe Band.

Bob Holles must have been of 1941 vintage, being well remembered by Pete Langley of that intake. His full name was Robert Owen Holles, *"after the poet"*, as he would say. Somehow, Owen became corrupted to 'Obadiah' and then shortened, so that young Holles eventually went by the nickname 'Obad'. He once made the mistake of mentioning that he had once won a Silver Spoon at school, for boxing. This of course catapulted him directly into the Company boxing team, where he learned the awful truth! There was a difference between what was regarded at his old school as 'the noble art' and the authorised thuggery that he now encountered in the ring at Arborfield! Apart from his writing, the last Pete Langley heard of Obad was that he had been 'done' for shooting seagulls from a cliff-top – with a Bren gun!

(The 'editorial comment' about Bob Holles' John Bull article is reproduced as a separate annex to this chapter.)

From School to College – part 1

In July, at the 'PoP', the Commandant announced that,

It may look a little spartan now, but some 40-50 years ago it was a most comfortable environment.

for the first time, apprentices would soon be attending at Reading Technical College to study for the Ordinary National Certificate (ONC) in either Mechanical or Electrical Engineering. Success at that level could then lead to further qualification at the Higher National Certificate (HNC) level. 1957 also saw the arrival of a number of boys from Chepstow, due to the fact that the teaching of Control Equipment Mechanics was transferred from that training establishment to the School here at Arborfield. The move had apparently caused much grief in the Electrical Department down at Beachley, as their proud boast about training *"future boffins"* would no longer be true.

One of those ex-Chepstow boys was David – or just 'Dave' - Howlett, who had 'signed on' (56B) the previous year at Chatham – confessing that he had always been *"nuts on the Navy"*! Following a train journey from Paddington, during which he sat on his

suitcase all the way, he had ended up at Beachley, starting to train as an Electrician, Vehicle and Plant, following similar footsteps to his elder brother Tony, already two years into his time at Harrogate as the other type of RE Electrician – Machinery and Heavy Plant. In the final analysis, Tony ended up in 'D' Sqn SAS, while Dave transferred here to Arborfield at the 3 Div stage and eventually trained as a Radar Tech – so much for career planning!

Dave has always said, *"God bless my Nan"*! This, down to the fact that his dear grandmother would, every Saturday without fail, post off a brown-paper wrapped parcel, tied with hemp string and sealed with the old-fashioned red sealing-wax. This parcel usually arrived at Camp on a Wednesday afternoon, its contents eagerly expected – a slab of bread pudding, cut into squares and liberally dusted with sugar; a half-crown postal order; five *Woodbines* – yes, they sold 'ciggies' in fives then - and a letter giving him all the news from home.

In the same year, a letter received by the School from LCpl John Weston, who had been a member of intake 52B, gave an insight into the conditions of service being endured in far-off Korea, where he was serving with soldiers from other Commonwealth countries near the town of Inchon. The harbour had proved too small for proper docking, and so, as John put it, *"We went ashore by landing craft, operated by the Yanks"*. Arriving later at the RAOC Vehicle Park, John was put in charge of five REME VMs and four local Korean fitters, working mainly on vehicle transmissions, shock absorbers and fuel systems.

Properly metalled roads were non-existent in that war-torn land, all transport being driven over dirt-tracks full of potholes, while the extremely cold temperatures caused constant problems, due to water leaking into petrol and then freezing. 'Starting up' each morning proved an arduous task. John was dismayed to see the miserable conditions under which the local people had to eke out a living, with only squalid huts as cover, some of them being constructed from old fuel cans. War-torn Inchon itself, despite being classified as a 'town', had been left in ruins by previous battles, and never rebuilt.

John continued with the story of one of the camp sentries, who had been knocked out by one of a local band of thieves, who then tried to make off with two six-volt batteries. Another sentry opened fire, but the thief got away – less the batteries, which must have been a heavy load to say the least! Compensation for the hazardous life-style inflicted upon the troops came in the form of free weekly issues – one hundred cigarettes, two bars of soap, some razor blades, matches and chocolate. Not surprisingly, this was one LCpl who was looking forward to returning home to a life of some normality and less danger!

Other correspondence received during that year gave evidence of the problems being encountered by the OBA in keeping track of its members. Cpl H Wilson of 55A wrote from 12 Armoured Wksp, complaining that he had 'paid his subs' upon posting from the School, but had received no membership details, badge or magazines since. A second letter, some six weeks later, thanked the Secretary for the subsequent receipt of the same items. Cpl Wilson explained that he had originally put the wrong British Forces Post Office (BFPO) number on his address, as

he had recently been in Tripoli (BFPO 57), attending his trade test, and had used this number rather than the correct one for his unit at Benghazi (BFPO 55). Now that he was in Germany, following the closure of the Libyan theatre of operations, he hoped that matters would now resolve themselves.

Every one's a record!

1957 saw the very first athletics meeting under the banner of 'Army Individual Championships (Boys)', which was held at Aldershot Military Stadium over a weekend in early July. As well as Arborfield, in their *"white vests with blue and gold bands"*, Harrogate and Chepstow also competed, along with Junior Leaders (JLdrs) from the RA, RAC, RAOC/REME, RAMC, R Sigs and Infantry. Because these championships had never been held before, there were no records to be broken, but of course every winner of each individual event automatically became that event's first record holder. Between the two age groups of 'Youths' and 'Juniors', the School was able to proudly come away with no less than eight winners medals.

A programme of events, issued for that athletics meeting, shows that the advertising of sports wear is no modern phenomenon, as the back page urged sportsmen and ladies to buy *'Joy and Tony Mottram'* tennis shirts and shorts, and *'Len Hutton'* cricket gear.

It must have been during the summer of 1957 that John Harte of 55B found himself touring the beautiful southwestern counties of Devon and Cornwall. No, this wasn't just another 'cream teas' holiday because, at the time, John was part of the Army Apprentices' Schools recruiting team. Although John confesses that he can't remember too many details of individual towns or events, he found the whole six-week period an *"enjoyable and educational experience"*. The recruiting team toured with an immensely long exhibition van that, on first glance, seemed far too long for the 3-ton truck that was designated to tow it. One wonders what became of the van – at least John has a photograph that proves its existence!

Mick Oulds turned up at the gates of Arborfield from the 'boondocks' of provincial Norfolk as a member of 57B. He reckons that the message above the camp gates could well have *read "Abandon all hope, all ye who enter here"*, but he may well be joking! *(Other less tactful apprentices said it should have read 'Arbeit macht frei', but perhaps that was a little too strong! Ed.)* During the trials and tribulations of his first six months in 'HQ' Coy, CSM Brady was inspecting Mick's boots one morning and begged the question, *"No relation to Sgt Tom Oulds, Irish Guards, are you, sonny?"* Mick could only stammer out the reply, *"He's my d-d-da Sir"*, and was immediately informed, *"See this 'ere nose sunshine, well it's your effing da that broke it for me, during the war in Italy"*. Not the most auspicious introduction, but Mick managed to survive.

One of Mick's best mates at the School was Andy Anderson, who Mick always reckons was a *"bit of a beatnik in khaki"*. They did their fair share of travelling round the country together in search of adventure – or more likely misadventure! Having already done the rounds of central London, such as Soho, Piccadilly and Leicester Square on quite a few occasions, on one leave period they decided to head up to Liverpool, where Andy is supposed to have had some old pals. However, their arrival wasn't greeted with much enthusiasm and, after a few days, they decided to head back south.

Hitch-hiking was the order of the day back in those times and, on their return trip, they were fortunate enough to be passed by an open-topped blue *Triumph* sports car, which then pulled over at the side of the road and waited for them. As an attractive young lady was driving it, they needed little encouragement to climb into the car for a lift. It came as a pleasant surprise to find that the lady was none other than the lovely Lita Rosa, quite a 'pop-star' in her day, and who came from Liverpool herself. An even more pleasant surprise awaited them at the end of their journey. No, don't read ahead too quickly, it was just a fiver pressed into each of their hands 'to help them on their way'. A generous gesture indeed.

A time of turmoil

September 1957 became a low point in the School's history, with the arrival of a particularly virulent 'Asian flu' (influenza) epidemic that not only swept the country, but also just about brought life at the School to a halt. The Camp Hall had to be quickly converted into a temporary convalescence centre full of beds, as literally hundreds of boys succumbed to this devastating outbreak. Those who were not themselves confined to bed were roped in as temporary medical orderlies, to look after and administer comfort to those boys who were bedded-down on doctor's orders. John Johnson (56B) was one Camp Hall occupant, his bout of flu proving so serious that he was later shifted to the MRS. He has been allergic to anti-histamines ever since!

This period inevitably lowered morale in the

The Military Band in 1957

School, while a few other 'incidents' that year gained some unwelcome publicity for the School in the national press. Not unexpectedly, this led to an outbreak of disappointing results for the Senior Division (or 6 Div), in both the technical and educational fields. Pete Gripton, then in 'A' Coy for his third term, remembers some of those incidents, which certainly added some 'spice' to the more mundane lifestyle that the boys were used to. No doubt more prank than criminal intent, 'raids' on the nearby *Rainbow Firework Factory* at Finchampstead and on local holiday camp '*California in England*' led to caches of fireworks and cigarettes being stashed away under the floorboards and behind the walls of certain spider-blocks.

Meanwhile, as reported in the *Daily Mirror* of October 10th 1957, a 'boy' who had been dismissed from the School for misbehaviour by Col Cole in 1955, had then gone on to somehow hoodwink his way into the RAF. The said boy, Ernie 'Paddy' Claydon, having subsequently deserted and gone 'on the run', found himself a reasonably safe hiding-place amongst some old pals back here at Arborfield.

Col Cole is quoted as saying, *"I must admit it is a funny story. I saw Claydon near the camp six weeks ago and recognised him, as I had dismissed him as being unsuitable in 1955. He could quite possibly have lived here if other boys were in on the secret."* No doubt the Commandant didn't really find the episode in the slightest bit funny, well not in the 'Ha! Ha!' sense, but maybe in the 'funny peculiar' sense. This was a clear case of his authority being flouted, with all the ensuing bad press coverage not being to the benefit of the School at all.

Many ex-boys will remember that, after the Wednesday pay parades of those notorious days, Claydon and his cronies went round collecting a tanner (sixpence) off every boy to keep him in beer and fags! It is also no secret that, on at least one occasion, he marched the Fire Picket squad down to their duties under the very nose of Provost Sgt Fred Silvers! The whole affair seems to have gone on for an incredible length of time, around six weeks.

Claydon's downfall apparently came about when he was spotted crossing from one spider to another, during a morning parade, by CSM John 'Daddy' Dunning of 'B' Coy. Upon being apprehended, Claydon gave a false name to one of the RP staff, who just happened to know the boy whose name had been given. The game was up and Claydon was quickly marched off to a local police station to await his inevitable punishment.

It must have been some time after this escapade that Col Cole took steps to alleviate the recent problems. Assuming that the boys probably had too much spare time on their hands, and thus being insufficiently occupied in the evenings, he swiftly ordered that there should be sessions of extra training, from 5 p.m. to 7 p.m. during the long winter nights. This move was resisted at first, not by the boys, but by those civilian instructors who had already taken part-time evening employment at local Technical Colleges. Eventually, however, the plan settled down and the Commandant was later able to declare it a *"great success"*.

A notable death recorded that year had been that of Brig Frank A Hilborn (Ret'd), who was the first Commandant of the School when it opened in 1939. Born in Somerset as long ago as 1882, he had been recalled from retirement to take up the appointment as Commandant here for a second time, from 1940 – 43. Even after that, he then carried on as Commandant of the Gordon Boys' School from 1943 - 53.

(Brig Hilborn's obituary appears as a separate annex at the end of this chapter.)

A right old scrape

John Stewart of 56B reckons that it must have also been sometime during the autumn days of 1957 that he and a handful of his mates got themselves into *"a right old scrape"*. Having suffered the attentions of some bullies from a senior intake for a while, they decided to wreak some sort of revenge by raiding the senior barrack room, where they then handed out a 'toothpasting' to some of the offenders. This involved beating at the base of their beds with broom-handles until the occupant came squeezing out from beneath the blankets at the top of the bed – literally just like toothpaste! Needless to say, some sort of retribution was expected from these senior boys, but instead, and to their utter dismay, John and his pals found themselves facing disciplinary action and a sentence of fourteen days jankers. At this point, the decision was made to go 'on the run'.

Along with his four fellow 'lawbreakers', John then spent many days on exciting escapades in places such as Maidstone, the Isle of Sheppey, Hastings and Brighton, finding such shelter as they could in

A/T/RSM Colin Drasutis 55B

abandoned caravans, seaside shelters, an old cow shed and the like. Apple-scrumping provided them with some much-needed sustenance, while some smooth talking pretence of being *"Queen's Scouts on a survival exercise"* actually persuaded some well-to-do people to provide a meal of tea and biscuits.

Eventually, of course, the adventure ran out of steam and three of the boys decided that it would be better if they headed back to Camp. John and another lad, 'Jonah' Jones, hitched along the south coast to Portsmouth and gave themselves up to the tender mercies of John's parents, who persuaded the two of them that it was about time they too returned to Arborfield to 'face the music'. John recalls being awarded an amazingly light sentence of only five days 'in the nick' for his misdemeanours. And, incredibly, this was immediately reduced down to only three days

because, at that time, the Guardroom was packed full of boys who had taken part in the raid on the local fireworks factory!

Things at the School weren't all bad of course, as borne out by the fact that by that same year, 1957, Mr Gerry Muldowney, an instructor in electronics and always the most Christian of gentlemen, had already been running the School's CF for around five years. Gerry was able to report, in a School magazine article, on the regular visits made by members of the CF to Battle Hospital, Reading, where the boys took part in prayer services in the 'old gentlemen's' ward. As many of these old gentlemen were ex-soldiers, the sight of a familiar khaki uniform brought them great cheer. Gerry remained at Arborfield for many years, eventually rising to Head of Department, and becoming most instrumental in the design of the computer system that was introduced some twenty years later. *(Since his retirement, Gerry has 'kept in touch' with the College. In fact, those of you who have read the latest issue (26) of OBAN may find that it was Gerry's fair hand that placed it in its envelope! Ed.)*

As part of the CF world, boys were encouraged to join in evening Bible Classes at Gerry's home, where, no doubt, generous helpings of tea and cream cakes helped the evening along – well, that is what was assumed by the non-attending boys! However, as recalled by Norman 'Dude' Dewdney, another of the 56B boys, it wasn't the bible lectures but the later return to barracks that would *"put the fear of God"* into him. His roommates, no doubt slightly envious of Norman's 'evening off' and perceived banquet, would prepare some sneaky surprises for him. These could include the stuffing of the six-foot ironing table into Dude's mattress cover, which was then tied so tight that it was almost impossible to remove the table.

Another prank was to somehow open Dude's locker – how *did* they do that? – and tie every item of its contents to the door, so that when the door opened, all of Dude's kit would end up on the floor. As all this occurred after 'lights out', with the room NCO bellowing for the noise to be kept down, Dude must have been going quietly bonkers at this stage! Quite how he put up with this so stoically, even he can't say, but he never bore a grudge and answered the call so well that he ended up as 'boy' RSM of his intake.

Around the same period, John Houghton of 56B, known to his mates as 'Doc', was back in the Fitters' Shop again at the end of 3 Div, when Capt Chivers told him to *"pack his toolbox"* and report to the Gun Shop. At long last, John was going to start training at his chosen trade of Fitter Gun – or Gun Fitter – or even 'Gunfighter' as some wags have often called them! Across the bench, Alan 'Spider' Dagless pricked up his ears – he was fed up with all the 'fitting and filing', so a change of trade looked very tempting to him. Fortunately, the need for Gun Fitters was quite strong and, in fact, a number of boys were actually allowed to change from the 'general fitting' side to the more specialized gun trade.

Doc was another victim of the previously mentioned flu epidemic. He recalls that both the MRS and the Camp Hall were so full of casualties that he was packed off to CMH Aldershot. He also sympathises with those who found attitudes outside of the School set against ex-apprentices. Upon his first posting, to Windsor, the first question he was asked was, *"Are you an ex-boy?"* His affirmative answer was followed by a feeling that 'his type' weren't welcome. Perhaps his young face and G-flog didn't quite go together! However, his spirits were lifted when he came under the wing of SSgt Vince – yes, the same one mentioned as the father of George Vince (57A). Doc remembers that he *"had a weather-beaten face, could practically turn his hand to anything and was protective of us boys straight out of Arborfield"*. But he never let on that he had a son there!

The 'Space Age' begins

1957 saw the world enter the 'Space Age', with the Russians launching their first satellite, the so-called 'Sputnik', into orbit in October of that year. The following month, Russian dog Laika became the first living creature to leave the confines of our planet in another rocket. Boys at the School must have been reading their *'Dan Dare'* comic strips in *The Eagle* with a great deal more credulity than previously! The editorial column of the School magazine that Christmas looked ahead with these stirring words:

> *"The apprentices of this school are the technicians of the future and will train the succeeding generation in the skills that they know. If these lads can look at the horizon and see the future, and can face it boldly and skillfully, this country and this world can strive continuously towards a united and*

full life, and even in the striving there is an unassailable virtue which we hope can be crowned with success."

1957 also brought the arrival of SSgt Buss RAEC to the PS and, as a 'schoolie', he had a most remarkable collection of medal ribbons. These were described by one boy as *"stacks on his left breast and one on the right"*. The individual one was of blue silk with a gold border, which turned out to be an American citation (Congressional Medal of Honour). It turned out that SSgt Buss had served with the Gloucesters in Korea and that medal had been won at the battle on the Imjin River, after which the regiment was permitted to wear, as well as their normal cap-badge, a second small badge on the back of their berets. It is believed that SSgt Buss was also the proud recipient of the MM for his Korean service.

SSgt Buss MM silencing the Chinese enemy

During that heroic Korean battle, when the Gloucesters were overrun by Chinese forces, Maj Anthony Farrar-Hockley was the Adjutant, until he realised that, with the radio almost dead, his position had become redundant. His last message to one of his subalterns, Lt Temple, was *"Guy, you will stay where you are until further notice. If your ammunition runs out, hurl bloody rocks at 'em"*. He then turned to Drum Maj Buss and ordered him to fetch his bugle and to play every call he knew – except of course 'Retreat'. Writing of his Drum Major's performance at a later date, Farrar-Hockley said:

"I could see his tall, lean figure, topped by a cap comforter. He always played the bugle well and that day he was not below form. The sweet notes of our own bugle, which now echoed through the valley below him, died away. For a moment there was silence – the last note had coincided with a lull in the action. Then the noise of battle began again, but with a difference – there was no sound of a Chinese bugle! There are not many Drum Majors in the British Army who can claim to have silenced the enemy's battle calls with a short bugle recital."

The School's Military Band had seen its usual turn-over of members, but was very much blessed by the August intake, which included at least eight boys who knew a little about music! String players were urgently required to form a School Orchestra, with classes to begin in December. Meanwhile, the Pipe Band was very proud of its achievements under Sgt Massie, its

Future Pentathlete A/T Jim Fox

Gordon Highlander Pipe Major. Another welcome arrival had been given to ex-Chepstow boy Arthur Gibson, who, having previously spent over six years at the Queen Vics, was already an accomplished piper.

OBAN No.3, published in December of 1957, welcomed the fact that the OBA continued to flourish, with an even larger intake of new members. That year's Reunion, held the previous August, had included a Friday evening in the form of a 'Smoker/Buffet' and had been claimed as *"an overwhelming success"*, due in no small part to the attendance of a *"token force of civilian staff"*. The Committee hoped that the same format could be repeated the following year.

It is a shame that some of the articles submitted in the very early issues of the *OBAN* gave no credit to their authors – no names or intake, in fact it is difficult to know whether or not they had been written by ex-boys, staff members, or even outsiders. One such article saw the light of day in the December 1957 issue, and gave a very interesting description of daily life in Kenya which, despite the author's naming it *"the land of sunshine"*, by that time had suffered the terrorist 'Mau Mau' uprising for some four years. Those troublesome times must have impinged upon the lives of a fair number of ex-boys at the time.

1957 heralded the arrival of a young fifteen-year old apprentice and budding sports enthusiast, Jeremy - or 'Jim' - Fox. Jim excelled at games and his mud-spattered frame could always be seen heading the field in cross-country events. This obviously gave him the inspiration to later become a member of the REME Modern Pentathlon team of 1962 and, in the following year, he went on to win the Army individual championship. Jim subsequently went on to appear in no less than eight World Championships and four consecutive Olympic Games. His successes included being the British individual champion on no less than ten occasions.

The *REME Magazine* of December covered the arrival, at Liverpool the previous September, of the NZ ship *'Captain Cook'*, which had returned men of all three services back to this country from 'Operation Grapple'. In the Army element were men from the REME Workshop that had been set up in 1956, part of the operation that assisted in the first British nuclear (atom-bomb) tests that had been carried out on the remote atoll of Christmas Island.

In January 1958, those REME Boys who had previously been at Blackdown with the RAOC, now found themselves re-located to Arborfield as the Junior Leaders Unit, based within the Depot REME. The announcement that the accommodation was suffering from dry rot was treated with some amusement! Their new locality, virtually 'next door' to the apprentices, engendered a certain amount of rivalry, in particular about 'who ruled Reading' or 'who ruled Wokingham', but most of it was fairly innocuous in nature.

Fall of the 'Mighty Atom'

The 'PoP' of February 1958 took place in dull overcast weather, accompanied by a bitterly cold east wind, in the presence of the reviewing officer, Maj Gen R A Bramwell-Davis CB, DSO, the GOC of Aldershot District. However, it is also better remembered as that notorious 'PoP', which was missed by the A/T RSM of the Senior Div, 55A, and whose name doesn't even appear on the list of those passing out, later printed in the summer edition of *The Arborfield Apprentice*. In his absence, the parade was ably taken by A/T CSM Ken Andrews of 'A' Coy, providing a *"good exhibition of drill and turnout"*. However, this had not been matched in the technical and educational fields, where the Senior Division's results had been disappointing.

It should have been James 'Jock' Massie's proudest day, leading the parade at the School's highest apprentice rank of RSM. Sadly for him, following the customary passing-out dance on the evening before the parade, Jock had been involved in the traditional Senior Div ritual, that of 'tipping' a number of junior boys out of bed. One unfortunate boy who suffered this indignity hit his nose on a bedside locker and the whole incident turned rather 'bloody'. So Jock, or the 'Mighty Atom' as he was dubbed in the *Daily Sketch*, was quickly sent off home to Aberdeen to await his first adult posting. This was another one of those unfortunate events that somehow made the national headlines. *(It was rumoured at the time that a boy at the School must have had a brother in the Press Corps! Ed.)*

Following that rather unpleasant incident, it would appear that 'the system' decided to tighten up on the activities at 'leaving dos'. Certainly, Charlie Leah of 57B intake recalls that, from the intake before his at least, the farewell parties were usually accompanied by members of the PS. Charlie remembers that, at his own Div's party in 1960, Provost Sergeant Fred Silvers was in attendance. Having just learned that he

A/T/RSM Drasutis receiving his award from Lt Gen Lathbury

was to be posted, Fred was 'in his cups' and lamenting the forthcoming move. He had always expected to see out his days here at Arborfield, and a posting would probably result in his 'acting' rank of Sergeant being downgraded.

(Stories concerning Fred Silvers are legion and a few of them can be found in a separate annex to this chapter.)

On March 8th, the School's Gymnastic Club performed at the Reading 'Festival of Queens', held at the Town Hall in aid of children's orphanages. They gave displays of groundwork, parallel bars and exercises to music. At the time, the Club was flourishing, with between thirty and forty members. They also boasted the *"best High Horse"* any gymnastic team could wish for – even Company Sgt Maj Instructor (CSMI) Stuart, the British Champion and Olympic gymnast had been to try it! As one young apprentice aptly stated, *"It's all right going up, but it's a long way down"*.

Two apprentices returning to their barrack room having just collected newly laundered overalls whilst four others make their way to dinner. Notice the two inside A/Ts about to play 'conkers' with their drinking mugs - many an unspecting apprentice was left carrying just the mug handle!

Please, Sir, can I have some more?

Paul Hudson arrived at the School as a member of 58A, an 'Easter Bunny' as he puts it. The first two Cookhouse dinners are forever etched on his mind. Turning up on his first day, Paul had just missed the official lunchtime meal, but was marched down to the Dining Room by Sgt Green. *"Are you hungry, son?"* asked another sergeant from behind the hotplate. At Paul's tentative *"Yes, sir"*, his plate was liberally filled with hot steaming food, which he actually quite enjoyed. 'This can't be bad', thought Paul!

The next day he joined the normal queue with other lads, only to find his plate about half-full, or even less, when compared to his previous meal. Like Oliver Twist asking for more, he questioned the Cook Sergeant as to why he couldn't have *"the same as yesterday"*. Came back the classic reply *"Because you're in the Army*

now, son, and only entitled to the basic amount". Ah well, no doubt Paul eventually got over it, he certainly looks well enough fed these days!

Another of that intake was Pat Gutteridge, who remembers boys' school as *"a hard existence, but a very rewarding one"*. It certainly served him well in his later civilian life, when he spent six years working 'under his own steam' in Saudi Arabia. Pat fondly remembers his 'C' Coy CSM 'Duggie' Huxley, who had the reputation of being the 'Singing CSM'. Well, that was the impression he gave, as his orders on the Parade Square always seemed to be tunefully sung, rather than the usual bellowing of other Sergeant Majors.

Pat's memories of Cookhouse food are less fond! To him, it seemed to always be a ladle full of the dreaded 'pom', a powdery and 'instant' version of what was supposed to be mashed potato. This was usually slapped on one's plate with a certain amount of distaste, accompanied by 'corned dog', as Pat so memorably puts it! The squares of margarine, floating in their tub of cold, greasy water, he'd rather forget about.

Ken Anderson was another of that 58A intake and, once settled in as a member of 'A' Coy a couple of years later, remembers his days as 'Assistant Cinema Projectionist'. A National Serviceman from the RAOC was running things at the time, and Ken was pleased to have been given the task of helping out with the preparation and showing of the films – anything was preferable to being caught for 'chairs'!

Before each evening's performance, it had always been customary to lower the lights and play the National Anthem, at which all the boys would stand to attention in silence. But with the current music scene being very much a 'youth culture' thing at the time, Ken recalls that he would often play one of the more popular 'skiffle' songs just prior to the Anthem. Jim Dale's *'Piccadilly Line'* was a classic take-off of Lonnie Donegan's *'Rock Island Line'*, its opening sound being the noise of a London Underground tube-train coming into Piccadilly Station. As this sounded just like the opening drum-roll of the National Anthem, no need to guess its effect on the assembled boys!

Ken went on to serve REME as an Artificer Radar and was one of the first ex-apprentices to gain an HNC in Electronic Engineering, as part of his artificer course. Some fifty years later, he was awarded a University of Gloucester Master of Science (MSc) degree in multi-media, the ceremony being held at Cheltenham's Town Hall. *(He is currently providing a lot of 'electronic effort' on behalf of the OBA, as we shall see! Ed.)*

On May 23rd that year, the School bade a fond farewell to Lt Col H Woolley, BA, AMIMechE, who had served his last four and a half years as its Chief Instructor. He had been posted to the ATS (Boys), Jersey, in October 1939 and took part in the evacuation of boys from Jersey to Arborfield during that year. He later served on the British Army Staff in Washington, USA, followed by postings in the UK, Australia, India and as Commander REME (CREME) in Austria. Lt Col Woolley's replacement was Lt Col R T Barfield, MIEE. 1958 was also memorable for the fact that A/T RSM Terry Fraser became the first apprentice tradesman to complete his ONC while still serving here at the School. The School was honoured to pay host to a goodwill mission from the Royal Thai Army during that same year.

The School Basketball team had suffered a rather depressing season, having failed to win even one of the Inter-School winter fixtures. However, they were cheered up on May 28th 1958, when they joined a party of almost two hundred School members on a visit to the Empire Pool at Wembley. Here they were treated to a Basketball match to remember, between the legendary Harlem Globetrotters and an opposing team of United States All-stars. The boys almost went cross-eyed, watching the intricate skills and clowning on offer, vowing to make their visit an annual event.

Another set of gates

The quality and elegance of the gates which now adorned the RMAS resulted in a prestigious follow-up order, this time for a set of four gates at All Saints Church, down in Aldershot. As this Garrison Church is the most senior in the British Army, the task was obviously treated as one of special significance. Still very much in evidence to this day, these gates are now a truly magnificent feature of the Church, and a credit to all those who played a part in their production. They were officially opened, on July 29th 1958, by Field Marshall The Earl Alexander of Tunis.

WO2 Ernie Burlison, who was near the end of his three years at the School and a *"full whack"* of thirty years in the Army, had supervised construction of those gates, although a photograph in the School magazine showed that *"big brother Lay was watching him"*! Chepstow could take great pride in this most excellent tradesman, for it was there that Ernie started his apprenticeship, between 1929 and 1932. He had been 'Mentioned in Dispatches', been presented the MSM, and been awarded both the 'Adjutant General's' and 'Quarter Master General's' certificates of commendation for good work. The School wished him 'Good Luck' in civvy street and only regretted that they had just missed out on another order – for St Peter's Pearly Gates!

The Instrument Section that summer reported that *"the inevitable change of military personnel"* had led to a re-shuffle. However, it also gloried in the fact that all the military staff were now ex-boys, in the shapes of Capt W Evatt, AQMSs L Nixon, R Janes and L Merrick, as well as Sgt D Robbins.

Just straighten that river, would you, Staff?

In the July 1958 fourth edition of *OBAN*, SSgt George

Apprentice Sergeants Mess 1958

Marshall, who had been a member of the 46B intake, published an article which vividly described his service in a very remote part of the globe, some 250 miles into the heart of the jungle of distant Borneo. This had all come about following an approach by the government of Sarawak, asking for some technical assistance from the military authorities in Singapore. The task in question was to remove, by explosive means where necessary, huge boulders from certain rivers, to make the rapids more navigable. This would then allow better access for the native craft, known as 'prahus', with the long-term intention of opening up the interior of the country to trade and cultivation.

Thus came into being 'Operation Coolcat', consisting of thirty men, spearheaded by the REs, with support from R Sigs, 'medics', the ACC and, last but not least, members of REME. George described the whole expedition in great detail, far too much to be included here. Two parties were used and, over the space of two months, successfully 'straightened out' nine different sets of rapids. Three other sets proved unworkable, as their rock barriers were permanently under the level of the fast-moving river itself. Eventually, after about fifteen weeks, and having exhausted their NAAFI supplies of beer and fags, the men were looking forward to a well-earned week's luxurious leave in Singapore.

Borneo was later to provide another 'trouble spot' in military history when, in December 1962, a coup in Brunei was initiated, with the evident objective of an Indonesian take-over. In 1963, Indonesian troops finally crossed the border, but the confrontation ended with the signing of a peace treaty in August 1966. Despite trying conditions and a mixed bag of problems, a good level of performance was maintained by the REME soldiers involved, which no doubt included the usual contingent of ex-apprentices.

While *OBAN No.4* marked yet another successful six months for the Association, it was also thought necessary at that time to issue, within its pages, *"Instructions for visiting ex-Apprentices"*. Apparently, a number of ex-boys, upon re-visiting the scene of their splendid past, had rather seen fit to abuse that privilege! In future, all such visits would have to be pre-notified and visitors were to report to the Guardroom both at the start and end of such visits.

If the OBA itself had been deemed 'successful', it certainly didn't seem that way for the Reunion weekend held in 1958. The Friday evening's 'Smoker' had clashed with the Sgts Mess regimental dance held at 5 Trg Btn, while the following morning saw a military parade held at 3 Trg Btn. Both of these functions would naturally have drawn their fair share of ex-boys. Apart from the Saturday night Dance, attendance had been most disappointing, but this could possibly be put down merely to 'bad planning'.

Although engagements had proved scarce at that time, the Military Band had improved wonderfully under Sgt F Backley, while the A/T Band Sergeant, Dave Precious, was doing a good job since his promotion. By now, A/T Cpl Domoney was leading the cornet section, so his musical career was on the right track. The clarinet section now numbered eleven, four of whom could also play the saxophone. The Pipe Band's strength had reached thirty-seven, with A/T Arthur Gibson of 'B' Coy having won the Piper's Trophy. A/T Pipe Major Mick Sloan, in his last term, thanked all members for their support during a happy stay.

Dancing the night away

Mr Fred Hall spent his days teaching in the electronics trades, but on some evenings also ran the School's Dancing Club, where his wife ably assisted him. *"To jive or not to jive"* had become the question of the day, with modern ballroom dancing having suffered a decline in popularity with the onslaught of rock'n'roll. But Fred took all this in his stride, ensuring that jiving was confined to only those tunes that were suited to it, with the foxtrot, quickstep and waltz still providing the bulk of the weekly dance sessions. Indeed, a current 'novelty' at these events was the 'Arborfield Progressive Barn Dance', which actually broke down into short sessions of each type of dance, including the 'jive'.

October 1958 brought the retirement of another 'old faithful' of the School. Mr F G 'Fred' Morris enlisted as a boy soldier with the AOC in January 1909 and, like many others of his trade, served his apprenticeship at Enfield. As a Staff Sergeant, he was attached to the Grenadier Guards in 1914 and served with them throughout the First World War. He left the Army in 1938 and was immediately employed as a civilian instructor at the Armourers' Training Branch (ATB). At the outbreak of the 1939 war, he re-enlisted and was a Captain by the end of that conflict. Those apprentice armourers who were taught by him remember his *"endless patience"* and have a great affection for him. After fifty years of loyal service to the Crown, Fred now looked forward to his latter days.

Many boys who spent their formative years at Arborfield during those late Fifties will recall the name of Stan Cocking. He was a WO2 in the RAEC, who definitely taught maths and possibly other topics. Whilst on his pet subject of trigonometry, with all its angles and areas, Stan had a little mantra that went, *"Some old hags carry a handbag 'til old age"*, which gives the three mathematical formulae for sine, cosine and tangent – don't worry if you don't understand it! Ken Anderson of 58A remembers Stan as a *"funny (peculiar) little man"*. He used to live – or so rumour had it – on a hedgerow diet of nuts and raisins, riding around the Camp on a racing-bike, with a sheet of cardboard stuffed inside either his BD blouse or tracksuit, to ward off the cold wind!

Despite the 'healthy' diet, Stan didn't look particularly healthy! If anything, he seemed rather frail and sickly, and is supposed to have collapsed one day during a 'PTI's Fun Run'. In the classroom, he would have an angled mirror on the blackboard, presumably to look out for any misbehaviour going on while his back was turned. Dave Howlett of 56B has the feeling that Stan could write on the board with both hands at the same time, which must have been quite a feat – especially if both sets of text were different ones! When on duty as Orderly Officer, he would lie in wait for boys breaking back *into* Camp, they were obviously easier to catch that way! The names of any lawbreakers would be duly noted down in Stan's famous *"little black book"*, in the manner of *"A/T Whosit, strolling across the Square, **both** hands in pockets"*.

'Doc' Houghton certainly recalls 'Stan' – a *"control freak"* he calls him. Not only did he live on his healthy diet, but also apparently he used to have his bed in the Mess positioned to face a particular point of the compass, in order to aid his circulation. *(And we all thought that this Feng Shui business was something new! Ed.)* Perhaps Stan, who was not the most popular of instructors, was the one recalled earlier by Wally Walters! In later years, it was rumored that Stan had been *"killed by a shark, whilst swimming off the waters of Hong Kong"* – but perhaps this was just wishful thinking by the boys who told the story!

Most of the Education Corps 'schoolies' are remembered as easy-going chaps. Many were National Servicemen who had finished their degree course and had to *"get some time in"* before reaching a certain age. They were very knowledgeable in many topics unrelated to the subjects being taught and had their own personal views on Britain's relationships with places like Malaya and Aden, views that certainly didn't come from any Army textbook.

The last 'PoP' of the year, held on a cold and wintry 17th December, was the first occasion on which the DEME, Maj Gen L N Tyler CB, OBE, had taken the parade. He congratulated the apprentices on their *"bearing, turnout and marching"* in such adverse conditions and welcomed the newly qualified tradesmen into the Corps, where he hoped they would find *"a full and successful career"*.

The Arborfield Apprentice of Christmas 1958 gave a glowing description of the WVS Club Room. This was a large comfortably furnished room in which could be found many amenities, including facilities for writing, books, daily newspapers, magazines and a good supply of small board games. There was also a radio and an electric gramophone, with numerous records. From this room, Whist Drives and tournaments of snooker, table-tennis etc were run from time to time on Sundays. Now those *were* the days!

At long last the RE had been persuaded to spend some money on the Miniature Range, much to the delight of the Shooting Club. It was now hoped to arrange fixtures against some of the local clubs. It was reckoned that past members of the School would hardly recognise the Range after all the improvements.

A/Ts to become 'VIPs'

The editorial in that same magazine reinforced the fact, as previously stated by the Commandant, that apprentices had suddenly become an admirable and very important part of the Army's future in terms of its tradesmen. The reason for this evaluation was that National Service was due to end some three years into the future, having previously provided the Army with a direct supply of many of its highly qualified personnel, especially in the more technical arms such as REME. Looking ahead to the years after 1962, the policy makers had suddenly awoken to the fact that these 'ready-made' technicians would then need replacing by the 'home-grown' variety.

The *REME Magazine* of December 1958 described the sporting prowess of one of Arborfield's best athletes. Cpl Brian Kitchener had joined the AAS in February 1953, going on to reach the rank of A/T CSM. He had captained the School athletics and cross-country teams and been a prominent achiever in

his chosen sports since an early age. Now a member of the Reading Athletic Club, Brian had received his Berkshire County Colours for both sports, as well as Army and Corps Colours for athletics. Having been posted to Gibraltar in 1957, he represented that tiny outpost at the Empire and Commonwealth Games, held in Wales during 1958.

Thirty-four boys from 2 and 3 Divs had, the previous February, started on the long trail leading to the award that HRH Prince Philip, Duke of Edinburgh, KG, KT, OM, GBE had instituted as a challenge to the individual and his personal achievement. Now, as the end of the year approached, all of the boys were halfway to their first 'Duke of Edinburgh's Silver Award'. To get this far, the lads had proven their skills in First Aid at Wokingham Town Hall, camped out on the banks of the Thames and undertaken many other individual pursuits. They were now looking forward to the next Summer's athletics season, which would see them setting off on the final section of their long pursuit of success.

March 1959 saw the fifth occasion of what had now become a regular event, the issue of the *OBAN*. It was reported that the OBA in 1956, eight years after its formation, had been reduced to a sickly total membership of only thirty. Thankfully, during the last three years, and due almost single-handedly to the efforts of the Assistant Hon Sec, AQMS Lawrence Nixon, himself an ex-boy, this had since grown to a far healthier total of 619. Lawrence had placed a notice in the October 1956 edition of the *REME Magazine*, urging all ex-boys to *"take advantage of the newly introduced subscription rates for life membership – for the sum of £1"*.

In that same *OBAN*, Col White, who had been Commandant at the School when the idea of a School cap-badge was conceived, recalled how it had all came about some twelve years earlier. He put down his memories in a short article that was aimed mainly at old boys of the School who had served here around the 1947 period.

(Col White's article regarding the School badge can be found in a separate annex to this chapter.)

Another tale from that *OBAN* concerned the lending of a white glazed one-pint drinking utensil from Cpl Fazackerley to one of his juniors, A/T 'Groggy' Orme. Spotting young Orme on his way out of the Cookhouse after tea one afternoon, Cpl F sharply reminded him, *"Don't forget my mug, Orme"*. Orme's reply of *"I don't think I could ever forget your mug, Corporal"* is reputed to have earned him seven days 'defaulters'. One wonders why? One other contribution to that *OBAN No.5* was under the heading *"Overheard in the Typists' Pool"*, and went along the lines of:

> Typist 1: *"I wouldn't have anything to do with that new chap in the Pay Office. He must have a dirty mind – he knows lots of rude songs."*
> Typist 2: *"Have you heard him singing them, then?"*
> Typist 1: *"No, but he goes around whistling them!"*

Some new accommodation

In an effort to improve the boys' living conditions at the School, there was some additional building construction in 1959. The new brick-built three storeyed 'HQ' Coy block, at the top of 'the Square', was finally completed and then occupied, while a new Education Block, which would incorporate both laboratories and classrooms, was still at the planning stage. The new block was described at the time as a *"promise of better things to come"*, and it was envisaged that another nine such blocks would be built in the future, at a rate of one per year, but history will show that this never did come to pass.

Older readers may remember that this 'HQ' block was built upon the site of a tall, old oak tree. Harold Price (42A) seems to remember that it was cut down between May and July of 1942, by Sgt Hotchkiss, the Provost Sergeant of his day. Alterations to the Cookhouse had also been made and a new 'self-service – help yourself' system had made for a happier atmosphere in the dining halls. To top it all, a new oil-fired central-heating system had replaced the antiquated coal-fired one, with some boys now actually having the temerity to now complain that they were 'too hot'!

In May's issue of the *REME Magazine*, it was announced that 'Saint Eligius' had been accepted as *"the Patron Saint"* for the REME. It was explained that many Regiments and Corps of the Army, as well as many civilian organisations, had adopted a patron saint. Originally, it was supposed, was that the organisation would then have someone to plead its case in heaven! But, latterly, the chosen personage would be someone whose history disclosed some connection with a particular craft, as well as displaying exemplary moral qualities. It was for these reasons that Eligius had been chosen.

Boys from the late Fifties will recall the old 'steam radio' that used to sit high on a shelf about halfway up each barrack room. At one point, it must have been early 1959, David 'Tubs' Harris of 'A' Coy (56B) had a flash of inspiration. Somehow he managed to link all the 'A' spider radios together with an old gramophone, of the 'sewing needle pickup' variety, and thus the whole block was soon reverberating to the hits of those days. The most popular tune seemed to be *'Little Darling'*, by a group called The Diamonds, accompanied by the wailing sound of six barrack rooms full of rocking boy soldiers!

Dave Harris, along with his reputation as a bit of a Cockney wide-boy, had another 'claim to fame' in that he had, somehow, wangled his way into running the Projector Room, used for showing films in the Camp Hall. The equipment was rather old-fashioned, even for those days, and the number of times a film spooled off its reel during a show was quite high – and, of course, accompanied by loud hoots of derision from the audience, accompanied by instructions to *"put a shilling in the meter"*! One of the 'tricks of the trade' in the Projector Room was maintaining the high-tension arc between two adjustable carbon electrodes, thus providing the light by which the pictures were transmitted, no easy task when a film reel had to be changed over at the same time.

The last Passing Out Parade to carry the .303 rifle

Another operation that took place in the Camp Hall, during those film-shows, was rather more dastardly! Senior boys, generally sitting to the rear on the sloping portion of the floor, would send one of their smallest members crawling down the slope to the rear row of the chairs *"down in the stalls"*, where the lowly Jeeps were located. A rope would then be surreptitiously tied to the back of one of those chairs and the other end dragged quietly back to the eager hands of a few of the senior boys. At a given signal, the rope would be given a sharp tug backwards towards the rear of the Hall. The unfortunate Jeep would then, much like the *'Wily Coyote'* character, in his incessant battle to get one up on his adversary, the resplendent *'Road Runner'*, find himself momentarily suspended above a gap of around eighteen inches, before plunging to the 'canyon' below! Not very intelligent – and likely to cause at least a few bruises to the backside – but that's what occasionally happened!

In July 1959, intake 56B was preparing for its 'PoP'. Many of them, on the electronics side, were to remain at Arborfield for up to another eighteen months on further training at the two adjacent 3 and 5 Trg Btns. For John Houghton however it meant a posting. Along with Roger Clarkson and Eric Pratt, both of whom had been back-squadded, he was off to Windsor to join the RHG. All three boys were summoned to the RCM's office, where they were vigorously lectured on *"... ... ... how privileged ... ... on being selected for attachment to one of the Army's most famous and senior regiments"*. Just a year later, while John was travelling by bus through Bovington, he spotted the newly commissioned Lt Sallis, resplendent in all his finery.

Despite his previous aversion to parades and drill, Tony Domoney had some regrets about not being part of the 'marching brigade' for his Div's 'PoP'. Instead of carrying his rifle on that parade, Tony was striding out at the front of the Band, swinging the mace with gusto in his role now as Apprentice Band Sergeant. The Band had certainly provided the impetus for him to continue as part of 56B, even stirring his efforts on the Fitters' course, where he had finished second in his trade behind colleague Dick Hampton. However, he always reckoned afterwards that his main achievement at boys' school had been that he learned to play the trumpet – something that was to continue to give him continual delight over the years ahead.

Another Apprentices' School is planned

During that last year of the Fifties, a fourth Army Apprentices' School, located at Hadrian's Camp, Carlisle, way up north in Cumbria, was under construction. The direct effect upon the three other Schools was one of a reallocation of trades. Arborfield lost the training of its previous Armourers, Fitters and Fitters Gun, but also expanded the numbers of personnel in the remaining trades. The first entry to Carlisle was not to occur until January of the following year. Over two hundred boys from Arborfield, plus eighty-seven new recruits, then joined the PS of civilian instructors and officers who were already 'in situ'. One of these officers was Capt Percy Chivers, who later designed and constructed the entrance gates for the new College.

Peter Church had joined Arborfield as part of intake 57B and, as a prospective Armourer, he found the thought of *"fiddling about with guns and firing them"* was an exciting prospect. He was one of those boys who later made the long trip north to Carlisle. He recalls his friendship with the legendary Jim Fox, another 'exile' from Arborfield, who went on to become famous as one of the Gold medal winning British Pentathletes team at the 1976 Olympic Games.

As previously mentioned, Jim had been an excellent athlete at Arborfield, always near the front at the cross-country running events, and eventually he ended up as the 'boy' RSM up at Carlisle. Peter recalls that he had never sought the limelight himself, but that *"something must have rubbed off"*, because at Carlisle he became one of only two Commandant's Orderlies. Kitted out in blue uniforms, they would strut about behind the Commandant on parades – and get an extra day's leave, which was most acceptable!

Arborfield received fifty-seven new Electrician apprentices, the overall result being a drop in the total population to 700. Thus it was that the new Commandant, Col R F D Legh, OBE (late RA) took over a slightly depleted School as 1959 – and the Fifties - drew to a close. But another wheel had turned full circle, as Arborfield had originally lost Electrician training to Chepstow back in 1948.

Another major change was being planned, with the number of intakes per year to be increased from two to three. In order to facilitate this, the most recent intake to leave the School did so before Christmas that year and was posted *en bloc* down to Blandford, Dorset, to do six weeks of Regimental Training. This was not part of any future policy, merely to make room for the accommodation of intake 60A, due to arrive in January.

Whither (or wither) the Old Boys?

Sadly, as the decade reached its conclusion, the OBA was in the doldrums and the planned 1959 Reunion for September 15th had to be cancelled. As explained in a letter from Col Cole to his predecessor, Col Magee, a mere fifteen old boys had notified their intention to attend and, of these, five were apprentices who had only recently left the School that July. The previous year's attendance had already been very poor, with quite a lot of money being lost. Despite being well publicised, this year's response had been equally abysmal, so the Commandant felt he had no other option than to cancel the weekend's event.

September 1959 saw the last edition of the *REME Magazine* under that particular title. As from the October edition, it would henceforth be known as *"The Craftsman"*, which, its publishers felt, would be a more appropriate title, especially so for those younger members of the Corps, who could more easily relate to a name that described their own state of affairs and aspirations.

On December 2nd that year, just like his namesake Fred Morris the previous year, the long career of Mr W H 'Bill' Morris finally reached its conclusion, when he retired from his position as Supervising Armourer Instructor. Bill had enlisted in the AOC way back in 1910 and, after serving his apprenticeship at the RSAF, Enfield, went to France in 1915 with the Durham Light Infantry (DLI). There he was wounded and evacuated, but went on to serve in far-off places like Turkey, Egypt, China and India – they certainly got about in those days! Upon retirement from the Army, Bill took up a post at Hilsea and became an instructor at the ATB. He also served as an ARP in Portsmouth and in the Hampshire Home Guard. During 1940, though still living on the south coast, Bill became responsible for the entire move of the ATB up to Arborfield. Awarded the BEM in 1950, his citation read that *"His influence, not only as an instructor but also as a man, has had far-reaching effects with apprentices"*.

The Press – some good, some bad

A newspaper cutting was received with some pride by the School during 1959, with the report that one of our ex-boys had been involved in the brave rescue of a man carried out to sea by a strong current at Portreath in Cornwall. Eighteen-year old Edward Bennett, home on leave from the Army, had assisted another youth in this splendid action. Edward had joined the School in February 1954 and attained the rank of A/T CSM of 'A' Coy, before passing out in July 1957. Rumour persisted at the School that 'Ben' Bennett had been one those boys who had been given the option of joining the School or going to Borstal! If true, then he had certainly made the right choice, and here was the definitive truth.

Other 'tales out of school' were being told during July 1959. Ronald 'Ron' Daykin had been told to take a Physics examination paper, but as he had been trained in one of what was termed the 'black trades', he took one look at the questions, decided that they were way above his head and handed in a blank answer sheet. This rather innocuous offence caused Ron, of 56B intake, to be placed under close arrest. Somehow, this became another story that was leaked to the press, and the daily newspapers gave much space to the fact that he had to share the Guardroom with another soldier, who had been accused of indecency. No doubt it was a typical 'storm in a teacup' episode and Ron was subsequently released.

Three young members of the same family also made the headlines in the Yorkshire press during December 1959. Glenna Clough was then a member of the Queen Alexandra's Royal Army Nursing Corps (QARANC), brother John, aged 19, had just finished his apprenticeship down at AAS Chepstow, while 'the baby' of the family, Terry Clough, had been here at Arborfield since the Summer of 1957. He was due to join the new School at Carlisle after the Christmas recess. Their father had served in the RAF during the war and was justifiably proud of the trio.

Annex to Chapter 5

RSM R L McNally MBE (Scots Guards)

In recognition of the valuable and unstinted service accorded by RSM McNally, both to the School in general and to the Association in particular, the committee invited RSM McNally to accept the first Honorary Life Membership ever to be offered by the Old Boy's Association.

This decision received unanimous approval at the GM and was kindly accepted later on in the evening by him.

RSM McNally enlisted in the 1st Battalion Scots Guards on the 23rd July 1924. He was promoted LCpl on the 11th June 1926; Sergeant on the 27th March 1931; CSM on 10th June 1937 and RSM on 23rd October 1940.

He served in Egypt during 1935/36 and with the British Expeditionary Force in Norway in 1940.

During his service, he represented the Scots Guards at Rugby, Cross-country Running, Athletics and Boxing.

After long service with his Regiment, he came to the School as RSM on the 5th May 1941. He was awarded the:

> Long Service & Good Conduct Medal (LSGC) in 1943
>
> CIGS's Certificate of Good Service in 1945
>
> MBE (Member of the Order of the British Empire) in 1946
>
> C-in-C's Certificate of Merit in 1953
>
> Meritous Service Medal (MSM) in 1953

RSM McNally left the Army on the 23rd July 1956, after 32 years service, to take up local residence and employment.

Of all individuals associated with the School, RSM McNally must have been the best known, and I am sure that all Arborfield ex-boys will concur that his standing as an RSM was respected by all concerned, both for his fairness and sincerity in a job which one does not normally associate with anything other than discipline.

We wish him a long and happy retirement and look forward to his presence at our annual reunions in the future.

(The above article was published in the very first edition of the OBAN in December 1956.)

RSM R L McNally MBE (Scots Guards)
An Appreciation

It is with regret that we shall have to say goodbye to yet another member of staff who has been with us for a long time, when RSM McNally leaves us this month. No member of staff has played such an important role in the life of the School over such a long period.

RSM McNally enlisted in the Scots Guards on July 23rd 1924. In the pre-war years he served at home and abroad with his regiment and, by 1937, had reached the rank of substantive CSM. During this period, he played an important part in the sporting life of his regiment, by representing them on many occasions in athletics, boxing, cross-country running and rugby.

After the outbreak of war, RSM McNally saw action with the British Expeditionary Force in Norway in 1940. After his return to the United Kingdom, he joined the staff of the School as RSM in May 1941, an appointment he has held ever since. He is now retiring after 32 years service.

Recognition for his distinguished military career is exemplified by the many awards which he received whilst on the staff of the School. These included the Long Service and Good Conduct Medal in 1943, the CIGS's Certificate for Good Service in 1945, the Member of the Order of the British Empire in 1946, the C-in-C's Certificate for Good Service, the Coronation Medal and the Meritous Service Medal, all in 1953.

RSM McNally has so identified himself with the activities of the School that, throughout the years, he has become an integral part of its traditions. He is deeply respected by all ranks and will be greatly missed by all who have worked with him.

At the time of writing, he is in the Military Hospital, Aldershot, recovering from an eye operation which will, we hope, improve his vision, which has been a source of worry to him in recent years. The best wishes of all ranks go with him, with the hope that he will return and visit us after he has retired.

(The above article was first published in the July 1956 edition of The Arborfield Apprentice, then reproduced in OBAN Number 13 of spring 1998.)

RCM J T Sallis (Royal Horse Guards)

When anyone holds an appointment for a long time, he is apt to leave a large sized job in the hands of his successor. Mr McNally was with us for fifteen years and now we welcome in his place Regimental Corporal Major J T Sallis, Royal Horse Guards. Already he has had a term with us and firmly established himself as a worthy successor. We may meet the RCM in an official capacity only too often, but in this account we are chiefly interested in the man and his career.

John Thomas Sallis was born at Cheltenham in Gloucestershire on the 6th March 1916. Educated there, he decided to make the Army his career. Being keenly interested in horses and riding, it was only natural that he should join the Royal Horse Guards. This he did without the bother of a recruiting office and he reported directly to the Horse Guards Depot, then at Knightsbridge, on 6th August 1934. To quote him, *"I literally gave myself up!"* Here, he did 10 months cavalry training and eventually moved with his regiment to Windsor.

This changing of barracks was done jointly by the Life Guards and Horse Guards. Each regiment occupied the barracks for one year, with the regiment at Knightsbridge being responsible for all ceremonial duties, such as the Opening of Parliament, Queen's Birthday Parade and the Horse Guards Parade at Whitehall. When changing over, the two regiments rode to their new homes, and one can imagine the magnificent spectacle as they passed each other on the Great West Road.

Training and duties continued until the beginning of World War II for Mr Sallis, who was at this time a Troop Corporal of Horse. This was a historic time for the Cavalry, as it underwent a complete mechanisation and re-training in the art of warfare. World War I had been the summit of the Cavalry's achievements as such, as a fighting unit.

At the same time, and for the duration of the war, the two Guards regiments were amalgamated into two regiments of the Household Cavalry. Mr Sallis remained in England with the second regiment, who were training and preparing for the major assault on Europe in 1944. His regiment went into France at Normandy on D-Day+21 and pushed on right through into Germany. The regiments were reformed after the war and Mr Sallis stayed in Germany until 1952. In February of that year he was posted to Cyprus, but returned to take up his duties here at Arborfield in June.

In twenty-two years of soldiering, including service under four sovereigns, Mr Sallis has seen many changes in military organisation and discipline. He recalls that it was an offence to shave the upper lip in the Horse Guard – an offence punishable by seven days CB! Walking out dress in those days included a bowler hat and either an umbrella or walking stick – a habit to make even the most broad-minded shiver.

Mr Sallis admits, however, that a well-groomed soldier still gives him pleasure, and that he cannot but inwardly smile at certain members of England's future Army who display 'Mohican' or 'Davy Crockett' hair styles. When one remembers that the RCM was brought up in the school that had the criterion of a correct haircut summed up by the phrase 'What's under your hat is yours – what sticks out is the Army's', one is not too surprised!

Thus we warmly welcome Mr Sallis and hope that both he and his family enjoy a long and pleasant stay at Arborfield.

(The above article was first published in the Christmas 1956 edition of The Arborfield Apprentice and reproduced in OBAN Number 16 in spring 1999.)

The School Badge
by Colonel J D White, DSO, MC

It has been represented to me that past and present members of the School would like to know how the School cap badge came into being. It is twelve years ago now since it happened but, to the best of my memory, the story is as follows:

As the older boys will remember, the General Service Corps badge was the one originally worn by Apprentices but this, having no particular relation to the objectives of the School, was not considered suitable. I do not know when a special badge was first suggested, but it was brought to my attention during my time as Commandant, and I suggested it to the Director of Military Training, who gave it his approval.

The next step was to produce a suitable design and suggestions were invited from all at Arborfield and, no doubt, at Chepstow as well. Quite a lot of ideas were forthcoming at Arborfield. I cannot remember the details now, but one design that I liked consisted of a quartered shield, bearing in the four quarters (1) a cross surmounted by a crown, to represent character and loyalty; (2) an open book, to represent learning; (3) the ancient Greek statue of a discus thrower, to represent physical fitness; and (4) a lightning flash, to represent technical skill.

Next, Colonel Cuddon, the then Commandant of Chepstow, and I were instructed to attend a meeting at the office of the King of Arms in London. Here we met the Inspector of Regimental Colours, who is responsible, among other things, for Army badges. I had with me the ideas from Arborfield and Colonel Cuddon had those from Chepstow. The shield idea was washed out because, it was explained, a shield charged with devices constitutes a coat of arms, which could be granted only on payment of a large fee. Neither Colonel Cuddon nor I felt able to pay £150!

We explained to the Inspector the aims and objects to be represented and left all the suggestions with him. The badge which you now know was the result, and incorporates features put forward by:

Civilian Instructor Mr J R Williams
2548288 A/T J W Davidson (42B)
2548159 A/T R T Janes (42B)
2549461 A/T D A Marsden (43A)
14469058 A/T J W N Pewsey (45A)

The ideas represented in the badge are explained to every boy on entering the School and are too well known to require repetition here. There is one point, however, which was brought out by Chaplain General Hughes in a sermon, which he preached in the Camp Hall, about the end of 1946, or the beginning of 1947. The gear wheel, he explained, represents not only technical knowledge and skill, but also co-operation. It is only by meshing or co-operating with others that it does useful work.

I have never forgotten those words and I commend them to you.

(This article is quoted verbatim from the pages of OBAN Number 5, issued in March 1959 and subsequently reproduced in OBAN Number 20, summer 2000.)

Fred Silvers (King's Royal Rifle Corps) Provost Sergeant

Many boys who served at the School during the Fifties will well remember the Provost Sergeant of those days, 'Fiery' Fred Silvers, he of the black bristling moustache and a temper to match, although not too many will recall any of his personal details. John Maddox (44B) had actually met him at the KRRC Regimental Depot in Winchester around 1949, just before Fred's Arborfield days. As John approached the Depot gates, he saw a *"seemingly demented"* Corporal yelling out loud at a couple of dejected riflemen. Yes, that was Fred all right, when he was a 'deputy Provost Corporal', but John didn't realise until years later that Fred had subsequently been posted to the Apprentices' School.

Considering how many years he spent at Arborfield, it is surprising that this is the only photograph that we could find of Fred!

Joe Kinson, however, was on the School's permanent staff from 1954 to 1957, and is thus able to cast a little more light on Fred's background details. Fred was a member of the KRRC (60th Foot). His three Sergeant's chevrons were woven of a black material on a red background, of a larger size than those worn by the apprentice NCOs, and his uniform always sported a black lanyard, black buttons and a black cap-badge – all matching his moustache! Joe recalls that Fred was less than popular with many boys but that, as Provost Sergeant, he had an unenviable task to fulfill.

Joe was to meet up with Fred again around 1961, now on route to join BAOR Germany and, despite his Regiment having suffered from an enforced amalgamation, Fred was still proudly wearing his KRRC cap-badge – he wasn't going to change that for anyone. Fred appeared a little non-plussed about the journey, explaining to Joe that he was heading for Bielefeld to join the administration staff responsible for

married quarters. Joe travelled with him to Harwich, then overnight with him on the ferry to the Hook of Holland, then finally on the train into Germany.

Ted Blowers was another PS member, from 1953 – 1956, so had plenty of experience of Fred's eccentricities. He remembers the huge wooden flower-boxes that Fred kept overnight in the Guardroom, having them carefully carried out for display each morning, they were his *"pride and joy"*. They actually contained geraniums, but Fred couldn't get his tongue round the name, as far as he was concerned they were 'germaniums'! Ted also recalls that Fred always had problems with words. Another classic, in that nasal twang of his, was the term 'gymnasshum', which no doubt referred to the Gymnasium!

Going back to Fred's flowers, there was one occasion when one of the janker wallahs kicked the head off a whole lot of them. In a flash of inspiration, and knowing that there would otherwise be great retribution, Ted came up with a cunning plan! Collecting a load of matchsticks, he carefully stuck these into the broken stems, then attached the flower heads back in place. A real good dose of water was then applied – and the unfortunate flowers actually held out until suppertime. The look on Fred's face as they then all sank gracefully down to soil level was something to be long remembered.

'Eggy' Egleton recalls that when he arrived at the School, as a member of intake 52B, Fred was on sick leave at the time, having suffered a stabbing by another member of the Provost staff! Gerry Berragan, who had joined earlier with 48B, remembers the affair very well. He was surprised that, as the incident had taken place on military property, the culprit hadn't been tried by court martial. Instead, he was tried by the local Magistrate's Court and received what seemed a fairly lenient sentence.

Ian Hume of 49A also remembers that stabbing, saying that it was not a particularly savoury incident to set before young boys undergoing training! The story is supported by Jim Baker of 46B, who recalls that his last meeting with Fred was in the Cambridge Military Hospital, Aldershot, in the summer of 1950, where Fred was then being treated for his *"multiple stab wounds"*. It sounds as if Fred must have enjoyed a pretty long sick leave!

Despite his lack of stature, Fred was quite vain about his appearance. His brand new dress uniform arrived in a box one day and Fred couldn't wait to try it on. There was a large mirror inside the Guardroom and Fred stood in front of it, preening himself, his normal beret discarded in favour his new flat peaked cap. Another of the Provost staff, a huge Welshman who answered to the name Taff Davies, walked in and shouted, *"Who the hell are you?"* Fred must have jumped a foot in the air and replied, *"Who do you think I am?"* Taff's response was immediate, *"God, Sarge, is that you? I never recognised you, you look so much taller"*. He then proceeded to put Fred's cap on at just the right angle, straighten his tie and smooth down his jacket, all the while remarking on how good Fred looked. He was actually taking the mickey, for the benefit of all the other staff, but Fred never did see it that way.

Greg Peck of 53B recalls Fred as *"the most feared of the PS after RSM McNally"*. He paints Fred as *"a dapper sallow-faced little man, of immaculate turnout"* – and the bane of every apprentice. Like every other boy at the School, Greg loathed the sight of an RP armband and wondered just what lower form of life could there possibly be? However, one incident that Greg remembers shows Fred in a somewhat different light to his usual 'fall-guy' image. Just prior to a 'PoP', boys of the Senior Div were leading the rest of the School on an impromptu 'conga' around the spiders, when suddenly the mood turned quite ugly when one senior boy was heard to shout, *"Let's get Johnny French!"*

Johnny French was an A/T Sergeant who had apparently upset someone, and the assembled crowd quickly took up the chant – no more *"Ee Aye Ee Aye Conga"*, but *"Let's get Johnny French"* – and went looking for him. Luckily for the boy in question, he had heard the first cries of the mob and got himself smartly down to the Guardroom for his own protection. When the mob arrived at the Guardroom in his wake, it was Fred Silvers who appeared on the verandah and stood there without comment, but facing down the boys in front of him. They gradually quietened down and Fred then reminded them that leave was coming up and, if they didn't behave, he would see that leave passes were cancelled *en masse*.

As two of his Provost staff came out of the Guardroom and stood either side of Fred, he then told the throng that, if they quietly disappeared, with no further nuisance, he would overlook their unruly behaviour on this occasion and not press charges on anyone. After some shuffling of feet and some under-

the-breath muttering, the boys decided that this was indeed the best course of action, and they gradually melted into the night and back off to their barrack rooms. Greg reckoned that it took a lot of courage on Fred's part to stand up and confront that gang of unruly teenagers.

Another PS member who got to know Fred *"fairly well"* was Brian Conway, an ex-boy himself of 42A, who later served here as a military instructor from 1954 to 57. Brian recalls one particular Saturday afternoon, after a typically *"heavy session"* in the Mess, when Fred made his way off through the gates on his bicycle in unsteady manner, steering single-handedly, with a bundle of clean laundry under the other arm. Now Fred had always been quite proud of his pocket watch, so when one young lad yelled across to ask him the time, Fred automatically reached for his watch and fell off his bike with a resounding crash! *"You bleedin' fool,"* shouted Fred, *"what you want to ask me the time for?"*

Fred was well known for taking 'Fire Picket', but never seemed to understand why he so often used to get his uniform soaking wet when conducting those infamous sessions! George 'Fleet' Fleetwood (56B) recalls one occasion of such a duty when Fred sent one lad off to get some rag, as the brass fittings of the hoses and standpipes required polishing. The unfortunate lad returned empty-handed some time later and, in his inimitable manner, Fred went quite mad. *"Get into the Guardroom and find me some rag"*, he bellowed. Some minutes later out came the same lad, proudly holding some rather splendid red rag in his clammy hands. Talk about 'red rag to a bull', the young fellow had only torn up one of the Guardroom curtains! A good example of obeying the last command if ever there was one.

Fleet himself became part of the 'Fred' legend, soon before his departure from the School in the summer of 1959. At the rear of the fire station was a small patch of 'garden' that Fred had nurtured, on the backs of his 'janker wallahs' and a supply of free manure from the adjacent stables. Fleet and another boy had been instructed to scratch out a number of small furrows and then to sow some seeds along them in the time-honoured fashion. Fleet's mate had other ideas however!

The furrows were duly scratched out and the individual seed packets proudly displayed at the end of each one for identification purposes. What Fred couldn't see was that **all** the seeds, from **all** the packets, had been deposited in the one large hole, prior to it being carefully filled in. We wonder what became of them? Another memory of Fred is recalled by Gerry Hincks, also of 56B – Fred doing an apparent 'war dance' on his beret, in frustration at seeing his beloved greenhouse virtually destroyed by a severe hailstorm, when they came down *"as big as golf balls"*.

One of Fred's more insidious duties was that of inspecting the boys, prior to their being allowed out into the world at large. Once the senior boys had gone past the 'School Mufti' stage of blazer and flannels, standard civilian clothes were then permissible. Now, it hadn't been too many years since the first 'teddy boys' had made their presence felt, with their drape suits, 'drainpipe' trousers with fluorescent socks, and 'slim jim' ties. So it was only natural that Arborfield boys, wishing to look their best for the young ladies of the outlying towns and villages, would endeavour to try and emulate the latest fashions.

Fred, of course, saw it all rather differently, and would be there at the Guardroom, ruler to the fore, ensuring that the boys' trouser bottoms were at least 16" wide. There was also a custom in those days that Arborfield boys would wear a slim bright red tie, it helped when attempting to come to the aid of one's mates should any fracas occur. Fred must have thought it was a symbol of being a Communist, the way he would rage against any boy actually wearing such a tie on his way out, so they were usually rolled up in one's pocket until the bus had been boarded!

George Vince, of intake 57A, recalls one occasion when Fred came a right cropper and had to be extricated, along with his bicycle, from 'A' Company's flower beds, by members of his own Regimental Police staff! Riding back from the Sergeants' Mess, where no doubt a certain amount of over-indulgence had been undertaken, Fred had failed to safely negotiate the corner of the Camp Hall road and found himself much closer to nature than was usually the case.

Mick Oulds' acquaintance with the 'dreaded Fred' began before he'd even crossed the threshold of the School to join intake 57B. Upon arrival at Wokingham railway station, he was greeted by what he describes as *"a dwarf with a large black moustache"*. Mick's 'great expectations' of a romantic start to his Army life were soon shattered by Fred's words, *"If yer for Arborfield, sonny, get yer arse into that lorry, quick!"* Mick is another who remembers the usual battle to get out of Camp in anything but the standard garb. His

usual trick was to cover it all up with a beige-coloured 'shorty' mac, they were very popular at the time.

Fred didn't make too many friends, that's for sure! He certainly came off second best on one occasion, as recalled by Eddie Cooper of 52A. Eddie's mate Bob Condon had an uncle, who had not only served in Fred's regiment, but had also been its RSM. Arriving as a visitor to the School one weekend, Bob's uncle was immediately recognised by Fred, who must have thought he was being checked up on. Fred was hopping about all over the place, *"Yes Sir, no Sir, three bags full Sir"*, completely subservient – much to the amusement of all the boys present at the time, happy to see Fred squirm for a change!

Whatever his reputation for 'fierceness', Fred must have had some milk of human kindness running through his veins, as borne out by Jim Cliff of intake 57A. Jim had travelled on a DC6 from Hong Kong on a flight that had lasted some thirty-six hours. He had then had to spend the night cooped up in a Reception Centre at London's Goodge Street, before being sent on his way to Arborfield to arrive very early one Sunday morning. His head *"still ringing from the drone of large piston engines"*, Jim hardly knew where he was, even wondering if he was still on 'Planet Earth'. Someone walked over and put his arms around Jim's shoulders, saying *"You look all in son, sit down over there"*. It was none other than Fred Silvers – Jim even has to add the word *"Honest!"* in response to we readers' looks of disbelief – and Jim always rather liked Fred after that.

Paul Hudson of 58A tells another story, again associating Fred with the Fire Picket. One evening, the gleaming *'Coventry Climax'* pump was wheeled out, with Fred yelling at the boys on duty to *"get it started then"*. Round and round went the starting handle, but with no apparent effect, the engine stubbornly refused to fire. *"Pull the bloody choke out, you morons"*, shouted Fred, *"pull the bloody choke out."* At this, one of the lads took him at his word and pulled at the choke knob with such fury that it did come out – all the way - followed by several feet of attached cable! *"Like this, Sarge?"* said the youngster, at which Fred did his famous 'beret dance', accompanied with much inappropriate language.

Another of that 58B intake, Geoff Earnest, recalls that Fire Picket drills under Fred's 'supervision' almost inevitably went wrong. With Fred's reputation and fierce temper going before him, a certain number of 'deliberate mistakes' were bound to occur, as the taunting of Fred became one of the customs of the School. *"Two lengths of suction hose, three lengths of delivery hose, branch pipe to work on 'B' Company Office"*. Fred's words ring down through the years, though Geoff doubts very much that the fire drills were ever brought to a satisfactory conclusion.

One day, Fred took it upon himself that he was just the right man to teach the Cookhouse staff the art of fire-fighting, especially in the maintenance and use of the fire extinguishers located in the kitchen. The staff all assembled outside and Fred duly demonstrated how the extinguisher should be activated – although he never actually set it off, this being *"only a demo"*. He then passed the appliance to one of the cooks, who just happened to be a bit of a nutter, to have it put back in its place on the wall. But the cook said, *"Is this how it's done, Sarge?"* - setting the extinguisher off and spraying Fred with foam!

Chris Jeffery of 59B remembers that, upon his arrival at the School, and having disembarked from the number 4 or 4a bus from Reading, he and some other boys were quickly assembled in front of the Guardroom. Out came Fred, all spits and snarls, snorting fire and brimstone, as was his fashion. Spotting that Chris was the tallest boy in the group (he was almost seventeen), Fred asked him, *"You done any boxing, boy?"* When Chris replied in the negative, Fred snarled back *"You bloody will"*! Chris is relieved to say that Fred's prediction never came true, though it was a close run thing.

One of the jobs of the Provost staff was to make sure that, after the weekly dances in the Camp Hall, none of the apprentices got into any shenanigans with the visiting girls! As soon as the last waltz came to a close, the girls were to be hustled away as quickly as possible onto their coach, before they fell into the clammy hands of the ever-hopeful boys. Ted Blowers was on duty with Fred on one such night, and his own *"bit of stuff"* had turned up for the dance. Ted could only inform her that he would see her afterwards.

As the evening's entertainment drew to a close, Ted dutifully escorted his girl onto her coach, then decided to stay there, offer his protection and *"say goodnight"*. In the meantime of course, Fred was dashing about like a mad thing, trying to split up any couple who looked as if they were enjoying themselves and screaming, *"Blowers! Blowers! Where the 'ell are you?"* Eventually Fred caught up with Ted on the coach and *"just about blew a gasket"* – and another part of Ted's

illustrious career came to a shuddering halt!

David Fisher (49B) recalls meeting Fred at Shrivenham in late 1965. By that time, Fred was preparing to return to civilian life and was having yet another attempt at passing his driving test, having already failed it several times. Imagine David's surprise when he next saw Fred patrolling the streets of Swindon, *"immaculate in the uniform of that town's only traffic warden"*. As confirmed by Brian Conway, who came back as an instructor for a second time between 1960 and 1967, Fred is next known to have been a traffic warden in the Winchester area around 1967. So perhaps he never did pass his driving test – and was looking for revenge on those who had!

John Maddox, who went on to become secretary to the Royal Greenjackets Association in the Cotswolds, actually attended Fred's funeral at a later date and, as he says, *"There will never be another Fred Silvers – the mould has been well and truly broken"*.
(These notes on Sgt Fred Silvers were concocted from the many stories sent in by ex-boys who remembered him only too well!)

Report from the Editor
referring to article by Robert Holles

The old school seemed a different place when Robert Holles, a *John Bull* writer, went back a few weeks ago. There was a television set in the canteen, sumptuous food in the mess, and a woman welfare officer to solve the boys' problems.

"Things were tougher in my day", says Holles, a sergeant major's son, who arrived at the Army Apprentices School, Arborfield, as a new boy in 1941. *"I was plunged straight into a room of older boys. My first spell of defaulters was a direct result of an old stager in the next bed shovelling his rubbish under mine"*.

After three years at Arborfield, Holles joined REME as an Armourer. In Korea, he was Armourer sergeant to the Glosters, and was saved from capture in the Imjin River battle by a dozen damaged rifles. Holles collected the rifles and returned to the workshop for new ones. While he was away, the Chinese struck. Holles told the story of that battle in his first British book on the Korean War, *'Now thrive the Armourers'*.

His first article for us – on Korean refugees – was scribbled in an Army notebook in a tent at Uijongbu. Later, he typed a final draft on a typewriter that he found on an abandoned American dump. *"The only snag"*, says Holles, *"was that the machine had Korean characters. We soon fixed that in the workshop"*.

Holles, a soft-spoken, studious man of thirty, left the Army last year to devote himself to full-time writing. His first novel was published a year ago; his fifth John Bull article begins in page 16. Now, at the three hundred-year-old cottage in Essex, where he lives with his wife and two young sons, he is busy on a novel about Army life. *"It begins where I did – at an Army apprentices' school"*.

(The above editorial comment was published in the 'John Bull' magazine of June 29th 1957.)

Obituary: Brigadier F A Hilborn, Ret'd.

It is given to comparatively few Army officers to be able, on retirement for age from the active list, to follow on for another twelve or thirteen years in employment which is thoroughly congenial to them. But I believe that such an individual was Brigadier F A Hilborn, of whose death on the 8th March at Bexhill, at the age of seventy-four, many of his contemporaries in the RAOC and the REME must have learned with much regret.

It was in 1922 that I first made the acquaintance of Frankie Hilborn. He was then the Adjutant of a Tank Training Battalion at Bovington, and working there in close liaison with the OC RAOC Tank Workshops (Maj B K Penn). He impressed me at once as a very competent regimental officer.

In 1927, he was transferred from the RTC (Royal Tank Corps) to the RAOC as an OME 2nd Class (Major). Thereafter I was in fairly frequent contact with him in the course of my service and found him very keen on the welfare of his staff, both military and civilian. He was essentially a 'happy warrior', always ready for a good bout of honest bandinage. I remember that, in 1935, when we were both in India with the IAOC, I visited his workshops at Allahabad Arsenal and, after my official inspection, he put on a brief but excellent display by his Indian Boy Scouts.

His very keen interest in boy training and welfare was plainly apparent and, after his retirement for age in November 1940, his employment as Commandant and Chief Instructor, Army Technical School (Boys) Arborfield (1940/43) and Commandant Gordon Boys' School, Woking (1943/53) gave ample scope for the exercise of his abilities in this connection.

It was a gracious gesture, and a fitting tribute to his memory, that a party of Gordon Boys – resplendent in their No.1 dress – attended the funeral service for Brigadier Hilborn at Golders Green Crematorium on the 12th March.

A.R.V.

(The above personal obituary was published in the REME Magazine of May 1957.)

The early 1960s saw a new accommodation block at the top of the square, SD uniforms and SLR rifles - and yes it rained occasionally.

Chapter 6

1960 - 64

A time of reorganisation

'Voluntary activities' quickly became the norm when they were introduced during the spring term of 1960, giving the large population of boys the chance to carry out a pastime, interest or hobby of their own choice, during any spare leisure time. This is possibly an astonishing thing to record now, when one thinks of the multifarious leisure activities available to the youths of today, with all their digital equipment, such as TV, computers, music centres, games consoles and video recorders.

Other changes were in the air too by 1960, with the number of intakes having been increased from two to three per year, and the corresponding number of 'Divs' from six to nine. The School population now included boys from 58A and 58B, plus the three Divs from 1959, 59A, B and C. The VM was now asked to undergo a two-week driving course as part of his training, sometime during what would now be his eighth term. The programme was also now to include extra military training, in the form of a full week of this activity in both the fourth and eighth terms, in addition to the initial draft training.

There were now to be three 'Wings' in each Company, plus the formation of a 'Senior Company' ('S' Coy) for the duration of the last two terms. 'S' Coy was formed on September 1st 1960, under the command of Maj J A Morton, REME, himself an ex-apprentice, though of the Chepstow breed. The ultimate aim was to get all of the most senior apprentices together under one 'umbrella' during their final phases of training, in order to acclimatise them to the sort of adult treatment they could be expected to receive, when taking up their follow-up postings. The 'guinea pigs' for this innovation were the boys of intake 58B. As the Senior Div, they were in fact now in their final term. Also, the School was now concentrating its training on the electrical and electronic trades, plus of course VMs. Those boys passing out in future years would be either VMs, Electricians REME (B), Control Equipment Technicians (CETs), Radar Techs, Tels Techs or Inst Techs. *(Note that 'Mechanics' had by now become transformed to 'Technicians' in all but the vehicle trade. Ed.)*

One of those Inst Techs was Barrie King of 60A, whose nickname of 'Titch' was most appropriate to his minute stature. Many years later he sent in a photograph of himself, published in *OBAN Issue 14*, where he stood on a chair next to Eric 'Lofty' Ricketts and still only just managed to match Eric for height. Looking at Lofty, it is easy to see how he became a Corps basketball player *par excellence* later in his career.

Barrie still likes to reminisce about those weekends when he could dress up in his best SD and walk sprightly down to the next village of Eversley. There, he would buy a pint of fresh milk for breakfast and then continue down to the A30, where he would endeavour to hitch a lift to his home of Bournemouth. With his 'little boy lost' appearance, Barrie could usually manage to get picked up and be transported home in time for his mother's tasty dinner. To ensure that he was back at Camp on time by the Sunday evening, he always caught the same train back, in those days when the train timetable actually meant something! Barrie recalls leaving home to the accompaniment of *'Sing Something Simple'* by the *Black and White Minstrels* on the TV, and still feels nostalgic whenever he hears that sweet refrain today.

Barrie eventually converted to Air Tech (Electric and Instrument), then finally saw out his days as Air Tech (Avionics), serving as an 'external validation' expert at SEME Bordon. *(I can vouch for that – we shared the same office! Ed.)*

Early in 1960, Col Legh had to spend some five weeks at hospital in London, leaving command of the School to his CI, Lt Col R C 'Reg' Barfield, REME. There was much talk in the air at that time about the School being moved from its *"untidy hutted accommodation"* to a more permanent location. Indeed, Col Legh recalls being driven by his wife down to inspect a derelict campsite near Andover, but this move never came to fruition.

In the May edition of *The Craftsman*, there was a report on the Corps Boxing Championships, held that year at the AAS, Arborfield. The attendance was disappointingly low, as was the standard of most of the boxing. The REME JLdrs were delighted to win a hat-trick of victories, whilst Cpl Phayer must have felt it was 'just like old times' as he won his light middleweight bout, having won the ISBA title at the School, as an apprentice, eight years earlier.

In that same year, it was decided that the 'Champion Company' Award would be presented for the last time, as this feature was now sadly to be discontinued as part of the fabric of School life. 'A' Coy was the winner of this final competition, but the Champion Company banner appears to have been lost, and is no longer in the possession of the School – perhaps taken as a treasured souvenir by one of 'A' Coy? June of that year saw RCM John Sallis relinquish his appointment, handing over to RSM J Stewart, of the Irish Guards. Another to leave in 1960 was Miss Gunning, the WVS lady, who had been here for five years, passing on the *"benefit of her feminine influence"* to successive intakes of apprentices.

Intake 57B passed out of the School on July 27th 1960, under the command of A/T RSM N W Lloyd. For a week before that parade, the weather had been poor, with rain threatening to spoil this *"crowning event of the term"*. Happily, the morning dawned brightly and, by the time that Senior Div marched on to the Square, the sun was *"beating down strongly"* on another fine spectacle. The spectators were probably unaware of the discomfort of the apprentices, who were all bothered by the irritating attentions of a large number of wind-borne tiny spiders. As detailed in the School magazine, later that autumn, *"not a muscle moved throughout their trying experience, for the discomfort was borne bravely – self-discipline indeed"*.

The Instrument Section was looking forward (?) towards its impending move to the northern outpost of Carlisle. Despite this *"looming like a large black cloud ahead"*, the boys were continuing to play their part in the rich fabric of School life. Even though the smallest section, they had recently filled no less than two of the six A/T CSM appointments, namely A/T CSM Tom Murray in 'J' Coy and A/T CSM Dave Harbron in 'C' Coy. The Section had been an integral part of the School since 1942, when the trade of 'Inst Mech' had taken its place in the REME structure. The last twenty years had seen many Inst Mechs – or Inst Techs as they were later to become – pass through the Section, training to tackle the multitude of problems and repairs that were their responsibility. Meanwhile, the Vehicle Department was being assisted by practical displays of products, provided by civilian firms such as *Ferodo* (clutch and brake linings) and *Timken's Ltd.* of Northampton (bearings).

'Captain Cat'

1960 also saw the publication of a book that went by the title of *'Captain Cat'*. It had been written by Bob Holles, an ex-apprentice Armourer from the 1941 intake. Bob was the same author who had previously written the *John Bull* magazine article during 1957. His lively book was written in the form of a novel, but was obviously based partly upon Bob's experiences whilst here at Arborfield. The fictitious military unit in his book became the '3rd Army Boys' Technical Training Battalion', and the book's flyleaf quoted that the author had produced *"a most convincing close-up of the influence of military training on impressionable boys"*.

Bryan Adams (42B) recalls that, following his boys' service, Bob had gone on to serve with

1960 School Cricket Team

This photograph of the School Hockey Team shows the Master Artificer (Mr Lilley) seated next to the Commandant. The Master Artificer, a REME ASM, along with a Lt Col Chief Instructor oversaw the trade training management of the 3 year apprenticeship. The photograph was taken on the sports field behind the Camp Hall - 'B' Coy lines are on the left and the Sgts Mess behind the team. All that now remains are the trees to the edge of the field.

the 1st Battalion of the famous Gloucestershire Regt in Korea, later writing an excellent and most descriptive account of their historic actions there in 1952. Bryan and Bob's paths later crossed briefly at Bordon, around 1956, when Bob was awaiting the completion of his *"twelve years with the Colours"*.

George Harold of 46A recalls that he met up with Bob Holles when posted as 'assistant Armourer' to The Gloucesters at Colchester in 1950. Bob was then the unit's Armourer Sergeant, and the pair stayed together, first in England, then followed by a term of service in Korea up until 1953. George remembers the book about those exploits being called *'Now thrive the Armourers'*. Paul 'Tug' Wilson (42A) says that the book would *"strike a chord with Armourers in general, ex-boys in particular and specifically 1941 Armourers of Room J5 in 'D' Coy lines"*!

Bob also went on to write *'Guns of Batasi'*, which was later made into a well-known adventure film starring Richard Attenborough. It still features in many a repeat showing on our TV screens. Bob also added to our entertainment, writing the scripts for a number of plays, for both the *BBC* and *ITV*, in the *'Armchair Theatre'* and *'Play for Today'* series during the Sixties.

David Cross of 42C has read *'Captain Cat'* on numerous occasions and, although he discovered bits here and there displaying the *"reality of boy service"*, he also found that it conjured up some unpleasant memories. David recalls that, in his opinion, boys were *"not treated to a very good standard of well-being"*. However, he survived it and today reckons that is why ex-boys still stick together so well! David now has three of Bob Holles' books in his possession, *'Captain Cat'* of course, *'Now thrive the Armourers'* and another by the title of *'Spawn'.(Any truth in that it is a nature book, dealing with frogs? Ed.)*

Whatever happened to the Old Boys?

Correspondence during the middle of 1960 showed that the OBA was sadly showing signs of becoming defunct. A letter from Sgt P J Cronshaw, then serving at Larkhill, Wiltshire, requested details of the Association and the possibility of his attendance at the next Reunion. The reply from Lt Col (Ret'd) Blunt, then Hon Sec, apologised that, due to a large number of other commitments, the School had been *"unable to fit in a Reunion this year"*. It came as no surprise that there was no Reunion the following year either. In another letter, dated May 1961, the Hon Sec was to report that all members of the Old Boys' Committee had left the School and added, wistfully, that *"there was no-one available and keen enough to serve"*. *(What one could term a 'blunt response' then? Ed.)*

Keith Thrower could hardly be surprised, having joined as a member of 60C, to be re-christened as 'Percy', after the famous gardener and TV celebrity of his day – it was a nickname that has stuck with him over the years. Being, in his own words, *"a bit of a swot"*, Percy was one of those boys who attended Reading Technical College for one day per week, as part of his ONC training. Sitting in class on one of those days, towards the end of his training in 8 Div, he was chewing the end of his 'biro' when the little blue bit at the end managed to come off and lodged down his throat. Percy coughed a lot, but the offending piece of plastic was hell bent on staying put! He was rushed, first to Battle Hospital, down the Oxford Road in Reading, then to the Royal Berkshire, on the other side of town. Under local anaesthetic, the offending 'blue bit' was finally removed. Percy enjoyed a couple of quiet days in bed, happy to be on a 'skive' that neither the CSM nor his OC could catch him for.

Edward 'Ted' Stanford was another of that 60C intake, later going into 'C' Coy, where his 'Room NCO', A/T LCpl John Taylor, sent young Ted over to 'A' Coy, where he was supposed to pick up a 'record stand'. Needless to say, Ted was still a bit green in those days and, after about an hour hanging around in the corridor, he was told *"You can go now, that must be a record, I've never had anyone stand there that long before!"* Ted obviously leaned a few tricks of his own, as do we all. When his Div joined 'S' Coy, he stayed with 'C' Coy as a SNCO. When 'C' Coy were on parade, Ted was a member of 'S' Coy – and *vice versa*. This went on until he was caught out by Maj J A N Sim MC, OC 'C' Coy, and of the York and Lancaster Regt, who threatened to reduce Ted to the ranks, before settling for *"a right rollicking"*.

The ownership of motor-bikes and cars was still 'illegal' in those days, but of course this didn't prevent boys from leaving their precious machines at garages and lock-ups all over the area. Ted's mate Paul Bosanko of 'A' Coy got caught out and had to bring his car into Camp, where it had to then stay until end of term. All the better of course, as a spare set of keys meant that they could pick up the car whenever they wanted, and drive out of the back entrance near the MRS. They would later return by the same route, parking the car up until the next time.

After their 'PoP' (in July 1963), Paul deposited all his kit into the back of his now legally-owned car and drove proudly out of the front gates. Ted has never seen him since! On the subject of that same 'PoP', Ted recalls that the Minister of War, John Profumo, was due to be the Reviewing Officer that day, but that the infamous 'Christine Keeler' affair led to the Minister's absence. During December 1960, the last 'call-up' papers were sent to those young men required for National Service. From now on, the Army was going to consist of 'regular soldiers' only.

The ones who got away!

Just prior to Christmas leave, members of the Angling Club spent an unforgettable weekend based at Deal, on the coast of Kent. Their first disaster was when they found that the 4,000 lugworms they had ordered as bait numbered a mere 100! Two hours were then spent, scouring the town for supplies. The coach driver was meanwhile preparing an 'all-in stew', which he somehow managed to burn! A/T Mack then lost all his tackle – his excuse was a monster cod, but everyone else knew it was seaweed. After hiring a *"leaky old tub"*, several members rowed it out a couple of miles to sea and actually caught some nice fish, despite looking as green as the sea on their return.

After a storm had blown up and one of their oars had snapped, our brave anglers then found their 'boat' shipping water and, after about two hours of hard slog, it finally sank in six foot of water just ten yards from the shore – but two miles down the coast. Other members quickly pulled them ashore. The fact that two rear tyres 'blew' on the return journey must have been 'the last straw'.

The 1960 Christmas Concert promised to be a gloomy affair. The Military Band was converting itself into a Brass Band, the Pipe Band and Scottish Dancers were unable to help, while the REME Staff Band, who had greatly contributed the previous year, was now away touring the Far East. But, thanks to a tremendous effort by BSM A Parker, Argyle and Sutherland Highlanders (ASH), members of staff and some ex-apprentices still in the locality, in the finest traditions of the theatre *"the show still went on"*. Another high spot on the entertainment scene was the arrival of some modern cinematic equipment, donated by the Nuffield Trust.

January 1961 saw the training of technicians and craftsmen come under the parliamentary spotlight, when the Minister of Education outlined his proposals in a report for *'Better opportunities in Technical Education'*. The report proposed that all apprentices should commence studying at a Technical College immediately upon leaving school. By virtue of the need for technicians to have a higher level of scientific and technical knowledge than the craftsman, the requirement for a higher entry standard was recognised. All the points raised by the report were sound and the School here at Arborfield was already following its broad recommendations.

Around that same time, the School's Dancing Club had moved its Tuesday evening venue to the Lecture Hall in the new Education Block, a much more compact hall for dancing. A new rock'n'roll group, the 'Red Devils' had been formed and proved a great success, driven along by the guitar of A/T LCpls Gajardo and 'Scouse' Burns. A 'big dance' was now being held in the Camp Hall on the last Tuesday of each month, in order to accommodate the 150 Club members. For the forthcoming 28th March dance, a guest band had been invited along – *'Preacher Hood and the Jazz Missionaries'*. Extensive advertising had been carried out in the hope of attracting more girls along – apparently they were a *"very scarce commodity in Arborfield"* at the time.

A *"very considerable boost"* to the Cycling Club had occurred the previous September, with a grant of £190 allowing the purchase of six gleaming new racing bikes. The winter term had then seen a period of relative inactivity as far as 'racing' members of the Club were concerned. But the 'touring' section did not join in this hibernation, enjoying two pleasant tours, one to Swanage in Dorset and the other to Marlborough, Wiltshire, during November. Now, on February 23rd 1961, the 'Bloodhound' Cycle Rally had proved an interesting innovation, ahead of what promised to be a busy season.

That year's spring term brought an interesting experiment, in the formation of a Church Committee. Run along similar lines to a civilian Parochial Church Council, its function was primarily to encourage apprentices to take a more active part in the running of the Church services. The boys would act as sidemen, read the lessons, take up collections and generally, it was hoped, improve communications between the Church and the School population. The Committee consisted of the Chaplain, Commandant, OC 'A' Coy, Administrative Officer, RSM and twelve boys.

March 16th 1961 saw the Corps Individual Boxing Championships return to the boys' school once again. Arrangements had been made for boxers from units in BAOR to enter the contest for the first time, and it was hoped that this would ensure a better standard of boxing, as well as a larger attendance than previously. Once again, the REME Staff Band provided the pre-fight and interval entertainment, while the presentation of trophies was shared by Maj Gen Redman (DEME), Maj Gen Stockdale and Brig Molony.

The birth of two new REME Training Schools

The following day, Saint Patrick's Day, may have been a great day for the Irish, but it proved an even greater one for REME. At Havannah Barracks, down at Bordon, a special parade set the seal on the amalgamation of Numbers 4 and 6 Trg Btns, which brought about the birth of SEME. As reported in *The Craftsman* magazine, this was *"the logical result of a process that, physically and geographically at least, had started some years before"*.

On April 1st 1961, the Apprentices' School's near neighbours, Numbers 3 and 5 Trg Btns REME, also amalgamated to form the newly designated School of Electronic Engineering (SEE). It's first Commandant was an old friend of the School's, Col Reg Barfield, who had been its CI after a lifetime in electronics. Both of these newly formed Schools would play their huge part in the future of most ex-apprentices.

News of Col Barfield's departure and 'new job' were reported as follows in the spring 1961 edition of *The Arborfield Apprentice*:

> *"Lt Col R T Barfield left this School at the end of the Easter term, after a very full three years in the Chief Instructor's appointment. It is gratifying to us, and must be to him, that*

he leaves the Apprentices' School on promotion to Colonel. Further, it is of more than passing interest that the SEE, of which he is to be Commandant, will be the receiving unit to which all of our Electronic tradesmen will be posted on leaving here. For the next three years therefore, he will be able to pass critical judgement on his own products!

The syllabus and curriculum to which the five trades in this School are now working is largely the result of Col Barfield's hard work and it can be truly said that in this field, as in many others, he has left his permanent mark on the School. We wish him the best of luck and hope that we shall see something of him in the future."

In that same copy of *The Arborfield Apprentice*, Maj Allan J Tucker, an ex-boy from intake 39B, and then OIC of the Electrical and Electronics (E & E) Department, wrote an article detailing the history of the REME cap badge. This had changed from its original 'four shield' style of the early days, when REME had been formed in the heat of battle during World War II, into the modern style 'prancing horse' design, which all apprentices would now be privileged to wear at the completion of their training.

(The Major's article regarding the badge can be found in a separate annex to this chapter.)

Also in that magazine, Col Legh reported that the Exhibition Hall in the E & E Department had been completed. This aimed at giving apprentices an idea of what life was like 'outside the School', and consisted of model workshops and weapon sites. A large mural had been painted, depicting a Brigade Group in action. Radar Techs were now receiving training on two new '4 Mk 7' equipments, while a complete set of electrical wiring from a *Centurion* tank was now being assembled as a training aid.

The School Athletics team could look back upon the year's efforts with *"some measure of pride of achievement"*. The season had, in fact, started badly, the state of the ground precluding the marking-out of the grass track until well after the summer term had started. The Individual Meeting of May 15th had brought an influx of newly discovered talent,

which then proved itself at Aldershot a few days later against other Boys' Units. A match was then arranged against the Athletics Clubs of Aldershot, Bracknell, Gosport and Southampton, where there were several outstanding individual performances.

At the Quadrangular Games, held at Chepstow that year, the boys came second to the home side, but had the satisfaction of leaving Harrogate and Carlisle trailing in their wake. As stated in *The Arborfield Apprentice*, no account of Athletics would be complete without a huge 'thank you' to Brig (Ret'd) N Rice, who had cheerfully performed as chief judge at all meetings and was always on hand to cheer and encourage the boys' performances.

On May 19th, 'D' Coy reported that they had sent *"a team of six"*, together with teams from other Companies, to take part in the 'Ten Tors Walk' in Devon. This was a fifty-mile course over Dartmoor and was entered by some eighty-four separate teams that year. The event started at White Tor and, even after only a few hours, several teams that had set off at a fast pace had already succumbed to the hot conditions, blistered feet or general fatigue. The overnight stop at the end of the first day was a period of utter exhaustion for most, but dawn the next day was the signal to rouse the weary bodies for the final effort. It was a very thankful 'D' Coy team that *"crawled home"* around five p.m. to qualify for the award of a medallion.

(This may well have been the fourth holding of the 'Ten Tors' event; it is thought to have started in 1958. An article in 'Soldier' magazine gave it great prominence and is reproduced as an annex to this chapter.)

May 27th brought a sad day for 'S' Coy, with the untimely deaths of two boys, Clive Rohan and Douglas Hawkins, in yet another motor-cycle accident. All boys of the Company attended the Military Funeral, held at Aldershot, to pay their last respects.

Between May 29th and June 4th 1961, boys from the School had played their full part in the Commonwealth Technical Training Week. Three of them were received by Prince Philip at London's Guildhall and the School Brass Band had the honour of leading the Army contingent into a march of all three services, plus a group of civilian apprentices, to a service at St Paul's Cathedral. In addition, several apprentices attended special shows and functions in Reading and at other centres.

The Craftsman of June 1961 featured a full-page report on the AAS, which started with the following words:

"Greetings to all ex-Apprentices. Inasmuch as this School trains and produces tradesmen exclusively for the Corps, and consequently has a considerable number of Corps personnel on its strength, as well as ex-Corps civilians, we have decided that a regular contribution ... should be made".

There followed a brief progress report on what was going on at the School, with a listing of the 'main players' in the various trade departments – Vehicles, Workshop Practice, Instruments, Electronics and Electrics.

The 'PoP' of July 27th was a proud one indeed for the 'Hattersley twins' of 58B. Both twins – and who could ever tell them apart? – had gone on to reach the rank of A/T CSM in their respective Companies. Between the pair of them, they had also picked up the Award of Honour, Commandant's Cup and Chief Instructor's Cup. The Commandant's Special Award was awarded to A/T RSM C Pike, another with a strong family tradition to follow, after his brother, the well-known 'Farmer' Pike of 57A, had commanded his own 'PoP' in December 1959.

You here again, Brian?

Geoffrey James was a member of 61B and, in the following year of 1962, proudly won the 'Best Bugler' award, thanks to the friendly and expert tutelage of Mr Brian Conway, who was also one of his civilian trade instructors. This was none other than the Brian Conway of 42A, who had previously returned here as a military instructor between 1954 and 1957, some of whose memories are featured earlier in this history. Brian had returned yet again in 1960, again as a 'motor vehicle mechanic instructor', and had then re-established the Corps of Drums. *(For a continuation of this story, move smartly forward to the chapter concerning 1997! Ed.)*

Brian's return to Arborfield may have given the appearance that he was a *"glutton for punishment"*, but he has always professed that he *"loved every moment of it"*. It's a good job too, as he was to stay on until 1967! During that time, Brian recalls that the new khaki No.2 dress was introduced, along with collar and tie, for all ranks. Any members of the Brigade of Guards were now able to wear their colourful dress caps for everyday use, while a sword belt with sword, as well as a red sash, would be worn for ceremonial occasions.

Brian was certainly courting trouble one day in the Sergeants' Mess. *"Could I have a packet of Guards please, Tom?"* he asked the bar steward. Now the bar steward in question was none other than Tom Drury, late Irish Guards and ex-QM, *"a huge man with the facial features of a heavyweight boxer"*. When informed that there were no *Guards* cigarettes available that day, and then asked would another brand do instead, Brian's response was, *"No thanks, I much prefer Guards, 'cos they're thicker"*! Unfortunately for Brian, he hadn't noticed the presence of 'C' Coy CSM 'Taffy' Hill, Welsh Guards, slightly to one side. There was no instant retribution, but Brian duly suffered for that remark on the next Wednesday morning PS drill session!

September 5th saw the arrival of 142 'new boys' representing intake 61C. It was only three weeks later that thirty of them were 'persuaded' to enter the Novices Boxing Competition, with two brave lads, A/Ts Burns and Groom, going on later to represent the School at the Southern Command Junior Championships. By October 31st, Junior Company ('J' Coy) had successfully passed the Annual Administrative Inspection, with great relief, and, on December 9th, 265 proud relatives braved the elements to attend the Parents' Day, watching their sons perform *"strange and difficult drill movements"*.

Anyone walking along the road near 'A' Coy lines on a Friday evening would be likely to hear the School Choir in Room 'A2', as it practiced its hymns for the forthcoming Sunday service. A total of twenty-seven tenors and basses would meet in the vestry, some fifteen minutes before the morning service, ready to play their part in the pastoral side of School life.

Although ex-RSM McNally had departed from the School in 1956 and had long since retired by 1961, John 'Doc' Houghton of 56B can still to this day entertain fond memories of him. Doc was doing a spot of 'courting' in the early Sixties and Marjorie, his wife-to-be, had become very friendly with the McNally family's youngest daughter, Ann.

Upon returning from Cyprus on one of his leave periods, Doc found himself invited to the McNally's

Apprentice Vehicle Mechanic learning how to carry out a brake overhaul

home in Reading. This naturally caused him some trepidation, having been made well aware of the ex-RSM's reputation from older ex-boys, but in fact the two got on very well. Doc recalls that Mr McNally came across as a very friendly type – and that he had a remarkable passion for cheese!

Making good its earlier promise of a 'regular contribution', the School published another report in the pages of *The Craftsman* in September that year. It particularly reported upon the departure to civilian life of WO2 J Pettit RAEC. 'Joe', as he was popularly and universally known, would be remembered by literally thousands of ex-boys, having started his life at the School as Sgt Pettit in the pre-war days of 1939. At that time, he was one of a mere half-dozen sergeant instructors, but had stuck around long enough to *"see his department grow up"*. Mention was also made of A/Ts Spurling and Barszac, who had won Gold Awards in the Duke of Edinburgh's Scheme, being presented with them at Buckingham Palace and Holyrood House

respectively.

A separate article featured an ex-boy who had excelled at cycling and who would be well remembered by boys at the School for his prowess at that sport. Cpl Pete Arnott was now at SEE and was the Army 1,000 metres Sprint and Time-trial Champion. He had joined the AAS during 1955 and taken up the challenge of cycling during the summer of 1957, going on to captain the School team. In addition to riding for SEE and the Army, Pete was well known in his home-town of Hull, where he rode for its Thursday Road Club, whenever service commitments allowed.

Educational changes

In the winter term of 1961, a new feature of apprentice life made its appearance, with the recruitment of three civilian 'Burnham' lecturers in the Education Department and a forecast for the future, that the staff would soon be composed half of civilians and half of

RAEC officers. By the end of the following year, the Education Department had said 'goodbye' to its last remaining group of Sergeants, Staff Sergeants and Warrant Officers. One of them, and perhaps the best known, WO2 C P Salisbury, had served for over seven years here at Arborfield.

Despite the sunshine, the 'PoP' of 14th December 1961 took place on a cold and windy day, with only a small number of apprentices passing out from intake 59A. They had been the first intake to join the School after the new policy of 'three intakes per year' had been introduced, which probably accounted for the fact that there were a mere fifty-six of them, far fewer than usual. But, by a quarter to ten that morning, the hustle and bustle, the shouting of commands and the stamping of feet had ceased – the School was 'on parade'. Despite their lack of numbers, Senior Div were determined to put on a good show, making their ceremonial departure through the gates to the traditional strains of *'Auld Lang Syne'*.

The Reviewing Officer that day was Maj Gen R B Stockdale OBE, Commandant of REME Technical Group (Tech Gp). His responsibilities for all aspects of the technical development, inspection and repair of the enormous amount of equipment that REME 'looked after' meant that he was closely interested in the technical efficiency of those apprentices now joining the Corps. The General was pleased to present the LSGC Medal to WO2 Boyd, an ex-apprentice of the School now based with the Army Work Study Group.

For his part, in his report to that 'PoP', Col Legh announced *"steady progress"* on the trade side of life. New radar sets had been received, while the Electricians' machinery bay had been further modernised and centralised in one building. Changes in the syllabus meant that Workshop Practice phase was more spread out over the whole length of the course. Engineering Drawing was to be brought forward, allowing the

Learning how to reseat engine valves in the Vehicle Training Workshop

Happy VMs working on a American Willey's 'Jeep' (Does anyone remember these sort of Jeeps in the Vehicle Shop). The Editor claims that Brian 'Roly' Wells and John 'Dinger' Bell were mates of his!

was *"marvellous"* all the time the lads were there and the evenings found a pretty tired bunch just about able to play a few hands of cards and take part in some less-than-energetic dancing.

Another deep freeze

That winter, between 1961 and 1962, provided some severe weather, which proved to be part of a pattern of cold winters in the early Sixties. As reported in an article in *The Craftsman* later that year, *"the best laid plans of mice and men ga'ng aft aglae"*. For, here at Arborfield, the first term of 1962 was delayed for a few days, as the underground water mains froze solid under the grip of 'Jack Frost'. This, of course, caused the two-year old central heating system to fail, with the usual dire consequences for all accommodation. The Garrison Works Officer (GWO) and his staff made great efforts to get things back to normal as soon as possible.

While this was going on, telegrams had to be quickly dispatched all over the country, warning 115 prospective students to delay their arrival, and to inform the present population that they could enjoy an extra week's leave – not too many complaints there, unless it was from long-suffering parents! No extra leave for the PS of course, those who lived locally were brought in to virtually *"man the pumps"* – or at least the mops – as 'Operation Cleanup' got underway. One outcome of the delay in starting the term was that Tuesday afternoon sport had to be given over to instructional activities.

The 'big freeze' was followed by a persistent epidemic of influenza and some scattered outbreaks of that *"most unpatriotic disease"*, German measles. One barrack room had to be converted into '*Emergency Ward Ten*', for the less severe cases, on a couple of occasions.

In an effort to encourage more serving apprentices

chance for the 'Senior Test' to be taken (and hopefully passed!) by the end of the fifth term.

Meanwhile, several new voluntary activities had been introduced, amongst them a 'Scientific Society', a class for learners of woodwind instruments and a Choral Society. A new 'Corps of Drums' had been formed, with thanks to Brian Conway, providing a drum and bugle extension to the Brass and Pipe Bands. September saw this extended Band commencing rehearsals for the Army Festival of Music and Drama. Unfortunately, bouts of bad weather meant that 'open air' rehearsals were severely limited but, even so, the Brass Band came first in its section, while individual performances on piano and euphonium won first and second places respectively.

On 28th December 1961, a party of fifteen apprentices left Newcastle aboard the '*SS Leda*' bound for Stavanger in Norway. These lucky lads were off skiing! *(And there's no 'v' in that either! Ed.)* They arrived to find lots of snow, yet strangely enough, it seemed a lot warmer than the England they had left behind. Their 91-mile journey to Sinnes was scheduled to take four hours, but the deep snow eventually extended this to almost nine hours. The last hour was undertaken on foot, through snowdrifts eight foot deep – and in the dark. Once the party had settled in, suitably 'booted and suited', basic skiing skills were first taken in, followed by some cross—country work. The food to join their 'OBA' upon leaving the School, Master Artificer A J Snape, himself an ex-boy, wrote an article in *The Arborfield Apprentice* of spring 1962. He wrote that it was a *"natural state of affairs"* that *"the ambition of most, if not all, apprentices, is to become ex-apprentices, putting as great a distance as possible between themselves and Arborfield"*. However, he hoped that the present boys would look ahead a few years, to the day when they would wistfully say, *"Remember old so-and-so; I wonder how he is making out?"* By joining the OBA, keeping in touch with old pals would be made that much easier.

His article was followed by another poem, entitled *"On being an Apprentice"* and written by *"Ex-Apprentice"*, which went like this:

"That common word 'apprentice', what does it mean to you?
Does it conjure up a picture of things you used to do?
Then let me say in passing, the picture you would see,
If by chance at Arborfield an A/T you would be.

You leave your home behind you, from those you love you part,
Then meet this new adventure with courage, stout of heart.
Your mark you are now making upon the world at large,
But don't just stand there dreaming – here comes the Duty Sarge!

You learn to chip and use a file and how to drive a car;
And while you have a 'spit and drag', the door you keep ajar.
Your head is crammed with all those things they feel you ought to know,
They tell you where and when to come – then where and when to go.

Make your bed and sweep the floor, place your kit on high.
You see it now, it's hard to win, no matter how you try.
But keep your head and try your best, give it all you can,
For here you stay, inside this place, until you are

a man.

It is here you serve your time out, you stick it to the end;
And as you pass from out the gates, now for yourself to fend,
You push the School right from your mind, the future lies ahead;
And as the years go drifting by, you'll find they've lost their dread!"

In the same magazine, WVS lady Miss K Mackay, who had arrived here late in 1960, was extolling the virtues of *"an amply furnished and well decorated room in the centre of the School"*. This was of course the WVS Club Room for which she was responsible. Since its inception in 1956, the 'room' or 'lounge' had become an integral part of the School, with its resident WVS lady always there to lend a sympathetic ear, as well as organising many facets of School life outside of the normal 'daily grind'.

Meanwhile, in *The Craftsman*, a brief notice urged all members of the Arborfield OBA to forward their current addresses to the Hon Sec of the Association. Provided there was sufficient response, steps would then be taken to re-activate the Association's activities, possibly by the return of an annual reunion. Sadly, this did not galvanise many into action and it was to be quite a while before the OBA was to fully rise back to a position of prominence in School life.

Music, sweet music

Musical pastimes were definitely 'on the up' early in 1962. The Bands were *"in the throes of intensive rehearsal"* for their many forthcoming engagements. A group of 'campanologists' (that's bell-ringers to thee and me!) had been formed and, after regular sessions at Arborfield Parish Church, were now fully qualified members of the Oxford Diocesan Guild. Under new management, the Jazz Club was leading *"a rather quiet life"* and hoped to organise a trip to see the immortal Ella Fitzgerald in the near future. Meanwhile, the School Choir wished their choirmaster, Maj Hinde, a speedy recovery from the hospital bed to which he had recently been confined.

Sporting activities were still to the fore too. In the North Hants (Hampshire) League, the Senior Basketball team was unbeaten and revelling in its top position. Fourteen School boxers had entered the Army Individual Championships, where winners' medals were taken at light middleweight and bantamweight. The School Hockey team had gone through the whole season unbeaten, even handing out a 4-1 thrashing to the old enemy, Chepstow, who they hadn't beaten in the previous nine attempts. And, despite the wet conditions that had prevailed for most of the season so far, the Soccer XI had lost only four out of fourteen games, winning the rest.

It had been a proud moment for A/T RSM C J 'Chris' Jeffery when he led his own intake (59B) off the square at their 'PoP' in April 1962. Chris had learned his military skills well, under the tuition of his two 'B' Coy CSMs, firstly WO2 'Daddy' Dunning of the Devon and Dorsets, followed by WO2 'The Beast' Roberts, Scots Guards. However, his pride was tinged with sorrow, following the sad death of one of his colleagues, whilst on their last term's military training.

During the 'civil defence' phase, A/T Stuart 'Ginge' Callender had suffered smoke inhalation from a smoke grenade, so severely that he died a few days later on March 16th. He was buried with *"full military honours"* at Aldershot Military Cemetery, and it was Chris who had the privilege of leading the burial party. The orders that Chris had to issue at the graveside will remain a sorrowful memory for as long he lives.

'The Beast' is coming!

CSM Roberts of 'B' Coy certainly tried to live up to his nickname of 'The Beast'. Even those boys from the other Companies had a certain amount of sympathy for their 'B' Boy counterparts! The CSM put the fear of God into everyone, not just his own apprentices. Every morning he could be heard marching down the road from the Sergeants' Mess, pace-stick open at the regulation thirty inches – tick, tick, tick with each stride. With the sound of his heel-plates and studs from his mirror-like boots, it was a sure signal to keep one's head down. *"Look out, 'The Beast' is coming!"*

Another who could scorch the paint off a door merely by breathing was Sgt 'Spike' Healy of the RA. During one particular drill session, when a young lad by the name of Bonnick just couldn't *"get it right"*, Spike really lost it! Literally *"frothing at the mouth"*, he threw his pace-stick down the rank, where it hit the unfortunate Bonnick like an arrow. Now in those days, such tantrums were looked upon as part and parcel

of the training system but, even so, Spike must have realised the seriousness of his action. He approached the youngster, asked if he was all right, and sent him back to his room. It was only much later that the rest of the squad learned that Spike had, that same evening after the incident, given Bonnick a ten-bob note to keep his mouth shut!

In June's issue of *The Craftsman*, another School article gave praise to the efforts of the Bands. The Brass Band had taken first place at the 1961-62 Army Junior Drama & Music Festival. At the above-mentioned 'PoP', the Bands had played a major part, with the Corps of Drums supported by some fourteen flute-players – or flautists, to use the correct terminology. Such was the rate of growth in Bands numbers at that time that it was mooted that the time could have been right for a take-over by the Army School of Music!

Friday 8th June saw the arrival of over a thousand young people at the village of Denbury in Devon. Included in those figures were five teams of six from Arborfield, attending the Army-organised 'Ten Tors' expedition. Before too long, the whole area seemed to be covered with tents of every size, shape and colour. With probably the hottest day of the year on parade, and the first leg being walked along hard-surfaced roads, many teams were forced to retire early. Despite the event ***not*** being a race, many treated it as such, which led to a fast drain of energy reserves.

By the time that Saturday evening came along, two of the Arborfield teams were also out of the event and, despite a cooler day on Sunday, the 'D' Coy team also found itself forced to bow out. So, in the final stretch, it was left to the boys of the 'B' and 'C' Coy teams to march home in style, which they did to the welcoming and inspiring sound of *"Here, here, the Reds are here!"*

A Quadrangular victory

On June 29th, a party of some ninety apprentices and staff caught the train up to the far-flung sporting arena of Hadrian's Camp, at Carlisle. Their purpose was to take part in the annual Quadrangular (Athletics) Games between the four Apprentices' Schools. Arborfield had not won this competition for a number of years, but had come a close second to Chepstow in 1961. Carlisle was again tipped to be the favourite team that year, being on its own 'track and field'. After around six events, Arborfield were in last position and things didn't look too good. However, after success in the 220 yards Junior Relay, a steady improvement took hold and the Arborfield boys surged into an unassailable position by the final event. Out of the full thirty events, the team eventually won ten and came second in nine, an excellent all-round performance.

Saturday 14th July saw a re-activation of some slight 'old boy' activity, in the form of a cricket match played against the School's First XI. The result wasn't too important (except that the old boys were soundly beaten!); the main point of the exercise was to advertise the fact that the OBA was still in existence. It was hoped that similar fixtures would become the norm, with a game of Hockey being arranged for November that year, but the idea seems to have stalled somewhat over the ensuing years.

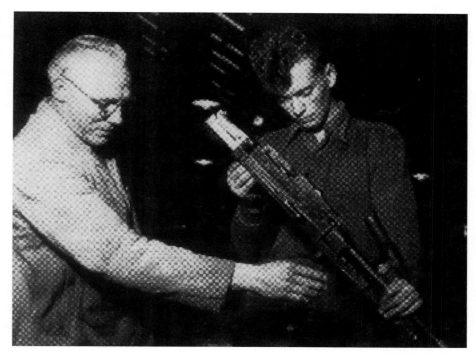

An apprentice Armourer learning all about the 'Bren' light machine gun

The overall picture of the cricket season had been one of considerable success, as the team did not taste defeat until the game that followed that against the old boys – perhaps the 'old codgers' had softened them up after all! The final game of the season, the traditional one against the PS, was spoiled by the elements, but rumours persisted of underhand methods by the staff side. Appealing against the fading light, they were allowed to 'bat on' against only the slowest of bowling, thanks to the sportsmanship of School Captain A/T Sgt Dunger, and finally passed the boys' total. The solace of a shared keg of 'best bitter' soothed the feelings on both sides!

The last week of July saw 'J' Coy off on a three-day camp at Hawley Common. A large heath fire had recently caused extensive damage to the camping area, wiping out the previously permanent oven and cookhouse. But two local members of the ACC were roped in from nearby Aldershot to assist, performing heroically over the next couple of days in supplying sustenance for the ravenous troops. One objective of the camp was to teach these new boys the elements of map reading. No one got hopelessly lost, so 'mission achieved'!

That autumn's issue of *The Arborfield Apprentice* gave news of the newest voluntary activity at the School, in the shape of the Gliding Club. As an encouragement to 'get involved', one of the sailplanes belonging to the Army Gliding Association had been on display at the August 'PoP'. For a subsidised sum, Arborfield boys could 'take off' from the airfield at Lasham, situated in the green and pleasant countryside between the towns of Alton and Basingstoke in Hampshire. Prospective members of the Club were reminded that, wherever they were eventually posted, be it to Germany, Cyprus or East Africa, there would always be the chance of carrying on at this exhilarating sport.

The same magazine reported on two 'PoPs', those of April 12th and August 1st. Those parades had been respectively reviewed by Maj Gen J F Metcalfe, CB, CBE, the GOC of Aldershot District and Lt Gen Sir Robert Bray, KCB, CBE, DSO, C-in-C of Southern Command. The Senior Div leaving in April had numbered only sixty-one, the smallest ever. The Commandant paid tribute to the departing SEO, Lt Col R D Wheal RAEC, who had been instrumental in raising Senior Test passes from between 40 and 50 per cent to virtually twice that level.

One of those 'PoPs' figures in the memory of John Swarbrick, who had joined intake 62A, but he cannot tell us which one! What he *does* recall is that the 'passing out' intake had decided to leave their mark on the School – by painting, in huge white capitals, their intake number on the Cookhouse roof! When RSM Stewart, *"smart as a button-stick"*, marched out to take up his position in front of the parade, his already green Irish Guards hat must have turned a few shades greener. Instead of calling the parade to attention, he barked out the words, *"The sun is shining and the birds are singing for you today, but before you (Senior Div) leave today, those words will be removed"*. And, do you know, they were!

John also recalls the Padre as being the Rev P W R Kennedy – a tall officer who wore glasses. He was more interested in doing God's work and *"looking after His flock"* than adhering to military discipline and procedures. When walking around the Camp, being saluted time and time again by all the boys who passed him by, the Padre would raise his saluting arm to his cap and just keep waggling his fingers until they had all gone past him, saying, *"Morning boys ... ... Morning boys"*.

A courageous rescue

Congratulations were in order at the end of August, when A/T R C Johnson rescued a woman from the sea at Peacehaven, Sussex, on August 30th. He was later the recipient of the Royal Humane Society's 'Award on Vellum' for this courageous action.

"The Army Apprentices' School extends a cordial invitation to Young Ladies to attend its Dancing Club every Thursday evening – FREE!" That's what the poster declared back in 1962 and, after a smooth chat-up line like that, how could they possible stay away? Coaches were laid on to make their way to Reading and Wokingham, to pick up those girls brave (or desperate?) enough to attend. Then it was time to jive, rock or twist the night away, to the tumultuous sound of the 'Red Devils', that group of apprentices who had formed this band and had now been playing to their adoring and spellbound audiences for the previous two years.

During 1962, the various chapels that existed for religious worship around the School were consolidated into a series of rooms in Stephenson Road – or Hilborn Road, as it later became. Many boys were not averse to now calling this thoroughfare 'Church Street'! The School Choir had enjoyed some remarkable success during the late Fifties, taking part in festivals at Sandhurst, Guildford, Aldershot and other locations,

on a regular basis. This was no doubt due to the efforts of its popular choirmaster, Maj George Hinde (RA), who had also been OC of 'A' Coy for the previous five years. Following his sad and untimely death towards the end of that year, his widow, Mrs Barbara Hinde, proudly presented a Book of Common Prayer and a Book of Altar Services to the School Chapel, both in her late husband's memory.

It was during that same year that another special trophy was presented to the School. This was 'The Award of Honour' and it was the gift of Maj Gen Sir Leslie N Tyler KBE, CB, BSc(Eng), CEng, FIMechE, a former DEME, when he was Colonel Commandant of the Corps. It was to be awarded each term to the apprentice who came nearest to achieving the School's aim of producing a *"well-educated soldier, tradesman and leader"*. Yet another award was presented by Brig (Ret'd) N Rice who, formerly as a Retired Officer on the staff, had done sterling work in the field of athletics training. His award was 'The Rice Bowl', which would in future go to that apprentice who had the 'Best Achievement in Sporting Activities'.

The School's first REME Commandant

As his three-year tour of duty ended, Col Dick Legh left the School in October 1962, having also reached the end of his Army service and a well-earned retirement. Col Legh's departure included 'dining outs' by both the Officers' and Sergeants' Messes, with the hand-over being conducted on the steps of the Commandant's office. He was then invited to sit in his staff-car, whilst the Senior Div apprentices used ropes to drag it down the main Camp avenue – a suitable exit for a popular Commandant.

He was succeeded by the first ever REME Commandant, Col J L 'Joe' Dobie, BSc, AMIEE. In his speech at his first 'PoP', Col Dobie referred to those training policy changes about to take place, whereby it was more realistic for apprentices to take the appropriate C & G courses, and to study for their ONC, rather than to take the traditional General Certificate of Education (GCE) subjects. C & G subjects were a logical extension to trade training and would therefore prove to be more 'in tune' with current industrial practice.

The October edition of *The Craftsman* contained an article that chronicled the career of Maj J A Morton of 'S' Coy. He had *"taken the King's Shilling"* at

The first Senior Company, October 1960

ARMY APPRENTICES SCHOOL, ARBORFIELD.

SENIOR COMPANY OCTOBER, 1960.

Schofield	Moor	Kew	Day	Ingomells	Dunn	Nixon	Yarwood
Smyth	Hammond	Luck	Sinclair	Bush	Keller	Hollingsworth	Mort
Care	Thomson	Knight	Elston	Morrow	Richardson	Bishop	Joh
Earnest	Hardy	Hurt	Owen	Allcock	Stevens	Smith	Biggs	No
Sgt Ballard	CSM O'Neil	Major Morton	Col Legh	Capt Churchill	Sgt Bell	Waite

Cirkut Photo—**P. J. HART,**
95. STREATHBOURNE ROAD
LONDON, S.W. 17.

Curphy	Skippen	Stott	Barber	Bradshaw	Clarke	
Woodward	Curry	Miles	Dambo	Hilton	Clarke	
Okai	Flaherty	Colley	Hoskins	Gibson	Austin	Abbott
...t	Murray	Kelsey	Lucas	Carter	Brown	Bond	Gutteridge

Helm	Smith	King	Wayland	Allen	Anderson	Ashby
Allen	Davies	Fraser	Akpan	Fowler	Leighton	Robb
Thomson	Critchley	Wilkins	Venner	Brown	Armstrong	Wiggins
Elliot	Gorham	Bartholmew	Mead	Irwin	Nobles	Hanron	Feulee

The new accommodation block caused problems for those on parade as they marched close to it, due to the echo of the beat of the drums from the Bands.

Winchester in 1927, before joining the Boys' Technical School at Chepstow. Prior to 1939, Maj Morton had served in Egypt, Palestine, Hong Kong and Shanghai with the RAOC. He then became one of those *"evacuated by the skin of his teeth from Dunkirk"*. In 1947, he volunteered to help form the newly constituted Territorial Army (TA), but spent three years in Australia, on an exchange posting at Melbourne. If any of this sounds vaguely familiar, it is because his son Alan was with him there, before himself joining the School here at Arborfield in 1951!

'Morton junior' had been a member of the Australian Army Cadet Force before 'coming home' to serve his apprenticeship. He reached the rank of A/T CSM and won a prize for Regimental Efficiency. Leaving the School in 1954, Alan served in Aden, Bahrain and Cyprus, around the time of the Suez crisis. By 1962, he was a SSgt Artificer Radio at the Trials Establishment Guided Weapons at Anglesey, North Wales. He was to later return to Arborfield and end his career as a civilian at what was by then the 'College'.

A rising star

In its November edition, *The Craftsman* magazine probably gave the first public news of a rising star in the sport of Modern Pentathlon. At the Army Championships, which had been held at Aldershot in September, LCpl J Fox, REME Training Centre, had amassed 3,901 points in assisting his unit's team to win the first prize. Individually, Jim also picked up the Junior Prize, for competitors under the age of twenty-one. Great things were in store for him in the years that followed.

That same month saw the Army Roller Racing Championships held at Arborfield. It was promoted at Bailleul Barracks in order to introduce the sport to the apprentices and junior leaders of the Garrison. Star of the show was ex-boy Pete Arnott, who won the individual titles at one mile and the 440-yard sprint, while the AAS won the unit competitions at the same two levels.

The hockey match that had been arranged between an old boys XI and the present School team had to be cancelled, due to a mixture of heavy rain and fog. A quickly arranged get-together over a glass of beer saw the renewal of some old acquaintances and the start of some new ones. The Commandant addressed the gathering of some fifty old boys and it was decided to hold a Reunion the following summer, on July 20th 1963.

If anything, the winter that year proved even more severe than the previous one, with pictures in the local newspapers showing the River Thames completely frozen over at Reading. The snow that had started falling on Boxing Day was to be still hanging around well into late March. The near-Arctic conditions finally relented, only for the subsequent thaw and

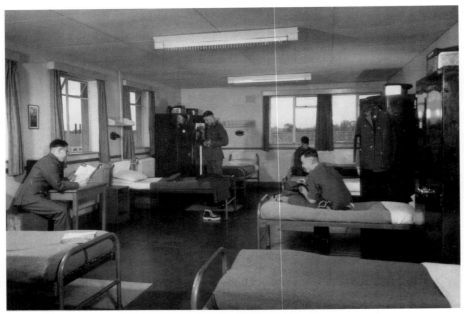

A barrack room inside the new block

'S' Coy scribes were reporting that three members of staff, Maj Morton, CSM O'Neill and SSgt Bell were so enamoured by their previous three years at Arborfield that they had all asked for another two-year extension on their tours. Not only that, but the OC had recently "acquired a new car, emblazoned with the Company colours". As the article went on to say, "Really, how loyal can you get?"

Another change of RSM occurred early in 1963, with RSM Stewart handing over to RSM H Simpson of the Coldstream Guards. Mr Simpson was later to recall that he had been involved in the changeover from the old boys' school cap-badge to the standard REME issue, when all the boys had been lined up on the Square to receive their new issue. The new RSM was himself an ex-Bandsman, so it was no surprise when he started dropping in on the Brass Band during their rehearsal nights. Following a busy Christmas period however, the Band found itself with too little to do during the 'big freeze', due to the lack of parades!

John Swarbrick (62A) certainly remembers his RSMs! He tells us that the new RSM was furious when he spotted the Cookhouse queue, with senior boys gypping their juniors in the time-honoured tradition. With "pace-stick waving and pointing", he ordered the disgruntled offenders to the back of the queue, before marching off in a rage. Needless to say, once he had gone and the queue moved into the Dining Hall and out of his sight, the "correct order of priority was quickly restored"!

Take-off time for Air Techs

There were changes too in the trade-training structure. The last of the Inst Techs were leaving the School and, in future, course loading would consist of forty-four per-cent VMs, eighteen per-cent Electricians and the remaining thirty-eight per-cent covering the three electronic trades. However, an adjustment to the September 1963 intake would see the entry of the first twenty-two Air Techs into the School. One of that

accompanying rain to result in playing fields being rendered impossible for use.

Ken Anderson's first posting after his training with intake 58A was to the Trials Section at the School of Artillery, Larkhill, on Salisbury Plain. However, after just a few months there, our young 'boffin' was sent off to Elliot Brothers of London on what was going to be a two-week training course. As the RA were unable to obtain a Field Artillery computer system (FADAC) from the US Army, who were currently trialling it, Elliot's (later to become GEC Computers) had been commissioned to produce a physical facsimile and interface it to a commercial digital computer. But when Ken arrived, he found that the system still had to be designed. And so, rather than attending a two-week training course, he actually spent the next nine months, in civvies, as part of Elliot's research and development team, being responsible for significant elements of both the hardware and software design.

The new system eventually became the widely used Field Artillery Computer Equipment (FACE). Ken can thus lay claim to being the first REME technician to have worked on digital computers in the Army and he is still working as a 'systems designer' some forty years later. As he puts it himself today, things have come a long way from the germanium transistors and iron-core logic of 1962 to the microprocessors and Large Scale Integration of the new Millennium.

In The Arborfield Apprentice of spring 1963, the

number, Frank Webb, a member of 63C now living in Nigeria, recalls that a film called *'Ten Feet Tall'* was made around that time, with most of its technical content based around this newly introduced trade.

'Paddy' Doyle was a member of 63A and, like Frank, remembers the shooting of the above film, but cannot recall whether or not he ever saw the final product. What he does remember well is *'The Reds'*, which was still the unofficial School Song in those early Sixties. Paddy says the first time he ever properly learned all the words was in the back of a 3-tonner on its way to Fleet, where he was to 'camp out' in the January snow as part of his survival training. He also recalls a couple of hot summers in '63 and '64, swimming in the static water tank besides the Chaplain's office at weekends, along with some serious sunbathing. Some of the lads later found out, to their dismay, that sunburn was deemed a 'self inflicted injury' and thus a punishable offence!

Another member of 63A was Bob Alleway, although he had headed north from Euston to join the School at Hadrian's Camp, three miles out of Carlisle on the Newcastle road. From what he was to tell in a copy of the *OBAN* almost forty years later, the escapades that took place at Carlisle have a familiar ring to them, being virtually a carbon copy of the Arborfield story! With Carlisle closing down only a few years later, after only a short life-span, the old boys from there have always been looked upon and welcomed as members of the OBA here at Arborfield.

Following his arrival and the routine 'shearing' by the Camp barber, Bob's first meal consisted of a mug of cocoa and a large hunk of bread and cheese. Coming from a *"small town in the Thames Valley"*, he had never heard such an array of almost uninterpretable accents that came from the assorted boys in his barrack room. And there, piled on a table in the middle of the room, was a heap of confiscated cigarettes.

The room NCO announced that there would be no smoking as from the next morning, so it would be better if the ciggies got smoked that evening. He then proceeded to grab a large handful of same! Bob, who had never smoked before, was a helpful lad and, wanting to look *"worldly wise"*, joined in the 'lighting-up ceremony'. It wasn't long before he was being sick in the toilet.

Bob was one of the tallest boys, so inevitably he was chosen as the right marker for drill sessions. It certainly didn't make him excel at drill though, his ineptitude was there for all to see. His drill sergeant remarked upon this in no uncertain manner, much familiar to many an ex-boy. *"Alleway, you'll never make a soldier as long as your fundamental orifice points south!"* (Well, it's definitely more refined than some I've heard! Ed.)

The same sergeant also introduced Bob to shaving. *"You haven't shaved,"* he told Bob on parade one morning. *"I don't shave"*, replied the unwitting young apprentice. *"Well, you're in the Army, so you do now"*, came the retort. Poor Bob thought it was best if he spent a few coppers on a razor that evening and, next morning, attacked his 'bum-fluff' with gusto. His drill sergeant was very pleased. The fact that Bob's face had *"more cuts than a butcher's chopping board"* was an irrelevant fact – at least he had shaved!

Back here at Arborfield around that time, in protest against the standard – or lack of standard! - of catering,

The Library provided ample reading material, but not a copy of 'Playboy' in sight!

a 'food strike' was organised. A boycott of the Cookhouse was supposed to occur, but some of the PS got wind of this and the word went out that it had better not happen – the phrase *"between a rock and a hard place"* comes to mind! In the event, a compromise solution was that a lot of boys went up to the hot-plate, received their ration of food – and promptly marched outside and dumped it in the swill-bins!

John Swarbrick cannot really remember whether the food was *"good, bad or indifferent"*, probably a mixture of all three. He certainly cannot recall it improving as a result of 'the strike'. On the subject of swill-bins though, he tells of the ancient civilian – looking a lot like *"old man Steptoe"* – whose job it was to empty those bins. He once saw the old chap picking up and eating a cold roast spud that had just been dumped from a boy's plate. *(Surely rationing had ended by then? Ed.)*

Family connections

Another 'father and son' article graced the pages of *The Craftsman* for January 1963. WO1 (ASM) F W Brotheridge had joined the Army at the age of fifteen in 1936, as a member of Chepstow's 38A intake. After a *"tough but enjoyable three-year apprenticeship"*, he passed out into the RAOC as a Fitter. Sent to France with the BEF, he later found himself *"on the wrong side"* of the German break-through.

With Dunkirk already part of history, he eventually escaped via the port of St Nazaire. Later, *en route* to the Middle East, 'F W' survived the disablement of his ship by enemy action. A mere six weeks later, he was heading to Malta on a convoy that survived a three-day running battle with enemy aircraft. It was about then that he decided a Naval career was not for him! At the time of the article, ASM Brotheridge was serving in BAOR, whilst his son Robert had, after four years with the Dukies, started his apprenticeship at Arborfield in 1961. Still under training, Robert hoped he was all set to *"follow in his father's footsteps"* and pursue a long career in REME.

January 1963 also saw the arrival at boys' school of A/T Terence Scurr as a VM apprentice, but he hoped to later become an Air Tech. He was yet another example of the old adage, *"like father, like son"*, as father George was serving as a WO1 at 26 Command Wksp. George had joined the ATS (Boys) on May 3rd 1939, joining REME upon its formation in 1942. He survived the

mining of a landing craft during a Commando raid on the island of Walcheron. As a Class 1 football referee, he had recently been appointed as a linesman at the Hibernian v Barcelona match. Another son, Ian, and only ten at the time, also longed for the day he too could join the Army.

February's issue of *The Craftsman* saw the first of a three-part article that dealt with the earliest Army Apprentice training, between 1907 and 1912. At the time, there was only the one training establishment and that was at the Personnel Ordnance College, Woolwich. Trainees were on the College strength, while the workshop and technical classrooms were at the Military Repository – familiarly known as 'the Repo'. Boys were apprentices until the age of eighteen, before 'joining the ranks' as gunners and drivers. Their training fitted them for appointment as 'fitters or wheelers'. Vacancies were few and only arose as the trainees were appointed as adult tradesmen.

Fire in the stores

In the early hours of Saturday 23rd March 1963, a lot of excitement was generated at the School when fire broke out in the QM's Stores. The prompt and efficient action by both the staff and boys kept damage to a minimum and prevented the fire from spreading to adjoining buildings. The QM had to be re-housed and rapidly set about getting re-equipped as never before! *(It is amazing what can be 'written off' in such circumstances! In fact there were allegations – unsubstantiated of course - that the QM's staff had been seen throwing ledgers onto the fire! Ed.)*

The event was obviously referred to at the 'PoP' in April, reviewed by the QMG, Gen Sir Gerald Lathbury GCB, DSO, MBE. He praised those who had acted so quickly in controlling the fire. He also paid tribute to the QM, Medical and Messing staff, who had coped so well during the appalling weather conditions that had prevailed during the early part of the year. In the School magazine a little later that year, there appeared an *"Olde English ballad, written for a one-string fiddle"*, which went something like this:

> *"Fire! Fire! Fire in the store.*
> *Play gently with the hoses,*
> *Until the embers are a'roar.*
> *Fire in the rations, quickly, break the door;*
> *The fire's melting all the gold*

Beneath the office floor.
Fire! Fire! Hurry!
Don't be slow,
Fetch the Company ledgers,
While the hut is still aglow."

John Swarbrick's recollection of the fire is that he sadly missed it! At the time, he was *hors de combat*, having been bedded down in the MRS with a nasty boil that had appeared inside his lower lip. *(No jokes about a stiff upper lip then? Ed.)* The boil later burst whilst John

Electronic Technicians in Mr Simpson's Class IVA

was eating a meal and he says that all he noticed was that the gravy did taste a bit funny!

On the same Saturday of 'the fire', the 'D' Coy Basketball team brought their sport to the forefront when they beat 'B' Coy from Chepstow to become Army Junior Champions. The season had been a busy one, following the formation of a new Arborfield Garrison League, which brought the chance of playing at least two games every week. This had certainly helped the team to develop. They had previously won the Aldershot District competition, playing at Fox's Gym in Aldershot, so when the Army final was played at the same venue, the lads considered it almost as a 'home fixture'. They were certainly not lacking in support and won that Championship by seventy-two to forty points.

How did I get here?

"Walking down the road from the bus stop, past the RSM's house, bag in hand, wondering how on earth I had got there." These words describe Trevor 'Pip' Piper's introduction to Arborfield, as a member of 63B. His experiences during the next three years largely follow the pattern of many who had gone before him, as well as many of those who followed him. One person who stands out in Pip's memory is Sgt Jim Shanley, his *"superb"* REME drill-sergeant. As Jim

told those apprentices under his tutelage, if he could do it *"with two toes missing"*, then they had no excuse for not being able to march along with the best!

As 63B entered its third term, Pip was glad to be able to get away from the Camp confines and out onto the adventure training that he loved – abseiling, canoeing, hill walking and parachuting. These pursuits took place mostly in the Brecon Beacons and Pip swore that every time the train emerged at the far end – the wet Welsh end! - of the Severn Tunnel, then sure enough, it would be raining!

Pip recalls being taught to drive in an old – nay, ancient! – *Austin K9* lorry, fully equipped with a 'crash' style gearbox and a front axle that was a good six inches wider than the rest of the vehicle, which certainly concentrated the mind. But his main passion was the coveted motorcycle, stashed away illegally at a house *"somewhere down the Nine-mile Ride"*. At his eventual 'PoP' in 1966, Pip remembers that, for the first time in years, a wet-weather programme had to be adhered to, due to the fact that it was snowing heavily at the time.

Trevor Taylor had joined up as a member of 60C, so would have been in 'S' Coy during 1963. He remembers that the School's fire alarm warning bell was always tested at mid-day, so that when he and his colleagues were on 'C' Coy verandah at 11.55 hours one Wednesday, waiting to be paid, the sound of the

The Cycling Club provided a great opportunity to get out of the Camp on sports afternoons and weekends!

Scouting and sailing

By the summer of '63, the 2nd Arborfield Scout Group had been in existence for around five years, its membership having fluctuated between ten and nineteen 'Scouts'. During the leave period, four Senior boys were fortunate enough to spend three hot, enjoyable weeks as part of the British contingent to the World Jamboree, held at Marathon in Greece – yes, that's the place it was first run, too! While those four were acquiring their enviable suntans, another four went hiking on the North Yorkshire moors, in a second attempt to complete the Lake Wyke

alarm gave them no immediate cause for concern. Not, that is, until a fire engine came flying in through the front gates! They later realised that there had been a genuine fire in one of the Workshops.

On another Wednesday, sports afternoon, as a member of the School shooting team, Trevor had been detailed to assist in some repairs to the miniature range. Armed with several pieces of wood, and an array of hammers and nails, he and his fellow marksmen were making their way to the range, when they met up with a particularly recalcitrant Jeep. The outcome of this meeting was that the unfortunate young lad later found his coveralls nailed to a tree. Even more unfortunate, he was still inside those same coveralls at the time!

Following lots of inactivity on the sporting front, due to unplayable pitches, fixtures had to be *"crammed in"* towards the end of the season. This did not halt the success of various teams. 'B' Coy's rugger side finally won the Youth Challenge Cup against a Chepstow side, after a draw and two periods of extra-time, then a replay. 'A' Coy topped the Aldershot and District League at soccer, with 'D' Coy as runners-up, and 'D' Coy had also won the Army Youth Cup at basketball.

Walk. Success was achieved, after some forty-five miles of crossing difficult areas of deep heather and peat bogs, in a time of twenty hours.

Also on the 'scouting' scene, 'Paddy' Wheeler had attended a reception at St James's Palace, where he had proudly received his Queen's Scout Certificate from HRH the Duke of Gloucester. It was hoped that several other Group members would soon join the ranks of the Queen's Scouts. Meanwhile, of the six most recent members to leave Arborfield, four had gone on to become Scoutmasters – the School was definitely *"doing its bit"*.

Despite *"another sailing season of poor weather"*, the Sailing Club's membership had managed to hold steady at around twenty-four keen members. A change in the sports afternoon programme meant that smaller groups were now sailing more frequently. By October of that year, nine members had been awarded their 'Helmsman' certificates, a much-coveted standard set by the Army Sailing Association. Outside participation saw some individual members occupied on deep-sea fishing off Iceland, others likewise off the Yorkshire coast, and one group sailing on a German lake.

In September, *The Craftsman* presented a two-page spread that dealt with the AAS under three separate paragraphs. The first gave a very brief review of the School's history since opening in 1939. The second paragraph dealt with the recent 'PoP' on the last day of July, honoured by the presence of Gen Atkinson, Director of the Corps. Then finally, the last report looked back at the Old Boys' Reunion that had taken place on July 20th. This had seen quite a revival in bringing old boys together, but sadly it did not last. The Reunion coincided with a 'J' Coy Parents' Day, followed by a cricket match against a current School team. The evening's dinner was enlivened by the later arrival of dear old Ben Cook, much to the delight of those who had served under him.

September 6th brought the news that ex-apprentice LCpl Jim Fox had won three individual titles – British, Inter-Service and Army – at the UK Modern Pentathlon Championships, assisting the REME and Army teams to win their respective Championships at the same time.

A dedicated Aircraft Wing

With the arrival of the first Air Techs, it was obviously necessary to have a dedicated 'Aircraft Wing', which subsequently came into being that same September of 1963. Initially forming only a small section of the Mechanical Wing, it offered a period of seven terms under instruction here at Arborfield, followed by a final two at Middle Wallop, Hampshire, for the completion of Class II and equipment training. The first boys to attend the adult School would not do so until the early months of 1966. The reception of the first Air Techs into the School proved a rather chilly one when, on receipt of one of the aircraft into the workshop, it managed to bring down a heating pipe!

October 14th was a date that will go down in history for the "martyrs of 61A and 61B", as 'S' Coy members became firmly established in their 'new quarters' at Bailleul Camp. Morale was exceedingly high, in spite of the ON/OFF technique of the highly efficient hot water system which, to no-one's surprise, was 'OFF' far more often than it was 'ON'! The Company Commander had always been of the theory that central heating was "cissy stuff", but two burst boilers later, even he agreed that perhaps it could just be a necessity! During the 'OFF' periods, the defaulter rate leaped up alarmingly, with a sudden rise in "horizontal champions".

During that October, shortly after the twenty-first anniversary of the formation of REME, HM the Queen appointed HRH Princess Marina, Duchess of Kent, as the Corps' first Colonel-in-Chief. The Princess was to take a great interest in her duties up until her death in 1968, and the Royal connection was later commemorated by what was then the AAC (Arborfield) being named after her.

Late in 1963, an interesting educational experiment

Foot Inspection for 'B' Coy boys on Thursley Common!

was conducted, which compared the results obtained by both formal teaching methods and scrambled textbooks against those from 'teaching machines', on which Capt John Birch RAEC had written what were termed 'programmed learning' courses. Interestingly, no significant difference in learning between the three methods was found, teacher and machine were shown to be complementary, rather than mutually exclusive. Whatever the thoughts on the subject at the time, this has been recognised as the School's first tentative step on the road towards what became 'computer assisted learning'.

Ordinary National Certificate? We could do that!

At the same time, consideration was being given to the School's running of its own two-year ONC courses and, by the December of 1963, a start had been made on the teaching of ONC Mathematics and General Studies. Simultaneously, a much-disputed and unpopular run-down of the trade of Electrician REME (which later had to be reinstated) meant that the number of potential Electricians had to be quickly absorbed into the other trade streams. This resulted in a concentration upon Radar, Tels and Control Equpt Techs, VMs and Air Techs. Much to the dismay of many VMs, they were now to take responsibility for 'vehicle electrics'. *(I well recall having to teach the subject to VMs at SEME Bordon, when posted down there at Easter 1964. It certainly wasn't the most popular phase of the VM syllabus! Ed.)*

On January 28th 1964, a Memorial Service was held at St Martin-in-the-Fields Church, Central London, for Maj Gen Rowcroft, who had died in the last month of the previous year. The list of those who attended, many retired and many still serving, would make up a 'Who's Who' of famous names, both from REME and the whole Army. The General's name still lives on in the name of the barracks in which the current ATFC is housed.

Bob Castell joined the School as a member of intake 64A. He remembers the Sixties for two main reasons. Firstly, as he puts it, that it was the era of 'free love', Carnaby Street, and the 'swinging scene', then secondly that he had joined the Army and unfortunately missed it all! Bob's father had been in REME since before Bob was born, so joining up seemed a logical step. What probably doesn't seem quite so logical, in afterthought, is that Bob swapped an idyllic existence in an apartment, overlooking St George's Bay, Malta, with its shimmering blue waters and sunny skies, for the rather different and intimidating scene of a cold January morning at Arborfield.

Bob boarded a RAF *Comet* for the flight to Lyneham, along with a Maltese boy who was also joining Arborfield. Together they travelled by train from *"the wilds of Wiltshire"* to Wokingham, where Bob dutifully phoned the School to let them know *"who he was, where he was, and where he wanted to be. Oh, and please could you send some transport?"* From the garbled response that came down the line, Bob definitely recognised the terms *"bus"*, *"bloody"* and *"get the"*, so it was an hour later that he and his pal walked through the gates to report to the Guardroom.

Having survived the initial shock of 'Jeepland', Bob then found himself wearing the blue shoulder flashes of 'A' Coy, and also learned the vagaries of Fire Picket. The burnt out remains of the QM's store had been left as a visible indication of what was ***not*** supposed to happen! Local, acting and unpaid *(the term 'unwanted' also springs to mind! Ed.)* LCpl Oxley had been seconded to the School for RP duties and was able to pass on his consummate fire-fighting skills to the boys. He told them not to use dirty water, as this was liable to ignite; hot water should not be used, in no way could it put a fire out; and for electrical fires the trick was to tie a knot in the cable to put out the fire! It is also alleged that he once had six GCEs, but that they had been taken away from him – for fighting!

The set-up at the School is something that Bob finds easy to recall. 'J' Coy – or 1 Div – was located in the block at the top of the Square (the block still survives). Divs 2 to 7 were located in the spider blocks around the Square, and constituted the four Companies, 'A' to 'D', dependent upon trade. *(This Company structure must have changed some time after Col Cole's tour of duty. Ed.)* Bob's 'A' Coy colour denoted him as a VM. During 8 and 9 Div, he remembers that all boys were eventually brought back together under the 'S' Coy banner, and housed in Bailleul Barracks.

Bob remembers that life was pretty hectic but, thanks to some *"excellent food and training"*, he gained confidence quickly. There was never time to become bored, though the frantic pace could prove a little confusing at times. Rushing into the barrack room one morning to get changed out of his sports kit and into his denims, ready for the day's work, his

Part of Ben Cook's legacy to Arborfield is the attractiveness of Nuffield Road with its trees and flower beds, as seen in this photograph of the view towards the front gates from the Workshops. A lasting memory to many Arborfield apprentices.

mate Pete Howes was seen changing into pyjamas and getting into bed. Upon being informed that he had about ten seconds to make it to the Education Wing, he replied, *"I knew I had to get changed into something, I just couldn't remember what"*!

Time passed by in a blur and it wasn't long before Bob joined 'S' Coy. He also remembers the re-badging ceremony that took place when the School was taken under REME control – *"it felt good to be wearing the chained horse at last"*. One of the benefits of being both a VM and a member of 'S' Coy was that he was now being taught to drive. He really wanted to buy a car to impress the birds, desperate to become part of that Sixties scene before it all finished! Bob still describes himself as one of the original 'virgin soldiers', and even now, some thirty-odd years later, with a brand-new computer and *Windows 98*, still reckons he has *"much to learn"*.

Suits you, Sir!

Local newspaper, the *Reading Mercury*, of February 8th 1964, published an article that made great play of *"a wonderful example of the new democracy in the Army"*.

For the past ten years, boys in their first two years at the AAS Arborfield had only been allowed out of Camp provided that they were suitably dressed in their 'School mufti', which consisted of a regulation blazer, emblazoned with the School badge and accompanied by grey flannels. In their final year, boys could then wear *"any reasonable form of civilian dress"*.

Col Joe Dobie had decided that a new standard pattern of 'walking out dress' should be introduced, with the revolutionary idea that the boys themselves be allowed to vote on what they considered the most suitable attire. With collar-less *'Beatle'* jackets and 'Italian style' suits the fashion of the day, a typically British compromise had to be eventually reached, the outcome of which was a smart looking suit that could be made up in only five weeks, at a cost of thirteen pounds and ten shillings (£13:50p). There was much excitement in the air amongst the budding 'fashion models' at the School, when it was announced that the new suits would be displayed on the TV programme *'Town and Around'*. But for reasons best known to the BBC, some professional models were eventually used. The contract for the suits went to the Garrison Tailor, Mr Norman Rose, who will be long remembered by

'Spud Bashing' whilst under canvas and out on field training

many ex-boys of the era.

In *The Arborfield Apprentice* later that year, one of the 'A' Coy scribes described the feelings of many boys as follows: *"Hurrah! At last we've got them! We've lost the blazer and grey flannels and 'got with it'. The A/Ts have exchanged their mufti for Italian suits, and their snub-nosed shoes for Cuban-heeled boots."* It was agreed that the suits weren't too bad for the price, the main complaint was the time it took for them to be measured, tailored and fitted. Many of the PS had been worried that the boys would turn into *"civilian yobbos"* once the booked out of Camp in this *"latest gear"*, but their fears proved groundless. *(Some old boys would recall being yobbos before joining up! Ed.)*

In the spring of 1964, there was yet another outbreak of German measles at the School – hardly life threatening, but still causing an isolation period of four days, followed by fourteen days sick leave. For one pair of bright young apprentices, Mother Nature seemed in no hurry to infect them, so they decided to give her a gentle push. They stood themselves under a hot shower until their skins were sufficiently tender, they then judiciously tapped each other's chests and backs with a stiff clothes-brush until they looked decidedly spotty!

After their attendance at morning sick parade, the MO was quick to send off our two skivers for the proscribed isolation period. The medicine they received tasted pretty vile, but they took it stoically, eagerly looking forward to their two-week reward yet to come. However, just as they thought they were

'on their way', they were paid a visit by none other than the Commandant, 'Colonel Joe' himself.

Yes, their little ruse had been well and truly rumbled! The Commandant's words went something like this: "Well boys, there are so many of you suffering from measles, it is no longer considered necessary to send you on sick leave. However, the MO has recommended that you have a fortnight of fresh air to recuperate. So I have decided to allow you fourteen days of potato planting in the field adjoining the MRS – which should prove quite easy for you – once you have dug the ground well!"

The Reviewing Officer for 61B's 'PoP' on April 17th 1964 was an old friend of Col Dobie's – and a naval man to boot. He had known Rear Admiral H.S. Mackenzie CBE, DSO, DSC when he commanded one of HM submarines. The Admiral's present appointment was 'Chief Polaris Executive', MoD, RN – 'Polaris' being Britain's strategic sub-launched nuclear weapon. Referring to the apparent anomaly of his *"reviewing a military parade"*, the Admiral claimed as one of his qualifications his *"abiding interest in the training of young men in the Services"*.

'Your loving instructor'

In the spring 1964 issue of The Arborfield Apprentice, the following rhyming verse, to just about any one of the many instructors at the School, was (strangely enough anonymously!) dedicated:

"He isn't a barman, he isn't a car man, not even a tram-car conductor;
He's merely the yob who's been given the job of being our tradesman instructor.
He stands on the dais with a leer on his face, whilst we carve our names on the ceiling;
His manner gets colder as he throws a boulder at us, with malicious feeling.

We don't mind the lashes, we don't mind the

gashes that he uses to rule us with violence,
But we reel at the jokes that he tries on us
blokes, whilst we sit and suffer in silence.
He's old and he's crusty, his voice none too
lusty, his snappers no good for a munch-up;
His pastime is torture, whenever he's caught
yer indulging in class with a punch-up.

'The Beatles' don't thrill him, 'The Shadows'
just kill him, their music is corny and rough,
But A/Ts forever think they're dead clever
– and smart and with-it and tough.
We jeer at this old 'un whose guidance is
golden; one day we'll get a big shock;
We'll learn to revere him, to love him and fear
him, in a full forty years on the clock.

When he's in the graveyard and we've started
to save hard, to purchase a house or a motor,
We'll wish we worked harder on that technical
cadre, whilst scaling promotion's slow rota.
So heed all you Jeeps, you 'orrible creeps
– pay heed to your loving instructor;
Don't make paper toys or kick up that noise
– such larking may be your destructor!"

The VM Department announced that its present title could possibly change somewhat in the future because, at the start of the next winter term, it would become responsible for training Air Techs (Airframe & Engine – or A & E). Two aspects of VM training had been dropped in order to provide staff and accommodation for this change. But this had in no way lightened the burden because it had coincided with the VM now becoming totally responsible for 'vehicle electrics', after the ill-fated abandonment of the trade of Vehicle Electrician (VE). From the previous winter term, all 6 Div VMs were now spending the whole of that term's training in the E & E Department.

School Padre, the Rev D G Bevan, BA, CF reported that *"seldom does a major Church Festival fall during School term"*. But 1964 saw such an occurrence, with the School *"in residence"* during Holy Week and Easter. Among the special services held was a devotional service on Good Friday and a celebration of Holy Communion on Easter Sunday, both of which were held in the Camp Hall. Earlier in the year, the Church Choir had enjoyed an outing to *'The Black and White Minstrel Show'* at the Victoria Palace in London,

organised by the Choirmaster, Maj Blakeborough REME.

On May 28th 1964, the Corps of REME was officially presented to its C-in-C, HRH Princess Marina, at Bordon, by the Representative Colonel Commandant Maj Gen Sir Leslie Tyler KBE, CB. It proved to be *"a unique occasion, attended by almost every notable Corps personality who was able to make the journey"*. The souvenir programme, with its gilt-edged cover, has become quite a 'collector's piece' in its time.

The Quadrangular Games, held at the end of summer term, was something of an historic occasion for the School Band as they combined their talents with those of the other three Apprentices' Schools. The four Bands gave a splendid 'massed band' performance at the Games venue, Bracknell Stadium. In the evening, the same combination did a 'Beating the Retreat' upon the square at Arborfield, then followed this up with a repeat performance for the people of Reading on the Sunday morning, in the beautiful setting of Christchurch Meadows. A special word of praise went to Arborfield's Bandmaster Parker, who had worked for six months in preparation for the extremely complicated operation.

The sports meeting included athletics, canoeing, cricket and cycling, with splendid weather conditions for the whole weekend. The canoe race started the event on the Friday afternoon, on the River Thames between Caversham Bridge (Reading) and Pangbourne, then back again, a distance of over ten miles. The final cycling race started at 6 a.m. on the Sunday morning, so did not draw too many spectators.

Wide-ranging activities

The summer 1964 edition of *The Arborfield Apprentice* gave a list of the School's *"active"* clubs and societies, showing the usual eclectic mix as follows:

Adventure Group; Angling Club; Archery Club; Art Club; Brass Band; Camera Club; Canoeing; Chess Club; Corps of Drums; Dancing Club; Drama Club; Gliding Club; Judo Club; Metalwork; Model Making; Motor Engineering Club; Pipe Band; Radio Club; Sailing Club; School Choir; Scientific Society; Scouts; Table Tennis Club; Weight Training; Woodwork Club.

The summer term had seen a lot of effort and

hard work in 'S' Coy, when it was decided to extend the 9 Div Military Training syllabus, in order to train a selected few up to the 2nd Class REME Certificate. This did not go amiss, as a total of twenty-seven apprentices achieved this distinction. Particular praise went to A/T RSM Hutchins, who qualified with a 'B' grading, before carrying off three of the major awards for his intake.

At the 'PoP' held in August that year, history was made when Air Marshall D J P Lee CB, CBE, Commandant of the RAF Staff College at Bracknell, was invited to be the Reviewing Officer, the first airman to act in that capacity. In his address, he said that his appearance at the parade was by no means inappropriate, in view of the commonality of technical training that existed between the RAF and REME and the steady tendency towards integration among all three services. The Air Marshall wished those passing out satisfaction and success in their careers and afterwards invited a number of them to flights in his own personal helicopter.

Douglas Beazer arrived at Arborfield to join intake 64C, little knowing that he would end up as the A/T CSM of 'C' Coy. He recalls the gypping that still went on in the meal queues, plus the ways that senior boys would subsidise their earning power by the 'pennies or bottles' method. This would be in the form of a collection of any spare change from the Jeeps or, failing that, sending one of those measly creatures to collect as many empty 'pop' bottles as possible, as these could be exchanged for cash at the NAAFI.

Another custom concerned the daily churn of milk, delivered to the top floor of 'J' Coy block. Before the milk was doled out, a mug inspection would take place. Woe betides anyone found with a chipped or dirty mug! Provided that the unfortunate owner could dash down the three flights of stairs and catch his offending mug before it hit the concrete floor, he could then have his milk ration. Needless to say, not many made it!

Members of the Scout Group had an evening out in October 1964, one that they may prefer to forget! Having forsaken their tea meal, they boarded the School minibus at 17.30 hours for the drive to the *Golders Green Hippodrome*, to see a presentation of Ralph Reader's *'Gang Show'*. The journey through London's rush hour traffic took them two hours, so they arrived only just in time for the start of the show. By the time the next three hours had passed by, hunger was definitely beginning to take its toll! It was then

the intention to stop at a café on the way back for a late supper, but they were astonished to find that there wasn't a single eating-place available all the way back to Arborfield. Arriving here at 00.30 hours, there was still a *"fearful seven hours to wait for breakfast"*.

On November 3rd, the Band and Drums were delighted to participate in a reception at Henley, held in honour of 'local girl' Mary Rand, triple medallist at the Olympic Games that had been held in Tokyo that year. One of Mary's medals had been the gold for her long jump, while Lynn 'The Leap' Davies performed similarly in the men's event.

The School's biggest audience?

On Saturday November 7th 1964, *"history was created"* when boys from the School presented a ten-minute impression of *'The life of an Army Apprentice'*, as part of the Army display in the Festival of Remembrance, held at the Royal Albert Hall in London. There were two public performances, one in the afternoon and another the same evening. HM the Queen, the Queen Mother, the Prime Minister, and many other distinguished guests were amongst the audience, which totalled some 7,000. More than thirty million people are estimated to have also watched the display on their TV receivers. This was the first time that apprentices had performed at the Festival; their enthusiasm and precision were a credit to their generation and a fine tribute to those to whom the Festival was dedicated.

(The full report on the above event is attached as a separate annex to this chapter.)

During the same year, the School finally obtained the authority to teach the ONC course 'in-house' in both the Electrical and Mechanical engineering disciplines. As a result, the Commandant was able to report at the year's final 'PoP' in December that, of the previous September's intake, about half had begun a course on which, if they were successful, would enable them to start an 'O1' course for ONC qualification in September 1965. This was a three-term General Engineering (G) course, which would cover English, Maths, Engineering Science, Workshop Processes & Materials, as well as Engineering Drawing.

Those apprentices who had achieved a high enough standard in their senior test examination, taken at the end of this 'G' course, would then be eligible to embark on a full ONC in their chosen trade-related discipline. Those unfortunates who had failed at this standard would instead start an appropriate C & G course. In addition, a number of boys entering the School were already considered sufficiently qualified to enter the ONC course, by virtue of their previously obtained passes at GCE level. At the same time, a number of well qualified apprentices were to be 'accelerated' by one term, allowing them to complete the General Engineering course in only two terms, rather than the more usual three.

The Climbing Club had a splendid weekend in the Wye Valley early in November. Accommodated at the nearby AAS Chepstow, they soon found themselves looking upwards at the sheer 250-foot high crags, rising straight up from the river. Blessed with exceptionally good weather so late in the year, the boys took full advantage of the conditions to graduate from 'nursery slopes' to some more difficult climbs.

In the Army Junior Bands Competition, A/T LCpl I W J Cleasby of 61C won his class in the Brass Section. It is good to know that 'Bill' was still blowing a mean trumpet as Hon Sec of the OBA some forty years later!

Following the Old Boys' Reunion, held in the School on November 21st that year, the Commandant later reported that "attendance was good" and that he believed "the Association would flourish", but perhaps he was overstating the fact somewhat, as numbers were actually falling and there were lean times ahead. One 'very old boy' who attended that evening was the Life President of the OBA, Brig J D White, who had recently celebrated his eightieth birthday. The youngest member present was a boy from 59B, LCpl Metcalfe.

Members of 'S' Coy bade a fond farewell to one of the stalwart founders of the Company, CSM F 'Big Frank' O'Neill, of the Scots Guards. Having completed his Army service, he had now retreated to the 'backwoods' of Shinfield Green, where he would play genial 'mine host' at the *Royal Oak*. A newly introduced 'gimmick' to improve drill movements was to have the accompaniment of a drumbeat. This proved quite successful until A/T Sgt Griffith managed to beat a neat hole in the skin of the drum!

The announcement of a 'room and garden' competition sparked off a flurry of enthusiasm and energy. Company lines began to look more chic every day, with extracts from *Men Only* giving way

CSM O'Neill Scots Guards

to oil paintings by numbers and some interesting models of ships and motor cars here and there. Some initiative was shown by some apprentices in the craft of 'pruning', as outside areas were transformed into something approaching *'Kew Gardens'* status – although the regular School gardener would most definitely argue this point!

The Arborfield Apprentice issued at the end of 1964 gave yet another notice extolling the virtues of the WVS Club, now firmly in the capable hands of the current incumbent, Miss Thompson. The Club Lounge opened during off-duty hours in the evenings and at weekends. It provided *"a nicely furnished lounge"* for letter writing, reading and listening to music. A good selection of indoor games was regularly updated, while competitions were often held at snooker, table tennis and darts.

—§—

Annex to Chapter 6

The Story of a Cap Badge
by Major A J Tucker, REME

On 1st October 1942, some 78,000 officers and men of the RE, RASC and RAOC replaced their existing cap badges with the one shown and, on that day, REME was born. This new corps of soldier technicians was responsible for the recovery, maintenance and repair of the majority of electrical and mechanical equipment in the Army.

At the height of the Second World War, over 160,000 REME cap badges were being worn by officers and men throughout the world. It was proudly worn throughout the major campaigns in Europe, the Middle and Far East, and was also seen in such widely diverse places as the island of Madagascar and the 'Pentagon' in Washington, United States of America (USA).

Here in Arborfield, the new cap badge was much in evidence when the Training Establishment REME replaced the former RAOC AFV (Armoured Fighting Vehicle) Mechanical School.

The soldier's badge was originally made of brass but, due to a shortage of raw material, for a time it was made, along with the badges of other corps, from a brown plastic material. Luckily, this economy measure did not last long and the badge, in its brass form, lasted until 1947.

Within the Dominions and Colonial Forces, sister corps were formed at various times between 1942 and 1945, and they adopted the same REME badge to suit their particular title.

The original REME cap badge was not, however, too popular in some parts of the Corps. Some wearers considered that the central symbol of a pair of calipers laid support to the saying 'Rough Engineering Made Easy'; others in the electrical and electronic side of the Corps were disappointed that the badge only incorporated a purely mechanical symbol.

During wartime, it was impossible to replace the badge but, with the advent of peace, consideration was given to a new design that was to be truly symbolic of the Corps. In 1947, the old badge was replaced by the one worn so frequently in this Garrison.

This present REME badge incorporates parts of the crests of both the Institute of Mechanical Engineers (IMechE) and the Institute of Electrical Engineers (IEE). The horse and chain are symbolic of 'power under control'; the lightning flash stands for 'electrical engineering'; the globe indicates that engineering is 'worldwide'.

The old cap badge, which was so proudly worn in wartime, is now a collector's item. The present cap badge is the one that all of you will wear, equally proudly, when you complete your training at this School.

(This article was first published in The Arborfield Apprentice magazine of spring 1961. Major Tucker was OIC Electrical & Electronics Department at the time. The article was reproduced in OBAN Number 6, issued in autumn 1994.)

A Thousand fall in on the Moor

An hour after dawn, a thousand gaily dressed young men and women, all carrying knapsacks, set off from the foot of Haytor Rocks on a fifty-mile march across the wild bracken-clad hills of Dartmoor.

They were taking part in the Army-organised Ten Tors expedition – the biggest youth event of its kind ever held in Britain and a gruelling test of endurance, determination and map reading that was to claim nearly 200 victims before the two-day trek was over.

The youths, with some sixty girls, came mainly from the west and south of England, but there were teams, too, from as far afield as Yorkshire, Cheshire and Lancashire. There were young soldiers from Regular Army and Territorial Army units, teams from almost all Junior Leader Regiments and Apprentice Schools, the Combined and Army Cadet Forces, Royal Navy, and Royal Air Force. Also represented were Police cadets, the three Women's Services and dozens of civilian enthusiasts.

They gathered at the foot of Haytor shortly after dawn to hear Maj Gen J H Cubbon, of 43rd (Wessex) Division-District, who arrived by helicopter to wish them good luck. At the sound of a trumpet fanfare, played by six bandsmen of the Junior Leaders Regiment, Royal Signals, team leaders opened their sealed envelopes containing the names of the ten tors, which they could then visit in any order. The girls – and boys under sixteen – had to cover a less strenuous course, which also took them to the tops of ten tors.

Hurriedly, the teams conferred, marked the tors on their maps, worked out the shortest routes to each and were off, most of them marching first by road to Widecombe and then through knee-high bracken and over rocks to the top of Bench Tor. Others decided on different routes and there were some who quickly paid the penalty for faulty map reading. One team became so hopelessly lost in the very first hour that it had to give up.

As the day wore on and the sun got hotter, some of the competitors – all carrying a sleeping-bag or blankets, food and cooking equipment – began to lag behind schedule and, by mid-afternoon, more than fifty boys and a dozen girls had retired with badly blistered feet. The rest battled on over the hills, flopping down for a few minutes rest and a drink of water at one tor, before wearily setting off for the next. One Royal Marine Commando team, hardened by previous tough training on Dartmoor, spurned a more comfortable, but longer, route for one that took them waist-high through the River Dart and saved nearly an hour of time.

At eight o'clock on the first evening, every competitor had to halt and all movement was forbidden until six o'clock the next morning. Some found shelter in haystacks and in farm buildings, but most slept out under the stars.

The first team home – at Hexworthy – was expected early in the afternoon of the next day. But the 41 Royal Commando team from Bickleigh made nonsense of that by arriving soon after ten in the morning, stopping 400 yards away from the finishing line to 'tidy up', then coming in 'at the double'! They had covered the course in twenty hours and twenty minutes.

Most teams completed the course by late afternoon. The first Army team home was from the Depot of the Somerset and Cornwall Light Infantry at Bodmin, in twenty-three hours forty minutes, followed by the Royal Army Service Corp Junior Leaders 'A' some ten minutes later. First home of the girls' teams were a civilian youth club, then a team of secondary schoolgirls and, third, the Women's Royal Army Corps from Guildford. The junior event was won by the Teignmouth Grammar School Combined Cadet Force. Every team that finished the course in thirty-six hours or less received medals and certificates.

The expedition was a triumph of organisation for the Junior Leaders Regiment, Royal Signals, who also provided the teams that manned the tops of the tors and arranged medical facilities in case of accident (a helicopter from a nearby Royal Naval Air Station was available in emergencies). They also held a 'jamboree' for all competitors after the contest.

The Army plans to widen the scope of the expedition in future years and, in 1962, hopes to attract more than 2,000 competitors from all over Britain and from France, Holland and Germany.

(This article is based upon that first published in 'Soldier' magazine and then reproduced in The Arborfield Apprentice of autumn 1961.)

George Riley – 'The Hanged Man'

The national newspapers had a field day in the early Sixties, concerning the controversial case involving an ex-boy of intake 55A, namely George Riley. It is impossible to say that the time he spent here at Arborfield had anything to do with George's eventual fate, one would certainly hope not. If it did, then obviously it can be put down as one of those exceptions that proved the rule. Certainly, there is no indication that a similar fate befell any other ex-apprentice.

Records seem to indicate that Riley never made it through his full three years of apprenticeship, he was apparently *"discharged, while in prison"* before the allotted period of time at the School. He was subsequently sentenced to death, and was duly hanged, for the self-confessed murder of sixty-two year old widow, Mrs Adeline Smith, at her home in the Copthorne area of Shrewsbury.

Talking to old boys of that era, Riley had always been considered one of the 'hard cases' of his Div, always *"up for a scrap"* and rumour had it that he habitually *"carried a knife"*. There is no doubt that he carried a fearsome reputation during his stay at the School and younger boys were wise to steer clear of him. Even so, the horrid event that led to his eventual demise must go down as one of the most unsavoury events in Arborfield's history.

Riley had certainly left 'boys' school' by the time of the incident, which didn't take place until October 1960. He must also have left the Army by then and returned to living at home with his parents. The local press described him as a *"typically excitable youngster"* but also reported that, on the particular Friday night in question, George had been indulging in some excessive drinking. He is reported to have sunk around nine pints and almost as many whiskies during the evening's 'entertainment'. Following his pub-crawl, he had also become involved in a fight at a *"works dance"*. His drinking partner had dragged him away from this fracas and later dropped him off outside of his home.

The case against Riley was that he must have entered the house of his neighbour, Mrs Smith, bent on stealing any ready cash, as he had drunk away most of his weekly wage packet. The unfortunate lady must have spotted George at his desperate search and, unthinkingly, had decided to tackle him head on. Perhaps she even recognised him and thought that she could reason with him. But George's drinking and fighting may well have left him all wound up and not in control of his emotions. The outcome was that his elderly neighbour suffered some vicious blows to her face, during an assault that was completely unnecessary.

Left lying unconscious and in a pool of blood upon the floor of her own bedroom, Adeline Smith succumbed to her dreadful injuries, while George left the house in a state of panic. He ended the night sleeping in the garage of his own home.

It wasn't long before the police came looking for him, as rumours began to circulate about his drunken actions of the previous evening, and the fact that he had been spotted lurking in the street during the early hours. Initially, Riley denied all charges but then, having been confronted with police evidence, confessed to the deadly deed, although he never actually signed the statement. His subsequent trial had to be heard in the neighbouring town of Stafford, as local feelings against him were running so high. He could only offer his *"drunkenness"* as a defence and was found guilty as charged. He later appealed, but this was turned down and he was hung at Shrewsbury.

The famous left-wing MP, Sydney Silverman, reported in the House of Commons, a week after Riley's sentence had been carried out, that the case left *"nagging doubts"* about its justice. According to Mr Silverman, young Riley, described in the press as a *"butcher's boy (or assistant)"*, had confessed to the crime only after the police had told him of overwhelming evidence that they supposedly held. He was told that his fingerprints, his footprints, and blood of his type were found all over *"the blood spattered room"* where Mrs Smith had met her violent death. Mr Silverman assured the House that there had been no such fingerprints, nor any footprints – and only a few spots of blood on Riley's trousers.

By the time of his appeal, twenty-one year old Riley had retracted his 'confession', telling the court that the bloodstains on his trousers had been the result of a bar-room brawl, a likely enough story considering George's antics in the early part of that Friday evening. The police officer in the case was suspended from duty when he was accused of tampering with witnesses, but was later absolved. Whatever the doubts these facts would have put into the jury's minds, it was all too late. Home Secretary R A Butler eventually made the decision that the jury's verdict should stand as correct. He was satisfied that Riley had rightly been found guilty and so the sentence, of *"death by hanging"*, was carried out.

George Riley's father, a former RSM, told the newspapers that his son had been convicted almost entirely due to his own confession, which had been made a mere seven hours after his arrest, and that there had been very little in the way of supporting evidence. Riley's solicitor later compared the case with that of Timothy Evans, who had been wrongly convicted of murder in the famous 'Ten Rillington Place' case of 1950. He too had 'confessed' to murder, but it was later proven that the culprit had been John Reginald Christie.

(The above story was gleaned from copies of newspapers sent to the editor by John Lee of 55A, backed up by more material later provided by the Shrewsbury Records and Research Service.)

Festival of Remembrance 1964

By Major J A Morton, REME

History was created on Saturday 7th November 1964 when, for the first time, the Army Apprentices' School presented a ten-minute impression of the life of an apprentice tradesman, as part of the Army display, televised at the Royal Albert Hall during the annual Festival of Remembrance. There were two public performances, one in the afternoon to all the Ladies' Branches of the British Legion, and the other in the evening. Her Majesty the Queen, Queen Elizabeth the Queen Mother and many other distinguished guests were among the audience of 7,000 packing the hall for the evening performance.

The work of more than half a term went into the ten-minute production by 100 personnel of the School. The Commandant, Colonel J L Dobie, was approached as far back as July by the Ministry of Defence and asked to give consideration to presenting an eight- to ten-minute display at the Festival.

Preliminary discussions were held with Mr Ralph Reader the Festival producer, Maj J A Morton REME and Maj F E White, South Staffordshire Regiment, who were given the task of producing and directing the display on behalf of the School. It was decided to adopt the theme of the life of an apprentice tradesman, during his three years at the School, covering all aspects of his work and leisure activities.

The display commenced showing long-haired recruits sheepishly following their new sergeant on first joining the School. This was immediately followed by twelve extremely smart apprentices, immaculately turned out, being marched on to the stage by the apprentice RSM. The marked contrast showed what good effect three years of Army training can achieve and brought tremendous applause from the audience.

The finished produce was a good cross-section from the more senior apprentices, depicting tough, intelligent soldier/tradesmen and potential leaders, ready to take their place as skilled craftsmen in the Corps of Royal Electrical and Mechanical Engineers, as electronic technicians, aircraft technicians and vehicle mechanics. The spotlights were then switched to various tableaux, highlighting the three main ingredients of the apprenticeship viz. technical, educational and military training.

This was achieved by showing apprentices appropriately dressed, engaged in such activities as workshop practice, electronic, vehicles and aircraft repairs, education instruction and culminating in a Bren group and Rifle section coming into action. Then, to demonstrate that a soldier must also be fit, tough and agile, some apprentices showed their skill at fencing, judo and physical training.

Adventure training also plays an important part in developing character and leadership qualities, and in lending excitement to recreational training. This was demonstrated by groups of canoeists, pot-holers, anglers, archers and horse riders, dressed and equipped at intervals across the centre of the arena. Her Majesty the Queen showed great interest in particular to the pot-holers, who looked uncommonly like a group of Welsh miners in their dress and equipment.

These lads were quickly followed by six well-groomed young men in School-mufti walking-out dress, marching in precision to the centre of the arena and halting very smartly. Then, to everyone's amusement, they all gave a jiving demonstration accompanied by one of the School's pop-groups, 'The Kingpins'; thus showing that it is not all work and no play at the School.

Whilst this was going on, the other apprentices removed their overalls and transformed themselves very promptly into the School Pipe Band, and so to the finale. All the participants marched off smartly behind the Pipe Band to the tune of 'Scotland the Brave', with the very smartly attired Drum Major in full Scottish regalia at the front. The tremendous applause from the audience suggested that all the very hard work, during the many evening rehearsals, had been well worthwhile.

After the display by the RAF, the apprentices had a prominent place in the arena for the community singing and remembrance service, with many close-up shots on the television cameras. It was a moving experience and undoubtedly made a lot of parents feel justly proud. Subsequently, the Commandant has received very many messages of congratulation, praise and appreciation, including one from the Inspector of Boys' Training (Army).

To take part in a performance before Her Majesty the Queen and a television audience of thirty million viewers is quite a test of a young soldier's versatility and courage. From the way they performed however, they might have been professionals. This was the first time ever that boys of the School have performed at the Festival. Their enthusiasm and precision was a great credit to their generation and a fine tribute to the memory of those to whom the Festival is dedicated.

(The above article was first published in The Craftsman magazine of January/February 1965.)

Seen from the Water-tower

By A/T Former

It was late 1940 and London was receiving its nightly visit from the German Air Force. As usual, the odd plane found its way across the Arborfield area, either *en route* or returning from, the Capital.

On this particular November night, at about nine o'clock, all was quiet in the School. An air raid 'warning purple' had been sounded and all lights were extinguished, except for the palest of blue emergency lights in the corridors.

Two adventurous apprentices (who shall be nameless) were, contrary to Standing Orders, sitting on the verandah roof of 'K' Block, watching the gun and bomb blasts over distant London. Suddenly inspired, they jumped down, duly filled a dustbin with stones and hoisted it up onto the roof.

A short wait for the sound of an approaching plane and then, at the correct psychological moment, one apprentice, with fingers in his mouth, let forth a piercing whistle, whilst the other, at the given pitch, dropped the dustbin onto the concrete path below.

The new Education Block can be clearly seen to the left whilst closer inspection shows that this was taken in a winter term, as the rugby posts are just visible on the sports fields

This view shows the Permanent Staff Block in the foreground, 3 Trg Battalion in Bailleu Camp at 2 o'clock and 'The GAPH' at 12 o'clock. Not many knew that GAPH stood for Garrison Area Picture House – the author admits that he thought is was 'the Gaff', assuming that it was a slang term for the stated title of 'Globe Cinema', run by the AKC.

Pandemonium broke loose in the Block, some sixteen apprentices in each room of the 'spider' hit the floor hard, to the great delight of the two perpetrators of this prank.

Suddenly, the air was blue with the venomous snarls of the CSM, who, at the precise moment of contact between dustbin and concrete, was opposite the entrance to Room K5, inspecting the blackout and security. Like all good soldiers, he flung himself flat in the corridor, but with disastrous results. The four filled fire-buckets were knocked over and the effect was pretty horrifying – especially to the apprentices on the roof!

Down they jumped and quickly disappeared into K5 through an open window, just a jump ahead of the CSM coming through the door. He ordered the NCO I/C Room to switch on the lights. The blackout shutters were immediately 'made good' and on went the lights. And there stood the apparition to end all apparitions – the irate CSM, water running from his clothes, hat knocked sideways, cap badge gone and absolutely red in the face.

But, I ask you, did anyone dare laugh? What do you think?

(The above article is based upon that published in The Arborfield Apprentice of spring 1963. The author's given name of 'A/T Former' could just be a cover for 'Former A/T' – what do you think?)

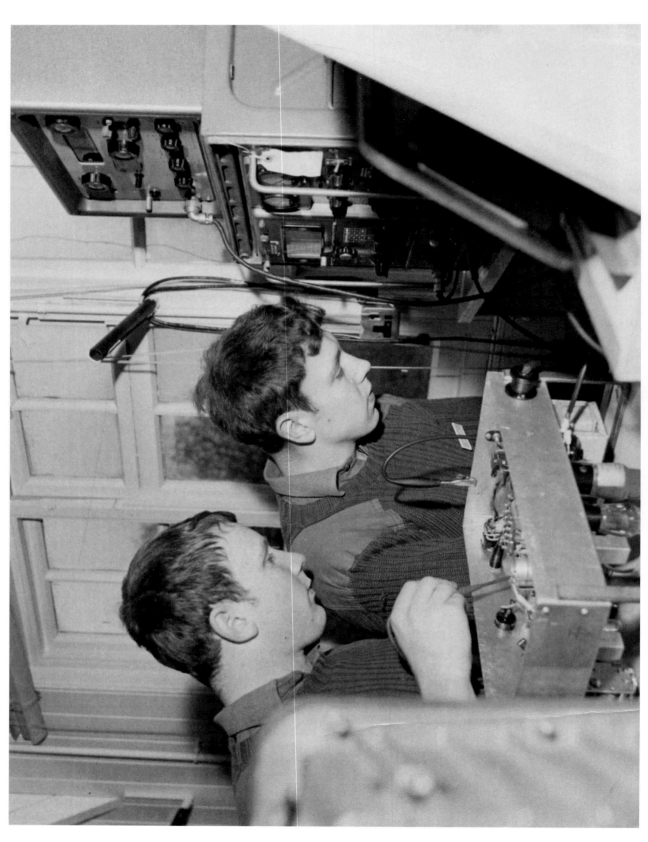

Fault finding practice for electronic apprentice technicians

Chapter 7

1965 - 67

The Olympian

The Craftsman magazine of March 1965 featured an excellent article by LCpl J R Fox, who had achieved a personal ambition the previous autumn, when he had represented his country at the 1964 Olympic Games held in Tokyo, Japan. On the journey out to the Far East, the first stop was at Rome, where Jim was surprised to find that the crew of stewardesses had been changed for Italian ones. Amazingly, there were another six touchdowns at various airports along the way, with a different set of young ladies coming aboard at each one – nice work if you can get it!

Ex-apprentice Jim went on to describe the receptions and training that took place during the ten days leading up to the Games and, in particular, the splendour of the opening ceremony. Jim's sport, the Modern Pentathlon, took place over the first five days of the Games and, despite a good performance, the team all felt that they *"could have done better"*. Upon returning home, the team took part in a reception at Buckingham Palace, hosted by The Queen. Jim describes how each athlete was greeted personally and how much he enjoyed the *"excellent buffet lunch"* – you can tell he's an ex-boy!

Moves and non-moves

One move that actually did take place in 1965 was when Col Dobie relinquished command of the School on February 12th. With due ceremony, he was dragged thorough the gates in a *Land Rover*, by VMs of 9 Div. The School wished him well and congratulated him on his promotion to Brigadier as DEME of 1 (BR) Corps. The Sergeant's Mess 'dined him out' in their usual inimitable style, presenting him with a silver salver as a token of their appreciation of his services to the Mess during his tour. In his speech of reply, the departing Commandant said that he had nothing quite so material to leave behind, but nevertheless left a tale which, although not suitable to be passed on to their grandchildren, the Mess members would remember for many years to follow!

The year 1965 saw a continuation of the discussions and proposals regarding the future of the School, which seemed to have dated back over a period of five years i.e. to 1960. These had been delayed back in May 1961, when a possible move to Barton Stacey is thought to have been mooted. This was probably the 'derelict' site that Col Legh and his wife had set their eyes upon in 1960. However, by the end of November 1964, it had definitely been decided that any 'new' School would still be located at Arborfield.

Meanwhile, Aircraft Wing had started to assert itself as a separate entity, following its initial 'bedding-in' period as part of Mechanical Wing. In May 1965 the Wing moved, *"bag and baggage"*, into Bailleul Barracks, but did not finally and completely break loose until a couple of years later. In August of that same year, stringent financial restraints dictated that a general embargo was placed on all major works services that had not already been put out to contract. This meant that the School was definitely 'staying put' for the foreseeable future.

The edition of *The Arborfield Apprentice* that appeared in spring 1965 reflected upon the fact that, of the original 115 potential tradesmen of intake 62A, a total of only eighty-seven had completed their apprenticeship. With much justification, Col Dobie had put this down to the exceptionally high standard that had to be achieved. The magazine also reported upon the 'PoP' of that same intake, where the Reviewing Officer was Maj Gen P H Man CBE, DSO, MC, the GOC Aldershot District. In his address, the General brought out the necessities of 'smartness', which was obviously a subject close to his heart. As he put it, *"A smart soldier is invariably a good soldier and a scruffy soldier an idle soldier"*.

Thankfully he had seen lots of smartness on that particular parade! This was in spite of the fact that conditions had almost forced a 'wet weather' parade to be held. But the General, himself a *"seasoned veteran"*, scorned the elements, carrying out a thorough inspection on the Parade Square. The rain, accompanied by a bitterly cold biting wind, caused quite a few 'lesser mortals' to keel over, with one

Alan Woolley, a 63C Radar Technician, working on a Green Archer mortar locating radar in the heart and heat of the Borneo jungle late in 1965. Prior to the deployment of a Mortar Locating Troop with three Green Archers, attack by Indonesian mortars had created a major problem for the British and Australian forces.

unfortunate young apprentice of 9 Div 'impaling' himself on his bayonet! However, he escaped serious injury, suffering nothing worse than a beautiful green and purple 'shiner', a proud badge to be worn for the next few days! The rest of the intake proudly passed through the gates to the traditional strains of *'Auld Lang Syne'* and flung their caps high into the air with the usual gusto.

Colin Newby was one of the first entrants that year, a member of 65A. But not for him the glories of promotion and high honours! As he put it himself, having finally joined the ranks of the OBA some thirty years later, he was one of *"the great unwashed"* – surely not, even during the 'Swingin' Sixties'? Colin goes on to say that he was *"good at his trade, good at education, good at keeping his nose clean (more or less), but not good at sports, hence remaining an A/T from start to finish"*.

Sports parades were obviously something that Colin dreaded, until he found out that the cross-country runners, once the parade had been dismissed, would quickly trot off to where they were *"out of sight and completely unsupervised"*. Thus it was that Colin took up the sport with some gusto. Wednesday afternoons during the late summer months would find him running *"at a brisk trot"* as far as the corner of the boiler-house, strolling across the sports field, then picking the succulent blackberries that grew in profusion on the hedges along the Camp's secluded rear perimeter road! This would end in *"a gentle jog"* back past the Guardroom, a quick shower, then some Egyptian 'bed pressing' until the sweaty sporty types also returned!

A road-run too far

The day eventually arrived when, on one cold January Wednesday afternoon parade, the ground was covered in snow. *"Ah, great"*, thought Colin, *"no cross-country today"*. But retribution had arrived in the form of new Company Commander, Maj Sim – *"supremely fit and determined to see the Company exercised"*. Proceeding to shout out drill commands that were completely unfamiliar to the boys, the OC finally got them into some semblance of order and doubled them off on a 'road run' – no escape this time Colin! However, the run eventually ended in farce, when the boys arrived at the ford through the River Blackwater. Maj Sim insisted that the boys wade across what had now become three feet of water, swollen by the melting snow.

This caused no end of confusion of course, as the ford was normally crossed by using the narrow bridge that ran alongside it. The leading boys were about halfway across when the Major told them to duck down and actually sit in the icy water! Several of them dutifully did just that, but the boys that had followed at a slower pace saw their plight and were most disinclined to follow suit. Maj Sim's dog then managed to free itself and run loose. Some boys tried to grab it, while others started 'ducking' their mates. By now, of course, total chaos reigned and most boys were no doubt able to slip across the bridge to the safety of the other side. The OC never did try that one again!

Around the time of his last year at Arborfield, Colin got involved in a bit of a 'kerfuffle' over some gypping in the Cookhouse queue. It was no doubt a case of 'handbags at fifty paces', but one of the PS Sergeants eventually decided to 'make an example' and randomly grabbed five apprentices – including Colin – and marched them down to the Guardroom. RSM Simpson thought this was all a bit of a joke, but the errant five were still placed on 'open arrest'. It was hardly justice, but it happened anyway – and all over trying to get to the front of the queue, where they could choose juicy chicken for dinner, rather than mutton or beef!

The spring term brought to an end the 'reign' of Maj Jim Morton in the higher echelons of 'S' Coy. He was departing the School after almost five years, having played his part in forming the original Company as an experiment in 1960. As reported in the latest School magazine by 'Nobby', Jim would *"mount his new steed and head in the direction of the rolling green pastures and comfortable offices at Salisbury and Southern Command"*. He was to be succeeded as OC by Maj D D Lister MBE.

(Jim Morton went on to serve a full forty years and died in 1977. A respectful acknowledgement of his career, written by his son Alan, an ex-boy from 51B, is included as a separate annex to this chapter.)

PS members were rightly proud of the exploits of their soccer side that season. They had gained top position of the 'B' Division of the Aldershot District Small Units League, with an enviable record of having won seventeen of their eighteen matches. Their goals tally was equally impressive, 114 goals scored and only twenty-six given away. Their only blemish was in losing to a team from SEME Bordon in the semi-final of the Commandant's Cup, but there was the extenuating circumstance of playing with only ten men! The unfortunate Cpl Baker had been injured right at the start of the game and, in those days, there were no substitutes sitting 'on the bench' to take over for him.

School Rugby was thriving early in 1965, the First XV enjoying *"its best season in many years"*. Having lost only one match during the winter term, to a very good side from Wellington College, the spring term was proving equally successful. Four team members had played in the final Junior Army trial, with one of the boys selected to play against the famous Blackheath side. Twenty team members were looking forward to a trip to Twickenham, for England's traditional 'Calcutta Cup' international game against the Scots.

April 14th saw yet another intake pass out of the School, those boys who had originally gathered together as 62B. Pride of place that day went to A/T RSM A McInnes, who walked off proudly into adult

service following his presentation with three separate trophies – namely the Award of Honour, Commandant's Cup and Chief Instructor's Cup. These trophies paid tribute to his highly effective efforts as both soldier and tradesman, with his leadership qualities also coming to the forefront.

Transfer of control to REME

That 'PoP' took place soon after Col G W Paris, MBE, AMIMechE, AMBIM, and again a member of REME, had succeeded Col Joe Dobie as the latest Commandant. The Apprentices' School at Carlisle had also seen the appointment of its first REME Commandant, Col Bill Kinchin, the previous year. This was a period of time that became of great importance to the historical existence of the School. In August of that year, as a result of decisions taken at the MoD, its sponsorship and control (as well as that of Carlisle) was irrevocably transferred away from the Inspector of Boys' Training (Army) to the DEME. Thus, both Schools now became a dedicated part of the overall REME training system.

(A brief history of Col Paris's career is included as a separate annex to this chapter.)

Following that historic transfer of control, the following message extract from Maj Gen L H (later Sir Leonard) Atkinson OBE, and DEME at the time, was sent to the two Schools. In appreciation of the DEME's message, the Commandant arranged for it to be published in *The Craftsman* the following month (November) and later reproduced in *The Arborfield Apprentice,* in its winter 1965 issue.

> *"On August 3rd 1965, the Army Apprentices' Schools at Arborfield and Carlisle were transferred to my control. I take this opportunity of welcoming to the Corps the apprentices and members of the permanent staffs of these Schools ... the ties between these Apprentices' Schools and the Corps are of long standing and have become progressively closer in recent years. Formal transfer of control will allow this process of integration to continue, to the material benefit, I am sure, of the Schools, the Corps and the students."*

A brief historical survey

This was probably a fortuitous time to reflect upon the School's already lengthening history and to look back on the events that had taken place during the previous twenty-six years. Maj C J Allin, BA, Dip Ed, RAEC, on the staff of the Education Wing, produced a paper that was entitled *"The Army Apprentices' School, Arborfield – a brief historical survey"*, apparently the first real attempt to put all that had happened since 1939 into a truly historical context. The paper was certainly a great effort and became the definitive forerunner of all the other 'histories' that were to follow, at somewhat irregular intervals, over the years that followed, including this present one. The full text of his historical document appeared in *The Craftsman* of January the following year.

Maj Allin introduced his paper in this fashion:

"Since the ATS (Boys), Arborfield, opened its gates for the first time on 1ˢᵗ April 1939, there have been a number of landmarks in the School's career. The present formal move to the control of the REME is the most significant yet for the future of the School. To reciprocate the good wishes of the DEME, on behalf of all members of the Army Apprentices' School, Arborfield, this short account of the School's first quarter century has been compiled."

His concluding paragraph, of the article itself, stated that:

"We have had a chequered past, meeting many difficulties and experiencing many memorable moments. Throughout its twenty-six years of existence the School has been constantly evolving and, with so much that is worthwhile and praiseworthy behind it, it looks forward to further success under its new badge."

The first Air Techs had arrived as members of 63C, their section located in just one classroom, with only a limited amount of training equipment, housed in a corner of building 'VM1'. This unsatisfactory state of affairs had continued for a few months until, in May 1965, the section moved to alternative accommodation in Bailleul Camp. This provided ample and comfortable classroom space and an aircraft hangar, complete with fluorescent lighting and central heating. At last, the availability of training staff and equipment was now keeping pace with the progress of the training cycle. The presence of Artificers Aircraft (Art Air), complete with their light blue Army Air Corps (AAC) berets, created the right atmosphere – all that was now needed to complete the scene were some 'running' aircraft!

Sunday 11ᵗʰ July saw a departure from the usual 'Sunday-morning-Service' routine when, for the first time in the history of the School, a public baptism was held. Rev R B Morris CF thanked Cpl Picton (PS) and his wife for allowing this Sacrament to be held in front of everyone, as a reminder of the importance of baptism in the life of the Church. As he wrote in *The Arborfield Apprentice,* in its summer edition, *"It's good that we should be reminded occasionally"*.

That same School magazine contained a two-page spread, reporting on the progress of the Saddle Club and splendidly illustrated with several photographs taken by members of the Camera Club. Facilities at Arborfield were ideal for those wishing to ride and some fifty boys were now taking advantage of the opportunity. The School had four horses of its own and hired another four, twice weekly, from the REME Saddle Club. The boys had an excellent instructor in Mr Bennett, who had arrived from the RMAS and had a lifetime's experience with horses. As reported at the time, he had *"forgotten more about stable management than some would ever learn"*.

At the beginning of the 1965 summer term, 'A' Coy welcomed a new 2I/C in the form of Capt R D King RA. The boys had been warned that he was *"a bit keen on athletics"* and so it proved! Hardly an evening went by when the Captain's track-suited figure of authority wasn't to be seen, descending upon the barrack rooms and chasing out the reluctant boys for training. 'B' Coy also had a change of face, when Maj H G Ferguson MC, of the Royal Northumberland Fusiliers (RNF) took over as Company Commander. He quickly proved that 'being new' was no handicap, handing out many a crafty trip and kick as he joined in with the boys during football matches!

When the going gets tough … … …

A team of 'C' Coy boys *"came, saw and conquered"* at what had now become the annual entry into the

'Ten Tors' event, held on Dartmoor. Records indicate that this was not the first time that the School had participated in this gruelling exercise. That year's apprentices were certainly not held back by superfluous gear! They carried a supply of dehydrated soup powder and solid fuel stoves, which they carted around in their 'ammo' pouches; they slept out in the open, protected from the cold night's rain only by sheets of polythene. At the 8th checkpoint, they were given some 'survival rations' by a kindly bunch of Royal Marines and, sufficiently refreshed, completed the final march to the finish at the 10th Tor.

Meanwhile, 'D' Coy boys of 6 and 7 Divs were proving the truth of another old adage – *"Ne'er cast a clout till May be out"*. They had gone down to the Black Mountains of Carmarthenshire for a spot of rock climbing and found the Welsh sunshine as elusive as ever! To rub salt into their wounds, host Mr Thomas, surrounded by his flock of faithful (though rather stupid!) sheep, and set against a sweeping backdrop of moor and mountain, invited the lads to partake of a swim in his sheep-dip on their next visit!

During the summer of 1965, boys from the School took part in the REME exhibition at the Aldershot Show, a public display of 'the tools of the trade'. The School was represented in all aspects of its life, trade, education, sports and hobbies. The most popular exhibit appeared to be the old *'Auster'* from the Aircraft Department, although it was later wondered just how long it took to get it back into working order! Tying for second place in the popularity stakes were Judo, Fencing and the Pipe Band – just how many photographs were taken of our kilted brethren? *(Perhaps this is where the story originated? When one boy was asked, "What's worn under your kilt?" he supposedly replied, "There's nothing worn under my kilt, it's all in good working order!" The old ones are the best! Ed.)*

The School's recently formed Sub-Aqua Club was involved in a treasure hunt that summer. They had been asked to assist in exploring a deep well within the grounds of historic Basing House. During the 17th-century English Civil War, Cromwell's 'Roundheads' had laid siege to the Royalist occupants of the house and later found that the expected booty had gone missing, with the well the most obvious location. The house's latest owner was now hoping to come up with an estimated two to three million pounds worth of goodies and was offering a ten-per-cent cut on what

was found! As reported in *The Arborfield Apprentice* at the time, only some old Tudor bricks and masonry had been recovered, but expectations were still high. *(Somehow, I don't think the boys hit the jackpot! If they did, it was never reported. Ed.)*

Another task that came the way of the intrepid divers was as an *"underwater salvage detachment"*! A canoe being used for a 7 Div training exercise had sunk in the Thames near Reading Bridge, and it was hoped that the skills of the sub-aqua boys could locate and recover it. Following some unsuccessful sweeps of the river, A/T Gibbs-Jones describes 'what happened next': *"I suddenly found a rudder lying on the bottom and, tracing along, came across the canoe on the river bed. I took my mouthpiece out and filled the canoe with air from my tanks and it rose to the surface"*. The canoe was subsequently recovered and later returned to Arborfield.

Despite a dreadful summer season as far as weather was concerned, the School cricket XI had enjoyed some successful results. Outstanding amongst these was the winning of the Quadrangular Competition held at Chepstow. First they beat Carlisle by seven wickets, then Harrogate by two wickets and, finally, the home side by seventy-eight runs. The most notable individual performance came from A/T RSM Whitaker, the School Captain, who took nine wickets for only nineteen runs against Harrogate. But probably the most popular victory of all, and to the *"absolute fury"* of the Cricket Officer, was the one later gained over the School's own PS side. With the winter coaching sessions ahead, under the expert eye of Ron Tindall of Surrey, the boys looked forward with great expectations to the following season.

'In-house' ONC training

In September 1965, the School finally embarked upon teaching the ONC 'in-house' here at Arborfield, in both Electrical and Mechanical Engineering. A total of thirty-one students had commenced the three-term course in Mathematics, Engineering Science, Workshop Processes and Materials, Engineering Drawing and General Studies. Prior to this, the reliance upon Reading Technical College had meant numbers were down to only four students. Dependent upon a successful examination result, students would then start the appropriate National Certificate at the start of their fourth term. Those below the required

The MI Room next to the MRS

ONC standard had the option of continuing at C & G level.

By the winter term, the Sub-Aqua Club was celebrating its first birthday and beginning to 'find its fins' in diving expeditions near Salcombe, Devon, and at Lake Mytchett near Aldershot. Two members had joined the nearby Reading Club on several dives off the coast of Cornwall, basing themselves at the picturesque resort of Penzance. Best of all was the day's course, run by the RE's Diving School at Marchwood, near Southampton, where they were able to familiarise themselves with a variety of equipment. Following a suggestion by a Club member, divers were later allowed to visit a lake at Bearwood, only a few miles from Arborfield, and owned by the Royal Merchant Navy College.

The winter 1965 edition of *The Arborfield Apprentice* commented upon the fact that *"there must be something about the ex-Apprentice, his bearing and his turnout"*. It had been most noticeable that the Guard of Honour, which had turned out for the Army Minister at the formal opening of SEE, contained several Technicians who had left the School only a few weeks previously. The editor of *The Craftsman*, REME's monthly magazine, had obviously been impressed,

as a photograph of that 'Guard' appeared on the front cover of the magazine's December issue.

Mr Harry Shaw, long standing member of the Sailing Club, used the School magazine to extol the virtues of dinghy racing – a sport that, as he put it, *"beats all bat and ball games into a cocked hat"*. As he also explained, the sport demands a great deal of mental and physical effort, while the presence of cheering spectators is replaced by the battle against the bitter and lonely elements of wind and sea. A cruise on the Baltic had taken place during the summer recess, while another from England's eastern coast, aboard the yacht *'Theodora'*, was eagerly anticipated.

That same School magazine took a nostalgic look back to some twenty years previously, commenting upon some of the quotations of that era as follows:

"The School Choir, 112 strong, gave a Christmas Concert in the Camp Hall" - perhaps we had a few more Welshmen in the School in those days. *"A/T Conway, the original Drum Major, has left us now"* – little did they know! *"Work has begun on the*

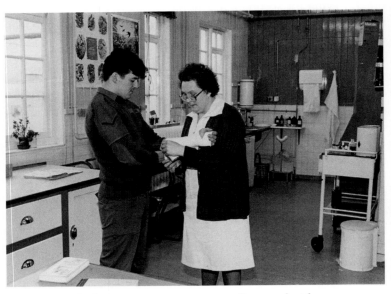

In latter years treatment was dispensed with much care by sympathetic mother figure nurses.

Company Gardens" – can we have a progress report in the 1986 edition? *"'D' Coy beat 'C' Coy at Hockey, by 8-2"* – this term 'C' Coy beat 'D' Coy 8 - 1, a slow business this team building, but it pays off in the end! *"In a (Sergeants' Mess) Snooker handicap, the RSM and the Provost Sergeant have already been beaten in close finishes, which says much for the efficiency of the handicapping"* – and for the moral courage of the handicapper!

A little nugget of information was included from the discerning pen of the Padre, Rev R B Morris. He explained that the derivation of the word 'magazine' came from the Arabic word *'makhzhan'*, still in use, which means 'a storehouse'. It was now used to indicate a periodical, containing miscellaneous articles, or a store of reading. The first publication of this kind in England had been the *Gentleman's Magazine* in 1731, so *The Arborfield Apprentice* could certainly be said to be upholding a long tradition.

December 16th 1965 was quite an historic day in the history of the School, as the final intake of GSC apprentices passed out on their way to adult service with the Corps. The weather proved very kind and a large number of spectators watched *"an excellent parade"*, reviewed by Brig K R S Trevor, the Inspector of Boys' Training (Army). Although re-badging was not due until the New Year, the whole of the previous term had seen the School under full REME control.

During winter term of 1963, the School had begun experimenting with 'teaching machines', with an in-house mathematics package being later written by members of the educational staff, under the direction of the SEO. Towards the end of 1965, the School had provided a display in programmed instruction at an Audio Visual Aids (AVA) exhibition in London. Now, in January of 1966, the School obtained six *'Auto Tutor'* and eighteen *'Grundig Master'* teaching machines. The former were used for assisting in the teaching of 'O' Level Mathematics, Electrical Science and slide-rule use, while the latter helped with English and Workshop Processes programmes. Besides evaluating the usefulness of commercial teaching programmes in their various disciplines, the School was to find them to be very useful in remedial work, for those apprentices who had missed normal lessons through sickness and for those who found certain aspects of the work more difficult than others.

England's successful World Cup year

In January 1966, *The Craftsman* magazine presented an article on the AAS Carlisle, which had just entered its sixth year of existence – still a Jeep in Arborfield's eyes! Located on the outskirts of the city of Carlisle, the School occupied a site through which passed some of the remnants of Hadrian's Wall, once built by the Roman forces on the northern perimeter of their far-flung Empire, to keep out the marauding Picts and Scots. It was this historic edifice that had given rise to the name 'Hadrian's Camp'.

Over the period 3rd – 5th February 1966, the School participated in a Recruiting Display down at the seaside resort of Bournemouth. Although its direct effect on recruiting figures may never have come to light, the impact on the packed audiences at the time was tremendous. The REME part of the display consisted, in the main, of short sketches, portraying the progress of a typical apprentice through his three-year stay at the School, depicting not only trade and education training, but also the importance of weapon training, physical fitness and drill. All in all, a cast of sixty-six boys – appropriate to the year! – was used to complement a three-ton truck, full of display equipment.

Canoeing had continued throughout the winter months, in the face of some very inclement weather. New members had quickly learned to endure the icy rigours of the Thames and a pair of Club enthusiasts had represented their activity in the Bournemouth display previously mentioned. The Canoe Club was now busily engaged in manufacturing ten double-seater canoes, of glass-fibre resin construction, which would then be offered for sale to Club members at a cost of £10 each. The Club as a whole was also looking ahead excitedly to their first entry into the long-distance Devizes-Westminster canoe race at Easter.

It was most fitting that the DEME, Maj Gen Atkinson himself, should be invited to review his first 'PoP' at the School, in the spring of 1966, when for the very first time, every single one of the graduating apprentices was now cap-badged as a member of REME. The Commandant, Col Paris, made the following statement, in reference to that parade:

"It is very appropriate that we have General Atkinson with us today. We have had many senior and important Reviewing Officers in the past, but none with a bigger interest in

RSM D M McMahon 1996-99

the School ... ... as the efficiency of his Corps rests, in no small way, on the type of apprentice we produce in this school and the standard of training they receive".

After a ten-year respite however, it was also the second time that a 'wet weather' routine had to be called into action, when the day of the 'PoP' dawned with a thick layer of snow covering the Parade Square. The unaccustomed procedure went very smoothly, much to the surprise of many pessimists! The departing intake, 102 strong when they arrived in May 1963, had later been boosted to 122 in number by other apprentices, 'back-squadded' from earlier intakes. But of this total, only seventy-five had survived to complete their trade training to the required standard, reminding everyone of just how hard one had to work to achieve that standard.

The DEME announced that he had attended some fifteen of the School's 'PoPs' during his career, with this one the third he had the honour of reviewing. He told the audience that he had it *"on good authority"* that the

School would be rebuilt in the foreseeable future. The living accommodation would be built nearby, while the instructional buildings would be *"rather closer to the SEE"*. He was right, of course, but only the passing of time was to prove how long that eventual rebuild would take.

Due to some dangerous conditions on the swollen River Thames, the Canoe Club had been unable to use the water until around four weeks before Easter. But they made as much use of this shortened time as possible, each crew paddling a distance of some 200 miles. When the Devizes-Westminster race took place, there were seventy-eight crews setting off at the start, but more than one half of these were to retire due to fatigue or boat damage. It is to their great credit that the two pairs from the School arrived at the finishing line in 17th and 23rd places – a considerable achievement.

April of 1966 saw the arrival of another replacement RSM, this time RSM D McMahon, who was the School's first RSM from the Grenadier Guards since dear old Ben Cook had departed in 1941, a gap of a quarter of a century. RSM Simpson left the School on retirement to civilian life in Yorkshire, with the best wishes of all ringing in his ears.

Crossing the Channel

Five apprentice members of the crew of the *'Billy Bray'* left Arborfield on April 7th, to join their boat, lying at its moorings at Hamble, down on the coast between Portsmouth and Southampton. They were up early the next morning, to literally 'learn the ropes', before setting sail. By early afternoon, however, they had become fog-bound and had to settle for finding an overnight berth at Yarmouth, just across the Solent on the Isle of Wight. The wind finally got up next day, a Saturday, quickly dispersing the fog. So, working in four-hour shifts through the whole day and following night, they eventually sighted the coast of France early on the Sunday morning.

After a brief two hours stopover at Le Havre, they weighed anchor for the return trip. By this time, however, the wind had died just about completely and, without sufficient fuel to motor, a log entry at 14.00 hours read, *"Speed half-a-knot. Overtaken by two jellyfish"*! It was to be mid-morning the following day, *"wallowing like a bag of dominoes"*, that they finally made their way back up the Solent, feeling rather pleased with themselves – very tired but definitely happy to be back.

Alec Powell was a member of that crew and, if his memory serves him correctly, he was accompanied by two mates, called Dick Menhinick and Hugh 'Lewie' Martin. He recalls the craft as a *"35-ton gaff-rigged ketch"* and believes that she still sails, but now under the name *'Ocean Blue'*. Alec also remembers that they were so late getting back to their mooring at Hamble that they thought they were in danger of being charged as AWOL and had to phone Arborfield to advise the School of their whereabouts.

The Athletics team had started its training in late April, with a heavy schedule ahead. At the first competition, held at the Aldershot and District Athletics Club, some fine performances saw the School win a narrow victory against four other competing teams. For the next meeting, at Reading's Palmer Park, the School entered a total of fifty-one athletes, with two fine individual wins in the junior hammer competition and the long jump. On June 8th, the boys were only just beaten into third place, in a meeting where all the other teams fielded adult soldiers. A couple of weeks later, ex-boy Sgt Hart-Ives, then in the team from SEE, set up a new unofficial Army record for the Javelin, with a throw of over 369 feet.

Andrew Dickson, another now settled somewhere 'in a land down under', relishes those days when a copy of the *OBAN* is delivered through his mail. He joined up here at Arborfield on May 10th 1966, a member of 66B, and recalls being lined up on the Square to be issued with all the *"new stuff"* associated with the transfer to REME. He joined the rest of his intake in their barrack rooms in the 'HQ' Block, by then firmly established at the top end of the Square. On the day that his squad passed out from 'J' Coy, it coincided with the football World Cup Final being shown 'live' on television. Andy recalls the excitement of that momentous occasion when England gained their famous 4 - 2 extra-time victory over the West Germans, thanks to a hat trick of goals from the legendary Geoff Hurst.

Andy's brother-in-law, Bob James, was also at the School at the time and often had a problem getting up in the morning. It thus became the custom for Andy to nearly beat Bob's door down before he managed to surface. One night after a particular attempt to finish off the whisky supply in Reading, Andy forgot to wake Bob, for which he assures us that he has never been forgiven! Andy had originally enlisted as a member of

66B but, having been relegated twice, he ended up in 67A, but still managing to become the A/T CSM of 'A' Coy and one of the growing population of Air Techs.

Anything England can do … … …

The World Cup wasn't the only soccer trophy on display that year, as the lads of 'B' Coy had excelled themselves in winning the Army Youth Challenge Cup. Along the way, they had beaten rivals 'D' Coy, a team from Harrogate, and another from the JLdrs Regt RA. In the final, the Arborfield boys *"had the edge in midfield and defence"*, going on to beat the Junior Tradesmen's Regt ACC by three goals to one.

The apprentices of 'J' Coy were constantly 'under invasion' during their first term. On most Wednesdays, in the interests of publicity and recruiting, they were hosting visits from schoolboys and their headmasters from all over the country. Despite the kudos that this ultimately brought to the School, those visits were not appreciated that much by the boys themselves, as it called for numerous extra drill sessions, used for demonstrations. With Saturday mornings reserved for the dubious pleasures of 'Company cleaning', followed by sporting activities in the afternoons, this left only Sunday as a time to perhaps rest and recuperate.

On May 23rd, a party of 6 and 7 Div boys from 'A' Coy found themselves at Cwm Gwdi, an exposed and bleak valley leading into the Brecon Beacons. The advantage of quick drainage was welcomed during the first few days, when the inevitable heavy 'Welsh rain' arrived. These days were spent on canoeing, caving and general 'limbering up' over the lower hills, in preparation for the more ambitious training to come. Later, whilst canoeing through the natural hazards of the Penybont Canal locks, the boys were hardly prepared to come under attack from a particularly militant swan, which took umbrage at - and attacked - each passing craft!

Rifle practice was finally achieved, despite the presence of many wandering sheep and a number of valuable ponies, which seemed oblivious to the shots whistling past their ears. The boys were thrilled to get the loan of a *Carl Gustav* rocket-launcher and a new General-purpose Machine Gun (GPMG), from a nearby Platoon of the Light Infantry Brigade, but this was only for 'dry training'. After the more arduous activities that followed, it was much appreciated that the end of 'camp' was a visit to the museum of the

SWB at Brecon, where the boys took their time to browse around the relics of Rorke's Drift and other historic battles.

Lean times for the OBA

A letter that had been sent out by the Hon Sec of the OBA on June 10th that year confirmed that the Association was still battling its way through the leanest of times. Due to a lack of staff, in the shape of old boys keen enough to give up their own time to help, it had ruefully been decided that it was now necessary to give up publication of the *OBAN*. Instead, any forthcoming reports, articles and notices would be confined to the pages of *The Craftsman*. Some earlier Reunions had been arranged, with varying measures of success, but once again the previous year's arrangements had had to be cancelled due to a continuing lack of interest and support.

The following day, June 11th, saw the REME Training Centre mark the occasion of the Queen's 'official' Birthday with a parade. Of the twelve detachments that appeared on the parade, the School provided no less than eight. Rehearsals proved long and arduous that summer, due to some extremely hot weather, but the eventual parade of over 600 soldiers proved a great success. The School Band led the way, fully maintaining its high reputation, while the apprentices' detachments did their duties in time-honoured fashion.

VM trade training 'farmed out'

Later that year, it became the policy that VMs would no longer continue to be trained here at the School. At the same time, new arrangements were being made for the final phase of equipment training, in the other trades, to be brought to completion at the appropriate adult REME School. Air Techs would, in future, exit to the Aircraft Engineering Training Wing (AETW), School of Army Aviation, at Middle Wallop, for their final two terms, while graduate Electronic Techs would continue their training here at Arborfield, but now at what had become the SEE in Hazebrouck Barracks. This had been formed from an amalgamation of Numbers 3 and 5 Training Battalions REME.

For a period of time, those boys completing their training at the AETW travelled there each week by bus, only returning to the School at weekends. The

first intake of Air Techs passed out in August 1966, with the staff having every confidence that they would carry the School's good name with them into the field of Army Aviation. Additional training equipment was continually being acquired from one source or another and it was hoped that the promised extra helicopters would soon materialise. During the late Sixties and into the early Seventies, it became the custom for Air Techs to receive their coveted light blue berets, when they returned to the School to participate in their 'PoP'.

An article in the summer's School magazine paid tribute to Band Sergeant Major (BSM) Parker, BEM. He had been appointed to his present position in 1957 and, in 1960, converted the Military Band to an all-brass combination. During his time at the School, he had already been instrumental (!) in teaching 200 apprentices to play on brass. At the same time, the Band had appeared three times at the Royal Tournament and won the Army Festival of Music Band section the same number of times. The BSM was looking forward to another two years at Arborfield before a welcome retirement.

From School to College – part 2

Two significant changes took place on September 1st 1966. The School relinquished that title and changed its status to become the 'Army Apprentices' College', a more-fitting title, which brought it into line with that of colleges of further education in the civilian environment and coincided with an increase in the number of ONC-qualified apprentices. This had risen to a present number of forty-six, with the prospect of an eventual target of between 120 and 150 being reached.

All apprentices at the College would, furthermore, now wear the REME cap-badge and, to celebrate this decision, a re-badging ceremony took place the following month. In the *REME Brochure*, which is published regularly, 'The Badge' is described thus:

> *"Upon a lightning flash, a horse forcene gorged with a cornet of four Fleur de Lys, a chain reflexed over its back and standing on a globe. Above, a crown upon a scroll bearing the letters R.E.M.E."*

And so it was that, on Saturday October 8th 1966, the music of *'Auld Lang Syne'* symbolised the end of an era. To its well-known strains, the College Flag was finally lowered, to be replaced by the REME Corps Flag, as the band broke into the Corps March. The Reviewing Officer on the day was Maj Gen A McGill CBE, the DEME (A) and, in his address to the parade, he summarised the history of the College, as well as dwelling upon the symbolism of the unique badge that had now been discarded. Two recent parades had been cancelled due to adverse weather, one to no less than snow in April, but this time the day stayed dry, though cloudy.

(A full report on this historic Re-badging parade is attached as a separate annex to this chapter.)

'A' Spider with the Cookhouse in the background. The black pipes carried the steam central heating supply to the barrack rooms and across to the Camp Hall. In the cold days of winter, escaping steam provided an evocative smell, still well remembered.

During the winter term of 1966, the *"eagle eye and quick brain"* of A/T Hatcher came to the rescue of the old replica School badge, which had now been replaced by the REME badge, in its position above the new College gates. The old badge had sadly come to rest behind the Guardroom, where rust and decay were definitely settling in. Young Hatcher removed it, no doubt on a dark night and, on the following morning, presented it to Capt the Hon A V Brooke RA, with the intention of it perhaps enhancing the premises of the Fencing Club in the old Bailleul Barracks.

The badge was apparently *"hung in the rafters"*, for no good discernible reason, and there it supposedly should have remained. It was to be quite a few years later when it again came to light behind a wooden cupboard, discovered by an A/T Gordon, and much to Victor Brooke's surprise, as he had forgotten all about its existence! Being now held responsible for the keeping of the College archives, Victor thought he'd now better hang on to it and keep it safe.

Senior Company bows out

In that winter's edition of the School magazine, an article entitled *"Arrivederci Sierra"* appeared. This may have sounded like the title of an Italian pop song but, in fact, referred to the pending disbandment of Senior Company. 'S' Coy had been formed in September of 1960, to provide the transitional phase from boys' service into adult service.

All serving apprentices (less a few NCOs in each Company) had thus been transferred to 'S' Coy at the end of their seventh term, in order to complete their training, during their eighth and ninth terms, as 'Senior Division'. This idea was a sound one, particularly in view of the fact that those apprentices in 'S' Coy were, in many cases, older than their adult counterparts in neighbouring service units. In spite of this profound logic, a decision from the Inspectorate of Establishments resulted in 'S' Coy being disbanded, on mainly economic grounds, at the end of 1966. The last 'S' Company Commander was Maj O H Thomas BSc (Eng), REME and the last CSM was WO2 A E Gillham of the Welsh Guards.

The CSM had first received news of his posting, in the summer of 1964, with mixed feelings. He had assumed that he would be moulding knee-high 'tiddlers' into shape, and was rudely awakened when he first caught sight of a *"row of great six footers, collecting their mail and foot-powder after a run and walk in battle order"*. Realising that these young men were adults, he subsequently treated them as such, with unbridled success.

He was later able to look back on several far-from-dull moments during his tour. Such as the fifteen-stone A/T who had to be coaxed down from a forty-foot scramble net, when he realised he had lost his head for heights. Then trying to establish how a *'chair, arm, easy'* had got to the top of the flag-pole on Bailleul Square; and attempting to (unsuccessfully) find the driver of an unregistered *Austin Seven*, found parked in one of the static water-tanks! Apprentices seemed to go where even the ubiquitous 'Kilroy' never dared to tread!

The Basketball team had enjoyed a most successful season, winning the Army Junior Championship and maintaining an unbeaten run against the other Apprentices' Colleges, a run that had begun before any of the current team had even joined up! Particularly gratifying was the defeat of RAF Locking, a feat which previous Arborfield teams had been unable to achieve. Entering the National Junior Championship, the College team made it all the way to the quarterfinals, competing against some excellent opposition. In the Army competition, reigning champions, the JLdrs Regt RE were disposed of at the semi-final stage, while old rivals Harrogate were the beaten opponents in the final.

At the 14th Modern Pentathlon World Championships, held in Melbourne between 6th – 10th November 1966, history was made in the shooting competition when the breathalyser and urine tests were used to check whether drugs or alcohol had been used! Thankfully, this did not affect the fine performance put in by old friend Sgt Jim Fox, who ended in a most creditable fifth place. His placing was the highest by a Briton since 1912 and it was hoped that he would soon replace the Hungarian competitor, Balczo, as the world's top pentathlete.

The Craftsman issued in December featured a 'PoP', just prior to the School becoming the College, where the A/T RSM Alan Flower, had collected the three major awards of 'Award of Honour', 'Commandant's Cup' and 'Chief Instructor's Cup'. Alan was now going on to fulfil his career as a Radar Tech with the Corps. It was unfortunate that, for the second time in succession, a wet weather programme was forced upon the disappointed participants.

Christmas recess proved a very rewarding period for the party of boys from 'B' Coy, who went off to Austria, for a few days of skiing at the village of Obergurgl – try saying that when on the *apfel brandy*! Trying their hardest to impress 'the locals' with their undoubted skills and daring, they floundered through some deep snow towards their hotel, little realising that the road was only a few feet away. The *piece de resistance* of the trip was performed by Tom Clarke, who skied swiftly, but gracefully, backwards down the slope to the road, where he was last seen, apparently making a spot-check inspection upon the tyres of a parked car!

Needless to say, the skiing lessons from instructor Maj Hyslop proved quite strenuous, so the boys were happy to participate in the *'apres ski'* activities at the local cellar bar, where they were treated to such local delicacies as *frankfurters* and *apfel strudel*. Postcards to home, and the presence of some pretty waitresses, added to their all-round sense of well being and enjoyment.

The Bell Tower

One lasting memento of the REME's previous occupation at the Woolwich Dockyard had been the acquisition of the old Toll Bell Tower (common to all Royal Dockyards), which had stood by the Dockyard gates, with the bell being used to toll for the commencement and finish of the working day. Originally intended to grace a museum owned by Woolwich Council, great efforts were made to acquire the historic relic. It was removed to Arborfield in 1966 and erected at the road junction opposite the College Chapel.

(During the consequent dismantling of the Bell Tower in 1982, it unfortunately toppled over and incurred considerable damage to its superstructure. It was then found that the base of the main support had been under attack from 'dry rot'. However, plans were subsequently put forward to have it reconstructed by our sister AAC at Chepstow, with its final re-erection, between the then College HQ and the Corps Secretariat building, not taking place until 1985. Ed.)

New Year's Day 1967 brought the re-designation of the Depot REME as 'The Training Battalion and Depot REME', representing a victory for its CO, Lt Col Arthur Reading. He and his staff had fought long and hard for the new name, which wasn't just a cosmetic exercise, but indicated the unit's vital role in the training organisation of the Corps. Since January 1961, when the basic military training for recruits to

REME was transferred from No.1 Trg Btn at Blandford, some 6,000 young soldiers had received training at the Depot. Its new title had been well earned.

In the February 1967 issue of *The Craftsman*, the AAC gave a progress report on its recent increase in the number of apprentices qualifying for the ONC. Two years previously, the maximum technical qualification that an apprentice could obtain, in addition to his trade rating, was an intermediate C & G Telecommunication Certificate. All apprentices now entering the College would study for the General Engineering Course (GEC) in Mathematics, Engineering Science, Engineering Drawing, Workshop Processes and Materials, which had started in September 1964. Now there were eighty-one apprentices at the College who were following the 'O1' (first year) course of their ONC education.

The next edition of *The Arborfield Apprentice*, that of spring 1967, reported on the visit to both Houses of Parliament by a group of apprentices from 4 Div. The visit was arranged by the resident Women's Royal Voluntary Service (WRVS) lady at the time, Miss Sally Blomfield, while the party was accompanied by Capt Foster RAEC and Padre Morris. Their tour guide for the morning visit was local MP for Wokingham, Mr Bill Van Straubenzee, who was described as being both *"amusing and informative"*. For most of the A/Ts it was their first ever visit to Westminster and all voted it a great success. After lunch they went on to spend an afternoon's visit to the Imperial War Museum. In April of that year, the first apprentices to have completed their whole ONC course within the College finally passed out.

The weekend of 27 - 28th May 1967 saw forty-eight Arborfield apprentices form part of a group of no less than 2,000 youngsters, up to the age of twenty, participating in the annual 'Ten Tors March' across the barren heights of Dartmoor. This annual event had first taken place in 1958 and the one of 1967 was treated to the worst weather in its history – never was the term 'Whitsun weekend' so incorrectly used! Fog and driving rain were the order of the day, as the earliest parties set off at 04.30 hours on the first morning. Two teams, one each from 'B' and 'C' Companies, were proudly presented with their commemorative medals

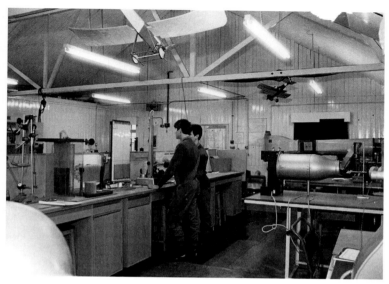

The Aviation Laboratory

on completing the arduous trek within the allotted time.

Pride tinged with sadness

LCpl John Kirton Carr had been an apprentice Air Tech (A & E) here at the College, from January 1964 to December 1966. On completion of his training, he was then posted to 10 Flight AAC, at Bulford Camp in Wiltshire. Tragically, John was killed there in a helicopter accident on June 6th 1967 and, shortly after his death, a fund was started by his friends and colleagues, who later presented a trophy to the College in his memory.

It was to be used as an award to the 'Best all-round Technician' in the Aircraft trade group, reminding all trainees of their future responsibilities and the contribution they would be required to make in the interests of flight safety. The trophy theme is the Army Air Corps Eagle, mounted on a letter 'C', and surrounded by a guard which symbolises protecting hands. John's parents sadly, but proudly, attended that first presentation, which went to A/T Sgt Clive Hugh Richardson, at the 'PoP' in December, later that same year.

The history of aviation in this country had always been closely linked with Army flying. The first British Military airplane to fly, Col S F Cody's biplane in 1908, was designed and built for the Army. It was the Army's considerable use of such machines, over the battlefields of the early First World War years, that was to lead to the eventual formation of the RAF. The present AAC was formed on September 1st 1957, since when it has continued to expand, with the helicopter having now become its primary aircraft. The Corps has since provided invaluable support to military operations worldwide, including Malaya, Borneo, Cyprus and Aden.

In the summer 1967 issue of *The Arborfield Apprentice*, Col Paris reported on the changes that were occurring in the boys' examination results. The College was now concentrating its efforts on Technical Examinations, with the result that 'O' Level successes had dropped considerably, but balanced by the news that ONC results were improving all the time. The January intake had been very small, totalling only thirty-eight new apprentices, but this had been expected, due to the transfer of VM training to the other College at Carlisle. With the VMs 'moving out', some buildings were now adapted, with wider doors, into aircraft hangars, for Air Tech training. Two instructors actually moved in, along with some *Skeeters* and a *Chipmunk*, but this was to be a short-lived change.

From the ranks of those apprentices 'passing out' of the College at the first 'PoP' of 1967, none could have been prouder than the A/T RSM, S J Vella. He had joined up in 1964 from St Aloysius College, on the sun-drenched island of Malta, and besides becoming the 'senior rank' of his intake, he almost managed a clean sweep of the available trophies. He won the Award of Honour, the Chief Instructor's Cup and the Senior Education Officer's Cup, as well as carrying off the awards for technical ability at his trade, Mathematics and English.

The living accommodation had been very much 'brightened up' that year, with the rooms being painted in varying shades of green, blue and *begonia* – yes, that's right, *begonia*! This latter colour had been dubiously greeted at first, but the boys eventually though reluctantly accepted it as 'warm and bright'. Pin-ups had been removed from all walls and ceilings, but a move was afoot to rectify this by the production of wooden frames on which pictures could then be mounted. Most beds were now covered by gaudily coloured rugs and bedspreads, draped over the usual drab grey woollen blankets, so the rooms certainly appeared brighter and more homely.

Far-flung activities

After nine weeks of the fourteen-week cricket season, only eight matches had been played, with a further seven having been cancelled due to the ever-pervasive rain. That same wet weather looked like wiping out the Quadrangular Games too. Harrogate had been due to host the Games that year, but instead asked for Arborfield to take on this task, as Harrogate itself was at the tricky stage of a rebuild programme. Some two weeks before the event, most of the sports pitches looked more suitable for swimming and canoeing only! Fortunately, a fortnight of dry sunny weather followed, allowing the Games to go ahead, despite the fact that rain fell once again for most of the Friday and Saturday.

At that time, each Company at the College was running weeklong Adventure Training sessions for apprentices from 4 – 7 Divisions inclusive, in areas as widely dispersed as Dover, South Wales and Salisbury Plain. These exercises included canoeing, caving, climbing and hill walking. During the Easter recess, six of the more adventurous apprentices completed a free-fall parachute course at Netheravon, the first of its kind, which confounded those so-called 'experts' who had confidently predicted failure.

In June 1967, the latest edition of *The Craftsman* was able to report to REME at large upon the high standards of the output from the College, both on the trade and sporting fields of achievement. Seldom had the College produced boys of such a high sporting success, the winter term had been exceptionally good. With education now producing students of ONC standard, this was not only a cause of satisfaction for the College, but also to the units who accepted their new adult soldiers – *"well-trained tradesmen"* and *"extremely promising Corps and Army sportsmen"*.

The above report must have caused a lot of pride in the chest of Lt Col Haworth, who had filled the post of SEO for the previous five years. He had been largely instrumental in the introduction of teaching of the ONC at the College and, alongside this Herculean effort, had also found the time to pass his Master of Education degree at Reading University. His widely read experience of educational processes had certainly kept the staff of his department on their toes and the Colonel now went off to an appointment as Inspector of Science on the Director of Army Education (DAE) Inspection team.

Digging for history

During six successive Sundays during June and July of 1967, some forty A/Ts became 'apprentice archaeologists', when they assisted at a 'dig' organised by Reading Museum. This took place at the Iron Age hill fort just outside the Oxfordshire village of Blewbury. The first Sunday's activities were curtailed by rain, but the rest of the dig was blessed by fine weather.

Intake 67A having survived to 9 Division

Hundreds of pottery fragments were revealed, along with 'post-holes' from some ancient structures. Some boys were also involved in the uncovering of a truncated human skeleton, while one boy was delighted to find a fragment of a bronze razor. Unfortunately, the most exciting discovery came to light just after the boys had finished their stint. This was a timber lacing construction, never previously discovered in Britain. However, the boys had thoroughly enjoyed their expedition, learning that their ancestors were much more sophisticated than they had been led to believe.

The College Sub-Aqua Club had, for its first couple of years, been associated with the local Reading Branch of the British organisation. This had proved less than ideal, due mainly to the distances involved in travelling. The College Club was now trying to become independent, but the purchase of an inflatable Dinghy, for use as a rescue boat, had rather deflated their available funds. It was hoped that a self-imposed tax of 'one pound per head per term' would soon help them find their financial feet – or flippers! *(Still no jackpot from Basing House then? Ed.)*

A life on the ocean wave

Still on a 'watery theme', a party of sailing enthusiasts had made the cross-Channel trip to Ostend from Dover during August 1967. Having driven across Belgium, they made an overnight stop at Minden in Germany, before a long trip north to the yachting haven of Kiel, and the British Yacht Club in particular. A busy day was spent on familiarisation and loading their vessel and the next morning saw the party sailing most of the day – and night – until they reached the little Danish harbour of Soby. The lads were able to grab just a few hours of rest, then a refreshing morning swim was followed by sailing to the island of Fyn. A nightspot known as the '*Casanova*' provided an entertaining evening for all concerned!

A full-on headwind delayed the next stage of their venture, but eventually the yacht made berth at Copenhagen and the boys were able to visit all the usual spots. Another sailing session brought the party to the quiet little Swedish town of Halsingborg. During the week that followed, the yacht met up with a strong gale, with waves *"that would not disgrace the North Atlantic"*, and even when the wind had abated, enough damage had occurred to cause thirty foot of mast to come crashing down. Fortunately, the rigging and sails were eventually sorted out, but the yacht was then forced to run under engine power – until it ran out of fuel! A Danish trawler came to the rescue and thankfully the trip ended with everyone safe and sound – with only a two-day drive home to contend with.

Kevin Meehan joined the College as a member of 67C, but he got off to a most inauspicious start! He was given a lift to Arborfield, all the way from his home in Kent, accompanied by his two younger sisters, with his father doing the driving. All had gone well earlier, as the party stopped at Wokingham and ate a hearty lunch at *'The Rose'*, in the town centre. After some self-confessed nervous moments in the confines of the 'gents', Kevin eventually got back into the car for the final few miles of his journey. He said his good-byes in the car, along with a few sniffles from his sisters, then bravely stepped out of the car, head held high, ready for the first step into a new life. Unfortunately, his father had parked rather too close to the edge of the road and poor Kevin found himself standing in a three-foot ditch! Thankfully, nobody saw the incident, so Kevin made his way through the gates and started his three-year apprenticeship as a Radar Tech.

Also joining with 67C was Jack Shram, who says that his intake, of 144 hardy souls, was the largest ever recorded at that time. He also recalls that his was the second intake to pass out from the School at the end of 8 Div, although he disputes that 67B was the first – he reckons that *they* passed out at the beginning of their 9th Div, that was to come in January 1970. Jack goes on to say that his intake, when they eventually assembled for their 'PoP' in April 1970, included the first of the two-year VMs that had arrived at Arborfield upon the closure of Carlisle.

Jack's three years – well, 8 Divs - at the School were mostly spent in 'A' Coy, where he studied and finally gained qualification as an Air Tech (A & E). He went on to serve until his 27th birthday in 1978, saying that it had been *"a great start to adult life and a good adventure"*. However, he was still in 'learning mode', as he wished to find out all he could about aircraft of the rotary-winged type. Seeing that his e-mail address includes the term 'London-helicopters', we can only assume that his plans came to fruition!

Smoking damages your health – and finances!

John 'Sailor' Sales was another 67C boy, joining the School on May 9th that year, following three years as an Army Cadet. The biggest shock to his system was to find out that he wasn't allowed to smoke during the furst twelve weeks of basic training. The usual talks were given by medical staff as to the inherent dangers of smoking, plus the dire warning that the first transgression of the 'no smoking' rule would be accompanied by a 'ten bob' fine, which would rise on each subsequent occasion. John was an addict already and could see no way of doing without a fag, but on a wage of three guineas a week, knew that he'd soon be insolvent if caught out!

In the event, John was caught out only the once, being sent to 'tap the boards' in front of his 'J' Company Commander, Maj Holdsworth of the Somerset and Cornwall Light Infantry (SCLI). *(The Somerset Light Infantry and the Duke of Cornwall's Light Infantry had been amalgamated in 1959, to form the SCLI. Ed.)* When charged with the contravention of Company orders, John pleaded guilty and was asked by the Major, *"Now, Sales, why do you think you shouldn't smoke?"* John thought carefully before replying, *"Because it's bad for my health Sir and I'm not old enough Sir"*. He was hoping for a reduced sentence, so that he could retain his scant resources. But the Major, carefully lighting up a cigarette of his own and blowing the smoke in John's direction, told him, *"Good answers Sales, but wrong! It's because I say you can't – fined ten shillings. March him out Sergeant Major!"*

John doesn't mention whether or not it was related to his smoking habit, but he had to retire from the Army on medical grounds as early as 1972, returning to his home in south Yorkshire. Partially disabled by an industrial accident, John is now a 'mature student' at Sheffield University and earns the bulk of his living as a professional gambler, even having written a book about his methods! *(Who says they didn't teach us much at boys' school? Ed.)*

The year's final edition of *The Arborfield Apprentice*, during winter 1967, reported on a successful 4/6 Div camp by members of 'D' Coy. They had been located near Bovington Camp down in Dorset, which had given them the chance to visit the excellent Tank Museum and also to watch a tank 'live firing' exercise. The night map reading exercises, undertaken in a variety of vehicles, provided some good results, but only on two occasions were the 'wounded' officers recovered. They had been waiting at their RV, which also turned out to be a public house, for so long that their wounds quite overcame them, after which they found some difficulty in speaking properly!

The 'PoP' of December 14th was reviewed by Maj Gen E F Foxton OBE, MA, the incumbent DAE. He had particular pleasure in visiting an establishment where so many RAEC officers were involved in the training system. In his address, the General said that, *"The Army today is tied up with the state of the national economy and some gloom is prevalent, due to reductions in the Armed Forces"*. But he also stressed the fact that there is still *"an extremely worthwhile job to do"*.

—§—

The School Athletics Team of Summer 1966 with Col Paris, Capt Daykin (to his left) and AQMS Evans (and to his right)

Annex to Chapter 7

Col G W Paris

(The brief career details below were first published in The Arborfield Apprentice, Volume V, Number 7, issued in spring 1965.)

Colonel G W Paris MBE, AMIMechE, AMBIM, commenced his career as a Cadet on HM School Ship 'Conway' and, having completed his apprenticeship at sea, obtained his Second Mate's Certificate. He then decided to leave sea-life and trained as an engineer at the Aeronautical and Automobile Training College, Chelsea. He later joined the staff of Laystall Engineering Co.

He joined the Territorial Army in April 1939 and was embodied into the Regular Army on the outbreak of war. He was later granted a commission as a Lieutenant Ordnance Mechanical Engineer 4th Class in the RAOC. He served with the BEF in France and, soon after returning to England, sailed for India. After completing the Armaments Course at Kirkee and the Instruments Course at Rawalpindi, he joined 59 Indian Infantry Workshop at Ahmednagar. His unit sailed for Burma in January 1942, where it joined the 17th Indian Division. He stayed with his unit in Burma and India until June 1945, when he was posted to the 19th Indian Division as CIEME. Whilst serving in Burma, he was 'mentioned in dispatches' and was awarded the MBE.

Upon returning to the UK, he commanded first 15 Command Wksp at Crawley, followed by 6 Command Wksp at Colchester. He came to Arborfield for the first time in January 1948, as a Senior Instructor in the Tactical Training Wing, HQ REME Training Centre. One of his tasks at that time was instructing ex-apprentices in REME organisation and Workshop Procedures.

Afterwards, he was posted as DADEME, ME7 at the Ministry of Defence and then sent to Woolwich to take command of the REME Scales Branch.

In 1954, Col Paris joined 40 Base Wksp REME Singapore as OIC Workshop Administration, where he and his family spent an enjoyable three years. On arrival back in the UK, he became ADEME EME Branch, HQ Northern Command and followed this up by commanding 48 Command Wksp REME in Cyprus for two years.

Before returning to Arborfield to take the post of Commandant at the AAS Arborfield, he commanded 34 Central Wksp REME Donnington.

First Impressions
or   When we were very young

The first impression I got when I arrived at the School was the way the buildings were situated and the colour of all of them. The next thing was the kind of uniform the boys wore and seeing them all dressed alike. Then at night, when we were in the barrack rooms, they were so cold and the blankets were very rough when they were over you.

The next impression I got was the getting out of bed so early in the mornings and having breakfast so early too. Also in the morning you had to move fairly fast and get your room tidy, so as to be in time for breakfast. And they ordered you round a lot!

The next impression was that there was a lot of noise in the dining-hall and so many boys at one table. There were no tablecloths and you had to eat what you had because there wasn't any more. Then the next thing was the funny feeling of getting into long trousers, after you have always been used to wearing short trousers.

Then the next impression I got was the way some of the Staff spoke and the different uniforms they all wore. Also I was not used to the orders they gave me. What also struck me was that you had to keep signing for nearly everything you received.

Then the most surprising impression I got was that you had to have a haircut and it had to be fairly short. Then you also had to clean your own kit and to make your own bed down – not for sleeping in, but for sitting down on, like an armchair.

I was rather disappointed and can't yet understand why we are not allowed out every night. Maybe it's an excuse for them giving us only four shillings a week. On the other hand, the length of leave sounds very promising.

The boys took a great interest in the 'new intake'. They seem to have inherited all the ways and feelings

of the intake before them, which they become as soon as another 'new intake' arrives.

Although glad when they leave, I should imagine that they gain much valuable human experience whilst here at the School. I also get the impression that every boy longs for the time when he will be in 'senior intake'.

Editor's note: Having talked to Junior Company, it seems that 'first impressions' haven't altered very much!

(The above article is based upon that published in The Arborfield Apprentice, Volume V, Number 9, issued in winter 1965 – and itself reprinted from the one of twenty-one years previously.)

Army Apprentices' College, Arborfield Re-badging Parade – 8ᵗʰ October 1966

The music of 'Auld Lang Syne' is a familiar sound on the Parade Square of the Army Apprentices' College, Arborfield. Three times a year it is heard on Passing-out Parades as the Senior Division marches off for the last time before its members join other REME units all over the world. On 8ᵗʰ October however, its playing symbolised the end of an era for the College, rather than for any of its students. To its strains, the College flag was lowered and replaced by the Corps flag, as the Band broke into the Corps march.

This incident formed part of a ceremonial parade to formally mark the assumption by the Corps of control over the fortunes of the College – a transfer of responsibility which was completed on 1ˢᵗ September 1966 – and to individually present to the apprentices of the College their REME cap-badges, henceforth to be worn instead of the Army Apprentices' School badge. This familiar design had, in any event, been outdated on 1ˢᵗ September by the assumption of the title 'Army Apprentices' College'.

The parade was commanded by the Chief Instructor of the College, Lt Col D A Brown REME and was formed of five Companies, the Brass Band, the Pipe Band and Corps of Drums. Altogether, over 700 apprentices were on parade, under their Company officers. Junior Company formed up as spectators. The Reviewing Officer, Maj Gen A McGill, Director of Mechanical and Electrical Engineering (Army)

inspected the parade, accompanied by the Commandant, Col G W Paris, and then distributed REME cap-badges to the Senior Company and to the Bands. Badges were presented to 'A and 'B' Companies by Brig T G Walker, Commander, REME Technical Training Centre, and to 'C' and 'D' Companies by Col G H Frost, Commandant, School of Electronic Engineering.

In his address to the parade, the Reviewing Officer summarised the history of the College and mentioned the symbolism of the badge which the apprentices had just discarded – with its design composed of the Cross of Christ, the Torch of Learning, the Crossed Swords of the Soldier and the Gear Wheel of Technical Skill. He was confident that the high standards to which these qualities had been displayed by apprentices and ex-apprentices in the past would continue to be upheld in the future. The Director concluded by wishing the College every success.

His words were heard by a large number of guests, who included Brig P G Palmer, Brig K F Kinchin from SEME, and many other REME officers. Present too was a large number of parents and friends, who helped to compose one of the largest gatherings ever seen at a parade of the College. Afterwards, lunch was served to many of the visitors, while distinguished guests were entertained in the Officers' Mess.

Recently, two parades at AAC Arborfield have been spoiled by bad weather and cancelled – in one case by a snowstorm in April! This time however, the weather, though cloudy, was dry, and it is to be hoped that the run of bad luck has been halted. The change in policy that the ceremony symbolised means that boys entering the College are now recruited directly into REME, instead of the General Service Corps as before.

(The above article is based upon that published in The Craftsman of January 1967.)

Major James Albert Morton

Senior Company Commander 1960 - 1965

If you were an Arborfield Apprentice in 1960, you will remember the School Curriculum being split into nine terms, with three intakes per year replacing the original two. This meant that the School would, from now on, have nine Divisions. 8 and 9 Divisions now formed the new 'Senior Company' and the first and only

Major James Albert Morton - Senior Company Commander 1960 - 1965

Company Commander was Maj James Albert Morton. This was a brand new venture for AAS Arborfield and 'Jim' Morton was chosen to set up 'S' Coy because of his wide military background and long experience in every aspect of REME.

Jim was himself an ex-Chepstow boy from 1927 intake who, at the outbreak of World War II in 1939, was a Corporal in the trade of Electrician. He was promoted to Sergeant to go over to France with the BEF and became one of the 'Dunkirk Veterans'. He then did his Armament Artificer Course and gained rapid promotion to WO2. He was given a wartime commission in 1944 and went over to France again on D-Day+6. He took his Workshop all the way from the beaches of France to a location in Hamburg, having been 'mentioned in despatches', en route, for an action against the enemy in Caen.

Returning to the UK from Germany in 1946, Jim started up the REME TA in Reading. He gained a Regular Commission and was promoted to Major to go on an exchange post to Melbourne, Australia. On his return to Blighty in 1951, he did one job in HQ Eastern Command at Hounslow, Middlesex, and was then promoted to 'acting' Lt Col as the CREME of 43 Wessex Division TA in Taunton, Somerset. He did this excellent job for four years but, sadly, in 1958 he had to drop down to a Major again, as MoD policy at the time deemed that he was 'academically not qualified' for a substantive Lt Colonel's post. He then went to No.6 Vehicle Battalion, Bordon as 2I/C, followed by a spell at HQ REME in Colchester, Essex, as DADEME (Tech).

Jim finally came to Arborfield in September of 1960 and there then followed, for him, one of his most rewarding jobs, as 'Senior Company' Commander. He absolutely loved ploughing back all of his valuable experience into the senior A/Ts, trying very hard to get them well prepared for a career in REME. He was a very popular officer in the School, a very strict disciplinarian in the fairest manner, and always looking after the welfare of those under his command. Upon leaving Arborfield in 1965, he did one final posting in HQ at Salisbury and, upon his leaving the Army in 1967, went to AETW, Middle Wallop, in a Retired Officer post. After forty years of excellent service, Jim was allowed to keep the title of Lt Col on retirement. Whilst serving in Middle Wallop at the age of 64, he had a massive heart attack in January 1977 and died instantly at his home on Porton Down.

Major Jim would have loved to be still around today to see what had happened to his Senior Company boys and to attend the excellent AOBA Reunions. But his spirit is still here in Arborfield and his son Alan (Algy) has carried on the family REME tradition by going from apprentice Tels Mech to Lt Col with all the stops along the way. May Jim Morton's fine military and personal legacy remain with us and all future apprentice tradesmen and women.

(The above article was contributed by Major Jim's son Alan (Algy) Morton 51B. and is a fitting tribute to a well loved Army Apprentices' School Company Commander)

I only asked for a new engine for my model aeroplane!

Chapter 8

1968 - 69

Changes and farewells

One rather startling and possibly controversial policy change that took place on Tuesday 9th January 1968 - whether for the better or the worse is perhaps a matter of personal conscience - coincided with the arrival of intake 68A. The change that occurred was in the decision to allow these thirty-four newly-arrived young apprentices, plus all those that were to follow, to partake in the smoking of tobacco, provided that they were (a) over sixteen years of age and (b) that they had their parents' or guardians' consent.

In March 1968, the College again changed its command. Col George Paris finally retired from the Army after a full twenty-nine years of industrious service, and left to take up an important appointment in the civilian world of industry. His last official act was the presentation of Hockey Colours to A/T McLaggen of 'A' Coy. That was closely followed by the presence of A/T CSM Stoddard of 'B' Coy, who presented the departing Commandant with a silver salver, as a parting gift on behalf of all apprentices.

The new Commandant, Col D A Brown CEng, MIEE, FIERE, AMBIM, was no stranger to the School however, having already served as its Chief Instructor and Deputy Commandant since September 1966. As a Captain serving at Agra in India in 1946, the Colonel had spent much of his spare time conducting visiting VIPs around the world-famous monument of the Taj Mahal.

In April of that same year, the first apprentices to complete their 'Arborfield ONC' passed out, having been taught for the whole of their course within the educational and technical facilities of the College itself. Thirteen, out of a total of fifteen, were successful, with one apprentice being 'referred' in Mathematics.

That year's spring issue of *The Arborfield Apprentice* was finally able to report that the Bell Tower was in position and now being used *"to call the faithful to worship on Sunday mornings"*. An object of much historical interest, it had begun its life at the Woolwich Royal Dockyard some 150 years previously, at the time of one of England's greatest heroes, Admiral Horatio Nelson. Several stories had surfaced as to its original use, but the most likely one is that its resonant sound was used to inform labouring gangs within the dockyard that a ship had come in for repair. The same article also announced that the Church had recently acquired a copy of a painting by Terence Cuneo, famous for his military works of art.

'A' Coy apprentices welcomed back CSM J Murrant, of the Grenadier Guards, after a prolonged absence due to his having attended an 'Equitation Course' – that's horse-riding to the uninitiated! In fact, the course must have been so successful that most mornings, the 'A' Coy boys fully expected to see their CSM come riding into Camp, hitch his horse to the crumbling rail of the Company verandah and vault over the same rail before striding into the Company Office, both guns blazing!

A/T Cpl Daniel of 'B' Coy reported upon his Company's team effort in that year's Ten Tors event. Good progress had been made for the first six miles, but then the inevitable rain began to fall and the boys were reduced to sloshing their way through one bog after another. At the end of a soaking day, the lads climbed into their sleeping bags, threw a groundsheet over themselves and huddled together for warmth and comfort throughout a very wet night.

An unappetising breakfast of cold bacon and beans was actually followed by the merest glimpse of sunshine, before it started raining again, with another seven miles still to go after the tenth Tor had been reached. Rest periods became longer and more regular and giving up seemed like a most tempting action. But the sound of voices over a microphone saw the team's faces light up and their legs gain renewed strength, as the boys realised that the finish was within reach. They were in fact the first team home, an experience that *"strengthened characters and powers of endurance"* but also taught another valuable lesson – that old Army adage, *"Never volunteer for anything"*.

At that same event, the 'C' Coy team obviously struggled without success, and one was afterwards moved to write of their epic effort as follows:

The Ten Tors Saga

Thirty-five had smelled a skive; volunteered,
or so they said,
For Ten Tors on the Moors.
For thirteen weeks they promised us
We'd miss parades without a fuss;
Not a word of wind and rain, round the Moors
then round again.

Didn't say we'd have no bed, just a plastic bag
instead.
Twenty-seven, sore afraid, opted to attend
parade.
Eight were left to carry on, wishing that they'd
not begun.
Came the day when fifty miles
Was our goal and, wreathed in smiles,
Off we went from Tor to Tor,
over that benighted Moor.

Mickey Jarvill trod the bog, sprained some
muscles in the fog.
We dragged him on as best we could,
Just like a twisted log of wood.
Hoppy, Dai, Lank, Titch and I
Sent him back to bed to lie.

But unbelieving with the dawn, came young
Jarvill all forlorn.
Tried to carry on again, but all his effort was
in vain.
At Checkpoint Seven, all was lost,
More than half the course we'd crossed.
With fifteen miles still to go, we just did not
want to know.
This whole experience had cost us dear -
The moral is, "Don't volunteer!"

The College Dancing Club was still very much a 'going concern' towards the end of the Sixties. Dances were now being held in the WRVS lounge, which had the advantage of being more spacious and of a more pleasing ambience than the previous venue, the College Lecture Hall – no surprise there! Regular coach services were being established to Frimley and Camberley, in the hope that larger numbers of young ladies would be encouraged to attend. Another attraction, of course, was that the College's very own 'Beat Group' was now providing the music, with 'twisting and shouting' now very much in vogue.

Years of service

On April 9th 1968, the Workshop Practice Department said a sad farewell to two of its oldest and most stalwart of friends. Between them, Mr Ernie Flear and Mr A D 'Tex' Rickard had given almost sixty full years of dedicated service to the College, having been instructors here ever since it was the original Army Technical School (Boys) in 1939. Indeed, their combined service in total was to add up to more than ninety years – a fact that was remarked upon in *The Craftsman* of August, later that year.

Ernie had enlisted in what was then the Royal Tank Corps (RTC) in 1920, serving in India and many other stations. He was called back to the Colours in 1939 and transferred to REME upon its 1942 foundation. Discharged as a Staff Sergeant in 1945, Ernie returned here as a civilian instructor right up until this year. Tex had himself started as an apprentice, with the RFC, in 1917. He later transferred to the RAF upon its formation in 1918, then changed the colour of his uniform when he transferred to the RAOC reserve in 1930. During the war, Tex was also called back to the Colours, serving both in France and the Middle East, and then being another founder member of REME in 1942. Like Ernie, he was discharged in 1945 as a Staff Sergeant, and joined Ernie here at Arborfield. As Tex liked to point out, there were not too many eligible to sport any one of four regimental ties!

Another 'old faithful' who had received his posting order for the Middle East was ASM Harry Evans, *"long, lean and bespectacled"*, who had spent so many years giving up his spare time to the training and organisation of the Cross Country team. Many ex-boys will remember him with respect and admiration. Amongst those also leaving the School around this time were two boys who were the first ever to have been 'advanced' by one term, having successfully completed their trade apprenticeship in only eight terms, instead of the normal nine. Another long-serving member of staff left on May 17th. Mr R L Atwell had joined the School after his 'demob' from the RAF in 1945 and seen twenty-three years of continuous service as a kitchen porter in the Cookhouse.

It was also time for change of staff in the WRVS lounge, as the College wished Sally Blomfield *bon voyage*, as she left to take up a post on an Educational Cruise Ship. Sally's exit made way for Helen Ayres, who joined Arborfield after a six-year stint at the Junior Tradesmen's Regt at Rhyl, on the North Wales coast. Later in that year, it was reported that the WRVS Club was then holding very successful fortnightly dances. This was no doubt due, in no small measure, to the regular attendance of a contingent of young ladies 'bussed in' from the 'Wrens' of Her Majesty's Ship (HMS) *Daedalus*, down on the Hampshire coast at Lee-on-Solent.

At the 'PoP' held on April 10th that year, Col Brown thought it appropriate to explain that the final two terms of equipment training, for those apprentices other than VMs, was now in the hands of SEE Arborfield and the AETW, Middle Wallop. He acknowledged the College's debt to both of these adult units, for their great help and the keen interest they had shown in the continuation training of apprentices. He added that the whole business of apprentice training was now very much a *"team effort"* within the overall REME Training Centre.

The Commandant was also pleased to report a closer and growing association with the local parish, following visits made to some old people by a small group of Church members. Dances had also been held, to which parish members had been invited. The College Choir had continued to progress, thanks to the efforts of the Choirmaster, Maj Whitehouse, with welcome assistance from BSM Parker and an equally devoted party of lady volunteers.

Ex-apprentices from intake 46A were no doubt devastated in April 1968, when they learned that one of their number had met a tragic death in a shooting accident at Chickerell Camp, Weymouth, in Dorset. Capt Michael – or 'Mike' - James Kelly was on the staff of the Trg Btn & Depot REME at the time. He had trained at boys' school as an Inst Mech and reached the rank of A/T CSM.

In February 1951, Mike had relinquished his trade background and transferred to the Regimental Duty (RD) roll. He was only twenty-five years of age when he was appointed as a Company Sergeant Major in July 1955, and was commissioned in August 1965. Throughout his service, Mike had been an enthusiastic shot and he was to pass on these skills in the training of many others.

Still time for sport!

In the first three games of the cricket season, the College batsmen had been unable to match the accomplishments and efforts of their bowlers. However, things improved against the JLdrs RAC from Bovington, with some excellent fielding at last giving the College team a victory. On this jubilant note, the team then travelled to Chepstow for the first of the Quadrangular Games. A splendid six-wicket victory was the outcome, and it was hoped that this would provide the necessary springboard to further success.

Amongst its many sporting successes, the College here at Arborfield was proud to have won the Army Swimming (Senior) Team Championships three years running, namely 1966, 1967 and 1968. Also, having won the Quadrangular Games in 1967, the question on

One should always keep a straight bat!

A selection of EIR apprentices

everyone's lips the following year was whether or not Arborfield could win it again. But the Commandant had announced that we could, so we did! The event was held at Harrogate, where everyone was accommodated, fed and entertained both efficiently and, it seemed, effortlessly. Some splendid new buildings formed a backdrop against which all the competitors made strenuous efforts to 'be the best', which is what the Arborfield team managed to be on the day.

So it was that on June 29th, A/T Cpl S Mansbridge proudly stepped up to receive the Quadrangular Games Trophy on behalf of the Arborfield team, for the second year in succession. Young Mansbridge was definitely of 'star quality', having already achieved the title of 'Victor Ludorum' at the REME Championships. Fourteen other apprentices had been awarded Amateur Athletics Association (AAA) standard certificates, during the College team's run of success. A railway dispute may have stopped the original transport arrangements for the long trip, but the hasty arrangement of a convoy of assorted vehicles to northern climes had certainly paid off.

The Craftsman magazine for June that year featured a famous 'sporting personality' of the Corps, who also happened to be an ex-apprentice from intake 57A. Cpl Brian Glossop had taken up the noble art whilst still serving at what was then 'the School' and for the past seven years brought great credit to the Corps through his boxing skill and sporting conduct at the middle-weight class. Once Brian had 'hung up his gloves', he was able to devote more time – and energy – to his second love, Rugby Union.

Although the Sub-Aqua Club had been in existence for about three years, it wasn't until July 1968 that it became fully operative, with a total membership of eight. The Club had contacted the 'Dolphins', a fourteen-year old established club at Aldershot, and arranged to use their training facilities. A sum of £100 had been granted from College funds, and the equipment subsequently purchased allowed for a successful visit to Weymouth that summer. This had inspired members to seek a large grant from the Nuffield Trust, for which hopes were high. Weekend visits to local gravel pits and lakes were now building up confidence and expertise, with proposed trips abroad to France and Malta in the pipeline.

The Reviewing Officer for the 'PoP' of August 8th was Maj Gen A McGill, CBE, who was DEME at that time. He began his address by stating that he had

also been a 'Reviewing Officer' the previous day, at the 'PoP' held at Carlisle. He had then had to travel virtually overnight in order to attend here at Arborfield. The General reminded all apprentices now leaving the College that they should not abuse their newfound freedom. He added that the reputation of the College was held in very high regard throughout the Corps, with many ex-apprentices progressing through to become either Commissioned Officers or Artificers. His final words reminded the boys that *"You will only get out what you put in"*, before he wished them *"God speed and Good Luck in the future"*.

The Commandant was again at pains to express his gratitude to both SEE and AETW for their continued support in the training of apprentices. He also congratulated Capt Burton of the RAEC, who had recently obtained his Bachelor of Arts Degree at London University, adding that this proved the fact that it wasn't only apprentices who passed examinations!

Death of Princess Marina

Tuesday August 27th brought the sad news that HRH Princess Marina, Duchess of Kent, and C-in-C of REME, had passed away. Condolences were immediately dispatched to her son, the Duke of Kent.

(A dedication to Princess Marina is attached as a separate annex to this chapter.)

Military Training had provided an active time during the summer months, when advantage had been taken of facilities in the Brecon Beacons and on Dartmoor. At the same time, training for the junior Divisions had carried on in the local area, where assistance had been gratefully accepted by the Berkshire CCF, for which the College was the sponsor unit. Indeed, a number of local youngsters had joined with the apprentices on their camping expeditions.

The boys from 'A' Coy had missed their early train on their way down to South Wales, much to the annoyance of Capt Vickers, who was supposed to be in charge of the move! While 6 Div gallantly *"braved the elements"* usually offered by the area, 4 Div paid a visit to the museum of the SWB in Brecon. Both parties were then pleased to welcome the late arrival of CSM Murrant, which had been delayed by floods! Later that month (September '68), 2 and 3 Divs were further north in Wales, making their way to the summit of Snowdon by various tracks.

For 'B' Coy, the 8 Div military training week on Hankley Common would be long remembered for its persistent rain – and by one member in particular, by the name of Dalton, for the copious amounts of beer he shifted at a local pub! 'C' Coy was maintaining its old traditions, being just about unbeatable at rugby, though it was usual that some of the team had to be released from close arrest in order to play! Over in 'D' Coy, its members looked back with pride on their performance at the 'Queen's Birthday' Parade, which had provided a *"fine, stirring sight"*. An intimate relationship with boggy Welsh hills had also instilled them with *"military fervour, knowledge and self-reliance"*.

It was reported that the Band has *"almost blown itself to a standstill"*, taking on such worthwhile external engagements as Carnivals, Fetes and Prize-giving ceremonies in the local towns of Abingdon, Basingstoke and Wallingford. Fortnightly dances were as popular as ever, helped along no doubt, by the presence of those parties of 'jolly Jill tars' who made things go with a swing. The musical standards of the Choir were continuing to rise under the guidance of the Padre and Maj Whitehouse, of the Royal Army Pay Corps (RAPC), who combined his duties with those of Paymaster.

Between August 25th and September 8th of that year, the College annual deep-sea adventure training exercise took place in the Baltic. The party of excited A/Ts assembled at the port of Harwich under the leadership of Maj R B Laurie REME, then sailed overnight across the North Sea to Bremerhaven, courtesy of the Swedish ferry *'Prins Hamlet'*. They were then transported to Kiel to pick up the seventeen-metre Bermudan rigged cutter *'Ragma R'* and sailed the following day for Faaborg in Denmark at around six to seven knots.

Further ports of call during the trip included Assens, Fredericia and Odense, before the lucky boys gained their first welcome view of the world-renowned *'Little Mermaid'*, perpetually seated on her favourite rock in the harbour at Copenhagen. They later enjoyed a bus-trip into the Danish capital city and a relaxing visit to the famous Tivoli Gardens.

Closure of the AAC Carlisle

One of the more stringent economies, as proposed by the *'Defence Review'* of 1968, was to be the closure of the AAC at Carlisle. A MoD letter, dated May 17th, had made the following statement:

"I am commanded by the Army Board of the Defence Council to inform you that the Army Apprentices' College REME at Carlisle is to be closed, and (that) the REME apprentice training is to be concentrated in one college at Arborfield."

Thus, after a life span of less than a decade and a throughput of 2,378 apprentices, the College at Carlisle was now to be amalgamated with that at Arborfield so that, in future, all of REME's apprentices' training would take place here. However, the overall total of boys at the two Colleges was to be reduced from 1,296 to only 850, which was predicted to still meet REME's long-term requirements. Asked to contribute an article to the last edition of *Hadrian's Journal*, the Carlisle College's in-house magazine, Col Fane Gladwin OBE, Scots Guards, Carlisle's first ever Commandant when it had opened in 1960, paraphrased a saying that he thought the Roman General Hadrian himself might have used. He said, *"Establishments that the Gods love, die young"*.

Protests from many local people in the Carlisle area, and from their two local MPs, were to no avail, as the necessary transfer arrangements were set in motion. The first of the new two-year VM apprentices, who arrived here at Arborfield in the winter term of 1968, were now joined by another forty-five boys from Carlisle. There was obviously a considerable reorganisation required in Vehicle Wing, where all the additional equipment, engines, assemblies and vehicles, which had been brought down from Carlisle, had to be quickly incorporated. It was a case of fitting a quart into a pint pot! Meanwhile, Aircraft Wing had already begun to re-concentrate its efforts back at Bailleul.

That influx of boys who would normally have gone to Carlisle had boosted numbers in 'J' Coy to a record-breaking 168. Naturally, an intake of that size severely tested the Company's abilities to cope, with doctors, dentists and tailors working flat out. Cpl Roberts, the Company Clerk, was duly praised for the amount of documentation he had to write out. Nowadays, even with a computer, he'd have gone down with what is now termed 'RSI' – Repetitive Strain Injury. Perhaps it wasn't allowed thirty-odd years ago! The following term was to see a far more manageable total of seventy-five arriving at the College gates.

The College Art and Pottery Club continued to be active, despite the counter-attractions of the outdoor summer activities. A number of entries were made for the local Arborfield Arts and Crafts Exhibition, with several prizes being won for both painting and pottery. Plans were also being made for entry to the Army Arts and Crafts Show, which was due to take place at Earls Court during the Royal Tournament. A coach load of Club members later went on to visit both the Art Exhibition and the Royal Tournament itself.

At the 'PoP' of December 12th 1968, the Commandant made mention of two welcome presentations to the College. Mrs Diane Williams, whose husband Tom had been, until his untimely death earlier that year, a Burnham lecturer in the Electronics Department, most generously presented a silver salver, which commemorated Tom's long and distinguished service to the College. This would be known as the 'Williams Prize' and would, in future, be awarded to a deserving Electronics Technician. Meanwhile, Lt Col A A W Hall, OBE, one-time OC of 44 Command Wksp REME, had also presented a trophy on behalf of his unit, a very handsome cup, which would now replace the Commandant's Cup.

Despite the impending closure of Carlisle, *The Arborfield Apprentice* that winter term was still 'advertising' the wide variety of trades that were taught across the whole system of apprentices' training. Here at Arborfield we had CETs, Radar & Tels Techs, VMs and the two different types of Air Tech. Chepstow could still boast of its Ammunition Examiners, Engine Fitters, Fitter Machinists, Welders, Carpenters and Joiners, Plumbers and Pipe Fitters, Bricklayers, Painters and Decorators, as well as its RE Electricians and Survey trades. Up at Harrogate, they were training Electronic Techs, Line Techs and Radio Techs, Telegraph Techs and Operators, plus Draughtsmen (Architectural). Those trade disciplines soon to return to Arborfield from their current College at Chepstow were Armourers, Gun Fitters and VMs.

In the 1969 New Year's Honours, ex-apprentice Cpl David Giles REME was awarded the BEM. David had completed his training at the College in December 1966 and was then posted as an Air Tech to AETW, Middle Wallop. His medal had been awarded in recognition of the amount of hard work he had put in at his job, often more than seventy hours per week. As reported later in the College magazine, *"this is an outstanding achievement for such a young man and should prove*

an inspiration to us all". Two other ex-boys, Stewart Slade and Timothy Eveleigh, were meanwhile making a good name for themselves as senior boys at Welbeck College.

Meanwhile, back at the Olympics

Having now reached the rank of Sergeant, old friend Jim Fox was back in the headlines, writing an article in the January 1969 edition of *The Craftsman*. At the end of September the previous year, he had been once again part of the British Olympics team that had set off that year for the 'big event' in Mexico City. Under strict orders to take things easy for the first five days, during which time nothing at all went on, once the training started, Jim found that any pre-conceived notions on how the altitude would affect him had to be quickly re-assessed.

The last of the three-year VMs completed their training and passed out from the College in the spring of 1969. Up until this time, they too had been eligible to take the ONC course. April 1969 saw one RSM from the Grenadier Guards hand over his appointment to another, with RSM Don McMahon giving way to RSM R Woodfield. RSM McMahon had enjoyed what can only be described as *"a most varied career"*, his service having included several spells of public duty that included no less than four great national occasions. He had attended the funeral of King George, in charge of the escort from Sandringham to Windsor; was a member of the bearer party at the State Funeral of Queen Mary; and was also on duty during the funeral of Sir Winston Churchill in 1965. Perhaps his happiest duty was at Her Majesty's robing room in Westminster Abbey at Queen Elizabeth's Coronation in 1953.

Born at Holt in Norfolk, Don had enlisted in the Army as long ago as 1945. He went on to serve in North Africa, Malta, British Guiana and the British Cameroons, before Arborfield completed his twenty-four years of service. He was greatly respected by the boys and the Senior Division that passed out that spring had requested that he be allowed to 'march off' their parade with them. This was the very first time that an adult soldier had this particular honour afforded him. An article entitled *'Speaking my mind'* appeared in the *Wokingham, Bracknell and Ascot Times* on April 17th 1969, which reported the occasion in the following manner:

"The Army appears to have changed more than somewhat since I did my stint. In those days the Regimental Sergeant Major was a force to be reckoned with; to be seen, heard, obeyed – and hated. We had our own nickname, albeit unprintable, for our RSM. When we sailed for the Middle East, he never came up on the deck of the troopship after dark – even though he could swim! At Arborfield Camp, things are different. At their passing-out parade last week, the apprentices especially requested that their RSM be permitted to march off parade with them, as a mark of respect and affection. Judging by the standard of the parade, Army discipline and training remains rigid, but the action by the apprentices show that somewhere behind it all there is the human touch."

The College Science Society had been entertained by films on a variety of topics, while also enjoying two visits to Reading Museum for evening lectures. Other lectures had been arranged within the College confines, one concerning *'Human problems in space-flight'* and the second on *'Britain's canal system'*. The latter had proved of considerable interest, as Society members looked ahead to assisting in restoration work along the Kennet and Avon Canal, which ran from Reading down to Bristol. One of the Society's new ventures that term was the study of weather patterns, no doubt brought about by the disbelief at the amount of rain that had fallen recently. It was rumoured that the College may soon boast a weather centre that could compete with the Meteorological Office at nearby Bracknell.

The Riding Club had gone from strength to strength, with over thirty apprentices now riding regularly. The College had also purchased its own horse, a sturdy mare called Liza, who was being kept very busy! She was looked after by the apprentices, under the guiding light of CSM Murrant, who had *"fired great enthusiasm"* amongst the riding fraternity, dividing his time between those just beginning at the sport and those experienced riders who wished to improve their skills.

The College Rugby Club was enjoying *"one of its best seasons ever"* as the spring term came to a close in 1969. The policy of fielding both a First XV and a Second XV every week had proved a sound one. Whenever a member of the 'firsts' had to miss a game, due either to injury or being selected for a representative

RSM R G Woodfield 1969-71

game, one of the 'seconds' was always available to admirably fill the vacant slot. Nine apprentices had been selected for the Army Junior XV, with the College Rugby Captain, A/T CSM Dalton, being chosen as Vice-captain of that same junior side. *(That wouldn't be the same Dalton who had shifted all that beer at camp on Hankley Common, would it? Rugger and beer do seem to have a close affinity! Ed.)* At the time, almost fifty young men were employed at the sport, training hard and playing cleanly, and certainly of the right mental attitude, boding well for further success in the games to come.

Driving and diving

Six boys from the Sub-Aqua Club left Arborfield as soon as the Easter 'PoP' had finished. They loaded up their vehicle and managed to get all the way to Yately before the roof rack collapsed! All the gear then had to be stowed inside the vehicle, which made for rather an uncomfortable journey. Once across the Channel to France, an overnight stop was made at the roadside. The lads were awakened next morning, not by the welcoming aroma of bacon and eggs, but by the horrible smell emanating from the nearby sewage works! Things could surely only get better after this inauspicious start and so it proved. A brief stop at Marseilles was followed by a move to La Ciota, further along the coast, with magnificent scenery only matched by the tortuous climbs and bends of the road.

After actually taking in some diving ventures, which were most enjoyable, the return trip brought our gallant group into Paris, where they managed to *"do some shopping"* and paid a visit to the famous Eiffel Tower. Later in the year, a dive near Lulworth Cove in Dorset took the boys down to a depth of some fifty feet. Here the boys were amazed to find so many shells – not of the 'fishy' type, but gunnery shells from the local Army firing-range! They also managed to rescue an old anchor from the seabed, which was taken back to Camp as a well-won trophy.

The Arborfield Apprentice issued in spring 1969 either had its wires crossed, or was suffering from a severe case of crystal ball gazing! It told of two sporting successes, the first in a winter games meeting at Harrogate on *"9 November 1969"* and the second at home against Chepstow on *"30 November 1969"*. It can only be assumed that these events had taken place in November of 1968 and the sentiments of the magazine's report remained true. On both occasions, the sports included were Basketball, Cross-country, Fencing, Hockey, Judo, Rugby, Shooting and Soccer, with a victory against Harrogate by 5 games to 3, while the poor lads from Chepstow must have returned home with a right dose of 'the blues', having been beaten in every single sport.

A/T Cpl Anthony Moogan had made a name for himself as he prepared to leave the College as a VM

Senior Company, having just 'passed out' and marched through the gates off the Square, celebrate in traditional manner by throwing their hats into the air. It looks in this photograph that they may have been slightly premature in doing so, as the gates behind them appear to still be open.

in April 1969. As an accomplished hammer-thrower, he had won that particular event at the Berkshire AAA meeting, followed this up by winning the Junior REME Championships, then made a record throw of 162 feet 8 inches at the Army Junior event. He was also a very good rugger player and had been awarded his College colours at that sport. Hailing from Pembroke Dock in South Wales, Anthony had completed his apprenticeship as a VM and was hoping to serve with the Corps in Cyprus.

Col Brown was pleased with a certain amount of progress from an organisation *"that is sometimes blamed for things which are not always its fault"*. He was referring to the Ministry of Public Buildings and Works (MPBW), which had recently made significant improvements to the NAAFI Clubs and Gymnasium, as well as to the living and workshop accommodation. He acknowledged that the work had been carried on under severe financial restraints and paid tribute to the MPBW staff for its excellent efforts on the College's behalf.

On Friday 27th June, the College was honoured by a visit from Gen Sir Geoffrey Baker, Chief of the General Staff (CGS). Arriving by helicopter, the General was officially on a visit to Arborfield Garrison but, due to his keen interest in apprentices' training, insisted on making a tour of the trade wings, meeting many of the instructors and apprentices at their place of work. Regardless of a very tight schedule, he also managed to visit the Camp Hall, where he met the Company Commanders and watched a display of PT.

The Carlisle Gates

To mark the occasion of the amalgamation of AAC Carlisle with the Arborfield College, a set of wrought-iron gates, brought down from the Camp at Carlisle, was erected here at what was still the main entrance, in Sheerlands Road. Designed by the well-loved Maj (Ret'd) P L Chivers REME, who had himself returned to Arborfield upon Carlisle's closure, these gates incorporated not only the famous *'Hadrian's Eagles'* but also all the regimental badges of those members of staff who had served at Carlisle. Percy Chivers had arrived here at what was then the AAS in the late Fifties, as a Captain in charge of the Fitters and Turners section.

These *'Carlisle Gates'* were formally 'declared open' by Brig G V Hayward, Commandant of the

REME Training Centre, on July 31st 1969, fittingly on the same day on which Carlisle held its very last Passing-out Parade. The standard flown at that parade is now held on permanent display in the present College. On that same parade were forty-four VM apprentices who had started their training at Carlisle, before being transferred here to Arborfield.

A new Colonel-in-Chief

Field Marshall HRH Prince Philip, the Duke of Edinburgh, was appointed C-in-C of the REME in July 1969, in succession to Princess Marina, who had died in 1968. That same month, Prince Philip visited Arborfield, when six of the College's senior apprentices were presented to him during his tour of SEE.

In the August edition of *The Craftsman* magazine, the official announcement was reported as follows:

> *"Her Majesty the Queen has approved the appointment of Prince Philip to be Colonel-in-Chief of the Corps, in succession to Her late Royal Highness Princess Marina, Duchess of Kent. All ranks received the news of this great honour with the greatest pleasure and we trust that His Royal Highness will enjoy a close and happy association with the Corps".*

August 1969 brought the retirement of a well-known and well-respected 'ex-boy', in the shape of Brig Joe Dobie. Although not an ex-apprentice, his term as Arborfield's first REME Commandant would long remain a highlight of the College history. Another of Joe's claims to fame was that, as an OME in 1938, he was chased around the Depot RAOC at Hilsea by the famous RSM Bennett!

A change in Military and Physical Training

The summer term of that year also saw a number of necessary changes to the College organisation, particularly in the field of military and physical training. The existing establishment was re-arranged into a Military Training Wing (MTW) so that, from now on, all military training would be organised under a centralised command structure, rather than being left to individual Company arrangements. This was in order to make the most economical and efficient use of the available resources and manpower.

With the advent of Military Cadres, it would usually fall to the Commandant of the day to stress the importance of this phase of training. Lots of time was dedicated to trade and education, with rather less time available for the purely military aspects. Even so, it was just as important to achieve equal success, as the whole purpose of the College, as had been that of the School that preceded it, was still to produce 'soldier/tradesmen' of the highest class. The Commandant would urge the boys to enjoy this *"pleasant break from normal training"* and, at the end of it all, they would be able to take their rightful place alongside the soldiers of other arms.

There was also change in the air regarding PT, the aim in future being to instruct this subject in a way which ensured that every boy received physical education to suit his own individual needs. The system consisted of carefully recording each boy's physical condition upon his arrival and then to monitor and record his progress throughout his time at the College. This system was researched and instituted by Maj J A T Brown, RA, the incumbent Military Training Officer, with able assistance from Quartermaster Sergeant Instructor (QMSI) Duncan. Its introduction aroused great interest in the greater APTC world outside of the College too. In fact the APTC had asked the College to give a presentation of the system at its next convention.

As well as the conventional aspects of military training, the College also continued its efforts to instill plenty of adventure and leadership qualities into the apprentices. Some boys had been sent off to Snowdonia, North Wales, for rock-climbing, while others travelled even further north, to the Cairngorms in Scotland, for a course in skiing. Officers and NCOs of the PS had attended the Army Outward Bound School, in order to gain qualifications that would enable them to take the lead on future expeditions.

Another innovation, during that year's summer term, was the REME exercise, 'Spring Entry', which took place on Hawley Common and was aimed exclusively at senior apprentice VMs. This particular exercise, during 1969, went on during three days of the most appalling weather but, to their lasting credit, the boys survived intact. Not one complained of either hardship, long hours, the strenuous work or field rations, and their enthusiasm was tremendous. As well as cross-country driving and recovery tasks,

Forward Repair Teams (FRTs) were set up and vehicles repaired, during a highly successful venture.

A most spectacluar take-off

The recently re-launched College Gliding Club had originally arranged for twelve places to be filled at Netheravon but, in the event, only six boys were found eligible to attend. Everything seemed fine as the first two days went quite smoothly, but then the third proved to be disastrous! The accompanying 'officer in charge' did a most spectacular take-off, which included an unplanned cartwheel and somersault, causing him to be rushed off to Tidworth Military Hospital in a 'blood-wagon'. A Mr Barrett, from the JLdrs Regt RE, Dover, kindly stepped 'into the breach' and the remainder of the course was salvaged, then finally brought to a satisfactory conclusion. The Club anxiously awaited the return of the OIC, if not in 'flying condition', then at least capable of fiercely waving a rampant crutch!

Two young apprentices, Peter Kaye and Tony Hutchinson, were fortunate enough to be chosen as members of an expedition party to Newfoundland organised by the British Schools' Exploring Society. This enabled them to spend six weeks on what A/T LCpl Kaye called *"the chance of a lifetime"*. During the expedition, the boys did research on the different types of bog encountered in that country – and no, they didn't mean toilets! One of the more pleasant parts of the trip was a visit to the island of St John's, where they met up with a fisherman by the quaint name of Abel Heinz. He was 'able' to offer them a good variety (57?) of locally-caught fish to supplement their rather boring diet of porridge (breakfast), cheese and biscuits (lunch) and stew (dinner).

Mike Wherton, a member of intake 69C and still today given to answering to the description 'stroppy Jeep', recalls that he was one of a large contingent of boys joining that term, some 340 in all, as the school-leaving age had been increased from fifteen to sixteen years. Mike went on to train as an Electronics Technician, rather unsuccessfully by his own admission, being more interested in the outside twin activities of *"birds and beer"* than anything the classroom could offer. However, he still went on to do the 'full twenty-two', ending up as a recruiting Staff Sergeant in London. Twice he failed Artificer selection, but on both occasions decided to 'soldier on'! *(Perhaps, coming from an electronics background,*

Blacksmithing was once an important part of the Army Apprenticeship - such skills proved of immense benefit for tradesmen out in their field units, no matter what their trade discipline.

he really meant 'solder on'? Ed.)

One of Mike's 'pet hates' at Arborfield had been his regular enforced visit to 'Charlie the Barber', who had been responsible for the haircuts of thousands of boys since the early Fifties. As far as Mike was concerned, Charlie must have learned his trade in the outback of Australia as a dubiously skillful sheep-shearer! The early Seventies, of course, was to bring back the fashion of 'long hair for men' with a vengeance, so the apprentices of those days would have stuck out from the civilian youngsters like sore thumbs. Mike also recalls the regime of 'Restriction of Privileges' (ROPs), more commonly known as 'ropes' by those boys who suffered this sentence. Serving on 'ropes' meant not being able to book out, no visits to the NAAFI Canteen, but lots of Cookhouse fatigues and other such dubious pleasures.

During the summer months, under the guidance of WRVS lady Helen Ayres, a party of apprentices undertook a social project on behalf of those handicapped children situated at Burghfield Hospital. They had been instrumental in making renovations to the children's playground and also assisted in exercising the limbs of those unfortunate children who were severely crippled.

The old tricks are best!

It is amazing to think that, in such 'enlightened times' as the late Sixties, young apprentices were still falling foul of some of the oldest tricks in the world! Stephen Budd of 69C wouldn't admit to being caught out, it was always someone else that was sent to the QM's stores to get a 'long stand' – which they usually got! Then of course were those essentials to be bought, on the orders of an A/T NCO no doubt, at the NAAFI Shop – jars of elbow grease, tins of beezing rings, and such like. Stephen - or Steve - or even 'Billy', as he was wont to be called by the other lads, became a member of the Corps of Drums, where he played the glockenspiel. He recalls that, prior to playing at a Royal Tournament, the band practiced for weeks beforehand, the tune in question being *'Yellow Bird'*.

On October 21st, forty American soldiers of *'The*

Midge - the College mascot

'Old Ironsides' were welcomed to the College and enjoyed being *"piped aboard"* by Pipe Majors Carver and McPhee. The American visitors were given an introductory talk by the Commandant, after which they were presented with a shield as a memento of their visit. They were then given a tour of the College, watching the apprentices at work and play, before being entertained to lunch in the Sergeants' Mess.

"The College flag has been lowered on the parade ground flagstaff for the last time and the final term at Carlisle is now over. All that is left to do is to close accounts, return stores and hand over Hadrian's Camp." Thus was reported, in October's issue of *The Craftsman*, the demise of what had been, for only too short a period, the fourth of the family of Apprentices' Colleges. The final parade there was attended by over 500 parents and friends of the apprentices.

In *The Arborfield Apprentice* of winter 1969, Col Brown was pleased to report that the Bands had taken part in a large number of outside engagements. These included the Basingstoke Carnival, where they had successfully combined with the massed bands of the Royal Marines, as well as National Cadet Sunday at Newbury. The Pipe Band had been honoured to play at the College gates during the Duke of Edinburgh's visit. A grand total of eighty-four apprentices now formed the Bands, of which the College was very proud.

The scribe responsible for the 'D' Coy notes in that magazine must have been in a very poetic mood! He told the story of the humble bumblebee, a creature of which it had been found aerodynamically unable to fly. Despite this, the bumblebee actually did fly, remarkably well in fact, and also managed to gather honey as it did so! This was all a lead in to the fact that 'D' Coy was flying high – and bumbling into a considerable amount of honey as well. This was borne out by the fact that the Commandant's Inspection had been cancelled, as the Queen's Birthday happened to fall on that very same day. Not only that, but the Company athletes had *"put up a very spirited performance – and come very close to second position"*! With the Company Dinner as highly successful as usual, the excitement factor was obviously running high in 'D' Coy!

The College reported its continued success with ONC courses, which had been introduced in 1965. Up to the present time, seventy-one ONCs had been awarded, with over half of these of a sufficiently high standard that their holders could be considered for entry onto a degree course. That quite remarkable level of attainment was something to which the College would continually aspire.

Departing through the College gates that year, leaving an almost unfillable gap, was the Paymaster, Maj Harold Whitehouse. Not only had he filled his official post most loyally, but he had also acted as Choirmaster and Organist, as well as being the musical director of the Garrison 'Gilbert & Sullivan Society'. Both he and his wife had devoted many long hours to College life, and would be sorely missed.

At the Christmas 1969 'PoP', the Commandant welcomed as a guest Mrs G Phelan, who had originally given to the College at Carlisle a trophy in memory of her son A/T Cpl Philip Phelan, an apprentice VM who had been tragically killed in a cycle accident the previous year. The first novice cyclist to receive the award at Arborfield was A/T Clive Hosking. Also on parade for the first time that year was a Shetland pony, 'Midge', which had recently become the College's new mascot. *(I have been unable to find a mention of 'Midge' after this occasion - wonder what happened to him? Ed.)*

—§—

Annex to Chapter 8

Her late Royal Highness Princess Marina Duchess of Kent CI, GCVO, GBE

Colonel-in-Chief, the Corps of Royal Electrical and Mechanical Engineers

It was with the greatest sorrow that the Corps heard of the tragic death on Tuesday 27th August of Her late Royal Highness, Princess Marina, our Colonel-in-Chief. The following signal was sent by the Representative Colonel Commandant, to His Royal Highness the Duke of Kent, immediately the sad news became known:

"The Colonel Commandant and all ranks of the Corps of Royal Electrical and Mechanical Engineers offer to your Royal Highness their deepest sympathy on the sad loss you have sustained on the death of your mother, Her Royal Highness Princess Marina, Duchess of Kent".

In reply, the following letter has been received from Sir Philip Hay, Private Secretary to Her late Royal Highness:

"The Duke of Kent has asked me to write and thank you for the very kind message of sympathy which you sent on behalf of all ranks of the Corps of Royal Electrical and Mechanical Engineers. His Royal Highness appreciates the message all the more because he was so well aware of his Mother" affectionate interest in everything that concerned the Corps. The Princess's connection as your Colonel-in-Chief was a source of much pride to her and the Duke would therefore be most grateful if you would convey to all ranks his very sincere thanks".

Her Majesty the Queen appointed Princess Marina to be the first Colonel-in-Chief of REME on October 25th 1963. So it was that, twenty-one years after its formation, the Corps was accorded the signal honour of having a member of the Royal Family as its head.

Princess Marina, the youngest daughter of Prince Nicholas of Greece, was born at Athens in 1906. In 1934, she became engaged to Prince George, the youngest son of King George V and, in November of that year, they were married in Westminster Abbey. Her great beauty and friendly nature very soon endeared her to the British people.

On the outbreak of the Second World War, the Princess devoted herself to the National cause and, in 1940, she became the Commandant of the WRNS. In July 1942, she suffered a great personal loss when her husband, the Duke of Kent, was killed on his way to inspect RAF units in Iceland. Much of her life following the end of hostilities was devoted to public duties. She was a knowledgeable patron of the arts and took immense interest in lawn tennis and, for over twenty-five years, she was President of the All-England Tennis Club. Skiing also held a great interest for the Princess and the Cup for the annual Army inter-service championship bears her name.

As Colonel-in-Chief, the Princess visited the Corps on a number of occasions and showed remarkable interest in its activities. On 28th May 1964, the Corps was formally presented to the Princess during a ceremonial parade at the School of Electrical and Mechanical Engineering, Bordon. Over 2,000 officers, soldiers, old comrades, wives and families attended on a gloriously sunny day.

During the parade, the Corps was presented to the Colonel-in-Chief by Major General Sir Leslie Tyler KBE, CB, Representative Colonel Commandant. In her reply to his address, the Princess showed a remarkable understanding and appreciation of the Corps, which was further exemplified later when she visited the various technical displays covering all facets of Corps activities.

In June 1965, Her Royal Highness dined with her officers at Headquarters Mess, where a representative gathering of regular and reserve officers was present. In May 1966, after arriving at Arborfield by helicopter, the Princess visited the Depot Sergeants' Mess and later attended a cocktail party at West Court.

In the summer of last year, Her Royal Highness toured Germany and visited the two regiments of which she was Colonel-in-Chief, the 1st Battalion The Queen's Regiment and the 1st Battalion the Devonshire and Dorset Regiment, and included in her tour a visit to 6 Infantry Workshop REME.

As recently as 9th May this year, Her Royal Highness made what was to be her last visit to the Corps. The Princess came to the School of Electronic Engineering, Arborfield. and later attended an informal luncheon party at West Court.

On all her visits to the Corps, Princess Marina expressed great interest in REME matters and everyone who had the privilege of meeting her was aware of the deep understanding and approachability. We sincerely hope that, in her association with the Corps, Her Royal Highness was aware of the pleasure she gave to its members.

The beautiful portrait of the Princess, which hangs in West Court, and the lovely antique silver gilt bowl presented by her to the officers of the Corps, will be constant reminders of her active association with the Corps.

(The above appreciation of Princess Marina was published in The Craftsman magazine of November 1968)

—§—

Sergeants Mess July 1970

Rear Row – Sgt P Mullins, ACC   Sgt B Jones, RGJ   Sgt A McLean, RGJ   Sgt R Bosley, Para   Sgt M Steel, RGJ   Sgt J Larvin, RCT,   Sgt L Scherer, REME
Fourth Row - Ssgt A Tredgold, Lt Div Sgt T Scott, REME   Sgt R Austin, R Hamps Sgt M Towell, RH   Sgt F Lunt, ACC   Sgt H Poulding, REME Sgt B Biggs, R Anglian Sgt C Biggin, ACC   CoH W Owen, Blues&Royals
Sgt H Dick, DERR Sgt H O'Neill, APTCC Sgt S Longman, D&D Sgt A Johnson, DERR Sgt A Wolsey, RA
Third row - Sgt R Riley, RCT Sgt V Emery, REME Sgt J Turnbull, REME Sgt G Willis, RCT CoH B Venn, LG   Sgt A Lloyd, REME Ssgt R Watson, RAOC Sgt J Millgate, R Anglian   Ssgt W
Bird, RAMC   Sgt P Hewlett, RGJ CoH J Edwards, Blues&Royals Sgt R Clarkson, REME Sgt W Lowrie, REME   Sgt B Pond, REME
Second row - P/Mjr R McPhee, QoH D/Mjr M Hudson, RNF Ssgt F Leonard, RCT Ssgt J Redfern, REME Ssgt G Swallow, REME   SSgt G Amos, REME AQMS T Lackey, REME   AQMS R Frost, REME CSMI D
McGregor, APTC AQMS B Ketley, REME Ssgt L K Anderson, REME Ssgt J Dixon, REME Ssgt R Nutt, REME Ssgt L Carter, REME Ssgt J Dorricut, REME   Ssgt F Peters, REME
Front row - CSM W Cook, Irish Gds CSM A Barrow, Gren Gds AQMS R Butterfield, REME ASM D Armstrong, REME   ASM G Walker, REME Cdr P Lemm, BEM, RAOC Col D A Brown, Comdt AAC   RSM R
Woodfield, Gren Gds Major R H Matthews, MC, RA ASM D Rich, REME ASM H Evans, REME RQMS E Murphy, REME CSM A Saundby, Coldm Gds CSM D Rickers, LI CSM R Lancaster, Gren Gds

Chapter 9

1970 - 75

Changes in Technician training

The first intake of the 'two-year trained' VMs passed out from Arborfield in April of 1970, having in fact spent only twelve months at the College, as their first year had already been served up at the now closed Carlisle. During that same year, the technicians' courses at the College were reduced from the previous nine, down to eight terms. Those graduate apprentices from 8 Div, who had already reached Class III standard in their trade, were passed directly into adult service. Those who had completed their ONC, but had not yet taken the Class III trade test (because their eighth term was devoted to education for ONC), were now attached to the adult units of either the SEE or AETW, depending upon trade, for their continuation training. This would enable them to pass their trade test, before proceeding directly on to adult service.

Also in 1970, away now from the pure training aspects of their full and busy lives, two young apprentices from the College, Paul Mackie and Pat Knowles of 'A' Coy, broke an existing world record. This they did by playing the mind-stretching game of chess, non-stop, for a total of fifty-two hours and forty-six minutes. In doing so, they also raised the sum of over £500, to buy a computerised typewriter for a disabled boy at the nearby Hephaistos School. Support for their worthy efforts came not only from local well-wishers, but also from as far afield as India, South Africa and Australia.

The College's apparent obsession with 'gates' showed no sign of coming to a conclusion! Yet another fine set was commissioned and then manufactured, this time for the adornment of Tweseldon racecourse, located on the outskirts of Aldershot. Of a more parochial interest, the College itself had also acquired a set of replacement main-entrance gates, rescued from the closed-down College at Carlisle – were these also to be known as the 'Carlisle Gates'? Once again, it was Percy Chivers who had made both these sets of gates. At the same time, St James Palace was also to get in on the act, requesting the manufacture of three new

'Colour mounts', to be used for the Queen's Colours in Windsor Castle.

During the period 1968 - 70, a College hovercraft project had been under way and, after many long hours of diligent work by both apprentices and interested staff, the innovative craft made its first public flight on June 1st 1970. One of those 'interested staff' was ex-58A old boy SSgt Ken Anderson, then instructing at the College and who had recently helped a civilian firm to develop a computer for the RA. Ken was already a member of the Hovercraft Club of Great Britain and had started up the Army's own such affiliated club. Ken had always been interested in such machines, ever since dabbling with model planes at school at Sandown on the Isle of Wight.

It had been Sir Christopher Cockerell's famous 'coffee-tin' experiment that had led to the invention of the hovercraft, which had once been a 'top secret' project, with only a handful of scientists, engineers and senior military leaders 'in the know'. The first craft was built by Saunders-Roe in 1959 and later versions had been adopted for military use by 200 Sqn, Royal Corps of Transport (RCT). Interest in small amateur 'sporting' hovercrafts had started around 1965 and it was the College here at Arborfield that hosted the inaugural meeting of the Army Hovercraft Club.

Another project, initiated by the 'boffins' of the Electronics Department, was the construction of a weather satellite tracking station. Again it was Ken Anderson who got 'stuck in' to the project, along with old friend John Pewsey of 45A, now serving at the College as an ASM. John had 'scrounged' a surplus 3Mk7 radar set from Old Dalby, while Ken had used his hard-learned fitting skills to file down the prongs of a tuning fork used in the machine's oscillator. On May 30th 1970, this too had become operational, and the first facsimile weather pictures were both received and recorded. The system drew great acclaim from the public when it was shown tracking American and Russian weather satellites at the Aldershot Military Show.

In July of 1970, Col E G Bailey, CEng, FIEE,

MBIM, became the newly appointed College Commandant. The Colonel had been commissioned into REME during 1945 and later went on to serve with distinction in Palestine, Germany, North Africa, Japan, Korea and Singapore. After leaving the College, 'Bill', as he was universally known, was later promoted to Brigadier.

That same month, the latest edition of *The Craftsman* publicised a new book that would be of immense interest to all ex-boys and members of REME in particular. *"Craftsmen of the Army"* was the title of a book that told the story of REME, from its inception until the present day. Compiled by Brig B B Kennett CBE and Col J A Tatman, the book's Foreword was written by Field Marshall Montgomery himself. *(The book proved immensely popular and a great source of reference. A second volume, updating the history from 1969 – 1992, was later published in 1996. Ed.)*

The College shows its quality

Another innovation at the College during 1970 was the establishment of an 'Evaluation and Quality Control' (EQC) cell, which set up a computer-aided test analysis system, in order to both assist with the development of course design and to promote a more modern style of instructional technology. The C & G examination was also now introduced for all trade disciplines, which would match the three-year training programme and bring about a closer relationship with the adult training schools.

At the same time, a revised education scheme, for both trade apprentices and junior soldiers, focused greater attention upon the educational support of training. Finally, the introduction of a General Engineering Certificate (GEC), precisely matching its civilian counterpart, together with the decision to raise the future school-leaving age to sixteen years, resulted in much robust discussion on the anticipated effect upon the number and quality of trainees.

The idea of 'quality control' in training establishments was comparatively new at the time. Most people already appreciated its use in industrial workshops and factories, on a sort of 'time and motion' basis, to ensure economic, efficiently produced, high standard goods. This was achieved by the feedback of information into the production organisation, regarding any faulty design features, duplication of effort or defects in manufacture. The Director of Army Training (DAT) had now decided that a system run along similar lines would be of benefit to training and the EQC cell was now about to either prove or disprove that decision.

Despite having only a limited staffing arrangement, the cell's 'brainpower' was greatly assisted by the acquisition of an advanced electronic calculator and immediate access to what was being described as a *'computor'* (sic). Where it had previously taken hours of diligent slide-rule work to analyse a set of test results, now this could be hopefully achieved in a matter of seconds. The measurement of student performance would presumably go a long way to remedy weaknesses and thus improve training standards.

Welcome to the enigma!

John Andrusiak (70B) has long harboured the opinion that the AAC was *"something of an enigma"*. To his mind, it endeavoured to impose many of the traditional values of a public school onto young men who were, in the main, from the 'lower classes'. As well as those disciplines imposed by members of College staff, he well remembers the self-imposed hierarchy within the ranks of the apprentices themselves and equates the Jeeps of Arborfield with the long-established 'fags' at such schools as Eton and Harrow. Nonetheless, John seems to have survived the regime as well as most – as testified by his thoughts that will be appearing later in this story, some twenty-five to thirty years after he passed out!

Joining on Monday May 4th 1970, John's apprenticeship *"as a mechanic"* was to last two years, rather than the full three enjoyed by the *"technician"* trades. Due to the restrictions of serving a shorter time (sentence?), John and his fellow tradesmen would only be able to reach the exalted rank of A/T Sergeant, the higher ranks being the exclusive attainment of the technicians. So it was that he left behind the *"pubs, clubs and coffee bars"* of his native Bradford, and his job behind the stall of the *"fruit and veg"* market. The anticipation was high as he cast off the past and ventured forth into an unknown world.

John travelled down by train from Leeds in company with an older boy, who was actually in 'Senior Div' at the time, so at least he had a companion who was able to fill him in on *"what it would be like"* – they even shared John's boiled egg sarnies! However, it was made very clear that, once they arrived at the College, all knowledge of each other must be disowned – from then on John would be on his own. In fact the older boy left the train at Wokingham, leaving John to travel onwards to Reading, as per his joining instructions. This John did, to find himself ordered onto the back of a 3-tonner for the final leg. Someone had a transistor radio playing and John listened to a song, popular at the time, called *'Spirit in the Sky'*, with the line, *"When I die and they lay me to rest, I'm going to the place that's the best"*! *(Was that prophetic – or not? Ed.)*

Amongst those boys who arrived as part of the next intake, 70C, was Graham Howland, from South Wales. He found things little different from many generations before him, with 'J' Coy, commonly known as Jeepland, providing its usual mixture of lifestyles. Firstly, the 'official' way, as demonstrated by the PS, then the way it really was, as dictated by the senior apprentices! Graham didn't try to fight 'the system' any more than the majority of boys, always finding it easier to go along with the quaint customs of the day – such as hanging from the beams by one's fingertips, singing those famous words, *"Beep, Beep, I'm a Jeep"*!

Following his move to 'C' Coy, one of his vivid memories is of the evening when a couple of lads, in a desperate effort to speed up the 'buffing' of the floor to a highly polished state, tied some dusters to the rear wheel of a *Lambretta* motor-scooter. This they then attempted to use as a mobile buffing machine. Needless to say, the results were fairly dismal, resulting in a hole in the linoleum and a room filled with two-stroke fumes! He also recalls a gardening competition, which his room would have won 'hands down' if it weren't for the horticultural eyes of Company Commander Maj Sim, Green Howards, who managed to spot that the splendid display had been augmented by a variety of plastic flowers.

Graham had a slight run-in with the Commandant one evening whilst on guard, when he refused to let the said gentleman through the Camp gates without his forgotten ID card. Col Bailey was forced to return to his quarters for the all-important document, meaning that he was eventually twenty minutes late for an all-important meeting! Graham also remembers standing at the bus stop up the hill, dressed in his civvies, waiting for the Reading bus, with his hands thrust deeply into his pockets against the cold wind. A PS Sergeant approached, and Graham quickly withdrew his hands, but was still greeted with a shout of, *"Are*

Col E G Bailey 1970-73

your hands cold, sonny?" When Graham replied in the affirmative, the response went something like, *"Well put them back in your effing pockets then!"* You can't win!

Getting out of Camp was fairly high on the list of Graham's priorities! He recalls that he joined the Science Society, which often enabled this particular priority to be frequently achieved. At those weekends, working parties would be sent off to clear weeds, nettles and other such undergrowth, along the banks of the Kennet and Avon Canal. This would then allow visits to a pub called *'The Cunning Man'* at Burghfield; indeed, Graham reckons he was pretty cunning himself! He also recalls the rigorous 'delights' of training for the Ten Tors event, marching up and down the Ridgeway north of Reading and striding across the Salisbury Plain.

Graham found that the three years at Arborfield passed quickly, with the final *tour de force*, his 'PoP', definitely the highlight of his tour. His parents attended that parade and there were tears in his father's eyes as Graham marched up to the stage afterwards, to be awarded the CI's Cup for technical ability. He still works for REME as a civilian, alongside serving members, at a local LAD near his home in Brecon.

The Donaldson Report

Another Parliamentary Report was issued in November 1970. This one was presented by the *'Committee on Boy Entrants and Young Servicemen'*, chaired by Lord Donaldson and hence, in common parlance, became the *'Donaldson Report'*. Its brief had been to investigate and assess those terms of service being offered. Public concern had been growing that a young boy, joining the Army at between fifteen and sixteen years of age, full of enthusiasm and unwilling to listen to the honest cautions of the recruiting staff, was able to 'sign away' a large part of his life, only coming to regret it at a later stage. One major criticism was that many boys didn't realise that their nine-year term started from the age of eighteen, and not at the age at which they had first joined as an apprentice.

Although Arborfield was **not** one of the establishments visited during the Committee's inquiries, but Harrogate was, one piece of quoted 'public evidence' concerned an apprentice who had joined up here as a prospective Air Tech in 1966. Finding the training difficult, and with his full agreement, he was consequently posted to Bordon, where he took and passed his trade test as a VM. Now, at the age of nineteen, and following service in Cyprus and Germany, it had suddenly hit home to him just how far ahead his service stretched. A letter from his father reported that he had met quite a few of his son's comrades, and realised that his son's case was not a unique one.

Under the *'Conditions for Leaving the Forces'* prevalent at that time, apprentice tradesmen (entering between the ages of fifteen and seventeen and a half) were debarred from purchasing a discharge during training and for four years thereafter. The Committee recommended that long term apprentices (i.e. those with two or more years' training) should, having reached the statutory age of eighteen, have the option of either confirming their original engagement, or reducing it to a period of training plus five years' service, or of leaving forthwith, without a punitive payment. Although concluding that the Services must continue to recruit boys, the main point was that, as eighteen was the new 'age of majority', it was at that age that boys should have the opportunity to alter any commitment they had innocently made on entry. Enlistment documents were, in future, to make perfectly clear to the boy the date of and his age at the end of his engagement.

When the *Donaldson Report* was published late in that year, it changed, and indeed made more liberal, the conditions of service that were to be offered to the prospective apprentice. A much larger turnover and wastage rate was anticipated – and indeed predicted - from the ramifications of this report. But, despite the greater ease with which the young entrant could now leave the College, at any time during his first six months of service, and was subsequently able to shorten his engagement, statistics showed that the overall effects on retention were not much changed. After an initial rush of applicants to serve as adults for the minimum three years only, the proportions of those wishing to serve either a three, six or nine-year engagement remained

Colonel Bailey with 1972 Aircraft Technician prizewinners.

at a fairly constant level.

It is gratifying that Lord Donaldson's report gave such strong support to our training system, with the following conclusion:

"In their own technological fields, the Army units struck us as being unsurpassed in their total further educational provision for Britain. The Armed Forces have for a long time been acknowledged pioneers in the field of industrial training and further education. It is high time that acknowledgement was made."

The final 'PoP' of 1970 took place on December 17th, with a total of sixty-one apprentices ably commanded by A/T RSM Peter Smart – 'smart by name smart by nature' – and an Air Tech. The reviewing officer that day was the GOC Southern Command and United Kingdom Land Forces (UKLF), Gen Sir Michael Carver GCB, CBE, DSO, MC, ADC and also the Colonel Commandant REME.

December's issue of *The Craftsman* had an article under the heading *"Arborfield Apprentices scupper the opposition"*. During the recent Army Canoe Championships, held on the River Trent at Nottingham, a team of six boys from the College paddled its way to victory. Of the eight events open to them, a total of six were won. The canoes had been purchased from a grant made to the College by the Nuffield Trust in 1968, and the boys spent most of their 'free' time out on the water in practice for their sport.

Faster turnover of RSMs

By the early Seventies, the appointment of RSM had ceased to be the long-term one that had been undertaken in Mr McNally's era. RSM Woodfield had hardly got his feet under the table, in a posting of less than two years, and that 'PoP' proved his last major function before he went off, on commissioning, as the Motor Transport Officer (MTO) with his battalion. His departure made way for RSM D Delgarno of the Scots Guards, in January 1971. RSM Delgarno himself remained here only until September of the following year, before handing over to RSM C Petherick of the Coldstream Guards, who had first joined the 1st Battalion at Windsor in 1953.

Field training was going well in Vehicle Wing, with ever-improving standards of apprentice participation.

Boys were taught to drive cross-country in *Rover* and *Bedford* vehicles, negotiating some quite spectacular obstacles. On a recent exercise, the standard of camouflage had proved so high that a *Sioux* pilot, practising tactical landings, actually dropped his 'chopper' in the section area. Having almost scalped a three-tonner, the pilot was asked to *"depart rapidly"* and not to repeat his 'Sitting Bull' performance again!

On April 1st 1971, the examinations for the ACE at third, second and first class were dropped, in favour of an alternative system. The two new qualifications were the Education Promotion Certificate (EPC), required for promotion to Sergeant, and EPC Advanced for those wishing to gain WO rank. However, this change did not impinge on the College at the time; it was probably not until the next decade that parts of the EPC training were first used for apprentices.

In October, *The Craftsman* magazine gave full two-page prominence to the 'PoP' that had taken place on August 12th. The College was graced by the presence of Maj Gen G H Girling OBE, the DEME(A), on what would probably be his last official visit. Despite the day having dawned *"grey, cold and wet"*, Col Bailey made a last-minute decision in favour of a standard 'dry weather' programme, as the rain eased off sufficiently to make another memorable occasion for yet another Senior Div. The General addressed the boys at the usual prize-giving ceremony, advising them to *"work hard, enjoy life and, above all, make friends"*. In his own humble opinion, as he told them, *"A man cannot have too many friends"*.

Many sporting activities

The winter term of 1971 had seen enthusiasm and competitive spirit at a peak during the annual Winter Games. There had been two such competitions, one at home to Harrogate and the second away at Chepstow. Each was held on a chosen Saturday and consisted of ten separate events. During the morning there were matches in Badminton, Basketball, Fencing, Hockey, Judo, Shooting (.22") and Squash; whilst after lunch came Cross-country, Football and Rugby. REME could certainly take heart for the sporting future, as the Arborfield boys were victorious on both occasions. However, it was noted that the sportsmanship and determination on display, by both the winners and losers, provided a wonderful advertisement for the principle of apprentice training as a whole.

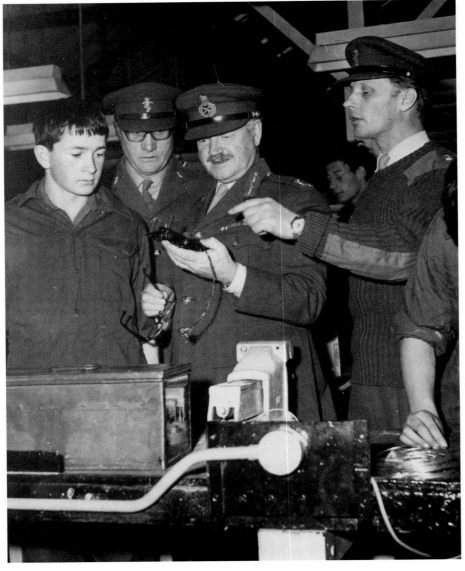

No Sir, I'm sure it's the other one you have to press!

placed upon the boys, whenever possible, to relax and get away from the classroom atmosphere. He enthused about the variety of hobbies and clubs that were available in the evenings and at weekends. On that very day, a Hobbies Exhibition had been laid on in the Educational Building, for the benefit of parental perusal.

The Commandant also praised the continued sterling work of the WRVS lady, at that time a Mrs E Jahans. Apart from her obvious 'mother hen' approach to the most-recently arrived boys, she was also responsible for organising many outings to such as the Royal Tournament and the Motor Show. Perhaps her most popular arrangement was for the regular Sunday visits to Streatham Ice Rink, where the boys not only 'got their skates on', but spent a fair amount of time on that ever-popular pastime, *"chatting up the birds"*.

Mrs Jahans sadly became ill during the spring recess, to be replaced at very short notice by Mrs Overton who, as Miss Blomfield, had served here from 1965 – 1968. For an interim period, the WRVS Centre was taken over and smoothly run by a number of 'College wives'.

One of the biggest sporting events of that winter term was the Army Roller Racing Championships, held locally at Bailleul Barracks. This is where the normal road cycling activities of the summer months are exchanged for the more static pleasures of the 'rolling road'. This is a testing experience, which makes great demands on the rider's stamina. The biggest advantage is that falling off the bike at zero speed is far more comfortable than hitting one's chin on the gravel of a road, at some speed in excess of 20 miles per hour! There were no hidden gradients or howling gales during the final fifty-metre sprint either!

After the 'PoP' held in December of 1971, Col Bailey informed the attending parents of the importance

Another enquiry

In January 1972, the AAC received a copy of yet another enquiry, this time into the opinions of young school leavers. This report had been carried out and submitted by Lt Col A B Edwards RAEC, as a Defence Fellowship thesis, but came highly recommended by the DAT as being *"of prime importance to the manning, recruiting and running of the Junior Training Organisation"*. In 1970, it had been estimated that seventy per cent of the Army's junior recruits had joined up at the age of fifteen. But the low birth rate that had been prevalent during the middle Fifties, combined with the raising of the school leaving age, was now predicted to cause manpower problems in future years. At the same time, the improved training currently being offered in civilian schemes could possibly neutralise some of the present attractions of the Services' apprenticeship schemes.

One of the establishments visited during the survey was the AAC at Chepstow, with the overall study showing that a vast majority of boys felt that they were more self-assured at the end of training, than they had been before starting. With facts such as these, the DAT and his staff hoped to maintain present recruiting levels as high as possible. An in-depth examination of young boys' attitudes towards their previous educational objectives would obviously help, but it was essential that joining the Services should be made as attractive a proposition as possible, through the medium of careers literature, liaison visits to schools, and such like.

In the spring 1972 edition of *The Arborfield Apprentice*, the 'A' Coy scribe found himself,

Now listen to me laddie, I'm a General and when I say that's my vice then it's most certainly my vice!

rather unwillingly, joining the ranks of what he termed 'typical Englishmen'. In other words, he started his article by mentioning the weather! *"Can anyone remember a soggier winter than the one that assaults us now?"* he asked. Ice and snow had been notable only by their absence, while the sun was only just remembered for its one brief appearance the previous November! It was all the more miraculous that the College had still been able to play so much non-aquatic sport. Our scribe continued with a word of apology to the poor typist who had probably suffered eyestrain

from his poorly produced manuscript. He gave the inarguable reason that Arborfield had recently suffered no less than eighteen power cuts within the space of a week.

One Thursday early in 1972, the veil of semi-obscurity that generally shrouded Aircraft Wing was blown away at around 09.30 hours, by the landing of three rotary-wing aircraft, arriving from the AETW at Middle Wallop. Two *Scouts* and a *Sioux* had arrived for the purpose of giving a party of Air Techs some 'air experience'. This was an integral part of their training in two respects. Firstly it gave the budding apprentices an introduction to the new, if somewhat noisy and slightly unstable, environment of a helicopter; secondly it gave them contact with those pilots who were themselves dependent upon the Air Techs' abilities to provide an airworthy machine.

It is pertinent here to remark upon the action of a brace of foolish young men who endeavoured to light up their cigarettes only a few feet from a fuel dump. They inevitably then found themselves in a serious airborne situation, even without the benefit of a rotary-winged aircraft. Fortunately for our two nameless heroes, this was due to a verbal blast from their instructor, rather than from exploding high-octane gasoline!

At work and play

Back on the 'work' front, Aircraft Wing was finally seeing the 'phasing out' of such ancient relics as its *Skeeter* and *Auster* equipments – much to the sorrow of some of the more mature instructors. The Wing was gradually warming up again, following the breakdown

SSgt Joe Redfearn of the Electronics Wing receiving his LSGC medal

of its central heating boiler during the winter. Rumour had it that the boiler had already been obsolete when installed ten years previously. The QM had supplied some paraffin-oil stoves during the emergency, the smell of which eventually led to the lighting of joss sticks in the classroom during one particular trade examination.

Vehicle Wing was busying itself with a start on the training of armoured vehicles, the necessary familiarisation on *Saracen* and *FV430 Series* vehicle, prior to the apprentices proceeding to SEME for their full equipment training. With the number of military staff leaving for *"short Mediterranean tours"*, the Wing was looked upon as the place to be if you wanted a six-month holiday in sunny Cyprus!

Following some winter training at the dry ski slope at nearby Aldershot, at the end of the spring term in 1972, sixteen apprentice tradesmen set off by road to Scotland. On the Friday night they slept at Army HQ, Edinburgh, before moving on to the pleasant resort of Aviemore. Here they spent a week living in caravans and skiing on the testing slopes of the Cairngorms. The week proved most successful, with everyone passing the Grade III test, while three of the party also went on to qualify at Grade II level.

During the Easter recess, the College soccer team enjoyed a short tour of the Channel Island of Guernsey. They drew one game and won the other two, one against the island's under-19 side. They continued to play well upon their return home and ended the season as champions of the East Berkshire League, Division III. From a possible sixty points for the season, the boys had amassed a total of fifty-three, a really first-class effort.

Over the period 20th / 23rd June 1972, the REME Tennis Championships were taking place at the Aldershot Officers' Club. As reported in *The Craftsman* later that year, *"the standard of tennis displayed by the apprentices was most creditable ... ... both they and their coaches are to be congratulated"*. The Plate Final was a keenly contested match between Cpl White of 3 Field Wksp and A/T Graham from the College, with the younger man taking the trophy. Another apprentice, A/T Hill, partnered a Capt March to win the Handicap Doubles tournament.

By the summer of 1972, the Science Society was proudly looking back upon a series of visits to places of variety and interest. Not least of all had been the Imperial War Museum and, in particular, its display of

Second World War German aircraft, including complete V1 and V2 machines. *(It's amazing how quickly those dreadful weapons of death and destruction had become mere museum pieces! Ed.)*

Society members had also made a trip down to the Motor Museum at Beaulieu, located in Hampshire's beautiful New Forest area, where the many historical vehicles were on display at an impressive new building that was now the National Car Museum. The Society was also proud that their Weather Station was now in full working order and that there was every expectation that it would soon be accepted as an official national weather recording station.

By the time that his summer leave arrived in 1972, ex-boy Vince Fuller of intake 57A had been raised to the adult rank of SSgt. But the spirit of adventure lived on, as Vince described in a letter to *The Craftsman* magazine. He had been asked, *"How would you like to go parachuting with the Bundeswehr?"* After three years of being a 'desk jockey' in Whitehall, this was an offer that couldn't be refused! Things didn't get off to a flying start however, as the first practice helicopter trip was abandoned due to mist and rain. But, by the end of his 'holiday', Staff Fuller had completed seven descents – one by night – from a French-German built C160 aircraft, and been awarded his bronze wings. The one thing he had found most difficult had been getting to bed before 2 a.m. – but the social life certainly cemented some lasting friendships!

The Westland Trophy

That summer's edition of *The Arborfield Apprentice* joyfully reported upon a ceremony that had been held at the AETW. Two ex-apprentices, LCpls Mark Plimmer and Frank Stringer, had been jointly awarded the coveted 'Westland Trophy'. This was a twelve-inch silver cup, donated by *Westland Helicopters*, not only for their outstanding examination results, but also for the necessary character, reliability and integrity required in aircraft servicing. The trophy had been proudly presented by none other than our own Commandant, Col Bailey, as this was the first time it had been won by boys from the College.

At the August 1972 'PoP', the reviewing officer was the QMG, Maj Gen Sir Anthony Read GCB, CBE, DSO, MC. In his address, the General told those apprentices who were passing out to enter adult service:

"You have lived in a disciplined community, where standards are kept high and nobody tolerates sloppy performances at anything. You have learnt to use the mind constructively and the body properly. This is the beginning of service to your Queen, your country, your unit and not only yourselves".

Flying high – and low!

Carrying on from the thriving Gliding Club, the College had seen a steep rise in the popularity of 'power flying'. Two apprentices, A/T Cpl French and A/T LCpl Haynes, had only started flying the previous October at nearby Blackbushe Airport. After some nine hours of instruction, each had now 'flown solo' and thus qualified for their private pilots' license, which were presented to the boys by the General at that 'PoP' in August.

It must have been a brave decision by one young apprentice, when he decided to 'have a go' at non-power flying, off the end of the lifeboat jetty at Selsey, on Sunday 15th August. If he could cover a distance of fifty yards, he would be awarded a sum of £1,000 – now that's a lot of NAAFI buns! Having built his own set of wings in less than four hours, he was then able to watch other competitors fail to make it. So now it was his turn – the money was his for the taking. He raised his wings, took a few sharp paces forward, and found that it only took 2.2 seconds to hit the water – which turned out to be pretty cold! He now has a certificate, signed by Patrick Moore, the famous astronomer, which confirms that *"Terence Raymond Arnell was an unsuccessful competitor in the Selsey Birdman Rally, 1972"*.

In October that same year, the REME Corps Swimming Championships were held at Aldershot. Despite the meagre swimming resources available to the College, a swimming squad had been set up only the previous April, with the express intention of entering this event, where it gained a reputable second place behind the team from BAOR. Great honour was then bestowed on the College when no less than five of its young swimmers were selected to represent the Corps, in its team to compete against the R Sigs. The REME team went on to win every single event, as well as winning the water polo by a magnificent 13 – 4. The whole of the Corps looked ahead to the facilities that would be offered by a swimming pool at the new

Arborfield Garrison Sports Centre, due to be completed the following year.

In the winter term that year, the College greeted its largest ever intake of *"277 bright, smiling faces"*, which brought the apprentice population up to a total of 966. The quality of this intake, despite its size, proved as good as any previous one. During that same term, A/T Cpl Hicks had been selected to take part in an expedition, organised by the British Schools' Exploring Society, which took place that year in Arctic Norway. That he was able to attend such a prestigious expedition was due, in no small part, to a handsome financial contribution from the REME Association.

Members of 'B' Coy were bemoaning the fact that the painting contract for 'D' spider had still not been completed. Alongside, in 'C' spider, a start had been made to tastefully decorate the newly painted walls with framed prints of 'Old Masters'. This was an effort to prevent younger members, completely against their will of course, to be forced to revert to full-colour lurid photographs from *Playboy* and *Penthouse* magazines for their artistic delights!

At the 'PoP' in December 1972, Mr Norman Groves enjoyed a fine ending to the year, when he returned to the College to be presented with his Imperial Service Medal. He had retired the previous year, following no less than thirty-two years service at the apprentices' establishments at Chepstow, Carlisle and Arborfield.

On January 21st 1973, newly arrived members of 'A' Coy got their *"first taste of soldiering"* in a hutted camp at Westwood, out somewhere on the Salisbury Plain. After their evening meal, having locked their weapons safely away for the night, the boys were able to spectate upon a *"realistic night exercise going on in the area"*. They watched the colourful parachute flares and tracer with lots of interest, whilst stuffing their faces with lemonade and *Smarties* – this was real soldiering indeed!

After a couple of days spent learning about ambushes and patrols, they got stuck into exercise 'Cold Crunchie', against 'D' Coy. A whole afternoon's march in full battle kit ended with a night of expectation, awaiting the enemy's attack. As this didn't take place until about fifteen minutes before dawn next morning, it must have been a long night!

After a breakfast of 'compo', a counter-attack against the 'D' Coy apprentices was launched. But, due to unforeseen circumstances (first his driver overslept, then his *Land Rover* got bogged down!)

the Commandant's view of this famous battle was severely restricted. The soldiering ended with a visit to Larkhill, where the boys were treated to a delivery of men and 105mm pack-howitzers, by *Sioux* and *Puma* helicopters. They then watched a demonstration of anti-aircraft fire, the very impressive *Abbott* self-propelled gun and, finally, heard the noisy roar that accompanied the firing of an *Honest John* missile.

Will the Old Boys revive?

That same year was to see a temporary revival of interest in the OBA, which had greatly lapsed since the last occurrence of a reunion in 1964. On January 26th 1973, there was a meeting of the OBA, at which the Vice Chairman, Lt Col D J Bowen, who was also then the CI of the College, commented upon the possible causes for the discontinuation of the Association's activities over the past few years. He also outlined some guidelines upon which the Association should be revived. It was thought that 'one-day activities', on a regular basis throughout the year, were preferable to an Annual Weekend, while some members were strongly in favour of including family members at Reunions, rather than continuing the previous 'stag' style arrangements. It was decided that these matters should be perused and another meeting held at some future stage.

February's edition of *The Craftsman* included an article under the heading *"A School for Bluebells"*, written by Maj Atkins RA. It was an affectionate description of his time spent as a Company Commander here at the College. Tongue in cheek, the Major asserted that *"Gunners run AAC Arborfield – or at least like to think that we do"*. At the end of his tour he was able to say that, *"Apart from commanding a Battery, the time spent at Arborfield has been the most rewarding and satisfying job of my career"*.

Maj Atkins found it fascinating to see the way in which officers, from all different arms, ran their separate Companies *"in the tradition of their own regiments"*, but that they all produced much the same quality of output – with the help, of course, of the REME and RAEC input on the trade and educational side! He found that the most satisfying aspect of the job was that, during a two- or three-year posting, it was generally possible to follow a new intake right through its training cycle, from *"immature young hopefuls to well-trained NCO material"*. In conclusion, he said that he had enjoyed his association with *"Bluebells in embryo"* and had the highest regard for the professional and human approach to training offered here at the College. *('Bluebell' is the recognised call sign for REME assistance, used over the Army radio net. Ed.)*

During the month of March that year, Col Bailey paid an inaugural visit to the DYRMS at Dover, at the invitation of its headmaster. The purpose of this visit was to present, to the boys living and studying there, an indication of the scope of training and wide range of sports and hobbies pursued at Arborfield. Accompanied by a party of around twenty-five *"keen and eager"* apprentices, the Commandant hoped that this goodwill visit would encourage the Dukies to continue their amicable long-standing association with the Apprentices' College, fostered over many long years with, of course, the possibility of gaining some well-motivated recruits. The party stayed on for an overnight sojourn, with a splendid evening enjoyed by all, thanks to the benevolence and liquid refreshment supplied in the name of one *William Younger*!

On Saturday 31st March 1973, the College held another 'Junior Company Parents' Days', for the new recruits of intake 73A. A programme printed for that event exists, annotated with pencilled-in corrections, which were then apparently used to update the programme in time for the 73B Parents' Day, held later on July 28th. Typically the day would start around 9.00 a.m. with visitors, including all sorts of relatives and family friends as well as the boys' parents, arriving for a 'coffee and biscuits' welcome at the NAAFI/WRVS Reception Rooms. A display of PT by boys of 'J' Coy would then take place at 11 o'clock in the College Hall, followed by the Commandant's address at the same venue. A Company parade and prize-giving ceremony would then lead up to lunch, attended by the boys and parents combined.

The afternoon would be reserved for parents/ visitors to tour classrooms, workshops, training areas

Prizewinners at a 1972 Passing Out Parade
- some of the trousers appear as shiny as the silver!

and boys' living accommodation. At 4.00 p.m., boys were then allowed to leave the College, in company with their families, as long as they were back in time for 'lights out' at 10.30 p.m. In later years, special dispensation would be given for boys to return home for the weekend with their parents. This custom for apprentices of the junior term lasted at least until the early Nineties.

More sporting activities

The Arborfield Apprentice issued in spring 1973 gave a brief mention of the efforts of one of the College's then PS members. This was Sgt Jim Fox, an ex-apprentice of 1957 and who had represented Great Britain in the 1972 Olympic Games at Munich, competing in the Modern Pentathlon. That same magazine also reported on some sporting successes by current members from the ranks of serving apprentices. At hockey, for instance, A/T Cpl Smith and A/T LCpl Farrell had been nominated to take part in the next Army Under-22 trials, while the Junior XI had recently fought their way through to the semi-finals of the Army Junior Cup competition. Meanwhile, the badminton team had been reasonably successful over the past two seasons, competing within the Berkshire Schools' League.

Staff of the Aircraft Wing, early Seventies

The sport of rugby provided some excellent results that term, with the College First XV winning all their games. In a match against Old Marlovians, an adult side, with the College in the lead by three points to nil and only ten minutes remaining, the game had to be abandoned when the ball burst! The annual matches against RAF Halton and RAF Locking produced scores of 24 – 4 and 43 – 0. The boys probably hoped at the time that they would get stiffer (and possibly prettier!) opposition if they invited the Dagenham Girl Pipers to come and play the next match!

At the end of the Easter term, some of the College Cycling Club made their way to the Channel Islands, to take part in the fourth staging of the Guernsey Festival of Cycling. They travelled by rail down to Portsmouth Harbour, after which they were at the tender mercies of the Maritime Sqn of the Royal Corps of Transport

(RCT) and onward nautical transportation by Landing Craft, Tank (LCT). Even the copious dispensation of 'Kwells' tablets didn't remove the impression that they would soon find themselves landing on the Normandy beaches, under the covering fire of tenacious German defenders!

Eventually, however, the boys found themselves disembarking at Alderney, where a further three-hour voyage awaited them. They were very happy to arrive at St Peter Port, where they could finally get themselves back onto the relative stability of two wheels! Training sessions then took place over the next six days, unfortunately with bathing facilities limited to five-minute showers, dictated by slot machines! There were some very soapy boys about, but they were still able to fascinate the local girls with their 'bubbly' personalities and 'scented' charms! And the racing?

Oh, that was completely ruined by heavy continuous rain and high winds – nothing much changes, does it? The boys happily left the island in good spirits, following a celebration dinner at which they were the guests of the Guernsey Velo Club.

Mr McNally's untimely death

It is always with regret that one records the death of a former member of the College, whether an ex-apprentice or member of staff, indeed there are far too many to detail here. But at that time, in 1973, we had to report the death of Mr McNally in a tragic traffic accident. On March 28th he had been waiting in a bus queue, at a busy junction in Reading town-centre, when the bus went off the road and managed to run him down.

As the School RSM for fifteen years, from 1941 until 1956, he had been one of the cornerstones upon which the standards of drill and traditions of smartness within the subsequent College had been mainly built. Since retiring in 1956, Roland McNally – and not many knew him by that name - had been employed by Reading County Council and working in the Shire Hall. Both in the May issue of *The Craftsman*, and in *The Arborfield Apprentice*, published in summer later that year, his Obituary was given the great prominence it deserved.

Lawrence Nixon (April 1942) sadly attended Mr McNally's funeral on April 4th, reporting that it was a memorable occasion at which the Scots Guards did our ex-RSM proud. Lawrence then went on to recall that, upon being posted back to the School PS as a substantive Armament SSgt, only three years after his boy's service, he was looked upon rather dubiously as a slightly less than *bone fide* Mess member! The RSM didn't see it that way however, in fact Lawrence and he became fairly good friends. On one occasion, Lawrence had the memorable role of taking one of the parades in Mr McNally's absence. He came to appreciate the RSM in many ways, and at the funeral, felt in a humble way that he represented the countless apprentices who had known and respected him during so many years here at Arborfield.

At the April 'PoP' that year, Col Bailey was proudly able to address the boys' parents, other relatives and distinguished guests once again. The Commandant emphasised the continuing diversity of College life in all fields, naming canoeing, gliding, power flying and sub-aqua diving as just a few examples of the extra-mural activities that were now available. He announced that, as from the following term, many apprentices would be eligible to enter the Duke of Edinburgh Award Scheme for the first time, and he looked forward to their future successes. He told parents in particular that their boys were being well looked after by Mrs Delgardo, the current WRVS lady, following recent extensions to the WRVS accommodation.

In April's edition of *The Craftsman*, it was announced that *"the technically minded youth of this country are now to be given a new challenge and another opportunity to display their natural inventiveness"*. This was in the form of the *British Petroleum (BP)* 'Build-a-Car' competition. The company would sponsor this, but the 'builders' would be able to draw upon REME advice. The AAC here at Arborfield would be building a car in parallel with the competition, but not as an entry – their car would be designed simply to show what could be achieved. It was also hoped that this would be 'on the cheap'!

The following month, the College again featured in the pages of *The Craftsman*, this time under the heading of *"Chess in REME"*. It stated that chess had become *"an absorbing hobby"* and that the AAC Arborfield was *"a leader in this activity"*. During the previous November, the College team had taken on a side representing the rest of the Army, going down to a narrow defeat. Having arranged a return tournament in March, the College gained its due revenge in quite an overwhelming victory. As stated in the REME magazine, *"What other unit could take on the remainder of the Army at any sport?"*

Walking for Charity

May 19th saw a party of thirty-two apprentices setting out from Henley Rugby Club on the Christian Aid Charity Walk. The walk took place in the Chilterns, over twenty miles, through some of the most attractive land in all England. The volunteers were split into small groups, before being set off at varying times. Fortunately, most of the checkpoints coincided with what turned out to be village pubs, so there was certainly no lack of liquid refreshment along the way. A spot of rain along the way didn't deter the boys, but there were a few who strayed off the beaten track at certain parts of the walk. Several young ladies, also out on the walk, were also led astray – but in a strictly

Hey, I used to have one of these!
Brig Garner and Col Bailey inspecting some practical work

cap' for cricket – complete with the 'ATS' insignia on the front, which at the time had caused some mirth amongst those who didn't know their history.

With the benefit of hindsight, it is interesting to note that in 1973, the College played host to two distinguished visitors from Iran. That was of course whilst the Shah of Iran still ruled his country, things have changed a fair bit since then! The first visitor, in February, had been Commander of the Iranian Ordnance Corps, while June 8th saw another visit, this time by General Oveisi, Commanding General of the Imperial Iranian Ground Forces.

In the summer 1973 edition of *The Arborfield Apprentice*, a number of ex-apprentices provided articles for the *'Old Boys' Corner'*. One of them, Sgt Riley, had left the College as an Air Tech at the end of 1967, then been posted to 70 Aircraft Wksp, Middle Wallop. Two short years later, he found himself posted to El Adem in Libya. Here, he managed to obtain a place on a challenging three-day RAF desert survival exercise. Of the original twelve members of the team, two had to be 'casevaced'

geographical sense, of course!

A letter addressed to the Commandant arrived from Poole, Dorset, on June 1st that year. It came from R Powell, who had been a member of only the second intake, starting October 1939. Unfortunately, his career had come to an abrupt end in February 1945, when a spinal injury led to his medical discharge. He recalled that, as a boy LCpl, he had been in charge of room 'G4' and that, during 1941 – 42, he had captained the School soccer team, leading to his name being put on the 'Honours Board' in the Camp Hall. *(What a shame that no trace can now be found of these famous old boards - Ed.)* Mr Powell was also presented with his 'School

to safety, so it had certainly been no picnic. A military uprising in Libya soon curtailed the British Army's presence there and Sgt Riley was then posted to BAOR, before eventually arriving back at Wallop.

What's in a name?

That same College magazine took a rather whimsical look at the titles that turned up on mail purportedly addressed to either apprentices or staff here at Arborfield. The first of these was a gentleman called *"A A College Esq."*, who had received a fair number of letters starting with the words, *"Dear Mr College"*.

There was also correspondence addressed to *"Mr J Spider"*, for *"Mr B Coy"* and a certain *"Major Green Howard"*. Some interesting spelling variations had seen envelopes for the *"Army Appetites College"* and the *"Army College, Poppingate Barracks"*. Perhaps the award for ingenuity must go to one young lady, obviously anxious to regain contact with an apprentice recently met (we won't ask why!). She optimistically addressed her envelope as follows *"To the soldier from Wooler who signed on for nine years, who drives a 1960 Wolsey with a radio and is on an electrical engineering course at the Army Camp, Reading"*! *(We wonder if they ever did meet up again? Ed.)*

At the August 1973 'PoP', the Commandant warmly welcomed Maj Gen A M McKay, CEng, FIMechE, FIEE, MBIM, then the DEME(A), as the parade's reviewing officer. The General was not only the nominal head of the Corps, but had also been a close personal friend of the Commandant for many years. Col Bailey aimed his own particular praise at the young men who had participated in that year's Ten Tors competition. This had taken place in the inevitable dreadful weather but excellent leadership qualities had been shown by the apprentices, in helping those less fortunate teams in an hour of need, sometimes at the cost of their own success.

During his address, General McKay stressed the enormous spread of interests and engineering disciplines that now awaited the new adult soldiers. He spoke about tanks, helicopters, guided weapons, guns, radar, advanced communication equipments, surveillance drones, electronic computers, heavy transport, hovercraft and sea-going vessels – to mention just the primary items! He advised that REME was responsible for the maintenance and repair of such equipment from *"cradle to grave"*, often a twenty-year life-span or longer, and that those boys leaving today would no doubt at some time in the future become responsible for the training of their own successors. He ended by thanking Col Bailey for all his hard work over the past three years, this being his final parade.

On Sunday August 5th 1973, four young apprentices left the College in drizzling rain, bound for the wilds of Dartmoor, where they were undergoing an expedition as part of the Duke of Edinburgh's Award scheme. Confronted with a fast-flowing ford, one young lad gallantly threw his rucksack into the stream as a stepping-stone – very helpful, but a lack of waterproofing didn't augur well for the next few days!

Not that it made much difference in the end, because the weather throughout the whole trek was abysmal, the rain coming down by the proverbial bucketful. Despite the discomfort, the boys were finally able to dry off their kit at Okehampton Camp and looked forward to the winter term, when they would be taking another trip, this time to the more northerly climes of far-off Snowdonia.

'A brief history' – the story so far

"In September 1973, the College received its first intake of young men who had all stayed at school until their sixteenth birthday, following the raising of the school leaving age." Thus ended the last paragraph of a small booklet entitled *"A brief history of the Army Apprentices' College"*. The author's name was not given, only the following printer's code, *"RR 25996/ 1/AAC 340 500 10/73 TP 8"*. The information given in the booklet was obviously an updated version of that paper written by Maj Allin in 1965, and itself used as a template during the following years, as other editions of a College history were eventually published.

Later in that same month, Col H K Tweed, CEng, FIMechE, FRAeS, MBIM, assumed command of the College. Col Tweed had 'joined up' as an engineering cadet in 1946, and was commissioned into REME during 1949. Following three years of service in Egypt, he had first arrived in Arborfield in 1953, at what was then No.3 Training Battalion. A wide variety of postings, including BAOR and Malaya, had preceded his move here to the College. At a presentation to the DAT on October 1st, he started off with the famous words, *"General, I have commanded this College for all of seventy-two hours, and that includes the weekend!"* Fortunately, of course, he had been well briefed by the CI, Col Barry Turner.

Changes on all fronts

For the new Commandant, there followed an intensive period of three years, during which further change and innovation considerably altered the contents of the laid down apprenticeship for both technicians and VMs. During the following year, working parties were to be set up, to examine the implications of the Technician Education Council (TEC) requirements for the College's technician apprentices. The TEC itself had only been established since March of 1973, following a recommendation of the 1969 *'Haselgrave Committee'*.

The three main aims of the College were still 'education, trade and military skills'. Education was provided by a Wing made up of three separate departments, General Engineering, Mathematics and Science, with a staff of twelve RAEC officers and some sixteen Burnham lecturers all under the control of the SEO, a Colonel of the RAEC. Trade training was split into four Wings, namely Workshop Practice, Vehicles, Aircraft and Electronics, each under the command of a REME Major, with the fore-mentioned CI in overall charge.

Military and adventure training were patently in good hands. At his very first 'PoP', held in December of that year, Col Tweed proudly reported that all of the young men leaving the College that day had succeeded in obtaining their basic REME Certificate in Military Skills. Ample opportunities still continued to exist in the field of outdoor activities and training, with boys able to participate in such diverse sports as abseiling, canoeing, hill walking, rock-climbing and offshore sailing.

Look, isn't that where the major dropped in?

During October 1973, one party of forty-two apprentices from 'A' Coy, well camouflaged as *"civilian tourists"*, had taken the cross-Channel ferry from Southampton to Le Havre. Disembarkation proved a difficulty, as the French Customs man proved highly suspicious of the pile of kit bags, bivvies, ration boxes and camp stores! He took some convincing that there were no arms or ammunition stashed away underneath. The boys' mission was to set up camp in France and to visit the Normandy D-Day landing beaches, tracing the steps of the Allied Forces' 1944 advance. Maj Sim, who had himself parachuted into France as part of those invading forces, led the recce party. He was able to give the boys a graphic description of the actions taken during those historic times.

Amongst other most interesting ports-of-call was the 'Pegasus Bridge', where the boys were shown the customary hospitality by Madame Gondre, whose family had owned the nearby café since the war. They were even allowed to camp out in the back garden, with staff members being accommodated in two spare rooms. It proved a memorable occasion. The party also viewed the world-famous Bayeux Tapestry, and the huge US War Cemetery, with its *"10,000 marble crosses standing coldly, row upon row, on close-cut grass"*. The last campsite was at Merville, overlooking what had been the German defensive emplacement – *"great slabs of cement, block-houses, ammunition pens and old gun positions"*.

Another party of eight boys was at the same time setting off on a trekking expedition in Snowdonia, as part of their membership of the Mountaineering Club, accompanied by the previously mentioned four boys who were practising for their Duke of Edinburgh's Gold Award.

The College musicians were in fine form during 1973, and well into 1974, being

Well Bluebell, when will my staff car be ready?
General Sir Basil Eugster's visit April 1973

much in demand at civilian functions far and wide. On Remembrance Day of 1973, the Brass Band and Corps of Drums were invited to 'do their stuff' at the Royal town of Windsor, where they rousingly led the Berkshire Yeomanry and Old Comrades in their ceremonial parade. On the same day, the Pipe Band was similarly engaged, leading the Royal British Legion parade through Basingstoke.

After an absence of many years, the College Christmas Concert once again took centre-stage towards the end of 1973. Despite a desperate petrol shortage, caused by another outbreak of anti-Western feelings in the Middle East, an audience of 1,000 still sat down to enjoy the show. That year, it was based upon a central television theme, including drama sketches, commercials, musical items and comedy. As well as providing a unifying activity for both boys and staff during term time, three local charitable organisations benefited by being awarded a share of 'the takings'.

The December issue of *The Craftsman* brought the sad news of the death of Brig 'Chalky' White, who had been the School's (as it was then!) second Commandant, between the years 1943 - 1947. He had gone on to reach the grand old age of eighty-eight years, having finally retired from the Army in 1947.

(The Obituary for Brig White is given in full as a separate annex to this chapter.)

On Sunday 20th January 1974, boys from the College took part in the fourth annual 'Wade Walk'. This twenty-mile sponsored walk is another event used to raise funds for local charities and other well-deserving causes. A sum of some £160 had been put together, going this year to Wokingham's Elderly Day Centre. Apart from the fact that all the participating boys enjoyed the walk itself, they were proud to be once again in the forefront of civic duties and the improvement of public relations.

Fuel economies and indigestion tablets

1974 saw the College still suffering from fuel economies, along with the rest of the country – although there was probably some regret that Prime Minister Edward Heath's 'three-day week' never quite made it as far as Arborfield! A 'Daylight Saving' scheme was introduced, which cut the lunch break by half an hour – no doubt thus increasing the NAAFI's

sale of indigestion tablets as boys hastened to bolt down their meal! *(Could it be that this is where the term 'fast food' originated? Ed.)* The afternoon tea break was abolished and – worst of all – there was to be no TV watching until after 18.00 hours! The *'Wombles of Wimbledon Common'* had to play all to themselves. *(The big tea-time hero in my day, the late Fifties, was 'Popeye the Sailor-man'. There would be a mad dash for the TV Room, to watch Popeye, in his continual battle to save 'Olive Oyl' from the clutches of 'Bluto'! Ed.)*

Some compensation for those trying times was gained by parties of apprentices, taking advantage of some complimentary tickets issued by an organisation called the 'Audience Participation Unit'. For only the price of the coach fare from Arborfield to the appropriate studio, boys were able to join the audience at a vast number of television programmes being presented around the London area. Amongst the shows seen were *'The Reg Varney Show'* at ATV Studios, Elstree; *'Bless This House'* at Thames Television; *'Doctor At Sea'* and *'The Freddie Starr Show'* at London Weekend; *'The Kiki Dee Show'* at the BBC Hippodrome, Golders Green; and *'Sunday Night at the London Palladium'* at … … … *(Only kidding! Ed.)*

In his address to the gathered parents and visitors attending the April 1974 'PoP', Col Tweed referred to the raising of the school-leaving age (to sixteen) that had come about in September 1972. The forecast then had been that previously high level of recruiting numbers would be drastically reduced. But, contrary to such expectations, the number of apprentices under training had not dropped significantly at all and the Commandant happily added that a reassuringly large intake was expected the following September.

Amongst the many arrivals and departures of PS personnel that year, it was a pleasure to welcome Miss Ayres back to the College, as the 'new' WRVS lady. Miss Ayres had spent a previous tour here, between 1967 and 1970, so would probably be well up to speed on any tricks that the new young boys thought they could get up to.

The spring term of 1974 proved a strenuous one for members of the Canoe Club, as they made preparations for the annual April race from Devizes, Wiltshire, all the way to Westminster in the capital city. The College had been entering a team now every year since 1966 and, indeed, had provided the winning individual canoe only the previous year, manned by A/T Sgt Greenop

Colonel H K Tweed 1973-76

and A/T Knight. The course stretches along 125 miles of water and is reputed to be the longest and toughest in the United Kingdom.

The training alone required a high degree of physical fitness, willpower and team spirit. It took place under the watchful eye of Sgt Syme, accompanied by his enthusiastic cries of *"Don't think of the pain, think of the glory"* and *"Come on, I'm not even sweating yet"*. Other supporting comments, along with responses from the boys, are deemed unsuitable for printing!

Also on the subject of canoeing, the College Chaplain, Rev Pratt, was proud to record that he had followed that particular sport for most of his adult life. He was fast coming to the end of his tour here at Arborfield, but was now looking forward to an even more challenging mission! He had been selected to accompany the famous Maj Blashford-Snell on his 'Livingstone-Stanley' expedition to Zaire, Central Africa. This would commemorate the century that had passed since Stanley's exploration of the Congo in 1874 and the famous search that Livingstone then undertook to find him.

The National Craftsman's Certificate

That same year, as a result of discussions with the City & Guilds of London Institute (CGLI), the National Craftsman's Certificate (NCC) was introduced for VMs. This nationally recognised qualification marked a further enhancement of the vehicle mechanic's apprenticeship. Meanwhile, yet another change of RSM took place in July of 1974, when RSM Petherick relinquished his appointment in favour of RSM H V Meredith, from the Irish Guards.

As was now the usual practice, May 1974 saw a grand total of eighty-five applicants for the annual Ten Tors expedition. Training sessions around the Farley Hill area and then, finally, on the moors themselves, eventually whittled this number down to less than a dozen. From this remaining number of hardy enthusiasts, a team of six, with two reserves, was selected. The Ten Tors in question were named *Steepleton, Silsden, Sitterford, Beardown, Gutter, Pugh, Lynch, Great Mist, Gren* and *Dinger* – a formidable mouthful, even when not having to walk round them all! The boys were proud to reach the finishing line to the applause of the assembled crowd, before making their way back to their tents with blistered feet and aching limbs – another 'mission accomplished'.

Early July 1974 was to see the opening of a newfound venture in the College. Following the 1973 Christmas Concert, it had been decided to form a Drama Group and, in January, rehearsals began for a stage presentation of *'The Long and The Short and The Tall'*. A wartime story, set in some far-eastern jungle, it proved a difficult rite of passage for the budding actors, due firstly to a shortage of volunteers and followed by several personnel changes. The final catastrophe was when one of the leading lights fractured his wrist on the assault course just four days before curtain-up! That the play ever made it on to stage at all was a credit to the cast of eight boys, though they will be the first to admit to the enduring assistance they had from the three gallant ladies 'behind the scenes', namely Audrey Ayres, June Eyre and Eugenie Gray.

Summer of 1974 saw the last edition of College magazine *The Arborfield Apprentice* in its previously long-established format, although the bright yellow cover must have been 'one in the eye' for traditionalists! Its contents were still of the time-honoured fashion however. The Pipe Band was happy to find that it remained still fully booked, with away trips to Hayling

Island and Basildon, Essex, in the offing.

The Band's scribe pointed out that the bagpipes had originated in Egypt around 1500 BC and then been adopted by the Romans when their influence began to spread throughout Europe. The Scots eventually used the music to stir men into battle, thus the pipes became known as 'an instrument of war'. *(Hands up all those who thought I was going to say 'torture'! Plus of course the inevitable question, 'What did the Romans ever do for us?' Ed.)*

At the August 'PoP', the Commandant gratefully received the presentation of the 'Cavalry Cup'. This had been presented by RAC members of the PS, and was to be awarded each term to the 'Best VM specialising in 'A' (Armoured) vehicle technology'. Another inaugural presentation that year was that of the 'BP Trophy', by the *British Petroleum Company*. This was in recognition of the College's technical involvement with the 'Build-a-car Competition' for schools, while the trophy itself would go to the VM who had achieved the 'Best Practical Training Result'.

Harry's 'Guide to Sailing'

On August 15th 1974, an enthusiastic party of boys joined the crew of the yacht *'Sabre'*, which was to be skippered by Mr Harry Shaw, an ex-boy with more years of 'life before the mast' than he'd like to remember! Harry's original experience, a crossing of the Channel to join the original 'Jersey Boys' back in 1939, obviously hadn't put him off sailing!

The yacht and its crew departed from Gosport, Hampshire, at 06.00 hours, to the skirl of the pipes being played by A/T Carmichael, one of the intrepid members of crew. A lengthy period of fine weather allowed for a smooth journey across the Irish Sea to the southwest corner of Ireland, before they headed for the Hebrides. During their trip, the boys excitedly sighted first a basking shark, then a school of leaping porpoises, a Russian trawler (spy ship?) and just one other yacht. The voyage was better known as Exercise 'Ocean Rock', which adequately described the small islet of Rockall, a mere twenty metres high and eighty metres in circumference – and 200 miles from anywhere – which was the planned destination! They actually missed out on some of the planned landmarks on the course, but the adventure was still voted a considerable success from the point of view of all concerned.

The Craftsman magazine of September 1974

gave news of the REME Pentathlon team, which was excelling in both Service and international competitions. Ex-boy, Sgt Jim Fox, had been awarded the MBE in Her Majesty's New Year Honours' List that year, reflecting a growing interest in this demanding sport. Jim also went on to win the Army Individual Championship Cup the same year.

Unbeknown to him at the time, a future Commanding Officer of the College was just starting his career that year, as a member of intake 74C. To this day, Derek McAvoy still reminisces over the 'bunkers', which were located outside the Technical Drawing Wing. 'Bunker running', up and down those steep slopes, was still much the fashion of leadership training demanded by the PTIs of the day. It was hard work, both physically and mentally, requiring good teamwork and a dogged determination to succeed. No doubt this had the desired effect on young Derek, but it is doubtful that he will be able to re-introduce this infamous 'sport' to a new generation of apprentices!

Another newly arrived member of that intake was promptly christened 'Gladys', due to his Seventies-style shoulder-length blonde hair! He was immediately escorted towards the barber's shop, where Charlie was apparently so impressed with the instant 'amputation' that followed, that the golden locks found an immediate pride-of-place on the shop wall. *"Hair today, gone tomorrow"*!

In November 1974, Lt Col Peter De La Haye RAEC, the SEO at that time, issued a paper which sought to establish the effects that TEC courses would have on the future of Further Education at the College. He noted that the TEC programme consisted of a phased operation, extending over a period of years, while any current technician awards would continue until the end of the decade. He urged that a College policy be formulated as quickly as possible, so that a College syllabus could be well in hand by the 1975 / 76 training year. He also encouraged DEME to form a working party to examine the overall effect of TEC on the complete REME training cycle.

A Royal visit

Another highlight in College life came towards the end of that year, with a further visit by HRH the Duke of Edinburgh, who, in his ceremonial capacity as C-in-C of the Corps, had been invited to review the College's winter 'PoP' on Monday December 9th. His visit literally got off to a 'flying start', when he personally landed a helicopter on the cricket field adjoining Hazebrouck Officers' Mess. Here he was met by three local dignitaries, in the shapes of the Lord Lieutenant of Berkshire, Maj Gen P G Palmer (representative Colonel Commandant REME) and Maj Gen A M McKay, DEME(A).

Later, whilst standing on the College saluting dais waiting for the march past, HRH turned and innocently asked Col Tweed what was the purpose of *"that old corrugated iron building"* at the far end of the square. When he was told that it was the College Gymnasium, which was to be used after the parade for the prize-giving ceremony, the Duke jokingly remarked, *"Well, I hope it lasts until then"*!

After presenting the prizes, Prince Philip addressed the boys, their parents and friends and members of staff. He explained that the Armed Forces were *"the nation's insurance policy"* and reminded the newest members of the Corps that this was *"not the end, but the beginning"* of their careers. There was much laughter when he also told the boys in particular that they had shown *"what splendid results can be achieved in perhaps not the most modern surroundings"*.

On December 13th, Mr Herbert William Lake was both pleased and proud to be awarded his Imperial Service Medal. Herbert had long ago entered military service as an A/T, being one of the very first intake (1923) at the ATS (Boys), Chepstow. After serving as a VM, he had joined the staff here at Arborfield on September 25th 1939, at the time that the School first opened. Since then he had continued to instruct in all aspects of Workshop Practice and Vehicle Technology for the following thirty-five years, encouraging

Members of the Drama Group re-enacting 'The Long and the Short and the Tall'

countless numbers of young apprentices on their way to becoming skilled soldier/tradesmen.

In that December's issue of *The Craftsman*, Harry Shaw provided an article that explained how he had come to participate in the 'Ocean Rock' sailing activity previously mentioned. He had been standing with *"a pint pot"* in his hand, pontificating to his military colleagues on the rather limited challenges presented by the current *"adventurous and external leadership training"* in the Army. He was then himself challenged to do something about it and, being no sort of shrinking violet, he immediately set upon the task with great gusto. At the conclusion of his article, Harry quoted the words of Doctor Johnson, when he had said, *"Every man thinks meanly of himself for not having been a soldier, or not having been at sea"*.

The Common Military Syllabus (Recruits)

A new training group system was introduced during 1975. This move was linked with the incorporation of the DAT inspired 'Common Military Syllabus (Recruits)' – or CMS(R) - and a rationalisation of the Workshop Practice training for all trades. A further step was taken when the Air Techs were enabled to complete their Class III trade course within the timetable and confines of the College.

In the Electronics Wing, a new syllabus termed 'Basic Electronics in the Seventies' was introduced. This latter phase marked a change in training philosophy – that of the existing 'Part to Whole'. Throughout the period, discussions were taking place between the College, SEE and AETW, with a view to co-ordinating and rationalising the College's proposed submission to the TEC for the running of both certificate and diploma programmes. These were designed to replace the two existing programmes, those for the C & G Technician Certificate and the ONC in Engineering.

At the end of February 1975, a party of apprentices from 'C' Coy set out on an exercise on the bank of the Kennet and Avon Canal. Here, they set about building a jetty, to be used for the paddle steamer owned by the Canal Trust. It proved to be a formidable task, as the baulks of timber to be used in the jetty's construction were extremely heavy. But necessity is the mother of invention, as they say. Finding the hulk of an old boat, half submerged in the murky waters, the boys managed first to refloat it, and then use its timbers to great effect on the resulting sturdy jetty that materialised. Due

credit was later given to the presence, only twenty-five feet away, of the local suitably-named watering hole, *'The Barge Inn'*!

It had long been the policy to produce a College magazine each term, but with publishing costs rising acutely, the spring 1975 edition of *The Arborfield Apprentice*, having been issued to cover the previous winter term as well, was also intended to become the final edition under that traditional title. Thus, by the following summer, the magazine was to see quite a change in its format, with its front cover now presenting it as *'The Journal'*.

In 1975, the College entered the field of 'Modern Pentathlon' for the very first time. It was an opportune moment, for HRH Prince Philip was not only REME's C-in-C, but also Patron of the Modern Pentathlon Association of Great Britain. For the past fifteen years, the sport had been well represented by REME personnel at Army, Inter-Service, International and Olympic level – who can forget the noble efforts of Sgts Derby, Fox, Twine and Younger? Jim Fox had been an apprentice, both here when he started in 1957 and then later at Carlisle. He had gone on to miss an individual Olympic Bronze Medal in 1976 by a mere seventeen points and was later awarded an MBE for his Herculean effort. The College now hoped to produce future Pentathletes to continue that proud tradition.

The College Cycling Club was able to report one of its most successful seasons on record. Taking part in the 1975 Army Ten-Mile (Adult) Championship, the College attained a creditable second place. Then, in the Junior Championships held at Harrogate in July, they swept the board in the 10, 15 and 25-miles individual Road Time Trials and won the 15-miles Team Time Trial, carrying off the Championship Shield for the fourth time in succession. They rounded off their memorable season by winning the Triangular Games 'Rose Bowl', a much-coveted trophy.

A change to the College magazine

Severe economies had dictated that the College magazine should now become *"home made"*, as the Commandant described it in his foreword. But, despite its rather 'down-market' appearance, when compared with previous publications, almost half of the contributions within its pages were from serving apprentices, which was very much to Col Tweed's pleasure. Thus it was that the very first issue of newly fashioned *The Journal* made its appearance in the summer of 1975, at a reduced price of 20p a copy, rather than the previous 50p charged for *The Arborfield Apprentice*.

One storyline in that first edition reported the success of a visit to sunny Malta for a sub-aqua expedition during April 1975. The experience gained there, in the crystal-clear blue waters, was far in excess of that normally gained in the UK, with a number of boys achieving a full ten hours of diving over the two-week period. Much closer to home, the hardy party of boys that visited the Peak District on a climbing exercise found weather conditions very much against them, cold and bleak with frequent flurries of snow. This inevitably made for quite hazardous conditions, but all of the boys performed well and were thus able to develop their all-weather stamina, technique and competence.

On May 22nd, Jim Fox had the honour of being invited to lunch with the Queen at Windsor Castle, in recognition of his fourteen years of achievement in the sport of Modern Pentathlon. He had recently been selected to represent his country in international competitions in Paris, Budapest and Sweden. The following month he was presented with the prestigious Baron Pierre de Coubertin Fair Play award at a ceremony in Paris, a great honour only awarded to *"true sportsmen throughout the world"*.

A certain newly arrived member of Junior ('J') Coy, A/T Murphy, struggled to come to terms with the age-old problem that had confronted many young apprentices over previous decades. It is the tradition and custom for the Horse Guards to have ranks appropriate to their military background. Thus, what is recognised by most as 'Sergeant', to them becomes 'Corporal of Horse'. Young Murphy suffered great difficulty with this, insisting on calling his drill sergeant by the reduced rank of 'Corporal'. This was tolerated for a time, but eventually the CoH blew his top, asking Murphy to explain his apparent rudeness. *"Well"*, explained the unfortunate Murphy, *"Oi thought your surname was O'Horse, Corporal, I mean, Sergeant"*. This story appeared in the first issue of *The Journal* and may not quite ring true to all ears but, as the storyteller remarked, *"Have you met Murphy?"*

A/T Seagrave of 'D' Coy had recently suffered severe injury from a motorcycle accident and now found himself at the Joint Services Medical Rehabilitation Unit (JSMRU), RAF Chessington. He enthused at the remarkable and effective treatment that was on offer, but added a warning that although it was relatively easy to get in, it was far more difficult to get out! Describing some of the horrific injuries that the doctors and surgeons had to deal with, he added that it had come as a salutary lesson to him that motorcycles can be pretty dangerous. Two other Arborfield boys were at the JSMRU at the same time, both having fallen victim to similar accidents.

Hard work, these hobbies

A/T Sgt Weyers extolled the virtues of belonging to the Corps of Drums, in his opinion *"the most hard working hobby within the College"*. Not that there wasn't a heap of fun to be had, as indicated by the numerous carnivals and processions held during the summer months. He recalled the Wokingham Carnival, where the Drum Major had been pelted with tomatoes, and on another occasion had led the Band up the wrong street in a strange town. Having worked so hard over a long period, young Weyers was looking forward to the Band 'disco', to be held at the end of term, as well as going to Wembley to see the Military Pageant.

Exercise 'True Grit' was to be a six-day climbing expedition, based in Derbyshire's Peak District, early in 1975. Two long-wheelbase *Land Rovers* had been duly serviced and loaded for the trip, but the 'best-laid' plans were suddenly dashed by an urgent request on behalf of Glasgow Corporation! The city's dustmen and street cleaners had gone on strike and any type of replacement vehicles was urgently required for rubbish clearance. Where better to get them from than Arborfield?

Luckily for the climbers, two smaller vehicles were quickly commandeered and, with a small trailer and the issue of some rail warrants, all of the boys finally made it to their destination. On the other hand, the cold weather they encountered on the gritstone outcrops gave them a far more demanding challenge than mere transportation difficulties. Their final day's climbing at Froggatt Edge was accompanied by an appalling blizzard and the talk turned to remarks about avalanches and survival techniques! This was a bit premature, the snow ceasing at a depth of two inches, but camp was struck pretty early the next morning, just in case.

For the very first time the College, represented by a team from 'B' Coy, took part in external tug-

The latest inmates? - No, just the Jeeps of 73C 4 Squad

of-war competitions. Working together in fine style, the team started off well by winning the Army Junior Championship at Aldershot. This set them up nicely for the Triangular Games, where they easily out-pulled the teams from both Harrogate and Chepstow. They then accepted an invitation to take part in an 'open competition', held at Ascot on July 5th. Again the team ran out worthy winners, with the highlight being the trophy presentation by a rather buxom young lady, going by the title of 'Miss South Ascot'. Later, at the REME Corps Championships, an exciting though gruelling afternoon ended with the boys narrowly beaten by a strong contingent from the SEME team from Bordon.

In July's edition of *The Craftsman*, old boy Bill Pusey of 46A published an article under the title of *"Down Memory Lane"*, which looked back fondly on his days at Arborfield almost thirty years previously. Despite the difficulties encountered in those days just after the war, it had still proved a rewarding experience. Another article in that same magazine told of another ex-boy, SSgt Charlie Brown of 56B, who had claimed a *"REME first"* at the British Army Training Unit, Suffield (BATUS) in Canada. Our *"intrepid hunting, shooting and fishing expert"* had crewed for a member of the Canadian Forces, and the pair had sailed home first in the Annual Regatta held at Trenton on Lake

Ontario. *(Well done, Charlie – or can we still call you 'Carlo'? Ed.)*

Life proved a tad difficult for those boys who went off on an 'Outward Bound' course later that year. The first sacrifice to be made was having to give up the dubious pleasures of smoking and drinking for the duration! After that, the physical efforts of two days' fitness training, followed by three days walking and camping on Dartmoor, must have seemed almost holiday-like. Another day was spent on a climbing exercise, with yet another spent working at a local hospital, helping with patients who were either physically or mentally handicapped, in some cases both. Canoeing on the River Dart and at Plymouth was to follow, with an afternoon of cross-country running and orienteering thrown in for good measure.

Caving and pot-holing later proved a demanding and very dirty experience, though the boys would probably have wished for a better cleansing experience than jumping off a thirty-foot high bridge into ice-cold water! With the final expedition taking the shape of a giant trek of one hundred miles across the open moors of Bodmin and Dartmoor, there is no doubt that the course gave all participants the chance to pit themselves against the elements.

Some hope for the OBA?

In September 1975, the Commandant received a letter from Col Dennis Bowen, an ex-apprentice and former CI at the College and now residing at the Army Scaling Authority in Woolwich. In his present post, he had come across a number of ex-boys of 1939 – 45 vintage, who were expressing a nostalgic wish to pay a visit to 'the old School'. In requesting permission for a visit, perhaps to coincide with a 'J' Coy Parents' Day, he recalled the times when, as the CI, he had tried to inject some enthusiasm into the OBA, along with another ex-boy, Charles Elsey (53A), who had done a lot of good work in this respect. *(Charles is still working away on good causes, looking after the pictorial archives at the REME Museum. Ed.)*

Although a Parents' Day trip was not deemed possible at that particular time, a visit by the Woolwich contingent was agreed and planned, to include a presentation of the College's present role, organisation and achievements, followed by a short tour of the present-day working environment. Col Tweed expressed his regrets that the OBA remained 'lifeless', stating that one main reason was the College's severe lack of the administrative capacity, which could have provided the necessary infrastructure for such matters. He looked ahead to the arrival of Col Barrie Keast as his successor, hoping that he may have some views on what should be done.

The autumn term of 1975 saw the accommodation of 'J' Coy *"bulging at the seams"*, following a huge intake of some 300 potential apprentices. The initial processing of such large numbers inevitably placed a considerable pressure upon the administrative machinery, with some long hours for the staff concerned. Accurate navigation through this hectic period was achieved by much sleight-of-hand with the military cadre programme, plus plenty of gazing into the fabled 'crystal ball'! When it became time for the boys' 'camp' at Crookham, administrative priorities quickly changed to the provision of supplies, such as fish and chips and chocolate bars. The introduction of many boys to 'compo' rations brought out many cooking techniques and recipes that Delia Smith '(or was it Fanny Craddock in those days?) has never even thought of, never mind tried!

The 1975 season for the Climbing Club closed on a note of great sadness, following the tragic death of Steven Cowie. Steven had been one of the Club's keenest climbers, possessing a great natural ability and lack of fear. For those who spent the final hours of his life at his side, they can have the great compensation that at least he died participating in a sport that he really enjoyed.

You mean motorcycling is now legal?

The variety of activities in which the apprentice of the mid-Seventies could take part was extensive and many 'old' ex-boys would express their delight that this had become the case. But a 'Motor-cycle Club'? Surely they hadn't spent all those long hours of yesteryear, sneaking out to ride their *BSAs* and *Nortons* from their illegal hideaways, only for the present boys to have a club of their own? But times change, things move on, and for 50p a week, that's exactly what the boys had now – and a good thing too, as borne out by the fact that all Club members were encouraged to attend road safety courses run by the Thames Valley Police, Traffic Division.

At the beginning of the winter term in 1975, the MTW was reformed, moving to 'I' Spider, Bailleul Barracks, on October 2nd. One section was immediately tasked with the organising and providing of instructors, for both apprentices and PS members. The introduction of the CMS(R) scheme, plus a new approach to the skill of shooting, had led to a great increase in the amount of military training required, with the time period to cover it now doubled from four to eight weeks. This new format was designed to ensure that all apprentices would subsequently receive the same standardised military training regime.

That winter's edition of *The Journal* reported that the Pipe Band was still a popular and going concern, with many of its varied presentations taking place outside of the College gates. One such engagement was at that year's Remembrance Day Parade in Newbury. After the initial playing through the town and then at the service, Band members were invited to attend a dinner, where they later gave a demonstration to the Mayoress and Charter Trustees of the town. The highlight appeared to be A/T Smith of 'C' Coy, whose undoubted talents at the 'sword dance' proved a great delight to the many young ladies in the audience.

Annex to Chapter 9

Brig J D White, DSO, MC

The death of Brigadier White at the age of eighty-eight represents the sad loss of one of the very few, if not the last, of those who saw service in REME and yet joined the Army before the First World War.

His service began in 1912, when he was appointed second lieutenant in the Middlesex Regiment (Territorial). He was posted to Gibraltar with the 8th Btn on the outbreak of World War I. He served with the BEF in France in the Middlesex Regt, 2nd Artists Rifles and attached to RE (Tank Corps). He was wounded twice, on the Somme and at Cambrai, and was awarded the DSO, MC and *Croix de Guerre*.

After the war, he was granted a regular commission in the Tank Corps as a captain. He applied for transfer to the RAOC in 1925, attended No.3 Ordnance Mechanical Engineering course at Woolwich and became an OME 2nd-class on March 24th 1927.

After a posting to HQ Northern Command, he served in India until 1935. This was followed by a year in Egypt and Palestine. On RHE as a lieutenant colonel, he was posted to Chilwell and later to HQ Aldershot Command as a colonel (OME 1st-class). On the outbreak of war he was promoted to acting brigadier and appointed POME Aldershot Command.

He embarked with the BEF as POME, was evacuated from Boulogne, returned to Normandy and was finally evacuated from La Pallice on 18th June 1940. Thereafter he became DDOS(E) and DDOS(E)(Org) Eastern Command until 4th November 1941 when he 'retired' with the honorary rank of brigadier. He was succeeded in his appointment by Brig Buttenshaw.

He was later offered re-employment and served as President of the Tradesmen's Interview Board until April 1943, when he became GSO 1 Tech of Northern Command, after transfer to REME. His last appointment was as Commandant Army Technical School (Boys), Arborfield, from 30th September 1943 to 10th May 1947. He finally retired on 1st November 1947. Our deepest sympathies go to his family at their sad loss.

Maj Gen W A Lord writes:
I first met 'J D', as he was known, when he came to Egypt in 1935 as SOME of the force assembled in Mersa Matruh to repel or hold the Italians. Typically he joined us in our meagre tented workshop mess, rather than live in more comfort at the HQ. I was to meet him on many other occasions after that. During his last appointment, my wife and I often stayed with the Whites at Arborfield. They were ideal hosts.
I have never met a gentler or more humane man. He was kindness personified but never hesitated to criticise when criticism was due. I grieve his death.

(The above Obituary was published in The Craftsman, issued in December 1973.)

—§—

Get on Parade!

Chapter 10

1976 - 79

Walking, shooting, swimming – life as normal!

The opening month of 1976 saw the annual charity event taking place once again, a twenty-mile round-trip known as the 'Wade Walk'. The start and finish line was at the Community Hall in Wokingham, with about ten per cent of the total *entourage* that year gathered from the ranks of boys here at the College. As well as these volunteer walkers, the College also contributed a large proportion of the route markers and radio operators on the day, which had by now turned into one of the 'social events' on the calendar. All in the name of charity of course, and from a total of some £6,000 raised that day, the College effort weighed in at around £300.

A new intake of eager young apprentices had arrived to fill the vacancies left by the previous 'J' Coy - with at least one notable exception. Having arrived at the College and been presented with a meal, this unnamed youngster decided he'd already seen enough of Army life and walked straight back out through the gates. He was most considerate however; he even left a brief note to explain exactly what was happening. On the negative side, however, he failed to leave the obligatory five-pound note that was his first day's pay, saying he needed that for the fare home!

At the winter camp held in Ashdown Forest, Sussex, two of the new recruits managed to 'break the ice' – literally that is, as they accidentally fell through the four-inch layer on the local lake. The anonymous member of staff who had gone to their assistance, having afterwards stripped off his wet clothes, was found to be wearing a pair of honey-coloured tights! That must have caused quite a stir – it's no wonder he remained anonymous! Another young apprentice, having 'bivvied down' for the night, decided he had the urgent need to 'spend a penny'. Having listened to the dire warnings about cold weather and camp hygiene, he wisely donned every stitch of clothing and steered well away from the tented area to do the business – only to fall into the nearby river!

In the January edition of *The Craftsman*, an obituary was published in memory of Percy Chivers, the skilled artisan and retired major who had so much to do with the design and construction of many fine sets of wrought-iron gates, both for the College and for the greater world outside, over a period of years.

(That obituary is published as a separate annex to this chapter.)

Just before dawn on March 1st 1976, the College square echoed to the tramp of many feet *(no, not the feet of many tramps! Ed.)*, as 3 Div assembled for their 'shooting camp'. A quick head-count and a check that all had their ear defenders, then it was off down to Bulford ranges on Salisbury Plain. There then followed four days of *"In the prone position, down!"* as the boys practiced their shooting skills. Probably the safest place to be was in the vicinity of the targets, as one wag was heard to put it! Friday arrived along with gale-force winds and lashing rain, so it was inevitably a *"happy bunch of campers"* that made their way back from Westdown Camp that weekend.

As the football season (1975 / 76) drew to a close, the College XI found itself in the exalted company of teams such as Liverpool, Sunderland, Hereford and Lincoln, in that they were all winners of their respective Leagues. The team had joined the East Berkshire 2nd Division, which consisted largely of works and village sides, the previous season. With only two games remaining, and positioned at the top of the table, the Arborfield lads found that they still had to face their closest rivals, the teams in second and third places. Both of these games were drawn, so the boys had their well-deserved triumph. Of a total of twenty-six matches, the boys had won no less than twenty, drawing another three and losing only three times, so they now looked forward to a season in the 1st Division.

In far sunnier climes, a party of the College's sub-aqua divers enjoyed two weeks swimming in the clear blue waters off Malta, between April and May 1976. Flying off from RAF Brize Norton, Oxfordshire, the boys reported the trip as a *"slick and efficient"* operation. Their whole stay at the George Cross island

Now look here lads, I want you to all sing, taking the timing from me!
Col Tweed bids farewell as he leaves in the summer of 1976

was a delight, with plenty of exhilarating diving at St George's Bay, Gnejna Bay, Paradise Bay and Anchor Bay among the highlights. The second week started on Monday 3rd May, with a ferry trip across from Malta to the neighbouring small island of Gozo, where the boys enjoyed the splendours of diving into and around the fabulous '*Blue Grotto*'. Their last couple of days were unfortunately hit by the arrival of some wet weather, which obviously prepared them well for their return to the UK, but overall the trip had once again proved a marvellous experience, especially for those novices who had been diving for the very first time.

An Old Boy returns – as Commandant

In June 1976, command of the College passed to Col B G Keast, CEng, MIEE, MBIM. This was indeed a 'red letter' day in the long College history, as Barrie Keast proudly returned as the first ever ex-Arborfield boy to take up post as its Commandant. Colonel Barrie had served his apprenticeship at what

was then the ATS (Boys) between 1945 and 1948, having been one of those few students selected for the previously mentioned Woolwich Arsenal Engineering Cadetship Scheme. Having completing his training in electronics as a Tels Tech, he went on to gain a HND in Electronics and Mathematics during 1952. Barrie was commissioned into REME just three years later, and then served worldwide in such places as Australia, Canada, Iran and the Middle East. During his service he held a variety of appointments at Field-force operational workshops, large static workshops, Research and Development (R & D) establishments and even some civilian firms.

Newly arrived from commanding the REME Wing of the RA Range in the Hebrides, Colonel Barrie made this initial statement in that summer's edition of *The Arborfield Apprentice*:

> *"In this, the first College magazine since I became Commandant, I would like to say how pleased I am to return to Arborfield and*

that I consider it an honour and a privilege to be selected for the post.

On learning that I am an ex-Arborfield apprentice, many people ask whether I have noticed any change since I first came here thirty-one years ago. Certainly, the buildings haven't changed at all! My first impression is that the present apprentice is every bit as good as we were, he eats well, is much better paid and works a lot harder. My strongest impression is that the place is smaller than I remember, but this may be due to the fact that I was some eight inches shorter when I first joined in 1945."

Computers? They'll never catch on!

The Colonel's subsequent tour of command back here at Arborfield was to be marked by two major events that were destined to have a significant effect upon apprentices' training. The first of these, during April 1977, was when the College took delivery of what was then classed as a 'powerful' mini-computer system and the second, in the following September, was when the new TEC courses were launched. The TEC was able to award the following qualifications: Certificate, Higher Certificate, Diploma and Higher Diploma. These would eventually replace the following technician qualifications: all CGLI Technician Certificates, ONC and Diplomas, HNC and Diplomas.

The computer, a *Data General 'Nova'* machine, was obtained as a consequence of much research and hard work, undertaken by members of the EQC staff. This all took place under the umbrella of a REME-sponsored project known as 'ASCOT RAIN', a pleasant sounding acronym which stood for 'ADP in Support of Control of Training'. The term 'ADP'

Colonel Keast executing a smart side-step as he inspects apprentices of 'C' Coy in 1976

was itself an acronym of those times, standing for 'Automatic Data Processing'. This was a now out-dated term which has long-since been replaced by the more familiar phrases of 'IS' (Information Systems) and/or 'IT' (Information Technology). The equipment (or hardware) was provided to enable the College staff to implement a system of Computer Managed Learning (CML), which was developed during the project.

Instrumental in the 'bedding in' of all this new technology was our very own 'Toy Soldier', W E N 'Bill' Pusey, ex-apprentice of 46A and now part of SEE's instructional staff. Due to the fact that SEE had no similar computing facility of its own, it had been authorised that the College's access to the new computer be shared by 'BAOR' – in this case, standing for 'British Army Over the Road'! For many months afterwards, Bill was to be seen, fair weather and foul, regularly traipsing the path between College and School. On these trips he would be pushing what appeared to be an old push-chair, which contained reams of computerised punch-cards and print-outs, containing the results and analysis of SEE's students. *(It is rumoured that the wheel ruts can still be seen today, whenever rain is expected! Ed.)*

Not unnaturally at first, the arrival of the computer was received with mixed feelings and not a little suspicion, by both the members of staff and students alike. But in the following year, at the summer 'PoP', the Commandant, in his address to the attending parents, was able to say with reference to the new technology:

> "It has not developed into a 'Big Brother' as some people feared, but rather a 'Man Friday' that has helped in the decision-making process, while in no way affecting the individuality of the apprentice".

A most welcome 'travel scheme' was introduced during 1976, whereby apprentices could choose to fly home on leave, rather than use the railway network, a system that had been in operation for many years. With the concessionary fares on offer from *British Airways* and *British Midland Airways*, the costs were not too much in excess of what had been paid out before. But the outstanding benefits were in the time reductions to places such as Teesside, Aberdeen and Glasgow. Thirty-five young apprentices took advantage of the new scheme for a 'trial run' and only two minor delays

were encountered, so it looked like it would provide a well-worth venture for the future.

Activities during a heatwave

The 'Summer of 76' will go down as historically one of the hottest on record, with large areas of the country suffering from drought-like conditions, as river beds and reservoirs dried up and cracked. The parched landscape began to look like something that wouldn't have been out of place in one of the desert regions of central Africa. Water shortages became the norm and, by September, standpipes were being set up in the streets of many towns and villages, as local inhabitants had to join queues in order to collect their water rations in an assortment of jugs, jars and buckets.

During that summer term, three intrepid civilian members of the Vehicle Wing instructional staff, Messrs Brown, Keep and White, volunteered to head off to Borth, located on the mid-Wales coast just north of Aberystwyth. The purpose of their mission was to assist the Adventure Training Officer, Capt Porter, on the supervision of a two-week External Leadership camp. As these posts had always normally been taken up by serving Sergeants from the military side of life, it was a great credit to these civilian instructors that they were able to successfully fulfil their tasks, supervising the boys at such activities as canoeing, mountain walking and rock climbing. They certainly must have thoroughly enjoyed themselves, as all three later volunteered to do it all again!

Other staff and apprentices of Vehicle Wing were, at the same time, involved in a 'community project' at the Crich Tramway Museum in Derbyshire. Here they had the task of building a ramp, which would allow 'ease of access' to the Museum café for wheelchair occupants, as well as the laying of a concrete floor and tramlines in a newly built vehicle display shed. The group's accommodation, during the period of their project, was provided by the Command Ordnance Depot (COD) at nearby Chilwell. During this same time, the boys were able to enjoy a visit to 38 Central Workshop REME, during which time they played a cricket match against that Workshop's civilian apprentices.

In July of 1976, members of the Rock Climbing Club once again dodged the RSM's drill parade, but were made to suffer for it, as they were transported all the way to North Wales in the back of a noisy old 4-tonner. Other expeditions during the year saw the boys enjoy some challenging climbs at the Avon Gorge near Bristol, at Swanage on the Dorset coast, and at Ambleside, up in the pleasant mountainous scenery of the Lake District. Swanage provided the most demanding adventure, as the boys found themselves climbing on sheer limestone cliffs, which dropped just about vertically down to the sea below. At Ambleside, the stark surroundings of an old stone hut, used as their hidey-hole, was ameliorated by a quick 'recce' of the local boozers, where they were able to pursue the twin pleasures of 'beer and birds'!

By the 1970s it was not unusual for apprentices to get involved with the local community as seen here working on a project to build a footpath for wheelchair bound youngsters.

That same summer term also gave much fun to those boys involved in archeology, of both the 'industrial' and 'field' styles. Boys of the Railway Group, for instance, spent many days assisting in the preparation for the many Open Days held at Didcot Railway Museum. None of the boys involved had yet qualified as either Driver or Fireman, (which was probably fortunate for the travelling public) but the boys lived in hope. The field archeologists who had planned to assist at a dig at the Saxon cemetery at Pewsey, Wiltshire, were disappointed when local heath fires near Arborfield demanded their being held back on stand-by as fire fighters. Work on an Iron Age site on Marlborough was hoped to compensate for this letdown.

Following that memorably hot summer, members of the Sub-aqua Club paid a most welcome 'cooling off' visit to Kimmeridge Bay in Dorset that September. The *Dorset Evening Echo* later reported that one of the diving party, eighteen-year old John Eccleston, had picked up a fossilised portion of an *ichthyosaurus*, a pre-historic reptile, which had roamed the area some 150 million years previously. John, who had joined the College as an apprentice VM in 1975, later presented his discovery to the Dorset County Museum in Dorchester.

On as many Sundays as possible, keen members of the Gliding Club set off to Bicester in Oxfordshire, where they were to partake in the exhilarating delights of soaring up into the blue skies, but without the assistance of an aero-engine. Learners at this exciting sport climb into their lightweight aircraft, then find themselves being winch-towed up at what seems an alarming angle, before completing a four-minute circuit of the airfield, finally landing and picking up the stomachs that had been left behind on take-off!

Olympic Gold for an ex-apprentice

At the Olympic Games held in Montreal, Canada, during 1976, the College was proud to acknowledge the success of Sgt Jim Fox, our well known ex-boy of 57B intake and now based at SEE, who had helped Britain's Modern Pentathlon team to the winning of a well-deserved Gold Medal. Already the proud holder of a MBE, Jim had long been a keen and accomplished member of the Corps team, which had provided many athletes who went on to represent their country at this exacting sport. He had already been part of the British Olympic team three times, in 1964 and 1968, and at those tragic Games held in Munich during 1972, when a number of Israeli athletes had been assassinated by terrorists. Here, Jim had finished in fourth place, just missing out on the bronze medal spot by a solitary shooting point.

Jim excelled at the five sporting disciplines: cross-country running, freestyle swimming, horse riding, shooting and fencing. By the time of the 1976 Games, he was arguably one of the fittest men in the country. It was during the fencing event that Jim involuntarily became involved in the exposure of one of the most notorious cheating scandals in Olympic history. He was amazed to discover that his Russian opponent was electronically registering 'hits' that had never actually touched him. It turned out that the Russian's foil had been rigged to a secret triggering device! On being caught out in this nefarious scheme, the Russian competitor was summarily bundled off on the next flight home to Moscow. Meanwhile Jim, along with his team-mates Adrian Parker, Andy Archibald and Danny Nightingale, went on to win the five-sport event and all pick up the well-deserved title of 'Olympic Champions'.

Following a hectic summer of engagements at carnivals and fetes, the College Band was delighted to provide a less formal musical feast, as escort for Jim Fox on his homecoming to Arborfield. The Brass Band, Pipe Band and Corps of Drums had been particularly busy that year. Between them, they had performed at the Lambeth Festival of Sport in London, various Royal British Legion events and a particularly fine Beating of Retreat, as well as all the usual College drills, Parents Days and Passing-out Parades.

On October 2nd 1976, the Combined Services Rugby team entertained the Japanese national side down at Devonport. It is well worth a mention here, as amongst the eight Army representatives chosen to play that day were three ex-Arborfield boys, namely the veteran SSgt Johnny Mills (1957 - 60), Cpl David Spawforth (1964 - 67) and Sgt John Morgan (1968 - 71). Johnny Mills had played for the Corps since 1962 and regularly represented the Army since 1969. David, or 'Spoff', had previously captained the College side and became the first known apprentice to represent REME at his sport whilst still serving here.

Later that month, the College's links with Iran were fortified by a visit from Brig Gen G H Alaee, who was Commandant of the Imperial Iranian Technical High School which, to some extent, was modelled upon the AAC, Arborfield. At the conclusion of his visit, the Iranian Commandant presented superbly mounted photographs of our own Queen and Prince Philip, the Shah and Queen of Iran, and a handsome decorative plate, all of which were then used to adorn the walls of our own Commandant's office.

The winter term of 1976 brought about the departure of Mr Bill Hall, who had served here as the Supervising Instructor of Vehicle Wing since 1971. Bill had joined up as an apprentice blacksmith at the AAS Chepstow as long ago as January 1933, continuing his service as a member of the RAOC after that. Following eventual war service in Egypt, Cyprus, Sudan, Libya and Italy, Bill had subsequently changed his trade to VM and transferred into REME just three days after its formation in October 1942. Seven years later, Bill left the Army and became a Civilian Instructional Officer. He had somehow, somewhere,

Look girls, the dance finished at 10 o'clock last night - you really must go now.

gained the nickname of 'Diesel Dan', but reckons that only certain National Servicemen of the time would know why! Bill went on to serve ten years down at SEME Bordon, prior to his last five years here at the College.

A sweet solution to a problem

Metalworking members of the Hobbies Club had been set an unusual challenge during 1976. Their objective was to produce, in alloy mounted on a shield, the crest of the Thames Valley Constabulary. The only 'blueprint' or plan available was a paper sketch of the coat of arms, so assistance was sought from 43 Command Wksp at nearby Aldershot, from where one of its apprentices eventually came up with a perfect wooden mould. The crest was subsequently cast from this, but then came the problem of 'how to cast the motto', as the letters for this were far too small to carve from wood. A brilliant solution was finally thought up by Mrs Sadd, cake-decorator *par excellence* and wife of one of the civilian instructors, who 'piped them on' with icing sugar! This ingenious idea eventually led to the successful production of the required crest.

Members of the Model Club were pleased and proud to be awarded first place, for the second year running, at the National Championships held at RAF Hendon in the December of 1976. However, the trophy which had been previously awarded had also proved to be 'rather odd shaped' (which was a kind description!). It therefore came about that the Club now decided to leave their mark on the International Plastic Modellers Society (IPMS), by purchasing and presenting a brand new shield to the President of the Society. Known as the 'Arborfield Trophy', it was indeed fitting that the first winners of the shield would be the College itself.

PS members of the Sergeant's Mess had been honoured in October 1976, by a visit from ex-RSM Bill Lee, late of the Duke of Wellington's Regt. Wined and dined as a birthday treat, Bill later entertained Mess members with his scintillating memories of his service during the years of World War I. Towards the end of that year, the Mess also entertained two Warrant Officers of the Australian Allied Forces for a while. Whether or not they learned anything of value was not made clear – but they certainly made a big impression on the prizes in the Christmas Draw!

For a long period of time, all metalwork training had been carried out in the A & G Wing, but during 1976, with the introduction of a common engineering syllabus, all Aircraft metalwork training was brought under the control of Aircraft Wing. A & G Wing would, however, continue to provide the basic skills and experience for blacksmithing, welding and general machine work.

The OBA - rising from the ashes

The welcome return of an ex-boy as College Commandant also saw the phoenix-like return of *The Arborfield Apprentice*. The magazine remained in its 'homemade' format, but the title reverted to the long established one of many a long year as the official School, and then College, newsletter. Barrie Keast's establishment at the College also became the catalyst for an upsurge in enthusiasm for the ethos and rebirth of the AOBA. Being a genuine 'old boy' himself, he now found himself in a position where he could greatly influence the future drive and direction of what had, much to his horror at that time, become rather a moribund Association.

Thus was held a meeting of interested parties on November 10th 1976, at which was discussed 'the way ahead'. Many kind offers of assistance had already been received from high-ranking officers in 'the world outside' and it was essential that there should be 'link men' in place at the various REME Training Centres. With the able support and dedication to the cause contributed by Harry Shaw, long serving member of staff and also an ex-boy of 39B vintage, letters were sent out to all those units where REME tradesmen were based, asking for their support in reviving the membership and existence of the OBA. To this end, an 'Open Day' at the College was proposed and accepted, to take place early in the following year.

1976 had seen the *Lynx* helicopter introduced into service with the Navy, which was followed in 1977 by its being sent to the Army's Intensive Flying Trials Unit (IFTU) at Middle Wallop. By this time, ex-54B boy Clive Soord had been given a short service commission and was posted to the REME element of the IFTU to 'head up' the avionics side of support to the new aircraft. Some time later, Clive was sent on a course at the REME Officers' School here at Arborfield, and took the chance to wander round the old boys' school. He found it *"an emotional and quite an eerie experience to walk among those spider blocks, which brought back so many memories"*.

That particular year ended on a sad note for the College, with the untimely death of Cfn Brian Swanson, REME, in a motorcycle accident near his home in Aberdeen. 'Jock', as he was popularly known during his time at the College, was on the last day of his leave, prior to a posting to what would have been his first adult unit, the KOSB. To an earlier generation of boys, this would bring back memories of another 'Jock', another motorcycle and, sorrowfully, another death – that of Andrew Grieve, almost twenty years previously.

Usually the gloomiest term of the year, instead the winter of 1976 / 77 proved a high spot for the soccer team of 'D' Coy, who triumphantly carried off the Army Apprentices' Football Cup. This was particularly pleasing for the Company Commander at the time, Maj Peter A'Hearne RA, as he had previously commanded a Company at the AAC Carlisle, that had also won the same trophy. Maj A'Hearne had served thirty-five years with the RA, but has a later claim to fame as an occasional TV star! A keen member of 'amateur dramatics', Peter has appeared as 'an extra' in several TV productions.

Returning from their three weeks leave, still *"full of the Christmas spirit"*, the members of 'C' Coy were horrified to find that, following some severe frosts, all the radiators in 'J' spider had inopportunely burst. Thus for a period of time, the Company became nomadic, with people moving around from room to room as drying-out operations were carried out. Spirits, possibly held over from Christmas, were raised again by the winning of the inter-Company Snooker Competition. The foul weather of that winter, rain followed by frost, more rain, then frost once again, certainly played havoc with the sports fields, so that training became confined to either road-running or use of the Gymnasium's indoor facilities for devotees of all sporting pastimes.

Historic meeting for Old Boys

On January 25th 1977, using the presence of now-legendary Jim Fox as a sort of talisman, a historic meeting of more than 150 ex-apprentices, representing all ranks, intakes and ages, took place at an 'Open Day' held in the College. There were large contingents from Bordon, Christchurch, Middle Wallop and Woolwich as well as Arborfield. Because of the numbers, that meeting had to be held in the Camp Hall, which certainly jogged the memories of many. Following a presentation by Col Barrie Keast, the assembly voted by an overwhelming majority to give their support to the OBA, not just in a tenuous way, but by making every effort to attend both future reunions and AGMs. Thus it was proposed to hold a 'Grand Reunion' over the weekend of 15th / 16th October later that year. Happily, this now annual event has continued ever since, with even the closure and eventual demolition of the 'old school' barracks unable to dampen the enthusiasm of those old boys who now regularly attend these nostalgic and happy occasions.

By the spring term of 1977, the pattern of External Leadership camps at the College had become well established. Some apprentices were returning for their third camp, with a fair degree of competence now having been achieved. For many of these boys, these camps had been their first experience of stress when facing a physical challenge, with the majority ably rising to the occasion in splendid fashion.

According to the programme for the 'PoP', held on April 13th of that year, it would appear that the 'Infantry Officers' Challenge Cup' was not awarded. In its place however, a new trophy, 'The Wavell Cup', was now being awarded for the 'Best Achievement in Adventurous Pursuits'. This had been presented to the College by the Wavell Memorial Trust, in memory of Maj the Earl Wavell MC, of the Black Watch, who had been killed in an ambush whilst serving in Kenya during 1953.

The Easter weekend of 1977 saw the Canoe Club once again taking part in the 'Devizes to Westminster' race. This long-distance competition is held over a four-day period, the daily consecutive distances being three of over thirty miles each, and a final one of seventeen miles, with three overnight stops at Newbury, Marlow and Teddington. Competing crews have to be 'self-supporting', meaning that they must carry all their own field camping and emergency supplies within the canoe. From an initial entry of sixty two-man crews, the College was proud to hold places 11 and 12 individually, with its other two crews assisting in the gaining of an overall third place for the College team.

On Thursday 12th May of that year, a group of twenty-five A/Ts was chosen to assist at the opening ceremony for the Folly Court Guide-dog Centre, to be performed by HRH Princess Alexandra. Designated as car-park attendants and ushers, the apprentices

The Inspecting Officer at the August 1977 Passing Out Parade

performed in their normally efficient and impeccable fashion, and the ceremony passed by quite uneventfully. However, following the departure of HRH, and with several hundred cars queuing up and attempting to leave the area, the heavens opened.

An initial downpour of hailstones, accompanied by some thunder and lightning, was quickly followed by torrential rain, which soon turned the whole car park into a quagmire. It is to the eternal credit of the young car-park attendants that they handled the whole business with such calmness and fortitude. Despite being soaked to the skin and mud-spattered from head to toe, they managed to ensure that every single vehicle was, somehow, either driven or pushed to safety and set safely on its way back home.

As from 1st June 1977, *British Rail* (as it then was!) announced that 'accompanied bicycles' could, in future, be taken on board trains, free of charge, for all journeys. This policy change was undoubtedly due to a pioneering group of boys from the College who, in April earlier that year, had left Reading Station *en route* to the Easter 'Festival of Cycling', held on the Channel Island of Guernsey. Each individual apprentice clutched a suitcase in one hand and carried under the other arm a hessian sack, inside of which was contained a bicycle. The boys had been quick to latch onto the fact that a hessian sack, whatever its contents, was classed as 'hand luggage' and thus permitted to travel for free! Needless to say, the concentrated riding that later took place on Guernsey provided an excellent preparation for the anticipated tough cycling season ahead.

In August 1977, former Commandant Col D A Brown was enjoying a period of 'loan service' to distant Iran. He used this opportunity to pay a visit to the Technical High School at Masjed-Is-Suleiman, where he presented a return gift from Arborfield to commemorate the 1976 visit from the Iranian Commandant. This consisted of a cast REME crest, in colour, mounted upon a shield of polished oak, together with a parchment scroll. All these items had been produced here within the College.

A letter received by the OBA that same month contained a request for details and information regarding the revival of interest in all things 'old boy'. It came from D J B Howes, who reported that he had joined as an apprentice to the RAOC on October 6th 1938, then found himself attached to the RASC Apprentices' School in Jersey, pending completion of the camp here at Arborfield. He finally arrived here in August 1939 and became one of the first members of REME, upon its formation in 1942. Yet another link back to the early days!

It was just prior to the summer recess that the Caving Club, having had two expeditions to Somerset during the previous term, set off to tackle some more underground work in Yorkshire. Here, they found that the caves differed quite a lot from those already encountered, in that lots of ladders and lifelines were required, in order to descend some vertical pitches. It proved an exhausting experience at first, but the situation eased with practice and familiarity. On Tuesday August 9th, their 'day of recovery' included a rugged walk up Ingleborough, which ended at a height of 2,400 feet – some recovery!

'An inexorable machine'

In the summer 1977 edition of *The Arborfield Apprentice*, Col Barrie Keast was able to look back on his first year as Commandant as *"an inexorable machine that regularly takes in the new intake, picks up a General at the right time and relentlessly produces a Passing-out Parade"*. He remained convinced that, despite the many recent swingeing cuts in the Defence budget, the Army (including the College of course) still offered a worthwhile career to young people, along with the opportunities for personal challenge. He went on to reassure all staff and apprentices that, here within the College, everyone would still be considered as an individual, able to develop his talents, even within the rigid framework of Army discipline.

Due to a variety of reasons, such as lack of training time and duty calls, the College Rugby team had suffered a frustrating season of mixed results during the autumn of 1977. Thus it was that the forthcoming winter games meeting with old rivals Chepstow looked a forbidding fixture, as military and adventure exercises again claimed a number of key players. One young apprentice, who had been pitchforked into the side as a last minute replacement, played excellently for the first twenty minutes, until felled by a well placed knee! Five minutes later he again went down, but picked himself up to tackle an opponent, the largest player on the field, who was heading at full speed for what seemed an inevitable try 'under the posts'. The try was averted, the game saved, although our unfortunate but gallant hero spent the rest of the game in the MRS. But, thanks to his brave contribution, in true Arborfield tradition, the game ended with victory by a score of 9 points to 3.

In *The Craftsman* of September 1977, the College was able to announce that, *"contrary to what many readers may have thought, the College is alive and well, still situated in the old and picturesque accommodation that generations of apprentices remember so well"*. However, evidence was now being gathered that the College would *"shortly"* be moving to a new home – or even to an old one as it eventually turned out! Col Keast was at pains to advertise the forthcoming reunion of its old boys and hoped that attendance would make it all worth while.

It is sad that the same magazine reported the death of Col Denis Bowen, who had done his best to bring attention to the moribund state of the OBA just a few years previously. Happily, those efforts had assisted in bringing about a revitalisation of OBA fortunes, so Denis left behind a proud legacy. Having joined as an apprentice himself (in 1939), Denis's potential was soon recognised and he was selected to attend an Engineering Cadetship at the Royal Technical College, Salford. He was to return here to Arborfield in 1965 as OIC Electrics Dept and then again in 1970, now as the CI – the first ex-apprentice to fulfill this prestigious appointment. Denis *"left the field of play"* having just watched the touring British Lions beating the All Blacks on their home soil in NZ, thanks to a live TV broadcast.

Welcome return to tradition

And so it was, as had been arranged in January earlier that year, that October 15th / 16th 1977 was to see the best attended Old Boys' Reunion (officially, the fifteenth) in many a long year. It took place within the original barracks, with many old boys, indeed some *very* old boys, amongst the ninety-three ex-apprentices who turned up, delighted to be quartered in their old familiar 'spider' blocks for the duration of the weekend. *(Was it only a rumour that the NCOs' bunk-rooms were allotted to the more senior ex-boys? Ed.)* A display of photographs certainly helped to jog memories of old faces and long-forgotten stories. The OBA post-bag must have bulged for many months afterwards, as letters of congratulation came pouring in, along with the enthusiastic forecasts of many more such occasions to take place in the future. The last reunion before this historic occasion had been more than ten years previously, so it was to be hoped that things could only get better from then on.

Following an afternoon of sporting engagements, the AGM was held in the Camp Hall. The old boys were then ceremonially 'piped in' to dinner, which was served with great skill by young boys then serving their second term. Guests of honour at dinner that Reunion evening were Maj Gen H McDonald Smith BSc, CEng, FIMechE, FIEE, who was the current DGEME and Brig P H Lee, Commandant of the REME Training Centre. The General later wrote to Col Keast, in words that virtually turned into a prediction:

> *"I thought that Saturday night's venture with the Arborfield Old Boys was a most successful occasion and that, given the continuing support and enthusiasm from yourself and your successors, the event will prosper. It was quite clear that those who were present enjoyed the occasion and will therefore be good ambassadors, by spreading the word amongst their friends and hopefully returning in future years."*

During 1977, the College Model Club was proud to once again win a prestigious award, for the third successive year, at the National Championships of the IPMS. The winning effort that year consisted of a *diorama* (a small scale model, seen through a viewing aperture) showing the scene of a heroic lifeboat rescue attempt, which had taken place in 1953. It recalled the desperate launch of the Arbroath lifeboat *'Robert Lindsey'*, during a tremendous storm and in almost impossible conditions. A full six of the crew of seven lost their lives on that terrible day, and it was to their lasting memory that the College's entry was dedicated.

That same year, 1977, had seen countrywide celebrations in honour of the Queen's Silver Jubilee, after twenty-five years since Her Majesty Queen Elizabeth II had succeeded to the throne, upon the death of her father, King George VI. During that nostalgic year, the Queen's Silver Jubilee Medal was awarded and that autumn's publication of *The Arborfield Apprentice* announced that four members of the PS had each been granted one of these coveted prizes. One of the medals was awarded to Mr T Latham who, as a member of the RAOC back in 1939, had actually helped to dig out the air-raid shelters – or bunkers - that could still be seen in parts of the Camp. Mr Latham had returned to Arborfield in 1946, joining Vehicle Wing as a civilian instructor, and was the longest serving member of the College staff when he retired after thirty-one years. Another recipient was a much younger Capt Robinson, 2I/C of 'J' Coy, who had himself been an apprentice here as a member of 60B.

A fishy story!

It was also during 1977 that the 'Great Fish' story finally came to a conclusion. It had long been rumoured that, deep in one of the College's massive 24,000-gallon static water tanks, there lived a monstrous fish. Many stories also told of unsuccessful attempts to catch this monster, and of the way that it had broken free of even the heaviest of lines and hooks - it was certainly a case of 'the one that got away'. Thus it was that the tank next to the Fishing Club hut became the first one to be drained, after many abortive attempts to start the pumping engine!

With only six inches of water remaining at the bottom of the tank, it was A/T LCpl Mason, suitably dressed in thigh-high waders, who made his grand entry. To many excited cries of *"There he goes!"*, *"It's a cod!"*, *"No, it's a roach"* and the like, young Mason made about ten splashing circuits of the tank before finally netting the elusive fish. It turned out to be a member of the carp family, measuring some twenty-eight inches and weighing in at around seventeen pounds, and a quick inspection of its mouth showed no evidence that it had ever been hooked.

The fish was eventually transferred to a new home in the lake at Bailleul. More water tanks were cleared in the days that followed, leading to a further very large rise in the lake's population, with a mix of roach and

Colonel Keast presenting the Commandants Cup in December 1977

rudd, carp and tench, a large catfish and several assorted goldfish! Amongst the other 'treasure' brought up to the light of day were many old bedsprings, bike frames, NAAFI beer mugs – plus around thirty empty wine bottles and even a six-foot locker! Rumours that the RSM was thinking of starting his own scrap business later proved unfounded!

On December 16th, Arborfield lost one of its longest serving officers, when Maj Ezra Rhodes started his second retirement, having been associated with the Garrison for the previous twenty years. Originally posted to the boys' school as Adjutant, he later became its Administrative Officer (AO) before retiring from the Army in 1962. Appointed as a Retired Officer (RO), Ezra filled the post of Project Liaison Officer (PLO) at SEE, spending four years in the job and seeing in SEE's *"first rebuild"*. In 1966, he was appointed as Garrison PLO, moving onto the staff of HQ REME Training Centre, where he was to spend his last eleven years, seeing the complete process of Arborfield's redevelopment all the way *"from the drawing board to bricks and mortar"*.

The happy feeling that usually heralds the approach of Christmas and the New Year was increased in 'D' Coy by the holding of a candlelit Company Carol Service, followed by a splendid buffet supper. The whole evening was much helped by a welcome visit from the Reading Branch of the Salvation Army Band, who enthusiastically played all the carols for the staff and boys to sing along to. The previous term, autumn 1977, had also seen the installation of a launderette. This had proved so well used and popular that lower charges were being considered its use for the new term. At the same time, the old and 'clapped out' Company television sets were replaced by new state-of-the-art versions, much appreciated by those boys who had 'twiddled and fiddled' with the tuning knobs of the old sets for too many years.

Raving and caving

Ten young members of the College Ski Club set off for Italy during that winter term, accompanied by two Club instructors and some members of their families. The trip took the form of a 'package deal', which had been arranged with a holiday firm. The flight itself, to the industrial city of Milan, proved uneventful, but the following coach journey to Livigno, up in the Italian Alps near the Swiss and Austrian borders, proved to be a seven-hour ordeal. Fortunately it took place mainly during the hours of darkness, so 'kipping' provided the best form of whiling away the time.

Apart from a few minor injuries, the following week's skiing turned out to be most enjoyable. With Livigno being designated as a duty-free area, whisky at only £1 a bottle proved a popular purchase! A *'disco'* evening rounded off the holiday with the opportunity for a good 'rave', while the *'grappa'* on offer was guaranteed to *"grow hair on a billiard ball"*. The return journey back to Milan was just as formidable, a 5 a.m. departure, followed by another boring seven hours on the coach. The tedium was not helped by the fact that they then had a five-hour wait at the airport, before their delayed flight home was allowed to eventually take off.

In complete contrast to the delights of a ski-slope, another party of boys had started the term with a trip to Derbyshire. As members of the Caving Club, they were enjoying a weekend at a cottage belonging to a local organisation. When they found that they had to share accommodation with a number of *"scantily dressed young ladies"*, it must have been a wrench next morning when they set off to enter the first cave, a small muddy one called Gautrius Hole. The grubby group of cavers that emerged quickly made their way to a 'wet' cave some distance away, where a stream was used to clean up. The intrepid group then tackled Knotlow Caverns, basically the remnants of some old lead mines, but also containing a number of natural caverns. Despite the cold and misty conditions, much valuable experience was gained prior to further visits that term to Monmouth and Yorkshire.

That old saying, *"It'll be all right on the night"*, was well to the fore as the end-of-year concert drew near. It was to be a Cecil B de Mille style production, with a 'cast of thousands', supported by an orchestra that would have graced any of Mr D'Oyly Carte's original efforts. In truth it was on a slightly smaller scale than that, but there is no doubt that the College's version of *'The Pirates of Penzance'* that year provided a tremendous performance. Star of the show was the splendid Maj Peter A'Hearne. He looked every inch the *'very model of a modern Major General'*, resplendent in scarlet and complete with monocle and medals. Everyone marvelled at his vocal dexterity, always managing to beat the orchestra by a short head. It definitely ***was*** all right on the night!

Incoming apprentices of intake 78A got off to a rough start as far as the weather was concerned. The continuing mixture of the winter's frost, snow and rain added an extra element of discomfort to the military cadre and dealt a heavy blow to the sporting programme. Added to this came the arrival of a pretty nasty bug, revelling in the unlikely name of 'red flu', which adversely affected around three-quarters of the junior Div during that first term. Even when that started to clear away, a fuel-tanker drivers' strike meant severe economies on the heating, ensuring that a fair number of chilly days still had to be endured.

The 'Old Boys' Award

The spring 1978 edition of *The Arborfield Apprentice* contained an article that set out to explain the objectives of the OBA. These were put down as *"fostering esprit de corps and comradeship"*, as well as *"maintaining and furthering the prestige and dignity of the College"* (or School, as it had originally been). However, the writer went on to say that perhaps the best example is by the way in which the ex-boy leads his normal life. Many former apprentices had already achieved success as soldiers, engineers, authors, teachers and sportsmen, the list being practically endless, but the common thread was that they can all be said to have greatly enhanced the reputation of Arborfield in one way or another.

At the previous AGM, the assembled old boys had unanimously voted to establish 'The Old Boys' Award'. This was, in future, to be awarded to either an individual A/T, or perhaps a group of A/Ts, who showed exceptional endeavour in any field, be it on the sports field, during military training, adventure training or whilst partaking in community service. The very first recipient of the Award was A/T CSM Barry Gee of 'D' Coy. In a letter of thanks to the OBA, he was quick to point out that the Award really represented the efforts of a large group of boys, of which he had merely had the honour and good fortune to be leading at that time.

An old favourite passes on

During March that year, a death occurred that would touch the hearts of hundreds of the earliest apprentices at Arborfield. After a long illness, Ben Cook – *"dear old Ben"* – came to the end of his final tour of duty. As described at the time by Harry Shaw, himself one of the first arrivals in August 1939, and then Hon Sec of the OBA, Ben remained in the memories of all those boys who had served under him as *"a great character"*.

Meanwhile, Bill Thomas of intake 44A was still serving, now as a Colonel in Bielefeld, BAOR, where his Adjutant was Maj Ross Bennett, another ex-boy from 1942. They had received a phone call from Maj Ken Head, another of the 1944 era, telling them of the sad news about Ben. That news quickly spread throughout BAOR, thanks to the 'old boys' net', and Ben's memory must have been toasted by the lifting of glasses in many a Mess that day. As Bill Thomas put it, Ben had been both *"feared and respected"* – but certainly never forgotten.

It was also in March that a copy of *Visor*, regularly issued as *'Service News for Northern Ireland'*, was put aside by an ex-boy. Phil Newton had been an apprentice of intake 68C and was now serving in Ulster with 702 Mobile Servicing & Repair Department (MSRD), a detachment of 70 Aircraft Wksp REME, based at RAF Aldergrove.

Phil was on a four-month tour in the Province, one of a team of fifteen REME personnel responsible for the 2nd-line maintenance of *Scout* and *Gazelle* helicopters. The inside page of the newspaper showed a photograph of the majority of the detachment. As if to underline the dangers faced by soldiers in Northern Ireland at that time, the front page reported the killing of two front-line soldiers, one shot and killed in Belfast and the other killed by a booby-trap explosion at Crossmaglen.

After staying on as the College RSM for almost four years, late springtime of 1978 saw the time finally arrive for RSM Meredith's departure. However, he managed to leave with his literary reputation enhanced in print, with an article in the latest College magazine, where he stressed the importance of safety awareness to those boys who had taken a liking to motor cycling. He also confessed that, were he himself still a boy, he would be into the College before you could say 'knife'. *(Revives memories of what Field Marshall Montgomery said back in 1946! Ed.)*

Appointments after that date became almost an annual event, with RSM L Perkins, BEM, Grenadier Guards, appointed that May, remaining in post for around only eighteen months. It was an amazing coincidence that RSM Perkins' own father had been a well-known RSM in REME many years previously, and it must have been a proud moment when he arrived here at Arborfield, virtually 'following in his father's footsteps'.

Apprentices from 'B' Coy had certainly been busy in the field of 'help thy neighbour', on both a parochial and worldwide mission. The Company had undertaken to build a concrete path through the trees at the Hephaistos School, so that children could move more smoothly in their wheelchairs when taking part in nature studies. The boys were assisted in their efforts by two ex-apprentice Sappers from Chepstow, who brought along their own concrete mixer! Meanwhile, over in Penang, Malaysia, a blind schoolboy had been boosted by the gift of £300, in order that he could move to a secondary school in Kuala Lumpur that autumn. Nearer to home again, the Guide

Civilian Patrolmen - It was never like this in Fred Silvers day!

Dogs Home for the Blind at Wokingham continued to receive support each Saturday from a dedicated Company team.

An article in that revered newspaper, *The Times*, published on July 7th 1978, announced the success of Lt D A Cory REME in being awarded a *"Bachelor of Science Degree, with First Class Honours, in Engineering by the Royal Military College of Science, Shrivenham"*. As followed up in *The Arborfield Apprentice* summer edition, it was an outstanding example of the sort of success that could be achieved by any of the apprentices from the College. Lt Cory had been here as 'a boy' in 'A' Coy from 1968 – 1971.

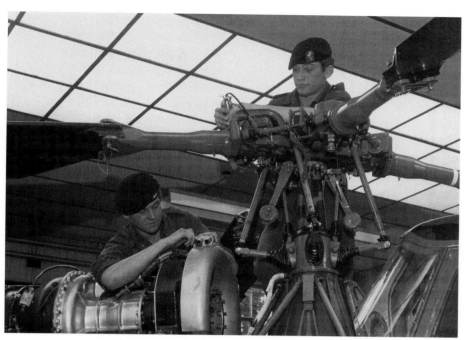

Apprentice aircraft technicians working on a Scout helicopter

One foot in the past

That summer magazine also took pleasure in some nostalgic looks back at past events at Arborfield. One article went into great detail, recounting the visit from Field Marshal Viscount Montgomery, hero of El Alamein and the following victorious desert campaign, to the November 'PoP' in 1946. Another story was a brief look at the life and times of the legendary Ben Cook, first RSM at the School, as it had been than, in 1939.

(The memorial article about Ben Cook is reproduced as a separate annex to this chapter.)

The College Bands were looking forward to busier and perhaps more demanding times, having had no outside engagements that spring term, but only having attended the usual College activities at the Officers' and Sergeants' Mess Dinner Nights. One big event looming on the horizon was to be 'Beating the Retreat' at Portsmouth, held on behalf of the REME Association. Normally accompanied by the REME Staff Band, this was the first time the College Bands had been asked to participate. However, the engagement nearly didn't take place, as the coach driver managed to get lost during his attempt to find the hotel. At least the boys on

board had a nice free sightseeing tour of Portsmouth! Two later engagements took place in London, one a two-day event at the Festival of Sport in Lambeth, the second at a garden fete, on behalf of the BBC Club.

Meanwhile, the College swimmers had been enjoying themselves, striking fear into all opposition. Having started the year with a win over Surrey University, they continued by beating RAF Halton and then gaining a narrow victory over Sandhurst. By June 6th, at the South East (SE) District Inter-Unit Championships, held at Aldershot, they were able to leave their closest rivals, the ACC Apprentices' College, trailing in their wake.

A letter, received in July 1978, paid tribute to the endeavours of an apprentice VM serving at the College. A/T Scrivenor had been on leave at the time and happened to be driving along the A43 near the Kidlington roundabout, on the outskirts of Oxford. Noticing a broken-down *Land Rover*, which was being utilised by a RAF Flight Commander on a reconnaissance mission, young Scrivenor had stopped to volunteer his services. As a result, the fault was quickly diagnosed and the vehicle was able to proceed on its journey. The letter, from Squadron Leader M J W Markey, asked for thanks to be passed on, in appreciation of *"a job well done"*.

On July 28th, a memorial service was held for A/T

'Charlie the Barber' showing the General his collection of haircut pictures!

Yet another letter, this one from Brig Bill Bailey of 23 Base Wksp, Wetter, BAOR thanked the Committee for having invited him along to that Reunion. As Commandant in the early Seventies, he had spent *"three memorable years"* and had been more than pleased to soak up the *"apprentice atmosphere"* once more. Of even earlier vintage, another ex-Commandant who attended that Reunion was Brig Joe Dobie.

One dark thought that must have been in the minds of many ex-apprentices, however, was that the old familiar barracks were now nearing the end of their useful life and were soon likely to disappear altogether. Would the OBA survive the loss of such a venue and continue to thrive in a new location? This question would only be answered as the following years rolled by.

Ian Budgen, who died a week after another of the College's motorcycle accidents, having never regained consciousness. One of his closest 'A' Coy friends, A/T LCpl Wood, unveiled a plaque to his memory in the College Chapel. Another letter, arriving in October the same year, told of yet another fatal motorcycle accident, this time on the Wokingham Road, that had taken the life of 'B' Coy's A/T Smalley. Another boy, A/T Roulstone and also of 'B' Coy, had been with Smalley at the time and the letter told of his calm and helpful manner as he attended to his colleague, before accompanying him to hospital, where his life, sadly, could not be saved. Young Roulstone was later nominated to receive the Old Boys' Award.

With the success of the previous year's revitalising Old Boys' Reunion still vivid to everyone's memory, it was gratifying to find that the October 1978 version was also well attended and just as enjoyable. Despite the thick fog that seemed to have enveloped much of southern England, over one hundred old boys had obviously seen the benefits of map reading – and carrot eating! - come to fruition, as they found their way through the College gates to partake of *"drinks and a substantial ploughman's lunch"*. Incoming members soon started filling up the Camp Hall, partaking in the convivial atmosphere of eating, drinking and greeting old comrades.

Old soldiers do it from memory!

Another 'old soldier' who attended that same Reunion was W A Arthur, BEM. He wrote to say how proud and honoured he had been to attend, having been one of the original PS members to arrive here at Arborfield, some forty years previously. He thought he was right in saying that he was the first military instructor, other than RSM Cook, to be posted here, under the command of Col Hilborn. Unfortunately, Mr Arthur gave no mention of his Christian name or rank, but mentioned that he had returned to his old Battalion of the SWB on the outbreak of war in September 1939.

Wally Footner (Oct '39) was delighted to attend his first Reunion that year. Walking through the old gates, past the Guardroom, then into the Camp Hall/ Gymnasium to 'book in', it seemed *"as if time had stood still"*. He was told his accommodation would be Room 'C5', in 'B' Coy lines, and was asked if he needed a guide – *"they were joking of course"*. He was even more surprised to find that old comrade Sam Coster was sitting in his (Wally's) bed-space! A lot of friendly banter obviously followed and the pair had great fun all weekend, reliving fond memories and re-enacting *("in a mature way of course")* some of their past escapades.

That Reunion's evening's entertainment was held in the old Camp Hall, with the old boys again accommodated in the original spider blocks. It was certainly an occasion to be remembered, eternally one would think in the memory of Harry Shaw. He suffered a bout of acute embarrassment when one of the *'cabaret artistes'* he had booked turned out to be a stripper, who did some amazing things with a large bottle of baby-oil! Then there was the lady with the snake, which turned out to have far more talent than its owner! Things did tend to change somewhat at subsequent Reunions!

As reported in the winter 1978 edition of *The Arborfield Apprentice*, the Sub-Aqua Club was still in fine fettle. Having enjoyed the usual Easter visit to Malta, the summer term had seen a continual pattern of pool training, which culminated in a week's diving at Fort Bovisand, Plymouth. Here, at the Joint Services Centre, they were pleased to meet up with ASM Alan Maloney, an ex-boy of the 58B intake. Club members were also grateful to find that RSM Perkins was able to offer a great deal of enthusiasm and practical experience, setting many newcomers on the way to safe and happy diving.

The College's tennis players had also enjoyed a good season. They had been able to complete all matches and championships on schedule that year. The Individual Singles Knock-out Competition was a hard fought battle between two excellent players, A/T Cpl Shields and A/T Baigent, won by the latter after three close sets. When the REME Corps Championships were held at Bordon, these two players teamed up in the Doubles and, for the first time ever, it was apprentices who won the event. It was no surprise when the pair later also won the Army Junior Doubles – an excellent achievement.

As 1978 drew near to a close, the Commandant was airing his concern about the position of 'President of the AOBA'. The Constitution demanded that there should be a Life President, but gave no indication as to the manner of his appointment. As far as could be gathered, the last Life President had been Brig (Ret'd) White DSO, MC, who had been Commandant between 1946 – 47, but the post had become vacant upon his death in 1973. Col Barrie now wrote to the DGEME, Maj Gen J V Homan, who had attended the recent

Reunion as guest of honour, to ask if he would take up the post, and that the post be automatically passed on to succeeding Directors on appointment. Unfortunately, this policy does not appear to have been taken up at that time.

The winter term, as far as the College Bands were concerned, was unusually quiet. The 1978 / 79 term was to prove an exception, however, in fact it turned out to be one of the busiest on record. The highlight was undoubtedly the notification that, in the three sections of the Army Music Competition, sponsored by *Soldier* magazine, the College had swept the board. Not only had they been voted 'Best Junior Band', but, individually, A/T Cpl Fadden had taken the 'Best Woodwind Player' title and A/T Feasy was the new 'Best Brass Player'. Other engagements that followed included a session at Bordon for the *'BP Build-a-car'* competition.

The Corps of Drums and the Brass Band were then invited to lead the Berkshire contingent of the Royal British Legion on parade at Sandhurst. Unfortunately, when the order came for the Bands to 'march on', no guides or markers had preceded them! Improvising a couple of marches around the square, the Bands awaited the outcome of heated discussions, taking place between their BSM and the Academy Sergeant Major. Apparently this was not a rare occurrence on a Legion-organised parade! When a representative from the Legion asked the Bands to perform again the following year, he was given the contact number – of the JLdrs RCT Band! As a fitting *finale* to the year, the musicians entertained Christmas shoppers at the Butts Centre in Reading.

Brief history - updated

It was around this time that an updated edition of *"A brief history of the Army Apprentices' College"* was published. Some hard working individual had obviously been very busy in adding in the relevant details covering a span of some five intervening years but, as far as is known, the author again wished to remain anonymous. The only information is once again given by the printer's code *"Rdg 39515/1/30/78 200 12/78 TP 12"*.

As the final year of the Seventies got under way, members of Vehicle Wing wondered whether they were going into competition with British Leyland. Having already been blessed with the services of an

Army Catering Corps cooks (chefs) hard at work preparing a 'PoP' breakfast treat!

'Austin' (Fred), a new member of staff turned out to be a 'Morris' (Jim). They eagerly awaited the arrivals of Messrs *Jaguar* and *Triumph*!

As if to prove that some things never change, members of 'D' Coy were dismayed to return from Christmas leave to burst pipes and a broken-down heating system! That was inevitably followed by rain, then more rain, then by even more rain! In fact most boys had forgotten just what sunshine looked like when it finally appeared at half term. All the more reason for praising the stoic endurance of 'J' Coy that year – out of a total intake of 110 newcomers, only five were unable to get through their first term.

The Canoe Club had some very mixed fortunes during the winter term. A/T Sgt Sutherland and A/T Cpl Smith had spent a week in Bonny Scotland, training with the Army slalom squad, and both impressed sufficiently to be chosen for the full Army team in the Inter-Services Championships. But, as often is the case, the good news was tragically balanced by the bad. An ex-boy of the College, 'Chalky' Whyte, drowned on the River Tay, whilst out training with the Army Long Distance team.

As a result of the Corps Badminton Championships, five young College players were subsequently selected to represent the REME squad in the Army Badminton League. For the second season in succession, the College had made a clean sweep of the Winter Games, beating Chepstow by 7 – 2 and giving a right old 'whitewashing' to Harrogate by 9 rubbers to nil.

Letters of invitation for the October 1979 Old Boys' Reunion were already being sent out during March that year. It had been anticipated that this would be the last ever Reunion to be held within the wooden spider-huts of the 'old school'. However, as the projected move had now been put back to some time in 1981, the 'Final Reunion' (in the original barracks, that is!) was now expected to take place in October of 1980.

On May 18th 1979, three six-man teams of apprentices set off on the traditional Ten Tors expedition across Dartmoor. Yet again, training had proved an arduous task, whittling down numbers from over one hundred original volunteers. Arranged by the Army, over a mixture of military and National Trust land, the Ten Tors is set over three separate distances, of thirty-five, forty-five and fifty-five miles. The College teams were attempting the 'Silver Medal' trek of forty-five miles, covering around thirty of these on the first day, 'camping out' overnight, before hitting the final stretch. Over 2,000 competitors took part in the event, with helicopters full of cameramen whizzing about overhead to record it. All three College teams successfully made it to the finishing line, with many vowing to return for an attempt on the 'Gold Medal' distance the following year.

It was also in May that the College Senior Fencing Team 'came off the fence' as it were, by winning the Army Championships. This meant that they would now go ahead and represent the Army at the Inter-Services Championships, soon to be held at Earls

Court as part of the Royal Tournament. This was quite an achievement for the College, as two of the six-man team were serving apprentices, A/T Sgt Kanuga and A/T LCpl Broadhead, both of 'A' Coy. In the individual events, young Kanuga had won the foil event and been runner-up in both the epee and sabre events, thus gaining the coveted award of Army Junior Champion-at-arms. It was fitting that the College team later went on to win the Inter-Services tournament in July, whilst on an individual basis, Kanuga achieved the ultimate of every Arborfield apprentice by becoming the A/T RSM for his intake.

Showing the flag

At the beginning of July 1979, Col Keast received a request from Lt Col Ferguson MBE, County Commandant of the Borders Battalion Army Cadet Force. Two young Arborfield apprentices, A/Ts P Kelly and S McLean, had been members of his Jedburgh detachment prior to joining the College, and the request was for them to join a training camp at Rowlston, on Humberside, in order to 'show the flag'. A letter of thanks later in the year proved what a good impression these two young men had made in assisting with the training of even younger Cadets. As stated by Lt Col Ferguson, *"each was given specific responsibilities, which they undertook with diligence and enthusiasm"*.

At Maidstone, Kent, that same month, a handful of boys from 'A' Coy marched a distance of 100 miles non-stop, in aid of the charity *'Action Research for Crippled Children'*. Not only did the team win the event, but A/T Cpl Mitchell covered the distance in only sixteen and a half hours, at an average speed of six miles per hour – didn't he do well? The event had been organised by Mrs George, mother of one of the 'A' Coy team.

The arrival in the College library of a climbing book, *'Classic Rock'*, in January 1979, had inspired the College Climbing Club to mount an expedition to the 'Black Cuillin of Skye'. In a sweep of six miles, the ridge encompasses some ten peaks over 3,000 feet, presenting a formidable challenge. Base camp established, with a fine view under a blue sky, the climbers of the advance party settled down to a good night's sleep. But that night, high winds and rain swept in at Force Ten. Over breakfast, the boys heard some tragic news coming in from that year's disastrous Fastnet Yacht Race, so they were grateful to at least be on *terra firma*. With the weather so poor, they could only settle down and await the arrival of the main party.

Once the complete team had assembled, they soon found that the approach to any section of the ridge involved some two to three hours 'flogging' across typical Scottish peat bog! In almost incessant rain and accompanying poor visibility, three days were then spent in individual parties doing 'recces' on different areas. Despite the treacherous conditions, the area eventually provided an exciting training ground, giving practice in basic mountaineering, route finding

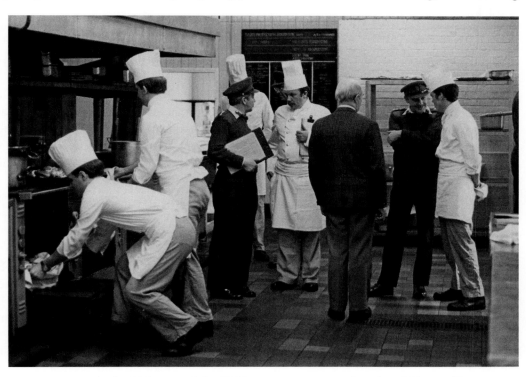

....and it look like one of the Old Boys is trying to get his plate full as well!

Weekly pay parade - it helped to have a name starting with a letter at the beginning of the alphabet.

and map reading. Last word however went to the local 'Skye midges', which fought their way through a bombardment of insect repellent to reach those parts that other insects could not reach!

The new TEC programmes for Aircraft and Electronic Apprentices were the culmination of an intensive period of preparations and negotiations. They provided Diploma and Certificate courses for technician apprentices, as replacements for the ONC and C & G courses respectively. Developments in TEC came about in September 1979, with the introduction of a seven-term TEC Certificate course for selected vehicle apprentices. An important aspect of this was to provide an additional source of candidates for entry to the Royal Military College of Science (RMCS) at Shrivenham, Wiltshire, through a commission in REME.

In the following month, October 1979, Col Barrie

Keast left on posting to 35 Central Wksp, Old Dalby, Leicestershire. He was greatly missed by the boys at the College. The fact that he had himself been an apprentice here, even though it had been some thirty-odd years previously, gave him a special bond, with the boys feeling very much that he was *"their own Commandant"*.

A hard act to follow

Col J D C Peacock, MA, FRGS, obviously had a *"hard act to follow"* when he arrived to take over as Commandant of the College, but he was well fitted for the task. Several years previously, he had served a tour as an instructor and Adjutant at the RMAS, as well as a couple of years as Chief Instructor at SEE. This had given him an insatiable appetite for training and his arrival here followed his own personal request to be considered for the post. As he stated at the time of his eventual arrival, to the editor of the College magazine, Bryn Richards, *"Our opportunity is renewable"*.

It was also the time for 'farewell' from the College RSM that month. Lincoln Perkins had joined the Grenadier Foot Guards some twenty-one years previously and had enjoyed the honour of being one of Sir Winston Churchill's coffin bearers at the famous statesman's funeral procession, following the great man's death in January 1965. Since then, Lincoln had acted as the RSM at the Silver Jubilee Royal Tournament in 1977, where he had met most of the Royal Family, and also been awarded the BEM. He had recently received his LSGC Medal at the August 'PoP' of 1979. Upon his posting to the DYRMS, his replacement, in the role of acting-RSM, was CSM D Cummins, also from the Grenadier Guards.

There was a third successive gathering of old boys over the weekend of 12th / 14th October, building upon the friendships, both old and new, that had been forged since the Reunions were 'reinvented' in 1977. The salute was taken by 'old faithful' Harry Shaw, who had done so much to rekindle the flames of eternal youth amongst members of the OBA. On the parade, the old boys' contingent, superbly led by Maj Bob McGrillen of 46B, included 'boys' from as far apart as Canada and Israel. A great tribute was paid to outgoing Commandant Barry Keast, for his three years of hard work on behalf of all apprentices, both past and present.

The final edition of *The Arborfield Apprentice* for that year, winter 1979, included an interesting article describing the history and concept of the 'Modern Pentathlon'. The author concluded by saying how fortunate was REME, in that Arborfield was now recognised as Great Britain's 'Centre of Excellence' for this most demanding of sports.

More changes ahead

The new Commandant's words about renewability proved to be very prophetic, for the next period of time, from then until July 1981, was perhaps the most significant in the history of the College up to that date. In addition to numerous far-reaching developments in the training of apprentices, the long-awaited move to a new, modern accommodation would take place, while at the same time the College was to be re-designated as 'Princess Marina College'. Other innovations were to include the inauguration of a College Council and the founding of a College Trust Fund, although this latter addition was brought about by the chill wind of more Government cuts in Defence spending.

Col John Peacock quickly discovered that it was traditional that the College Commandant takes command of the Garrison Remembrance Parade. Having himself never commanded such a large parade, he wisely deferred to the 'expert' in these matters, CSM Cummings, who was also acting-RSM. After the first rehearsal, the CSM wisely and politely told the Colonel, *"That was first rate, Sir, absolutely 100 per cent – now if, on the actual day, you can give it about ninety-seven per cent, it will be perfect"*! This very tactful and diplomatic reply informed the Commandant that perhaps his performance had been just a little bit 'over the top' and he rightly took the advice to heart. It is therefore understandable that there was a touch of regret in his heart when the CSM returned to 'B' Coy, and the 'real' RSM arrived to take over the post.

Col Peacock's philosophy was that the College was **not** just another means of recruiting tradesmen for REME. He saw the term of apprenticeship as being *"training for life"* and, in particular, laying the foundation for future Artificers of the Corps. He was very keen on the development of leadership training, saying that it was all very fine for someone to be an expert tradesman, but in order to wear the badge of Staff Sergeant or above, it also required the qualities of being a leader of men. During his time at the College, leadership cadres were introduced, by which anyone with outstanding potential would be quickly identified.

As the Seventies finally drew to a close, one sports-mad apprentice had a lucky escape, following a nasty injury in a College rugby match. Cpl K Lang, ACC, one of the PS, quickly realised the serious nature of the accident, and rushed to the young lad's assistance with basic first aid. Then the boy stopped breathing and Cpl Lang applied mouth-to-mouth resuscitation until a certain amount of breathing and consciousness returned. The fortunate apprentice was quickly taken off to hospital, where he later went on to make a complete recovery, while Cpl Lang received the GOC's Commendation for his quick thinking, efficient action and first aid skills.

—§—

Annex to Chapter 10

RSM Cook, Grenadier Guards

A certain American magazine used to publish an article every month under the title *'My Most Unforgettable Character'*. There are many that would be on my short list, but probably the final selection would be Ben Cook. Ben was born early in this century, joined the Grenadier Guards in 1918 and died in March of this year (1978). He was the first RSM of this College, or Army Technical School as it was then called, starting his duties in April 1939 with the first intake.

I well remember my first view of him. A tall imposing figure in the serge service dress of that time, complete with knee-length puttees, the whole topped with the No.1 dress hat, affected then only by the Brigade of Guards. A voice best described as 'gravelly', certainly deep, and years on the parade ground had perfected his technique of throwing it long distances. He demonstrated this once by giving

RSM 'Ben' Cook
photographed in front of the old Remount Stables

the 'Quick March' to an apprentice by Workshop Practice. We remained there and watched the A/T until he was about to disappear round the back of the hospital (MRS). Then Ben bellowed the 'About Turn'. To our inner glee, the A//T did not appear to hear, but continued for a pace or two, before turning about smartly and returning towards us. Sound travels at a relatively low velocity or, as Ben put it, *"You have to allow for it to get there"*.

Ben spent little time in his office, he was everywhere in the School at once, or so it seemed to us. From *'Reveille'* to *'Lights Out'*, no place was safe from him; no window through which he may not peer; and no road which may not be suddenly enfiladed end-to-end by his caustic comments!

Ben's disciplinary methods were unorthodox to say the least. Doubling round the square was for minor offences, whilst other offenders were told to put themselves in the Guardroom, with the addendum sometimes *"and throw away the key"*. His stick was frequently applied to the rumps of transgressors, but occasionally he would make the punishment fit the crime. For example, one A/T, who carelessly discarded a toffee paper, had been observed by Ben at a range of two hundred yards. He was told to go all round the School, pick up all the spent matches, scrub them with a nail-brush and present them, neatly packed in a box, later that evening. *"And don't go buying a box from the NAAFI and striking them"*, added Ben, *"I can tell"*. He probably could.

Ben Cook descended on my room several times. One Sunday morning, just before Reveille, he stamped into the room and, in sheer terror, we all leapt from our beds. *"What are you doing out of bed,"* shouted Ben, *"causing a disturbance after Lights Out? Get back into bed at once!"* This we dutifully did, just as the first quavering note of the bugler sounding Reveille came floating across the square. *"Get out of bed you lazy, idle lot,"* shouted Ben, whacking the recumbent forms with his stick. Those of us with a well-developed instinct for self-preservation grabbed our towels and dashed for the showers, leaving any slower brethren to face his wrath.

In the fullness of time, Ben was commissioned, becoming first 'QM', then later 'Agricultural Officer'. At that time, during the Second World War, Britain was very short of food and it was decided to bring the School grounds under cultivation. Ben threw himself into this task with his customary energy and, using a horse-drawn plough and squads of off-duty A/Ts, soon had a thriving farm on the go.

Needless to say, the apprentices would have much preferred to spend their Saturday afternoons in some other pursuit; they could not be relied upon to furnish one hundred per cent co-operation. However, there was one advantage to these fatigues and that was the promise of refreshments. At some point in the afternoon, the Cookhouse would send out an urn of sweet tea and a tray of slab-cake for the hungry workers.

On one such occasion, faced with a more-than-usually idle and recalcitrant squad of puffing boys, Ben opined that the only one who had worked hard enough to deserve refreshment was the horse! He accordingly fed all the slab-cake to the lucky animal, much to the chagrin of the apprentices. There are many stories such as this; perhaps some day a writer will try to collect them all into a book. *(It's funny you should say that! Ed.)*

Many years after these happenings, I was recovering from an operation in the Cambridge Military Hospital when I heard a voice ring out down the long corridor. *"I don't want that muck! Bring me some beer!"* Yes, it was Ben all right. Coming out of the Bramshill Hunt one night, he had been struck by an ill-driven car and badly injured. He recovered and, I believe, took to drinking Guinness instead of beer.

More years were to pass before I saw him again, both of us now being civilians. He was still engaged on his agricultural duties, white-haired now but still erect and soldierly of manner. He insisted on calling me 'Sir', an accolade I tried to persuade him I didn't deserve, but without success. Eventually his last, long illness removed him from the scene. And now he is gone.

From some of the above, the reader could be forgiven for summing up Ben as a harsh man, but he would be wrong. Underneath the bluff exterior he was a kindly, even sentimental man. Any military organisation that takes discipline lightly is merely an armed rabble and bound for destruction. The disciplined professional will always beat the enthusiastic amateur, almost regardless of numbers. In war, in the final analysis, only discipline and leadership matter.

One can get all this from reading military history of

course, but Ben knew instinctively what others have to learn from books or bitter experience. It was discipline and leadership that Ben provided and, hard as he drove others, he drove himself even harder. Ben, and others like him, laboured to produce an Army that saved our country from one of the vilest tyrannies the world has yet seen. Let that be his epitaph.

(The above article is adapted from that published in The Arborfield Apprentice of summer 1978, a few months after the death of Ben Cook. It had no author's name attached, but could have been written by any of those who served under Ben's stewardship and certainly provides an eloquent obituary for that great and stalwart servant of Arborfield.)

Maj P L Chivers
Major Ezra Rhodes writes:

It is with regret that we report the death of Percy Lionel Chivers, a civilian instructor of the Apprentices' College, Arborfield. Born of military family in January 1914, his father was the Director of Music at the Royal Military Academy at Sandhurst. Having enlisted at the age of fourteen as an apprentice Blacksmith at Chepstow, Percy served some forty-eight years as a soldier, officer and, subsequently, civilian instructor.

He was a highly skilled and competent artisan who, during his service and particularly in the latter years, has left many fine examples of his skills by way of wrought-iron gates. At the Garrison Church, Aldershot; Yorktown gates at the Royal Military College, Sandhurst; the National Army Museum; and finally, as a very last act, wrought-iron altar gates for St Andrew's Church, Aldershot. During his last twenty years of military and civilian service, he devoted his energies to passing on his skills to young apprentices at both Arborfield and Carlisle.

Percy was known and appreciated not only for his skills as an artisan and instructor, but also for his efforts on the field of sport – as an official, umpire and organiser, to which he devoted unstintingly incalculable hours of his time. A kindly and considerate man, of whom it can be truly said:

"Large was his bounty and his soul sincere".

(The above obituary was published in The Craftsman magazine, issued in January 1976.)

With the old buildings starting to look tired, it appears that we won't be marching along here for much longer!

Chapter 11

1980 - 84

Great expectations

Colonel Peacock was fiercely, and rightly so, proud of his role here at the College, insisting to the various posting branches that only the very best quality of NCOs and officers should be posted here. One such new arrival, in January 1980, was RSM D P Yorke, from the Coldstream Guards. He was destined to become not only the last RSM of the Army Apprentices' College, under its then current title, but also the first RSM of the re-named Princess Marina College, in May of the following year - a rare distinction indeed.

Another member of staff at the time could certainly be described as 'one of the best'. At the spring 'PoP', WO1 Edmondson (ASH), was presented with the MSM. He had previously fought with The Cameronians across northwestern Europe between 1944 – 45 and was later one of the first British soldiers to disembark in Korea in 1950. He later went on to serve on three operational tours in Borneo. Now on the Long Service List, WO1 Edmondson had been at Arborfield since 1977.

Not only did the Commandant demand a high standard of staff, but also that the work they carried out should be of an equal standard. In a phrase, he expected *"lots of effort during a short, but intensive, tour"*. It was during Col Peacock's time that the number of teaching periods was increased from nine to ten per day but, as a direct result of this, half-term periods were now also able to be increased, from a mere 'long weekend' to a full week-long break. This gave everyone the chance of a well-earned breather after the hectic time that had preceded it.

Paul Hudson of 58A had passed out of Arborfield in 1961 and not been back near the place in almost twenty years. But, at some time during 1980, he found himself in the locality and, having recently heard about the planned rebuild, decided to pay a somewhat nostalgic visit to his old stamping ground. Upon first sight, he was amazed to find the 'old place' still standing, although with a slightly different colour scheme to the one he remembered. All the old 'tin huts' were displayed in a delicate shade of what could only be described as *cream*! Despite this shock to his system,

the outcome of his visit was that he promptly arranged to attend the 1980 Old Boys' Reunion, the very last that would be held in the old accommodation. Needless to say, like many others who attend 'for the first time', Paul has gone on to be present at each reunion since then.

In February 1980, the College ran an inaugural two-day leadership assessment cadre for senior apprentices, based upon the well-tried principles and practices already used at the Regular Commissions Board (RCB) and Artificer Selection Board (ASB). It was a highly successful period of experimental learning, both for the boys and serving PS concerned, heralding the start of formal developmental training in the art of leadership for all apprentices. From that February until the following October, a one-week introductory leadership cadre was introduced for all technician apprentices in their fourth term, and for all VM apprentices in their third term. In the training of craft apprentices, the College took over the examining of CGLI Part 2 for VMs from SEME, Bordon, in April of that year.

In *The Arborfield Apprentice* issued for the spring term 1980, an article appeared which informed current apprentices at the College of the activities of its Old Boys' Association. It covered how the original setting up of the OBA had occurred in 1948 and went on to give details of reunions, awards and the newsletter. Finally, the article encouraged the present boys to think seriously about joining the OBA in the future.

(The same magazine carried a poem entitled 'An ode to the OBA', under the anonymous banner, which is (mostly!) reproduced as a separate annex to this chapter.)

Success on the soccer field

Company Commander of 'A' Coy, Maj J B Hyslop, Duke of Edinburgh's Royal Regiment (DERR), claimed to have the best soccer team he had seen in fifteen years. His skillful side had good reason to be pleased, having pulled off a most creditable hat-trick of victories that season. Not only had they won the

Apprentices' Cup, but had gone on to achieve 'the double' of finishing top of the SE District League and winning the SE District Cup. One of their most remarkable victories had come in the Cup semi-final, against 'the cooks' from Aldershot. Three down at half time, with their 'goose' seemingly well and truly 'cooked' the boys had fought back with four second half goals to gain their place in the final.

The Brass Band had enjoyed a successful, though fairly quiet, winter term. Following weekly rehearsals at Slough, they had provided the backing music for an entertaining version of *'The Wizard of Oz'*, put on by the *Generation Theatre Group*. Some of the lads were to get a bit excited at the sight of young girls running around in somewhat skimpy costumes, with a few burgeoning romances boding well for the future! The Pipe Band had supported the Remembrance Day parade at Newbury, while the Brass Band and Corps of Drums performed a similar function at Bordon. Meanwhile, the arrival of Pipe Major Wilson (KOSB), with his *"bright red tartan trews"*, brought a welcome splash of colour to the scene.

The staff of Vehicle Wing was trying to run down their equipment holdings, in preparation for the impending move across to the new College accommodation. The only trouble was that they were suffering from an influx of new equipment for training purposes at the same time! Batches of new universal engine stands, new engines of both 1100 cc and 1300 cc types and two huge crates, labelled *'Foden Gearboxes'*, had appeared. As for the latter, everyone seemed very reluctant to even touch them, never mind start opening them! The 'old relics' of the *Bedford RL* line were almost at the point of disappearing, to be replaced, hopefully in time for the big move, by the more up-to-date *Bedford MKs*. The Wing OIC, Maj Kempson, was meanwhile combining his trade duties with his other favourite pastimes of football and parachuting.

The College boxing team had been in great demand that season, showing off their skills of the 'noble art' at many civilian 'Boxing Dinner Shows' at such places as *The Hexagon Theatre* at Reading, Eastleigh and Newbury Town Halls and at the *Wantage Lions Club*, to name but a few. Such was their reputation at the time that the match against Chepstow was called off, after their (Chepstow's) Boxing Officer decided that they weren't sufficiently strong to challenge us! Their boys were now hard at training, in order that they could bring themselves up to standard for a forthcoming challenge.

The recipe for Arborfield's undisputed esteem was put down to *"hard training and doggedness"*.

Meanwhile, the hockey team had its best season in years, ending in their winning of the Junior Army Cup. All but two fixtures had been won that season, an excellent achievement. Just prior to the Cup Final against the old enemy, Chepstow, the team was devastated when one of its best defenders managed to break his collarbone. Despite this, the lads outplayed 'Chep' in the first half, leading 1 – 0, only to be hauled back to equality four minutes from time. Extra-time then had to be played, but without further addition to the 1 – 1 score-line. And so it finally came down to the dreaded penalty shoot-out, from which the Arborfield team emerged triumphant by three shots to one. It had taken many years to win this particular competition; in fact ever since the then School's opening in 1939, so that victory proved especially sweet. The Hockey Officer, Maj Peter A'Hearne RA must have been extremely proud of his boys.

A retiring sort of fellow!

At the end of April 1980, the College Chaplain, Rev Thomas Lovegrove MC, retired for the third time – this time he intended it to be for good! The Padre had joined the Royal Army Chaplains Department (RAChD) as long ago as at the outbreak of the Second World War. He later arrived uncomfortably early upon the blood-stained Normandy beaches, a mere fifty minutes after the first troops had waded ashore under a withering hail of fire. Issued with his own *Jeep* for transportation, he used it on various occasions, ferrying wounded men back from close to the enemy lines, under the most severe of conditions. Complaining that the *"steering felt stiff"* at one point, the Padre discovered that a land mine had wedged itself under the front of his vehicle! His constant bravery was rewarded with the MC, and he later received his decoration from General Sir Brian Horrocks 'in the field' close to Nijmegen Bridge.

After being wounded, then shipped home for a period of recovery, he had insisted upon being sent back into the thick of the action to continue his life's mission. By now he had his own driver and one day they came upon a German Field Hospital. The hospital's commander, seeing the Padre's unusual uniform, assumed him to be a high-ranking officer and immediately surrendered the entire unit. He took his first retirement, from the Army, to become a full-time

Welcome to Legoland! The gates at the entrance to the Princess Marina College

minister and then in 1975 retired for the second time. However, he carried on as a part-time pastor at Windsor Baptist Church and took the post of Officiating Chaplain here at the College, until finally calling it a day this year.

The summer term of 1980 had brought great sadness to members of the Workshop Practice Wing. In June, OC Lt Col Jim McLeod, who was only fifty-three, died after a short confinement in the military hospital at Aldershot. Jim had joined as an apprentice at Chepstow in 1942 and will be well remembered, not only by many REME personnel, but also in the wider Army world, for his great services to swimming over the years. This was reflected by the large cross-section of people who attended his funeral.

Within a week came the news that Mr Ken Ward, Supervising Instructor in the Drawing Department, had also died. Ken had also enlisted into boys' service, at the Military College of Science at Woolwich, and moved here to Arborfield in May 1960. Despite being plagued by illness and obvious pain over a prolonged period, he remained at work until only two weeks before his death.

On a lighter note, one member of staff was delighted by a visit from the Rt Hon Barney Heyhoe MP, Under Secretary of State for Defence (Army) in July. Despite a busy schedule, the Minister had time to stop and check some A/Ts' filing for 'squareness', as well as shaking the hand of Mrs Carol Davies, on duty in the Tool Store. It is rumoured that she hasn't washed her right hand since!

'Trip of a lifetime'

In the summer edition of *The Arborfield Apprentice*, pride of place was given to the efforts of the College Climbing Club. Two years previously (1978), thwarted by some appalling weather conditions, Club members had returned from an unsuccessful expedition to climb the Eiger. Many critics had said that attempting this level of climb, with only junior soldiers, was vastly over-ambitious. However, August 1980 was to prove the critics wrong, as members of 'Exercise Alp Two' not only scaled the Eiger, but also the Wetterhorn, the Monch, the Jungfrau and, finally, as possibly the 'icing on the cake', the highest mountain in Switzerland, the Matterhorn. A/T Cpl G Bateman was undoubtedly correct in his assessment when he later described it as *"the trip of a lifetime".*

On the eve of the August 'PoP', just as he was about to take his place in the adult Army at the end of his apprenticeship, a promising soldier and tradesman sadly met a tragic death. A/T LCpl David Patchett was killed when the car he was driving was involved in an accident at Winnersh, on the outskirts of Reading. Naturally, a great gloom descended upon his colleagues in 'D' Coy, but they were greatly heartened when David's father, in spite of his own obvious deep distress and grief, asked that the following day's parade should go ahead as normal. This it duly did, with one of the young apprentices declaring afterwards, *"Dave would have been proud of us today"*.

The College Appeal Fund

The autumn term gave forecast of a chilly financial climate to come, as economies enforced by the Defence budget took their inevitable toll on monetary matters. In common with all other military units, the College had to bear its fair share of cuts. The mainstream of training itself had been protected, but cutting back on most other activities, especially those which involved transportation away from the College confines, in support of such pastimes as 'adventure training', proved indefensible. A rise in apprentices' subscriptions to the President of the Regimental Institute (PRI) Fund, plus some heavy inroads into this fund, alleviated the situation, if only on a temporary basis. For the longer-term benefit, however, the Commandant eventually

Gunfitters of Intake 81C

decided that it would be judicious to set up the 'College Appeal Fund'.

The Fund's target was, and remained so right through until 1991, the raising of £50,000 by appealing to various sources. These would include the College's own Old Boys' Association, several traditional service institutions, other grant-making trusts, contacts in commerce and industry and, last but not least, the parents of the apprentices themselves. The apprentices, of course, would continue to be the only direct beneficiaries. It was hoped, indeed intended, that the investment income from such a fund would be sufficient to raise a sum that would be double the amount which boys already contributed and, if this proved to be the case, be also sufficient for the College's purpose for the foreseeable future.

More power to your computer!

A significant consequence of the introduction of TEC courses at PMC and, indeed, throughout further education generally, had been the need for a dramatic increase in student assessment and administration. The answer for the PMC appeared to lay with an expansion of the by now well-established computerised testing system, and so additional funds were provided by the Army Committee of Instructional Technology (ACIT) to enable the original system to be upgraded, in order to cope with the expected additional workload.

Following an extensive period of research and evaluation, the required enhancements to both computer hardware and its software were completed in September 1980. This not only gave the computer the necessary power and storage to handle TEC matters, but also provided many additional facilities, including the ability to automatically generate examination papers, either randomly or to a stated specification, selected from electronically-held question banks.

The new system, now to be known as 'SPEC' (Student Performance Evaluation by Computer), and running on a *Data General 'Eclipse'* mini-computer, aroused considerable interest throughout the three services, as well as in several civilian technical training establishments. Its practical success at the College was followed by the implementation of similar systems at SEE and SEME, as well as at the Apprentices' Colleges at Chepstow and Harrogate. Indeed, 'SPEC' and its successor 'SPEX' (son of SPEC!) were to continue in use until the late Nineties. *(From one who knows! I ran the SEME version of SPEC/SPEX until it was subsumed into the new 'TAFMIS' system, conveniently at the time of my retirement. Ed.)*

1980 saw Table Tennis showing a healthy rise in popularity, with three College teams regularly competing in the Bracknell and District League.

Armourers of Intake 81C

Towards the end of June, twelve boys took part in a forty-eight hour sponsored table tennis marathon. Garrison Commander Brig Palmer and Col Peacock got the event under way and popped in occasionally to monitor progress. A sum of over £1,000 was raised, half of which went to Guide Dogs for the Blind. The other half, in the form of a large cheque, was handed over personally to Jimmy *'Jim'll fix it'* Saville OBE, who received it on behalf of Stoke Mandeville Hospital.

End of an era

One weekend in October that year saw the final Old Boys' Reunion to be held in the original barracks, which must have brought a few tears to many eyes. For the old boys who gathered at Arborfield, it was to be the last time they would sleep in the old wooden spiders and attend the get-together in the Camp Hall. Some would no doubt say *"about time too"*, as the actual accommodation was hardly in keeping with the times, but nostalgia isn't like that and for the thousands of apprentices who had passed through those famous School Gates, it truly was the end of an era.

The Arborfield Apprentice of winter 1980 carried an article written by 'Charlie the Barber', who had been operating (without anaesthetic!) here for many years. Along with his wife and young son, he had emigrated to Brisbane, Australia, soon after The Queen's Coronation in 1953. As part of the continuing celebrations of that Royal event, Her Majesty sailed off on the Royal Yacht, with one of her main ports of call being the eastern seaboard of Australia. Here, Charlie and his family were determined to see her, as they were missing 'the old country' very much.

Charlie carried a hand-bell and, as the Queen passed by that evening, he rang it furiously. Her Majesty, fully regaled in diamond tiara, must have heard the noise, and she smiled radiantly as her car passed by. As Charlie now put it, in the College magazine, there are not too many who travel *"19,000 miles to see the Queen"*! Australia's charms obviously didn't quite work out for Charlie, and he was to return to 'Blighty' after only a couple of years.

By the time that the next edition of the College magazine (spring 1981) made its usual welcome appearance, Col Peacock was announcing that, once the College had moved into its new home, it would henceforth be known as 'Princess Marina College', in memory of REME's first Royal C-in-C. The Commandant also looked back fondly to a Joint Services expedition in 1969, when he had made the first ever journey down a long glacier in northern Greenland and named it 'Princess Marina Glacier'. At the same time, he also set his sights firmly in a forward direction – to the time when the College would enter *"several million pounds worth of shining new concrete, steel and glass"*.

Col Peacock was also pleased to report on the highly successful inauguration of the College Appeal Fund. Launched just the previous Christmas, it had already been whole-heartedly supported by most parents. The Corps had not been slow to help either, with future prizes and awards to be funded by the REME Institution and REME Association. However, the Commandant recognised that outside help would only continue to arrive if self-help was seen to be generated from within the College. Sponsored events to this effect had already stimulated interest and imaginative ideas for the future would be in continual demand.

Living up to his name!

For a short period early in 1981, 'B' Coy found itself severely undermanned, for two significant reasons. The first had seen a drastic and complete change of staff in only three weeks. The Company Clerk, Cpl A J Keast, perhaps should have known that, with a name like that, he may have had something to live up to. He may even have guessed that he would end up as 'acting' OC, 2I/C and CSM of the Company – but not all at the same time! However, he lived up to his famous name, took it all in his stride and coped admirably, even though it meant coming in early to work, in order to keep things ticking over. Apart from a lack of hot water, the other main talking point – and the second reason for 'undermanning' – was that abnormal numbers of 'B' Coy apprentices were under detention for various reasons. At one point, it seemed that the Company flag was going to be unfurled outside the Guardroom! Things eventually settled down of course, they always do, but it had certainly been touch and go for a while!

In early 1981, a working party was set up to consider the future training of apprentices up to TEC Diploma standard, the result of which was the phasing-out of the seven-term and eight-term Advanced Diploma courses, and their replacement by a single seven-term Diploma course. The first of these new courses began in September, later that year. That same intake also saw the re-introduction of Weapons apprentices, the training of whom had been moved to Carlisle way back in 1960, but had not then returned to Arborfield upon the closure of Hadrian's Camp in 1969. Potential Armourers and Gun Fitters were now to follow a six-term apprenticeship, based upon CLGI 200/205, at the end of which period they would undertake 'continuation' trade training at SEME for a period of approximately twelve weeks.

On March 1st 1981, a fifteen-strong team set out on the 'Wade Walk' of twenty miles around Wokingham, under dull, cloudy skies. This was to be their final training session for the world-famous 'Nijmegen Marches', held in Holland later that same month. After a little over three-and-a-half hours, the team collected their certificates, before proceeding on the journey back to Camp. Yes, you've guessed correctly, they had to walk! To rub salt into their wounds, just a mile short of home, the heavens opened and everyone got an early shower!

The team that later went to Holland was twelve strong, made up of volunteers from both the boys and staff. The team was led by the imposing six-and-a-half feet tall CoH Andrew Rhymer. The march proved to be an experience *"enjoyed by all"*, despite a number of attempts to break the world record for blisters! The first three days started off at 03.00 hours, while the last began even earlier at an unearthly 02.30 hours. Those four days were really hard work, with a total of 100 miles covered altogether, but the climax made it all worthwhile, when crowds lined the streets up to fifteen deep to cheer home the gallant marchers.

As that year's soccer season drew to a close, team members gave credit for any success to their team coach, Mr Len Burdett. Born in London in 1913, Len had played for his local team, Walthamstow Town, at the tender age of eleven. On leaving school in 1928, he had joined the famous amateur club, Walthamstow Avenue, gaining six England amateur international caps, before being snapped up by Tottenham Hotspur the following year.

Along with the many thousands of his generation upon the outbreak of war, Len joined the Army in 1939. Originally this was with the RA, but he transferred to the APTC in 1941. Eventually he turned from the playing side to a coaching position, and ran the Army team between 1948 and 1950. In the early Sixties he helped as part-time coach at Reading Football Club and, at the same time, joined the staff here at Arborfield, until retiring in 1978. But he had maintained his close connection with the College, continuing to pass on his considerable knowledge and experience to its soccer squad.

On May 27th 1981, a party of boys from 'D' Coy was transported to the middle of Salisbury Plain, where they were to take part in a TA exercise. They arrived at Westdown Camp in somewhat confused fashion, not really knowing what they had let themselves in for. When a good meal was followed by a visit to a make-up artist, no doubt a few dark thoughts began to surface, but things then began to look clear. They were to be 'casualties' for the Medics or, as one boy so aptly put it – *"cannon fodder"*! However, acting comes naturally to most apprentices. So, with the 'make-up' in the form of wounds and bandages, 'playing

HRH Prince Philip opens the Princess Marina College

however, although the occasional apprentice was still to be seen wandering along the narrow corridors, looking for the way out. The stiffness of the return-springs on various fire doors caused the odd bloody nose too! The initial lack of a telephone was a frustration for some – and a blessing to others, who enjoyed the respite from its incessant demands. Eventually a landline and field telephone link back to the College HQ was set up, which eased the situation somewhat. Electronic Techs were gauged to be visibly shorter after the daily trudge between their new place of work and their sleeping quarters, and they looked forward keenly to the eventual 'big move'.

dead' must have seemed an ideal way to pass the time, whilst being treated by the female nurses proved quite enjoyable too.

The big move and change of title

After prolonged months of delay, as well as many hours spent in deliberation over plans and preparation by the members of the 'College New Build Co-ordination Committee' between 1975 and 1981, the long promised new College premises had at last taken shape in Hazebrouck Barracks, adjacent to the SEE. Capt (Ret'd) R F 'Ron' Sherriff, the Project Officer and Secretary, is well worthy of a mention here, in respect of his sterling work on that Committee.

The move had finally begun in March 1981, with the Electronics Wing being the first occupants of the new multi-million pound complex. Looking back over that initial move, the things that were best (or worst?) remembered were the little incidents like crushed fingers and cracked shins, causing even the formerly most placid members of staff to be seen stamping their feet!

Most of the foreseen (and lots of unforeseen!) problems were overcome

The formal change of College title took place on June 1st 1981, it being now named after the late Princess Marina, Duchess of Kent, who had been the first C-in-C of our Corps. The Princess had been born into the Royal Family of Greece, daughter of that country's Prince Nicholas and his wife Helen, Grand Duchess of Russia. Marina was a cousin to our own HRH the Prince Philip, Duke of Edinburgh. In 1934, she had married HRH the Prince George, Duke of Kent, and brother to our

I've always wanted to grab hold of its tail!

own late King George VI. Whilst on active service with the RAF, Prince George was tragically killed in an air crash during wartime 1942. As Patron of many organisations, Princess Marina played a prominent part in public life. She became the C-in-C of the Corps of REME in 1963 and retained that appointment until her death in 1968.

The new-build project obviously took an extremely long time to plan and prepare, before even a single brick could be laid and, during this protracted period, a few other dramatic changes were also taking place, which would have far-reaching effects on the College. Firstly came the raising of the school-leaving age, followed by the news that the Army apprenticeship itself was to be drastically reduced from its present three to two years, while the future new Weapons apprenticeship had still not then been finalised.

On top of all this, the very equipments on which the trainees studied and worked were themselves undergoing much change and renewal. But there comes a definitive time, in any project, when ongoing changes in the final specification can no longer be tolerated and decisions not only have to be made, but adhered to. So it will have come as no surprise to find that the new College, both in its buildings and training equipment, once taken into occupancy, proved to be rather less than a 'perfect fit'.

Col Roberts drives out in style

A new home at last

The final move of the main College was completed in early July 1981 and, on Monday 13th July, PMC finally became 'fully operational' within its new location. Its purpose-built buildings now provided training and living accommodation for up to 850 apprentices, as well as for an establishment of PS. (Aircraft Wing was destined to remain at Bailleul Barracks until as late as September 1985.) The event was seen at the time as one of the most significant in the College's history, ever since it had received its first intake, as the Army Technical School (Boys), way back in 1939. It was a proud moment indeed for the Commandant as his wife performed the opening ceremony, cutting the traditional ribbon in front of the new College HQ.

The change of location was itself a considerable achievement; over one thousand personnel, plus all the equipment for such a complex institution, all moved within the space of a fortnight and with very little outside assistance. There will always be one outstanding memory for those boys who moved the Library – some 10,000 books, in what seemed almost as many boxes, which weighed far more than they had any reasonable right to weigh! One wag remarked afterwards that he'd often wondered if his Certificate of Secondary Education (CSE) in English Literature would prove useful – and now, he was pleased to say, it had! One unforeseen benefit of all the hard work was that boys who hadn't been near the library before suddenly discovered that there were books in there worth reading! As a consequence, the library lending rate increased quite a lot.

Despite the pride and enthusiasm generated by the move, there was also an inevitable tinge of sadness in the minds and memories of many onlookers, as the old metal-clad wooden buildings, which had stood the test of time for over four decades, were finally and irretrievably bulldozed to the ground. Prior to this 'bringing down of the curtain', the Corps

Photographer had been busily pointing his camera in all directions, in order to make a permanent record of over forty years of history. Some of the 'ancient artefacts' that were discovered behind the panelling of the old huts were quite amazing and even the Commandant was overheard to later admit that it was a pity that a museum had not been arranged in which to house the various finds.

Like everyone else in the College, the Padre had also been forced to move. Unlike everyone else however, John Holliman would virtually have had to build his new Church himself, were it not for, as the *Beatles* would have put it, *'a little help from his friends'*. The efforts of numerous volunteers were truly magnificent. The old Dental Centre on Biggs Lane, into which the faithful would soon be called, rapidly became transformed into an attractive little Church.

Listing all those voluntary helpers would probably take as long as the building conversion itself! However, a special mention and vote of thanks must be made for Maj Mike Smith-Rewse, of the Gloucestershire Regt, whose previously undiscovered talents as a carpenter were a revelation, indeed some would say that they bordered on the miraculous! It must have come as no great surprise to the congregation when, on the Sunday morning just before work was completed, the Padre solemnly conducted his Communion service over a *Black and Decker 'Workmate'*! After all, as most were quick to recognise, Jesus had himself started his working life as a carpenter.

Within the College itself, sleeping quarters were now provided by well-constructed modern 'Company Blocks', with apprentices assigned either four or eight to a room, and plenty of space allowed for their beds and lockers. The more senior boys earned the right to a single room. A central catering facility, one of the largest in the British Army, provided meals for both the PMC and the neighbouring SEE. A modern Medical and Dental Centre was to be shared by the College with the rest of the Garrison. The new College had its own NAAFI complex, which included a shop, games room, cafeteria and lounge, with a separate office for the WRVS lady, by now affectionately known as the 'Regimental Mum'.

When Lt Col Frank Benfold MBE retired in 1981, he was serving on the staff of the Director General Electrical and Mechanical Engineering (DGEME) at Andover, Hampshire. On his final interview, the Director told him that, of all the Corpsmen he had met,

Frank was undoubtedly the first to have specialised in three separate trades. Frank had joined up as a General Fitter in October 1942, later obtaining his Class II trade classification whilst serving in Egypt. Changing his trade to VM, he had quickly qualified as Class I, before attending a Leading Artisan Staff Sergeant (LASS) course at the tender age of twenty. After service in Cyprus, Korea and Japan, Frank was selected to attend the first Aircraft Artificer course in 1957 and ended up as an Artificer Aircraft, which of course became his third trade, with commissioning duly following in 1964.

Blowing hot – and cold

During that summer's leave period, the College Band embarked on an extensive tour of the USA, travelling some 12,000 miles through nine different States, in what turned out to be a highly successful venture. A party of fifty-three staff and boys had departed from the US Air Force Base at Mildenhall in Suffolk on August 18th. Prior to their leaving, the Band had 'posed' for a magnificent colour photograph, which later adorned the front cover of *The Craftsman* magazine in the following November.

Upon their arrival in America, the boys were delighted by the hospitality shown by their hosts, as well as their magnificent transport, which consisted of four well-equipped and self-contained minibuses. One of the highlights of the trip was undoubtedly marching through Disney World, at the head of the Character Parade, at which the Band was received with rapturous applause from the enthusiastic crowd.

In somewhat colder conditions, the Sub-Aqua Club had been away exploring the deep waters off the Outer Hebrides. Meanwhile in Europe, another party of boys, representing the College Climbing Club, whilst climbing on the steep slopes of the 'Jungfrau', heard some frantic cries for help. Despite the difficulties and danger involved, the group's subsequent actions were paramount in saving the life of an Austrian climber who had fallen and suffered injury. Sgt Challinor, an experienced climber of the APTC, was praised for his *"cool and decisive leadership"*, while two apprentices, A/T LCpl Spencer and A/T Willis, displayed *"practical skill and teamwork"*. All three members were duly recognised by the award of the GOC's commendation, for their conduct during the incident, a further example that exemplified the best traditions of the College.

The Pipes and Drums together with the Military Band escort the Permanent Staff Sgts Mess out of the old Camp and onto their new home in what was 5 Btn Sgts Mess....

.... and the College Gates are now closed after the relocation of the College to Hazebrouk....

.... with the Barrack Rooms and Spiders looking strangely quiet.

On July 18th 1981, another group of hardy volunteers left the College, on their way to participate in the annual Nijmegen Marches. Their first day began with a 3 a.m. wake-up call and an early breakfast and was followed by a mile walk, just in order to reach the official starting line! During the subsequent four-day exercise, with a challenging distance of twenty-five miles to cover each day, many firm friendships were struck up between the boys and their counterparts amongst the Dutch, French and American services. Team morale remained high throughout the whole period, with marching songs being bandied about from one group to another. *(No doubt 'The Reds' figured somewhere in that repertoire? Ed.)* The boys were heartened by the fact that, no matter how early they started off each day, the local population was always there before them to cheer them along their way. Despite the inevitable blisters gathered along the route, it proved to be an unforgettable experience for everyone.

Col Peacock was justifiably proud of all these achievements, as he looked forward to continuing similar adventures during the coming year. In the pages of the College magazine, he reminded all boys to try to make full use of the vast opportunities on offer, as they were unlikely to come their way so easily during their later adult service. He particularly urged the College clubs and organisations to start their planning early, as half the fun of any trip was to be found in the preparation. Atlases, route maps, pictures and guidebooks provided an encouragement to travel, to see the world and experience the thrills of exploring new countries and meeting new people.

Closer to home, another party, made up of twenty-two apprentices from 'C' Coy, set off on a 1,245 mile round trip, during which they would attempt to climb, one after the other, all of the *'Three Peaks'*, these being the three highest mountains in Scotland, England and Wales respectively. This is not to be confused with a similar 'civilian' expedition that also involves sailing yachts up the coast between the same three locations. First on the list was Scotland's Ben Nevis, which proved a fairly easy ascent, despite the 04.00 hours start time and the plague of tartan-clad midges! The party then sped southwards into the English Lake District for an evening's hike up Scafell Pike in the gathering mist. The following day saw a long drive down into North Wales and the eventual long haul up Mount Snowdon, where the boys were kept cool by the persistent rain. Despite the unfavourable conditions encountered throughout the exercise, with all three peaks shrouded in mist, the whole endeavour was completed in only thirty-two hours. The Welsh language name for Snowdon *is 'Yr Wyddfa'*, which translates to 'burial place', but happily it didn't turn out that way for the boys! Possibly the worst aspect of the whole expedition was the transport. This took place in an ancient *Bedford*, which added no less than a further twenty-one hours to the total time. Second on the list of 'forgettable moments' were the constant mutterings of the OC to the effect that *"This is the life!"*

A Royal Wedding

On July 29th 1981, the whole country seemed to be celebrating the Royal Wedding, between HRH Prince Charles and Lady Diana Spencer, who became the Princess of Wales. Not to be left out of things, a 'summer fair' was organised here at the College, with a huge barbecue open to all civilian staff and their families, accompanied by lots of sideshows and fund-raising efforts.

As a focal point on the day, the Commandant gave an address, at which he read out the 'Oath of Allegiance', which is supposedly spoken by all soldiers when they 'sign on'. He then asked all apprentices and PS to join him in re-affirming this oath. Later, in the Sergeants' Mess, several members were to congratulate him, saying that they had never heard the oath read out in public before. This reading of the oath was later incorporated into the end-of-term prize-giving ceremony.

That Summer term had seen the usual squad of between forty and sixty A/Ts undergoing athletics training, as part of what was known at the time as 'The Running, Jumping and Throwing Club'. The start of the season generally sees a bunch of flabby pallid individuals, the first sight of which would make any self-respecting OIC Athletics *"rush off, flog his wheelchair and volunteer for something less dangerous"*.

However, during the season that follows, an amazing transformation takes place, with muscles being honed to perfection, rippling under the College athletics strip, and each apprentice seemingly grown to ten feet of golden haired and bronzed beauty. The College magazine was possibly overstating the case somewhat, but competition definitely brings out the best in those boys who excel at athletic pastimes.

All of the season's coaching, training and effort was geared to entering a team for the Junior Army Major Unit Championships, as well as for the Triangular Games between Arborfield and its archrivals, Chepstow and Harrogate. That season also saw the team compete in the Berkshire County Junior Championships, with other friendly competitions arranged against such worthy opponents as Wellington College, the Metropolitan Police College and RMA Sandhurst. This obviously paid off, as nine members that year gained their Army Junior Colours, with one boy even representing the Army at Senior level in the shot-put. He was kindly described at the time as the *"biggest, most sun-tanned VM"* in the College!

A 'College Council' is set up

Following what he thought was an isolated, but nevertheless serious, incident of bullying, the Commandant moved quickly to dispel any possibility of further outbreaks, by having the dozen or so offenders summarily discharged from the service. This unfortunate occurrence consequently led to the setting up of a 'College Council', made up of several boys who had reached senior apprentice rank in their respective Companies, the boy-RSM, PS RSM and the Commandant himself. The purpose of the Council was basically to find out, at first hand and as early as possible, what was going through the minds of the boys, and to attempt to nip any future problems 'in the bud'.

As the Commandant was to explain some years later, the Army system of punishment at that time, the early Eighties, seemed to award a first offender a relatively minor punishment, with increasingly stiffer penalties for any further transgressions. He was thus quite surprised to find that, from his Council meeting, the representative senior boys 'on the ground' recommended that any first offence should be punitively dealt with. They were of the thought that the previous 'gently, gently' approach caused an offender to become conditioned to breaking the rules, whereas the 'hit them hard' approach would act as a far greater deterrent. Despite some misgivings, it was the boys' approach that was adopted.

A very big 'feather in the cap' for the College during the summer term was the attendance by twenty apprentices from assorted Companies at a three-day 'bash' with the LAD of 29 Commando Regt RA at Plymouth, Devon. Here the boys discovered the dubious delights of patrolling on Dartmoor, both under a noonday sun and during the darkness of night. Then there was the notorious 'scramble course' – doubling for 400 yards, plunging 300 feet down over rocks and trees, diving through the river, scrambling up another 400 feet of rocks and trees, back down for another river crossing, up to the start point and collapsing! Except that there was no time for collapsing – because instead the boys then faced a two-mile run, followed at the ultimate stage by the steepest hill one could imagine!

After all that, it was back to 'the citadel' and the dreaded assault course. But having already undergone the previous part of the training course, this final stretch, which consisted of filthy water in the tunnel, oozing

Is it just rose tinted spectacles - or were the wooden Spiders more comfortable than modern brick built barrack rooms?

mud, broken glass, wet ropes and slippery planks, seemed like 'a piece of cake'! After all, these lads were from the Apprentices' College – and when the going gets tough, it's the tough that get going!

Very important visitors

Since his arrival at Arborfield, Col John Peacock had always insisted that the reviewing officers at apprentices' 'PoP's' should be of no less than three-star status. For the first 'PoP' to take place within the new College, he had actually left the issue of his invitations rather late. So he considered it most fortunate indeed to finally arrange for the parade to be reviewed by no less than the Chief of Defence Staff himself, Admiral of the Fleet Sir Terence Lewin, GCB, MVO, DSC, DSc. The Admiral was most impressed by what he saw here at Arborfield and wasn't afraid to say so. As possibly the last reviewing officer to still have personal experiences of World War II, he had that generosity of spirit that was so often found in the senior officers of his generation.

1981 had been designated as 'International Year of the Disabled'. Following a request set up partly by Capt Jim Fox, the College's and REME's own Olympic hero, it came as no surprise that it was Arborfield Garrison that hosted the very first 'Armed Forces Wheelchair Marathon' in September of that year. Apprentices from the College had long played their part in assisting local charities and community projects, and at this inaugural event, the College entered six separate teams, out of a total of fifty-seven.

In October 1981, the Commandant produced a paper of his own, in response to the conclusions of an 'Aircraft Apprentices Study'. This had been based upon recruiting figures and demographic trends, arguing that there would be sufficient adult recruits to the Air Tech trade to meet the full requirements of the Corps for the foreseeable future. Col Peacock, however, was advising that further research was required into details of birth rates, along with relevant dates, before any reduction in – or even a complete loss of - apprentice training at this trade was approved.

The main thrust of his argument, of a more parochial nature, was based upon the possible dilution in the 'ethos' of the College. There is no doubt that the Air Tech trade group had provided many a high quality apprentice over recent years, reaching many of the senior rank A/T positions and winning a good proportion of the College awards. Air Techs certainly made a disproportionate contribution to College life, far outweighing their mere numbers. As far as the Commandant was concerned, the loss of the source of such talent would prove a hard one to bear.

November 7th 1981 brought another get-together for old boys, although due to the recent move of the College, the normal full weekend Reunion was not possible. An afternoon tour of the new PMC buildings was first on the agenda, followed by the AGM and a buffet supper. The 'old school', with its large barrack rooms of around twenty young boys allocated to each, had gone and the new smaller rooms were a lot cosier. But in some cases, there were now stairs to climb, and some of the old boys were now truly becoming less sprightly in that particular department!

The winter 1981 edition of *The Arborfield Apprentice* gave a fascinating report on the origins of the term 'Jeep' (in the singular) or 'Jeeps' (plural). Someone had argued that the latter stood for 'junior entry, everyone's personal slave', but this is probably a case of the phrase being invented to fit the acronym. Far more likely was that story told by the venerable Harry Shaw, who remembered a character in the old *'Popeye'* cartoon strip, a baby who was at the crawling stage only, and whose sole expression seemed to be 'jeep'. Some parallel, between the extreme youth and monosyllabic language of the child and the tender age of the latest recruit, seems to have been given a permanent place in history!

Long service and good conduct

Another item of both current and historical interest again saw the light of day during 1981, namely the LSGC Medal, which was awarded that year to WO2s Fairbairn and Padwick, both of them Coldstream Guards and then serving here on the PS. The Medal had been instituted in 1830 by order of King William IV, in recognition of meritorious service. It was awarded to soldiers of the British Army, who had served for either twenty-one years in the infantry or twenty with the cavalry. Its issue was limited to Warrant Officers, Non-Commissioned Officers and 'men of irreproachable character'. The earliest version of the medal featured a trophy of weapons on the obverse and the inscription *'For long service and good conduct'* stamped on the reverse. A plain crimson accompanying ribbon was used.

The original design was to change slightly during Queen Victoria's reign, the sovereign's head first appearing in 1901. During the First World War, the ribbon was given white edges, to prevent it being confused with that of the Victoria Cross. In 1930, the medal acquired its present title and has remained unchanged ever since. It is now awarded to officers and soldiers who have completed a minimum of fifteen years exemplary Regular Army service, or its equivalent, over the age of seventeen and a half years. Only those personnel who are in every way worthy of the distinction, and whose personal conduct has proved to be irreproachable throughout their service, are considered for this prestigious award.

That same year finally saw the retirement of Mr Cyril Rapley, one of the College's longest serving members, from his seemingly 'permanent' job in the Admin Office. Cyril's major claim to fame was the fact that, having once been a keen motor-cyclist and then later suffered the loss of one leg, he still continued to ride to and from work, albeit now in a motor-cycle and side-car combination. Cyril also had an almost superhuman memory for detail, able to call to mind a vast miscellany of facts and figures on demand. It wasn't for nothing that he was called the 'human computer'.

The indoor sport of Table Tennis was going particularly well in the College. The season began in October 1981, with three teams being entered in the Bracknell and District League. Considering the high standards set by their civilian counterparts, these youngsters were able to 'hold their own' in commanding fashion. This was highlighted by the fact that two young Arborfield apprentices were selected to represent the Army team at RAF Stanmore, against opponents from both the RAF and RN.

The Freedom of Wokingham

That same month, the College was chosen to represent REME, when the Corps exercised its three-year old right as 'Honorary Townspeople', to march through the neighbouring town of Wokingham. In June 1978, following a meeting between His Worship the Mayor and the Commandant REME Training Centre, it had been proposed that REME be given 'The Freedom of Wokingham' on October 21st of that year. A document was duly drawn up, which included the following statement:

"Know all men by these presents that we, the Mayor, Councillors and Townspeople of the Town of Wokingham, in recognition of the close ties of lasting friendship between our town and the Corps of Royal Electrical and Mechanical Engineers, and of the most excellent civic links thus formed, do hereby grant and confirm to The Corps of Royal Electrical and Mechanical Engineers the status of Honorary Townspeople, and the freedom of entry to the Town of Wokingham, under arms and in full ceremonial."

Thus it was that, three years after the inaugural occasion, it was the College that now provided one Company, comprising four officers and over one hundred soldiers, to march through the town, accompanied by the College's own Pipes and Drums, as well as by the REME Staff Band. Following the ceremony and a lavish lunch reception in the Town Hall, the Corps reciprocated that evening with a cocktail reception in the HQ REME Officers' Mess at West Court.

In November 1981 the College finally thought to enter a team for the SE District Patrol Competition, from which it had previously been conspicuous by its absence. From an initial squad of around twenty volunteers, a final team of eight apprentices was selected, under the command of Sgt Isom of the PS. Training had started in September, with Monday evenings, Thursday afternoons and most weekends devoted to the required marching, patrolling, crawling and shooting. As was to be expected it rained just about every time the lads went out, which proved to be just as well, as they were all well used to the rain by the time the heavens opened on the day of the competition. The patrol itself finished at 03.00 hrs, followed by a forced march over 10 km at 06.00 hrs. After all the sweat, tears and just a little blood, the Arborfield team finished a most creditable third, ahead of all other apprentice teams.

The final month of 1981 saw RSM Yorke depart from Arborfield, his replacement being RSM A 'Tony' Fox, another from the ranks of the splendid Coldstream Guards. 1982 certainly started on a high note, when Mrs Peggy McMaster, our resident WRVS lady at the time, was made a Member of the Order of the British Empire in the New Year's Honours List. She had been more affectionately known by all the boys as 'Mrs

Mac' since her arrival in 1979, and there could not be a single apprentice who hadn't benefited from her tireless efforts on their behalf. She proudly took her place in the Investiture at Buckingham Palace on March 2nd. Mrs Mac's work at the College was the very epitome of voluntary service: *"To labour and not ask for any reward"*.

Touring with the Bands

Meanwhile, the College Bands set off on tour once again, this time to visit BAOR in Germany, performing to their usual high standard at several REME units in the north of that country. A rather rough ferry crossing gave one of the Band the ideal chance to make a detailed study of the ship's plumbing system! However, this inauspicious start was soon forgotten as the tour got into its swing. As well as the obvious delights of making music and entertaining, 49 Field Regt RA gave them the opportunity of a 'cabby' in *FV432* Armoured Personnel Carriers (APCs), while 71 Aircraft Wksp provided some exciting helicopter tours.

A concert, presented in the shopping centre of Celle, a fine old German town full of mediaeval-looking buildings and 'home' to many military units, was thoroughly enjoyed and applauded by hundreds of local people, as well as many members of forces' families. The 'big day' of the trip was at Fallingbostel, a small town further north, where the Band entertained more civilians outside the town's 'Rathaus' (town hall), before marching in style up the sloping cobbled road to 7 Armoured Wksp REME for its 'Open Day'. This event ended with the College Bands 'beating the retreat'.

Col Peacock, writing in *The Arborfield Apprentice* of the 1981 winter term, reminded 'his' boys that nearly sixty per cent of all REME Artificers at that time had previously exited through the gates of the College. As the ratio of adult to apprentice entries was approximately 60:40, this meant that the likelihood of an ex-boy reaching the senior ranks was twice that

NAAFI Break

of adult entries, a pretty good record for the College to have maintained. As Commandant, Col Peacock was also proud to report on the unmitigated success, so far, of the College Appeal Fund. Thanks to a lot of effort from the old boys, institutions within the Corps and present boys' families, the Fund then stood at some £7,000. Charitable status was now being sought, which, if granted, would prove an important consideration for tax purposes.

The first intake of 1982 numbered a meagre total of thirty-seven boys, proving to be the smallest 'J' Coy on record. There were so few of them that they tended to 'rattle around' in their accommodation block, so it was decided to close down the top floor as an economy measure. One of those boys who had joined as a member of 82A was Danny James, who trained here as a Gun Fitter for the requisite two years, but recalls that on his subsequent posting to BAOR, was used as a *"jack of all trades"*. Later, during service in Northern Ireland, he volunteered to handle guard dogs and, in 1988, voluntarily transferred to the Ulster Defence Regt (UDR). Whilst at the College, Danny had been part of 'C' Coy, whose OC at the time was Maj 'Monty' Montgomery of the RTR. During leadership training in the hills of South Wales, Monty's ritual was to make the boys wash in cold running water, drawn from whatever source was to hand.

Action Man (or just plain knackered!)

Danny can remember one particular early morning when Monty, in his usual gung-ho style, woke the boys up at 6 o'clock and had them in for a 'quick dip' in an ice-cold pool, situated below a mountain waterfall. They then went off hill walking in the Brecon Beacons, their challenge for the day to scale Pen-y-fan, the region's highest peak. As Danny describes it, *"A mountain goat couldn't hold a candle to Monty, he was off like a rocket"*. By the time the peak was attained, the boys were on their proverbial knees, but Monty still appeared *"as fresh as a daisy"*.

Early in 1982, PMC lost a couple of its 'driving force', in the shape of Messrs Sid Bradford and Bill

Hayles, who both ended their long careers whilst acting as Driving Instructors at the College. Sid had joined the Army in 1934 and ended his military service in 1956 as an ASM in REME. Bill had also seen many years of service, having been with the BEF at the start of the war and going on to serve in many different countries. Like Sid, he had arrived here at Arborfield in 1977.

Meanwhile down at Bordon, ex-boy Pete Gripton of 56B was coming to terms with the arrival of the SEME Computer system, based very much upon that already in use at the College. The hardware was delivered in March 1982, but the system was not 'up and running' until July that year, when the equipment had passed stringent tests by the Central Computer and Telecommunications Agency (CCTA). During that time, Pete made several trips back to his 'ancestral home' in order to learn just how the system was used here at Arborfield. He then set about the task, in conjunction with *Data General* personnel, of re-writing much of the software for the particular requirements of the SEME Training Validation Department. 'Computer based training' was certainly spreading throughout the Army during that aptly named '*Information Technology Year*'.

Conflict in the Falklands

In the shadow of the invasion of the Falklands Islands by Argentine troops on April 2nd, HRH the Prince Philip, Duke of Edinburgh and C-in-C of the Corps, arrived on another visit to Arborfield, in order to officially open the new PMC buildings on Thursday 15th April 1982. Here, he unveiled a commemorative plaque in the main entrance hall of the new College HQ, as shown on the cover of *The Craftsman* in July that year. Brilliant sunshine accompanied Prince Philip during his tour and he later observed that both the Commandant and RSM must have been praying hard at Church the previous Sunday! Later, in the College magazine, the Commandant was to express his relief that, after all the effort and preparation, some roles played in the background and others in the limelight, the event had gone so successfully.

In the audience on that auspicious day was Ianto Metcalfe, an ex-boy from 39B intake, who had travelled all the way from his far-off home in New Zealand for the occasion. Meanwhile, a newspaper article in the *Middlesborough Evening Gazette* of 22nd April proudly pointed out a happy coincidence that had a 'local' flavour. It turned out that the staff RSM Fox and the 'boy' A/T RSM, Chris Keating, both of whom had participated in the above parade, were from the neighbouring town of Stockton-on-Tees.

It was Prince Philip's second visit to Arborfield within the space of four years. On April 27th 1978, he had been the guest here of the Training Battalion and Depot REME. The Battalion had moved into Rowcroft Barracks in October of 1977, from their original home in Poperinghe Barracks, which had then been demolished to make way for a new Garrison by-pass road and housing estate. At that time, entrance to the Depot was through the main gates of the old AAC site.

The war in those distant ocean-swept Falklands Islands of the South Atlantic inevitably involved members of REME and, as far as can be established, at least thirty-seven ex-apprentices served there, mainly attached to units of the Royal Marines. Thankfully, none lost their lives, although one of them, ex-boy Cfn Andrew Owen was severely burned at Bluff Cove on the supply ship HMS 'Sir Galahad' on June 8th, whilst serving with the LAD of the Welsh Guards. It was barely a week later that the Argentine invaders were forced to surrender. Later, whilst recovering in Woolwich Hospital, Andrew was greatly cheered to receive a huge hamper of gifts from local people and schoolchildren in Wokingham.

(A brief story about Andrew Owen, containing further details, is included as a separate annex to this chapter.)

Two other REME tradesmen, LCpl A R Streatfield and Cfn M W Rollins, were killed in that attack by Argentine bombers at Bluff Cove. REME also lost two more members, Cpl J Newton, serving with 22 SAS and Cfn A Shaw, attached to 3 Parachute Regt. A tribute to them all was paid in *The Craftsman* issued in August that year.

Writing about that conflict later, the Commandant touched upon the subject of courage, much in the way that his predecessor Col Hilborn had many years ago when he encouraged the 1939 boys with the words *"Courage mes enfants"*. Referring firstly to Cfn Owen, Col Peacock stated, *"Clearly he was not short of courage when courage was called for. Members of the College have every right to be proud of him"*. Then he continued on the same theme, *"Perhaps 'Courage' is the key word to come out of that war. Courage displayed by sailors, soldiers and airmen throughout*

the short-lived campaign. From the early actions on South Georgia, through the daring raid on Pebble Island, the air raids at San Carlos, the phenomenal victory at Goose Green, the horror of Bluff Cove and the final assault and victorious entry into Port Stanley".

A study too far?

It was around that time that yet another 'study' was taking place into the 'junior' Army training programme. Chaired by Gen John Groom, an ex-Sapper, the eventual *'Groom Study'* was heading for a conclusion that went along the following lines: *'if an infantry soldier could receive the required leadership and military training in only one year, why could not technicians be likewise trained in a similar period, leaving any further training to the adult training units?'* This proposal was evidently fought off at the time but, ominously as it would prove for the College, the ideas behind it were never completely dropped.

The spring 1982 edition of *The Arborfield Apprentice* provided an article which looked back nostalgically upon three of the College cap-badges worn by previous apprentices. Firstly came the badge of the RAOC, as it was this Corps to which the original boys were intended to go. That badge lasted from the inauguration of the ATS in 1939 until the formation of REME in 1942. The GSC badge followed this from 1942 to 1947, then finally came the unique AAS badge, introduced in 1947 and which remained in service until the 'School' became a College in 1966. At the time of the article, all three badges could be seen displayed on guidons in the College entrance hall.

In that same edition, A/T LCpl Langley told of his inevitably mixed feelings, leading up to what was going to be his first parachute descent. *"You wake up in the morning with a strange feeling running through your head, a feeling of giddiness and excitement. Then the thoughts turn to questions – 'So I'm really going to jump am I?' 'What will it feel like?' 'Will I remember my drill, my count?' 'Why did I volunteer for this stupid game anyway?'"* He then went on to describe the events leading up to the take-off, firstly the climb, then his attachment to the static line and, finally, the jump! *"You fling your arms and legs out, as you have practiced so many times on the ground. You're falling faster and faster. You feel the tug on your shoulders and look up to see a large orange and white canopy, the plane going away. 'I've done it! I've done it! Damn, I forgot to count!'"* But he **did** do it.

Another young apprentice, A/T Steven, described the *"chance of a lifetime"* he had been able to take, when serving as a crewmember on a very large sailing ship, the *'Sir Winston Churchill'*. He went on to say that it had certainly not been a 'luxury cruise', but was very rewarding and a lot of fun. Whilst on watch, climbing the masts to reef the sails proved a terrifying experience, but one not to be missed. The food was good and regular, while everyone was free to make their own drinks and sandwiches when on duty. The whole trip was truly memorable, but young Steven still felt relieved to reach port in one piece, having been awarded his 'competent crewman' certificate. Even if he never sailed again, he would be able to look back and say, *"I tried it the hard way"*.

Ex-apprentice - and now Sgt - P Russell of intake 65C found his name in the news that summer. He had been awarded a Commendation from the GOC Northern Ireland, for his outstanding performance as an Avionics Tech with 655 Sqn LAD AAC since January 1981. The Commendation read *" ... ... your devotion to duty, professional expertise and cheerful example in maintaining the very high level of aircraft availability, which operations in Northern Ireland demand, has been of the highest order"*.

Achievements one, two, three

In the summer 1982 publication of *The Arborfield Apprentice*, the boys of 'C' Coy were rightfully proud of the fact that they had achieved a notable hat-trick of victories in the College Athletics Championships. Some members of the Company had also been out on field exercises at Sennybridge, which had only recently been vacated by echelons of the Falklands Task Force following their 'warm-up' exercise. And, as a proud addition to their accomplishments that year, once again the challenge of *'The Three Peaks'* had been faced and overcome. (*"Why do you climb a mountain?" "Because it's there." "Then why climb three mountains in just one weekend?"* Lost for words!)

At the summer 'PoP', Col Peacock was delighted to welcome a very special visitor, Lt Gen Sir Stuart Pringle Bt, KCB, then Commandant General of the Royal Marines, as the Reviewing Officer. It was purely coincidental that the General attended here so soon after the recapture of the Falkland Islands, where

the Royal Marines had played such a significant role. The General had lost one of his legs in a bombing attempt on his life, presumably by a unit of the IRA, at Dulwich (London) the previous year. The Parade itself had to be curtailed somewhat, as the General was unable to remain on the saluting platform, at the standing position, for too long. But prior to that, Gen Pringle had made a special point of stopping to speak to every single member of the Senior Div.

During the summer recess, four brave lads from 'D' Coy gave up their leave to attend 'Outward Bound' courses at Ullswater and Eskdale in the Lake District, and Aberdovey (or Aberdyffi to the locals!) on the western coast of mid-Wales. Although at times the weather did its utmost to thwart their efforts *(doesn't it always? It's not known as 'Wet Wales' for nothing! Ed.)*, all appeared none the worse for their experiences and looked forward to the next External Leadership (EL) camp, where they hoped to show off their newly honed skills.

The latest arrivals in 'Jeepland' ('J' Coy) had some welcome news of a change of scene when told that they would be attending the Army Air Display at Middle Wallop for three days. Although it turned out that they were required to fill in as car-park attendants and litter-pickers *(some things never change! Ed.)*, they still found plenty of time to look around and enjoy the show. It was also discovered that a *Bentley* could sometimes be parked where once only a *Mini* would go, but perhaps we shouldn't expand on that! Their efforts proved 'a nice little earner' too, as they earned the sum of £900 towards the College Trust Fund.

In August of that year, Barry Reeves BA submitted a report *"in part fulfillment of the requirements for the degree of Master of Arts in the University of London"*. Members of the College between September 1979 and September 1981 would recognise the author as none other than their SEO of those two years, Lt Col B Reeves RAEC. In that post, he had been intimately involved in the development of leadership training. Barry had now undertaken to study the *"reactions and attitudes of Army Apprentices"* in respect to their training for REME. His study tested certain hypotheses, using multi-choice style questionnaires, most of which were rejected! Barry's final words indicated that, as a study of job satisfaction, his task was necessarily incomplete. Back to the drawing board eh, Barry?

During the 1982 summer term, the College bade its farewell to Mr Mike Kapuscinski of the EQC

Department, where he had been looking after the SPEC computer system since 1977, following a most interesting previous career. Mike had joined the Polish Army as a cadet at the tender age of only thirteen, being eventually commissioned into its Armoured Corps. Captured by the German forces in 1939, he was sent to a prison camp in Romania, from which he bravely escaped, crossing Europe to join the French Army as a tank commander. Having then been wounded, and after France's capitulation, Mike made his way across the mountain passes of the Pyrenees to Spain and managed to talk himself aboard a coal ship across the Bay of Biscay, eventually disembarking at the port of Plymouth.

He soon found his way up to Scotland, where he joined the First Armoured Division of the Free Polish Army. Needless to say, when the Allied invasion of Europe took place in June 1944, Mike was right there in the front line, taking part in the capture of Caen and the closure of the Falaise Gap. He was to end the war participating in the capture of the German submarine base at Wilhelmshaven. Following service in the British Army from 1947 right up to 1969, Mike eventually found himself instructing in Arborfield's Vehicle Wing in 1972. Showing the 'slight of hand' at which he became adept, Mike joined the EQC in 1975 and proved himself a 'keyboard wizard' for the few remaining years of his service.

The 'demon barber' retires

It was also during 1982 that the College finally said goodbye to Charlie, the 'demon barber' who had so terrorised apprentices with his instant applications of 'short back and sides' styles of coiffeur whilst serving for nearly thirty years with REME. That was 'only joking' of course, as the boys sincerely wished him a long and happy retirement. Charlie had himself joined the DYRMS – or Dukies – as a young lad of eleven years of age in 1924, prior to serving with the Royal

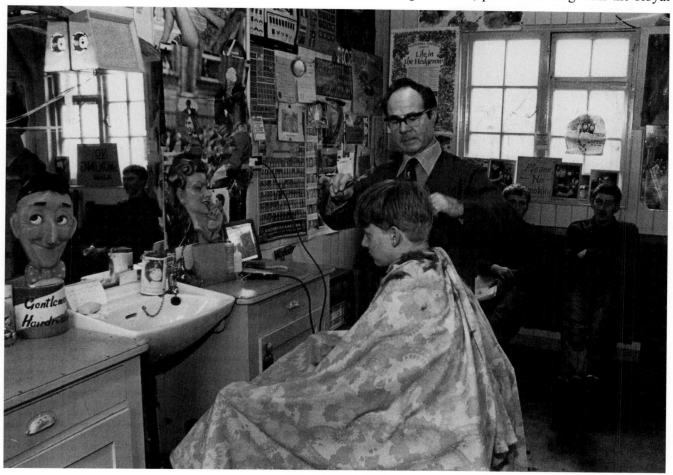

Something for the weekend, Sir?

So this is Legoland!

For tens of thousands of ex-boys, the shape of the buildings in the new Army Apprentices' is light years away from the warm and familiar Spiders built in 1939. But will they stand the test of time?

Hampshire Regt.

His first association with REME came at the Depot in 1949, after which he later spent two short years with his family in Australia. Having got to know the Garrison barber at Tidworth, who subsequently moved here to Arborfield, Charlie was then offered what turned out to be his final job. A proud moment for Charlie was when he was presented to Prince Philip at the parade to open the PMC.

On Wednesday 20th October 1982, PMC was happy to host a get-together of the Worshipful Company of Turners, which had maintained a long and happy affiliation with REME since shortly after its formation in 1942. Some time towards the end of the decade, the Company was to make an annual award of its Silver Medal, a monetary reward and a certificate, to the apprentice who achieved the 'highest standard of craft skills during training'.

The last 'PoP' of that year, held on December 17th, saw the attendance of another Falklands hero, Maj Gen Jeremy Moore KCB, OBE, MC, as the Reviewing Officer. During his speech, he mentioned that, as Commander of the Land Forces, he had spent a lot of that encounter 'flying tactically' in helicopters, by which he meant *"you are so low that you have to lift up to get over a sheep"*! The General presented the LSGC Medal to Sgt Young (ASH), a member of MTW. Following the Prize-giving Ceremony, the General was then introduced to Cfn Andrew Owen, the ex-apprentice who had been injured at Bluff Cove. Having been recently awarded the 'Atlantic Sword' by the City of London, at the Victory Parade, the General took off the sword and casually handed it over to Andrew, asking him to keep it safe until his (the General's) departure.

Reunion in 'Legoland'

In *The Arborfield Apprentice* issue of winter 1982, there was a look back to the Old Boys' Reunion of the previous October. This was the first time that a *"full-scale reunion"* had been possible in the new buildings, which had already been christened '*Legoland*' by some of the more irreverent apprentices! For the first time, much pleasure was gained by the evening's use of the Garrison Bailleul Sergeants' Mess for dinner, complete with candelabras and the Mess silver, making it a thoroughly memorable occasion. But there was an even longer peek into the past, with the reproduction of a photograph which was finally reckoned to have been taken as long ago as 1939.

It had been brought in by 'Hoppy' Hopkins, an ex-boy who left Arborfield at the end of 1941 and was now a Senior Lecturer at SEE. The photograph showed a group of apprentices gathered in front of the old oak tree that used to decorate the top end of the Parade Square. The writer wondered what had happened to all those members of 5 Wing, 'B' Coy, familiar enough faces, but with now forgotten names? To how many distant corners of the world did they scatter – and how many great stories could they tell? Indeed, how many of them, like that oak tree, would never be seen again?

A heartfelt request by the REME Mobile Display Team caused much scratching of heads and frantic planning just prior to the Christmas recess, when the Model Club was asked to produce a new display model for their mobile caravan. With a deadline of late February 1983, there was much work to be done but, in true Arborfield manner, the target was reached. The model produced was of a *Centurion* tank being pulled out of the mud by a second *Centurion*, in its Armoured Recovery Vehicle (ARV) role, complete with figures representing individual members of the recovery team. The Display Team received this with much delight, knowing that it would provide an excellent talking point around which future recruitment would be greatly assisted.

On Tuesday 11th January 1983, eighty-eight young boys arrived, eagerly wanting to be turned into soldier/ tradesmen. With all the usual settling-in procedures behind them, the second week saw their 'Junior Cadre' start in earnest. It was unfortunate that several of those 83A boys were later struck down by some mysterious 'bug', seeing them fall prey to the tender mercies of the medical staff. But their eventual Parents' Day turned out to be a splendid occasion. PS members took the opportunity to interview the parents, to ensure that they were fit enough people to look after their young charges during the forthcoming leave period!

The beginning of 1983 also witnessed the moment of Col John Peacock's departure. He had found his three-year stint to be *"very stimulating, immensely satisfying and great fun from beginning to end"*. His successor, Colonel S J 'Sam' Roberts, BSc(Eng), CEng, FIMechE, FIEE, FBIM, thus became the sixteenth Commandant. *(He could also have been the seventeenth, if the first Commandant's 'double tour' is classed as two separate appointments. Ed.)* Col Roberts had just completed a tour at HQ DGEME, Andover, having spent most of

Enjoying the benefits of the Library under the watchful eye of Victor Brook,
the Honourable Viscount Alanbrooke of Brookeborough

his career with the 1st and 4th Armoured Divisions in BAOR, with brief interludes in Hong Kong, Canada and here at Arborfield.

(A brief look at Col Peacock's career is attached as a separate annex to this chapter.)

The new Commandant's tour was to be epitomised by his policy of 'MBWA', which, as he was quick to explain to everyone, stood for *"management by walking about"*. All staff were encouraged to actually walk around the College, to observe and make themselves seen, and to both listen and be listened to. Col Roberts, as a Corps player himself, certainly made an impact upon the fortunes of the College Squash Team. In February, the Army U-19 Championship was won in fine style and there was already a marked increase in standards all round.

Later that year, members of the Climbing Club spent the first week of their Easter leave up at a favourite spot, namely the remote Cairngorms. The weather was extremely kind (makes a change!) and gave good opportunities for climbing experience on snow and ice. Most of the climbs had to be preceded by lengthy walks, up to some thirty kilometres a stretch, but that year's party had the benefit of being accompanied by LCpl Hiett of the ACC. Not only did

he join in with all the hard work of walking and climbing, but he produced all the meals too. Not a bad chap to have along!

The College had to make do with a combined spring/summer issue of *The Arborfield Apprentice* in 1983. In it, the Commandant was telling of his impressions of his tour so far, during which he had certainly not been disappointed at all. After one particular tour of the College, one visiting senior officer had remarked that *"this must be the best technical college in the country"*. True of course, but another more 'tongue-in-cheek' way of looking at things came a few pages later, when a 'mock' VM exam paper was supposed to have contained the following question:

Q. Draw, with great difficulty, a sectioned view of a Bedford RL engine, and explain why you are unlikely to meet this engine ever again in your service career.

A 'taste of the future'

That same magazine contained a contribution from two apprentices, giving observations of their temporary attachment to an adult unit, 12 Air Defence Regt at Kirton-in-Lindsey, up in north Lincolnshire, a few miles south of Scunthorpe. This 'posting' was an attempt to give apprentices a 'taste of the future', by seconding them to a regular unit to gain experience. A/Ts Mullin and Harry were definitely in favour of their 'away trip'. They had taken a serious look at the *'Rapier'* system that had scored numerous hits on Argentine aircraft in the Falklands the previous year, but had still had time to note that the small village contained four pubs!

A cold winter's morning earlier in the year had led to the decision by boys of 'D' Coy that their 'Company Outing' would be a little different that year. Thus it was that, one Saturday early in June saw 100 assorted apprentices, members of staff and 'affiliated personnel' boarding two coaches bound for 'a day trip to France'.

It is not known how many portions of frogs' legs and *escargot* were devoured that day, as the town of Boulogne suffered its Arborfield invasion. What is known is that everyone was safely accounted for when the two coaches set off on the return trip. One happy band of travellers sang all the way home, to the twang of A/T Sgt Tolson's guitar, while it is believed the second party just got their heads down and kipped the journey away!

In *The Craftsman* magazine of June 1983, a certain Mr T Godwin had written to say how disappointed he had been that, at the last Old Boy's Reunion, there were so few of his 62B/62C colleagues in attendance. This brought to notice that, at the time, it was mainly down to the old boys themselves to spread the word and assist in recruiting new members. Later years were to bring more sophisticated recruiting methods, but that 'old boy network' still remains the best method of all.

The Ten Tors walk took its usual place on the College itinerary in 1983, with eleven actual finishers, while the challenge of walking 'Offa's Dyke' was taken up by another party of eager volunteers that summer. In ancient times, Offa, King of Mercia, had constructed a bank and ditch to mark the boundary between England and Wales. Now, some 1,200 years later, the Offa's Dyke path runs about 180 miles, from Sedbury Cliffs, near Chepstow, all the way up to the estuary of the River Dee at Prestatyn, North Wales. Setting off in high spirits, the nineteen-strong party of apprentices, along with five support staff that included RSM Tony Fox as expedition leader, reached Monmouth at the end of the first day. Eighteen miles had been covered, the weather hadn't been too bad, but blistered feet and sweat rashes *'sur la derriere'* were the order of the day.

Covering an average of about the same mileage per day, the party trekked its way north in a mixture of fog and sunshine, until one day's slog of twenty-seven miles in the hot sun brought the possibility of sunburn. After that, however, the weather gradually turned for the worse, and the temperature dropped as they found themselves once again enmeshed in fog. With one day and only fourteen miles to go, the boys enjoyed a splendid late-evening barbecue and a lie-in until six o'clock on the last morning. As the weather warmed up again and the hills became a memory, the whole group finally dropped rucksacks and posed for the obligatory photographs. On morning assembly back at Arborfield on June 27th, the Commandant awarded the boys a 'Certificate of Merit' for their fine effort.

It was also in June that four apprentices of the Climbing Club set off for Cornwall to gain experience of cliff climbing. An introductory session of 'rock scrambling' was accompanied by some unplanned knowledge of seawater on the first evening, before the following morning saw the first ascent. This took place on 'Commando Ridge', suitably named after the training that had taken place there during the Second World War, and provided some severe climbs.

The evening was spent at Sennen Cove watching one of the PS members try out his windsurfing techniques. The following day, the boys themselves had a go – but minus the sails. One invaluable lesson was learned on a subsequent climb, when A/T McArthur found the penalty of climbing with the rope between his legs! Before returning, rather regretfully, to Arborfield, the amusements and 'talent' of St Ives were explored.

RSMs? They come and go

August 1983 heralded the arrival of a new RSM, when the third successive member from the Coldstream Guards, RSM J H 'John' Todd took over the appointment from RSM Tony Fox. The incoming RSM had been none too impressed when he first heard of his posting here to Arborfield, as it had long been his dream that promotion would bring with it the treasured post at the Guard's Depot, at Pirbright. But '*Arborfield*? *Princess Marina College*?' Where is it and what is it, were the questions John must have asked himself. However, his impressions of PMC were immediately enhanced upon arriving at the Guardroom and being challenged by a very smart young REME soldier, wearing green flashes upon his epaulettes. Following a close grilling by the Commandant, and two weeks spent in preparation for the next 'PoP', John decided that perhaps there was another life outside of the Household Division after all!

'Civic duties' were well to the fore once more during 1983. Local newspapers were happily reporting the opening of a new six-metre riverside footbridge across a ditch at Waterloo Meadows, Reading. The *Reading Waterways Trust* had provided most of the materials, but it was the efforts of twelve young Arborfield apprentices, over two successive weekends, that had provided the labour. Technical advice – and the concrete mixer – was on hand, courtesy of RE

LCpl Wooton from his Depot at Hawley. As quoted in one story, *"They built the bridge in a sort of super Meccano-style at the College and then transported it to the site"*. The Mayor of Reading later invited the boys to a reception at the Mayor's Parlour.

A telephone call, received on August 19th, confirmed that the PMC Cycle Team had not only cycled 2,000 miles non-stop through France and Italy, but had completed their journey within the target time of six days. This was not only a personal achievement for each team member, but also assisted the charity 'ASBAH' to raise much needed sponsorship funds towards the treatment of sufferers of spina bifida and hydrocephalus, two very debilitating diseases.

The team's journey, starting of course from Arborfield, took them in relay form via Southampton, by cross-Channel ferry to Le Havre. Despite the support mini-bus deciding to have a punctured tyre, steady progress was then made, on through Paris and Lyon. On one particularly straight stretch of road, one unfortunate rider actually fell asleep, but luckily fell into the soft landing of a roadside bush! Undeterred, the lads continued their epic journey via Turin, Genoa, Rome and Naples, and on to their final destination, Palermo, on the sun-drenched Mediterranean island of Sicily.

During a hobbies evening, it was remarked that the College had never had a 'regimental style picture' to its credit. The OC 'C' Coy, Maj M J Mockridge, Scots DG, nominated himself to organise a project by which such a 'College Painting' could be produced. Arriving here in early September 1983, artist Ken Howard proceeded on the necessary artwork. Completed by the end of that month, the watercolour on a theme of 'Soldier Tradesman' was surrounded by line drawings of typical College activities and a motif of the famous entrance gates. A number of prints were made for general sale, while the original painting was hung on general display in the main entrance of the College HQ building.

The one-year Apprenticeship

The winter term later that year was to see more significant changes. These would include the reorganisation of training programmes, as a result of the Home Defence requirements for trained soldiers in the Composite General Reserve Companies. Also came the arrival of the 'one-year' apprenticeship,

following the closure of the REME Company at the RAOC Apprentices' College, Deepcut, while the established seven-term technician apprenticeship was now being further reduced, to six terms.

Those REME Junior Craftsmen from Deepcut commenced their training at Arborfield in September 1983, on a one-year course that would lead on to a choice of Clerk, Metalsmith, Recovery Mechanic, Storeman or Vehicle Electrician training. It was Col Roberts' policy to integrate rather than segregate, so these young men completed the same CMS(R) syllabus as the remainder of 'J' Coy. Forming up on September 14th 1983 were 165 'new boys' – 149 of them being apprentices and the remaining sixteen PS. With no trade training whatsoever in the Company, all effort was put into military endeavours, which included learning the College song! 'J' Coy started off with the concept of five Platoons of approximately thirty apprentices each and, after initial 'teething problems', soon settled down to its function.

At the invitation of the DAE, Her Majesty's Inspectors from the Department of Education and Science once again visited the College for a period of five days during the latter part of September. This is an event that takes place approximately every four years and, as on previous occasions, their report proved more than satisfactory. The Inspectors took note of the fact that the Army's recently devised Junior Army Education Certificate (JAEC) was to be introduced for certain categories of General Trades apprentices in their second term (Jan 1984). This development was welcomed, as it would provide a useful incentive for those apprentices involved. On a completely different subject, the one factor that apprentices had frequently commented upon was the excellent quality of the food provided – indeed, it was described as being *"appetising, with attractive garnishes, available on a self-service basis"*. *(All together now, "It was never like that in **my** day!" Ed.)*

October brought the twentieth annual Old Boys' Reunion. Many members met up on the Friday night, where old friendships were renewed and new acquaintances made. Over 100 hardy old boys assembled for the next morning's parade, but some wet weather caused its cancellation. At the AGM that evening, President of the Association, Maj Gen T B Palmer, told the meeting that the OBA was *"part of the essential family business of the Corps"*. The evening's dinner was again held in Bailleul Sergeants'

Mess, while there were sufficient fit bodies around on the Sunday morning for the traditional church service.

It is likely that 1983 saw the introduction of EPC training here at the College, certainly all the training pamphlets that were used by Maj Knowles RAEC point to that date. The two subjects that were deemed suitable for apprentice tradesmen were at the basic level only, as the EPC was aimed at the attainment of adult sergeant rank. The advanced level, that up to WO status, was not used. Thus it was that classes in 'Military Calculations' and 'The Army in the Contemporary World' started to become part of

Goodbye Mrs Mac

the 'J' Coy scenario. The remaining two subjects of the EPC, 'Military Management' and 'Communications Studies' were to be left until later adult training.

That winter's edition of *The Arborfield Apprentice* saw the Commandant looking back on yet another year of change and challenge at the College. He now assumed that, following the passing of the *'Groom Study'* cloud, the College would hopefully be allowed a period of some stability. *(Come along, Sir, you didn't really think you'd get it? Ed.)*

A coveted 'Sword of Honour'

Mr J A Wedgwood, Chairman of the *Southern Electricity Board*, presented a cup to the College, to be awarded to the best Electronics Technician and, on December 16th 1983, A/T LCpl K Milner of 'C' Coy became its first recipient. In the same year, three ex-apprentices passed out with commissions into REME from the RMA at Sandhurst; the three new officers were Richard Mitchell, who had won the coveted 'Sword of Honour', Alan Powell, who received the Anson Memorial prize, and Paul Martin. The Sword of Honour is awarded to the Officer Cadet who is considered to be the best in his intake, so the fact that it went to an ex-boy proved a great honour for the College. 2nd Lt Mitchell had started his career as an Avionics Tech as a member of 77C, after an eight-term diploma course.

Meanwhile back here at Arborfield, a team of

three boys from 'D' Coy had volunteered to compete – or maybe even complete! – in the Wokingham Half Marathon, held on February 19th 1984. Guest runners at the event were to include Lewis Collins from *'The Professionals'* TV series, Phil Parkes the West Ham goalkeeper, and Jimmy Saville – perhaps Jim could *'fix it'* for 'D' Coy! Ideal weather accompanied the lads as they set off from the *'Molly Miller'* area, on a route that took in Barkham Hill, Sindlesham, Arborfield village and Finchampstead, before returning to Wokingham. All three competitors made it round the full thirteen miles, afterwards enjoying a quick visit to the *'Two Poplars'* watering hole before heading back to camp.

Remembering the past

It is to his eternal credit that Col Roberts took upon the task, with a reconstituted and enlarged magazine committee, of researching the historical story of the College and to present this in regular articles in *The Arborfield Apprentice*. This was no doubt largely instrumental in providing some of the material for the eventual College History that you find laid out in these pages.

Despite the poor employment situation in the country as a whole, which seemed fitting in *"the Orwellian year of disaster"*, recruitment was very low and still falling rapidly during 1984. This was attributed mainly to a raising of entry standards for apprenticeships, as dictated at Army Careers Information Offices, without due reference to REME. Thus, many 'possible' apprentices were being hived off to wear other cap badges. Indeed, the PMC population in the summer term that year was at its lowest point in the forty-five years of School and College history. However, the production of a new and more attractive College brochure, accompanied by some fairly aggressive advertising, plus various representations at outside schools and career conventions, resulted in an upsurge in enquiries and many firm acceptances for future terms.

On a slightly sadder note, the College now said a fond goodbye to Peggy McMaster, the well-known Mrs Mac of the WRVS, who was about to move on to a well-earned retirement in Winchester. Also leaving us that year was the ever helpful and smiling Joe Surtees, retiring from the Turning Shop of A & G Wing to the open spaces of the North Wales golf courses.

Joe had joined the Army way back in the pre-war days of 1937, as an apprentice Artificer with the RA, going on to serve during the war in India and Burma, followed by a gruelling stint with the UN forces in Korea. After fifteen years with the RA, he then transferred to the REME for the next seven. Following a period of instructing at Carlisle, then at Portsmouth Dockyard, Joe finally arrived here at the College in 1966. Joe's contribution to the College had been considerable over the years, particularly when the service of his two sons, who eventually both passed through the College, is taken into account.

An increasing use of the latest microcomputer technology, both in equipment design and management, resulted in a corresponding increase in the overall use of computers at the College. Extra local-area networks had been delivered, catering for the Education, Electronic, Vehicle and Aircraft Wings, as well as in the EQC Department. Even better monitoring of apprentices' performance, accompanied by the finer tuning of trade and education course contents, was looked upon as the way ahead. Wastage rates had already shown signs of improvement, following some trade course restructuring in September 1983.

In place of parents

One thing that Col Roberts thought would improve life at the College was to get the Company Commanders more involved in the day-to-day life of the young apprentices under their command. Seeing that these gentlemen were in all respects *in locum parentis*, the Commandant found it strange that they could remain desk-bound for long periods, with no regular contact with the boys. Thus it was that these 'acting parents' were encouraged to get out into the Training Wings and Education Wing, in order to better understand and appreciate what the apprentices got up to during their working days.

Members of 'B' Coy had begun their Basic Military Cadre (BMC) just after half-term, managing to scrape through their Battle Fitness Test (BFT) after some extra running and training during that half-term. A hard week's effort was put in at Longmoor Camp (near Bordon), which included a weapons test and refresher training on Fieldcraft, First Aid, Nuclear, Biological and Chemical (NBC) Warfare, as well as Battle Drills, Ambush Techniques and Patrols. All the boys were relieved to catch the truck back to Arborfield – although the unpleasant surprise that awaited them, an unheralded trip to the 'gas chamber', almost had them dashing back south!

Apprentices participating in the Duke of Edinburgh's Award Scheme were very busy in 1984, especially in their 'Service to the Community' section. Some boys assisted the *Great Western Society* at Didcot, playing their part in restoring an old (railway) tank engine that had been built in Swindon during 1929. Oaths and well-skinned knuckles were apparently order of the day! Other boys were engaged in draining a Nature Reserve in the Vale of Pewsey, Wiltshire. This Reserve had an abundance of rare and beautiful plants and wildlife, the drainage being necessary to prevent the site from becoming a marsh. One boy, A/T Park, later received the Old Boys' Association Prize for the excellent work he put in on this project.

An ex-boy's diligence and attention to detail was reported in the authoritative *Army Air Corps Newsletter* during 1984. Cpl Iain McFadzean (intake 80C) had been carrying out a routine inspection of a *Lynx* helicopter, whilst on his tour of duty in Northern Ireland. This was at night and *"under difficult conditions"* but, even so, Iain spotted damage to the aircraft's tail rotor control rod, an item that he was not officially required to check. He quietly but pointedly advised the pilot of the damage and thus a potential hazard was duly recognised and then remedied.

March's issue of *The Craftsman* pictured two young soldiers who had made their own small piece of history. Brothers Michael and Richard Vaughan had recently been posted to Waterbeach, Cambridgeshire. Michael had been an apprentice, having joined at Chepstow in 1977, and was now a LCpl with the RE, while Cfn Richard Vaughan had followed a slightly different path, joining the Arborfield College in 1980 and graduating as a REME VM.

An 'introductory' College history

Every year, almost since 'time immemorial', the *'Journal of the Royal Electrical and Mechanical Engineers'*, or *'REME Journal'* as it is usually recognised, is published. The 1984 edition, issued that April, was numbered '34'. Amongst the many interesting articles in that particular *REME Journal* was one submitted by Capt (Ret'd) D B 'Bryn' Richards, Dip Ed Tech, entitled *'Princess Marina College, a brief historical survey'*.

Inevitably drawing upon data originally published in 1951, 1965, 1973 and 1978, Bryn had updated those editions during 1981, eventually producing a glossy-fronted small booklet entitled *"A Brief History, 1939 – 1981"*. It would appear that this booklet was not published until June 1984, accompanied by a foreword by Col Sam Roberts. Bryn's article in the *Journal* was a slightly later version and obviously the forerunner of the eventual edition that was to commemorate the College's Jubilee Year five years later. Bryn's final paragraph in that article read as follows:

> *"A lot of material has been lost, hopefully not forever. If any reader has anything to contribute to the history of the College, would he please write to the author, who is the College archivist. In particular, personal reminiscences would be welcome, in order to put some fat upon the skeleton history reproduced here."*

In June 1984, nine *"indomitable ladies"*, ex-members of the ATS, came together at Arborfield for a nostalgic meeting, to *"meet again and rediscover the ground on which they had served"*. Their title badges had caused great confusion during the early days of the war, when the boys from the 'Army Technical School' must have cringed every time they 'walked out' with those brass shoulder flashes on display.

On June 24th, a 'fortieth anniversary' memorial service was held at the small military cemetery in Lenham, Kent. On that same date in 1944, at 05.45 hours, tragedy struck fifty-two REME soldiers, when a V1 flying bomb had been shot down by the RAF, only to strike the Nissen hut where the men were sleeping. That sad event had been recalled by Paul 'Tug' Wilson earlier in this history.

A narrow escape

A coach load of Arborfield apprentices had a very narrow and fortunate escape in July of that year. They were travelling up to North Yorkshire for a sporting weekend on Friday 13th – lucky for some! – when the coach brakes are believed to have failed on a downhill road. The vehicle subsequently hit a bridge, near to their destination of the AAC at Harrogate, suffering frontal damage and demolishing some thirty feet of wall, but fortunately causing no serious damage to any of the passengers – only shaken, not stirred! Needless to say, the boys were happy to transfer to another coach and continue the short remaining distance. They were then able to enjoy the weekend's annual Triangular Games against Harrogate and Chepstow.

Maj Colin Scragg (RTR) had just completed his first term as Adjutant of the College in July, when he was handed the privilege of becoming the 'Bands President'. He was *"perfectly honest"* when he said that he didn't realise the implications of the task! All apprentices are naturally under the utmost pressure in academic and military terms, as well as upon the sports field. But despite this, Band members *"emerge as a colourful spectacular, pleasing to both the eye and the ear"* – that is how Colin described things, and it amazed him that the boys could actually live up to their deserved reputation, whilst still managing to cope with all the normal everyday pressures. The 'musical maestros' were certainly a great credit to the College, which benefited enormously from the dedication and musical ability of the Band participants.

On a pleasant summer's evening in late July, the College Barbecue was held. To add to the fun and salmonella, each Company and Trade Wing were asked to enter a team to assemble and propel a raft across the College lake. Rules were made and instantly broken, some rafts took on the appearance of battleships – and sank just as quickly! But amid the scenes of chaos and general confusion, the race actually did take place, with the team from 'B' Coy eventually emerging as the winners.

For many years, apprentices and staff at the College, who had chosen climbing as their organised activity, had used The Alps as their major objective. August 1984 proved no exception, as the climbing party set off to tackle the peaks of the Italian Dolomites, in the South Tyrol region. Their journey across the Channel proved incident free – except for A/T Green's phenomenal run of luck on the ship's fruit machines!

Some of the climbs ahead of them were already steeped in military history, being the routes taken by alpine troops during the First World War, carrying ammunition and supplies to gun emplacements on top of the mountains. Over the next ten days or so, the boys made full use of their chance of climbing experience, making an impressive list of peaks that succumbed to their youthful energy. The trip was eventually curtailed by a day of incessant rain, but as the lads made their way through Austria, there it was snow that had fallen, presenting them with a very scenic journey back towards the Channel.

The summer that year saw a plethora of posters all around the College, all in full colour and advertising the fact that PMC was hosting the Army Cycling Festival. Eight months of preparation had resulted in around 150 riders descending on Arborfield for nine days of cycling events. These were held over many different distances around both the local roads and others much further afield. Venues included the track at Palmer Park in Reading and that at the Transport and Road Research Laboratory at Crowthorne. Other road-based events were held at Newbury and Maidenhead, with the final thirty-mile course based upon the triangle between Yately, Hook and Odiham – with diversions!

On September 3rd, Col Barrie Keast, ex-Commandant, finally retired from the Army after forty years of loyal service. A photograph in the following month's edition of *The Craftsman* shows him departing from the REME Wing, Royal School of Artillery, Larkhill. He is precariously perched upon a *"chair, arm, easy"*, above the driver of a *Tracked Rapier* vehicle. Many ex-boys will recognise the important part he played in reviving the OBA to the splendid position in which it survives today.

College Gates – the saga continues

On the architectural side, PMC was soon to be enhanced by the erection, at the main entrance, of the supporting pillars for the College gates. *(The original 1939 gates had meanwhile been 'found' at the side entrance to the WO's and Sgts Mess, in the old School, so these were now lovingly repositioned at their original site – see 1985 for more details. Ed.)* The existing gates, inherited upon the closure of the Carlisle Apprentices' College at Hadrian's Camp, were now to be re-hung at the new entrance, with wicket (or side) gates added by the wonderful wrought-iron craftsmanship of Mr Fred Sadd, from the Blacksmith's Shop. Entrance gates have become an integral part of the College history, for all apprentices have passed through them with awe on entry, then again, with much satisfaction, when leaving on the completion of training.

Indeed, the gates were proudly adopted as the official emblem of the OBA and, at the summer term 'PoP' in August 1984, they were ceremonially opened by Maj Gen T B Palmer, CB, DGEME. But the year was to eventually end upon rather a sad note 'gatewise', when on December 27th 1984 at around 04.15 hours, a car driven by a lady driver overshot the junction of Biggs Lane and Princess Marina Drive, and just about demolished the gates. As one wag put it at the time, *"That must have been the re-opening ceremony!"* Happily, the driver suffered only from slight shock, although her car was a write-off, its velocity having carried it up the lamppost at the top end of the lay-by!

RSM John Todd had received news of this event in an early morning call from the Guardroom. In his own words, he *"chickened out"* of reporting it directly to the Commandant and, even then, waited until around 6 a.m. before informing the College Adjutant, the previously mentioned Maj Colin Scragg. Drawing straws as to who should inform Col Sam, the task went to the Adjutant. It was much later that the RSM confessed to having 'rigged' the short straw! Fortunately, the news was received with a calm shrug of the shoulders and eventually the gates were repaired by 43 Command Wksp and re-hung at a later date. Perhaps the A/T who had been on duty in the gatehouse came off worst, as he had imagined the incident was the start of a full-blown attack by the IRA. *(Brings back memories of the 1955 raid and its aftermath! Ed.)*

The College gates also feature on the 'standard' of the OBA, which was generously donated to the Association by Vince Lutman of 54B. Vince is now retired from the Army and runs a hotel in Germany, where many soldiers go for winter training. The formal presentation of this standard was held at the College, during the Reunion parade held on October 13th 1984. It has a claret background, emblazoned with both the College gates and the 'OBA' title in gold. The border and tassles are also in gold and the standard has since been proudly carried on parade at every Reunion since its presentation. On the day, the standard was proudly carried by John Northam (47A), having been fittingly handed over by Vince Lutman himself. A full-colour picture of the standard was displayed on the front cover of *The Craftsman* in March the following year.

Collecting trophies seemed to be quite a popular hobby for ex-apprentice Cpl John Cole. The former 'boy RSM' had passed out in August 1980, but not before picking up the Award of Honour, the Commandant's Cup, the CI's Cup and the SEO's Cup! Not content with that impressive haul, the *Soldier* magazine of September 10th 1984 told of a further award that had just come his way.

Serving a six-month tour of duty with the UN Forces in Cyprus (UNFICYP), John had spotted some cracks in certain helicopter parts. Should those parts have been fitted, a flight safety hazard would inevitably have occurred. For his quick thinking and powers of observation, he was given a Commendation by Brig P R Duchesne, Chief of Staff with UNFICYP.

No 'ageism' here!

That year's Old Boys' Reunion was another most successful event. Intakes represented extended as far back as the greybeards of 37C (RAOC Depot, Hilsea) and as recently as the rather sprightlier (and still serving) 62C! Notably, there were several ex-Carlisle boys there, now officially taken under the Arborfield wing. Ex-boy Brig Gerry Berragan proudly filled the post of Reviewing Officer (more about him later!) and the Old Boys' Platoon on parade was ably led by the ever-young Walter McCormick of 38C. Following the evening's AGM, the assembled throng made their way to Bailleul Sergeants' Mess for dinner, only to be denied attendance due to a bomb scare! No such device was found, the delayed meal eventually went ahead, with the false alarm presumably being blamed upon one of the old boys reverting to type!

'Food, glorious food'!

It was at that Reunion that Harry Shaw relinquished the post of Hon Sec of the OBA. In recognition of all the hard work and sterling 'dedication to the cause' displayed by Harry over many years, the old boys presented him with a pair of crystal decanters, suitably filled, one with sherry and the other with whisky. Harry's replacement was Mick Sutton (50A) of the College's A & G Wing, who shortly afterwards passed the baton on to Sam Weller (54B).

On November 10th 1984, a team of apprentices performed a gymnastic display at the Royal Albert Hall, in front of HM the Queen and other members of the Royal Family, on the occasion of the annual Festival of Remembrance. This event was televised on *BBC1* and, coincidentally, on that Saturday and the one preceding it, 'J' Coy had appeared live on the *'Noel Edmunds Show'*, competing to see how many 'passengers' could be carried within the confines of a *Land Rover*. Restricted by their own self-imposed safety rules, the number of boys on the vehicle reached 141, but they had to settle for second place, eleven passengers short of the winning team. The following week, on November 17th, the College again entered the annual *'BP Build-a-car'* competition, held at SEME, Bordon. The team of six apprentices, led by AQMS Davis, as well as the 'home-made' car, appeared on both *ITV's 'Southern News'* and the *BBC's 'South Today'* programme.

In that same month, the College was invited to represent REME at the Garden of Remembrance Service, attended by HM Queen Elizabeth the Queen Mother. This event took place at St Margaret's Church, close to Westminster Abbey. Japanese tourists seemed to rate the boys as second in importance only to the Changing of the Guard, much to their pride and delight. They joined soldiers from the past and present, representing all Regiments and Corps of the British Army, some of which had long ago been disbanded.

You are what you eat!

It was also in November that an article appeared in the *Evening Post*, highlighting the changing face of 'Army Grub'. In the recently published *Egon Ronay Guide*, the master gourmet heaped praise upon Army cooking, following a well-publicised visit to the College. Instead of the old 'bangers and mash', accompanied by watery cabbage and woody tasteless carrots, the boys of today look forward to a menu showing such delights

as *'Saute Kidney Turbigo'*, *'Lamb Cutlets Milanaise'* or *'Rainbow Trout in Almonds'*. This was undoubtedly a far cry from the days when one would ask the cook, *"What's this, Sarge?"* The cook sergeant's reply of 'Bean Soup' would then get the witty response, *"I know it's been soup, Sarge, but I want to know what it is now!"*

The editor of *The Arborfield Apprentice* was pleased to say, in one of the 1984 editions, that he had been overwhelmed by the amount of material received for publication. The magazine tries to reflect on all aspects of College life, and the fact that most of the articles and stories had been written by the boys themselves was a source of great satisfaction. *(From the point of view of this particular scribe, the College magazines, along with regular issues of the OBAN, have been an invaluable source of information - I can only hope that I have done justice to the many boys — and ex-boys of course — who have submitted so many well-written anecdotes. Ed.)*

In the winter issue of *The Arborfield Apprentice* for 1984, the Commandant was pleased to report that, of the 199 apprentices who had joined the previous term, 189 were now moving on to their second term. This indicated a wastage rate of only five per cent, which must have been one of the lowest in the College's history. An attendance of over 1,000 parents and relatives at the recent Junior Company Parents' Day was an indication of the great interest being taken in the apprentices' progress, a healthy sign indeed.

Supporting trades

The one-year 'supporting trades' course was gradually being refined, striking a happy balance between educational, military and trade-associated training. The first intake of apprentices on that course had now passed through the College and integrated into adult service. They comprised the Clerk, Driver, Storeman and Recy Mech tradesmen, those often 'unsung heroes' who are rather taken for granted, noticed mainly when they are conspicuously absent. The College was also looking forward to the arrival of the medical and dental apprentices, due to join the one-year scheme the following year.

At the beginning of that winter term, all the sixth-term lads from 'C' and 'D' Companies were taking part in 'Operation Gannet'. Along with some 300 other Junior Soldiers from other units, they were off to

Denmark to act the part of battle casualties. Arriving at RAF Lyneham, they found a six-hour wait ahead of them, due to a mix-up over time zones. Their long flight in a noisy old *Hercules*, sustained only by orange juice and biscuits, was enough to make most of them feel like **real** casualties! Touching down on a cold wet morning, they were met by a gang of long-haired guys, claiming to be soldiers, who transported them to their accommodation in a Danish Naval Base.

As the exercise started, fake injuries were applied, ranging from cut fingers to gunshot wounds. The lads didn't mind too much, being well looked after by a crew of QARANC ladies! The highlight of the whole event, for around ten lucky 'casualties', was being airlifted out by a *Chinook* helicopter, racing from one part of Denmark to another at high speed. The only real-life threat to health came A/T LCpl Fraser's way, hit by an attack of tonsillitis. However, this didn't prevent him from joining the rest of the team on a spot of well deserved 'R & R' on the streets of Copenhagen.

During 1981, the Fencing Club had had to vacate its old fencing room in the Sergeants' Mess, Bailleul, which they had been using since 1969. Following the 'big move' to the new campus in the summer of 1981, a new venue was urgently sought and the fencers eventually found a spot right above the Band Block. With the room's slippery floor, and hobbies night also giving the coincidence of band practice, attempts at fencing became *"something like the Battle of Bannockburn on ice"*! Thankfully, a permanent home in the College HQ building had since materialised and the fencing team was then able to get back to its rigorous training routines.

The year's final issue of *The Craftsman*, in December 1984, brought a long article written by 'Sgt S Johnson'. He had been given his first Army uniform in March 1941, as a member of the Dukies, which was then temporarily located at the Saunton Sands Hotel in North Devon. He told the story that the school had been forced to move from Dover, when it came under shellfire from the German gun emplacements at Calais. Steve Johnson had joined Arborfield in February 1946 and well remembers his 'PoP' being honoured by the visit from 'Monty', or Field Marshall Viscount Montgomery of Alamein, as he eventually became, in February 1949.

Steve's first posting was to Colchester, in his trade as a turner. His first job was to service water-trailers, recently returned from Palestine and containing many different foreign coins. His subsequent life in the Army took Steve to many distant places, much like so many of his contemporaries. Swapping to a civilian career, he became Barrack Warden, and then Estate Warden, for the British Forces in Antwerp during the early Seventies. While there, Steve attended an 'unveiling ceremony' at Waterloo, by no less a personage than the current Duke of Wellington!

—§—

Some Reunion photographs from later years

Annex to Chapter 11

Colonel John Peacock

Colonel John Peacock took over command of the Army Apprentices College, Arborfield, from Colonel Barrie Keast, on Wednesday 17th October 1979, at the start of a three-year appointment as the College Commandant.

John Peacock (48) started his career as a National Service officer in 1951, in Britain's British Army of the Rhine, with a commission in the Royal Electrical and Mechanical Engineers. He has been back to Arborfield, REME's home, twice before his present appointment. One of those occasions was to complete a Guided Weapons course, after which he went to Guided Weapons Regiment, Royal Artillery, in Germany, from 1960 – 62. The dates of his other appointments are as follows:

From 1962 – 64, he served on the staff at the Ministry of Defence, again working with Guided Weapons. From 1965 – 68 he was an instructor at the Royal Military Academy, Sandhurst. Then, for a year, he commanded a REME Workshop in Sharjah, on the Persian Gulf. In April 1969 he went from the heat of the Middle East to the cold of the Arctic, when he served with 'Exercise North Peary Land', a Joint Services expedition to the northernmost tip of Greenland.

In September the same year, after the Arctic trip, he was again employed on the staff of the Ministry. 1971 saw him, now as a Lieutenant Colonel, take command of the REME in the Hebrides, off the western coast of Scotland, a job he thoroughly enjoyed. In 1973 he returned to Arborfield as the Chief Instructor at the School of Electronic Engineering. In 1976, he was in charge of Engineering Support of the Army in Germany, whilst at Headquarters BAOR. It was from this post that he arrived to become the College Commandant.

John Peacock's claims to fame are his activities for Arctic and mountaineering expeditions. While at Sandhurst as an instructor, he went on two expeditions to the western coast of Greenland. This was later followed by the previously mentioned Exercise Peary Land.

His major contribution was towards the Army Mountaineering Association's build-up and the actual expedition that led to the successful conquest of Everest in 1976. This had begun in 1973, with a training programme in the western Himalayas, followed by a venture on Mount Nutze, Everest's neighbour, on which many problems were met and overcome. On the 1976 conquest, Colonel John played his part, as Chairman of the planning committee.

(The above article is adapted from that published in The Arborfield Apprentice of spring 1980, a few months after Col Peacock's arrival.)

An ode to the OBA

"What makes the PS tremble so?"
Asked the Colonel on parade.
"It's bitter cold, it's bitter cold"
The Colour Sergeant said.
"What makes the RPs faint and fall?"
Asked the Major on parade.
"A touch of sun, a touch of sun"
The Colour Sergeant said.

For the Old Boys are returning,
They'll be here by and by,
They'll vandalise the Guardroom
And drink the NAAFI dry.
They'll leave a bill for damages
At least a mile high,
For the Old Boys are back here in the morning.

"I saw them here a year ago"
Said the Captain on parade.
"And yet you lived to tell the tale?"
The Colour Sergeant said.
"I've seen them come, I've seen them go"
Bragged Lieutenant on parade.
"Their going's good, their going's best!"
The Colour Sergeant said.

For every year they do it
And every year's the same,
They get up to their dirty tricks,
To them it's just a game.
The QM's staff are shaking
For they think they'll end up lame,
For the Old Boys will be at it in the morning.

"What is that mangled lump of tin?"
The RSM then prayed.
"It's what's been left of the Sergeants' Mess"
The Colour Sergeant said.
"What makes the Padre look so white?"
Asked a Sergeant on parade.
"He's been through hell and just come back!"
The Colour Sergeant brayed.

For the Old Boys now are leaving,
Victorious from their fight,
Their former home resembles
A demolition site.
Apprentices' knees are trembling,
They'll need a beer tonight
After seeing what the Old Boys did that morning.

(The above poem is adapted from that published in The Arborfield Apprentice of spring 1980, by an anonymous author.)

Andrew Owen

After leaving the College, Cfn Andrew Owen was posted to the LAD of the Welsh Guards, stationed at Pirbright. He gradually became adapted to life in one of the Household Division's Battalions and made a great friend of another of the attached REME personnel.

Following the outbreak of hostilities in the Falkland Islands, which had started with an Argentine invasion on April 2nd, Andrew accompanied the Welsh Guards when they were sent off to the South Atlantic. He was on board the *'Sir Galahad'* on June 6th when it sat waiting in Bluff Cove, awaiting the troops to disembark and be taken to Ajax Bay. The medics had fortunately already landed there and now ammunition was being loaded into small boats.

As Andrew waited, alongside his REME friend, two missiles narrowly missed the *'Sir Galahad'* but, unfortunately, a third one made contact and the ensuing explosion blew Andrew back into the ship. When he gathered himself and got to his feet, he was on fire. He and another casualty got themselves to a sprinkler and managed to stand underneath it for some time. He was quite conscious all the time and gave a vivid description of the way that helicopters were used to blow the small boats, full of survivors, away from the flames of the stricken ship and then seeing the injured men safely ashore.

Eventually, a chopper picked Andrew up and took him to Ajax Bay, where he realised just how badly burned he was. From the islands, he was flown to Montevideo and transferred to the *'Uganda'*, playing its role as a hospital ship. He was later shipped to Ascension Island and then onwards on a return flight to the UK. After a night's stop at Wroughton (near Swindon), he was taken to the Burns Unit of the Queen Elizabeth Hospital, Woolwich, where he is now receiving skin grafts and gradually making his way towards recovery. He was saddened to find that his REME friend was killed in the explosion.

When Prince Charles visited the hospital he spent five minutes with Andrew and was greatly interested in his story. Andrew would like to thank the people of Wokingham who very generously gave him gifts of cake and fruit, as soon as they heard that he had been a Falklands casualty.

(The above story is adapted from that published in The Arborfield Apprentice of summer 1982, by an anonymous author.)

Rotary wing aircraft like these Sioux and Scout helicopters were the workhorses for the Army Air Corps, seeing service in many parts of the world

Chapter 12

1985 - 89

Another ex-boy makes General

The year 1985 provided a pleasant and happy note on which to begin, both for his previous Corps as a whole, and for the College here at Arborfield in particular, when Brig G B Berragan (late RAOC) was selected to become the Director General of Ordnance Services (DGOS), Logistics Executive (Army) – or LE(A), in the rank of Major General, the post to be taken up later in that year. An ex-apprentice from the 48C intake, Gerry had joined up at the tender age of fifteen, and now joined ranks with Maj Gen (Ret'd) Peter Baldwin (42A and late R Sigs) as one of our illustrious two-star old boys. Passing out from what was then still the 'School' here at Arborfield in 1951, Brigadier Gerry had firstly been commissioned into the REME, before later transferring to the RAOC, where he was currently holding the post of Director of Supply Management (Army) or DSM(A).

In that same January, the College gladly hosted a 'getting to know you' visit by representatives of the press from north of the border Kilmarnock, as well as Carlisle and Bolton. Each of these press officers subsequently went on to produce lengthy and favourable reports about the College in their respective newspapers, accompanied by numerous photographs of industrious apprentices from their appropriate local areas. This was a continuation of the intensive recruiting campaign previously begun by Col Sam Roberts, which was now obviously paying off, with all three intakes for the year ahead looking to be well filled.

On Sunday 3rd February, a special service of dedication was held in St Eligius Church, Arborfield, when the parents of the late Sgt Keith Baker, REME, presented a new Lectern Bible. Keith had been a 75C intake ex-apprentice Tels Tech,, where he had attained the rank of A/T Sgt, and had gone on to also reach the same adult rank of Sergeant. Having passed the RCB in July 1984, Keith had been due to join the RMAS, but then was tragically killed in a climbing accident in the Swiss Alps only a few days later. After the sad service, A/Ts of 'A' Coy gathered together in the WRVS lounge

and entertained Mr & Mrs Baker to coffee.

The Bell Tower rises again

As previously mentioned, it had always been the intention to re-erect the famous old Woolwich Bell Tower, and this plan finally came to fruition in February of 1985. After various meetings and attempts to raise funds for the project, it was eventually decided to completely rebuild the tower, as an identical replica of the original eighteenth-century Old Tower.

The woodwork was completed to the highest standard of craftsmanship, which was a great credit

The Woolwich Bell Tower

to the staff of our sister College at Chepstow, while the metalwork was superbly copied by Messrs Horton, Hunt and Spreadborough, three civilians of the College's own A & G Wing. The footings were dug out by the combined efforts of boys from 'J' and 'A' Companies, with the final placement being made with the assistance of No.1 Training Regt RE, based at Hawley. The bell was to finally ring out its resonant message again, after an absence of four years, five minutes prior to the College and Garrison Church service on Easter Sunday that year.

(An article regarding the history of the Bell Tower can be found in a separate annex to this chapter.)

February 15th 1985 saw the start of another four-day expedition by the College Climbing Club. This was essentially a training exercise, held in preparation for a visit to the Alps later in the year, and was to be followed at Easter by similar training in the Cairngorms. The first exercise took place amongst the challenging, and sometimes treacherous, ridges of Snowdonia.

An imaginary line, if drawn due south from Mount Snowdon itself, would encounter nothing as high until reaching the Pyrenees on the French-Spanish border, so the trip proved a demanding but rewarding expedition for all concerned.

Meanwhile, the Orienteering team was enjoying a fine run of success that spring. The undoubted highlight was their attainment of second place in the Junior Army Championships, held at the Minley and Hawley training areas. First place went to the JLdrs of the RAC, but the College team had the satisfaction of being ahead of both the other apprentices' teams from Chepstow and Harrogate.

Around the same time, the College had sent off a squad of skiers to enter the REME Championships in Bavaria. Their 700-mile journey took them via London to Ramsgate, then by sea-ferry to Dunkirk, across northern France and on into Belgium. A burst radiator hose on their transport was quickly sorted out with the aid of a Swiss Army penknife, water was scrounged from a local farmhouse, while some compensation was later gained at a stop in Mons for a helping of

Beats me Sir!   Major General Homan with Major Scragg RTR examining the plaque at the Front Gate

'*bratwurst and pommes frites*' in the market square. Following this, the party eventually carried on through Luxembourg into Germany. Believe it or not, the tale that was later told about the whole adventure seems to concentrate on the varying types of food scoffed by the boys, rather than the thrills of the skiing – but then, boys will be boys, and will also eventually become ex-boys! Oh, and they did manage to bring back some duty-frees!

Past members of the Band during the Forties would no doubt be mortified to know that one of their Maces had been found to have deteriorated into a very poor state during the intervening forty years. However, it had now been superbly restored, through the combined generosities of '*Potters*' (its original presenters) and Col Sam Roberts. This Mace was now to be mounted for safe keeping in the Commandant's office, only being removed for ceremonial use on Passing-out Parades.

The spring term of 1985 saw some exceptionally cold weather here at Arborfield, with sub-zero temperatures making two consecutive weekend training exercises particularly uncomfortable. Despite this, the all-night patrols, attacks and ambushes continued as normal, demonstrating the general improvement in military training standards brought about by the CMS(R) regime. This was now being completed in 'J' Coy, with worthwhile continuation training under the auspices of the senior Company Commanders. The PS members of the MTW provided control of the whole cycle in an objective manner.

The spring 'PoP' provided a proud moment for A/T RSM Anthony Poulson, as he was presented with the Commandant's Cup as 'best soldier and leader' by the Reviewing Officer that day, Lt Gen Sir Geoffrey Howlett. What made the occasion so special was that Anthony had grown up here in Arborfield and had gone to school locally before joining PMC at the age of sixteen. Passing his apprenticeship with flying colours, he now intended to pursue his chosen career as a VM.

Restoration of 'The Gates'

An incredible total of over 10,000 apprentices had passed through the famous old gates between 1939 and 1981, when the new accommodation of PMC was first occupied. As a permanent memorial to those ex-boys and staff over those years, the old entrance to Rowcroft Barracks was now restored to its former 1939 glory.

These old gates, albeit in a shortened form, had long since formed the entrance to the WOs' and Sgts' Mess in Sheerlands Road.

Now, with much gratitude to the skills of Messrs Les Shearer and Fred Sadd, the arch and gates had been lovingly rebuilt. This could not have been achieved without able assistance from personnel of the 'A & G' Section and 43 Command Wksp, Aldershot, all under the guiding supervision of Maj (Ret'd) R F N 'Ray' Eke MBE, DFC. Fred Sadd was also able to cast two 'torches of education', using the originals as patterns, while Aircraft Wing made two sets of replica 'flames' from fibre-glass. The grand opening was timed to coincide with that of the Corps Museum on Friday March 22nd 1985, which was attended by a most distinguished gathering. A plaque explaining their history was mounted on one of the support pillars and unveiled by Maj Gen J V Holman CB.

A fair number of old boys were present for the ceremony and, in 'intake order' (Jeeps at the end!), they were:

Peter Spargo (39A), Harry Shaw (39C), George Dixon (43B), Keith Evans (45A), Andy Brown and Dave Armstrong (46B), John Northam (47A), Gordon Littlecote (47B), Les Shearer (48B), Mike Sutton (50A), John Weston (52B), Sam Weller (54B) and Dennis Farrell (55A).

(An article regarding the history of the College Gates can be found in a separate annex to this chapter.)

Between the 13th and 20th April, the Ski Club was fortunate enough to enjoy the best snow conditions in Europe, at Tonale, to the north of the Italian industrial city of Milan. Most of the party took advantage of lessons laid on at the local ski school, gaining a fair deal of knowledge from the experienced instructors at the resort. Indeed, several boys had reached two or three gold-star standard by the end of their week's stay.

Doctors and Dentists!

As a consequence of the previously mentioned '*Groom Study*', May 1985 heralded the addition to College strength of both RAMC and Royal Army Dental Corps (RADC) JLdrs, following the closure of their own training unit, the RAMC JLdrs Division, at

Keogh Barracks, Mytchett. They would now go on to complete a one-year course at Arborfield towards Combat Medical/Dental Technician trade training. The subjects of Anatomy and Physiology were now to be used towards an Army career, rather than in their previous pursuit of the fair sex! History was thus seen to turn full circle, in the fact that once again there were three different cap badges being worn by College apprentices, just as it had been back in 1939. On the subject of cap-badges, the spring 1985 edition of *The Arborfield Apprentice* featured a centre-page spread of no less than forty different cap badges, as worn by current PS members of the College on February 1st that year.

In an effort to strengthen these newly-forged links, at a 'PoP' that took place later that year, the post of Reviewing Officer was taken up by Lt Gen Sir Cameron Moffat KBE, QHS, MB, ChB, FRCS. He was, at the time, the Surgeon General and Director General of Army Medical Services (DGAMS).

That same month of May saw the departure of Fred Sadd, whose name, like that of Percy Chivers, will forever be linked with the history of the College gates. Fred had joined the Army as a boy of only fourteen and, at the age of eighteen, was part of the BEF that was sent to France right at the outset of World War II. Fred had arrived here as a Blacksmith Instructor in 1967 and certainly left his mark upon both staff and apprentices during his subsequent service. His wrought-iron skills are evident in many places, both here within Arborfield and in the greater world outside. Amongst the many examples of his skill and work that are on display are those at St George's Chapel, Windsor; Coventry Cathedral; the Palace of the Shah of Iran; and HQ Thames Valley Police.

On the evening of May 31st, one unfortunate young apprentice from 'D' Coy managed to slip over on the washroom floor. Falling onto the back of his head, he suffered a serious cut and was soon bleeding profusely. He was lucky in the fact that A/T CSM A Collingwood was on hand, as the CSM immediately applied pressure to the wound and rushed the young lad off to the MRS. There, he maintained the pressure whilst an ambulance was called and the duty nurse bathed the wound. The patient eventually had to be taken to the *Royal Berkshire Hospital* in Reading with an almost negligible blood pressure, before being finally stitched up and given a major blood transfusion. A/T CSM Collingwood's calm and efficient action was later recognised and rewarded by a GOC's Commendation.

The times they are a 'changing'

An article, written for the College magazine, illustrated some of the many changes thrust upon the daily life of an apprentice since the 'early days' of 1939. A/T Bryston had arrived here on transfer from the JLdrs RAC, astonished to find carpets on the floor and lots of locker space! A meal at the Cookhouse bought him further delights, such as having his cutlery already laid out for him and then to have his dirty plates collected from him after the meal. When he mentioned that at Bovington they still did 'Cookhouse fatigues', he was asked, *"What are those?"* In the words of the Bob Dylan song, *'The times they are a'changing'*.

On a gloriously sunny first day of June 1985, the College hosted the sixth occasion on which the Inter-Service Triangular Games were held, with the visitors being apprentices from HMS Collingwood at Gosport and No.1 School of Technical Training at RAF Halton. With two previous wins each for the Navy and RAF teams, and only one for the College, it was obviously time to balance the equation, and this Arborfield did on the day, much to the pleasure of the Commandant, who proudly presented the overall Winner's Cup to the home team. The five sporting disciplines contested that day were Athletics, Shooting, Swimming, Tennis and Tug-of-war.

Saturday June 29th brought another edition of 'COLLSAM' – no, this was nothing directly to do with 'Col Sam', but the shortened name given to the annual College Skill-at-Arms Meeting. This provides good competition between the Companies and is organised like a 'mini-Bisley', with rifle, pistol and SMG events. The most popular shoot, the Falling Plate Competition, rounded off the day, after which the Commandant was faced by an impressive array of cups, medals and shields, to be distributed amongst the winners of what had proved another successful event.

A telephone request from the headmaster of a local school at Coley, in Reading, was followed up by no less than thirty hand-written letters from a class of his pupils. They had recently completed a project on the 'history of archery', and now wondered if the College Archery Club could entertain them with a practical demonstration. Thus it was that on the afternoon of 4th July 1985, two young apprentices, accompanied by Sgt Stannard of the PS, were greeted by what seemed a multitude of children, sheltering under the shade of an old oak tree in the school grounds. The young men's demonstration of their archery skills was cheered enthusiastically by the children, and was followed by an excellent 'cream tea' in the staff room. It was only a couple of weeks later, when the College archery team competed in the Junior Army Competition at Bovington, Dorset, where they finished in a creditable second place.

The White Shield and Halton Bell

The College had competed regularly at athletics against RAF Halton, with the winning team being awarded the 'White Shield'. This trophy commemorated two former Commandants, our own Col J D White (1943 - 47) and Air Commodore H G White, who had commanded Halton during the same era. The runners-up, however, received the 'Halton Bell', which had an interesting, if rather murky, past. It had been originally used at Halton, ringing out to indicate the final lap of the longer athletics events, and was known to have been used as recently as 1961. But, by 1969, it had somehow disappeared. It was only to re-appear in 1977, when Col Barrie Keast, Commandant here at the time, spotted it on display on a shelf behind the bar, in the old Sergeant's Mess at Bailleul. No doubt it had been 'lifted' at some time as an unofficial 'souvenir' trophy. Following discussions with the present-day RAF Commandant, the Halton Bell now once again fulfills its runners-up function as mentioned earlier.

On July 6th 1985, one of the most important events on the Garrison calendar was once again celebrated, the REME Corps Open Day. As was the tradition, the College gave its usual worthy support, providing the manpower and expertise that would be difficult to find elsewhere. One of the undoubted highlights of the event was provided by the Pipes and Drums, marching around and exuding all the skill and panache of a regular regimental band. Apart from the salesmanship and good humour, brought by the apprentices to the many varied stalls around the arena, the College also provided a breathtaking Gymnastic Display that delighted the large attendance.

Just a week after the above event, a bittersweet moment arrived for the wife of Mr Douglas Crowhurst, a civilian instructional officer from the A & G Wing. Diane Crowhurst had originally been married to Mr Tom Williams, an instructor/lecturer in the College

Electronics Wing from 1955, until his death in 1968. At that time, she had proudly presented the 'Tom Williams Salver' to the College in his memory. Now married again, this time to Dougie Crowhurst, she had been invited to re-present the salver to the best A/T CSM in the Drill Competition. This she happily did, its first recipient being A/T CSM Wood of 'B' Coy. It is sad to relate that Dougie himself died, just over two short years later.

After a number of years *"in the doldrums"*, the College Caving Club enjoyed something of a revival in August 1985, setting out for an enjoyable week's pot holing in Yorkshire. Meanwhile, members of the Climbing Club made their way to the Bernese Alps, via a ferry crossing between Ramsgate and Dunkirk and then a long drive across Belgium and Germany. The famous 'trinity' of peaks - the Eiger, Monch and Jungfrau – lay in the largest continuous major range in the Alps. They were soon to become the scalps on the belts of the happy bunch that returned to Arborfield. It hadn't been that easy to get there though – Swiss border officials were relentless in extracting a £20 tourist road tax for the bus and trailer! After the glory of the 'trinity' in three consecutive days, thoughts then returned to the trip home. Should they call in at Düsseldorf, for duty-frees, town-centre nightlife and a cookhouse meal?

August also provided a splendid outing for the Canoe Club, which had decided to take up the challenge of several French rivers, which included a selection of rapids and weirs. The first of these came during some exceptionally wet weather, when the roads they were travelling on, themselves turned into torrents of muddy brown water! Once the lads got their canoes launched out onto some 'real' water, concentration became increasingly difficult due to the distractions provided by riverside French beauties, many of whom preferred to sunbathe *au natural*! After completion of their main targets, the party decided to push south to the Mediterranean for some sea canoeing – and a certain amount of relaxation in the sunshine!

There was an air of excitement in the air that same year, as two *Lynx* helicopters swooped down and landed on the College football pitch. After boarding and a twenty-minute flight under clear blue skies, the party of twelve 'C' Coy volunteers, all of them Air Techs by trade, deployed onto the airfield at Fleetlands, Portsmouth. They were there to demonstrate how, with the aid of the Air Corps, a Vehicle Checkpoint

(VCP) could be speedily set up and manned. This was, at the time, an almost everyday occurrence in the 'bandit country' of Northern Ireland. A thrilled crowd of some 3,000 spectators watched, as a very realistic depiction of such an occurrence was acted out, with two 'terrorists' being quickly apprehended, while a third was 'shot' after trying to escape. The apprentice 'actors' were applauded off the arena, before setting off on a tour of the Naval Yard, and then being flown back to Arborfield.

An exercise in defence

For some during that year, summer leave was extended, thus enabling PMC personnel, both apprentices and staff, to participate in Exercise 'Brave Defender', which was thoroughly enjoyed by all concerned. The exercise was designed to test the nation's civil defences against possible foreign infiltration and acts of sabotage across the downs and plains of Southern England.

'A' Coy was deemed to have acquitted itself well, defending its base at Thatcham against all sorts of insurgents; 'B' Coy reported that the period between 'startex' and 'endex' should be known as 'durex' – it was after all an exercise in protection! ; the boys of 'C' Coy reckoned that they had filled more sandbags, dug more trenches and laid out more barbed wire than had been seen at the battle of Leningrad; while 'D' Coy were deployed in three separate Platoons to areas of North Kent. All in all, the exercise provided a large arc on the learning curve of life.

All too soon, it was 'hand-over' time for yet another Commandant. Due to the exigencies of the service, Col Sam Roberts had been 'short toured' and thus passed over his command to Col A A Soar, BSc(Eng), MIProdE, MBIM, who joined the College from 32 Base Wksp, Bicester, on September 16th 1985. Like so many Commandants before him, Col Roberts had experienced much change at the College during his foreshortened tenure. He achieved almost all of the aims he had set himself upon arrival in 1983; he will long be remembered for his 'open door' system, which meant that anyone, regardless of age, rank or position, was always welcome to go in and discuss their problems. He also led the successful drive that had seen an increase in the College strength from 400 up to 750 in only two years. He left the PMC to join the LE(A) down at Andover in Hampshire.

As Col Roberts left, driven through the recently restored College gates in a 1927 *Austin*, he was firmly convinced that the quality of apprentices passing out was still as commendably high as it had ever been. He believed that the balance between trade, education, military training and character development was now *"just right"*. External visits to military units and manufacturers were making courses more motivating and interesting. Despite some understandable initial doubts, 'contract' driver training for REME one-year apprentices had proved beneficial, while a better liaison between the Trade and Education Wings had reduced duplication and amalgamated theory and practice better together. All courses were now very intensive and precisely met the 'Charter' of the College.

During the month of September, Aircraft Wing was finally 'dragged screaming' into the new College environment. Its 'purpose built' accommodation had been taken over by A & G Wing but, after something of a struggle, Aircraft Wing gained tenancy of its own hangar, plus one other room set aside for repairs. However, the remainder of the Wing had to remain scattered between various locations, given up by the Vehicles, Electronics and Education Wings. This presented a number of administrative problems of course, and the precarious situation was to remain so for a number of years afterwards.

We've got our beady eyes on you!

October 19th 1985 saw the OBA Reunion take place once again, this time under the watchful eyes of no less than five Commandants and the present DGEME! Newly arrived Col Soar was there of course, as well as his recent predecessor, Col Sam Roberts. Going back a little further, the gathering was graced by the presence of three other ex-Commandants, Col David Brown (1968 – 70), Brig Joe Dobie (1962 – 66) and Col John Cole (1955 – 59). The DGEME at that time was Maj Gen Terry Palmer, who attended also in his role as President of the Association.

Another ex-Commandant, Brig Bill Bailey had managed to get his wires crossed, having arrived a week too early! *(We've heard of 'better late than never', but 'better early than never' was stretching things a bit too much! Ed.)* So enthusiastic were the Old Boys to show their paces on the Saturday morning, that more than sixty of them marched around the Square, under the authorative guidance of Maj Harry Bray, ex-46A.

The October issue of *The Craftsman* reported

upon the success of the PMC Trust Fund, which had been set up in early 1982. The scheme had already raised the princely sum of £19,000, which had gathered an interest of some £4,000. This had been mainly allocated to help finance a number of College adventure-training activities and to purchase associated specialised equipment.

In that winter's edition of *The Arborfield Apprentice*, 'old faithful' Harry Shaw wrote an interesting article on a hobby that had become increasingly popular at that time. With a history that dated back to the start of World War II, Harry was obviously well equipped to be 'OIC War Games'! The derisive description *"playing with toy soldiers"* may have been mentioned, but Harry explained that it was certainly much more than that. The 'game' dated back to the *'Kriegsspiel'* of the Prussian Army, at the time of Kaiser Friedrick Wilhelm, and was designed to provide an excellent introduction to the problems of fire and movement during battle conditions.

A great attraction of the modern system is that it can be either as complicated or as simple as the players' desire. A lot of satisfaction could be gained, simply by making up the scale model and making the figures and weapons as realistic as necessary – or it could even be played with mere counters. As Harry remarked, it was impossible to detail all aspects of the War Game scenario in such a short article. But if any boy fancied himself as a latter day Hannibal or Rommel, or was a dab hand at the precision painting of 20mm figures, then he was welcome to trot along to the Education Block on a Monday evening and join in the fun and fantasy.

On Friday 8th November, the A/T RSM and the four Company A/T CSMs attended the Field of Remembrance Parade, where these young apprentices were again reported as *"stealing the show"*. Two days later, the College Square was the scene of the Garrison Remembrance Day service, where all the major units were represented. A/T RSM P R Dawson laid the College wreath and the Chaplain concluded his address by reading *'The Story of the Poppy'* by Col John McCrae. Its poignant message made a lasting impression on everyone:

"In Flanders' fields the poppies blow,
Between the crosses, row on row,
That mark our place; and in the sky

The larks, still bravely singing, fly,
Scarce heard among the guns below.

We are the dead. Short days ago
We lived, felt dawn, saw sunset glow,
Loved, and were loved, and now we lie
In Flanders' fields.

Take up our quarrel with the foe;
To you from failing hands we throw
The torch; be yours to hold it high.
If ye break faith with us who die,
We shall not sleep, though poppies grow
In Flanders' fields."

In January of 1986, the England under-21 hockey squad embarked on a short tour of Malaysia. Included in that squad for the first time was an ex-Arborfield apprentice, Cfn K D Jordan, who had been trained as a Gun Fitter from the 83C intake. Currently serving with the KOSB at Colchester, Essex, young Jordan had skillfully represented both the Army and Combined Service teams at hockey during his time here at the College. In March of the same year, the College's own hockey team won the Junior Army Cup, beating the 'old enemy' from Chepstow after an exciting penalty shoot-out at the end of extra-time. Special mention must go to A/T LCpl Pearson, who not only saved a penalty during the game, but also saved another three during the shoot-out. Thus the College was able to boast its fifth claim on this trophy since first winning it in 1980.

A freezing interlude

Usually, any really bad weather at the turn of the year tends to be gone by the beginning of February – but it certainly wasn't the case this year! The Padre had obviously indented on the wrong form, because the great 'Ordnance Depot in the sky' delivered two inches of snow on February 2nd, then followed it up with twenty-eight consecutive days of frost. That extensive freeze-up certainly played havoc with some of the winter sports fixtures, the soccer team for instance ended up at Easter having to play seven matches in only fifteen days, in order to complete their season!

On February 20th 1986, the fortieth anniversary of his joining the Army coincided with the retirement from that same body for Maj Harry Bray. Having

General G B Berragan with HM The Queen

caving and climbing. Despite all this adventurous exercise, the highlight of their trip appeared to be an 'Egon Ronay' lunch of good old Army stew, followed by a steaming hot cuppa tea!

Sunday 16th March saw a sporting event that would live long in the memories of those who witnessed it, one that Arborfield couldn't possibly lose. The famous Bill Shankly, when manager of an all-conquering Liverpool, had once described football as *"not a matter of life and death, it's more than that"*. Well, to the boys of 'A' and 'B' Companies that day, it was all a matter of who would win the final of the Army Youth Challenge Cup. First blood went to 'B' Coy after half an hour when the 'A' Coy goalkeeper nipped smartly between two defenders and rammed the ball into the net – his own! With a huge crowd roaring the two sides on, it wasn't until fifteen minutes from the end that 'A' Coy finally saw their superior strength force an equalising goal.

They continued to look the stronger team, but still couldn't find a winner and so the match went into extra time. The boys of 'B' Coy defended resolutely and the deadlock remained unbroken, meaning that the outcome would now rest upon the dreaded penalty shoot-out. After five attempts each, the sides still remained level with five goals each and now it became a matter of 'sudden death', first one to miss loses! The 'B' Coy man lofted his shot over the bar, and then it was the turn of A/T LCpl Mitchell of 'A' Coy. All he had to do was slot the ball home and the Cup would be won. The crowd sent up a mighty hush, you could hear a pin drop as he stepped forward to place the ball. His aim was true and 'A' Coy had done it. Their supporters went wild with delight and an epic match ended in a famous victory – and a valiant defeat.

Intake 86A was continuing in the same vein as thousands of its predecessors – drawing their kit, some of which actually fitted; having their medicals, *"Cough please"*; and the dreaded visit to the barber's chair, *"What's under yer hat is yours, the rest is coming off!"*

joined the ATS (Boys) on February 20th 1946, as an apprentice Armourer with intake 46A, life had now completed its full circle for Harry. He had attended and passed his 'Tiffy' course at Bordon back in 1960 / 61 and then been commissioned into REME during 1970. Harry had proudly spent his last two years of service back here at Arborfield, as OIC A & G Wing, during which time he had happily played a large part in the restoration of the College gates.

Sarah Fryer and Mandy Burton felt very privileged during the spring term. As resident clerks in the Pay Office, and at their personal request, these lucky young ladies were allowed to accompany 'J' Coy on their EL exercise at Vauxhall Camp, Monmouth, where they bravely joined in the activities of hill walking,

The usual terms of endearment echoed around their ears, *"Get a move on"*, *"You idle lot"* and *"Double away"*, yes life still continued as normal at Arborfield. Then it was time for Exercise 'Milk Teeth' *(wherever do they think these names up from? Ed.)*, sleeping out in the open for the first time and having to cook for themselves. A 'stretcher race' was organised, but not with the usual type. One 'gung ho' member of staff actually borrowed several stretchers from 'P' Coy of the Parachute Regiment – great long things, weighing 140 pounds each and to be carried a distance of two-and-a-half miles! *"We'll make these lads into soldiers if it kills them!"* - a threat or a promise that must be seared into the memory of many an ex-boy!

One of Col Arthur Soar's first official tasks was to sign the Unit Historical Record (UHR) on April 1st 1986. He was able to report that recruiting remained buoyant and that the College strength numbered a healthy 796 apprentices. The absorption of JLdrs training, on behalf of the RAMC and RADC, had gone extremely well, with the first junior soldiers for these Corps maturing and graduating into adult service that same month.

A General returns

The 'PoP' that took place on Friday 18th April 1986 was another particularly nostalgic occasion for the Reviewing Officer, who was none other than our own Maj Gen Gerry Berragan, DGOS, who had started his Army service here as an apprentice in September 1948. The programme of events for that day gave a potted history of the General's career.

(The relevant potted history can be found as a separate annex to this chapter.)

The 'merry month of May' proved just the opposite for the usual Ten Tors expedition. The College had opted to raise their sights from the 'short' 45-mile distance to the more gruelling 55-mile route. Despite a gloriously sunny Friday, whilst the teams expectantly made themselves ready, the day's weather proved to be nothing but a 'red herring'. Come Saturday morning and the event started in driving rain, which continued for the whole day, causing a thirty per cent drop-out rate in competitors – and who could blame them? The depleted Sunday field eventually contained only two of the six original Arborfield entries, A/T Cpl Powell

First commissioned in February 1954

and A/T LCpl McGill, who showed a great amount of *"gritty determination"* in actually running the final 900 metres, to finish just within the prescribed time.

It was also in May 1986 that the newly arrived RSM A Milloy, Scots Guards, took over from RSM Todd. The outgoing RSM certainly went off in some style! Having long luxuriated in his fond attachment to a magnificent moustache, he had volunteered – in the name of charity of course – to have it shaved off on the evening before his departure. Two young A/Ts from 'A' Coy took on this dreaded task, wondering if their careers hung in the balance! All went well however, with little blood spilled, and a sum of over £350 was raised, being donated to two of the RSM's favourite charities.

The untimely death of Capt (Ret'd) Walker occurred the following month. He had been a member of the Education Wing staff ever since 1968, the first four years as a serving officer in the RAEC and the remainder as a respected civilian lecturer. He would be particularly remembered by past Aircraft apprentices, for the keen interest he took in their careers and personal welfare whilst they were here in the College.

A taste of 'REME life'

A four-day exercise was reported upon, entitled *'REME Life'* and designed to show those VMs who had reached the dizzy heights of 6 Division, what it might be like 'in the field' once they had qualified to serve their future adult units. After an early breakfast and the washing of mess tins, jobs were allocated, to the accompaniment of such remarks as *"I can't do that, can I?"* Well, not only **could** they, but they had to! An exploratory look at the bulky blue-bound Electrical & Mechanical Engineering Regulations (EMERs), a sort through the toolbox for something suitable, some frayed temper followed by a touch of panic, an improvised solution, and it was all over! Some jobs even lasted until daylight arrived, and it finally sunk in just what the boys had let themselves in for. They even have a name for it nowadays – 'Culture Shock'!

By the time that summer's edition of *The Arborfield Apprentice* made its appearance, the Commandant was able to reflect upon yet another term, the third in a row, of regrettable weather. Happily, this had not prevented the College from gaining success in sports competitions, with a particularly high standard having been achieved. At the Tri-Service Games, held at HMS Collingwood, the College emerged as easy victors, while back on home ground, in the Triangular Games, the Arborfield boys were able to win six out of the twelve sports that were contested. Seven of the College's athletes had later gone on to be chosen to represent the Army at Junior level.

Bands President Maj Colin Scragg was preparing to hand over his role to Maj I C Park (ASH) that summer, full of trepidation due to the fact that no less than twenty Band members were set to leave that same term. He reiterated his opinion that, of all extra-mural activities, it was the displays by the Massed Bands that *"did most to enhance the prestige of the College"*. He urged both his successor and the College at large to ensure that the Bands' strength be immediately rebuilt, reminding one and all *"what a sad place the College would be without them"*. Amongst the vacancies that would now arise were included drums and side drums, the pipes, bass, cornet, glockenspiel, tenor horn and saxophone.

The highlight of the term for one party of apprentices had been their visit to West Berlin, still in relative captivity behind the Iron Curtain at that time. Having been amazed at the large number of *'young ladies'* along the Kurfursten-Damm, waiting for taxis that never stopped, the boys enjoyed a day in the Eastern Sector, wearing their uniforms, which proved a great attraction to the 'locals'. However, shopping in East Berlin proved a non-event; *Harrods* it certainly wasn't - there was hardly anything on display! Even the seemingly simple task of ordering a coffee proved difficult, as it would take fifteen minutes to make! Returning through 'Checkpoint Charlie' gave the boys a chance to visit the Museum, while they were surprised to find that the music concert being advertised for that evening starred *Queen* and *Marillon*, two of the 'hottest' Western rock-bands of the day. A visit to 14 Field Wksp gave an opportunity for the party to have lunch with the DGEME, and the week's visit was finalised with a boating trip on Havel Lake.

More success at sports

On June 15th 1986, a party of keen cyclists set off for Clapham Common, from where they were to set off on the London-Brighton Charity Bike Ride. As they arrived, surrounded by thousands of bikes, they felt a little conspicuous, climbing down from the back of a 4-tonner! The back-up car and its crew accompanied the cyclists, with staff member Mr Mike Mullett kept busy with his repair-kit, aiding the odd hapless broken-down cycle – or cyclist! - along the way. Arriving at the sea-front at Brighton, the back-up crew ordered ice creams all round as they awaited the arrival of the brightly-dressed Arborfield boys. However, poor A/T Taylor had been abandoned with a puncture some twelve miles short of the finish, and a frantic search had to be made before he was eventually found – sleeping against a concrete post on the promenade!

At the Triangular Games mentioned earlier, held between the 11th and 13th July, the Harrogate team had arrived early on the Friday evening, ensuring that the Junior Ranks Club (JRC) was packed out and that there were a few bleary eyes the following morning! The Chepstow lads then arrived at around 8 a.m. on the Saturday, swelling the total number of competitors to some 500. Morning drizzle made it difficult for those sportsmen involved in outdoor events to stay on their feet, but some afternoon sunshine eventually arrived to lift the spirits. The Athletics competition was held a few miles away, at Bracknell Sports Stadium, where a total of seven College records were broken. A 'disco' was held for all apprentices that evening, while the Officers and SNCOs of the PS entertained their counterparts with a barbecue at the Sergeants' Mess.

The Eighties were definitely proving to be a decade of sporting prowess at Arborfield. As well as those sports already reported upon, *The Arborfield Apprentice* that summer also gave articles regarding the Climbing Club, Fencing, Swimming, Tug of War, Lawn Tennis and Orienteering. The Lawn Tennis players were rightly proud of their newly constructed *"green and red courts"*.

In July, the College held its now annual Barbecue. A new addition that year was a Shield, kindly presented by Tony Clarkson, landlord of the *'Bramshill Hunt'*. This was won by the current Champion Company, 'C' Coy, having won both the tug-of-war and five-a-side soccer events and sharing the 'It's a Knockout' competition with 'B' Coy. That knockout game consisted of a water race, balloon race, ski race and bicycle race. Competition of a different kind was enjoyed by families and staff alike, who took full advantage of all the side-stalls on offer, while children had great fun on a variety of rides, roundabouts, trampolines and so on.

On Saturday 9th August 1986, 'J' Coy held its Parents' Day, after the completion of thirteen weeks of training. This was an opportunity for a unique occasion for four members of the Corps, two near the end of their military careers and the other two just beginning. WO1 (ASM) B P Cooper, ex-62A, was due to retire in November, while his son A/T A S Cooper had just joined intake 86B. WO1 (ASM) R S Cooper had joined two years later than his brother as a member of 64B, and his son A/T Cpl G P Cooper was about to start his final term as an apprentice Armourer of intake 85A. Thus, all four members of this proud family had started their careers here at boys' school.

Towards the end of September that year, the College was saddened to hear of the death of Douglas – or 'Dougie' - Crowhurst. Born in 1924, Dougie had joined the RASC as a junior soldier just before the outbreak of war in 1939. After the war, he transferred to REME and had become WO2 Artificer Vehicles (Art Vehs) after serving a full Army Career. Employed for a while at 13 Command Wksp (later 43 Command Wksp) at Aldershot, Dougie had joined the College as an Instructional Officer in September 1965 and

subsequently gave twenty-one years of dedicated skill, training and encouragement to those boys who passed through his hands in the Fitting Shop.

The 'Fifty-year' apprentices

On 1st October 1986, SEME hosted a most nostalgic event for the fiftieth anniversary of the first recruits for technical apprentice training. Those young boys had joined up at Bramley and Hilsea in Hampshire in 1936, many of whom were later to become founder members of REME in 1942. Eddie Walters, employed at Bordon as a civilian instructor, had the idea for the reunion and, eventually. With great assistance from the REME Manning and Records Office (RMRO) and the *Daily Express*, the event came into being. All in all, ninety-six old soldiers attended, honoured by the presence of Maj Gen Boyne DGEME and Maj Gen Berragan DGOS, himself an ex-Arborfield boy. Eddie, representing his group of colleagues, presented a magnificent silver rose bowl to the DGEME, on behalf of the Corps, with the words, *"We left the family, we travelled far and we've been away a long time, but by golly it's good to come home"*.

In the winter edition of the College magazine, some long overdue recognition was given to the exploits of Electronics Wing. Its very name was a dead giveaway for what it purported to achieve and its students were then resident from the start of 2 Div until the eleventh week of their sixth term. Basic Electronics theory was backed up by various experiments and practical fault-finding, as well as by visits to friendly local electronics firms. When not to be found missing, off training for his BFT, the OIC Wing at the time was Maj Bill Cleasby, an ex-apprentice of 61C, with his trusty 2I/C another ex-boy, Capt Brian Glossop of 57A. Bill's name crops up later in this history, as he went on to become, amongst other things, Hon Sec of the AOBA.

That magazine was again based around a sporting theme. Climbers from the College had once again been practicing their skills in the Alps and the Lake District. The Cricket team had finally, for the very first time, triumphed at the Triangular Games. The intrepid Canoe Club had participated at the Army Wild Water Championships on the River Swale, at Richmond, North Yorkshire, while other sports getting a mention included Caving, Cycling, Orienteering and Squash. The Inter-Company Novices Boxing event had proved an excellent one for 'B' Coy. Its team contested ten out of the twelve bouts, winning no less than six different weight divisions.

An event that had gained a certain respectability at the College was the Cross Country 'Tin Hat' Race, 'voluntarily' entered (*oh yeah?*) by ALL apprentices. Custom dictated that the start of the race began on the Parade Square, by the Commandant's blowing of a bugle! This would set off a mad rush by some 450 pairs of legs to be the first to the far corner. By the time the first man reached the Pavilion, the whole cavalcade would already be stretched across about 500 metres, but there was no giving up, everyone had to finish the run. The result was decided by taking the finishing positions of the apprentices in each Company and dividing that by the number of runners. At that term's event, it was 'A' Coy that won the award of two Tin Hats.

NAAFI gets spruced up

The spring term of 1987 had obviously seen a refurbishment of the NAAFI Club. Describing this, one young apprentice reported that *"after coming back from half term, I thought I was dreaming. Entering the NAAFI main doors, I noticed that the walls were not their usual drab white – but brilliant, bright white".* Within the canteen, new refrigerated cabinets and computerised drinks machines had replaced the old pre-war types. One machine now dispensed such delicacies as sausage rolls and alongside was a 'do-it-yourself' microwave oven in which they could be heated up.

The Tavern Bar now looked more like something you'd find at *The Ritz*, with old-fashioned wooden tables and straight-backed chairs now replaced with Formica-topped low tables and comfortable easy-chairs. Our apprentice reporter was obviously most impressed by all this. Settling himself down with a couple of tipples, he found it so comfortable that he had to be almost carried to his bed at locking-up time! A definite contender for the *'Satisfied Soldier'* scheme.

Vehicle Wing was continuing its successful policy of sending off its almost-qualified apprentices on detachments to units of the Regular Army. This was a method of preparing its students for the type of working environment within which they would soon find themselves. The Units visited included the Irish Guards at Chelsea, the Life Guards at Windsor, and the Scots Guards, recently returned from peacekeeping duties in Northern Ireland. An early return to PMC

was forced upon A/T Wheeldon – he came back in an ambulance, covered in spots, due to a dose of chicken pox. Meanwhile, upon their arrival at 37 Sqn RCT, three hardy VMs were first briefed on all the important stuff – like the location of the bar and the WRAC block!

The Commandant always knew when 'end of term' beckoned, as the editor of *The Arborfield Apprentice* would start hanging around his office, dropping hints that the magazine was 'just about ready', and all that was needed was the Commandant's *'Foreword'*. Col Soar happily obliged again that spring, firm in the knowledge that it had been another fruitful term.

The College Soccer team had achieved promotion to Division I of the Reading Combination League for the first time; the Rugby team had achieved a similar 'first' by winning the Army Under-17 Junior Cup; while the Chess Club had once again regained the title of Army Junior Chess Champions. And. of course, there had been the little matter of another 104 ex-apprentices enjoying the traditional 'PoP' and then taking their first steps into the challenge of adult service.

March 1987 brought the terrible news of a tragedy at sea, when the ferry *'Herald of Free Enterprise'* sank, with a disastrous loss of lives, at Zeebrugge. What made this most poignant from the College's point of view was that we lost one of our favourite sons, in the shape of Maj Jim Stanyer, who had started his all too brief life as an apprentice here in September 1954. It was ironic that Jim should lose his life in a shipping accident, as he had previously sailed across countless thousands of miles during his career in REME. He had been one of the first students at the Joint Services Adventurous Training Centre (JSATC) down at Gosport in the early Seventies, going on to qualify as an Ocean Yachtmaster. Jim had long been a keen supporter of offshore sailing and was a regular instructor on courses run at JSATC.

Continuation of sporting success

The College Cycling team reported a successful season in 1987. It had started off in March with the Army Spring Cup, held at Chepstow, followed by both the Berkshire 25- and 50-mile rides in May, the London-Brighton race in June and the Festival of Cycling, held at Folkstone, in June / July. A/T CSM McLeish of 'D' Coy enjoyed a lot of personal reward, ending the Festival with two gold and three silver medals, and along the way becoming both Army Junior Road Race Champion and Army Junior Track Champion. Awarded his Army senior colours, he later represented the winning Army team in the Inter-Services Track Races, held at Brighton at the end of June.

If cycling had been 'successful', then athletics provided an 'out of this world' season that same year. The Inter-Service match, held at RAF Halton in early June in some cold, wet and blustery conditions, provided the College with a good win, despite their being hard pressed by the team of 'jolly jack tars' from HMS Collingwood. Having lost by a single point to Harrogate in the previous year's Triangular Games, the College now gained sweet revenge on Harrogate's home 'cinder' track, winning no less than seventeen of the nineteen events.

The climax of the season, the Army Junior Championship, had eluded Arborfield since 1979. But there was to be no stopping them this season. Even though the age-limit meant a large number of first-string athletes had to drop out, their keen, eager replacements lived up to the task in hand. Taking the lead from the opening event, the College went on to add the term 'Army Junior Champions' to what had been a memorable year.

August 7th 1987 saw a party of climbers set off from the College, including four serving apprentices, two recent ex-apprentices, as well as some more experienced personnel. After some early practice and first-time experience on steep ice, the team challenge was to attempt the famous 'Trinity' of mountain peaks, namely the Jungfrau, Monch and Eiger.

It was Doctor Mike Motley, previously on the Arborfield staff but now based at Chepstow, who became a casualty during his descent from the first climb. He had complained of feeling a little unwell some time earlier, but now fell and injured his knee. Four hours later, he was being speedily whisked away in a Swiss air-rescue helicopter. Mike proved his fortitude by volunteering to serve here again later in his career! The second peak was accomplished the next day, with all of the serving apprentices proudly posing for photographs on the summit. The Eiger was eventually considered too difficult for the serving boys, due to their inexperience but, even so, the whole exercise had proved well worth the effort.

Towards the end of August, the Canoe Club set off on what they described as their 'Grand European Tour'. Their arrival in the Schwartzwald (*Black*

Forest, but no gateaux! Ed.) was greeted by some torrential rain, so the boys spent a day canoeing along the River Neckar in conditions more suited to the Amazon. Their next phase was to be held at Augsburg, on the Olympic Slalom Course. Never have so many knees knocked together, so loudly, for so long! But most boys completed one or more parts of the course, so that their previous nervous silence soon gave way to light-hearted banter once again. A three-day stopover at Lake Chiemsee allowed plenty of canoeing and mountain walking amongst the magnificent scenery, set in the foothills of the Alps.

A broken ignition key then became something of an embarrassment, but a steel replacement eventually saw the party driving through Austria and on into northern Italy. A series of seemingly endless tunnels, broken only by many nerve-wrenching hairpin bends, ended with their welcome arrival at the campsite of Carazei, high in the Dolomites. Some hill walking to a height of some 3,000 metres above sea level confirmed that the air is definitely rarified at that height!

Surviving on a diet of salami, *"stinky cheese"* and hard Italian bread, the boys eventually earned a day's outing in the uniquely spectacular canal-based city of Venice, before reaching their final campsite on the banks of the huge inland Lake Garda. After a few days of climbing, windsurfing and lots of *gelato* (ice cream), the party began the long trip home through Germany and Belgium, sustained by a visit to the beautiful mediaeval city of Bruges.

Col Soar was justifiably proud of the sporting achievements that had been gained by the College. Apart from the athletics glory, 'D' Coy football team had gone all the way to the final of the Army Youth Cup, while fencing, swimming and canoeing had also proved prominent that year. In the summer edition of *The Arborfield Apprentice*, the Commandant stressed that such success, no matter how great or small, was due in no small measure to the continuing efforts of the College staff, who provide such excellent support and encouragement to the boys under their supervision.

In September 1987, another College stalwart reached his final retirement age of sixty-five. Peter Spargo had joined the ATS (Boys) here at Arborfield in the very first intake of 1939, returning to the College as a member of its civilian instructional staff in 1960. An article in that summer's edition (1987) of the College magazine gave tribute to Peter's long service and a brief description of his career. He was to return the

I know we're not Sappers but we can still lay a bridge!

For this to happen, it was recognised that there had to be a well-developed application of a 'Systems Approach to Training' (SAT) in place. Fortunately, the College, with its long experience of this system, combined with an established computer-based validation set-up, was ideally placed to cope.

Despite these 'behind-the-scenes' manouvres, Monday 21st March 1988 dawned brightly and cheerfully on the eager faces of a party of boys, as they assembled outside the Guardroom to pick up transport for a MTW exercise. Two glorious days were then spent on Bulford ranges, completing a round of weapons training, but the end of the shooting session also saw off the good weather! The next morning, as they started off on a forty-kilometre walk on Salisbury Plain, the boys could hardly believe the driving wind and cold rain that accompanied them. All but two of the squad, genuine injury cases, eventually struggled to the tank crossing below Westdown Camp, where they were delighted to be picked up in the new *Warrior* APCs.

The next couple of days were spent at the village of Imber, where our intrepid troops were to spend their time on tactics, trench digging and patrolling. During this time, they were introduced to a vast array of night-vision devices, which included both thermal imagers and image intensifiers. Their amazement at the way that night could be turned into day soon turned into concern, as they realised that camouflage was nowadays just as important by night as it had always been by day. Their final fast withdrawal from the area, under the threat of attack by the enemy (staff members), was so realistic that there was lots of urgency in their movements. Judging by the nodding heads on the buses, on the return journey home, the exercise had provided plenty of exercise and excitement, as well as a feeling of utter contentment that they had survived it all – and lived to tell the tale!

following year, receiving his Imperial Service Medal from Maj Gen Dennis Shaw CBE, DGEME, on the occasion of the April 1988 'PoP'.

(A copy of the relevant article can be found in a separate annex to this chapter.)

'Contracting' on the horizon

By that month of September, it was becoming increasingly obvious that the Government of the day was keenly pursuing its policy of 'contracting out'. The control of many Army functions had already been handed over to civilian firms and institutions, as a means of achieving manpower and financial savings. Due to continuing pressure on both of these resources in the Individual Training Organisation (ITO), it was decided that the implications of contracting out the military and civilian educational and instructional functions, within the ITO, should be closely examined. Two major areas were selected for investigation: Army Apprentices' Colleges and certain technical Arms and Service Schools. The 'pilot' establishments for this study were to be SEME, Bordon, and the ACC College at Aldershot.

Many concerns and objections were raised across all training units, with most of them being common to all units. It was taken as read that the current standards and results of training must be vigorously retained.

A severe case of 'numbus bumbus'

The Easter weekend of 1988 saw the College Canoe Club embark once again on, this time the fortieth anniversary of, the Devizes to Westminster canoe race, that gruelling four-day event, consisting of 125 miles of non-stop paddling. The first stretch of thirty-four miles, along the Kennet and Avon Canal, saw the boys end up at Newbury, suffering from the dreaded 'numbus bumbus', an affliction that apparently grips all would-be canoeists!

Another thirty-six miles of canal ended at Reading, and then the boys were at last onto 'moving water' along the River Thames past such lovely spots as Henley and Marlow, then on towards London. A third leg of thirty-eight miles, with the boys now suffering a variety of wrist problems and blisters, brought them to Teddington, ready for a 05.30 hours start the next morning, on their final seventeen-mile dash down to Westminster. As explained by a previous competitor, the bridges down to Westminster make a spectacular backdrop, it's just that there are so many of them! But finally, reaching the steps of the old Greater London Council building to cheers and applause certainly lifted the spirits. After the medals had been awarded, the boys were grateful for the chance of devouring a huge and hearty breakfast.

The end of the 1987 / 88 soccer season saw an exciting finale, as the College looked forward to an appearance in the Army Youth Challenge Cup Final (SE District) at Aldershot. The opposition that year was provided by apprentices from the ACC. A crowd of some 800 spectators cheered on every move, as the two sides battled to a half-time score of two goals apiece. Arborfield must have thought the game was won when they went ahead in the 72nd minute, but a soft penalty allowed the ACC back into the game. 3 - 3 now and all to play for as the match went into extra-time. It was then that the skill and endeavour of the PMC side came to the fore, as they relentlessly tore into the opposition defence. First one goal, then another, until, with the match already wrapped up, a superlative individual opportunist sixth goal ensured that victory would go to the College XI.

New School at Wallop

The Craftsman magazine of April 1988 reported on the parade that had been held the previous January at Middle Wallop, when the AETW was re-designated as the School of Aeronautical Engineering (SAE). This brought the unit into line with the other two adult training centres, SEE at Arborfield and SEME at Bordon. Thus, on leaving the College in future, Air

Techs would go back to school! Originally set up to meet the demands of the expanding AAC, which came into being on September 1st 1957, the 'Wing' in its title had led many to believe that it was merely an off-shoot of that Corps. This, despite the fact that it was a REME trade school, commanded by a Lieutenant Colonel. Its new title finally gave the establishment the status it deserved.

The final intake of the REME 'One-Year Apprenticeship' began its mission in life on May 2nd 1988, as 144 *"innocent civilians"* spluttered their way into action. Scalped, uniformed and 'rifted' across the Parade Square, the familiar pattern of training soon sorted out the men from the boys. The term sped by in frantic fashion, helped along by some excellent weather, for which the apprentices were extremely grateful. Not so one PS member, who kept muttering such things as *"If it ain't raining, it ain't training"*!

A final farewell was bidden to WO2 Henry Ravai of the RRF, who was retiring to his native land of Fiji after more years in 'J' Coy than other staff members were prepared to remember. The final few weeks of term were taken up by the normal rehearsals and exercises, before Blenheim Platoon won the Drill Competition and the accolade of being *'Victor Ludorum'*.

Established at the College for only around four years, the sport of orienteering had become extremely popular by 1988, with its required map-reading skills providing an obvious military asset. The College team had indeed established itself most successfully. They dominated the Junior Army Championship, winning for the third successive year, and came fourth out of eleven teams at the SE District major units meeting. On Easter Sunday, a College team of eleven boys entered an international Festival of Orienteering at Goodwood, West Sussex, with A/T Cook of 'A' Coy leading the field on the first day from A/T Hall of 'C' Coy. A French runner provided some serious opposition at the start of the second day, but young Cook stayed calm, ran his own race, and was rewarded with another fine victory. As well as providing the event winner, the College also claimed fourth and fifth places on the combined times.

Soon afterwards, the PMC team was extremely privileged and honoured to receive an invitation to visit the country of Sweden, in order to train and compete with one of that country's Infantry Regiments. During their stay, the apprentices received some first-class coaching and participated in three Swedish national

Keith Evans greeting Princess Alexandra

and one military orienteering event. As well as the obvious enjoyment of their sport, the boys were also able to spend a very interesting morning at a College of Further Education. Here, they were impressed by the way that computers were being used as an aid to learning, as well as for administrative purposes.

Awards and trophies

Early in that year, the *Worshipful Company of Turners* decided to inaugurate an annual award to the College. The Company's Silver Medal, together with a monetary award and certificate, was to be awarded to that apprentice who achieved the 'highest standard of craft skills' during his training. The first recipient of this prestigious award was an aspiring Armourer, A/T Timothy Leak, in February 1989. The College Commandant was also pleased to receive the '*Litster Trophy*', awarded by the *Livery Company*.

In the summer 1988 edition of *The Arborfield Apprentice*, A/T Robinson gave his account of '*Life as a Medic*'. It didn't sound too much different from stories told elsewhere in this history, except for the fact that if he actually went on to enter the 'medics', young Robinson would at least have the chance of some

revenge! Along with some colleagues, he had attended Saighton Camp in Chester to do 'casualty simulation' for the TA RAMC who were based there. Putting on some shabby bloodstained clothes, and being administered with very realistic 'wounds', the boys then spent three days generally lying about! Our man Robinson found it an enjoyable experience, one that he wouldn't mind doing again, though he got hardly any sleep and found the food *"even worse than the College's"*.

Although Hockey is not traditionally regarded as a 'summer sport', the College entered two teams for a six-a-side tournament, as part of the REME Corps Weekend. The PS side, with plenty of experience available, did extremely well until good old '*anno domini*' took its toll. The A/Ts' side, however, made an immediate impact upon the competition, with their youthful vigour, speed and tenacity. They surprised everyone by going through the initial league stage, then winning their way through the quarter-finals and semi-finals to contest the final against a strong side from SEE. Here, skill and experience finally came into their own and the boys were beaten 0 – 2, but not before they had been treated with plenty of respect by their more accomplished rivals.

Getting up early on those cold, dark winter mornings had certainly paid off for the College swimmers. Now that the sun had decided to rise at a reasonable hour, their trips to the pool seemed a lot less arduous and treacherous. The first event to be entered was the Junior Army competition, where all opposition was left trailing in the wakes of the Arborfield boys. They picked up sixty-seven points, against the JLdrs from RAC Bovington, the second team, whose haul was a mere forty-three. Lots of personal best times were recorded. Then it was on to the Tri-Service Games for another convincing win, much to the horror of RAF Halton, who had trained really hard that season. The Triangular Games brought a further triumph and a total of seven apprentices were later awarded their Junior Army colours.

Set your sights high

Leaving the College after his two-year stint, A/T RSM Smith felt that he had enjoyed *"just about everything"* that the College had to offer. Having joined up at Christmas 1986, his rather unimpressive early exam results meant that he was initially offered the chance of becoming a Recy Mech. Accepting this, young Smith worked hard and, by the end of 'J' Coy, was sufficiently advanced to change his employment to VM. This was his chance to prove his worth so, making up his own motto of *"Be enthusiastic in everything"*, he went on to gain good results at trade, education and military training, so good in fact that he also advanced up the ranks.

He was very proud of his feat in gaining the top rank of 'Boy RSM' and, writing in the College magazine, he urged all boys to follow his example, try as hard as possible, and take advantage of the endless opportunities ahead of them. His last bit of advice – *"Set your sights high"* – which brings back memories of a similar exhortation by 'Monty' in 1942 - was proved by the fact that he was awarded both the *BP Trophy* as 'Best Vehicle Mechanic', and the Commandant's Cup as 'Best Apprentice'.

The College magazine that summer gave its usual round up of events from the Companies. 'A' Coy, despite a perceived notion of not being able to 'pull their weight' at sports, managed to do just that by winning the Tug-of-War at all three weight categories. 'B' Coy boys were treading very warily that term, having been hit by three new arrivals in the form of OC, 2IC and CSM! 'C' Coy was busily engaged in following that great bastion of Australian culture – the TV serial *'Neighbours'*. If they missed it at lunchtime, a special effort would be made to catch up with the evening programme. Lastly, 'D' Coy bemoaned the fact that, having won at Cricket, Tennis, Orienteering and Drill, and coming second in Athletics and Skill-at-Arms, they had still lost the Champion Company competition to 'Charlie' Coy.

Col Soar's time here had proved a comparatively quiet one, as far as any serious changes were concerned. But, in his final script to *The Arborfield Apprentice,* he was able to write of his pride in all that had been achieved on the sporting scene. The efforts of all concerned had not only maintained but enhanced the College's reputation as *"a superb competitor in any event, whatever the field"*. The Commandant went on to say that much of the success was due to PS commitment, evidenced not only in the winning of trophies, but also in the plethora of hobbies and pastimes, particularly the adventurous expeditions, that were usually organised outside the confines of the working day.

Centre of interest - and opportunity

During the year, PMC had become the centre of interest for all sorts of study groups, as a result of imminent Defence cuts. The latter part of 1988 witnessed yet more changes in staff. RSM Milloy gave way to RSM N F Hartley, Coldstream Guards, while Col P H Kay OBE, BSc(Eng), CEng, FIMfgE, FIEE took over as Commandant and looked forward to celebrating 1989 as the College's Golden Jubilee year. The new Commandant gave his initial thoughts in *The Arborfield Apprentice* of winter 1988. He summed up his first impressions in a single word – *"Opportunity"*. He had never seen so many facilities available in a single institution in his whole career. However, he reminded everyone that these did not come cheaply, with the College then costing just a little under £20 million per year to run. His predecessor had told Col Kay that he would have lots to smile about, as long as the boys continued to acquit themselves well. He was happy to report to Col Soar that he was still smiling!

Exercise 'Bonnie Dundee' saw the College take up its role in the large United Kingdom exercise in Home Defence. One wag in 'A' Coy said that the purpose of the exercise was to *"defend truth, justice, the British way of life - and my Mum"*! The official line was that it was designed to test the *"ability to mobilise, deploy and defend key point installations, both during the transition to war and in war itself"*.

However described, the exercise saw apprentices from the College dispatched, on all sorts of transport, to all corners of – I was going to say Kingdom, but in fact it turned out to be Scotland! Places mentioned by the boys on their return included the Isle of Lewis, Stornaway, Benbecula, Edinburgh, Dalbeattie, Dumfries and Galloway, while transport was provided by bus, truck, train, *Hercules*, *Chinook* and landing craft! All in all, the *"short vacation"* provided a welcome break in routine and proved worthwhile and enjoyable – especially once it was over!

After the four-week summer break, the budding Air Techs of 87A were back to raise the blood pressure of their instructors. Climax of the term in Aircraft Wing came with the arrival of a *Lynx* helicopter from the AAC at Oakington, near Cambridge. Due to typically English weather difficulties, it arrived late but at least it looked just the same as the photographs! Fifteen-minute flights, six passengers at a time, were organised; even some members of the Pay Office, complete with handbags, were accommodated. Some of the students had a go at 'marshalling' the aircraft during its take-off and landing. Later in the term, a visit to SAE Middle Wallop was undertaken, giving the lads a chance to see real 'loadsamoney' Air Techs.

Overseas expeditions

Two expeditions that year gave opportunities for apprentices to revel in the thrills of overseas travel once more. One group set off on a three-week visit to Morocco. Arriving at Marrakech, they had to hire taxis to take them to their hotel, to which the lads later gave a star rating of minus five! They made their way into some splendid mountainous country and actually found that they needed axes, boots and crampons to achieve the snow-covered peak of Toubkal. Returning to lower levels and desert surroundings, they tried their hand at camel riding, before spending a day in sardine-like conditions on a bus to Agadir. The journey proved a dangerous one as they hit snow and ice, but it actually ended with some time spent on a sun-drenched beach. Their flight home was delayed by striking Spanish air-controllers and the lads had to spend a long time sitting around at Lisbon before finally receiving permission to return to Heathrow.

October saw the College Hockey team in fine form. Having lost the first match of the season against Sandhurst, they had remained unbeaten since, winning seven and drawing another two games. The culmination of this effort came in the Army Junior Cup. In the preliminary games they effortlessly disposed of all opposition by scores of 6 – 0, 7 – 0 and 4 – 0. A tighter semi-final saw Harrogate beaten 2 – 0 and the lads closed down the final against the JLdrs Regt RA by another fine score of 4 – 0. College goalkeeper A/T Smith reckoned he touched the ball no more than seven times throughout the tournament!

In the end-of-term 'grudge clash' against the College PS, OIC Hockey Maj Butler had an unfortunate meeting between his face and the ball, resulting in a dash to the MRS, where the skillful medics managed to save his good looks. As if to rub salt in his wound, it was the boys who ran out winners by a score of 6 – 2. Three of the team were afterwards selected to play for the Army U-21 side.

In *The Craftsman* issued that October, Steve Johnson (46A) gave some details of his service on Christmas Island, on the thirtieth anniversary of the last live dropping of an H-bomb. He had arrived on that remote atoll in April 1958 and recalls a later visit by the Royal Yacht *Britannia*, bringing HRH Prince Philip to meet the troops. Steve found life quite primitive on the island; accommodation was of the tented variety, while spares were at a premium. Drinking water was scarce and, although the Navy occasionally provided some fresh water, mostly it was into the sea for a salty wash! The two bomb tests eventually took place in September and Steve was allowed a stopover in Hawaii at the end of his twelve-month tour.

Over the weekend 7th / 9th October, a light shower of rain was the only thing that marred the parade held during the annual Old Boys' Reunion. 155 old boys marched proudly onto the Square, accompanied by the boys of 'A' Coy, and led by the stirring sounds of the College Band and Pipes and Drums. The salute was taken by ex-Commandant Col (Ret'd) John Cole, escorted by Col Phil Kay. The ex-apprentices looked as indefatigable as ever, although their drill was by now showing a little sign of rustiness. *(Let's put that down to the rain, shall we? Ed.)* However, their lifting elbows showed not a sign of rust at the inevitable session at the bar that Saturday evening!

Sadly, as the year drew towards a close, November 3rd brought the accidental death of A/T LCpl Anthony Chorlton, who somehow managed to fall to his death from the high-speed train that was carrying him home on half-term leave. This unfortunate accident cast a deep shadow over the College and Anthony's fellow apprentices. He was given a funeral, with full military honours, at his hometown of Ashton-under-Lyne, near Manchester.

A great fight-back

Aldershot Military Stadium provided a fitting backdrop to the Army Apprentices' Football Cup Final on December 4th. It was a bleak Sunday afternoon and the Arborfield boys were tense, remembering their defeat of the previous year. Once again Harrogate provided the opposition and a rather defensive game saw the first half end in a scoreline of 0 - 0. With only fifteen minutes to go, Harrogate scored and began to celebrate what looked like being another victory. But PMC weren't finished yet and forced an equaliser to send the game into extra-time. Then, under the floodlights, the Harrogate goalkeeper sent a clearance soaring into the evening sky, only to find it flying back past him from the head of A/T Isbister, hero of the hour. Arborfield had won the Cup!

The winter term had seen a fairly large involvement by the College with the Berkshire Award Group of the Duke of Edinburgh's Award Scheme. They provided two bases during a map-reading exercise, during which contestants had to complete certain tests. One test was a casualty simulation, where entrants had to prove their first-aid skills, while the second involved the crossing of a *"snake infested pit"* to retrieve a pot of gold – in this case a box of *Mars Bars*! This good public relations exercise was followed, on December 12th, by the College's hosting of the annual award ceremony. The highlight of the evening was when A/T Buffery was presented with his Gold Award by the Lord Lieutenant of Berkshire, to background music provided by two of the College pipers.

Another group of apprentices, during their ten-day EL exercise in Wales, took time off to join wardens from the Brecon Beacons National Park in a variety of tasks. These were aimed at improving both the environment and tourist access to local attractions. The boys, all members of 'J' Coy, were involved in the re-building of a riverside path at a well-known beauty spot, which had been eroded by natural river action and by the tramp of many feet. *(No, we've heard that one before! Ed.)* Three bridges were also replaced over local streams; all the building material literally hauled in by the boys, as vehicular access was restricted. A number of stiles, gates and signs were replaced, along a stretch of the famous Offa's Dyke footpath.

Saturday 17th December provided the culmination of a fine season for the College Rugby XV. Things hadn't looked too bright at the start of term, with a full twelve first-team regulars having moved on to adult service. Thankfully, the College trials in September had brought some noticeable new talent to light. Two College records were broken against the JLdrs RAC, a score of 94 – 0 and a personal haul of forty-four points by A/T Sgt Webster.

Six of the squad were regular members of the Army Youth team, with A/T SSgt Jeffery as its captain. In the semi-final of the Army Youth Cup, AAC Aldershot had been thrashed by forty points to nil, so now, a week before Christmas, it was the Cup Final against Harrogate. 300 enthusiastic College supporters made the short trip to Aldershot and, after a closely fought battle, PMC lifted the trophy by a score of 15 – 13, the first time they had won the Cup since 1971.

More than eighty old-age pensioners (no, they weren't all old boys!) attended the College for a traditional Christmas dinner. As well as all the Christmas goodies on offer, the young soldiers had also organised a collection, so that they could send all the senior citizens home with a miniature spirits bottle each. To complete the seasonal atmosphere, Pipe Major Stuart Burns of the Royal Scots Regiment (RSR) played the pipes whist the pudding was served. Unfortunately, the College magazine reported this as *"the Pipe Major piped in the desert"*! *(He was a long way from home, and known as 'Sandy'. Ed.)*

On Thursday 22nd December, another 135 apprentices passed out of the College on their way to adult service. Reviewing Officer that day was Lt Gen Sir Peter de la Billiere KCB, CBE, DSO, MC, and GOC SE District. A former SAS chief and the man who had masterminded the never-to-be-forgotten raid on the Iranian Embassy in London, Sir Peter was the nation's most decorated General. He was to claim a further place in history when commanding the British Forces in the Gulf War, just a couple of short years later.

Golden Jubilee Year

1989 saw the start of the fiftieth year since the establishment of the College, its glorious 'Golden Jubilee' year. While PMC still undertook its normal daily routines, and presented its face to the outside world as all 'peace and calm', underneath that seemingly placid façade a great deal of hectic activity was taking place. Many organising committees were being set in place to organise the forthcoming celebrations. The first of these was to be the Golden Jubilee 'PoP', which took place on April 21st 1989.

The Reviewing Officer at that parade was Maj Gen A S J Blacker CBE, the Representative Colonel Commandant REME, and the day was certainly full of a sense of *"past and present"*, visible in the attendance of so many ex-Commandants invited along for this momentous occasion. These included Brigadiers Dobie and Percival, along with Colonels Brown, Cole,

Keast, Peacock, Roberts, Soar and Tweed, a veritable roll call stretching back many years. One of the rarest sights that day was College RSM Hartley in *"full dress uniform"*, as he received his LSGC Medal from the General.

Incorporated into the normal 'PoP' that day was a proud contingent of old boys, which included amongst its ranks a number from the original intake of 1939. One of these stalwarts was Keith Evans, who had joined in 1945 as an Inst Mech and was now back at the College in his role as a Maths lecturer. Peter Spargo was also on parade, as would be expected from such a staunch member of the OBA, who still meets and greets lots of old friends and colleagues at the annual reunions. There was a great deal of local media interest and Association Secretary Sam Weller made his TV debut on the *Southern News* that very evening.

To commemorate the occasion of its Golden Jubilee, the College commissioned a painting by the military artist, David Rowlands. The centrepiece of this painting depicted the scene of a typical Passing-out Parade and, around its periphery, it contained several scenes of College life that had occurred over the years. They included the 1942 visit by 'Monty', showing Col Hilborn and RSM McNally. From the Fifties were bench-fitting and PT; the Sixties scenes showed apprentices working on vehicles and a helicopter; and from the Eighties, an ARV lifting a power-pack and a scene depicting computer technology. Needless to say, the original College gates also figured prominently. The original painting was hung in the PMC foyer, but many members of the College, both past and present, were able to purchase 'limited edition' signed prints, which are no doubt proudly displayed in many locations world-wide. One such print proudly hangs in the foyer of the REME Museum, where it is admired by many thousands of visitors.

Another highlight of the Jubilee celebrations was the presentation of a hand-made plate by John Northam to Col Kay. John was himself an apprentice at Arborfield between 1947 / 1950 and was now an instructor here. One of his extra-mural activities was the running of a Ceramics Club, and it was these talents that had led to him making and painting the commemorative plate.

History - topped up!

It was also during that Golden Jubilee year that yet another, believed to be the fifth, *'Brief History'* of the College was published. In his foreword to that publication, in very similar wording to that used by Col Roberts in 1984, Col Phil Kay wrote:

"Before Captain (Ret'd) Bryn Richards set about the compilation of an article, which appeared in the 1984 REME Journal, very little had been officially recorded on the fascinating stories surrounding the history of the Apprentices' College at Arborfield. Spurred on by his findings, more detail and personal experiences emerged to add to the already comprehensive outline entry. As the College Archivist, we are indebted to him for (his) diligence in unravelling the facts of the past and continuing this work through to the Golden Jubilee Year."

Because of the loss of many of its top runners upon posting, the College entered a severely weakened Cross-country team for the British Army Championship held at Aldershot, early in 1989, gaining only fourth place in the Junior section. Consequently, the next few weeks were spent on some very tough training in anticipation of the forthcoming REME Championships, to be held at Bordon. Despite being the only junior team in the race, PMC gained a creditable second place behind the strong SEME team. This fine effort soon paid off, when the College was asked to provide a team to travel to Germany and compete for the BAOR Championship, held at Detmold. The course proved exceptionally difficult, with lots of hills, but out of fifteen major unit teams in the race, PMC came in third. The celebrations that followed can be safely left to the imagination!

On June 3rd 1989, a party of ninety willing volunteers travelled up to London to watch the first rehearsal for the Queen's Birthday Parade. An early highlight of the day was the rush to be 'searched' by the young Women Police Constables (WPCs) at the entrance to the Parade Square! On marched the Divisions of the Welsh, Irish, Grenadier and Scots Guards, followed by men from the Coldstream Guards, trooping the colour in full ceremonial dress, polished boots like mirrors and all brasses and buttons sparkling. The drill on display was of the highest calibre and, after the mock inspection, on rode the Life Guards and the Blues & Royals. Overawed A/Ts later returned to Arborfield, very much reminded that their own drill could perhaps do with just a slight touch of improvement!

The weather during that summer of 1989 will be long remembered, for its above average sunshine and temperatures. It certainly seemed to make a difference on the sporting scene, especially to the College Athletics team, who set a record that may only be equalled, but will never be improved upon. They remained unbeaten by any other Junior Army side throughout the whole season. Their achievement was closely followed by that of the Cycling team, who, at the Army Festival of Cycling, a nine-day programme of time trials, track and road racing, triumphed in all the Junior events except one. Orienteering too was on a high note, with victories in both the REME and Junior Army (Night and Day) Championships.

For the athletes, the auspices were good when the season started with a success over the RMAS, with another victory following in the Tri-Service games, held at HMS Collingwood. The boys were then well-deserved runners-up in the Corps Championships, against mainly adult opposition, which proved an excellent warm-up for the Triangular Games, won by a squad *"finely honed and buoyant with confidence"*, against Chepstow and Harrogate. The team then marched on as winners over the Junior Leaders from RAC Bovington and the RCT Colerne. The season reached a fitting climax with a well-fought victory in the Junior Army Championship. The boys' main strength was that they had worked as a closely-knit team on every occasion.

Another special event took place that year, when Col (Ret'd) John Peacock, who had served as Commandant from October 1979 to January 1983, returned to the College to present a splendid sword, his own personal possession, to the Apprentice Drum Major. This sword, which normally hangs in the Commandant's office along with the Mace, was now to be worn by the resident Drum Major on all ceremonial parades.

The 'Hathi' Project

In Vehicle Wing, a College engineering project got under way. The challenge was for apprentices to restore a British Army 1925 *Thorneycroft* Breakdown Truck back to working condition. Only twenty-five of these vehicles had ever been built, being used mainly by the RA as gun-tractors, between the wars. Its special significance is that it was the first positive attempt to design a four-wheel drive vehicle for the Army. They were very powerful and effective cross-country vehicles, but required much skilful maintenance. Commercial variants were tested in India and South Africa, while some went later to the Australian Army.

Known as the *'Hathi'*, from the Hindustani word for 'elephant', only one such vehicle had been adapted for breakdown work. It was used throughout the Second World War by the RN at Portsmouth before being sold off for use in timber-felling work, plus the occasional recovery task, in the Hindhead area of Surrey. It eventually became, to use Army parlance, 'BER' (Beyond Economic Repair) and, in 1987, was offered to the Corps Museum for its Historic Vehicles collection.

The task of restoration was taken up by the College as a 'hobbies night' project under the guidance of Maj Derek Millman and presented *"a tremendous challenge of engineering skills"* to those apprentices who would afterwards become involved. The project was to be sponsored by the REME Corps Museum with a watching eye being kept by the firm of *Vosper Thorneycroft*. An offshoot of the company had originally built vehicles at Basingstoke, but this enterprise was subsumed first by *AEC*, then later

The Hathi - battered, bent and bereft of bits

Princess Alexandra with Col Kay and some happy Apprentices

by *Leyland*, and vehicle production transferred to Watford.

The College vehicle club certainly faced a daunting task. The old vehicle was *"battered, bent and bereft of bits"*. Perhaps the hardest part would be the removal of extraneous fittings and the relocation of some original parts, which had been moved when the vehicle was converted for tree pulling. However, it certainly provided a worthwhile project and, provided that things worked out, would eventually represent *"an important part of REME's and the Army's technical heritage"*.

A very special Reunion

As had become the custom, the OBA held their annual reunion in October 1989, with the programme of events over the weekend following much the normal format. The Saturday morning parade was reviewed by the DGEME of the day, Maj Gen Dennis Shaw, CBE. In the evening, however, instead of the normal 'men only' (or ex-boys only, to be exact!) formal dinner, a dance

was held in the College Gymnasium, accompanied by the serving of a splendid buffet supper. This was much enjoyed by the wives of the old boys and everyone agreed that the event was such a great success, that perhaps the same format should be used in another fifty years!

Amongst the many delighted participants in that Reunion was Bill Tingey, who 'came home' especially from the other side of the world (NZ) to attend, mainly due to the efforts of Jim Silby, who had also been one of those original boys of 39A. Bill had recently had his memory stirred by a photograph in the Corps Magazine of a Chelsea Pensioner, Dave Slane. Bill's initial thought was that he had also been one of the first intake, known to one and all as 'Slasher'. It eventually turned out to be another Slane, who Bill then recalled as having been pitted against in the boxing ring, where they had *"punched each other to a standstill"*. After their bout, Ben Cook had told them that it would be *"a sign of weakness"* if they reported sick the following morning!

The programme produced for the reunion that year contained a reminder to all old boys of the objectives of their Association. These were, and remain:

"To foster esprit de corps and comradeship among all old boys of the College; to maintain and further the prestige and dignity of the College; to assist old comrades who have fallen on hard times."

While the old boys were enjoying their special reunion that weekend, four of the present young apprentices were bobbing about on the ocean, learning the skills and perils of offshore sailing. Their first challenge involved *"chasing around the Solent"*, getting as close as possible to several buoys on the way round, whilst filling in questionnaires and splicing a rope!

A cross-Channel trip then gave the boys an opportunity to see Cherbourg, before they headed off to Alderney. A sudden storm blew up and it was a case of struggling into foul-weather gear and dashing for harbour, where they reconciled themselves to a couple of long evenings *"in the pub"*, waiting for the storm to abate. Finally, storm or no storm, the return trip had to be made. Despite their navigation system failing, and not a sight of another friendly vessel, they eventually reached their home port of Gosport, where they found that the next expedition might well be in the Bermuda Triangle!

A helping hand

During late October, a deterioration in industrial relations between the Department of Health and the Ambulance Unions had resulted in men and women from all three Services being deployed on the streets of the UK in support of the sick and needy. The dispute was to last a full six months, with REME and RAMC units playing a major part in the success of the whole operation. Needless to say that, with apprentices from both Corps here at PMC, Arborfield was able to provide much-needed backup with both manpower and a certain amount of training.

The winter term had seen the College Hockey team playing in the SE District League for the first time and games against some of the adult sides proved very tough. As a junior team however, PMC still had no rivals, as proved by another Army Junior Cup victory

at Aldershot in November. Once again it was a story of great defence, with no goals given away during the preliminary rounds, although the first game had seen only a single goal scored against the apprentices of the ACC. The opposition in the final was provided by old foes from Chepstow, whose goalkeeper had an inspired game. Full time ended in a 0 – 0 stalemate, but extra-time saw PMC gain a well deserved 2 – 0 success.

'D' Coy looked back on 1989 with some satisfaction, having regained the title of Champion Company. 'A' Coy reckoned to have abolished slavery – the sort where Senior Div throw rubbish all over the place, so that 2 Div can find it, pick it all up and make the Company lines 'spick and span' once again. With rubbish bins every five steps and contract cleaners 'on the case', the lads were considering entering the next 'Homes and Gardens' competition! Boys from 'B' Coy had enjoyed a weekend training exercise on the south coast, with visits to *HMS Victory*, the D-Day Museum and Royal Marine Museum at Portsmouth, and the Submarine Museum at Poole. 'C' Coy had looked forward immensely to the Christmas party, having been promised a *"bus load of WRACs"*. Nobody had told them that it would be a mini-bus, but the 'disco' was a success and great fun for the outnumbered seven girls who did turn up!

As a fitting close to the Eighties, PMC had been honoured by a visit from HRH Princess Alexandra on October 29th of its Golden Jubilee year. She spent the afternoon meeting staff and apprentices at their place of work, taking much time in chatting and shaking hands. The College had been named after her mother, the first C-in-C of REME, while Princess Alexandra herself had a daughter by the name of Marina. Thus it was that during her tour she officially, and with much personal pleasure, named the College Hall as 'Princess Alexandra Hall', unveiling a plaque to commemorate the auspicious occasion. It was fitting that Maj Mike Costanzo hosted her visit to Electronics Wing, while she toured A & G Wing with Maj Roger Nickson, as they were both ex-boys, of intakes 53B and 56B respectively. The Princess also had time to see the progress being made on Project *Hathi*.

Annex to Chapter 12

The REME Bell Tower

In the December 1966 issue of *'The Craftsman'* magazine, there appeared an article written by one of the Officers of HQ Technical Group REME. This recorded an outline history of the Woolwich Dockyard, from its beginnings in 1510 – 11, as a Royal Dockyard of King Henry V111, up to its closure on 18th September 1869. This was followed by its subsequent ownership by the War Office, until it was finally evacuated in 1966 and handed over to the Borough of Greenwich.

Whilst under War Office ownership, the site had been used largely for the storehouses and workshops, under the Ordnance Department of the Royal Arsenal. RAOC units continued to reside there until the 1960s. A nucleus of Scales Branch (E) was first housed there upon the formation of REME in 1942 and, latterly, Guided Weapons Branch and Scales Branch (E) became the main residents of the site. Both of these units were part of Tech Group REME.

Curiously, the Commanding Officer was allowed to retain the appointment of 'Superintendent of the Royal Dockyard', an historic title that had been handed down from those days when Woolwich had been an active dockyard on the Thames, along with both Deptford and Chatham. With the final evacuation and cessation of this appointment, the last Superintendent obviously felt it within his powers to dispose of the Toll Bell.

All Royal Dockyards had such a Toll Bell, which was rung at the commencement and finish of work. There is no indication on the Woolwich bell, either of its age or foundry of casting. The age of the tower, as it was acquired from Woolwich, is also unknown. The one old sketch in existence is of the entrance to the Dockyard, and shows a much taller, though less ornate, tower. Suffice to say that both the bell and its tower were presented to the Corps by HQ Tech Group, on its departure from the Dockyard in 1966. The tower was then moved to the Army Apprentices College at Arborfield, where it was erected behind 'C' Company lines, as a permanent reminder of the historic link between the Corps and the Woolwich Dockyard.

On the move of the AAC, by now renamed Princess Marina College, in 1982 to its present accommodation, attempts were made to move the Bell Tower too. However, the wood was found to be well rotted and additional damage unfortunately occurred during its dismantling. In 1983, an approach was made by the College to HQ 11 Engineer Group RE, for its assistance in the restoration of the tower. Although they agreed to provide cranes and such, they confirmed that a new tower was required, but that they did not have the facilities to work on such large timbers. An approach to our sister AAC at Chepstow met with a more sympathetic response, and we are most grateful to them for reproducing an identical tower, in pitched pine and oak, within a matter of six months.

The whole top-heavy structure weighed some two tons, which obviously required a substantial foundation and support. For the eventual provision of this, we are eternally grateful to Maj (Ret'd) Ray Eke, the Project Liaison Officer of Arborfield Garrison, for his tireless work in the subsequent design and construction - not to mention the able assistance of pick-and-shovel assistance by countless Apprentices!

On 27th/28th February 1985, with the help of two cranes from No.1 Training Regt RE, the wooden pillar, the bell housing and, finally, the copper clad roof, were erected opposite the Guardroom of PMC. As had become customary in the old Army Apprentices College, the bell is again to be rung to call people to church. It was heard for the first time in its new location on Easter Sunday, for the College end-of-term church service.

(The above article is adapted from the one published in The Craftsman magazine of June 1985.)

The College Gates

The original entrance gates (main and two wicket gates) and arch stood where what is now an emergency entrance/exit to Rowcroft Barracks, in Sheerlands Road. The arch, in open ironworks, had the words 'ARMY TECHNICAL SCHOOL (BOYS)', which was the title of the first establishment.

On 1st February 1947, the School changed its title to 'ARMY APPRENTICES SCHOOL ARBORFIELD'. The arch was covered in sheet metal, giving it a solid appearance, and the new title was superimposed on this. On the 19th August of the same year, the School adopted its new badge and this too was added above the arch. (This very badge at present rests in the Library.)

It was on 3rd August 1965 that the Inspector of Boys' Training (Army) officially handed over to DEME the control and sponsorship of the School. As a result of this, the word 'SCHOOL' was exchanged for 'COLLEGE', and the old badge above the gate was exchanged for a REME badge in September 1966.

One of the economies of the 1968 Defence Review was to be the closure of the Apprentices' College, Carlisle, in 1969. The gates from Carlisle were hung at Arborfield that same year. They were designed and made by the late Maj (Ret'd) Percy Chivers REME.

The original gates were removed to an entrance further up Sheerlands Road, to the left of the then WOs' and Sergeants' Mess, after a small reduction in width by Mr Leslie Shearer, of Workshop Practice Wing. They were to serve as security gates and they were never opened from the day they were hung until their removal in January this year (1984).

It is at this point that some confusion has arisen over the terminology 'Carlisle Gates'. For a special set of gates was made by Percy Chivers, to mark the amalgamation of the College (Arborfield) with Carlisle, and erected opposite the old Guardroom. They incorporated the famous 'Hadrian' eagles and the regimental badges of those members of staff who served at Carlisle. (Unfortunately, eager 'collectors' have removed all but one of these badges.) These gates were formally opened by Brig G V Hayward, Commandant REME Training Centre, on 31st July 1969, the day on which Carlisle held its final Passing-out Parade. (The gates now repose in the present Guardroom cycle shed.)

The arch, too, was beginning to show signs of weathering, so the sheet metal covering was removed, and the open ironwork reappeared, reading 'ARMY APPRENTICES SCHOOL ARBORFIELD'. This was now updated to display the word 'COLLEGE' instead of 'SCHOOL'.

The intention is to return the original gates to the former College (or School!) entrance in Sheerlands Road. Then, on the approach road to the new College, construct new pillars to hold the entrance gates, originally from Carlisle. The Carlisle 'memorial gates' will then be re-positioned on the grass triangle in front of the present dining-hall and HQ Building.

(The above article is adapted from the one published in The Arborfield Apprentice in spring 1984.)

Major General G B Berragan

Major General Gerry Berragan was born in Carlisle on 2nd May 1933. During his early childhood he lived in India, before his parents returned to England and settled in York. He started his career as an apprentice in what was then the Army Apprentices School, at Arborfield, in September 1948. He earned his Good Conduct Badge (1st class) in August 1950 and, in the same year, was appointed as Captain of the School cricket team and awarded his colours. He passed out of the School as a Class III Vehicle Mechanic in June 1951, returning here as a Craftsman after a four-month spell of rheumatic fever and being medically downgraded.

A posting to 14 Command Wksp at Ashford saw Gerry get himself fit again, enough to gain prowess on the rugby field. He was then included in a batch of VMs sent off to serve in Austria. Passing his First Class Trade Test, Gerry was promoted to Corporal and medically upgraded again. He then returned to the UK to attend a WOSB at Barton Stacey and, having passed for selection, went off for officer training at Eaton Hall in Cheshire.

It was during that period that Winston Churchill used the Army to break a petrol-tanker driver's strike. At the Regent Fuel Depot at Barking in Essex, he was allotted to drive a 2,000-gallon articulated petrol-tanker. He says that it was a great experience at the time, with a great reception received from a grateful public. The sixteen-week course at Eaton Hall was intense, but Gerry sailed through it all, after all, three years at Arborfield had prepared him well. The vast majority of the other cadets were young National Servicemen who had completed a mere few weeks of basic training.

Gerry was first commissioned into REME in February 1954 and attended a Young Officers' course at Arborfield and Bordon. Finding that he had a few spare months before joining his first unit, he qualified as a parachutist after two weeks of 'P' Coy at Aldershot and four weeks at Abingdon. However, he was not to join the airborne forces until 1963. During his subsequent tour with the 7th Hussars in Hong Kong, where future DGEME Pat Lee was the OC LAD, he was successful in obtaining a regular commission and transferred to the RAOC in 1956.

He went on to serve with that Corps for the next thirty-two years in the United Kingdom (UK), Belgium and Germany.

In 1966, following a tour with the Territorial Army (TA) Parachute Brigade, he attended the Army Staff College and subsequently the National Defence College in 1972 / 73. His appointments in the rank of Major included DAQMG HQ Northern Ireland, OC 4 Guards Brigade OFP and DAAG AG9. As a Lieutenant Colonel he served as CRAOC 3 Division and AQMG HQ Northern Ireland.

On promotion to Colonel in 1978, he was appointed Colonel Ord 1 in HQ DGOS and this was followed by promotion to Brigadier in 1980, as Commandant of COD Chilwell. Following closure of the depot in March 1982, Gerry attended the Senior Course at the Henley Management College, prior to becoming Commandant at COD Bicester. His final appointment as a Brigadier was as a Director of Supply Operations (Army), which he assumed on 24th June 1983, a date well remembered for the historic fire that occurred at COD Donnington.

Gerry attended the Senior International Defence Management Course in the United States during 1985 and, on September 2nd of that year, at the rank of Major General, he was appointed Director General of Ordnance Services.

He was awarded the CB in the 1988 New Year's Honours List and had the honour of accompanying HM the Queen, in her role as C-in-C of the RAOC, throughout her visit to the Command Ammunition Depot (CAD) Kineton in March of that year. Retiring in June 1988, Gerry remained as Colonel Commandant of his Corps until its amalgamation into the RLC, at which point he became that Corps' first Colonel Commandant until 1998.

He and his wife, Anne, have three sons and live in their own house at Hungerford, in Berkshire. Gerry retains an active interest in sport, which includes sailing, skiing and an enthusiastic, if not very skillful, game of tennis, while other interests include home computing. He is Chairman of Army Gliding and Admiral of RAOC Sailing.

When Gerry was selected for promotion to Maj Gen in 1985, he received a letter of congratulation from Col Sam Roberts, Commandant of the College at that time. Gerry's subsequent reply, the full text of which was printed in the spring 1985 edition of 'The Arborfield Apprentice', included the following message:

"I am sure that the firm foundation for my Army career was laid during my three years at Arborfield from 1948 to 1951 and I hope that my case, together with others, will provide the proof that the opportunities for advancement in the Army today are unlimited."

(The above was adapted from a 'potted history' written in the programme for the Passing-out Parade at Arborfield in April 1986, and supplemented by memories passed on to the editor by Gerry himself, in the latter months of 2002.)

An 'original' apprentice finally retires
Mr Peter Spargo

On 21st June 1939, 7597097 Apprentice Tradesman Spargo P S joined the Army Technical School (Boys), Arborfield, in the very first intake (39A) at the age of 15, as an apprentice General Fitter. During his time at the School, he achieved the highest A/T rank obtainable during those days, A/T LCpl, but was reduced to the ranks immediately prior to passing out, for unspecified misdemeanours. On leaving the School in September 1940, Peter continued his trade training at 51 Trade Training School, Aldershot. Postings to the Leicestershire Yeomanry and 11 AA Wksp RA followed.

In 1943, Cpl Spargo attended an Artificer Gun course of 6 months duration at Croydon, on completion of which the newly promoted Armament Artificer SSgt Spargo was posted to Falmouth, as a member of a Periodic REME Examination (PRE) team. He vividly recalls applauding the American and British Forces from the cliff-tops, as they sailed off for the invasion of France, blissfully unaware that he was to follow only a week later. Upon arrival in France, on 21st September 1944, Peter was attached to 370 LAA Battery RA as the resident 'tiffy' (Artificer). He remained with that unit throughout the war in France, Belgium and Holland, then finally into Germany. He was one of those troops who arrived at the infamous Bergen-Belsen concentration camp, only two days after it had been 'liberated'. Peter stayed at Belsen for three weeks, with direct responsibility for maintaining the camp water supplies.

After the war, Peter was posted to 4 Training Battalion REME here at Arborfield, employed as an Armament and Wksp Practice instructor. In 1951 he was sent back to Germany (BAOR) as WO I/C Wksp Detachment at 5 AGRA (AA) Wksp, followed by a tour in 23 Base Wksp REME. He returned to the UK in 1956 and served with 55 Training Regt RA, LAD REME and 17 Training Regt RA, LAD REME. 1957 saw him gain dual qualification as Artificer Weapons (Art Wpns) and Art Vehs. In 1960, at a time when there were 'more chiefs than indians', Peter took advantage of redundancy terms being offered and retired from the Regular Army. Nevertheless, he continued to serve in the Territorial Army as an Art Wpns until 1966.

Peter Sydenham Spargo joined the civilian staff of the College as an Engineering Drawing Instructor, Grade III, in 1960, gaining promotion to Grade I in 1981. He retired at the age of 65 on September 6th 1987, having served 48 years either in, or closely associated with, the Corps. He actually retired from the same unit as that which he first joined in 1939. Peter was a very popular member of staff and, during his 28 years service at the College, made many close friends. He will be missed for his keen sense of humour, his sincerity, his friendly and good-natured attitude. There was also his tactful and diplomatic approach, his many military anecdotes, his ability to be elsewhere whenever needed and his unswerving ability to cadge cigarettes!

On the sporting scene, his enthusiasm for the lunchtime volleyball sessions was second to none. It can be said, without fear of contradiction, that what Peter did for lunchtime volleyball, 'Jaws' did for swimming! After a successful retirement party, Peter was towed out through the College gates in a wheel chair by all members of A & G Wing and other friends, off to a well-earned retirement.

(The above article was extracted from that published in the summer 1987 edition of The Arborfield Apprentice.)

Ode to the Apprentice

"To all you budding Craftsmen,
Be warned and be aware;
The bed of roses you've lain in
May not exist 'out there'.

For when you've got to Six Div
And you're keyed up, ready to go,
Just don't rush in, in double time,
Just take things nice and slow.

For you'll soon find in your Units,
Though here you were the 'bees knees',
There'll be someone watching for your first mistake.
So be quiet – don't even sneeze!

You must accept, as an ex-A/T,
That though you've done two years,
There's an awful lot still to be learned
To catch up with your peers.

So once you're finally accepted
And become just 'one of the crowd',
Be you 'Black Hand Man' or 'Wobbly Head'
You'll have reason to be proud.

But until you've reached this point, be sure
To take in all you hear;
Don't let the wide boys lead you astray
And in BAOR – WATCH THE BEER!

In a few years' time you can nod your head
And shout to Fred or Smiffy,
'Back in '85 I was a mere A/T
But I'm soon to be a Tiffy!'

And if you've made it this far, be certain
That what you learned while you were a 'brat'
Is available at your finger tips,
Or at least 'under your hat'.

For the few who linger longer,
With shoulder rank in mind,
You'll be on the road to a new kind of life,
Leaving lots of pals behind.

You may even be posted back here –
A 'staffer' then you'll be;
You'll watch the new boys passing out
And think 'Twenty years ago that was me!'

(The above poem is based upon that published in the winter 1985 edition of The Arborfield Apprentice by 'Anon'.)

—§—

With a range of equipment and tools, the envy of many civilian colleges, the practical aspects of trade training at Arborfield gave apprentices a unique and enviable advantage over their civvie counterparts.

Chapter 13

1990 - 94

Close to a contract

As PMC entered the year 1990 and the last decade of the twentieth century, its staff were preparing both themselves and the College for the fundamental change in lifestyle that had been 'brewing' ever since certain preliminary studies undertaken in 1987. This would entail the handing over of responsibilities for training to a 'contractor'. The College, of course, was not to be just 'sold off' in any shape or form. However, the MoD had decided, in its wisdom and on a trial basis, to replace the existing staff of Burnham Lecturers, Instructional Officers and Military Instructors with contract personnel, under the supervision and management of a civilianised system. Naturally enough, there was much concern for job security and the possibility, in some cases at least, of redundancy. In the event, many staff members were later able to 'swap' from their original posts to become employees of the contractor and, in fact, continuing to teach apprentices in the same subjects as they had in previous years.

As A/T Edward Winterbottom signed on in January 1990, his intention was to become an Air Tech. He hoped to eventually take his 'Tiffy' course and perhaps go on for a Commission. He certainly had some history on his side, as both his father and grandfather before him had served in REME. Frank Winterbottom had enlisted in the RAOC on September 11th 1939 and promoted to SSgt the following day, due to his civilian qualifications. He transferred to REME on its formation and reached the rank of Captain, before retiring in 1962. Just prior to that date, his son Glynn was called up for National Service. However, Glynn had recently married and felt that he would be better off in 'regular' employment, thus he signed on for nine years. He was at Arborfield when the amalgamation of the two Trg Btns into SEE took place in 1961. Having left the service as a WO2, Glynn was back in uniform in 1990 with the Royal Anglians. Yes, son Edward had something to live up to, let's hope he made it! *(Who was it we wonder who first coined the phrase 'Royal Angle Irons'? Must have been an ex-boy! Ed.)*

A question of sport

In that spring's edition of *The Arborfield Apprentice*, no less a person than the Commandant himself found himself wondering just how the College managed to fulfil its primary role, that of training the potential SNCOs and Artificers for REME and the SNCOs for the RAMC and RADC! Having read the College magazine for himself, he expressed no doubt tongue-in-cheek 'shocked surprise' that he had found it *"full of accounts of mountaineering expeditions, Atlantic crossings by yacht and Sub-aqua diving, to mention just a few"*. He calculated that those A/Ts and JLdrs who **didn't** like either heights or water had managed to spend the whole term playing every other conceivable type of sport! He reflected, naturally enough, that it was these very activities that publicly distinguished the Arborfield old boy from his contemporaries, and hoped that these qualities would continue to be carried forward into adult service.

The magazine certainly did appear to be like that popular weekly TV programme – '*A Question of Sport*'. Apart from the few stories that appear below, the range of sports and hobbies covered was pretty far reaching. Both the Basketball team and Orienteers had reported a busy season, while the Rugby side could only look back on a period of mixed results. Small-bore shooters and footballers were featured and even the infant Judo Club had *"started to thrive"*. Hockey and Cycling also continued to play their part in the rich tapestry of everyday life, while the pursuits of Cross-country running, Volleyball and Sub-Aqua diving vied with Tug-of-War to draw the apprentices' attention to their particular sport.

The same College magazine reported on Exercise 'Caribbean Sea' – those boys did get around didn't they? At Heathrow Airport, the boys were startled to hear that their flight had been overbooked – in accordance with the presumed normal practice! A few well-chosen words obviously did the trick, because the next thing they knew they were 'upgraded' into Club Class – and at no extra expense. Their luxurious flight behind them, the boys' first two days were spent

Nineties Tug of War

in the superb weather and facilities accorded by Fort Lauderdale, Florida, before the intrepid crew set off to sail down to Miami. There then followed two nights of *"Latin-American bands, firework displays, mountains of fried chicken and pitchers of beer"*. No wonder our sailors were glad to set sail and leave!

Returning to Fort Lauderdale, the lads were just in time to catch the arrival of the leading contenders in the *Whitbread* Around-the-World Race and had the privilege of being invited aboard two of the British boats, *'Rothmans'* and *'British Defender'*. A few 'salty stories' were swapped between the crews, whilst several 'wets' were demolished along the way. Finally the College lads got under way again and had an uneventful and calm crossing to Nassau, capital of the Bahamas. Their vessel must have felt a little small and humble, being tied up alongside some of those huge luxury cruise liners.

The western tip of Grand Bahamas Island gave another port of call before a day was spent snorkeling amongst the colourful coral and fish of all shapes and sizes. Nightfall brought the start of an 800-mile journey to Bermuda, two boring days with very little wind, followed by another five 'hairy' days, during which a 'Force 8' was encountered. Clothing and sleeping bags managed to get a little soggy before the weather happily relented for the last two days. This was finally *"sailing at its best"*, with flying fish a common sight and even the company of a school of dolphins for a while. The stay in Bermuda was only to last a day, which was just as well, with beer at over two pounds for a small bottle!

The latest *Defence White Paper* quoted a large increase in the number of women joining the Army, rising to an indomitable force of 6,000 in the Regulars and another 4,000 in the Reserves. On the 'home front' of PMC, the number of attached WRAC officers was soon to rise from five to seven.

In safe hands

The year's first edition of *The Craftsman* featured a short article under the heading *'In Safe Hands'*. A photograph showed Lt Col Dorward congratulating Lt Col Bowles on his appointment as CI of the College. The significance of the article was that both Colonels were ex-boys, hence the title! Mike Dorward had joined as a member of 60A and trained as a Radar Tech, while Martin Bowles was a *"veritable Jeep"*, having joined in January 1964, at the tender age of fifteen. He had been present when the School changed into a College in 1966, before qualifying as another *"Wobbly"*, as those of an electronics background are lovingly known.

It was during 1990 that Mr J D Kirwan took it upon himself to write a short history of the Aircraft Wing, covering the period since its conception in 1963. At the time, he was a Supervising Instructor in the Wing, having previously served as its first ASM from 1965 – 66. He looked back upon the many different types of aircraft that had been used for instruction, including at one time a *Gloster Meteor* jet fighter. Originally, a Captain had been in charge but having gained acceptance as a Wing in 1967, a Major was then considered necessary. For a short period in 1979, no officers had been available for the post, but the Wing still survived. Mr Kirwan looked ahead towards a *"rather vague"* future, due to the threat of contractorisation, but hoped that those high standards set in the past would continue for a long time to come.

During renovations to the ablutions in 'D' Coy's living accommodation, the top floor TV lounge had been used by the building contractors to store their supplies of bricks, tiles, pipes and cement.*(Any truth in the rumour that they also stored vast supplies of tea, coffee, sugar and milk? Ed.)* Even after their eventual departure, the room still looked like a redundant building site. Eager volunteers – yes, real ones! – soon turned up to assist in the sanding down, papering, undercoating and painting, until the room had been converted into a suitably comfortable *'des res'*. Officially opened by Col Phil Kay and christened with the odd glass of Port, the room was re-named as the *'Cavillery Lounge'*. For those who puzzled over this name, it was pointed out that the OC was a Gunner and the 2I/C was in the Blues and Royals! *(Work it out! Ed.)*

Paradise Lost - and regained

"Another rainy day in Paradise" - that's how the College Climbing expedition looked after a week's endeavours. Its members had left Arborfield on April 18th 1990 and soon found themselves on the French Riviera beach at Nice, under clear blue skies and awaiting the ferry to transport them across to Corsica. Following their arrival at this 'Island of Beauty' however, they encountered some appalling weather as they drove up into the mountains. Heavy rain turned to snow and three inches of the white stuff caused serious doubts as to whether or not the minibus could keep going. The snow eventually turned back to rain to ease the transport problem, but the intended campsite at Zonga was then found to be closed and the lads had to settle for an alternative one at Porto Vecchio. Then it was time to try some climbing but once again the rain set in, allowing only twenty metres of visibility. Unfortunately, the weather was to continue like this for days, and the situation was not at all helped by the discovery that Corsica was home to several species of venomous ants and snakes. Some serious searching of sleeping bags became the order of the day!

At last the weather changed for the better and there followed some superb climbing in glorious sunshine. Just when things were 'on the up' however, team leader Capt Neil Malpas slipped off a ledge, breaking an arm and badly injuring his leg. Fortunately, with the assistance of the rest of the group, Neil was able to walk to the minibus and be driven to hospital. It was four hours before he arrived there and he later said, *"the general anaesthetic was a welcome relief"*. Neil lay in hospital for a week, not too impressed with the local medical facilities, but at least cheered by daily visits from the climbers, who were at last enjoying some long technical climbs. All in all, the expedition had been quite an eventful one, despite the early weather conditions and the accident. Would they do it again? – you bet your life they would!

The April issue of *The Craftsman* magazine reported on a trip that had been undertaken by members of the College Canoe Club. They had left Brize Norton on a rainy, wet day and arrived at RAF Akrotiri on the 'sun-baked island of Cyprus', only to find it was a rainy, wet day there too! However, the lads didn't let this get them down too much, spending the first day driving between Dhekelia, Episkopi and Akrotiri, picking up all the canoes and equipment required for their expedition. After a few days of splendid canoeing around the coastal waters, the apprentices were able to find some entertainment at the fun-filled resort of Aiya Napa – but, as was stated in the report – *"that, gentlemen, is a different story"*!

During the first week of May 1990, the Sub-Aqua Club embarked on a diving expedition to the Kyle of Lochalsh, up on the northwestern coast of Scotland, close to the Isle of Skye. This was to include diving onto shipwrecks, exploring cliffs and caves, as well as learning to cope with the cold water conditions. The denseness of the seawater was a novelty to some and they found it difficult to actually sink down to the required depths. Despite these teething problems, the novices soon buckled down to training and made good progress. Crabs and lobsters were plentiful, as were sea urchins and starfish. One wonderful moment came when they visited an island in the loch and made friends with some local seals!

Life in the Band

An article in *The Arborfield Apprentice* poured scorn on all those who thought that joining one of the College Bands was just a way of skiving off from other duties. The author reminded any such suspicious readers that, while **they** were out with their mates during evenings and weekends, the Band boys were as likely as not putting in a few hours of practice. One of the Band's engagements that term was at Bulford Garrison. After a ninety-minute journey, the particular Officers' Mess for the evening venue was conspicuous by its absence, resulting in the Band's minibus trying to turn round in a field where the only sign in sight read *"Keep off the Grass"*. Needless to say, the vehicle bedded itself down for the duration and some exasperated brass players and pipers found themselves covered in mud splashes, as they eventually returned the bus to the safety of dry land!

The proper destination was eventually found and the lads just about had time for a *"wash and brush up"* before their evening's musical appearance. They 'did their stuff' with the usual aplomb then cleared away their instruments and made their way back to the bus. By the time they had returned to Arborfield it was well after midnight, probably a two good hours after the rest of the College had hit the sack. A letter on the Band notice-board a couple of weeks later thanked the boys for their splendid effort – and notified them that they had been pre-booked for a return appearance the following year! That's life in the Band.

Due to the forthcoming contractorisation, both the CI and the SEO were inevitably to spend many hours, totally involved in the writing of a *'Statement of Requirement'*. Perhaps it was their efforts upon this lengthy task that distracted them and led to a certain amount of confusion at the summer 'PoP' that year, reviewed by Vice Admiral Sir Godfrey Milton-Thompson KBE, QHP, FRCP, the Surgeon General. The weather was glorious and the side of the Square was packed with a large congregation of proud parents – but they were not necessarily the right ones!

After a hasty public announcement that the Training Battalion and Depot was also holding a parade that same day, there was a lot of muttering and some hasty checking of invitation cards. This was followed by the sudden exit of about thirty parents, who were last seen rushing through Arborfield Garrison, trying to find their way to the REME Depot!

'D' Coy spent the summer's half term on Adventure Training up at Glencoe in bonny Scotland. After a twelve-hour journey, some horrible weather forced the lads to abandon some climbing plans and do a spot of sightseeing in nearby Mallaig instead. Their main social activity that evening was all about the usual comparison of midge bites! With the weather eventually relenting, some climbing and fishing was enjoyed until, on their last night, a friendly barman allowed the lads to watch TV, as England beat Egypt at soccer. A 'late night' was the inevitable conclusion and the long journey home next day was usefully employed in catching up on some sleep.

A useful teaching 'aid'

A couple of years previously, as the OC 'D' Coy post had been traditionally handed over to a 'Gunner', it was deemed appropriate that a large gun, of some sort or other, should be displayed in the foyer of the Company block. The Royal Artillery Institution at Woolwich was approached and the long-term loan of a 68-pounder Russian brass *'Corronade'* (c.1837) was duly arranged. As part of the loan package, it had been agreed that the College would construct a gun carriage, but this turned out to be a lot more complex than had originally been thought. 43 Command Wksp personnel were tentatively approached for assistance, and they kindly took on the task, as long as the project could be considered as a 'teaching aid'! Thus it was that in June 1990, the splendidly mounted gun finally made its debut on display. In time honoured tradition, a bottle of 12-year old Highland 'lubricant' duly changed hands.

The cricket season had started as long ago as November 1989, with the indoor cricket league. Long hours of practice had finely-honed the PMC team in readiness for the Army Cup Final on July 18th, played at the grand setting of the Army Officers' Club at Aldershot. After an opening stand of 139, the College XI went on to amass a score of 258 for five wickets off their statutory thirty-five overs. It was the highest score ever recorded in the competition's long history. This was obviously all too much for Chepstow, who were subsequently bowled out for a mere 114. It had been a splendid victory.

It was fitting that, as the first hockey season of the new decade approached, the College could reflect upon their most successful side, which had been quoted as *"the outstanding team of the last decade"*. It had been season 1979 / 80 that saw the first winning of the Junior Army Cup, under the tutelage of Maj Peter A'Hearne RA, who had now returned to PMC as PRI. That first victory had been followed up by three further successes in 1981, 1982 and 1984, then subsequently each season from 1986 right up until the current one of 1989 / 90. Eight victories in only ten seasons was definitely an excellent record, and one that seemed hardly likely to ever be bettered.

War in the Gulf

Following the replacement of RSM Hartley by RSM M Burns, freshly recruited from the Irish Guards, another serious event was soon to relegate 'contractorisation' to the back pages for a while. On August 2nd 1990, the Iraqi military forces of President Saddam Hussein crossed their southern border in an invasion of its close neighbour-state Kuwait and, as did the rest of the world, the College watched events unroll with baited breath. The 'excuse' for the invasion had been a long-running dispute over the ownership of the Rumailia oilfield, which straddled the border between the two countries.

Soon, having swept through the relatively weak Kuwaiti defences, Saddam's armoured brigades stood at the gateway into Saudi Arabia, a country with an area almost as big as Europe and floating upon a sea of oil that the Western world needed, in order to survive.

Here in London on September 11th, Prime Minister Margaret Thatcher ordered defence chiefs to send 7,000 ground troops and at least 100 *Challenger* tanks to join American and other western forces in the desert. It was to be the biggest deployment of British troops since the South Atlantic Falklands battle in 1982.

Sixteen members of PMC, including apprentices and staff, were involved in a sixteen-day caving expedition in southern France during the first half of September 1990. A twenty-seven hours long trip, undertaken in two rather uncomfortable mini-buses, was brightened up by their first view of the breathtaking scenery that surrounded the campsite. Some of the deeper caves each required a tiring six hours of exploration, but the magnificent combination of stalagmites and stalactites, pools and chambers, was soon to leave the cavers with a lasting impression. The party was also able to spend some time in the outdoors of course, including a canoe trip down the River Rhone in two-man Canadian kayaks. At the end of the trip, each individual felt that he had been challenged in one way or another, even if only to try out the local lingo!

Despite the 'threat' that had been caused by the uncertainties of a future contractorisation, the College continued to advertise itself, as indicated by a notice in *The Craftsman* magazine of October 1990, under the heading *"Engineering Apprentices in REME through Princess Marina College"*. The notice, placed on behalf of REME, announced *"sandwich engineering apprenticeships, lasting approximately six years, to young men who are physically fit, of good character and interested in an exciting, challenging, well-paid and worthwhile career. Initial training of two years is carried out as a junior soldier (at PMC), followed by up to three years' on-the-job training in the Army, serving mainly in Germany and other overseas stations"*. The three intakes per year, in January, May and September, offered training in the three Technician trades of Aircraft, Electronics and Instruments, as well as the Craft trades of Armourer, Gun Fitter and VM.

At that year's Old Boys' Reunion, during the evening's usual splendid dinner, 'Percy' Thrower of 60C found himself sitting alongside a member of the PS. During their subsequent conversation, Percy was told the story of *"some A/T who had once swallowed three ball-point pens"*, some thirty years previously, presumably in an effort to get off a Saturday morning RSM's parade. As Percy's memory got into gear, he recalled that he had once, completely accidentally, swallowed the 'blue bit' from the end of a battered old biro. Now, he reckoned that the tale being told, rather than proving 'hard to swallow', must actually be about him! He wondered how many pints it had taken for his slight accident to develop into this full-blown horror story! That's how legends are born!

Every year, a 'Patrol Competition' is held at the Bordon and Longmoor training area, down in 'deepest Hampshire'. This examines the required patrolling skills of fitness, navigation, marksmanship, first aid and leadership. 1990 was no exception and, following some intense training sessions, PMC entered a team from each Company over the weekend of 7th / 8th November. Against such formidable competition as boys from the Junior Infantry Battalion and the Parachute Regt, the College team from 'D' Coy eventually ran 'the Paras' a close second by a mere two points, with the trip back to Arborfield filled with many wistful sighs of *"if only"*.

The Geoffrey White Library

On Saturday 15th December 1990, during the customary 'J' Coy 'Parents Day', a special and poignant event took place within the confines of the College Library. The mother and brother of a former apprentice, 2nd Lt Geoffrey Alan White, who had been killed in action during the 'almost forgotten' Korean War of the early Fifties, ceremonially handed over his medals and citation to REME.

Geoffrey had enlisted as an apprentice Armourer at Arborfield during its early days in October 1942 and had been subsequently commissioned into the RAOC. He had been seconded to the 1st Battalion of the Middlesex Regt, in order that he should gain experience as a Platoon Commander. Thus, in August 1950, his unit became one of the first British contingents to disembark in South Korea, as part of the UN Forces that were fighting in that far-off country. Sadly, Geoffrey was killed in battle some twenty-five days later and was posthumously awarded the American Silver Star for gallantry, having sacrificed his own life for the welfare of his men. The College Library was duly renamed the *'Geoffrey White Library'* in his memory and honour.

The story of Geoffrey White came to light following many hours of research by old boy John Northam, after he had come across the minutes of the fourth AGM of the OBA, which had been held as long ago as September 1951. The Vice President of the day had read out the citation in what seemed an almost casual reference, but now John puzzled over the fact that a boy who had left the School in 1945 should then have received this gallantry award from the American forces. Thanks go to John for discovering all the facts upon which the story has now been recalled and published.

(Further details can be found in a separate annex to this chapter. John Northam's own story of his research was published in The Arborfield Apprentice of autumn 1990.)

That same edition of the College magazine proved that, despite what old boys are always saying about the fact that it 'was a lot harder in my day', for the boys of whatever era they serve, some things remain very much the same! One unnamed apprentice, having just passed through 'J' Coy, expressed it like this:

"I quite enjoyed 'J' Coy, it was quite an experience. There were times when I hated it and hated the platoon staff, but after the initial shock of military life, I got into the swing of things. Everyone got to know my name quite quickly, as I was always being shouted at in drill. (Sounds familiar? Ed.) When doing drill, I felt as though I was being watched closely for little mistakes, while others weren't, as my name got shouted quite frequently. Maybe it was because they had got to know my name, or maybe they pick on you to see how much you can take. This made me more determined I was going to pass out of 'J' Coy even if it killed me."

The College is 'contracted out'

Late in 1990, the inevitable contract to provide the College's civilian teaching staff was won by 'SERCo', a private company that was already well known to the MoD in various other fields. The company was well placed to understand the needs of the College, as it had a number of retired Army officers (one late REME) on its board of directors. The contract was signed to start on 25th March 1991 and thereafter to run for an initial period of three years. The time prior to that date was filled with all the rigmarole of staff selection and much detailed planning. This change inevitably saw the loss of the majority of the REME staff from PMC, thus ending a long-standing tradition and period of continuity.

The *SERCo* contract manager in the College was to be an ex-REME officer (although not, unfortunately, an ex-apprentice), while the senior member of the contract staff was a retired RE officer, who had served as a Company Commander down at Chepstow. There were many 'teething problems' of course, as apprentices had to become used to being taught by contract staff, some of whom had little background knowledge of a military-style ethos and infrastructure. But, generally, things went very well and later, after the first twelve months of the contract, most would agree that it had proven to be a substantial success.

Meanwhile, events were fast moving towards a conclusion in the Middle East, following the build up of coalition forces in Saudi Arabia. After a spectacular Allied air offensive by aircraft and unmanned *Cruise* missiles, the first land skirmishes took place on January 29th. Any last chances of a negotiated peace came to nothing and, on February 24th 1991, battle-tanks of Britain's 4th and 7th Armoured Brigades raced across the Kuwaiti border to join the Allied invasion. At 2 a.m. on Thursday February 28th, just one hundred hours after its start, President of the United States, George Bush, appeared on TV to announce to the world that the Gulf War was over, the Iraqi forces had been routed and that a cease-fire had been called. *(It was to be the President's own son, George 'Dubya' Bush, who ordered US and UK troops across the Iraqi border early in 2003. Ed.)*

With fuel prices rocketing at home, the first REME soldiers had already been deployed to the Gulf during the previous September (1990). By the start of the land war, officially termed *'Operation Desert Storm'*, with their friends and families at home here in Britain snowbound, some 3,700 REME officers and tradesmen were embroiled in the dispute in the heat of the desert. An accurate figure for the number of ex-apprentices who took part is not known, but a large number of old boys, in rank from Craftsman to Major, spent some time in this theatre of war. Although British and REME casualties were thankfully light, two REME NCOs sadly lost their lives, though neither were ex-boys from the College.

February's edition of *The Craftsman* gave notice of a fund-raising effort by the College, one that raised over £400 for the 'Soldier in Need' appeal. During an adventurous training camp, whilst the young apprentices trekked across the Black Mountains in Wales, two hardy PS members ran the same distance in five hours and twenty minutes. The gallant pair had been sponsored by apprentices, civilian and military staff alike for their splendid effort.

It was probably with slightly anxious feelings that a party of College skiers set off for a week's expedition to the Army Mountain Training Centre in mid-February. The purpose of the exercise was to introduce the boys to 'Nordic skiing', which can be likened to 'running on skis'. They were relieved to arrive in the Harz Mountains of Germany to find plenty of snow on the ground. After a week of 'blood, sweat and tears', fifteen out of eighteen of the Arborfield contingent passed their Bronze Proficiency test. It had certainly been physically demanding, but also most exhilarating and rewarding.

Messing about on the river

That year's Good Friday saw the Canoe Club about to once more compete at the annual Devizes-Westminster race. Disaster struck when two of the A/Ts developed injuries and a third had to return home on compassionate leave. Fortunately, Cfn Heaps, an ex-boy RSM and veteran of the race, stepped in to provide a total of four two-man crews. With around 600 competitors, the start was a little confused, to say the least! At the beginning of the final stage, a missing paddle almost caused A/T Cooper a coronary, but the 'boys done good' in the end, with a creditable overall fifth place by the time the teams all crossed the finishing line.

A small party of College orienteers took the one-and-a-half hour flight from Heathrow to Gothenburg, Sweden, on April 19th 1991. The flight with *'SAS'* was noticeable not only for its short duration, but also for the beauty of the stewardesses! They were in Scandinavia at the invitation of the Swedish Army and experienced a week's sport that proved far more demanding, both physically and technically, than anything they had encountered back home in England. Not only that, they found that the beer was so expensive that they spent more time walking than drinking!

Having seen the initial 'bedding-in' of the SERCo contract, Col Phil Kay now decided that it was time for him to 'hang up his boots' and to retire from the Army. He had been given the difficult task of steering PMC through a period of great change and upheaval, a task he had carried out with an abundance of skill and enthusiasm. Col Kay's *"swan song"*, in May 1981, coincided with the first 'PoP' on which apprentices carried the SA80 rifle. Rain had earlier threatened the parade, but it still went ahead and, afterwards, the outgoing Commandant was driven out through the gates in a *Ferret* Scout Car. He was succeeded as Commandant by Col P H Gibson BSc(Eng), CEng, MIEE, FIMgt, who came to Arborfield 'hot foot' from the rigors of the Gulf War, where he had served as Commander Maintenance.

In his first '*Foreword*', to *The Arborfield Apprentice* of spring 1991, Col Gibson felt that, despite having arrived three weeks late for the start of term, he had rapidly achieved enough knowledge about the place to pass his end-of-term exams! He had found the opportunity to speak to many apprentices and JLdrs, sometimes in their Company blocks, at other times during sporting events and even once halfway up a mountain in Wales! After a chat with the newly arrived Garrison Commander, after his initial visit to PMC, the Commandant could only agree that *"the place and the people give me a warm feeling"*.

'I served at Arborfield'

A poem donated anonymously to the summer 1991 edition of *The Arborfield Apprentice* was dedicated to all ex-apprentices:

> *The soldier stood at the Pearly Gate,*
> *His face all scarred and old.*
> *He stood before the man of fate*
> *And sought admission to the fold.*
>
> *"What have you done," St Peter asked,*
> *"To gain admission here?"*
> *"I served at Arborfield" he said,*
> *His eye wet with a tear.*
>
> *Then the famous Gates swung open wide,*
> *As St Peter tolled his bell.*
> *"Come in my son, come in," he cried,*
> *"You've had your share of Hell!"*

Aircraft Wing had recently put up the 'Under New Management' sign, as a result of the *SERCo* contract. Initially, there had been concerns that the new instructors would be unsympathetic about the pressures put upon apprentices by military staff in the Companies, a feeling that must have spread across other trade wings too. Some of the 'new' instructors, however, looked very similar to the old ones. Indeed, a very close glance would in fact prove that they were one and the same! Many of them had merely transferred from MoD to *SERCo* so, thankfully, a good continuity was maintained. Not only that, a large number of staff at the College had always been made up from the ranks of ex-soldiers and, as such, they were very aware of the special needs of young soldier/tradesmen.

MTW was keen to advertise just who they were and what they did. They formed a large element of the PMC and would play a part in the development of every A/T and JLdr who passed through their capable hands. There were four separate sections to the Wing, namely PT, Military Training, EL and Medical Training. The military training personnel were themselves split into five parts, each one relating to the College terms i.e. from 2 Div to 6 Div. Within the EL Section, at that time, students were expected to take part in three exercises during their apprenticeship. These were, in chronological order, 'New Venture', 'Mixed Effort' and 'Last Chance'; each one designed to test an apprentice's ability within *"an unfamiliar and potentially dangerous environment"*.

A/T Cpl Derrick was one of those almost unfathomable characters who find an irresistible thrill in jumping out of what is presumed to be a perfectly serviceable aircraft! Representing the College at the British Army Parachute Championships, during the summer recess, he won two Silver Medals in the Junior Army Accuracy and Novice events. This involved jumping from a height of 3,500 feet, 'free falling' for 1,200 feet and only then 'pulling the cord'. He had only started training in September 1990, but since the moment he had looked up and seen the red, white and blue nylon canopy above him, he had never looked back – up yes, down maybe, but definitely not back!

Over the period 15th / 18th July, PMC entered a team of twelve young soldiers into the Junior Army Skill-at-Arms Meeting. This was held at Pirbright ranges, under the auspices of the Army Rifle Association (ARA). Prior to this competition, much practice had to be held to ensure that the boys' could compete on a 'level playing field'. With so many other calls on their time, this proved immensely difficult, but eventually they made their way to the competition. On the first afternoon, the electrical target system broke down, but the next day saw the apprentices come second in a snapshooting contest. Considering the limited training, the team made a good showing throughout the rest of the meeting.

Threatened by closure

Following the letting of the contract, the College was obviously not going to be allowed any quiet period of consolidation! An exercise by the name of *'Options for Change'* was flavour of the month within Government circles and the MoD was now ordered to consider the whole future of its apprentice training, as carried out by the Army. This study continued throughout the second half of 1991 and, at one time, it was even being strongly rumoured that the College would soon have to finally 'lock up shop' and perhaps close its famous old gates for the last time.

Project *Hathi* was continuing to gather pace, much to the amazement of all those original 'doubting Thomases' who were now hastily revising their former opinions. The particular vehicle had been originally retrieved from a forest, where it had been used for winching out timber as recently as 1985. It may also been one of a pair of such venerable vehicles that were later used to haul boats out of the water at Portsmouth Harbour.

Despite still having no engine, much repair work had been carried out on radiators, jibs, bulkheads and bodywork, so much so that the vehicle had been proudly displayed at the *Thorneycroft* Veteran Vehicle Rally on June 23rd. With no prospect of an original 1920s' engine being found, it was decided that a *'Big Ben'* type from the 1950s had to be fitted. Marginally larger than the original engine, this meant that the vehicle chassis would have to be slightly modified, but at least this would mean only minor departures from originality.

College hockey players were still at the zenith of their powers. Company hockey continued to be played with spirit and enthusiasm, with the 'A' Coy team winning the SE District League. The College side won both the Army Junior Cup and the Army Youth Cup and enjoyed two famous 'away' victories, over the Royal Navy in the Sultan Games and against the RAF Halton team. Six apprentices represented the Army at U-21 level, while A/T LCpl Hornby and A/T Hughes were in the side that won the Inter-Services Championship at Plymouth, coached by QMSI Sadd, a College PS member.

At the 'PoP' held on August 9th 1991, the College said its farewell to Marie de Rancourt, the incumbent 'College Mum' who had served an extensive seven-year tour at the College, out of a total nineteen years in the WRVS. She was presented to the Reviewing Officer, Maj Gen Rob McAfee, Director General Army Training (DGAT). Marie's replacement was to be Pauline Coombs.

During the OBA Annual Reunion of that year, held as usual during the College's half-term break in October, the Commandant briefed those attending on the options that were available for PMC and explained his hopes for the future. He mentioned that, should the College manage to survive, the present-day 'political correctness' (PC) meant that the arrival of the first female apprentice was now only a matter of time. There are no prizes for guessing that this caused great amusement to many of the assembled ex-boys, tinged, no doubt, with some feelings of envy!

A proposed 12-month course

In December of 1990, the Executive Committee of the Army Board (ECAB) had met to decide the fate of all Army Apprentices' Colleges. ECAB subsequently sent two recommendations to the Secretary of State for Defence. The first, which had advised that apprentice training should continue, but be reduced to a single year, was the one accepted and this new course of training was eventually to commence in September 1992.

Under this scheme, PMC would undertake to teach only basic military and technical training, with the final months of a boy's (or girl's) apprenticeship to be undertaken (up until C & G and BTEC qualifications) at one of the three adult training schools of SEME, SEE and SAE, Middle Wallop. BTEC – the Business Technician Education Council – had been brought into being some time around 1983 / 84, by an amalgamation of the old TEC with the Business Education Council (BEC).

During that winter's half term break, *"for want of something better to do"*, members of the Canoe Club willingly went off on another military canoeing expedition to the Mediterranean island of Cyprus. All the vital equipment necessary to the expedition's success was taken along – sun cream, shades, shorts, flip-flops and cameras! With their accommodation conveniently located just above the cookhouse at Dhekelia, the boys soon set off to get a taste of the local scene, starting with a crash-course in Finnish from some pretty female tourists. With a free weekend available, this was filled with an acclimatisation session in the island's capital, Nicosia. Oh yes, they did eventually manage to fit in some canoeing too!

'A' Coy had an excellent exercise that term, held at Shorncliffe TA Base. They had gone down there to do some shooting and, to their delight, found 'D' Coy already there – employed on digging trenches! Their up-beat mood continued when they found that they would be taking part in many different types of shooting, at static targets, moving targets and pop-up targets. Walking around, with guns blazing from their hips, they felt much like the old gunslingers from the Wild West! Then it was 'down to earth' with a bump, when the 'March and Shoot' section began with an assault course, followed by a one-mile fast march and a map-reading test. A First Aid test quickly followed and then it was into respirators and NBC suits for the always-unwelcome entry into the gas chamber. Thankfully, they were still able to hang on to glorious memories of the shoot-out!

The weekend of October 11th – 13th saw yet another successful Old Boys' Reunion. One moment of good-natured ribaldry occurred when the Commandant pointed out to a certain uniformed Sergeant Major that his collar-badges were mounted the wrong way round! This was an oversight that was to cost the unfortunate

gentleman a pint or two in the bar later that evening. Col Gibson himself filled the spot of Reviewing Officer for the Old Boys' Parade, which was commanded by Mick Harold of 53B, with the banner being carried by another of equal vintage, Mike Constanzo.

This sporting life

The Arborfield Apprentice of winter 1991 contained the usual *potpourri* of sporting tales and a list of the sports held in the College over the years would make the ideal basis for a 'Sports Encyclopedia'. The 'usual suspects' were there of course, in the shape of Association Football, Rugby and Hockey; Cycling, Orienteering and Sub-Aqua – these had always been fairly common contributors to the magazine's pages. Recent additions and newcomers included Badminton and Squash, now becoming big-time sports, both here at PMC as well as nationwide.

On December 6th 1991, Maj Gen Heath CBE, DGEME, reviewed the final parade of the Trg Btn & Depot REME, as Rowcroft Barracks was officially vacated, ending thirty years of REME Adult Recruit Training at Arborfield. One week later, the Depot REME was established as an independent command within the PMC. But the way was now clear for the boys' school to move back onto familiar territory.

January 1992 saw the completion of a full *"fifty years with the Army"* for Harry Budd, one of the College lecturers. Originally a Dukie and then training here at Arborfield as a member of 42A, Harry still insists that he was a 'Radio Mechanic', rather than a Tels Mech – but what's in a name? He was one of those boys who had suffered the dispersal of 1944, joining his first REME unit in 1945. In later years, having completed his Artificer course, Harry has happy memories of a twenty-five day cruise from Southampton, via the Suez Canal, Aden and Colombo, to his posting with 12 Infantry Wksp in Malaysia. This was followed by other periods of service in Germany and Singapore but, by 1964, he was back at Arborfield, as ASM in charge of the Tels Department at SEE.

After three years with the Signals and another three at Chatham with the

Col Kay is 'clapped' on his way!

Sappers, Harry finally hung up his medals in 1972 and started a 'new life' at what was then the AAC Arborfield as a civilian instructional officer. He thought that there had been little change in the last twenty years, even contractorisation had gone smoothly and Harry believes that *"the very high standard of training in the College continues"*.

That month's issue of *The Craftsman* brought news of another ex-boy, this time at the start of a promising career. 2Lt David McEvoy had joined the College in September 1984 and reached the rank of A/T CSM. He had also obtained a BTEC National Diploma and qualified as an Air Tech, and was posted to what was still AETW (now SAE). Having completed his training in 1987, he went on to pass an All-Arms Commando Course. Having been selected for and passing the RCM, he then joined RMAS in September 1990. Here, David achieved the best results of his course and was presented with the Queen's Medal.

Not the dreaded 'flu' again?

January also brought with it a familiar problem, when a flu epidemic had around half of the new intake bedded down in the MRS. Rumours abounded that 'J' Coy would have to be quarantined, but it never quite came to that. By the time that Exercise Milk Teeth came along, a good dose of fresh clean overnight air had apparently cleared everyone's germs away. Some would say that they (the germs) had met an icy death, as many apprentices awoke on the first morning to find that their water bottles had frozen solid overnight!

From 1st – 7th February, along with some JLdrs from the RAMC, several apprentices boarded the *'Princess Maria Esmeralda'* at Dover, *en route* to Ostend in Belgium. They were all off to Rheindalen in Germany to try their hands at the sport of 'Luge' (or tobogganing). This had been started in the Alps in 1883, but it wasn't until 1957 that the World Tobogganing Association was founded, with the sport becoming a Winter Olympics event some seven years later. The track our intrepid adventurers would be using was at Winterburg.

When the would-be tobogannists eventually got to the top of the novices' course, there was a mixture of feelings, ranging from wild excitement to severe apprehension! Those who actually made it to the bottom were obviously ecstatic, but a large proportion had crashed out at high speed on the way down. After a couple of days in practice, a competition was held, but

Col P H Gibson 1991-94

it was a team of Sappers that won most of the medals. It had certainly proved a week of hard knocks but the party returned to Arborfield in good heart, saying that it had been *"the most exciting sport any of us had experienced"*.

February 7th saw another 'official ceremony' within PMC, when Maj Gen D Shaw CB, CBE, REME's Representative Colonel Commandant, cut the ribbon and formally opened the new Depot REME. Here, it would continue to perform many of the functions of its predecessor, the former HQ and Depot Coy of the Trg Btn.

The College Electronics Wing always swore that it could be easily recognised by the 'wobblyheads' that ran it! In 1992, apprentices joined the Wing at the beginning of 2 Div and stayed there until the eleventh week of their sixth term. Here, they slogged away at learning basic electronics theory, backed up by various practical experiments and fault finding. Interspersed with this were visits to local electronics firms and adult REME units. Head of the Wing at that time was Mick Harold, himself an ex-boy of vintage 53B. At one time,

Mick had advanced to become a Major in the RAEC and had held the post of Deputy SEO in the Education Wing, so Arborfield had become 'a way of life' for him. In later years, his 'seating plans' at the increasingly well-attended Old Boys' Reunion dinners became a thing of wonder!

April 1992 saw a change of RSM appointment once again. RSM Burns had served for almost two years, but now handed over the appointment to RSM D Murray, Scots Guards, for the next eighteen months. On 6th April, as a result of the Logistic Support Review, a new organisation was formed, entitled the Directorate of Equipment Support (Army), or DES(A). The ES task range was to embrace the activities of inspection, repair, recovery, equipment management and modification, as well as the management and procurement of technical spares, the majority of these being the responsibility of REME.

Old Boys here, there – and everywhere

Two days later, Maj Gen Mike Heath arrived at Arborfield to officially open the new Corps 'Pictorial Archive'. This is situated adjacent to the REME Museum and contains a veritable wealth of archive material in the shape of photographs, maps, films, videos, blueprints and posters. The Archive was set up with the enthusiastic assistance of two ex-boys, John Dutton and John Northam, who also created, within the archives, a photographic display that illustrated the history of apprentice training in Arborfield. Yet another old boy was Curator of the REME Museum at the time, in the shape of Lt Col (Ret'd) Larry Le Var, ex-47A intake.

Meanwhile, down at SEME Bordon, a rather unique occasion was taking place, when one ex-boy handed over command of Vehicle Engineering Wing (VEW) to another. Lt Col Pat Hassell had been a member of intake 54B, which had a strong claim to fame in that it produced three Lieutenant Colonels amongst its ranks. Pat Hassell had been one, while the others were Bob Gregory and Bernie Turnbull – quite an achievement. Lt Col Pat went off to Chertsey, with some wag at SEME offering this advice to his underlings – *"Hide your cigarettes!"* Pat's successor at Bordon was Lt Col Gordon Mead, of 1958 vintage, who sadly died whilst serving at SEME a couple of years later.

Old Ben Cook would have been a proud man on Saturday 9th May, when a small band of 'A' Coy apprentices set off to Wokingham to do some voluntary gardening. This was as part of their 'service to the community' effort and they had been given the task of clearing out the rear of a property that looked more like an African jungle than an *'olde English'* garden! A variety of implements was used for the task – shovels, forks, saws, shears and machetes, you name it, those boys had it. Unfortunately, as is common on our 'sceptred isle', the rain set in and it wasn't long before our gardeners were soaked to the skin and they were glad to call it a day by lunchtime. They returned to base, wet, hungry and tired – but happy.

The following weekend, it was time once again for the Ten Tors event, when all those hours of winter training would now end up in the 'proof of the pudding' test. The Commandant made a personal appearance to see the teams off and to wish them luck – but luck quickly deserted the 55-mile team, as two unfortunate members suffered injuries that left them unable to continue and they had to be 'casevaced' out by helicopter. The rest of the lads were so demoralised that they also 'dropped out' shortly afterwards. All

A/T/RSM Hurd August 1991

eyes turned now to the 45-mile team, who finished the course to tumultuous applause from the gathered throng. Tiredness was replaced by bravado and pain by elation, as the lads congratulated each other on a job well done. The 'pudding' had been well and truly eaten!

"Well done the boys!" That phrase obviously suited the Ten Tors team, but it was also the first phrase of a magazine article about the College Rugby XV. Having shown plenty of latent talent early in the season, this had been honed into excellent skills by season's end. Great determination and team spirit were the other factors that led to the Army Junior Cup Final at Aldershot. Here, a team from the JLdrs RA at Bramcote was put to the sword and PMC came proudly away as Junior Army Champions. The team was then to face the same problems as every other rugby side the following season – that the International Board had introduced wholesale changes in the laws of the game, in an effort to produce a faster, more open style of play.

Mission of mercy

An edition of *Focus*, the in-house magazine regularly issued by the MoD, featured the efforts of John Stewart, an ex-boy of intake 56B, who had just returned from a 'mission of mercy' to the war-torn African country of Malawi during 1989. By his own admission, John had been a *"bit of a lad"* in his younger days, when he was an apprentice Gun Fitter here at Arborfield. But since becoming a committed Christian in later life, he had then realised that there were millions of unfortunate people in the 'third world' who would always need the help of those who were better off. At the time, John was still working as Head of Media Resources, at the School of Signals, Blandford in Dorset, and living in nearby Corfe Mullen.

And now, in May of 1992, John was about to start work on fund raising for another mission, this time to the Albanian capital of Tirana. Since the fall of the Communist regime in that desperately poor country, times had become even more difficult for certain of its citizens, particularly young children at two orphanages, where supplies of the basic things in life, such as food and medicine, were desperately required.

At the end of May, the College Swimming team was competing in the Junior Army Championships at Bovington. From the start, it was obvious that the three Apprentices' Colleges were the strongest teams on display and, as the event progressed, it came down to a straight fight between Arborfield and Chepstow in the final event, the four-by-50 metre medley relay. PMC had to beat the old enemy by two clear places to win. A fast and furious race reflected the high standard of the competition and the PMC boys, by sheer effort, finished first in a nail-biting finish. It was then discovered that the Chepstow team had been disqualified, due to an illegal changeover, and so Arborfield were duly declared 'Army Junior Swimming Champions'.

The official statement on the restructuring of Army Apprentices' training was read out in the House of Commons, by the Minister of State for the Armed Forces, on June 5th. It read as follows:

> *"We now propose that all apprentices should undertake a common one-year foundation course at a single Army Technical College (ATC), with one wing at Arborfield for the technical corps and another at Aldershot for the ACC and Adjutant General's Corps (AGC). I have already announced the proposal to concentrate the training of junior leaders at Harrogate. No final decision has been taken on possible future uses for the remaining college at Chepstow."*

Rebirth of the 'OBAN'

1992 also saw the most welcome revival of *'OBAN'* – the *Old Boys' Association Newsletter*. Published as 'Number One', its front cover was a nostalgic facsimile of the first ever *OBAN*, which had been issued in December 1956. Sadly, both the OBA and its *OBAN* had gone into the doldrums around 1963 - 64. PMC Commandant Col Gibson, in his other role as Chairman of the OBA, took much pleasure in the Newsletter's phoenix-like reappearance. In a message to all its readers, he spoke about the forecast reduction in the size of the Army, accompanied as it was by the proposal that the other two Apprentices' Colleges, those at Chepstow and Harrogate, should both cease functioning. In future, RE and R Sigs boys were to be trained here at Arborfield, under the banner of the 'ATC'.

His main message to the worldwide population of ex-apprentices was as follows:

"It gives me the greatest pleasure to be allowed to write the 'Chairman's Message' in this, the first issue of the Arborfield Old Boys' Association Newsletter for a very long time. One reason, of course, is that any association as large as ours should have some means of communicating with its members. Another reason though is that the next few years are to be a period of considerable change within the College and the Junior Army, and I shall need your advice and involvement."

Editor John Northam (vintage 1947 and also Membership Secretary at that time) made this impassioned plea:

"Gentlemen, if we are to survive as an association and go from strength to strength, we really do need to spread the word, especially in the light of the inevitable changes about to come in apprentice training. There must be thousands of potential members out there; we need to communicate more with each other, to consolidate and build on what we have – hence the reason for this newsletter.

However, we do need your contributions, which could include anecdotes or any topic of general interest to Association members, or even just news of yourself or any other old boy you may have met up with."

In *The Arborfield Apprentice* that summer, there was a nostalgic peep into the past by the editor, illustrating some of the 'beneficial' changes that had taken place over the years. He quoted a standard letter that the Commandant of 1953 would send out to all parents, regarding the subject of 'punishment':

"It is my opinion that for certain boys, the best form of punishment is a few strokes of the cane, rather than confinement to Camp or detention. This is only awarded by me with your consent, after my personal investigation of an offence, and is given in the presence of a senior officer".

A proforma would accompany the letter, whereby the parent could sign to agree the punishment. The magazine editor also quoted the pay rates for those days as follows:

During first year: 2s. 6d. a day   (that's about twelve pence!)
During second year: 3s. 6d. a day   (seventeen pence)
During third year: 4s. 0d. a day   (a whopping twenty pence!)

Thoughts turn to a 'full history'

In June 1992, yet another updated version of the 'brief' College history was published, due mainly to the efforts of Maj Mike Costanzo, himself an ex-boy of 53B, who was then serving at the College as OIC of the Electronics Branch. Under the guidance – or was it a whip? – of Col Peter Gibson, Mike had added the relevant information, required to cover the time since the previous 'Jubilee' issue of 1989. In a foreword to the new (sixth) edition, the Commandant stated:

"You have in your hands the updated edition of 'A Brief History' of Princess Marina College. We have not changed Bryn Richards' original manuscript, only added a few paragraphs to it. The booklet now tells the story of fifty-three years of the College's existence, ending in REME's own Golden Jubilee year."

This new publication obviously became the inspiration behind the plan to now compile a 'full' history of the College, although a variety of reasons seemed to conspire against that plan being put into practice over the following few years. It was to be well into the 'New Millennium' year of 2000 that the project actually became a reality.

The College Band had enjoyed another busy couple of terms. They had been delighted to play at a Rugby tournament, held within the Garrison as part of the 'REME 50' celebrations between the Corps side and representative sides from the REME equivalents from Australia and NZ. Their biggest 'gig' came when they were an important part of the Lord Mayor of London's Procession, appearing on national TV. And, at the end of June, the Band happily played host to Helen Simpson, a young lady who was to spend three weeks rehearsing and playing with the Band as part of a 'work experience' programme. During her stay, Helen was also allowed to visit the REME Staff Band and the KOSB Regimental Band at Blackpool.

Members of 'D' Coy were enjoying some pleasant days out during that summer, both on general educational visits and trade-related ones. One party went off to the Imperial War Museum, where they were relieved to be quietly ushered past the long queues waiting outside. 4 Div boys visited RAF Brize Norton, where they were fascinated by some non-destructive testing in the 'Wheels and Tyres' bay, while a group from 3 Div travelled down to RAF Odiham in Hampshire. Here they found the place looking very 'spick and span', with everyone walking round in best dress. *"Very nice"*, they thought, *"they've made a special effort for us"*. Their visit had coincided with that of a VIP! Whisked sharply out of sight, the boys were treated to a tour of some stripped-down *Chinook* and *Puma* helicopters.

Tennis provided the high spot of the summer term, as the College team swept aside all opposition. Starting with the Tri-Service Games at HMS Sultan, the home side were beaten 0 – 3 and RAF Halton went down by 1 – 2. Despite some terrible weather at the fiercely contested Triangular games, PMC first put paid to Harrogate by 3 – 0 and then Chepstow by 2 – 1. Finally came the Army Junior Championships, where the College enjoyed their finest-ever display in that particular competition, providing both the winners and runners-up in both the Singles and Doubles, as well as the winner of the Singles Plate.

Adventurous training continued to provide both challenge and enjoyment for all those who became involved. In June, PMC had contributed the seventh leg of sailing on *'Master Craftsman'*, as part of the REME's fiftieth birthday celebrations, on the Great Lakes of Canada. Then, in August, Exercise Alpine Challenge saw College climbers back on familiar territory in the Swiss Alps. There were several *"difficulties and setbacks"* encountered along the way, but overall the trip had proved to be both exciting and educational – as well as rather nerve-wracking at times!

In the August 1992 issue of *The Craftsman*, PMC was proud to supply an article that declared that *"Orienteering continues to be one of the most active and successful sports in the College"*. In the period between September 1991 and June 1992, College orienteers had participated in over fifty separate events and enjoyed some considerable success. Highlights of the season had included a visit to Leeds, during a very foggy November weekend, for the British Schools Championships. At the end of May they had competed at Alcester (near Stratford-upon-Avon) in the Junior Championships, taking the title for an unprecedented seventh consecutive year. Another occasion took the team to Somerset, for the UKLF and Army Championships, while the Junior Army Night Cup was retained for the third consecutive year.

Uncertain lies the road ahead

By the autumn of 1992, the future of the College, as well as that of the rest of the Army, was still a matter of conjecture and, indeed, this unresolved situation was to continue until well into the following year. The first few REME female apprentices had been planned to arrive here in May 1993, in order that the College could gain some measure of 'experience' in their requirements, prior to the expected arrival of larger numbers of R Sigs girls in the following September. But recruitment

RSM Murray Scots Guards 1992-93

417

Our number may be reduced but we're still as smart as boys of earlier years.

of the requisite numbers had proved impossible at that time, and so it wasn't until September 1994 that female apprentices would be admitted to the College for the first time.

September of 1992 saw the publication of the College's new one-year prospectus, for Engineering and Supporting Trade Apprenticeships in REME. It explained that, in civilian terms, this consisted of an initial period of one to two years (still the case at that point), depending on the trade chosen, covering military, trade and education training at PMC. This was to be followed by 'on the job experience' of between two-and-a-half to three years as an adult in the field force Army. Finally, a more advanced training package of approximately six months would be completed, bringing the technician/tradesman – or tradesperson? - up to Class I standard.

The 'one-year only' scheme was designed specifically for young men to enter REME between the ages of sixteen and seventeen-and-a-half, as JLdrs, in those trades where costs and facilities did not allow a full six-term trade training course to be completed at the College. Only the following trades would form part of this one-year scheme: Clerk, Driver, Metalsmith, Recy Mech, Storeman and VE.

During the period 16th – 18th September, it was the turn of REME to host the biennial Army Engineering Symposium. The aim of this high profile event, sponsored by the Director of Army Recruiting (DAR),

was to inform delegates of how the Army goes about recruiting, training, retaining and employing its engineering graduates in the three Army engineering corps. The Symposium itself was held here at Arborfield, within PMC, with presentations taking place in the Lecture Theatre and demonstrations and displays in the Princess Alexandra Hall. As was reported in *The Craftsman*, it was difficult to describe the complete transformation of the hall. On Monday it was a mere gymnasium, by Tuesday it had been carpeted and decorated and laid out with all the elements of the three individual corps' displays. It was no small feather in the cap of the College, to be chosen for an event of such complexity and size.

At the 1992 Old Boys' Reunion, Larry Le Var of 47A took over the reins as Hon Sec of the OBA from Sam Weller (54B). Sam was presented with a gift from the Committee as a token of thanks for all the hard work he had put in over a number of years previously. Paul 'Tug' Wilson (42A) attended that Reunion, happy to bump into Dave Smart, an old Dukie and fellow apprentice, who he hadn't seen since 1944! Paul had gone into Aldershot Military Hospital in January of that year and, on returning to the School, found that the dispersal had removed everyone from the premises! *('Tug' then went to Ashford – fully reported earlier in this history. Ed.)*

A return to the flock

The subsequent autumn *OBAN* reported the welcoming of Lawrence Nixon (April 1942) back 'into the fold' of the AOBA. Lawrence had recently retired from what he called *"my second job"*, where he had been responsible for the training needs of over 20,000 employees at a large electronics firm. Having been on holiday in Yorkshire that year, he had called in on old pal H W (Bert) Kelly, an ex-boy of 39A, who had also been the WO I/C Fitter Gun section here, between 1954 and 1959. He was delighted to find that Bert was in proud possession of the splendid and decorative 'Jubilee Plate', which commemorated the College's Fiftieth Anniversary.

Lawrence had been an apprentice Instrument

Mechanic here from 1942 - 45, returning as an Armament Artificer SSgt from April 1948 to October 1949. He recalled attending the first-ever Old Boys' Reunion during his return tour. Following a further three years on the sunny island of Malta, Lawrence eventually joined the PS here between 1953 and 1958. It was during this latter tour that Lawrence, in his position as Assistant Hon Sec, helped put the AOBA onto a firm footing and the OBAN into existence.

Lawrence had thought that he was too late to attend the 1992 Reunion, but fate had decreed otherwise. Bert Kelly obviously knew all the right strings to pull as he made late arrangements, which ended up with the pair of them being able to come down to Arborfield for a nostalgic weekend together. Lawrence remembered that back in 1948, even the oldest 'old boy' was then relatively young but that, today, he was in no doubt whatsoever that he had truly joined the ranks of the '*Old*' Boys.

The autumn 1992 edition of *The Arborfield Apprentice* reported further progress on the prestigious Project *Hathi*. An 11.3 litre straight-six *Thorneycroft* engine had now been acquired. Rescued from a scrap-yard at Newcastle-under-Lyme, Staffordshire, the £1,000 cost had been borne by Corps funds for the REME Museum. Restoration work was continuing on the vehicle's bodywork and around 500 man-hours had so far been spent, just on building the enormous radiator. It was certainly proving to be a 'labour of love' for those apprentices working on the project. After all, the old vehicle was now getting on for seventy years of age, and who wouldn't like to look 'in their prime' at that time of life?

Mid-November saw the Princess Alexandra Hall hosting the Army Cycle Roller Championships for the second consecutive year. With PMC having won the Junior Trophy for the past three years, hopes were high that a fourth successive victory would come along. But opposition was very strong that year and it was Harrogate who finally ended the College's winning streak.

Meanwhile, the College Rugby team was trying to live within a new set of laws, as laid down by the International Board. These had been set to encourage a faster and more open style of play – and PMC weren't found wanting! Having lost some very good players from the XV that had won the Junior Cup in March, their *"squad system"* then fully justified itself. In the early-season Army Youth Cup, they beat the young

chefs from Aldershot by twenty-six points to twelve. Then they literally 'ran away with the game' in the Final against Chepstow, coming up with a magnificent tally of fifty-seven points, against which the 'Beachley Boys' could not offer a single response.

Consider yourself proposed!

On November 29th 1992, representatives of PMC and the OBA played a prominent part in the inauguration of one of its ex-apprentices as the '*Portreeve of Ashburton*'. This was a small town in Devon, located just off the A38 between Exeter and Plymouth. The quaintly named post was similar in function to that of a Mayor, and was defined in the *Concise Oxford Dictionary* as 'Chief Officer of Town or Borough'. Bill Ward (47A) had proudly accepted his nomination for this position, and then had written to ask Col Peter Gibson would he be able to officially propose him. The occasion that followed was marked by a parade, at which the OBA standard was carried by A/T CSM Michael Dingley of 90C ('A' Coy), accompanied by the stirring sound of music being played by the College Band.

At the turn of the year, ex-boy Lt Col (Ret'd) Peter Daykin of 46B, along with his wife, attended a New Year's Eve wedding in distant Bangkok, where his son married a girl from Thailand. During his trip, he visited the site of '*The Bridge on the River Kwai*', as well as two of the war cemeteries in the area. Peter had joined the boys' school just after the end of the war, so had strong memories of those times and the plight of the prisoners of war at the hands of their Japanese captors.

Both Peter and his wife were very moved at the thought of some forty-eight REME personnel who had perished, their graves each bearing an engraved plaque with the early REME badge. As he wrote in *The Craftsman* of April 1993, "*we should never forget the courage of those founder members of our Corps*" and hoped that they would be remembered in prayers, some fifty years after those terrible events,

As if to show that life must contain as many 'downs' as 'ups', the PMC football team during the 1992 - 93 season started off quite badly – and then got steadily worse! Many of the side that year were inexperienced youngsters, as the more seasoned players always seemed to be away on one duty or another when it came time to kick off each Sunday. An upsurge in form towards the end of the season was not quite enough to prevent the College team from finishing bottom of the Reading and District League.

In contrast to the poor football season, the College Table Tennis team was able to report a 'champion' result in its Division of the Bracknell and District League. They had entered three separate teams and, in the final account, it was the 'A' team that found itself in a great battle with two other sides, from Broadmoor and Wokingham. The last match of the season proved to be a 'crunch' game played against Broadmoor, with the PMC side the eventual 6 - 4 winners and worthy champions.

For the party of expectant boys taking part in the College ski trip to France in late February 1993, things got off to a most inauspicious start, when they learned that the travel firm they had booked with had subsequently gone bust! However, within the space of about three hectic hours, a viable alternative had been found, a briefing held and, instead of the original hotel in Avion, the boys found themselves now booked into a purpose-built self-catering resort at Puy St Vincent.

Not arriving at their destination until late in the evening, the boys could hardly have been surprised to find that their hastily re-arranged sleeping conditions were far from perfect. But the requisition of a couple of spare mattresses, hastily thrown onto the floor, solved the initial problem. Thankfully, the trip had only one way to go after that and, by the end of the week some brilliant times had been enjoyed on the slopes – with video evidence recorded and brought back to prove it.

External visits continue

Closer to home, other parties of apprentices were dispatched on various training visits during March. One group, consisting of Armourers and Gun Fitters, visited the Royal Ordnance Factory (ROF), at Nottingham. Here, they were given a basic history of the ROF, from its founding in 1916 right up until the present day, followed by a video presentation of the products now being turned out, which included the Army's *Combat Engineer Tractor (CET)* at a cost of £1 million each.

The second group, made up of Air Techs, made a shorter trip to RAF Brize Norton, in neighbouring Oxfordshire. After a visit to the very large NAAFI, the apprentices were given a tour of the undercarriage bay before moving on to the Engine Flight. Here, they were able to investigate the very *VC10* aircraft recently used by the Prince and Princess of Wales on their state visit to Korea.

In the spring 1993 issue of the *OBAN*, Colin Gribble of 78C was moved to write a letter from BAOR. In essence, he thought that the younger and still-serving members of the Association would probably take little part in its activities until well after they had left the Service. Nostalgia is something that usually comes with increased age, especially when one gets to miss the comradeship of one's working life. Colin hoped that this would indeed be the case for him, looking forward to the time when he, along with many others, would truly feel the pull of the College as one of its old boys.

Meanwhile, the College magazine contained some vivid descriptions of a 'survival weekend' inflicted upon members of 'D' Coy, and hosted at the nearby Bramley training area by 21 SAS. After a brisk PT session, class participation was then demanded in a demonstration of how to 'slaughter, skin and butcher' a live sheep! As pointed out by the SAS instructors, anything that could walk, crawl, fly or swim was suitable as food – or bait. The true survivor was expected to catch his own breakfast, using the well-known methods of *"mangle, dangle, strangle or tangle"*.

Overnight shelters – or 'bashas' – were constructed from any available vegetation and metal debris found in the vicinity. One such shelter proved so successful that the hard-to-please instructors ordered it to be left intact, as a demo model for future courses. The night's entertainment was provided by the headless antics of the chickens, which were shortly to figure as the apprentices' evening meal. The next morning brought a study of improvised weapons – consisting of an array of rocks, clubs and sharp edges hardly likely to win friends and influence people!

Finally, the boys were given an insight into the work of police dog-handling teams. Given the chance to sprint away from 'the scene of crime', hotly pursued by the well-trained dogs, it soon became clear that our four-footed friends were in charge! The short trip back to what now seemed like the luxurious comforts of PMC, with its excellent food and comfortable beds, made the boys realise how fortunate they were that the exercise had only lasted a couple of days. Never had *Mars Bars* or NAAFI buns tasted so good!

In April 1993, *The Craftsman* magazine reported on the achievement of 2nd Lt David Hall, who had been awarded the Queen's Medal on passing out from the RMAS. He had proudly received his reward from HRH the Duchess of Kent at the Sovereign's Parade the previous December, due to his having achieved the highest overall marks on his commissioning course. David had joined PMC as an apprentice Inst Tech in 1987 and, having served first at Catterick and then in The Gulf, was selected for commissioning in September 1991.

A welcome reprieve

By May of 1993, as reported in *OBAN Issue 3* by the Commandant, the College had seen the collapse of the previously floated proposals to convert Arborfield into a combined ATC. A commonality of certain trade training between REME and the other technical corps had led to the serious possibility of amalgamation of all three Apprentices' Colleges, on site here at Arborfield. But, following opposition from both the RE and R Sigs, and a clear lack of the funding that would be required for such an ambitious venture, those plans had now been shelved. However, it couldn't have come as any surprise that those two other Apprentices' Colleges at Chepstow and Harrogate *were* still to close. With many welcome and audible sighs of relief, PMC was thus saved as a going concern – well, at least for the foreseeable future.

The Director General Equipment Support (Army), otherwise known as DGES(A) as a replacement for DGEME, was now vigorously persuaded that the new and unloved 'one-year apprenticeship' should not be allowed to continue. Thus, all those original one-year boys who had started their training courses in September of 1992 were quickly converted back to a two-year apprenticeship. Much 'burning of the midnight oil', though in an obviously good cause, must have taken place, as existing programmes, syllabi and schedules were scrapped, then hastily re-arranged.

Studies abounded at that time and one, the *'Postgate Study'*, now came up with the conclusion and recommendation that the PMC should be moved back to its original site of what had now become known as Rowcroft Barracks. However, this could obviously not happen without the building of a large amount of new technical training accommodation. But if the move *was* going to happen, then at least it was good to know that the College would find the old gates still in place!

The next few months saw some firm and far-reaching decisions finally being made. Foremost amongst them would be the move of the SAE from its Hampshire home of Middle Wallop to Arborfield. Here it was to be amalgamated with the SEE, thus forming the School of Electronic and Aeronautical Engineering (SEAE). SEME was to remain in its long-held location at Bordon, although it would now become just a 'Wing', under the leadership of Headquarters REME Training Group (HQ RTG), based here at Arborfield. With this expansion of SEE into the larger SEAE, that Hazebrouck accommodation still housing the present PMC would become untenable, thus the need to move back to the Rowcroft site became increasingly essential.

Later that year, Col Gibson was able to report on these proposed changes to the old boys, via the pages of their *Newsletter*:

> *"The changes are more easily described than achieved and staff are busy preparing for the move and re-writing syllabi. However, the future of Apprentice training in the Corps is now secure and the way forward is clear. I have no doubt that the College will maintain its high traditions and standards and will continue to make a considerable contribution to the performance of REME, in support of the Army as a whole".*

Up for a challenge

During a weekend in June 1993, a team of boys from the College, calling themselves 'The Pythons', entered an exercise called 'Snowdon Challenge', in aid of sufferers from Multiple Sclerosis (MS). There was an evening get-together at the pretty little village of Beddgelert on the Saturday, where the boys received advice from previous entrants.

Sunday morning started with a big breakfast at a local pizza restaurant, from where the team made its way to the start line of the well-worn Ranger's Path. The task in hand was to carry volunteer MS sufferer Pam up to the summit of Mount Snowdon. This ascent was achieved in around two hours. Much effort had to be put in, but there were plenty of organised drink-stops en route. Pam was delighted to have fulfilled her ambition of reaching the mountain top and the boys joined in her happiness with a photo session at the summit.

On August 1st, two teams, one each from 'B' and 'D' Companies, spent a few hours walking around the South Downs. They were taking part in the City of Chichester and Royal Military Police (RMP) Marches, an internationally renowned event. The Army was well represented, especially on the 40km event, which many units used as training for the forthcoming *'Nijmegen Marches'* in Holland. The route wandered around the many hills that surrounded the ancient but pretty city of Chichester in Sussex, with its famous eye-catching Cathedral. The 'B' Coy team had to compromise between those who just wanted a 'Sunday stroll' and those who wished to make a fast time, eventually coming home in four hours twenty minutes, just fifteen minutes behind the dedicated boys of 'D' Coy. In lovely sunshine and sat on the grass at the end of their efforts, the boys enjoyed a feast of beef-burgers and ice cream - plus the odd glass of 'amber nectar'!

Later that month, the College Climbing Club went off to pastures new. Having already accomplished many peaks within the bounds of the UK, 1992 had seen the Club off to Europe and the Alps. But this year it was decided that *"Mexico would be interesting"*. The first few days were spent in Mexico City on 'acclimatisation duties' i.e. chillies, tacos, tortillas and re-fried beans! Needless to say, a couple of the party later suffered the infamous 'Montezuma's Revenge', prior to the ascent of a volcanic crater going by the name of 'Poppocateptl'. A planned climb up the mountain 'Iztacchivatl' then had to be abandoned, after news came through of some recent violent avalanche activity towards its summit. An alternative visit, to the famous holiday-resort of Acapulco, proved irresistible to most of the boys before the time came to return home.

The Sub-Aqua Club also went abroad that August, to experience some warm water diving off Spain's Costa Brava. Their delayed flight from Gatwick didn't take off until the early hours, so at 5 a.m. on August 17th, their first 'dive' happened to be into the luxury of their beds! Following that, the boys soon got themselves accustomed to the local waters and it wasn't long before some of them had the excitement of a 'wreck' dive.

Two minor injuries were picked up in the form of bites – one from an octopus, the other from a grouper – while it was generally found that conger eels had a great appetite for 'compo' sausage! During one afternoon's dive the weather 'turned English', in the form of heavy rain, which later developed into a storm of hailstones as big as golf-balls. But the last day was spent in typical apprentice style – poolside and surrounded by admiring lasses!

A number of apprentices again took the chance to join in what was now becoming quite a popular and rewarding pastime, namely 'Battlefield Tours' of the sites of famous battles of the First World War. One such group found itself at Ypres, near the France-Belgium border. During the day, the boys visited many of the Commonwealth graves and saw some of the authentic trenches that had been 'home' to the soldiers of 1914. This brought home the harshness and hopelessness that must have been felt at the time. Towards the end of the day, the boys visited a War Memorial called the Menin Gate and had the great privilege of being invited to join in a special ceremony alongside a party of visiting ex-servicemen.

Old Boys – spreading the word

During the later months of 1993, *OBAN's* editor, John Northam, along with his wife Judy, made a long trip to see old friends in the Far East, then completed their tour by visiting Australia and NZ. Since the *OBAN's* re-appearance in 1992, many welcome letters had been received from NZ, written by past apprentices who had settled there, with the result that the Northams had received 'open invitations' to visit many of them. This they did most happily and, as a result, were greatly instrumental in the eventual setting up of the British Services ex-Boys' Association (BSXBA) in that far off corner of the globe, which has since gone from strength to strength.

Upon their arrival at Auckland Airport, they were slightly concerned that their expected host had not met them. Then June gave John a nudge and whispered *"There's a chap over there holding up a copy of the OBAN – do you think it could be him?"* Indeed it was, and over the next ten days, Eric Corscadden (Apr '42 or 42A, whichever you prefer!) and his wife Yvonne took great pleasure in entertaining Judy and John, including vast quantities of superb food and 'New World' wine! They later had the pleasure of meeting up with Noeline, widow of 39A's Bill Tingey, who had sadly died earlier in the year.

Another of the old boys met by Judy and John that year was Joe Culley, who had been a member of the 44A intake and was now a thirty-year resident of NZ.

John took great pleasure in recording some of Joe's memories on tape, which inevitably included a few stories about Ben Cook and Gilbert - the NAAFI slab cake and the 'horse in the water' episode amongst them. *(It must all be true then! Ed.)* Joe also remembers 'scrumping' for apples over at Farley Hill, and his trip up to London to celebrate VE Day, stopping overnight at the services' *Union Jack Club* near Waterloo Station. He and his pal 'Gabby' Williams were absent for three days, getting back to Arborfield too late to be charged, as by then the Commandant had initiated the big let-off – another great escape. As Joe succinctly put it, *"If you are going to be a criminal, be a big one!"*

At the Old Boys' Reunion of October 1993, Padre Broddle, the AOBA Chaplain at the time, introduced the old boys to two specially written prayers that he had written on their behalf. The Old Boys' 'Grace' was said and heard for the first time at that Reunion dinner, whilst the Old Boys' 'Collect' was spoken at the first dedicated old boys church service the following morning.

(This 'Collect' for the old boys, along with those of the College and of the REME, is published as a separate annex to this chapter.)

In the *OBAN Issue 4*, Larry Le Var reported on the all the hard work that had gone into organising what had been his first Reunion as 'Hon Sec'. In particular, he was startled at the large amount of voluntary activity that had been found necessary within the College, to make the event such a successful occasion. The list of 'mother's little helpers' included the Commandant, Adjutant and RSM, all of the CSMs, many Mess Staff, Regimental Restaurant (that's Cookhouse to **really** old boys!) Staff, the WRVS lady, the Band and – last but not least – those apprentices who had been on hand to carry bags and suitcases, parade on the Square and wait on table during the evening's excellent meal.

In the same magazine, David 'Titch' Schofield (65A) wrote up his thoughts on that recent Reunion. He had arrived by train at Reading Station, to be met by his brother Ken, another ex-boy from the earlier intake of 62C. They managed to get lost, whilst trying to find their way out of town, until Ken's *"ancient love life"* came to the rescue – he suddenly recognised a street where one of his old girl-friends used to live. Ken had attended the previous year's Reunion in a wheel chair, and it had taken a tremendous amount of effort - and

pain – to 'get on parade' again this year.

Frank Reynolds had served here at the College as its QM(R) from 1988 to 1990. Writing as an ex-Harrogate boy in that same OBAN, Frank said that, *"If you delete Wokingham and insert Harrogate and substitute Betty's Tea Rooms for Smokey Joe's, it would bring a touch of class to its pages"*. Frank is now an 'Honorary Old Boy', so may just get away with that statement – but only just! He went on to recall memories of his apprenticeship at Harrogate – *"endless bull, long parades, non-stop blancoing, interior economy, no money, appalling food and bullying"*. He ended by recalling his boys' service as *"bloody awful"*. Come on, Frank, you obviously went to the wrong place!

College history - thoughts turn into action

At some point during that year, the Commandant decided that it was about time that the 'full' College History should finally be put together. The 'slippery baton' was duly passed to Victor Brooke, or to give him his due title, Viscount Alanbrooke. Victor had previously served as the 2I/C of 'D' Coy in the early Seventies, as 'Capt The Hon A V H Brooke RA'. He had left the College towards the end of 1972, in order to attend Teachers' Training College at Cheltenham. This had obviously proved reasonably successful, as Victor was now serving as a lecturer at the College! He had been given dispensation from his normal duties to concentrate the effort required to collate all the necessary archival data. Sadly, Victor was unable to complete the task, due mainly to health problems but, nevertheless, did a sterling job on the initial job of information gathering before his eventual retirement in 1997.

December 1993 saw the arrival of yet another RSM at the College, the last of a long unbroken line of RSM appointments from the Guards Regiments to grace the Barrack Square at the boys' school. He was RSM J F Rowell from the Grenadier Guards.

Mountain biking was a sport that was becoming very popular at the turn of the year; it had also just become officially recognised by the Army Cycling Union. Just before Christmas leave, an event at Perham Down, near Andover, had proved almost impossible in constant rain, with only two juniors finishing. Needless to say, they were both from PMC, in first and second place! *(Who said they could walk – or ride - on water? Ed.)* Further events were now in the pipeline and the weekend of 19th / 20th March was eagerly anticipated, as PMC were to play host to the Army Spring Cup.

With the demise in the number of Junior Army units, the Army Apprentices' Football Cup competition, played at Aldershot over the first weekend in December, saw only four entries. As well as the 'home' side, Arborfield, Chepstow and Harrogate provided the other three teams. The final was contested by PMC and Harrogate, producing a comfortable victory for PMC, with A/T White recording a total of thirteen goals during the weekend's games. Arborfield's footballers had achieved some notable representative honours that season, under the tutelage of the veteran Chris Eade, who had tasted much previous success at SEME Bordon.

A booklet entitled *'An introduction to Aircraft Training'* was issued during January 1994. The intention was that it would be presented to all those apprentices just commencing their aircraft training, but the first issue was also given to all serving apprentices of that trade in the College at that time. The booklet was a general guide to what Air Techs could expect during their training course. This would include a visit from a helicopter, a familiarisation flight and initial contact with AAC aircrew members. A trip to Brize Norton would give a close look at the Transport aircraft and equipment used by the RAF, followed by a trip to see an AAC unit, along with it's REME support, in action.

In the spring 1994 issue of *OBAN*, Col (Ret'd) John Peacock, who had been Commandant between 1979 and 1983, was moved to write of his pleasure in seeing the revival of the Newsletter. This, despite the fact that most of the contents were from old boys from long before even his time at the College. He rightly assumed that 'nostalgia' takes a while to take hold on many, so that it would still be some time before there were regular contributions from the Seventies and later. John certainly looked back upon his time here as the *"high spot"* of his Army career, though doubtless he saw it from a different perspective to the boys. He congratulated the editorial staff on the Newsletter and wished the *OBAN* a long and prosperous future.

It was also in early 1994 that Judy and John Northam were trying to realise their long-held ambition of moving down to the West Country, while Brian Hornsey of 54A was preparing to take over the editorship of the *OBAN* from them. Brian was eminently suited to the task, being self-employed as a Publications Consultant at the time, with access to his own computer system, which included the necessary 'desk-top publishing' (DTP) software.

Chepstow's long history draws to a close

The weekend of 5th / 6th March brought the last gathering of competitors for the annual Triangular Games. In fact it sadly turned out to be a little less than 'triangular', as Chepstow had been unable to provide a team, owing to the fact that the Beachley site, lying under the shadow of the Severn suspension bridge, was finally closing down after a history dating back some seventy-five years. It was also the very first time that the sport of Karate had been represented, in the form of an exhibition match between PMC and the AAC Harrogate. The sport was still in its infancy and yet to be officially 'recognised', but the fine bouts on display that weekend certainly added to its growing prestige.

The 'Pilgrim's Way' winds its way from the gates of Winchester Cathedral all the way to the spires of Canterbury Cathedral, a distance of some 156 miles. Originally well-trodden by the religious pilgrims of earlier centuries, it was considered that if the journey was made three times in one's life, then your sins would be forgiven. The question now was, would it work on 21-gear mountain bikes?

Well, over the Easter weekend of 1994, a team of eager cyclists from PMC set off to find out. The first day's journey ended in a dreadful mixture of rain, hail and snow, before the cold and weary boys were able to recover with an overnight stay at the Guards' barracks in Caterham. The last eighty-five miles were then completed the following day. The average speed for the journey was twenty-one miles per hour, but the boys reckon that this would have been much faster if the Padre had been ten years younger!

During April of that year, as part of his data gathering and research for the College history project, Victor Brooke received a letter from David Wright, an ex-boy of the 48B intake. In fact the letter was hand-delivered by David's grandson Justin, who was himself serving his apprenticeship here during 1994. David's letter remarked on his disbelief at some of the changes at Arborfield since his day, such as the absence of *Reveille* or muster parades! No doubt young Justin had been forced to listen to many long stories of what it was like in Granddad's day!

In the spring edition of *The Arborfield Apprentice*,

an article recorded the first-ever event held at Arborfield of the 'Modern Triathlon'. Some competitors were obviously keen to do well at this new sport; others had been dragged along rather unwillingly! The afternoon's entertainment began with eight lengths of the swimming pool (200 metres), which suddenly looked a very long way indeed. This was followed by pistol shooting – the targets were only six feet away, but of miniature size, while the air pistols certainly took some aiming. The third section was a three-kilometre run through what turned out to be a mud bath. Still recovering at the completion of this inaugural event, the boys were given the good news that more were being planned!

The same magazine gave the chance for several Jeeps of intake 94A to let off steam and describe their first few weeks of basic training. In the time-honoured manner of many thousands of their predecessors, these young men found that *"life in the Army is not exactly as portrayed by the Army Careers Office"*. Being supervised all the time, twenty-four hours a day, came as a big surprise, but drill, PT and skinhead haircuts soon transformed our errant schoolboys into hardened apprentices. *(I was going to say squaddies, but perhaps it's too soon for that! Ed.)* The general feeling was that, although they wouldn't like to do it all again, they were glad to have done it and were definitely wiser for the experience.

The 'Hathi' gets a move on

Labelled as *"impossible"* in its earlier years, the restoration of the veteran *Thorneycroft Hathi* vehicle had now become an *"attractive, forward looking project"*. One of the biggest problems had been that the 'downdraft' carburettor on the modern engine would not fit within the bonnet profile. However, visible progress was now so obvious that it was making every spare minute's effort into a satisfying contribution. Wings, wheels, tyres, exhaust and silencer – all were now being worked on, with A & G Wing's contribution

Where the hell have you done with my Staff Car RSM? Col Gibson is driven out aboard the 'Hathi'

a vital one. The Commandant had taken a personal and active interest in the project and looked forward to the moment when the project would reach its inevitable triumphant conclusion.

In June 1994, Col Peter Gibson left Arborfield to take up his new appointment as OIC of the RMRO at Glen Parva Barracks, Wigston, just outside Leicester. It was fitting that Col Gibson's tenure came to an end by his being ceremonially 'towed out' by the *Hathi*. One of those attending the event was the son of its original civilian owner, who also enjoyed a brief ride.

By now, work on the project had been long taken over by instructors, rather than the apprentices and indeed, the project was now rather intermittent and running out of steam. The College's forthcoming transformation into a non-technical training unit, plus the move back to Rowcroft, meant that a new home for the *Hathi* was becoming essential. It was therefore eventually taken, still in an unfinished state, down to Bordon, where a Mr Richard James and his son, Simon, undertook to provide the necessary *"labour of love"*, provided that the REME Museum would still cover any major expenses.

Another 'Old Boy' takes command

Col Gibson's replacement was Col M C Dorward MBE, MIEE, MIMgt, himself an old boy of the College, intake 60A, and destined to become the last ever 'Commandant'. There must be a saying somewhere, how does it go? *'Don't the Commandants look young nowadays?'* One of Col Mike's first activities was to contribute an article to the latest edition of *OBAN* under the heading *'Personality Slot'*, where old boys are encouraged to provide a potted biography of their career, including photographs of 'then and now'.

After the previous year's successful initial attempt at the *'MS Snowdon Challenge'*, PMC decided to enter a team again in the middle of June. MS is a condition that affects the function of the central nervous system; it can affect either men or women, often in the prime of their lives, without warning. Symptoms vary greatly but usually consist of problems with balance, the function and movement of limbs, speech and visual impairment. Even with advances in medicines and technology, no cure seems available either now or in the near future. *(My own niece has been diagnosed as having this disease and I know how shattering it has been for her and her parents. Ed.)*

The Challenge in 1993 had involved carrying an MS volunteer on a stretcher up to the top of Wales' highest mountain. This had changed in 1994, where a four-and-a-half-mile course over the rocky marshland and muddy terrain of Snowdonia had been laid out. The challenge now was to carry the volunteer in a specially designed wheelchair. This was achieved in good time, with all sponsorship money going to the Reading Therapy Centre for MS sufferers.

During the last week of July, the Army Lawn Tennis Championships were held, on the immaculately kept lawns of the former Royal Aldershot Officers' Club. Despite increasing military commitments for the 'leaner, tauter Army', there was a good turnout, but entries for the Junior Army competition were well down on the previous year. It was encouraging, therefore, to find enthusiastic squads entered from both PMC and AAC Harrogate. A/T Dunstone did Arborfield proud by winning the Junior Army Singles title, beating his fellow apprentice from PMC, A/T Cook. Not content with this fine effort, he then joined forces with A/T LCpl Joyce, and the pairing lifted the Junior Army Inter-Unit Doubles trophy for PMC.

In July's edition of *The Craftsman*, Maj (Ret'd) A'Hearne felt moved to respond to a previous issue, in which it had been argued that perhaps it was time for apprentices' training to be left purely in civilian hands. Peter A'Hearne was well qualified to present the case for continuation, having spent ten years as a Company Commander in three Apprentices' Colleges. For many years, PMC had produced one of the lowest wastage rates in the Army and was currently receiving as many applicants as it could handle.

In that same month, the Apprentices' College at Chepstow finally closed down, and a new Apprentice Training Wing was set up at Minley, situated in North Hampshire. As part of that unit, 82 Sqn RE, with a long and chequered history dating back to 1914, maintained its name. It had arrived at Chepstow in October 1991, on the disbandment of the JLdrs Regt at Dover and was destined to eventually form the RE contingent of apprentice training here at Arborfield a few years later.

A homecoming beckons – as first girls arrive

Meanwhile, back here at Arborfield, other most pressing tasks were now to hand, not least of all the preparation and planning for the forthcoming move of the College to its new (old?) home. There was also the

Girl Apprentice Vehicle Mechs

implementation of Total Quality Management (TQM), a strategy that was definitely the 'buzz word' at the time, not only at PMC, but in most spheres of the REME training system. Added to this were the preparation of eighteen-month courses for VMs, Armourers and Gun Fitters. With the introduction of internal validation procedures, a review of the CMS(R) scheme and the need to react to a move towards Agency status – by no stretch of the imagination could life at PMC be described as being dull!

As previously mentioned, female apprentices had been expected at PMC in 1993, but this had been then somewhat delayed. However, history was finally made on September 10th 1994, when the first young girls joined 'Blenheim Platoon' for training. Five of these girls went on to complete their basic training and one of them, A/T Nadine Mackenzie, proudly achieved the status of 'top recruit'. *(Is there a moral in this tale? Ed.)*

(An article written by Nadine can be found as a separate annex to this chapter.)

The arrival of the first girls brought about the issuing of an *'Annex to Joining Instructions'*, which was aimed specifically at female apprentices. In respect of *'Training'*, it stated that:

"The basic recruit training programme is a busy one. The first term lasts fifteen weeks and is devoted to basic military training, but includes one week of adventurous training in Wales. The hours worked are quite long and arduous, and there is little time off. The working day starts at 6.00 a.m. and 'lights out' is at 10.30 p.m. The syllabus includes drill, weapon training, physical training, first aid, education and map reading. In the evenings, some time is spent upon cleaning the accommodation, washing, ironing and preparing locker layouts.

There are numerous sporting competitions and apprentices are introduced to a variety of outdoor activities. As a general rule, Sundays are kept free for relaxation and personal administration. After the fourth week, limited 'walking out' is allowed, subject to training requirements. During her second and subsequent terms, she will find she has much more time for individual study, recreation and walking out."

One is tempted to ask *"just how did the boys react to the introduction of females into their previously male-only ranks?"* Indeed, an article published around that time humorously puts the point from 'an ardent naturist's' perspective, under the heading *'A spot of Ornithology (or not?) at the College'*:

"This Autumn sees a welcome addition to the College in the form of the female Green Finch (Latin name: Femalus Apprenticus). The female of this species is far more attractive than her male counterpart, especially around the head feathers, and she tends to keep her plumage in tip-top condition. Her eating habits are somewhat more refined and her outward appearance is far less aggressive than the male.

At the moment they are only arriving in twos and threes, but it is hoped that, if they settle here successfully, more will follow in the coming months. Of course, some of the older males are finding it difficult to adapt to the new arrivals, and feel that they simply won't fit into the environment. They obviously feel that their dominance is being threatened, as research indicates that the females may prove more intelligent than the males."

The autumn 1994 edition of *OBAN* published an obituary in memory of Bryn Richards. Although he had not been an ex-boy himself, Bryn became heavily and heartily involved in OBA affairs and was extremely proud when he was awarded with an 'honorary OBA tie' in recognition of his esteemed services. Bryn had devoted a full twenty-two years to the benefit of the College, four of them whilst in uniform, followed by another eighteen as a Burnham Lecturer. Amongst his many achievements was the writing of a couple of versions of the *'Brief History'*, which certainly form the framework upon which this extended version so reverently hangs.

(Bryn's obituary can be found as a separate annex to this chapter.)

Another article in the same *OBAN* reflected upon a donation that had been made to the REME Museum on August 8th, by John Shaw, an ex-boy of 46B vintage. John had collected a variety of military items over the years, many from his own apprentice days. They included a full complement of personal kit, from tin helmet to boots and a set of '1937 pattern' webbing. *(Are you sure you weren't one of those 'spivs' you mentioned earlier, John? Ed.)*

He also handed over many documents, contemporary literature, cigarettes, light fittings, an electric iron and playing cards from those distant days. Also included in the collection was a framed collection of cap badges, as worn by the PS members of the time. John was given a tour of the present-day College and entertained to lunch. Especially happy that day was John Northam, who had last served with his namesake

John Shaw hands on his memorabilia to the Museum

at 21 Command Wksp, Burscough, Lancashire, in 1950 - and who accompanied his 'old mate' during his nostalgic visit.

New contract in the offing

By the autumn of 1994, the contractor (*SERCo*) was reminding its staff of the forthcoming battle to retain the contract for a further period. An issue of the *'Invitation to Tender'* was due in October that same year and *SERCo*'s technical and financial proposals had to be with MoD Contracts Branch by January 1995. After technical evaluation at HQ RTG, which would include PMC input, and then a clarification period, the financial evaluation was due the following July, with the new contract set to be awarded in September 1995. The starting point for this new contract would then be March 1996, five years after the beginning of the first one. All of these timings were set out in a newsletter issued by *SERCo*, which also asked all staff for some *"really innovative ideas"* to be included in the re-bid proposals.

That same newsletter provided news of yet another example of the longevity of the College's old boys' links throughout REME and beyond. Maj (Ret'd) Jack Easterbrook CEng, MIEE had joined the ATS (Boys) on the 21st February 1944 and gone on to train as an apprentice Electrician. Now, more than fifty years later, his career was ending in retirement from his post, within the *SERCo* organisation, as Head of the Electronic Science Department at SEE. In 1949, Jack had attended and passed the ASB and, at the age of only twenty-one, returned to Arborfield to commence Artificer Control Equipment Course No.5.

After commissioning in 1961, he returned to Arborfield in 1964 as OIC Radar Section, being present at the formation of SEE on September 15th 1965. Taking early retirement in 1976, Jack took up a post as a MoD Burnham Lecturer at PMC, where he continued in employment for a further seven years, before returning to SEE in 1983. After becoming a redundant civil servant, he was then snapped up by *SERCo* to continue in his original post until finally retiring on September 30th 1994.

That winter's edition of *The Arborfield Apprentice* gave some A/Ts the chance to 'enthuse' about their week's EL. Although a recognised term for 'external leadership', it was also used as 'extra large', as the boys had to cope with 'EL' hills, 'EL' bergens and 'EL' blisters! However, these difficulties were overcome as the boys pursued the usual mixture of hill walking, canoeing, caving and climbing in an unusually sunny South Wales. 'What goes up must come down' – an old adage that was tested to the full by a session of abseiling. A/T Geary described the thrill and excitement of *"being up against the sides of cliffs, just hanging on by ropes"* whilst A/T Shaw found that caving was going through gaps that he thought *"only rats went through"*.

A/T Cpl Preston of intake 92F had enjoyed a session with *"the real Army"*, on secondment to the Irish Guards, based at London's Chelsea Barracks. Upon arrival there, he found that he was due off to Canada only a few days later. A nine-hour flight took him from RAF Brize Norton to Edmonton, in Alberta. A variety of different weapons passed through his hands, while a fair number of miles passed under his feet during early morning PT runs. But it was not all work, and he found time to visit Jasper National Park in the Rockies, coming across some *"pretty awesome wildlife"* in the shape of grizzly and black bears, elk, deer, moose and buffalo. All this on top of horse riding and white-water rafting, definitely an experience not to be missed.

As one career was just beginning, so another came to a sad end on October 14th 1994, when Lt Col Gordon 'Taff' Mead died, after a fighting battle against cancer. Gordon had joined as a fifteen-year old in 1958, rising to the rank of A/T CSM. Enforced service with the Commandos early in his career suited him perfectly, his postings including some of the world's 'hot spots', in Aden, Borneo and Malaya. Gordon was an 'acting WO2' when he was commissioned, missing out on the treasured rank of WO1. When pressed on the subject, he would retort, *"I simply didn't have the time, boyo"*.

Gordon was always *"passionately Welsh"* and enjoyed a wide variety of sporting pastimes. No doubt he would have been most disconsolate about the current state of Welsh rugby! He had won his first skirmish against the dreaded cancer, but it was to prove all too much for him at the end. Gordon died in his post, as CI at SEME, following the merger of the two training sections, Vehicle Wing and General Engineering Wing, and was buried with full military honours in the Military Cemetery at Bordon. *('Taff' was a 'young lad' under my supervision, when I was an A/T JNCO in HQ Coy in 1958. Ed.)*

Memories are made of this

The Old Boys' Reunion of October 1994 provided an emotional return to his roots for another 'Preston', in the shape of ex-apprentice Gerry Preston of 44B. After twenty-six years of living in Australia, Gerry had finally come back to Arborfield to celebrate the fiftieth anniversary of his intake. As he was to say after that memorable event, *"It was hard to describe one's emotions"*. He had kept in touch with old comrade Ken Jenner over the years, and it was Ken who had made him aware of the significance of the date. He had been sent some recent *OBANs* by John Dutton, and been made especially welcome over the Reunion weekend by Larry Le Var.

In some ways, it was also a fifty-fifth anniversary, as Gerry, to his surprise and great pleasure, met up with some even older friends from the Dukies. He was most impressed by the spirit of the present-day apprentices - *"as strong as ever"* - and he paid a nostalgic visit to the REME Museum, where the vast range of displays rekindled many fond memories.

Gerry also recalled some of the words that had been spoken by 'Monty' during his 1946 visit – *"Learn*

1994 Prizewinners with Brig Palmer and Col Dorward

not only your own trade well, but also those of your mates, as best you can, he may not always be there". Heeding this advice had paid off for Gerry at his many endeavours over the span of his career. He had served the "full twenty-two" after becoming a 'Tiffy' and for a number of recent years had been involved in the communications world of the Flying Doctor Service 'down under'. *(Gerry was also instrumental in the setting up of the South Australia branch of the REME Association. Ed.)*

Mike Wells found himself at first rather disconcerted when he attended the same Reunion. Mike had been a member of intake 49A and, although he had returned to Arborfield on many occasions since then, these had generally been bound up with his involvement with the REME Rugby Football Club. Having at long last decided to return to the OBA fold, he spent the last pre-Reunion fortnight *"on a blissful mental high of recollection. Names, faces, and events which had been dormant for ages, sprang to vivid life again."* But when Mike arrived, he couldn't even find the road past the Camp gates, the road he had so achingly trudged along all those years ago, having missed the last bus from Reading.

Having eventually found his way around, and met up with old chum Bernie Shrubsole (also 49A), it still took a few drinks at the bar before the first glimmerings of hope began to raise themselves. Mike realised that his was not the only 'carrot top' that had now turned to 'salt and pepper'. And it wasn't long before he felt about seventeen again, freely chatting about the likes of Biddulph, McNally, Brady, Weston and company, as though they were in the same room, rather than mere faded spectres from the past.

Another attendee at that Reunion was Dudley Martin, previously a 1938 Hilsea boy, who had joined the School here at Arborfield in 1940. He certainly found the occasion a memorable one, especially as he had fallen flat on his face, coming down the steps after the AGM! Dudley wishes it had happened **after** having a drink, rather than **before**, thinking perhaps that there were some members present who thought he might have been groveling at the feet of the Committee! It was Dudley's own fault, he confesses, he had merely miscounted the steps. Thankfully, there was no harm done, just a few bruises and perhaps a slightly damaged pride.

The *OBAN Issue 6* of autumn 1994 gave the chance for Frank Bennet to display some old photographs in the *'Personality Slot'*. Frank had joined the AAS (Boys) in October 1939 and one photograph, taken on Christmas Day that same year, down at his home in Sandwich, Kent, shows Frank resplendent in his SD, complete with tin hat and carrying his gas-mask. Another photo showed Frank and old pal Ron Holland from the same intake, when they were serving together with the 'Chindits' in India during 1945. They had lost touch after that, but happily had been able to get together again many years later and had attended the 1993 Reunion.

Big Macs - and Big Ben

It had long been an ambition of the College that the apprentices should get out and learn a little about life, either by spectating at important events or visiting historical monuments and buildings. Thus it was that, on December 1st 1994, a party of youngsters attended at the Houses of Parliament at Westminster. They were most fortunate to have had their visit arranged by a real 'Peer of the Realm', in the shape of Viscount Alanbrooke of the MEW. PS members enjoyed a three-course meal in the House of Lords' restaurant, whilst the younger element went off to find the local *McDonald's*! After that, there was a visit to *'Big Ben'* – up 292 steps to witness the working parts and a further forty-two up to the Belfry and the four clock faces. The party was fortunate to be in the Belfry as the bell announced the time as 4 p.m., with a four-hundredweight hammer hitting a thirteen-and-a-half bell, it proved to be a noisy experience!

Just a few days later, on December 6th, PMC held its annual boxing competition, for apprentices aged between sixteen and eighteen. All must have entertained the same mixture of emotions, ranging from confidence, fear or pure disbelief at being there in the ring! But the amount of enthusiasm was evident and a responsive audience cheered the combatants on. Next morning's sore faces of the boxers were matched by the sore throats of their supporters. In the event, the 'A' Coy squad managed to beat the squad from 'B' Coy by seven bouts to five.

Annex to Chapter 13

2nd Lt Geoffrey White, RAOC (1927 – 1950)

On 7th October 1942, Geoffrey White was enlisted into the Army as an apprentice Armourer at the Army Technical School (Boys) at Arborfield. He was subsequently commissioned into the Royal Army Ordnance Corps and was then seconded to the 1st Battalion the Middlesex Regt for experience as a Platoon Commander. On 29th August 1950, his Battalion disembarked at Pusan as one of the first British units with the United Nations forces in Korea. 25 days later he was killed in action.

By direction of the President of the United States of America, under the provisions of the Act of Congress, the Silver Star for gallantry in action was awarded posthumously to Geoffrey White. The citation reads:

"Lt White, while serving with the 1st Battalion the Middlesex Regiment, attached to the United States 1st Corps, distinguished himself by gallantry in action against the enemy in Korea on September 22nd 1950.

Lt White was ordered to lead his platoon of 'D' Company in an attack on a hill near the Naktong River. This hill was strongly held by an enemy force, supported by mortars and self-propelled guns. The attack was successful, in spite of the precipitous slope and intense enemy rifle and automatic weapon's fire. Reaching the crest of the hill, Lt White's platoon encountered intense fire from an enemy position on a previously hidden spur of the hill. Undaunted, and thinking only of the best method of silencing this enemy fire, he directed his men forward into positions, while continuing to stand in full view of all members of the platoon and in full view of the enemy. In the course of this action, Lt White was mortally injured.

The success of the platoon, in capturing its objective in the face of such odds, was very largely due to the leadership of this officer who, throughout, took no account of his personal safety and thought only of his duty

and the welfare of his men. The courageous devotion to duty and gallant sacrifice of Lt White reflected great credit on himself and the military services of the United Nations."

Geoffrey White's mother, brother and several old comrades are attending today's parade, during the course of which Mrs White will hand over her son's medals to the Royal Electrical and Mechanical Engineers. After the display in Princess Alexandra Hall, the medals, citation and an account of the battle will be placed in the College Library, which will be renamed the 'Geoffrey White Library'.

(The above article was published in the programme for Junior Company Parents Day, which took place on Saturday 15th December 1990.)

Females to the Front
A/T Sgt Mackenzie writes:

"I arrived at Princess Marina College in September 1994 and was shocked to find that I was one of the seven first female apprentices. This was to me surprising, but I put it to the back of my mind and concentrated on passing out of basic training. This proved to be excellent and I enjoyed every moment of it. In December, five of the females passed out. I was lucky enough to win the best recruit in Blenheim Platoon. The next intake, in January 1995, also had female recruits, and a few more than my intake. The majority of them also passed out and one of them won a prize at her passing-out parade.

From the start of my time at the College, life has been very enjoyable. I have been able to travel, even in the short time that I have been here. For example, in February last year, there was a Careers Convention in Belfast. With another female apprentice, I attended this, in order to contribute a female's opinion to potential apprentices. This was good experience and I felt privileged to be chosen.

During the Easter recess, I was lucky enough to take part in Exercise Snow Eagle at Vancouver, in Canada.

Since I joined the College, I have also had the opportunity to participate in a number of sports. I therefore took the time to learn to play tennis. This resulted in myself, along with a few others from the College, taking part in the Army Junior Tennis Championships. I won the title of Junior Army Female Tennis Winner, 1995. Not only have I taken part in different sports, but I have also experienced caving, climbing and canoeing activities.

Overall, my time at Princess Marina College has been a great experience. I have now reached the rank of A/T Sergeant and feel quite proud to be the first female member of the College to reach this rank."

(A/T Sgt Mackenzie is modest. She did not mention that she received the Award of Honour as the Best Apprentice of her intake [total 76] on her Passing-out Parade in April. She is currently an Electronics Technician at SEAE.)

(The above article is based upon that published in the August 1996 edition of The Craftsman magazine.)

In Memoriam – Bryn Richards (PS)

Bryn devoted twenty-two years to the College, four in uniform as assistant to the SEO and eighteen as a civilian Burnham Lecturer. Bryn was helpful to everyone, a good friend and a perfectionist. The many tasks which he took on all bore his hallmark of dedicated enthusiasm. His activities at one time encompassed teaching in, and civilian management of, the General Studies Department, Chief Librarian, member of the New College Build Co-ordination Committee, editor of the College Magazine and OIC of the Model Club, together with a variety of other minor commitments.

It is probably not surprising that, during his service to the College, Bryn suffered two heart attacks. However, after each one he returned, phoenix like, and continued to give of himself. In the ten years before retirement, he was the College Archivist, in which capacity he is well known to many 'old boys'. During this time, he wrote 'A Brief History' of the College and two updates to the original. He was delighted to participate in OBA affairs and was extremely pleased when he was awarded an 'honorary OBA tie' in recognition of his services to the Association.

He retired in 1991 to Berkhamstead, looking forward to a happy period with his wife Norma, in which to develop his artistic and handiwork activities. However, trouble with his heart re-emerged and he had to undergo a by-pass operation. It was just as he was beginning to feel better, after a long struggle back to health, that he suffered his third and final heart attack – on his feet, on the go, just like him. He leaves a widow, Norma, and two sons, Vaughan and Brent, plus a granddaughter, Paris, to all of whom the OBA send their sympathy and warmest appreciation of Bryn's services to the College.

(The above obituary was published in the autumn 1994 edition of the OBAN.)

Collects and Graces associated with the College

Princess Marina College Collect

*Teach us, good Lord, to serve thee as thou
deservest;
To give and not to count the cost;
To fight and not to heed the wounds;
To toil and not to seek for rest;
To labour and to ask for any reward
Save that of knowing that we do thy will,
Through Jesus Christ our Lord.*

Amen.

The REME Collect

*O God of power and might,
Whose all-pervading energy is the strength of
nature and man,
Inspire, we pray Thee, us Thy servants of the
Royal Electrical and Mechanical Engineers,
With the quickening spirit of goodwill,
That, as honest craftsmen,
Seeking only the good of all in peace and war,
We may glorify Thee,
Both in the work of our hands
And in the example of our fellowship,
Through Jesus Christ our Lord.*

Amen.

Arborfield Old Boys' Association Collect

*O God our Father,
We pray for all who have served their country,
Remembering especially the families of the
Arborfield Old Boys' Association,
Rekindle our courage to face the future
As we did in our youth,
Strengthen our will to seize the moment
As we did in the past,
Enliven our minds to the needs of others
As loyalty and discipline taught us.*

Amen.

Old Boys' Grace

*For the spirit of adventure which took us into the
service;
For the grace of God which brought us through
safely;
For the comradeship which draws us together;
For the blessing of good food;
For these and all his other mercies, God's name be
praised.*

Amen.

Old Boys' Grace at the 40th Reunion Dinner

*Almighty God, we give thnaks this night
For food and wine and perhaps the odd pint
For friends and collegues old and new
Apprentice boys through and through
We celebrate this time to share
In stories based on yester-year
And while the lamp is fully swung
With tales and deeds of 'when we were young'
You may look with envy at the Apprentices today
No bed block for them, just a simple duvet
And as the night begins to wear on
With wine and food and perhaps the odd song
The noise will grow loud, our balance will sway
And before you know it it'll be a new day
So now I ask with one accord
That you all say amen, to give thanks to the Lord*

Amen.

*(These Collects are copied from various Orders of
Service, as published by the present College.)*

—§—

The Military Band in 1975, with then A/T/Cpl McAvoy (front right), latter CO of the ATFC

Chapter 14

1995 - 96

Last post for the Band?

After three weeks of Christmas recess, the New Year of 1995 was welcomed in at the first 'assembly' by the Band's brass section playing a rousing rendition of *'Fight the good fight'*. The College Band was still in great demand and, on January 20th 1995, its combined sections of pipes, drums and brass played for the belated Bailleul Sergeants' Mess 'Christmas Ball'. *(How late can one get? Ed.)* By far the biggest engagement for some time took place on March 25th, when the Band participated in the annual concert given by the Swindon Male Voice Choir at the town's Wyvern Theatre. After the concert, the boys were treated to an evening meal at a local pub, which just happened to be owned by one of the choristers.

Apprentice Pipe Major Walker's experience of life so far had dictated that any hobby that involved more learning than the everyday trade and education lectures should be considered a complete 'no-no'. That was until he joined the Band! His thoughts were quickly blown away by the great example set by the Pipe Major – *"the real one"*. His Black Watch hackle and temperament ensured that all of the young pipers were kept strictly on their toes. Sadly, however, the writing was definitely starting to be written on the wall, as far as the Band's future was concerned.

Writing in the College magazine later in the year, A/T Nicholls recalled his arrival at PMC on 10th January 1995. Some of his mates from home had already become members of the Queen's Own Highlanders, so he had some reasonable idea of what he faced. After his initial seven weeks of training, he arrived back home for the first time, with the first telltale signs of maturity already showing. His parents were amazed to find that their son now actually cleared up after himself! What this young apprentice had quickly learned was that, not only could he now feel more of an individual, but that he was far better suited to also act as part of a team.

In that same month of January, a group of ten ex-apprentices, most of them accompanied by their ladies, met together informally to celebrate the fiftieth anniversary of when they had joined up. That had

been in February 1945, and the old boys were of intake 45A. The 'reunion' had first been suggested by Eddie Broomfield, now living in the Worcestershire town of Malvern, and then set up by Keith Evans, still working – just! – at the College. On parade that day were Eddie and Keith of course, plus Denzil Keep, John Dewar, George Oliver, Dave Richards, John Venn, Doug Kew, Eric Brown and Stan Rycroft. They had a great time together, following their reception at Hazebrouck Officers' Mess and a tour of the REME Museum

At a meeting held on February 3rd, the 'way ahead' for the College magazine was held. The Commandant, in particular, felt that it should reflect issues and events that would be of interest to readers not only of the present, but also of the past and future. However, historical content was to be balanced with contemporary material with which the modern apprentice could relate. A 'memo' sent out in the same month reminded all of its recipients of what must have been a long-standing tradition regarding the 'Official Guests' to be invited to the next 'PoP'. This was that consideration must be given to the following criteria regarding such guests: *"They should be those who have done the College a service; they should have connections with College life and training; they could be in a position to assist the College in the future"*.

Completing the cycle

The Arborfield Apprentice issue of spring 1995 saw the welcome return of an article by the Commandant, a tradition that had been sadly missing over the previous few years. As an ex-boy himself, Col Mike Dorward looked back on his first six months with pride, feeling that he had finally completed *"the full cycle from apprentice through to Commandant"*. Upon taking over at the College, he had been anxious to establish whether or not any great change had taken place in the quality of apprenticeship. He was now convinced that the courses were definitely harder than they had been in his day, but that the training received was still an excellent *"head start in life"* for those embarking on an Army career. The Colonel also undertook the challenge of trying to boost College numbers, with PMC presently some twenty-five per cent under-recruited.

With so many AGC personnel now on the College staff, it was thought that a brief explanation as to the AGC's role should be included in the latest publication of the College magazine. The Corps had only recently been formed in April 1992, following an amalgamation of the WRAC, RAEC, Army Pay Corps (APC), Army Legal Corps (ALC) and RMP. It was now divided into four branches – Staff and Personnel Support (SPS), Educational Training Services (ETS), Provost Branch (still RMP) and Army Legal Services (ALS). Their combined roles are as support to the rest of the Army, both in peace and at war.

At the beginning of 1995, financial restraints were leading to proposals to cease 'Education for Promotion' for both Junior and Senior NCOs, which would effectively end all education for soldiers. However, with standards in the general education of young people being judged to be falling, the Army was very much concerned about its own educational

requirements. With leadership having always been based upon the twin components of 'Training' and 'Education', the standard military view was that there was a *"continuing requirement for a clearly defined, progressive educational programme for its soldiers and junior officers"*.

Spring term saw the departure of another 'old faithful' member of the civilian staff. John Courage had joined what was then the AAS Arborfield as an apprentice VM back in 1947 and followed his three years of 'boy's service' with twenty-three years in the REME, spending most of his time in the Far East – Hong Kong, Korea, Malaya and Singapore. He came back to the College as an instructional officer in Vehicle Wing in 1973, quickly gaining promotion to the A & G Wing, where for the remainder of his service he attempted to inculcate apprentices into the 'black arts' of bench-fitting. His sympathetic approach to students' problems had won him the nickname of 'Gentle John' and, upon retirement, he was heading to France to spend time languishing besides some tranquil vineyard.

Members of 45A some 50 years on now with their wives

New skills take wing

Another Wing at the College was fast becoming 'bedded in'. The Maths, Science and Computing (MSC) Wing had been set up in support of training and to meet the additional academic requirements of BTEC and CGLI examinations. Computing skills, as well as the teaching of the same, had been developing greatly over the previous two years, coinciding with the technological breakthroughs that were fast becoming 'the norm' in the outside world. Written paperwork was tending to decrease in the classroom and most communications were now being relayed across electronic computer links. The arrival of the 'Pasco' system from America had allowed a good interface with the College's network, providing instant calibration of results, displays in graphical format and the ability to 'freeze' or store the required information.

The Military Education Wing (MEW) had also been set up to provide support in aid of training, this on the technical and trade training side of life. The main thrust of the Wing was to cover such syllabus components as Communication Skills (CS), Study Skills (SS), the Soldier in Society (S-in-S), IT (yes, good old computing again!), Leadership and Basic Presentational Skills (BPS). Broken down into the requisite sub-components, the skills taught included such subjects as revision and exam techniques; note taking and information retrieval; the writing of letters, incident reports and memoranda; and, last but not least, Army organisation.

On April 3rd, several members of 93B set off for the East End of London, where they were to take part in a 'Science and Technology' event at Tower Hamlets. Sponsored by the local Education Partnership, one aim was to improve the awareness of local pupils towards scientific subjects. A further objective was to encourage more female pupils to consider future science-based subjects, which caused a certain amount of merriment amongst the boys. One unconsidered side effect of this particular event was the vast improvement in make-up techniques amongst the girls, prior to their "meeting the Army"!

The presentations given by the young apprentices included a wind tunnel, displaying the effect of 'drag' on vehicles; an experiment to show how resonance affects electronic components; and a computer-based electronic circuit design package. Overall, the exercise proved a valuable experience for both the apprentices and the children concerned.

Drumming up a free drink!

Even with the restrictions upon their time and the uncertainties facing its future, apprentices were still finding time to join the Band and make every attempt to become as proficient as their predecessors had been. A/T Kaye had joined the Corps of Drums with no previous knowledge but could soon boast that he had enjoyed entertaining the SNCOs and Officers at their Mess functions. He also described how it could sometimes occur that a free drink could be obtained on the Drum Major's tab! A/T McIntosh was another with no previous musical experience, but he had now learned to play not only the pipes, but the sleigh bells and cymbals, and had even taken part in a concert, held at Reading's Hexagon Theatre.

Mother Shipton's Caves at Knaresborough, just outside Harrogate – that was as far underground that A/T Harrison had ever previously been when he set off for his EL training in Wales. Choosing 'caving' as his activity, his initial nervousness soon gave way to discomfort as his boots filled up with icy-cold water. He then got into his stride – or rather his crawl – as he progressed through the narrow passages. The names of 'Letterbox' and 'Cheese-press' indicate just how narrow! Despite some worries about getting stuck, all the caves and passages were successfully navigated – mostly in total darkness – and the whole effort was looked back upon as 'something of an experience'.

Geoff Currie had been a member of intake 62B, training here as a Radar Tech for three years, followed by another nine months at SEE, before being unleashed onto the outside world. His first 'real' posting had been to far-off Malaysia, and then on to Sarawak for a six-month tour. As he remarked many years later, this made *"a sensational impression on a relatively naïve nineteen-year-old"*. A subsequent year in Singapore had led to Geoff's love of the 'tropical' lifestyle, even though the rest of his engagement led to terms in the German cities of Dortmund and Düsseldorf. Geoff served only until 1972, but had an interesting tale to tell concerning his later civilian life.

In 1995, he had found himself driving down the eastern coast of Tanzania (previously Tanganyika), *"following in the footsteps of Arab traders, English missionaries and German colonists"*, as he later so eloquently put it. He had passed through many

What a pity the photographer who asked these girls to pose for the photograph was not mechanically minded!

villages and ports, obviously once wealthy, but now in severe decline following the loss of traditional trading commodities, namely ivory and slaves! Near to the border with Mozambique, he came across the small historic port of Mikindani and noticed a beautiful, though dilapidated, German-built palace, around one hundred years old.

To cut what must have been a pretty long story short, Geoff has now converted the old palace into an 'African Country House Hotel', which overlooks an idyllic lagoon on the Indian Ocean – and invites any old boy who wishes to take a holiday there, to get in touch! He adds the wonderful names of the local beers – *'Kilimanjaro'*, *'Safari'*, *'Tusker'*, *'Serengeti'*, plus perhaps the best, the powerful *'Bingwa'* – as a temptation to those who may wish to take him up on his offer!

The return to Rowcroft

In June 1995, some three months later than originally planned, the main elements of the College moved from Hazebrouck back to its spiritual home at what was now Rowcroft Barracks, to where it had all begun fifty-six years previously. As the saying goes, *'What goes around comes around'*. Intakes 95B and 95C thus became the first apprentices to occupy the site at Rowcroft since 1981.

This return journey was not to the original old wooden spider-blocks of course, as these had all been long since demolished, along with most of the infrastructure, in the early Eighties. Some sections of trade training had to continue operations at Hazebrouck, which caused considerable problems in the schedule of managing a split site. Course timings had to be adjusted, so that any moves between sites could still take place during 'natural' break times, while physical training had to be provided for on both sites. Eventually, of course, these difficulties were overcome with the proverbial good humour and perseverance of both the staff and apprentices.

The barracks at Rowcroft had been extensively re-furbished, even the Cookhouse had now been extended and totally re-equipped, and later, as 1995 drew to a close, a brand new MEW was well on its way towards completion. This was to comprise both classrooms and staff rooms, a 170-seat purpose-built lecture theatre, plus a library and resource centre, all of which went towards providing some tremendous extra assets to the daily routine of College life.

Unfortunately, as happens during most moves of accommodation, certain things tend to either get lost or, at the very least, mislaid. 'Mislaid' is the term that best describes the data that had been dutifully collected towards the College history. Without a natural home having been set aside for such items at the new barracks, most of the collected data was bundled up and stored away within the vast archives cavern of the REME Museum, where it sadly did nothing but gather a thick layer of dust for the next few years.

To change - or not to change?

The summer edition of *The Arborfield Apprentice* published an article by A/T Carter, which indicated the change of lifestyle enjoyed by the modern apprentice, when compared to those of the 'old school'. He was led into Block 16, his home for the next fifteen weeks and then, after tea and biscuits, shown to his room. Some things never change though, for, as he says, *"The kit hardly fitted me; my shoes one size too small, my jumper two sizes too large"*. Sounds like the QM staff were still intent on sticking to tradition! His final words were, *"Fifteen weeks is the turning point, then you know you're in the real Army"*. Many old boys will be counting their fingers and thinking, *"Fifteen weeks – that would just about have seen us through the initial drill sessions!"*

The same magazine published details of success *'on the piste'* for some of the College's hardier members, who had braved some snow-covered slopes in Bavaria and Canada during skiing expeditions. One party of boys, along with experienced supervisors of course, joined the REME Ski Meet in Bavaria, while 'Exercise Snow Eagle' took place during April and May at the resort of Whistler, far away in the Canadian Rocky Mountains, north of Vancouver.

The aims of these expeditions were to increase apprentices' all-round experience, the novices up to bronze standard, and any existing skiers to silver standard. A successful time was only marred by a number of minor injuries, which included one snapped tendon and the loss of four teeth! Despite having been booked into the 'lowest class' type of accommodation, the party was delighted to find that such amenities included cable television, washing machines, tumble dryers, refrigerators, freezers, microwave ovens, jacuzzis and very large bedrooms.

Meanwhile, another party, this time of intrepid 'apprentice yachtsmen', took the long flight across the Atlantic to Miami, Florida. Having prepared their yacht for sail, the boys then had time to sample the sights of Miami for a few hours, paying a visit to the original *'Hard Rock Café'*. On setting sail, a trip of ten hours duration saw them landing at the atoll of Bimini. A further stormy passage took the boys to Nassau, capital of the Bahamas, where an unfortunate failure of the yacht's starter motor then caused some delay. The yachting adventure over, the boys returned to Florida and were able to visit Orlando and Tampa Bay, as well as taking in a tour of the world-renowned Everglades. How does the song go? *'Some guys have all the luck!'*

In the summer 1995 edition of *OBAN*, an extract was printed from the first Reunion and AGM of the newly formed BSXBA, which had been held in the far-off reaches of NZ the previous October. Its proud members had been delighted that very day to receive a phone call from John Northam, passing on 'official' good wishes from the Arborfield OBA, whose members were holding their own Reunion that same weekend. John had experienced some difficulty in locating the Reunion site at Taupo, but eventually had the number passed on to him, having first phoned Ianto Metcalfe in Taumaranui. Of the twenty attendees at Lake Taupo, no less than eight were ex-Arborfield 'brats'.

The 'Modern Apprenticeship'

With the REME Training Organisation having found that it had been underfunded by several million pounds for the financial years 1995 / 96 onwards, hurriedly organised 'scoping studies' were now being used to identify those areas where substantial savings could possibly be made. The HQ RTG Group Management Board, which had met in November of 1994, had tasked PMC to identify any areas where such savings could be made. It was most unfortunate that certain factors mitigated against the College, the outcome being that, in future, the College's input to training was to be drastically and irrevocably reduced.

Despite the figures produced to prove the value of the prevailing system over many preceding years, it had been decided that financial factors were now to reign supreme. Thus, as part of the Government's 'Modern Apprenticeship' (MA) Scheme, and with the adult trade training centres having a certain amount of spare capacity, the College would now only be required to undertake a two-term 'foundation' phase.

The adult schools of SEAE and SEME would then complete the trade training phases, a plan that had been lurking in the background ever since 1992. The overall apprenticeship would then be completed by a period of consolidation training in the field environment, followed by an 'upgrading' course of around six months, again at one of the adult training centres. Along the way, the apprentices would continue to be offered training towards their BTEC and C & G qualifications. Strong arguments were put forward that the REME apprenticeship should remain attractive; it had to continue to offer the appropriate civilian qualifications and move quickly towards National Vocational Qualifications (NVQs), in order to remain competitive against its rivals in the engineering world.

As an ex-boy himself, Col Mike Dorward could hardly pretend to have been pleased that this unwelcome change had taken place only months after his arrival as Commandant, but the pressure to change had proved to be irresistible. However, there was some consolation in the fact that the PMC had twice fought off the Army Board's proposal that apprentice training should be dispensed with altogether. At least the revised course continued the very essence of apprentice training, albeit in a much-reduced format, while the most valuable asset of all – the apprentice himself (or herself!)– would still be retained. Thus it was that intake 95C was destined to be the first to embark upon this new two-term course, providing the largest 'J' Coy in the College's long history.

A letter dated 1ˢᵗ June 1995, explaining some of the reasoning behind the restructuring of the REME apprenticeship, was sent to all parents by the Commandant. He reported that the drawdown of troops from Germany, plus the 'contracting out' of many REME functions, had generated a fair amount of spare capacity in the adult training schools. He went on to describe the sort of apprenticeship that was now on offer, but also reassured parents that REME would continue to meet all its promises and obligations regarding the current population of the College.

Col Dorward reiterated that the aim of the College remained unchanged and confirmed that it would continue to give its apprentices *"a head start"* in their careers and early advancement. He was also able to confirm that he had the firm assurances of the Commandants of the adult schools that *all* parts of the MA scheme would continue to be properly delivered.

Despite the obvious and natural fears, that the

Col Dorward 1994-95

new training package may not have proved to be as attractive to prospective recruits and their parents as previously, the initial reaction in fact proved to be surprisingly favourable. The last intake of 1995 was to contain 159 apprentices, a good percentage of whom (fifteen in number) were females. This was, no doubt, assisted by the aggressive recruiting campaign that had been recently instigated at the Commandant's bequest. A three-day Careers Fair, held in Northern Ireland at Belfast, had generated tremendous interest, and this was later followed up by presentations to Civilian Careers Advisors in Edinburgh, Dundee, Glasgow and Nottingham. Return visits to the College by those same Careers Advisors had also borne fruit.

Towards the end of June, a party of apprentices was chosen to take part in a parachute-training week at the Joint Service Parachute Centre (JSPC) at Netheravon, Wiltshire. The purpose of this effort was to hopefully have a team in place to compete for the Army Championships, to be held in August later that year. Despite the sun shining brightly that morning, strong winds caused a delay in proceedings, but eventually each of the six trainees made around twelve descents, depending upon their individual competencies.

The culmination of a lot of *"wheeling and dealing"* finally paid off, when members of the PMC Sub-Aqua Club set off to 'The Rock' of Gibraltar during their summer break. Leaving the UK basking in warm and pleasant sunshine may not have seemed a good omen and, indeed, torrential rain during the first two days made the boys think that they had arrived in monsoon season! But clear blue skies eventually developed and a multitude of wrecks, both small and large, at a variety of depths, proved good sport and an exhilarating experience for the fortunate party of boys.

Gloves were found to be an essential accessory during the dives, with numerous spiny sea urchins lurking in the shadows, waiting for unsuspecting hands to be laid upon them. A healthy respect of all nooks and crannies was also required, as there were a number of quite large octopuses (or, argumentatively, octopi?) scrabbling about, some *"bigger than a dinner plate"*, especially on the reef. As well as these exciting underwater activities, the boys were also able to pursue some 'overwater' tourism, with dolphins swimming in the wake of their boat and a visit to meet the world-famous Barbary Apes on 'The Rock'. The culmination of their expedition was a splendid evening at *"a local Chinese"*.

A strong recruiting drive

The continual drive to increase recruiting figures led to a party of apprentices attending an Army Careers Convention at the Army Training Regiment (ATR) Bassingbourn, up near Cambridge, at the start of July. High on the list of their priorities was the construction of a 'Go-kart' track, which was later put to some good use. The A/Ts also learned the art of making sure that all the school children entering the area just *had* to pass in front of the REME Display Stand. The week was helped

December 1995 Passing out Parade at Princess Marina College. The Square may be different but the evolutions are the same!

along by the provision of a minibus, which took the volunteers into Cambridge city centre each evening, where a variety of nightlife provided a welcome break from their hard-working days.

During the weekend 7th / 8th / 9th July, PMC played host to the REME Association's '50th Anniversary' celebrations, but unfortunately the College Band was otherwise occupied! They had been booked to pay a return visit to the *Sue Ryder* home at nearby Nettlebed. By now, Band numbers had fallen drastically and it was feared that their performance would be similarly diluted. These fears came to naught however, with two excellent marching displays – and a heartfelt request for a third performance, after the failure of some other participants to turn up. Band members were delighted at the overwhelming reception and ovation they received. The following weekend the Corps of Drums excelled themselves at the Sergeants' Mess Summer Ball.

Over the third weekend in July, a party of PMC canoeists set off to compete in the Army Championships. A stop at Symond's Yat, in the Forest of Dean, gave them the opportunity for a last 'full English' breakfast before they crossed the Welsh border into Monmouthshire. The initial Sprint events were held over distances of 500 metres and one kilometre (km), followed the next day by Marathon events at 8km, 12km and 14km. Despite some crews coming under attack from an angry swan, and fierce competition from four other Junior units, the combined results over the two-day meeting meant that PMC won

the Junior Army Championships for the second year running – or should that be 'second year canoeing'?

July's edition of *The Craftsman* brought another entry from 'old soldier' Steve Johnson, in which he reminded readers that the following month would bring the fiftieth anniversary of VJ Day. The end of the war against the Japanese forces had been brought about by the dropping of two atomic bombs, a subject that had close personal memories for Steve. He had been present during the later A-bomb and H-bomb tests on Christmas Island in 1958. Steve, an ex-boy of 46A, had contributed a number of articles to the REME magazine over the years, and now looked forward to retiring in 1996, from his then post as Estate Warden at Arborfield.

The autumn 1995 edition of *The Arborfield Apprentice* saw the welcome return of a written version of 'the speech'. Lt Gen Sir William Rouse, the QMG, had made this speech after the 'PoP' of August 18th. He was able to report that, *"historically, apprentices from this College have done extremely well in the Army"*, and gave the career of the Commandant as an example of this, returning as he had after a gap of thirty-five years.

The same magazine contained an article written by A/T RSM Carolan of intake 94A, in which he described how he and a party of apprentices had gone to Reading one weekend, to assist in packing food pallets for the '*Feed the Children*' project. The voluntary staff at the Charity's depot were delighted to see the arrival of so many willing hands, and it wasn't long before the

WO1 RSM R L P Matthews REME

Arborfield contingent were hard at work. They had to go through hundreds of MoD 10-man ration packs, checking for any damage or spillage, before re-sealing them and packing them away into their boxes. One priority was to ensure that there were no pork-related products in the packages, as the pallets were destined for scattered Muslim communities in such war-torn countries as Bosnia, Somalia and Sudan. *(Shades of the Indian Mutiny? Ed.)*

The summer term had certainly proved a busy one for those with an 'orienteering' bent. It had started in March at Anglesey, North Wales, before continuing with a three-day event near Catterick in Yorkshire, where PMC again became the U-21 Army team champions. This was followed by a week in Scotland, with the benefit of 'letting the plane take the strain' between Heathrow and Edinburgh. Then it was off to Belgium by ferry, where the party stayed in a Belgian-style Youth Hostel and took part in three days of individual events. The final tour took the team to Sweden, along with the official British Army team. For their short stay, the apprentices were all classed as 'officers', each with their own personal accommodation and separate

toilet – luxury indeed! As well as the sport, where they were able to pick up some good tips from both the Swedish and British Army teams, some time was found for shopping and sightseeing.

First RSM from REME

September 1995 saw the final break in a long line of tradition at the College. For the previous fifty-six years, ever since its original inception, firstly the School, and latterly the College, had its appointment of RSM filled from the notable ranks of the Guards Regiments. RSM Jeff Rowell, Grenadier Guards, was the last such proud holder of this post, and it is to his eternal credit that, before he moved on to pastures new, he had diligently compiled a list of all College (and School of course) RSMs up to that date. This had been published in the spring 1995 edition of the College magazine.

Before departing to the AAC, the newly commissioned Lt Rowell wrote a fond farewell note in *The Arborfield Apprentice*. He remarked that nothing could ever surpass the honour of being the College RSM. He had marched off his final 'PoP' with very mixed feelings and later congratulated all participants for an outstanding performance. Jeff handed over his duty to the very first RSM from the Corps of REME, in the proud shape of RSM Roy Mathews. Roy's first task appears to have been to make preparation for the Old Boys' Reunion that was to follow only a few weeks later in October.

September 1995 finally brought to an end the career of yet another old boy, in the shape of Maj (Ret'd) Stan Rycroft. Joining up as a member of 45A, Stan had completed *"fifty years of dedicated service to REME"*, the first forty in uniform, then most recently as a lecturer on Health & Safety matters at the School of Equipment Support SES(A). Just prior to his departure, Stan's achievements were recognised by the award of a DGES(A) Commendation.

Gates and gardens

As part of the seemingly interminable restructuring and inevitable downsizing, the rank of the Commandant's appointment was now to be reduced to Lt Col, with Col Mike Dorward himself 'moving sideways' to take command at SEAE. Before his departure, he was able to report that the old College (or should we again say School?) Gates had now been hung on pillars at the original camp entrance in Sheerlands Road. A 'Memorial Garden' had also been constructed, on the site of the old Rowcroft Guardroom and Church of England Chapel. Thus it was that, at their Reunion in October 1995, the old boys were able to proudly march through those gates and hold a dedication 'Drumhead' service in front of the freshly planted garden. It is reassuring to report that a large contingent of some 250 old boys attended that Reunion, with a complement of around 175 sitting down to dinner on the Saturday evening.

(Further details regarding the Memorial Garden can be found in a separate annex to this chapter.)

It is fitting here that mention is made of an article in the next *OBAN*, describing that 1995 OBA Reunion. As has since become the custom, an ex-boy from an intake of fifty years previous was 'invited' to write it. *(There is no truth in the story that anyone failing to respond positively to such an invitation is then dumped in a static water-tank! Ed.)* The ex-boy on this particular occasion was none other than 'Mac' McNally (45A), son of the old RSM so fondly remembered by all the boys who served here during his fifteen-year tenure.

Fred Ford (39A) later wrote that it must have been a bit more difficult for Mac than the other lads, being an apprentice under the very eyes of his own Dad – and the RSM too! One big advantage however would be that he never felt homesick. As Fred put it, *"many of us frequently sobbed under the blankets at night"*. Mac went on to write that the year 1995, as well as being recalled on behalf of his intake, had also been *"particularly poignant, with the fiftieth anniversaries of VE and VJ Days"*.

Mac was both surprised and delighted that he actually found his way to the Reunion, now being held at the original site of the old School. He thought that, fifty years on, it was most appropriate that *"things had turned full circle"*. He went on, *"Down the slope, past the old stables and cabbage patch, memories flooding back of Ben Cook, the old shire horse Gilbert being given our cake and bucket of tea at break time"*. What made the Reunion very special for Mac were the dozens of old boys who came up with their humourous stories and fondly-held memories of both his mother and father. His Mum had always told him that she had never been short of partners at a REME dance, since there was always someone eager to show how well

they had benefited from her teaching.

That article by Mac also brought some fond memories back to mind for Allan Tucker, of intake 39B. Allan recalled that he must have been one of Mrs Ada McNally's first dancing partners, courtesy of the RSM himself. As Allan recalls the event, it was the very first dance to be held in the Gymnasium and he (Allan) had been detailed to act as the Master of Ceremonies (MC). 'Bandy' Nel had issued his instructions, but it was the RSM who told Allan that it was customary for the MC to be *"first on the floor"*. Protesting that he couldn't dance only brought this smiling response from the RSM – *"Mrs McNally, take care of this will you?"* Which, of course, she proceeded to do, nimble of foot and with great aplomb!

I've missed the bus!

Also attending that 1995 Reunion was Fred Ford of 39A, who struggled to come to terms with the changes to the Rowcroft vista that had taken place since his day. He looked in vain for the *"double-decker red buses"*, picking up apprentice boys just up the road from the Camp gates for their trips to Reading. Fred found it ironical that the Memorial Garden should stand on the site of his 'fall from grace', having once served seven days detention in the Guardroom under the baleful watch of Sgt 'Grockle' Hotchkiss, due to his third smoking offence. And he still finds it unfathomable that a grown man could spend Saturday and Sunday afternoons creeping around the ablutions in gym shoes, looking for the telltale signs of blue smoke drifting either under or over the toilet doors!

Another 39A apprentice, Alastair 'Geordie' Hall, also made it back to Arborfield for that 1995 Reunion. Although it had by now been long demolished, Geordie could still close his eyes and visualise the old Camp Hall (or Gymnasium, or Cinema, depending upon your individual preference!), where he had delighted in the black and white film-shows of those days, playing to *"sell-out audiences"*. One lesson that had been well learned by Geordie was that it was far better to attend Church service on a Sunday morning than to come face to face with the mountain of spuds to be peeled for that day's dinner!

At the age of seventy-plus, Geordie was still able to recall the three rounds that he went with 'Champ' Chamberlain, the Rocky Marciano of his day, and to call to mind the stamina that they both must have had.

Col Dorward gives the College Key to Lt Col Mount

at the end of Winter term 1996. In the interests of energy conservation, it was hoped that the last one to leave would switch off the lights and heating!

(An article commemorating the closure of Vehicle Wing is included as a separate annex at the end of this chapter.)

Life still goes on

Despite all the 'chopping and changing' in the air, life still went on pretty much as normal, as members of 95A were soon to find out on their EL training. One group was up in North Wales at Capel Curig, while other apprentices were at Crickhowell in the South. A sign outside the northern campsite read *"All water must be boiled before drinking"* – but this hardly applied to the copious amounts of water swallowed while the boys carried out their caving and canoeing activities! This was all part of the overall fun, which also included hill walking, rock climbing and abseiling at both locations. Some warm sunny weather – most unusual for Wales! – at Crickhowell gave rise to a fair amount of sunburn, with many PS members taking on the appearance of well-cooked lobsters. Meanwhile at Capel Curig, came what the lads referred to as *"the white stuff"* – a hard night's snow providing a good depth of twelve inches! But both parties were to arrive back at Arborfield having immensely enjoyed the challenge.

But he is not too certain of another event that may or may not have taken place. As he put it many years later, *"Did Sir Malcolm Campbell come and relate to us of his world speed attempts?"* Having attended that Reunion, he remarked upon the fact that *"the old camaraderie was still there and that the unique bond between us had survived"*. And so say all of us.

Dudley Martin, proudly displaying his 'H38' identification tag, also enjoyed that Reunion. He found the dinner *"tremendous – a far cry from the 'armoured cars', lardy cakes, kippers and stodgy duff"* that had been served up at Hilsea in 1938, although he hastened to add that it *"did us no harm at all"*. (Dudley did have to explain afterwards that the 'armoured cars' he mentioned had been suitably disguised as meat pasties!) He was absolutely delighted to meet up once again with old friend Alan 'Paddy' Loftus, who had taught him so much about the gear changing and air-intake controls on the motorcycle. He added that Alan *"did not look a day older"*!

Along with the plan for apprentices to carry out their trade training outside the College, came the inevitable final phase of existence for Vehicle Wing. Originally it had planned to move to a shiny new building in Rowcroft, but the Wing now found itself scattered across a number of buildings at Hazebrouck. Even this was, of course, 'temporary', since the Wing was now destined to close its doors for the last time

Lt Gen Sam Cowan CBE, the Inspector General Training (IGT) visited PMC in September 1995. His 'three-star' status counted towards the total of thirty-three 'stars' for VIP visits that year. Thankfully his visit went well, as he was the very General who would have such a big part in deciding the future of the College. The following month, the Commandant said his farewell as he departed for SEAE. He wasn't allowed to go quietly however, being challenged to cross the only-partially finished footbridge that joined Rowcroft and Hazebrouck. Showing off his remarkable EL skills, Colonel Mike managed to complete the course but admitted that, to use his own phrase, his *"abseil into SEAE territory was something less than glamorous"*.

Following Col Mike Dorward's departure,

command of the College was, for a short term, put into the capable hands of its Deputy Commandant, Lt Col Bob Mount CEng, MRAeS, MIMgt. Lt Col Mount 'picked up his quill' to continue the tradition of providing his one and only introductory article for the spring 1996 edition of *The Arborfield Apprentice*. He was able to announce that intake 95C had arrived with a strength of 165 prospective apprentices, the largest 'J' Coy in College history.

(A brief appreciation of Mike Dorward's career and term as Commandant is attached as a separate annex to this chapter.)

That same College magazine saw the publication of an article by RSM Matthews – much to his surprise! He described his pride in being the first REME soldier to fill this post and was at great pains to explain the difference between the two terms, 'Sergeant Major' and 'RSM'. The former term had become the normal way of referring to the long line of previous incumbents, but REME had traditionally referred to this rank as 'RSM' – so 'RSM' it was now going to be. Roy went on to say that any further discussions on this point could be made by still calling him 'Sergeant Major' – as long as the obligatory bottle of port was carried by the offender!

John Andrusiak, previously mentioned as a new apprentice in the 70B intake, had more recently been reading his latest copy of *OBAN* during 1995. What staggered him was the fact that, for so many ex-boys, of twenty or more year's seniority to him, the College (or School) still remained absolutely intact in their memories. He wrote to *OBAN Issue 8* himself with these words: *"It is almost as if a place, which no longer exists, is still there in all our minds as a form of virtual reality"*. *(I am confident that most ex-boys would not disagree with that! Ed.)*

Get the right message across

During November that year, the College conducted an *'Apprentice Evaluation Survey on Training'*, with all apprentices except those of 95C, who were still in their first term, asked to take part. The survey showed that a sizeable minority, about one third, had not originally had REME as their first choice, while almost a quarter had failed to be allocated to their first choice of trade. These facts did not show the Army recruiting process in a good light. Sizeable minorities were not fully aware

of either the REME trade structure, the career structure, nor even what was required of them to reach Artificer rank. Even fewer apprentices, almost half of those surveyed, were unaware of the opportunities and their potential for commissioning. It was recommended that these failings should be vigorously addressed in the future.

Mid-November brought a shock to the system for those apprentices sent off to Winterbourne Gunner, just outside of Salisbury. The aim of their weekend training was to enhance their skills and add to their almost non-existent knowledge of NBC warfare. As the coach approached the Training Centre, the

My trousers are a little short Mum,
as I've grown so much since I came here.

adrenaline was pumping and morale was high. But the sub-zero temperature and the sight of their tented homes for the next two nights brought a chill to their spines. The following morning was a time for learning in the classroom, before the inevitable 'practical' side saw the apprentices herded into the gas chamber! It was only for five minutes but it was long enough for most. They were glad to get onto the coach back to Arborfield, their brains swimming with such phrases as 'Immediate Action Drills', 'Decontamination', 'NBC First Aid' and the use of 'Combo Pens'.

It was also in November that an ex-boy from 55A, Dave Levitt, was on holiday in Thailand. He visited a cemetery at Kanchanaburi, close to the site of the world-famous 'Bridge on the River Kwai'. Dave paused a while to take some photographs. There were graves denoting the last resting-place of thousands, from Britain, Australia, Holland and America. Dave found the graves of several REME personnel, which brought memories of his own father. The elder Mr Levitt had also been a prisoner there, had survived the ordeal, only to die afterwards as a result of ill health, due to the torture that had been inflicted upon him.

A letter dated November 17th gave thanks to PMC for allowing a 'weekend pass' to A/T Townsend of Hazebrouck Company ('H' Coy). As the only 'serving' member of the Royal British Legion branch at Teynham and Lynsted (near Sittingbourne in Kent), it had meant a great deal to the other Legion members to have had him 'on display' at their annual Remembrance Sunday parade. He had borne the *"close scrutiny and inspection"* of the 'old soldiers' with good humour and re-assured them that, in his own humble opinion

Opening of the Princess Marina Hall by DGES(A)

at least, the standards within the services were as high as ever.

November also saw *"the end of an era"*, with the formal closure of REME training at Middle Wallop, with the SAE now closed to become part of the new SEAE. SAE itself had only been formed since 1988, when it took over what had previously been the AETW. REME involvement in Army aviation had first started in 1957, when it took over certain responsibilities from the RAF. The famous light blue beret had been introduced in 1958, to assist in making pilots, ground crew and technical support into a close-knit team. SEAE (Air Systems Branch) would now continue to produce the required future tradesmen in accommodation vacated by PMC.

There's a first time for most things

The 'PoP' that took place in December 1995 was memorable for a number of 'firsts'. It was the first parade undertaken by apprentices at Rowcroft Barracks for seventeen years and the first time that 'J' Coy had been on parade with their seniors. It was the first time that a female A/T Sgt had been on parade; the first time that a Lt Col would attend the parade as Commandant; the first ever REME RSM was 'in charge'; and the first-ever female member of the Band was on parade. Sadly, there was also one major downside to all that, in the fact that it was also the very last time that an Apprentices' Band would play on such a parade.

The programme for that 'PoP' gave a brief history of the College Bands. A 'Fife and Drum Band' had been formed in 1941 and, over the years, had evolved into 'The Corps of Drums', 'The Pipes' and 'The Brass Band', all composed of volunteer apprentices, giving up much of their spare time in pursuit of this rewarding musical hobby. Up to only a few years previously, the combined Bands had totalled some sixty-five members but, sadly, as College numbers fell, so also did the number of Bandsmen. As the programme concluded, *"the Band as you see it today is performing for the last time"*.

On December 14th 1995, the entrance to College HQ was formally opened at a brief ceremony. After the last fifty years of peace between the two countries, it was perhaps fitting that a visiting senior officer of the Bundeswehr (German Army), Brigade-General Bernd, was invited to 'cut the ribbon'. He performed this traditional task and then joined in a toast with a glass of champagne. Also present on the day was the Commander RTG, Brig J B Palmer.

Over the Christmas and New Year's break leading into 1996, yet another diving expedition, split up into two separate one-week sessions, was undertaken by Arborfield apprentices of the Sub-Aqua Club, this one at Hurghada, an 'up and coming' diving resort on the west coast of the Red Sea. The boys were more than happy to leave behind the cold and damp of the UK season, and instead to delight in the different culture and stifling heat of distant Egypt.

Hurghada proved a strange mix of large, modern Western-style hotels along with an 'Indiana Jones' type of market town. The crime rate was around zero level, but the boys quickly decided that local styles of punishment would not suit them back in the depths of Arborfield! The diving proved to be exquisite, with an amazing variety of reefs, coral pillars and even a coral garden, all at depths of only five to fifteen metres and in brilliant visibility.

Princess Marina Hall opens

The New Year of 1996 saw the opening of 'Princess Marina Hall', the first new building to have been erected in Rowcroft Barracks since the completion of what had then been the REME Depot. It was a superb building that housed the MEW, with a magnificent library and high-tech lecture theatre, and enabled the College to maintain its links with the name of the Princess. The library complex includes IT systems and areas for private study. The official opening ceremony, held on February 2nd, was performed by Maj Gen P J G Corp, DGES(A), following a short service and the 'blessing' by the Padre, the Reverend Paul Thompson. The VIPs of the opening party were 'piped aboard' on their approach, by the College Pipe-Major, SSgt M J Elder of the Black Watch and, afterwards, the ceremony was concluded by a formal luncheon in Hazebrouck Officer's Mess.

1996 also brought inevitable change on the musical front – the College Band had finally lost its 'Brass element'. A sad thing to happen, because each element of the combined Band - Brass, Pipes and Corp of Drums - had always magnificently supported each other, when one group or the other found it did not have sufficient numbers. With a lot of hard work and practice, a new format, composed of just eight pipers and eight drummers, was eventually put together. It

took much 'heart and soul' to give up so much spare time, but these sixteen young apprentices were to be the last in a long line of tradition.

As a sign of the difficult times that the College, indeed the Army, was living through, the following message appeared in the national press, under the heading 'Army about-turn on new recruits':

> "Junior leaders courses are to be re-instated, Apprentices' Colleges revitalised and vocational training offered to recruits, as part of an overhaul of Army recruiting to solve the manpower shortage. Measures being considered include a £100 bonus or a weekend's leave for every friend that soldiers persuade to join up. The Army is also considering the use of NVQs as a way of proving an individual's worth to future employers. A plan to close High Street Recruitment Centres, and move their role to Job Centres, may also be scrapped".

On February 5th, PMC held a 'civilian day' in aid of charity. The theme of this was that both apprentices and members of staff each paid the sum of £1 for the 'privilege' of wearing civilian clothing for the entire day. One of the Commandant's last official duties was the pleasant one of handing over a cheque for £364 to the 'Rotary Convoy of Hope', a charity associated with the Prince's Trust. The money was to be used to assist in the next mission to Croatia, to provide medical aid, food and life saving equipment to the unfortunate victims of that country's civil war.

In March, another Triangular Games competition was held, at the RE Camp of Gibraltar Barracks in Aldershot. Apart from the RE and REME teams, the other Corps represented were the Royal Logistics Corps (RLC) and R Sigs, so perhaps it should have been more correctly called the 'Quadrangular Games'. With the RE having held the trophy for the previous two years, the Arborfield team were determined to 'bring it back home'. The five main sports of the event were Basketball, Football, Hockey, Rugby and Volleyball and, on the opening day, PMC was able to win through to the Finals of each of these. On the following day, three of those five Finals were won. With the amalgamation of all apprentices' training now firmly in sight, this would probably be the last ever sports event of its kind.

Under new management

On April 1st 1996, the RTG, comprising SEAE, SEME Bordon, the School of Equipment Support – or SES(A) - and, of course, PMC, came under the control of the newly formed Defence Agency, known as the Army Individual Training Organisation (AITO). This was aimed at providing all of the Army's training requirements. As part of the new organisation's official launch the following month, the Minister for the Armed Forces paid an official visit, meeting both students and instructors here at Arborfield, from both SEAE and the College. The stated mission of the RTG was now to *"provide and deliver apprentice, technical, management and military training for the Group's internal and external customers, to agreed standards, in the most cost effective manner"*.

At a ceremony held on April 25th, Maj Gen P J G Corp, the DGES(A), unveiled a plaque to formally open the new Aircraft Hangar at SEAE. At the accompanying parade, two companies wore the traditional dark blue berets of REME personnel, while the remaining two wore the light blue versions. The companies actually swapped positions during the parade, to signify the merging of the two previous schools. Col Mike Dorward was 'on parade', clearly proud of his new command.

Resources were *"stretched to the limit"* in Rowcroft during April. A total of five intakes of apprentices, covering the period from May 1994 to December 1995, were all due to pass out and move on to further training. Planning had clearly started as early as possible but, for the two parades of April 13th and 19th; there were still many last-minute preparations for the arrival of parents and guests.

The first 'PoP' combined the final intake (95A) of the two-year apprentices, and 95B, which was the first of the new eight-month intakes, but who had spent one year at the College as a transition measure, along with 95C, the first intake that had completed just eight-months here. The second parade consisted of the *"old stalwarts"* of both 94B and 94C, less their VM members, who weren't due to pass out until later that year.

Both of the above parades saw very high standards of drill and turnout, under the eagle-eyed supervision of RSM Roy Matthews and ably led by A/T RSM Simpson. The College Pipes and Drums proudly played on both of these splendid occasions and were privileged to accompany the REME Band for the second parade. With so many changes going on, however, it was difficult to predict any sort of 'steady period' lying ahead for the College. The forthcoming 'PoP' for instance, due to be held in August 1996, would be the last of those for REME apprentices alone, as the College looked forward to welcoming those newcomers from the R Sigs in September. In future, two new grades of provisional tradesmen would be added to those passing out from the College, namely Tels Techs and Tels Operators, on the first stage of their careers with the R Sigs.

The programme for those April parades gave news that, despite the difficulties imposed by the short eight-month course, the College's firm intention was to retain both 'The Pipes' and 'Corps of Drums'. They had always been an integral part of the College heritage and both remained extremely popular with current apprentices.

Chips with everything!

On April 26th, that week's edition of the magazine *Electronics Weekly* published a glowing report on the progress being made by the President and Chief Executive Officer (CEO) of the *Altera Corporation*, one of America's fastest growing semi-conductor 'chip' manufacturers. *(The chips, to give them their full name, were 'programmable logic modules'. Ed.)* The man in question just happened to be Rodney Smith, and it was fitting that the article came out in 1996, as this was the fortieth anniversary of Rodney's entry into Arborfield as a member of intake 56B.

Arriving here from his hometown of Oldham, Lancashire, and then going on to train as a Radar Tech, Rodney became one of the first apprentices to attend Reading Technical College as part of his ONC (Electrical Engineering) Course. At the end of his three-years at what was then the AAS, Rodney gained the CI's Cup for Technical and Educational Ability. Leaving the Army at the nine-year point in 1967, Rodney had moved out to the US in the early Seventies and helped found the *Altera Corporation* at San Jose, in California's 'Silicon Valley', during the Eighties.

Editor of this history, Pete Gripton, was also one of those who studied for his ONC at that time, during an eighteen-month period that followed 56B's passing out in the summer of 1959. Apart from the sense of freedom encountered by attending 'Reading Tech', surrounded by civilians, some of whom were quite pretty young ladies, there was also the subject of food! Having caught the bus into Reading in the morning, first port of call was the *'Joe Lyons'* teashop in Broad Street for a bacon and egg breakfast. The lunch-hour at the College gave the opportunity to nip into town and enjoy a pie and a pint at one of the myriad of hostelries along the way.

But, best remembered of all, were the 'late meals' on offer at 3 Battalion cookhouse in the evening. Special dispensation had been given for a late 'dinner' to be laid on for the small party of boys arriving back from their 'studies'. With the helpful attitude of the duty cook, who was usually a LCpl from the Pioneer Corps who answered to the name 'Chunky', the boys in fact had great fun cooking their own supper. This would consist of plates full of sausages, bacon, eggs, beans and the inevitable chips – the works, in fact. This would be washed down with pints of ice-cold milk, drained off from the churn in the massive walk-in refrigerator. Happy days!

A final grounding

Aircraft Wing closed its doors for the last time on April 30th 1996. It had always been the most 'junior' Wing in the College, having originally formed in what had been 'the School', as a part of the Mechanical Wing back in 1963. It broke away as a separate entity in May 1965 and co-located, with the rest of the College, to Hazebrouck in September 1985. Unfortunately their planned accommodation at that time 'went missing' and the Wing had instead been dispersed over four seperate buildings. However, the staff was still able to look back proudly to those days when the Wing had provided a 'full house', in the shape of the apprentice RSM and all four A/T CSMs. A week later, the 'handover' from PMC to SEAE was commemorated by the presentation of an aircraft propeller to Lt Col Cameron, the CI of SEAE.

Electronics Wing was also in 'shut-down' mode, even though it had only recently had to move to a new home during the previous autumn term. It was generally agreed as being a rather sad time, since electronics had been taught at the College (or School in its day) ever since staff member Ron Taylor of 45A had been in short trousers. In those days, of course, electrons were still being handled by glass-envelope vacuum valves, rather than by the new-fangled transistors. As the time

for closure drew ever nearer, members of staff were investing heavily in the National Lottery, hopefully waiting for Mystic Meg to announce that *"a bunch of ageing lecturers are about to win the Big One"*.

Sadly, many old customs and occasions within the College were also coming to a gradual and grudging halt. On April 4th 1996, for example, the final A/T Sgts' Mess Dinner was held, another casualty of the 'two-terms only' foundation course. There would not be sufficient A/T Sergeants available in the future to make this a worthwhile event. The end of the current term would also see the very last of a long line of A/T RSMs pass out of the College. For the reasons mentioned, adult RSM Roy Matthews had decided that the Mess Dinner would be allowed to take place within the confines of the main Sergeants' Mess, to try and make the occasion as memorable a one as possible. Just ask any of those who attended, and they are sure to tell you that the aim was definitely achieved.

It was intake 94B that was to leave Arborfield with the no doubt unwanted description as *"The last complete intake to serve the full apprenticeship at PMC"*. It was thus fitting that one of their officers, Capt A K Browne, should say a few words about them in the College magazine. He described them as *"relaxed, quietly confident and unusually mature"*. Their great strength lay in unit integrity and, at the end of the day, they had become true comrades and friends, a most important part of soldiering.

Army Apprentices' College – Part 2!

Lt Col Bob Mount's short tenure ended at half term, when he took an appointment at the neighbouring SES(A). He had served at PMC for three years in total, although his actual command of the College was regrettably short. Fortunately, he had a *"sunshine break in Cyprus"* as part of the package deal! Lt Col N Moore MBE, BSc was the new CO – yes, even the old and well-renowned appointment of 'Commandant' had now sadly disappeared too.

Yet another of those seemingly endless reviews, this one into the whole business of Army apprentices' training, had been carried out, with its final decision recommending that the centralisation of all such training should now be undertaken on a combined basis here at Arborfield. The official statement was given in the House of Commons, by the Minister for Armed Forces, on April 16th. Before his final departure, Lt Col

Mount announced the news to College staff, saying that *"Whilst it is sad that apprentices' training will cease outside Arborfield, I am sure you will all be pleased that the future here at PMC is now assured"*. His final departure through the College gates was led by his *"young officers"*, as he was chauffeured away in a vintage automobile.

Thus it was that in May 1996, many Royal Signals staff arrived, in readiness for the arrival of their first apprentice intake in the following September. At the same time, the title was to be changed back to the old familiar 'Army Apprentices' College'. It was also decided that the 'new' College blazer badge would be based upon that one so well remembered and loved by many earlier generations of apprentices; but with the word 'School' deleted and replaced by that of 'College'. Driving into Rowcroft one day, Larry Le Var was delighted to see that a very large facsimile of that same 'old school' badge was now adorning the 'welcome' sign to the new College. Each individual apprentice however, on arrival at the College, would now wear the cap-badge of his or her parent Corps.

During that same month of May, great foresight was shown, by the setting up of a 'Heritage Action Team', whose terms of reference were stated thus:

"With the closure of the remaining apprentices' training units, Arborfield will become the focus for apprentices both past and present. If we are to continue to turn out high calibre young men and women, they must have a clear vision of the origins of their parent Corps and the history of apprentices' training; it is all part of the undefinable 'apprentice ethos'. Some of this can be achieved by presenting apprentices with clear examples of the past achievements of both their Corps and other apprentices/ apprentices' colleges; by ensuring that they are aware of their heritage as both apprentices and soldiers."

The Team was directed **not** to teach a formal Corps history *per se*. Instead, it was to concentrate on such disparate subjects as gates, guardrooms, museum items, pictures and displays, prizes and awards, written archives and the almost spiritual relationship that had always existed between the College and its Old Boys' Association.

New horizons

Reorganisation brought new aims, and these were clearly laid out by the Course Development Team. The main aim, that of the 'Army Apprentices' Scheme', was *"to produce technicians and tradesmen for the Regular Army, who have begun the preparation necessary to reach Senior NCO and WO rank"*. The College's stated aim was *"to develop, in young men and women, the military knowledge and education to prepare them for a successful career, as potential leaders and managers, in specific technical trades for the RE, R Sigs, RLC and REME."* Other declared aims covered the individual subjects of Military Training, Leadership and Initiative Training, and Education.

It must have been staggering news to the serried ranks of old boys, both very old and recently new, that the above objectives were to now be attained in a mere two terms of fourteen weeks each, a total training time of only twenty-eight weeks. Due to the shortened period of time that an apprentice would now spend at the College, an even greater emphasis was now to be placed upon the two separate training modules of Leadership and EL.

The first module would concentrate upon the principles of, approach to and styles of leadership, with such confidence-building exercises as map reading and route planning, night navigation and competitive physical tasks. The latter module aimed to develop the individual apprentice's character, improve his (or her) personal organisation, self-confidence and determination, during the official pursuits of hill walking, rock climbing, canoeing and caving.

Technical Education was now underpinned by three requirements: to meet the needs of the contributing Corps; to facilitate success in Phase 2 (adult school) training; and, finally, to provide a tangible qualification linked to the MA Scheme. The core skills to be taught included communication, information technology, working with others and problem solving. Monday evenings were designated to the familiar pursuits of 'Hobbies', which included the following activities: Badminton, Band, Canoeing, Cycling, Go-karting, Karate, Motorcycling, Sub-aqua, Weight training and War Games. Weekend activities were to be closely monitored and supervised, and required to include such items as discussion groups, command tasks, sports and community service.

Old Boys in far-off places

In the May edition of *The Craftsman* magazine, a letter was published, reinforcing the good news about the growing strength and popularity of the 'BSXBA', which had been set up, halfway around the world, in NZ. This Association encompasses the majority of ex-boys from RAOC/REME who have now settled in that far-off country, and includes apprentices from both Arborfield and Chepstow. Long may they survive and prosper.

A great honour came the way of A/T David 'Dai' Davies on May 25th of 1996, when he was selected to represent his country at Rugby (the sport, not the town!) in an Under-19 match against Portugal. Hailing from Pencoed, near Bridgend, Dai had begun his apprenticeship in September 1994 and was due to pass out as a VM in August. When asked how he felt about his selection, he simply replied, *"Excellent, Rugby is my life". (Look out Dai, there may be a few ASMs around who will dispute that claim! Ed.)*

That same month saw what could be possibly the last time that the College would enter a team for the annual Ten Tors event on Dartmoor. Restructuring of the College meant that the College would now be hard pressed to participate in future. College teams had enthusiastically entered this event ever since 1964, a proud tradition which now sadly appeared to have come to an end. Starting at 07.00 hours on a Saturday, the set route was to be completed by 17.00 hours on the Sunday. It was cool and dry, with not too much wind, when the lads set off, but after that it was all downhill – or *not* downhill, if you get my meaning!

Around midday, the wind picked up and some horizontal rain began to make for uncomfortable conditions. The restless night that followed was spent trying to contain all the leaks that appeared in their tents. Foul weather then continued to plague the event, with the high points of the moor at times under six inches of snow, winds gusting to sixty miles per hour and a chill factor considerably below zero – and all this in the 'merry month of May'! Cancellation was inevitably the only option - perhaps an omen that, for Arborfield at least, this was a good time to draw down the curtain after all.

Over the weekend of 13th / 14th July 1996, with the kind permission of RSM Roy Matthews, the Sergeants' Mess hosted an 'unofficial' reunion for intake 56B, on the fortieth anniversary of them having come together.

Admittedly the whole intake did not turn up, but those who did, along with their wives, enjoyed a thoroughly good trawl through the old memory banks. This was helped along by the photo-album brought along by Pete Gripton, who had put together a priceless collection of photos, all of which appertain to his intake. Dinner in the Mess, with Roy and his wife as guests, was followed by – well, you know what! – and then a splendid 'full English' the next morning. (It's only a rumour, but Norman Dewdney is believed to have taken home a supply of cold fried bread from the breakfast table – just like the old days!)

On July 29th, a party of four Burnham Lecturers paid a 'recce' visit to the College, in preparation for their subsequent 'posting' to Arborfield as part of the R Sigs contingent. A 'thank you' letter was duly received from this group of 'refugees', who both appreciated their whistle-stop tour and looked forward to their subsequent arrival here the following September.

The *MS Challenge* was taken up once again in July, based this time at Capel Curig, deep in the heart of Snowdonia. Accommodation was provided by ten-man tents, erected by the local TA unit. The College team was very keen to beat the record time of one hour forty-eight minutes set by a RE team of 5/9 Commando Sqn. Gritting their teeth, and sustained by a supply of *Mars Bars*, to help them *"work, rest and play"*, the team battled through bogs and across streams, sometimes chest deep in the icy water. Their passenger, a brave young lady called Alison, came very close to going for an unintended swim, but sportingly didn't complain too much. As the team approached the end of the course, they crossed the final stile and

For over 60 years Arborfield has continued to consistently produce the smartest soldier tradesmen!

Helping with the 'Feed the Children' campaign

sprinted the last twenty metres. One hour forty-seven minutes – the fastest time of the weekend and in fact the fastest time ever!

Harrogate's final parade

August 2nd brought the final graduation parade at the College in Harrogate, when seventy-five apprentice tradesmen of 94C marched into the history books as its last intake. The intakes for 1995 were going to train at Blandford in Dorset, leaving the future of the Yorkshire-based site still in a state of uncertainty. A forty-seven year legacy of apprentices' training had come to completion.

An article appearing in *The Craftsman* magazine of August 1996 paid due tribute to the history of firstly the School and secondly the College, in producing some outstanding sportsmen in all fields. Except that now, the term 'sportswomen' was definitely to be added. A/T LCpl Storme Alexander – what a splendid name! – had excelled at the game of basketball, representing not only the College, but also the Army and Combined Services, in their Ladies' teams. As well as her chosen sport, Storme also enjoyed athletics, especially sprinting. Despite her extraordinary achievements so far, she was still aiming high and dreaming of playing for England.

In the programme for the August 16th 'PoP', a page appeared for the first time stressing the importance of gaining 'Civilian Trade Qualifications'. It stated that every young person entering PMC on an apprenticeship had the opportunity to obtain a nationally recognised trade qualification. Indeed, it was one of the pillars

around which their training would revolve. Over ninety percent of all apprentices go on to obtain a civilian qualification, many of them with Credits and Distinctions. Not only fitting in with their Army careers, these would prove a valuable asset upon their eventual return to civilian life and employment.

Old comrades at work

That summer's edition of *The Arborfield Apprentice* saw Lt Col Nigel Moore reflecting upon his first few months in charge of the College. The thing that struck him most forcefully was the *"immense change"* that PMC had endured over its recent history. As little as eighteen months previously, its future had been unsure, with a two-year apprenticeship on a split site and a massive building programme in the offing. Six months later the whole course was down to a mere two terms and there seemed to be no money available beyond 1998. If anyone had asked the CO or his predecessors whether the College could possibly survive those levels of change, the answer would definitely ***not*** have been in the affirmative!

Another article in that magazine gave Owen Nichols the chance to look back a few years. He had joined the PMC staff in January 1987, following some nine years teaching at Reading Technical College. But his first memories of Arborfield dated back to around 1952. He had then been in a party of Chepstow apprentices, sent here to spectate at a prestigious football match. Owen recalls that the coach got lost on its way here and that the 'rent-a-crowd' were consequently late for the game! Whether or not his side won or was beaten, he has no idea. The whole article was a composite one, by members of the MSC Wing, and included two other contributions from ex-apprentices, John Peters (42A) and Keith Evans (45A), both having returned to their roots here at Arborfield after many years of varied service elsewhere.

That summer's issue of *OBAN* gave news of a typical piece of old boy camaraderie. John Sullivan, one of our earliest members from October 1939, had read a letter in the previous *OBAN*, which mentioned the name of Bill Tate from Wrexham. John had obtained Bill's number and called him, to ask if it was possible to pay a visit to Ron Le Rendu (also of 39B), who was currently in hospital in nearby Oswestry. This of course Bill did, taking along a book for Ron to read and cheering him immensely. Bill later sent John an aerial photograph of the old camp.

On October 5th 1996, during that year's Old Boys' Reunion, the CO made a special presentation of a watch to Mrs June Northam, in recognition and gratitude from the AOBA for her services in assisting and organising the membership administration, along with husband John. June and John had also been heavily involved in the production of the *OBAN*, ever since its re-introduction in 1992. June had spent many a long evening typing and re-typing, proof reading, checking grammar and spelling mistakes. (*I know the feeling myself! Ed.*) It is true to say that, without her immense dedication, and along with John's profound enthusiasm, the *OBAN* would certainly not have flourished in the way it does today.

The *OBAN* that followed that Reunion was, as custom now dictated, reported upon by one of the 'fiftieth anniversary' boys, in this case Tony 'Digger' Head of 46A. Upon arrival at Arborfield for that Reunion weekend, Tony had found it hard to understand at first all the talk about a certain 'Jewish' boy – he certainly couldn't remember who it could have been. Even so, all he could hear from his old colleagues was *'Jew member this'* and *'Jew member that'*. It eventually dawned on him that what they were actually saying was *"Do you remember ... ...?"* (*Bring the old hearing aid next time, Tony! Ed.*)

Tony certainly enjoyed the parade, commanded by Maj Robin Cooper, a mere Jeep from 64B, with the standard bearer for the day being Alan 'Algy' Morton of 51B. Tony compared it to the four hours that he and his mates had stood on the Square during 'Monty's' parade in 1946. The present length of time that his 'bunch of oldies' stood to attention, waiting for their increasing girth and decreasing hair to be inspected, seemed like the proverbial *"piece of cake"*. His memory even strayed to that long distant Sunday morning when he had actually eaten his way through eleven plates of porridge for breakfast – his wife still doesn't believe it to this day!

Another whose memory may have 'strayed' a little was Fred Wells of 44A, who had later assisted in that 1954 polio outbreak in Kenya. He had only recently become acquainted with the OBA, through a photo that had been published the previous year (1995) in *Yours* magazine. This had persuaded him to make contact and 'rejoin the ranks'. He was also going to inveigle his elder brother to rejoin too, after all, it was he who had brought Fred to Arborfield from the R Sigs in the first place!

That same month of October saw the threat of even more trial and tribulation, with the whole of Arborfield Garrison now being subjected to a *'Competing for Quality'* (CFQ) feasibility study. Many long-standing Garrison activities were to be examined for exposure to competition, to see whether or not private sector contractors could more efficiently run them. All this would inevitably impinge on aspects of College life, like it or not!

During that month, Arborfield Garrison was (again) invited to take part in the *World's Largest Coffee Morning*, to raise funds towards the Macmillan Nurses Cancer Relief Appeal. Many units, large and small, took part but, as reported later in one of the monthly editions of *The Craftsman*, *"the stars were the Army Apprentices' College"*. Over £400 was raised by the College, in an entertaining variety of ways. These included eating crackers and then blowing up balloons, eating baked beans, with the only available implements being toothpicks, and finally, members of the civilian staff dressing up as collection boxes.

Sad news of a favourite son

Towards the end of October, an article in the *Daily Mail*, by the respected sports journalist Ian Wooldridge, paid tribute to our own Olympic hero, Jim Fox (57B). Jim had been a Sergeant at the time of his sporting triumph, eventually retiring after twenty-six years service in the rank of Captain. He had just recently been elected chairman of the British Modern Pentathlon Association (BMPA), which had fallen on hard times.

Unfortunately, it wasn't only the BMPA that was suffering, as Jim himself had fallen prey to ill health. Some muscle-wasting disease had hit him hard, causing a severe lack of mobility and a forward-leaning gait. But Jim bravely told Ian to publish details of all the 'medical stuff', as he was embarrassed that at meetings in London, people had looked at him with an unwritten question in their eyes – *"How can this guy have got so drunk so early in the day?"* Taking up the challenge on behalf of the BMPA was a brave step indeed, one that deserved to succeed.

On Remembrance Sunday, the College's Princess Alexandra Hall had the honour of being chosen as the venue for the Garrison Parade, which was followed by a wreath-laying service at the Garrison Church of Saint Eligius. The ceremony was accompanied by the

Pipes and Drums of the AAC, with all of Arborfield's disparate units being represented. Following the morning service, the College also provided platoons for a second wreath-laying ceremony, this time at the War Memorial in Arborfield village.

The Norman Fursden Award

In the last issue of *OBAN* for 1996, Lt Col Moore was moved to write about an award that had become a tradition in the College:

> *"The Norman Fursden Award has its roots in the Old Boys' Association Award, which itself goes back to 1981 (as far as I can trace at the moment). The Award was renamed in late 1986 in honour of Norman Fursden, an old boy who left a sum of money to the OBA, to cover the cost of the Award on a recurring basis. The Award was aimed at apprentices who, by their personal endeavour and actions in the eyes of the community, Garrison or the College, enhanced the prestige and reputation of the College.*
>
> *Acts of heroism, voluntary and noteworthy effort by individual apprentices in aid of the local community, Garrison or College, in conjunction with satisfactory endeavour in all aspects of training, would merit a recommendation for this Award."*

The CO was also proud to say that many fine sporting traditions were being upheld. That season had seen success for the College in the Quadrangular Games, where the team had already been in an unassailable position at the end of the first day.

The same issue of *OBAN* included a letter from John Pewsey of 45A vintage, who had been involved in the competition to design that old 'School Badge' of so many years ago. John recalls that he won the vast amount of 'five bob' (25p) for his efforts. In a later copy of the *OBAN*, John was incorrectly mentioned as intake 45B. He says that the error is *"quite understandable, because Chalky (Col White) probably shuddered at the mere mention"* of his (John's) name – and probably *"heartily wished he'd been back-squadded to at least 50A, after he (Chalky) had retired"*!

Having been a keen cross-country runner in his youth, John can also remember a dark secret from his past – he used to 'run' *Woodbines* from the nearby *Robinson Crusoe* shop back to the 'fag barons', once collecting a total of seventy-three days 'jankers' for his many indiscretions. But John's main (who said only?) claim to fame was that he had happily married Molly, daughter of the famous Ben Cook and, at the time of writing, the couple could boast an innings of almost forty-five years not out!

Brian Conway (42A) was amazed to find out from an old comrade, Tug Wilson, that the OBA was still thriving! Since then, he had been catching up on recent copies of the *OBAN* and noted the remarks about a film called *'Ten Feet Tall'* being made around 1963. As Brian had been an instructor here at the time, he was equally amazed that he knew nothing about it. Brian himself had spent the whole of 1995 trying to trace another film called *'Stepping Toes'*, made way back in 1936, which contained scenes of the Dukies' Band. Unfortunately, no progress was made on that film, but Brian did later receive a couple of 'stills' from the film, thanks to the Dukies' own old boys' setup.

December 22nd 1996 saw the passing away of Col Richard 'Dick' Legh, OBE, who had been the last non-REME Commandant at what was then 'the School', between November 1959 and October 1962. He had reached the ripe old age of eighty-five years.

That December saw the final two-year apprentices, those of intake 95A, leave the College. They had studied military skills, military education, leadership, technical studies and vehicle mechanisms. Along the way, they had pursued a wide variety of sports and hobbies, from cycling to football and from go-karting to playing in the Band. But, on Sunday, December 15th, they marched smartly and proudly from Hazebrouck Barracks for the last time, from the end-of-term church service to the gates, with the route lined by their junior colleagues.

That event marked yet another *"end of an era"* as the last of the Hazebrouck accommodation had been finally handed over to SEAE, meaning that the site of Rowcroft Barracks was once again the sole home of apprentices' training in Arborfield. Formal approval had been given to the College's new (or should that be old?) title of 'Army Apprentices' College'. The old REME Officer's School was now transformed into the combined College Maths Department and Military Training Wing. A new Gymnasium was to be built, while the blocks at the top of the Square would be converted back to barrack accommodation. The old gym was to be converted to lecture theatre and church, WRVS facilities were to be expanded and it was hoped that an all-weather floodlit sports area would be constructed.

Under four cap-badges

The fact that the newly designated AAC was eventually to be responsible for the training of apprentices under four different cap-badges brought a fundamental reorganisation of its command structure. It was decided that 'cap-badge integrity' at Company level was the way ahead, signalling the end of a dedicated military training company. Thus it was that, on December 19th 1996, 'J' Coy was disbanded and re-titled 'Carlisle Company', with its new role dedicated to the training of future REME soldiers.

The name 'Carlisle' was chosen, to acknowledge the AAC that had existed at Hadrian's Camp, Carlisle, between 1961 and 1969 and which had been mainly dedicated to training REME tradesmen. The event was celebrated by the holding of a Formation Parade, reviewed by Brig (Ret'd) Kneen, who had the honour of being the last Commandant at Carlisle. His speech served to bridge the discontinuity of the twenty-seven year gap between 1969 and 1996, and gave Carlisle Coy an identity with their predecessors. Also in his speech, the Brigadier identified the qualities required by those apprentices back in the Sixties, which he declared are still relevant today, namely those of *"Courage, Loyalty, Initiative and Determination"*.

The 'PoP' programme of December 20th gave further evidence of the College's changing role. A short article reviewed the history of The Royal Signals, which had formed on June 28th 1920 by separation from the Corps of Royal Engineers. First known as the 'Corps of Signals', it was awarded its 'Royal' status by King George V in August that same year. Its role is to provide Command, Control, Communication and Information systems for Field Force units, HQ, military establishments and Joint Service operations. It also provides the support, co-ordination and technical supervision of all Army communications. The Corps' C-in-C has been Princess Anne, the Princess Royal GCVO since her appointment was approved by The Queen in June 1977.

During that same year of 1996, it was reported that the Army had scaled down its traditionally rigorous basic training, due to the fact that today's young men

(and women of course) are 'not as tough as' their predecessors. The 'sink or swim' attitude of forcing all recruits to meet tough fitness standards straight away was now to be dropped. There must have been many old boys having a quiet chuckle at the thought! Modern recruits are in future to be brought gradually onto a regime of physical exercise, being initially allowed to use 'training shoes' and only given boots when judged ready for them. Just think, one used to wear plimsolls only when on sport or sick parade!

Along with this news came a new style of training for female soldiers. When they were first introduced, little consideration had been given to those physical differences between young men and women. Due to the fact that the female physique is generally slighter than the male counterpart, they had been found to be more prone to injury. A new system of 'Gender Fair Training' was to be introduced, but the College felt that it had already made much progress towards the declared aims of the new policy, so the guidelines were to be immediately implemented as far as practicable.

As that year drew to a close, an old acquaintance was resumed out in Perth, Western Australia, between Pete Gripton and Tony Domoney, both ex-boys of 56B. Having had a brief phone conversation some weeks earlier, while Tony was in England, it transpired that he would shortly be returning 'down under', where he lived but half-a-mile from Pete's Mum! Pete himself was due to arrive in Perth just before Christmas, so a meeting was definitely in order. A great night out was enjoyed, along with their wives, at a local Italian restaurant, over several bottles of the finest Aussie red wine. A long way from home, but the Arborfield spirit was still strong.

Tony was able to explain that his experience in 'the Band', whilst at boys' school had certainly paid off on a personal basis. Wherever he had travelled around the globe, he had always been able to find small bands and orchestras where he could *"ply his trade"* as it were, by joining in as a reasonable accomplished trumpeter. He also recalled having *"worked on some gates"* with another lad, possibly by the name of 'Humphries', who was also something of a long-distance runner. *(These would no doubt have been the Aldershot Garrison Church gates, manufactured in 1958. Ed.)*

Annex to Chapter 14

Incident Report
By Lord Alanbrooke

"I have the honour thus to write, last night on guard I saw a light.
I was outside the brand new MEW, the light inside was ghostly blue.
I did not like the look of it one teeny-weeny little bit!
I found the door was open wide and, cold with fear, I went inside.

The door slammed shut behind my back, my radio hit the wall a smack.
Now trapped and incommunicado, I wished I had a loaded Spandau!
But being skilled at unarmed combat, I braced myself to fight a wombat,
But nothing stirred, no voice was heard, but wait a bit, there's something weird.

The library door is swinging wide, I cannot quite see what's inside.
I lean towards the source of light and shudder at the spooky sight.
The vaulted pride of glazed roof has vanished and, by God, oh struth,
I see a ghostly barrack room, complete with prehistoric gloom!

Four baleful bulbs illuminate some inmates in a gruesome state,
Each soldier thinking it a farce, actually cleaning bits of brass!
The need for this eludes me quite, all my best brass is nice 'stay-brite',
But they must do this 'ere the sun has its Antipodean journey done.

Not only that, but they appear to have to wear all sorts of gear.
You'd probably think that I was fibbing, if I told you it was bits of webbing.
Yet draped around this sombre room, drying in its fetid gloom,
Were braces, gaiters, packs and pouches, painted green with blanco washes.

Just then a smell assailed my nose, of scorched trousers I suppose,
And burning Kiwi, boots and sweat, and sixteen pairs of unwashed feet!
I backed out slowly to the night but, on my way, I caught a sight
Of a picture on the wall, which to me explained it all.

The brand-new MEW is built just where the huts of old 'D' Coy appear.
The library thus bestrides the site where grisly tales might well you fright.
The moral then is clear to us – when out on guard, don't make a fuss.
Just walk right past the brand-new MEW, for fear these spirits you may view!"

(Lord Alanbrooke was formerly Captain the Hon V Brooke RA, 2I/C of 'D' Company during 1969 to 1972 – this being the period that 'D' Company occupied the spider at the bottom of the Square. The 'brand-new MEW' is the Military Education Wing. Ed.)

The Planting of the Memorial Garden

On September 20th 1995, the Memorial Garden was planted out on the site of the old guardroom at Rowcroft Barracks, to commemorate all past apprentices who had graduated into the adult Army.

Carol Crail of Craimore Garden Designs provided the horticultural intelligence in the project. She planned, selected and bought some 150 plants and, with the very able assistance of her father John Moir (39B) and John Northam (47A), set to with a will.

Some dubious relics (bits of plumbing, some red-painted and blue-tiled bricks) were excavated by John Moir, while digging holes for the trees to be sited at the rear corners.

It was a treat to see our esteemed Membership Secretary in his shirt sleeves, diggin' away, certainly with a lot more enthusiasm than he would have done some 50 years ago as an A/T. I think the occasion must have carried him back to the old days, as he was observed at one stage dressing the *Hebe Buxifolia* shrubs by the right, across the centre of the plot!

A ceremonial tree planting was kindly carried out by the AOBA Secretary, Lt Col (Ret'd) M W Le Var.

A plan of the garden has been supplied to the Corps Museum, detailing the names of the plants, for anyone interested.

In conclusion, I have to say that I felt quite guilty just standing there 'skiving' all morning, taking the photographs. It gave me plenty of time to reflect upon all the activities that must have taken place on the site over the years.

Brian Hornsey (54A)

(The above article was published in the OBAN, issued autumn/winter 1995.)

Colonel M C Dorward MBE

Michael Charles Dorward 23744520 joined the Army Apprentices School, Arborfield, on 13th January 1960, having enlisted the previous day. Following recruit training, he joined 'B' Company to begin training as an Electronic Technician.

A studious chap, he excelled in Maths. However, despite achieving A/T Sergeant rank with 'exemplary' conduct, his leadership was considered to be only 'adequate'. Although not a superstar at sport, he represented his Company at soccer and shooting, and gained the Duke of Edinburgh Gold Award.

The changes wrought on him by his apprentice training can be judged by the fact that, between July 1960 and November 1962, he gained an inch in height to six foot two inches and put on seventeen and a half pounds, to a mighty weight of thirteen stones and one pound!

In December 1962, he transferred to the School of Electronic Engineering, to complete his training as a Radar Technician. For some reason, he did not at that time receive an Army Form C7013 (Certificate of Apprentice Training). When this error was discovered in 1994, the Army Board wisely ordered him to return to the (now) College as Commandant, in order to complete his apprenticeship.

Thanks to the unstinting support of his dear wife, Mary, Colonel Mike has finally passed out of the College, and this dinner marks that achievement. We thank them both for all they have done for the College over the past years and wish them the best of luck for the future. ON! ON!

(The above appreciation was published in the programme for the Ladies' Dinner Night, held at the Hazebrouk Officers' Mess on Friday 13th October 1995.)

My first impressions of Army Life by A/T Hudson

Well, if first impressions were anything to go by, I think I would have gone home on the third day! No longer was I being pampered and fussed over by parents, but instead I was being screamed at by Corporals who I'd only known for a few days.

I had to say 'goodbye' to jeans and baggy jumpers and dress identically to everybody else. Our uniforms had to be immaculately ironed because we were inspected every day. The first few weeks, I thought everyone in the Army was totally weird, they got up at 06.00 hours, marched everywhere around Camp and did everything to perfection.

I had been used to rising at 09.30, with a lazy swagger, rather than a fast walk or march. After a while at the College, I noticed how proud everybody was, of where they were and of what they were doing, so it began to rub off.

Physical training was what I was dreading most and I had every right to after our first run! It was only two-and-d-half miles but it felt like ten. During it, I thought, "I'm going to die". It wasn't much like school's physical education; it was much more intense and strict. We even had inspections of our PT kit to make sure it was cleaned and ironed correctly. At the time, I couldn't see the point, since it was going to get creased and mucky anyway. I thought all the PTIs were totally mad, they did PT every day and seemed to enjoy it.

I didn't think I was going to last two minutes in the Army, it was just so incredibly different to anything I had ever experienced. We were told to do so many things, in such a small amount of time, that I thought the NCOs were asking for a 'Mission Impossible'. Time always seemed to be of the essence, I don't think I sat down and had time to myself during the whole fourteen weeks of basic training.

There was so much to learn every day, my brain had to be constantly switched on, no more 'Neighbours' or 'Home and Away' on television, but everything seemed exciting and new.

When we first had 'Skill at Arms', I didn't think I'd ever remember all the rifle's characteristics – but I did. The NCOs seemed to have a unique way of teaching, very different from the teachers at my senior school. They made the lessons interesting and it was fun to learn. I respected the NCOs, not just because I was supposed to, but because they earned it. They were just so clever and knew so much.

I didn't want to change my attitude or my way of life to the extent that we had to, because I never saw myself enjoying 'the Army way of life'. But the change was quite gradual and I hardly noticed myself settling in to routine. I often wonder where I would be now if I had left the Army because of my 'first impressions'. Now I know I could be in no better place and, dare I say it, I actually love the Army way of life.

(The above article was published in the spring 1995 edition of The Arborfield Apprentice, showing that even though the time spent here at Arborfield had been drastically reduced, the mode of life certainly hadn't changed too much!)

Princess Marina College Vehicle Wing Closes

Head of Wing: Mr W D Weedon
Training Managers: Mr R Large, Mr A Robinson

Recent statistics obtained from REME Manning & Records Office indicate that some thirty-two per cent (approximately 1,268) of the serving vehicle mechanic population (including Artificers Vehicle) are ex-apprentices and, as such, they may be interested to learn that Vehicle Wing, the last of the Technical Training Wings, is to close in December 1996. This is when the final two-year intake of VM apprentices (intake 95A) complete their apprenticeship.

It is understood that Vehicle Wing was formed in 1945, as part of the then Army Apprentices' School *, and has trained some thirty per cent of the Corps annual requirement of VMs ever since (a total of fifty-one years).

Originally, the length of the apprenticeship was three years, reducing to two years in 1966. Now, apprentice VMs will only complete two terms in the College, before being transferred to SEME Bordon to follow the identical basic VM course as the adult entrant.

Pictured below are some of the lecturers and staff of the Vehicle Wing, the majority of whom were officers, WOs, SNCOs and ex-apprentices themselves, prior to becoming civilians employed by SERCo Defence Ltd. No doubt many of the lecturers faces will be familiar to ex-apprentices who have passed through Vehicle Wing, not only in recent years, but even those who are approaching the end of their careers. Some lecturers have taught in Vehicle Wing for over twenty-six years! In fact the average number of years' service within, and working for, REME is twenty-six.

The majority of lecturers are being transferred back into the Civil Service as Instructional Officers Grade 1 at SEME. A few of the remaining staff have secured alternative jobs within the Garrison, but some have been made redundant. These lecturers wish all ex-apprentices every success in the future and trust that the technical skills taught in Vehicle Wing, and indeed other technical departments in PMC, have stood them in good stead.

(* I think you'll find, Bill, that in 1945 we were still the Army Technical School (Boys) – but what's in a name? Ed.)

—§—

The layout of Princess Marina College bore no resemblance to the symmetry of the original Army Apprentices' School. No wonder it was nicknamed Legoland!

The old Camp Hall – to the left the two main entrances whilst, to the right, is the entrance to the old Projection Room, which later became offices for the PT staff. Further to the right is the Hall's side entrance and, on the extreme right, can be seen the edge of the Guardroom.

Chapter 15

1997 - 99

Female 'old boys' – how confusing!

The CO was delighted to report, in the *OBAN Issue 11* of 1997, that the first two female 'old boys', namely Cfn Boyle and Cfn Ellis, had recently joined the ranks of the OBA. *(A confusion in terms? Yes, definitely, but I'm sure they'd hate to be called 'old girls'! Ed.)* At the same time he was pleased to announce that OBA membership had now risen to a record number of 662, with a target of 1,000 members the aim for the forthcoming 'Millennium' year of 2000. It was surprising that amongst the many recent 're-entrants' were a handful of old boys from as far back as intake 39A! John Northam, Membership Secretary, never ceased to be amazed that, from the telephone messages he received, after chatting for only a minute or two, boys who had left from twenty to fifty years ago were now recalling events *"as though 'twere only yesterday"*.

Meanwhile, Hon Sec of the OBA, Larry le Var, was himself in reminiscent mood as he thought about the fifty years that had now gone by since he first walked through the famous gates. Just before the occasion of the last 'PoP', the QM had managed to get the arch above those very gates repaired, so at least the College now looked at its best. The Parade Reviewing Officer was The Earl Howe, Parliamentary Under-Secretary for Defence. This was quite a coup for the College, indicating the high level of support for what was being achieved amidst the climate of almost continuous change. The College was buzzing, rather like the set of the popular TV series *'Soldier, Soldier'*, with apprentices everywhere doing drill, PT, fieldcraft, or just marching between classes.

With the early chapters of this history recalling the strong influence exerted upon the boys' school by the DYRMS (or Dukies) at Dover, it was refreshing to find that this fine old school was still fully operational. This was borne out by an advertisement in February's edition of *The Craftsman*, extolling the virtues of the place. Catering exclusively for the sons – and now daughters, of course – of members and retired members of the Armed Forces, the DYRMS happily blew its own trumpet, by offering a *"caring family atmosphere"*, as well as small average class sizes and an excellent pupil to teacher ratio.

Honker's final contribution

As a strong reminder of that school's fine history, and its place as one of the various 'feeder' systems for Arborfield, January 12th 1997 brought the sad news of the death, at a mere sixty-seven years, of Thomas Leslie Pearce, or 'Honker' to many of his dearest friends. Tom had been a Dukie and had joined the AAS (Boys) directly from there in 1944. Tom had not only been an ex-boy, but an active one, writing many articles and letters in the pages of the *OBAN* over his last few years. His final contribution, although it hadn't been planned that way, appeared in *Issue 11*, as did his obituary, kindly written by Peter Darton of 43A.

Tom had originally served as an Armourer, but had converted to become an Art Radar by the time he left the service. He had then taken up with the civil service, initially with the Atomic Energy Commission at Aldermaston, before joining the European Aircraft Project. Here, he taught himself French and an adequate German. Tom also worked on the *Challenger* project at ROF Leeds, before coming back to REME at Electronics Branch, Malvern. When he finally became very ill, he fought it with his usual 'no fuss' manner and sense of humour. He was certainly one of *"the old school"* in more ways than one.

On the morning of March 15th 1997, A/T Stojanovic was one of a group of ten R Sigs apprentices who set off to an airfield at South Cerney, near Cirencester in rural Gloucestershire, to participate in 'Exercise Snow Drop'. This was a 'one-jump' parachute course, held at the home of the RLC Parachute Display Team, known as 'The Silver Stars'. It was to be 17.00 hours before he boarded his light plane, referred to as '*Miss Piggy*' because of its pink colour. The jump came as the plane reached about seventy m.p.h. and a height of 3,000 feet – *"a great experience"* as our novice later called it.

The adventure had proven to be so good that all ten young fledgling parachutists returned to the airfield the very next day to do it all again. It will probably come as no surprise that young Stojanovic was later awarded the 'Rice Bowl', as being *"the best in sporting activities"*, at his 'PoP' in August that same year.

A new command structure

April 1997 saw the functionality of the College come under the command of the Initial Training Group (ITG), based at Upavon, on Salisbury Plain. To complete the integration of the College into the full Government MA system, boys from the RE and RLC were then due to join us on 4th May 1998. *The Craftsman* magazine that month announced the future formation of an Army Foundation College (AFC) in September 1998. This would most likely be located on the site of the old AAC at Harrogate in Yorkshire, offering a forty-two week course for young soldiers destined for 'front line' roles. AFC funding was to be provided through a Private Finance Initiative (PFI) and a total of 1,300 student places would be on offer.

Apprentices here at Arborfield were now to undertake a seven-month course only, consisting of two fourteen-week terms, interspersed by leave periods. The first term was to be predominantly devoted to CMS(R) training, in line with that conducted at the ATRs. The term would also include a one-week EL exercise and a Basic Leadership course. In their second term, the students would then receive a measure of technical and military education, the aim being to provide the basic educational foundation for subsequent trade training. As from January 1997, the internal structure of the College had changed too, with only three designated training Companies, namely those of 'J' Coy, 'A' Coy and R Sigs, each one responsible for both its Junior and Senior divisions.

Also during that second term, the apprentices would now complete a further EL exercise, an Advanced Leadership cadre, and a final military exercise prior to passing out. During their leave periods, boys and girls alike would have the opportunity to take part in a large variety of adventurous training exercises across the globe, in such far-flung places as Nepal, Austria, Cyprus, Spain and Bavaria. All of these were helped on their way by non-public funding from the College Trust Fund and the continuing generous contribution of the OBA, while being organised and led by members of the College's military and civilian PS.

The CO, writing *in The Arborfield Apprentice* for spring 1997, reported on the successful 'PoP' of the previous December. It had been held during inclement weather, but in front of a massed crowd of some 1,500 spectators. The end of that year had seen the final closure of the College trade training wings and the completion of the relocation of the College, *"lock, stock and barrel"*, back to its traditional home. Lt Col Nigel Moore proudly announced that the names of 263 (Harrogate) Signal Sqn and Carlisle Company now bore the flags of their forebears at those two former Army Apprentices' Colleges.

The half-term break that spring reported on nine young apprentices who had taken part in a five-day sailing expedition on the Solent. They had been split up across three separate yachts, along with some experienced yachtsmen, and soon set about making everything *"sea-shape and Bristol fashion"*. A short trip from the JSATC Gosport to Cowes gave them their 'sea legs' and these were most necessary next day when they set off for Southampton on rough seas. Navigational skills and knowledge of sailing were gradually built up over the length of the venture, until the final part of it came down to the inevitable cleaning of their accommodation – it was time to return to Camp!

National Vocational Qualifications

During 1997, the Military Studies Department (MSD) was deeply into the trialling of Key Skills, as laid down as part of the NVQ assessments. The skills 'units', as deemed essential by both employers and colleges, were indicated as Communication, Application of Number, Information Technology, Working with Others, and Improving own Learning and Performance. To achieve these units, a student would have to fulfil the following criteria:

> *Communicate effectively with a range of different people, when discussing or writing about complex subjects; interpret complex information, including numbers and images; make calculations; make appropriate use of IT; plan, organise yourself and work with others.*

A memo sent out on May 26th invited respondents to a 'Core Skills Brains Trust' regarding the above criteria, but was obviously a bit 'tongue in cheek' and in typical boys' school style! It read:

1. Fed up? Confused? Ready for some constructive dissatisfaction?
2. OK. Come to the meeting in MSD. Bring your teddy and be prepared to throw it in the corner.
3. Also, bring along your worries, ideas and those boring Halifax shares, and give them to your Uncle Arnie.
4. Remember, *"Let's do it, lets NVQ it!"*

Where did all those years go?

The Craftsman magazine that had been issued in April published a couple of photographs, spanning a lengthy gap of forty-one years, under the heading *'Ex-apprentices never die – they just re-unite'*. The first photo showed three young men, A/T Mike Roberts, LCpl (ex-A/T CSM) Alan Morton and A/T CSM Frank Townsend, as they had been, in their prime, back in 1955. Alan had by then left the School, as it was then still, but had just returned on a visit, proudly displaying his neatly pressed BD and newly won Lance Corporal's stripe.

The second photo was taken, as well as could be remembered that is, on 'the same spot' during the Old Boys' Reunion of 1996, showing three 'slightly more mature' retired officers. The common factor that had brought the three boys together in the first place had been the friendship between their respective fathers, all of whom had served together at Bordon. Thus that 1955 photo commemorated the fact that, like their fathers before them, these three buys also happened to be together *"at the same place, at the same time"*. Coincidentally, all three boys later went on to serve as Tels Mechs.

On May 31st 1997, a large party of apprentices formed up to go on a fact-finding expedition to France. Their mission was to find out all they could about the D-Day landings of June 6th 1944, as part of their College military studies. Having crossed the Channel by ferry from Portsmouth, their first destination was the port of Arromanches to see the remnants of *'Port Winston'*, or *Mulberry Harbour*, the 'floating dock' system that had proved so invaluable to supplying the food, fuel and ammunition supplies for the invading forces. They later visited *'Sword Beach'*, the easternmost of those Normandy beaches where the British Second Army landed and the future destiny of Europe began to be shaped.

A final port of call was at *'Pegasus Bridge'*, just outside the town of Caen, where they had the good fortune to meet up with Maj John Howard, the officer who had led the battle to take the bridge from the German defenders. Then it was back to Cherbourg for the return trip, and a rough Channel crossing must have made the apprentices realise just what those invading troops had gone through so many years ago.

In June 1997, the *Hathi* vehicle project hit a snag, when Richard and Simon Jones found they could not undertake the construction of the complex body panels that were now required. A local firm at Bracknell came up with the most economical quotation for the work and promised that it would be delivered back to Bordon in time for the C-in-C's visit there in July. Thus it was that, when HRH Prince Philip, Duke of Edinburgh, saw the *Hathi* at SEME, it was accompanied by a photograph of King George V and Queen Mary, inspecting just such a vehicle during one of their visits to 'Army Manouvres' in the early Thirties. HRH was suitably impressed.

On August 1st that same year, HRH paid an official visit to SEAE Arborfield, again in his capacity as C-in-C REME. The weeks that led up to that visit must have been nerve-wracking enough for the five apprentices who had been 'detailed' for the honour of meeting the Prince, but perhaps the worst aspect of it all was that they would be personally inspected by the RSM before the presentation! Despite their being called *"flaming' donkeys"* (*nothing new there!*), our 'famous five' were eventually allowed to take their place in front of their C-in-C and managed to answer his questions without muttering or stumbling over their words, which had been their biggest worry.

'Vital to the Army's needs'

At the 'PoP' of August 15th, for those leaving the College having been members of 96C, it was fitting that the Reviewing Officer was an ex-apprentice from Harrogate. Maj Gen J D Stokoe CBE addressed those passing out with the following words of encouragement:

"Some of you go to join the Royal Corps of Signals, others to the Royal Electrical and Mechanical Engineers – Corps vital to the

Army's needs – both at home in this country and on operations – wherever they may be sent. Our technical corps enable the Army to fight – whether providing the nervous system to communicate with and direct its forces, or keeping its equipment in fighting condition – if that support fails, then the body of the Army withers and dies. Those serving today feature large in the Army's exploits on the battlefield – you are now a part of that."

August 20th found eleven apprentices setting off for a fourteen-day trekking expedition in the Sierra Nevada mountains of California. Upon arrival in the US, they picked up two 'people carriers' (the new posh versions of mini-buses) and headed towards the splendid beauty of Yosemite National Park. The main purpose of the venture was to climb the 14,496 feet to the peak of Mount Whitney, but a certain amount of acclimatisation was called for, before that could be achieved. The final trek of twenty-two miles brought them to their 'start point' and the ascent was begun at 03.00 hours. Altitude effects caused problems for quite a few of the party, but they were assisted and encouraged by their mates, as team spirit prevailed and all personnel reached the summit by midday.

The descent proved rather less arduous and, as they walked off the mountain, they had a few chuckles at the sight of so many overweight Americans, trudging on their way up! A total time of thirteen hours saw the party, tired but happy, back at base altitude. All the hard work was then rewarded by a shopping spree in the heart of downtown San Francisco, followed by a trip to the famous island prison of Alcatraz. *(The guy who said, "It's just like Arborfield" will remain nameless. Ed.)*

In the autumn 1997 issue of *OBAN*, the deaths of two former staff members were sadly reported. Brig Edward L Percival, DSO, had been the Commandant in charge of the School, as it had then been, from 1949 to 1952. Born in 1905, the Brigadier had reached the ripe old age of ninety-two. He had been awarded the DSO in 1941, when commanding the 2nd Battalion HLI in East Africa, and a bar to it in 1945 when in command of the 6th Battalion during the North Western Europe campaign. In all, 'Ned' Percival, as family and friends knew him, served in the Army for forty-one years. A far more untimely death, at an early age, was that of Capt Michael Burns of the Irish Guards, who had been a popular RSM here at PMC, serving from 1990 to 1992.

That *OBAN* also announced that RSM Roy Matthews (REME) had been replaced during August. The RSM had already reflected, in an earlier College magazine, that *"that time"* was approaching, the time when his twenty-two years of Army service finally came to an end. After his uphill battle to end the habit of his being called 'Sergeant Major', roles would now reverse once again in the reinstatement of the 'household' tradition, as he had been succeeded by RSM Phil Rooney of the Welsh Guards.

Links across the decades

The same issue of *OBAN* saw the continuation of a tale that tied together four separate decades – the Forties, Fifties, Sixties and now, with a great leap forward, the Nineties. Geoffrey James of 61B had been reading an earlier

Some things never change! Can't you stand on your feet Clements?

OBAN, when he came across a letter written by Brian Conway, of 1942 era. Geoffrey recognised the name as that of one of his old instructors, after a gap of more than thirty years. Brian had long since left the service, in September 1967, subsequently going on to train as a civilian lecturer. Following later service in Libya, the Bahamas, Oman and Nigeria, Brian had finally settled on the island of Cyprus. Geoff and Brian have now been able to renew their original acquaintanceship, which reinforces the feelings that all ex-boys have always had for the 'old school'.

As the CO looked out of his office window to see some old boys arriving for their annual Reunion in 1997, he could only hope that *"the apprentices of today"* would prove to be *"as loyal, dedicated and successful as their predecessors"*. He mused that the only predictable thing about College life at the present was its sheer unpredictability! The Pay and QM staff of the College had recently been centralised at Garrison level, though, despite this being such a culture shock, the personnel involved had gone out of their way to make the transition as smooth as possible.

One of those old boys was Frank Fendrick (45A), who couldn't really work out why he had returned! He had always held it against his father that he had allowed Frank to leave school (the DYRMS) and join the AAS (Boys), rather than staying on in sixth form and going on to Sandhurst. He'd always thought he should have been an *"officer and a gentlemen, instead of a craftsman and a paratrooper"*! Poor Frank, he never did enjoy Army life, saying it was *"almost a complete waste of my life"*. So it begs the obvious question - why did Frank attend that Reunion? Well, he must have heard somewhere a quote by Allan Tucker (39B), who said, *"The tone and humour of the (OBAN) letters fill me with such a sense of fellowship that I cannot imagine any ex-boy not wishing to be a part of it"*. (And so say all of us. Ed.)

All change on the OBA front

1997 saw John Northam retire as the Honorary Membership Secretary of the OBA, heartened by the way that both the Association and its *OBAN* had developed since their respective re-launches. John also took upon the task of reporting that year's Reunion in the *OBAN*, celebrating the fiftieth anniversary of his 47A intake. It wasn't to be too long before he and June were able to fulfill their dreams of moving to the 'West Country'. They are now happily settled down in Taunton, in the heart of Somerset – *"where the cider apples grow"*!

The immense task of 'filling his shoes' was taken up by the not unknown figure of Col (Ret'd) Peter Gibson. It was a tremendous asset to the Association that someone who had served here as Commandant at the College, but was not himself an old boy at that time, had now become one of the most important 'Old Boys' of all time! All ex-apprentices wish Peter well in the task of gathering even more old boys into the OBA. A further change that year was when 'Larry' Le Var stood down from his role as Hon Sec. Larry added a few well-chosen words of his own in the *OBAN*:

> *"When I watched the 1996 reunion parade, I felt proud to belong to such an elite group who had served their country so loyally in peace and war, and who continue to contribute so much to society in their later years."*

Larry's post was taken up by self-confessed Jeep, Maj Bob Hambly, whose sell-by date only stretched as far back as to a vintage of 64A – he was virtually a *Beaujolais Nouveau*! Bob was serving at the time in the Army Careers Office in Reading, his duties covering the counties of Berks, Bucks, Oxon. & Herts (Berkshire, Buckinghamshire, Oxfordshire and Hertfortdshire).

Another challenge was taken up in 1997, the idea of producing a modern videocassette, based upon some of the old films and newsreel items that had been taken during preceding years. John Smithson, ex-46B vintage, had been connected with the film and television industry for many years and, provided that he could get his hands on the relevant material, was prepared to take on the job of cleaning and editing it, in order to provide a lasting memento of some of the activities here at Arborfield. John hoped to have the completed video ready for the following year's Old Boys' Reunion.

As the sun set on the evening of Friday 24th October, sleep was hard to come by for the group of excited apprentices who were off for a week's walking and climbing 'holiday'. After a bus ride to Luton Airport, they boarded the plane to Barcelona, their flight being followed by a two-and-a-half hour train trip into the Pyrenees, the mountainous area between Spain and France. Another train then took them to a small monastery at Nuria, at the base of Puigmal. Breathing proved difficult in the thin mountain air, but the team achieved the height of almost 3,000 metres and enjoyed a lunch at the summit, basking in sunshine. The next couple of days were spent hill-walking and, as you'd guess, the weather turned nasty! Their last day was spent on a bus that took them slowly across the Catalonian countryside to the ancient cathedral town of Girona.

"Can you imagine walking up and down three different mountains, a distance of twenty-five miles, in the moonlight as well as daytime, in the wind and rain, and all in under twelve hours?" The question was asked by one who did it! The venture was undertaken in mid-November of 1997, in aid of the Gurkha Welfare Trust, and took place on three peaks, Ingleborough, Whernside and Pen-y-Ghent, all situated within the Yorkshire Dales. Following only a short orienteering course in the local area around Arborfield, three teams, made up of eighteen apprentices, achieved the challenge only nine weeks into their CMS(R) training.

The Honourable Viscount Alanbrooke of Brookeborough, known to his many friends simply as Victor Brooke, retired from the Civil Service and the College in November of 1997. His association with the College had been long and rich, since joining the staff here in 1978. Victor had been latterly employed as the College Historian, as well as being a Burnham Lecturer with the MSD. His retirement party was in the form of an informal lunch, attended by many friends and colleagues, both past and present.

Farewell old friend

November's edition of *The Craftsman* contained an obituary for General Sir John Hackett GCB, CBE, DSO, MC, who had died on September 9th at the age of eighty-six. Sir John was recognised as *"the cleverest soldier of his generation"*. His intellectual attainments had been combined with an excellent record of military leadership and gallantry that stretched back prior to the Second World War. He had been captured at the Battle of Arnhem, but subsequently escaped. After that war, he became into closer contact with REME, and will be remembered by many REME officers as the Commandant of the RMCS. Towards the end of his tour, during the period 1961 – 1966, he was appointed as a Colonel Commandant REME, taking a keen interest in both the Corps and its members.

In *The Arborfield Apprentice* issued in December 1997, an article tried to explain the thesis behind the Government's MA Scheme. It was intended to provide the skills and knowledge required by young people embarking on careers in industry. The Army, along with many other employers, had now taken this 'on board', offering NVQs to all personnel as part of their career development and MAs to young people under twenty-five years of age. This new system was not based merely on 'time served', as in previous times, but entirely upon individual achievement or demonstration of competence.

1997 had seen the College deliver 600 apprentices, most as usual to SEAE and SEME, but now some also to the R Sigs Phase 2 training centre at Blandford. This output was expected to increase to 900 the following year, when the College would have the additional task of training RE and RLC apprentices.

(The February edition of The Craftsman contained a contribution from an anonymous author, entitled 'The Brat', and was obviously written by an ex-apprentice from the May 1957 intake. It is included in its entirety as an annex to this chapter.)

Over the weekend of 7th / 8th March 1998, apprentices from the College again showed their willingness to assist those other members of society less fortunate than themselves. Fifty-two boys and girls took part in a sponsored twenty-four hour Triathlon – the swimming, cycling and running event that proved a shattering experience for one and all. But at the end of the day, a total of some £1,278 was raised, and a cheque for that amount was handed over to the *Guide Dogs for the Blind Association*.

In that same month, *The Craftsman* reported on the radical changes that were taking place within the Instruments Career Employment Group (CEG). The increase in sophistication and number of laser and thermal imaging equipments now demanded that Inst Techs become electronically trained, to support systems that were now predominantly electronic in nature. The 'old days' of working merely on binoculars, compasses, optical range-finders and artillery dial sights were fast disappearing, with 'Optronics' now being used as the generic term to describe the ever-widening range of instrument systems.

On Sunday April 19th, several A/Ts found themselves in the intense heat of the desert in Egypt, land of the Pharaohs and Pyramids. They had arrived at Sharm-el-Sheikh, on the Red Sea, to sample the delights of diving in its warm waters. Two young girl apprentices in the party were fortunate not to be sold off for the price of a couple of camels – well, that's the story put out by the boys! Ras-ma-hamed is one of the top ten diving sites in the world, and the party was soon enjoying the underwater world of sharks, barracuda and turtles. All the sunshine must have gone to the heads of several of the party, because they arrived back in England at 02.00 hours wearing only T-shirts and shorts, finding it rather on the chilly side.

Times of constant change

The CO also wrote in the College magazine mentioned previously. He was already looking back on some twenty-one months at Arborfield, commenting that he had hardly had time to draw a breath! The only thing constant about his tour so far was the inconstancy! For example, in the previous eight months, no less than one third of the total College military staff had moved on to new appointments, with their replacements now hurriedly going through the learning process, while civilian personnel also seemed to be on the same merry-go-round.

New buildings had been sprouting up all over the place and planning had begun towards an impressive new Gymnasium. Despite the short and intensive course that was now the norm, sporting and adventurous activities had continued to thrive. A great deal of effort was now being put into the planning for the arrival of RE and RLC apprentices in May 1998.

Another edition of the *OBAN* made its entry in spring 1998. Editor Brian Hornsey (54A) continued his description of Arborfield's local hostelries, most, if not all, of which will have been visited by apprentices and ex-apprentices at one time or another. The *'Bramshill Hunt'* is the closest to Camp and, no longer on the 'main road', it relies heavily on Garrison custom. Brian also included the *'Swan'*, the Arborfield *'Bull'*, the Barkham *'Bull'* and the *'Black Boy'* at Shinfield, all of which will stir the memories, if not the taste buds, of Arborfield boys everywhere.

Those RLC apprentices who had arrived to form the St Omer Sqn, provided nine entrants to the Ten Tors event between 12th / 17th May, picking up on a College tradition that had been thought lost for good. Amazingly, considering the prevailing conditions

that usually accompanied this event, the weather was extremely hot that year. This was *"ideal for Officers' suntans"* but hardly what the team wanted for a strenuous 55-mile trek! After an excellent start, one of the lads unfortunately pulled his hamstring and, despite desperate efforts to make up time, the team had to call it a day after forty-five miles – still an extremely good effort.

In the June 1998 edition of *The Arborfield Apprentice*, the Pipe Major explained just how difficult it was to train a volunteer piper nowadays. The main requirement had to be keenness and dedication, as there were only some fourteen weeks available to learn 'from scratch' to reach some level of adequate performance. At that time, there were just seven such 'learners', and the Pipe Major hoped to have this 'Magnificent Seven' available to form the Pipes section of the College Pipes and Drums at the 'PoP' in August.

Although time was now at a premium in the College, apprentices were still doing their best to continue their pursuit of 'the sporting life'. There had been a revival of the College basketball team, with matches against other local teams, both military and civilian. The College had also managed to put together a football team, with a number of players being chosen to play for the Army Junior team, while the swimmers were the current holders of the Minor Units title. Fourteen members of the College had been to Bavaria, trying out the fairly new fast and furious sport of ski biking, while other expeditions of note were the sailing trips in the Baltic and the Solent.

A 'Sapper' in charge

The summer of 1998 had marked the departure time for Lt Col Moore, who went off to take up a Staff appointment at Andover. On June 19th he was given a traditional 'College farewell', being applauded out by all personnel, piped out by the Pipe Major and driven out in an *"antique vehicle"*. The speed of his exit journey gave him plenty of time to reflect upon his time here! He handed over command of the College to Lt Col J W Mitchell RE, this change of cap-badge reflecting the ever-widening training role, as the College finally relinquished its previous 'REME only' role.

Writing in the *OBAN* during autumn 1998, the new CO said how much he had enjoyed attending his first Old Boys' Reunion, and how delighted was Brig Tim

Tyler, the Commander of RTG and Arborfield Garrison, who had been the Reviewing Officer and dinner guest. He went on to express this view:

"The benefit to the College of the Association and of the reunion event is, of course, to serve both as a reminder and an example of the wider family of the British Army. For young apprentices, it is a family that will come to include chums, units, Corps and many Service charities and associations, including the AOBA. It is vital that apprentices gain a feel for this wider family during their short time at the College, since it underpins so much of the Army ethos".

The CO reported that up to 650 apprentices at any one time were then completing the new eight-month foundation course, so the College was running *"at full capacity"*. On a personal side, he looked forward to the honour and challenge of being the first 'Sapper' in command. As a short term measure, to help out the wider Army training organisation, he announced that the College now had a Platoon of Infantry under its supervision, which had certainly thrown up some interesting times for the staff!

Old Boys - at home and abroad

Just preceding another get-together of the Arborfield boys, ex-RASC 'Jersey' boys held a nostalgic reunion of their own on that island during the week September 19th / 26th. The highest rank achieved by those boys who joined up in Jersey in 1938 was by Maj Gen (Ret'd) Peter Blunt CB, MBE, GM, who was now the local mayor – or '*Connetable*', to use the correct phrase. The General proudly took the salute during a parade, which was followed by a church service. During the celebrations, the old boys presented a nominal roll, photograph and shield to the Jersey Museum in St Helier. As reported by the Chairman of the Jersey Boys' Association, it had been *"a very emotional week"*.

Some fifty-five years after entering boys' service here in Arborfield, the latter months of 1998 saw Norman Donnithorne set off on a tour of the Far East, Australia and NZ. Ostensibly, the trip was to celebrate Norman's and his wife's Golden Wedding Anniversary, but Norman was just able to convince his good lady that

some fishing and a drink with old comrades may just take precedence! Around the same time, a letter from Eric Corscadden (42A) announced that the BSXBA were due to hold their annual reunion in Napier (NZ) to coincide with Armistice Day, November 11th.

Much like John Northam, five years earlier, Norman had set off with the addresses of nine NZ old boys clutched in his hand, and was in fact able to make contact with three of those on his list. First came Denys Goldfinch, who lives in Auckland and, himself an ex-Chepstow boy, is currently running the ex-boys' association in those parts. Norman was also able to deliver the recently made video, '*Arborfield Apprentice*', to Andy Rackstraw of 55A vintage, at his North Island home at Upper Hutt. His final meeting was at the South Island town of Nelson, with another ex-Chepstow boy, Jeff Trowe.

That video, '*Arborfield Apprentice*', had been well received by members of the OBA. It contained scenes of the 1997 Reunion, with some of the old boys at that Reunion vividly recounting some of their memories. However, the main bulk of the video was made up from two films recovered from the Museum Archives, '*Soldier Apprentice*' from 1951 and '*Apprenticed to Adventure*', made in 1962.

'Live life to the fullest'

The 24th of October 1998 was not only the day of the annual Old Boys' Reunion, but also one of sadness and pride for the Schofield family. Just a year earlier, Ken Schofield (62C) had lost the valiant battle for his life, but not before nurturing a number of acorns into small trees. During that 1998 Reunion, a service of dedication was held in the Sergeants' Mess, attended by Ken's widow Sylvia, his son William, and younger brother David, also an ex-boy from 65A. Between bouts of heavy rain, and with the brave assistance of the Padre, one of the small oak trees was planted in the Memorial Garden in a lasting tribute to Ken's memory.

In memory of Ken, who was always younger brother David's role model, the following poem by Amanda Bradley was read out, by David, at the service:

If you treasure the beauty that shows all around you
And try to add some of your own,
Enjoy the companionship others can give you,
Yet value your moments alone.

If you honour opinions that differ from yours,
Yet stand up for what you believe,
Admire the accomplishments others have made
And take pride in what you can achieve.

If you love those around you and love yourself too,
If your spirit is eager and free,
Then you know what it means to live life to the fullest
And be the best 'you' you can be.

That same heavy rain had caused the normal parade to be cancelled that year, to be replaced by a 'wet weather' service that was held in the College Gymnasium. Ray Derrick of 44B was enjoying a quiet pint in the Sergeants' Mess on the morning of that Reunion, when all his fears came true! As a cry rang out across the room, *"Anyone from '48 intake here?"* Almost automatically, Ray unwisely raised his hand. The cry had come from *OBAN* editor Brian Hornsey and he explained to Ray that it had now become the custom – nay, the duty – of a *"fiftieth anniversary member"* to write a report on that year's Reunion. Ray realised that he had actually **volunteered**, something he had been studiously avoiding since leaving Arborfield in 1947! Needless to say, the article that later appeared in *OBAN Issue 15* was a credit to his intake, with the reassurance that he wouldn't have to do it again - until 2047!

Those apprentices who had formed the May 1998 intake left in December the same year, full of enthusiasm in now moving on to the next stage of their careers. For the RE contingent it was on to nearby Minley and, for R Sigs, the delights of Blandford, down in Dorset. The RLC members went off to their new home at Aldershot, while for the REME personnel it was either a case of staying on here at SEAE Arborfield or moving down to SEME Bordon, depending upon each individual's trade discipline. As that December 'PoP' was the first on which Sapper apprentices were represented, it was appropriate that Brig Albert Whiteley CBE, the Engineer-in-Charge, took the salute.

Just prior to the annual 'Juniors v Seniors' rugger match here at Arborfield on December 16th, ex-apprentice Brian Glossop of 57A, now working for an insurance group, presented a new playing strip to the SEAE team. Brian had played regularly for SEE (as it had then been) until retiring as a Captain in 1987 and, during his REME service, had won colours at both rugby and boxing.

New contractor takes over

On 1st January 1999, a new contractor, namely *Vosper Thorneycroft*, perhaps better known for its shipbuilding activities down on the south Hampshire coastline, assumed the responsibility for the delivery and administration of technical training in support of trade at the College, SEAE and SES(A). They were also contracted to provide the Garrison's QM functions, administration offices, primary health care, postal and messenger services. This followed a statement in Parliament on August 4th 1998, after a CFQ competition had identified a range of activities deemed suitable for 'private sector' involvement. The official 'Vesting Day' was hosted at SEAE on Friday 8th January. A spokesman for the company explained, *"We have established a good working relationship with the Army at Bordon and are confident that we can also apply our management expertise to the benefit of the Army at Arborfield"*.

The building of the College's new Gymnasium, some three times the area of the original, was completed during the first half of 1999, with its official opening held at the August 'PoP'. In the summer *OBAN* later in that year, the Commandant was raving about its facilities, which included two new squash courts, areas for weight training and cardio-vascular exercise, as well as a 'fearsome' climbing wall.

At the same time, the **old** gymnasium, now known as the 'Beachley Centre', had been refurbished to provide a range of new facilities, including a new chapel, classrooms, a large cinema/lecture theatre, and office space for use by the College padres. 'Beachley', of course, was the name of the camp of the 'old enemy' – Chepstow – thus highlighting the fact that the College was now both PC **and** fully multi-cultural! The addition of an all-weather AstroTurf football and hockey pitch, close to the location of the old 'Square', will enable Rowcroft Barracks to boast really first-class sporting amenities.

Arrivals and departures

January 4th 1999 brought the arrival of a new apprentice at the College, A/T Glyn Parry. Glyn's claim to fame, according to the staff of the Haverfordwest Army Careers Office, was that his enlistment had been the fastest on record. Glyn, a former pupil of Cardigan Secondary School, had walked into the Haverfordwest office at 10.30 a.m. on December 15th and, at 12.00 hours on December 18th, he was enlisted.

In May 1999 came another example of the old saying – 'It all starts and ends at Arborfield'. It was certainly true for Larry Le Var, who had started his career here as an apprentice in 1947 and was now bowing out from his role as Director of the REME Museum. On May 28th he was given a *"final Corps farewell"* by around 120 friends and colleagues at a buffet party, held in the Vehicle Exhibition Hall. He was driven away from the Hall in the Museum's oldest (even older than Larry!) historical vehicle, the previously mentioned 1925 *Thorneycroft 'Hathi'*. Larry's position was taken by another ex-boy, Lt Col (Ret'd) Bill Cleasby MBE, of intake 61C, who also succeeded Bob Hambly as Honorary Secretary of the OBA. Bob had been forced to step down from his position, due to the increasing pressure of his work in the world of recruiting.

In the *REME Journal* that year, Brian Baxter, deputy curator of the REME Museum, was able to put the final few words to the tale of the *Hathi* project, which had begun at the boys' school several years previously. It had made a *"star appearance"* at the 1998 Basingstoke Festival of Transport, collecting the prize for the *"best Thorneycroft vehicle present"*. As far as was aware, the vehicle was the last survivor of the thirty or so originally built, making it one of the rarest military vehicles in existence. Great credit lies with those who first undertook the painstaking work at Arborfield, and those *"gifted enthusiasts"* who had later brought the project to fruition.

Issue 16 of OBAN, in the spring of 1999, published a resumé of the career of Charlie Ashdown, detailing his career record between him joining up as a member

OBAN editor Brian Hornsey of 54A (on right) greets an old colleague some forty-three years later

of 42A until his eventual retirement from the Canadian civil service in April 1992. That record of fifty years 'on duty' is one that seems typical of many ex-boys and a fine target to aim at for the current apprentices, both male and female. Charlie had eventually moved to live in 'the States', where he still contributes a prodigious amount of 'copy' to the pages of the *OBAN*.

Editor Brian Hornsey was delighted with a contribution for that *OBAN* from Nick Dunmore of 88A. At the time, it was possibly the first 'old boy' article submitted by a former member of PMC, rather than the many letters from ex-apprentices of ATS, AAS and AAC times. Nick had been one of the very few Armourers to pass out from his intake and, at the time of writing, was serving in Londonderry, Northern Ireland. He recommended the post to any future Armourer interested in learning about the *"more diverse side of the trade"* – far more than could be picked up on a Class 1 course at SEME Bordon, according to Nick!

Brian also welcomed a contribution from the pen of Steve Budd, almost thirty years after he had joined as part of 69C. Steve hoped that Brian could decipher his handwriting, which had always been described as *"atrocious"* since his days here at Arborfield. Steve's letter was basically a plea for information, as he was trying to trace his two uncles, Harry and Bruce, who he thought had both passed through the College (or School, of course) in their time. Steve's own father had also been an apprentice, though in his case he had been at Chepstow. *(The 'Uncle Harry' would surely be the same Harry Budd who joined up early in 1942? Ed.)*

If you want to get ahead – get a hat!

Although he didn't realise it at the time he joined up as a member of 61B, Brian Hutchins was not only destined to attain the rank of Colonel, but by 1999 he had become the 'Senior Serving Old Boy' and taken up his post as Vice Chairman of the OBA. Some years earlier, Brian had been gypped in the canteen queue at Electronics Branch, Malvern, by Alan 'Algy' Morton of 51B – old habits certainly die hard! Alan had warned Brian to 'get fell in' by joining the OBA, but it was to be three tours later before he finally got *'a round tuit'*. Imagine his surprise when, on attending his first Reunion, instead of an anonymous position somewhere in the centre ranks of the parade, Brian found himself in the honoured position of Reviewing Officer.

Not only that, but he would have to wear a hat!

Now there's a story that goes with the hat that Brian wore. It had originally been purchased by Larry Le Var to be worn at a ceremony held to remember those who had fallen in the Gulf War – this at a time when Larry had lots of hair (or so he says!). At a subsequent OBA Reunion, Larry had again worn the hat – a bowler – but this time craftily padded out to stop it falling off. Now it was time for Brian to 'take the parade', similarly attired in 'padded' bowler. He spent the whole parade, tortured by the thought that he may have to doff his hat in salute, thus causing scraps of programme to flutter and scatter all over the parade ground. In the event, he got away with it!

Whilst sitting in his pew at the Sunday morning church service at that same Reunion, Brian was musing on something that didn't seem quite right. Perhaps it was that the service was actually taking place in a church, or maybe he couldn't find the halfpenny to put in the collection plate. Then it suddenly dawned on him - he hadn't been marched to church! Brian's retirement date was due to hit him in August 1999, so he was anxiously searching around for another 'senior soldier' to act as his successor.

That summer's edition of *OBAN* published a letter from Tony 'Dom' Domoney, an old boy from the 56B intake. Tony had started his days as a 'general fitter' and gone on to have a musical outlet too, by joining and then later becoming an A/T Sgt member of the School Band in those days. Tony went on to transfer to the Army Air Corps in 1960 and, after a year at Middle Wallop, just scraping through his course, he went on to wear his light blue beret with much pride on a posting to Nairobi, Kenya, in 1961. He did some more training in England, plus a six-month stint in Cyprus with the UN, but the *"Africa bug"* had bitten deep and was calling him back.

So, when he left the Army in 1967, Tony then enjoyed a long romance with the 'dark continent' of Africa over some thirteen years. Although working as an aircraft technician, he also enjoyed the privilege of working alongside game rangers, biologists, zoologists and other specialists. He got caught up in 'game counting' as well as the catching and relocation of wild animals, and Tony reports that he was once charged by a bull elephant! The beast just *"flapped its ears, trumpeted and thundered towards him"*, before stopping just three metres short, having a quick smell, then turning into reverse. It must have recognised Tony as an ex-boy!

He eventually took the immigration path to Australia in 1980, but continued his travels after that with contracts in Zimbabwe and Saudi Arabia. Throughout his long career in 'aviation', mainly on the safety and airworthiness side, he has always put any success down to the *"excellent training and disciplines"* knocked into him during his apprenticeship here at Arborfield. Tony finally made his first ever Old Boys' Reunion in 2000, when he was able to 'fill in' for Pete Gripton (also 56B), who had booked his place but then found himself unavoidably unable to attend. It was unfortunate that Tony found himself the only member of his intake present that year, but perhaps he didn't look hard enough, as Russell 'Jock' Dodds – who was also from the Band – reckons he was definitely there that weekend!

Trouble in the Balkans

In his 'Chairman's Message' to that *OBAN* of spring 1999, Lt Col Mitchell reported that staffing problems continued to play havoc with programmes and schedules, with several members of the College staff having been called away on duty to the Balkan state of Kosovo at very short notice. However, he was gratified to hear from the various adult training schools of how well the ex-apprentices were doing. It went a long way to allay fears that 'foundation' training wasn't the 'full monty', to use a current phrase. The tenuous balance of education, military training, leadership, initiative and character training was working well, and the CO was able to assure the old boys that *"the quality of apprentices now is just as high as it ever was"*.

The CO also reflected on the recruiting difficulties encountered during periods which were 'out of cycle' with the school year. The September intake is inevitably filled with those youngsters who have just left school, while the January intake catches those who just fancied a short breather after leaving school, or who had to retake their examinations. By the springtime however, pickings were usually very slim. This showed up in the small May intake of that year, following the similar pattern of previous years.

Bill Cleasby, who had recently become the Hon Sec of the OBA, could rightly be accused of the age-old custom of gypping. As a *"product of the Sixties"*, as he described himself, he had now leapt from the Jeeps' table at Reunion dinners directly to the top table, something other members of his intake (61C) would

take a few more years to achieve. Bill said that it said a lot about the depth and strength of the Association that this was the case.

The College's adventure training staff made a successful move, still within the confines of the Welsh borders. With the Cwrt-y-gollen camp area at Crickhowell being sold off by the MoD, training facilities had now been established at Sennybridge, which was better placed to provide the required support for climbing, caving, canoeing and mountain walking.

Also in Wales, but this time in the northern reaches of that country, a party of apprentices again took part in the '*MS Challenge*', a charity event held over three days. With MS sufferer Geoff in the specially adapted wheelchair, the boys found it hard going, with most of the ideas and practical suggestions actually coming from Geoff himself, who had completed the event several times before. The event was to raise money of course, and at the 'PoP' of August 12th, a cheque for £1,000 was handed over to Geoff himself, who had been invited along to the College as the principal guest for the day.

A proposal to extend the College course length from two to three terms was examined in 1999, but was not likely to be implemented until possibly the September of the following year. Both the AG and Director General of Army Training and Recruiting (DGATR) had visited the College however, and were keen to see the College develop along the lines suggested. Course Design work is aimed at developing the current course in line with the aspirations of the constituent Corps, reflecting changes in technology and reacting to national standards within the realms of vocational education.

Another wet weekend

The Old Boys' Reunion in October 1999 was, for the second consecutive year, badly hit by wet weather, hopefully nothing to do with the Sappers having taken over the appointment of CO! Despite rumours to that effect, Lt Col Mitchell was able to report that, *"the weekend proved to be the usual combination of pomp, pageantry, comradeship, discomfort and good humour"*. The Parade and Dinner were both splendidly addressed by a particularly relevant 'reviewing officer'. This was Maj Gen (Ret'd) Peter Baldwin, CBE, who had himself been an apprentice here, of 42A intake. He may not have been a star at *"taps and basins"* in those days, but he certainly proved a star entertainer that weekend.

Peter had left boys' school around the end of the war, no doubt feeling, as with many boys of that time, a little relieved that it was all over at last – the war that is, not just Arborfield! In December of 1945 he had been posted to the Sudan EME as part of that country's Defence Force. As Cfn Baldwin, he had taken his first tentative step up the promotion ladder, little realising that he would end up so near to its top! A contemporary photograph, taken during 1946, shows Peter proudly standing in front of the statue of another General, the legendary 'Gordon of Khartoum'. In later years, this edifice was removed and now stands in the grounds of the Gordon Boys' School at Woking. *(There is no truth in the rumour that you are now 'Baldwin of Gerrards Cross' is there Peter? Ed.)*

Reporting on that year's Reunion fell to the pen of Gordon Bonner of 49B, who had finally returned to Arborfield fifty years after first joining. Driving up from the A30, through Eversley, and then turning onto Sheerlands Road, he stopped outside the old gates, which were sadly now surrounded by barbed wire. Everything seemed so much smaller to Gordon – the width of the road, the width of the entrance – but the welcome he received at the Beachley Centre was as large as ever. He was quickly 'booked in' and then escorted to his room by *"a delightful female apprentice"*, so some things had definitely changed - and for the better he thought! He eventually met up with old pals Ernie Towser and John Cassells, thinking how wrinkled they looked! So began another enjoyable weekend, steeped in nostalgia and memories of long ago.

Pete Henry was another of that 49B intake to attend the '99 Reunion. Pete had gone on to serve in the RE after his boys' service. As to why this had happened, he has an interesting theory. He explains that Sappers tend to be either *"mad, married or Methodist"*. On leaving the School in 1952, Pete certainly wasn't married, nor was he of religious bent!

Following some operations and courses of radiotherapy and chemotherapy, Pete had made it well known to his surgeons, doctors and nurses that he would be there at *"the fiftieth"*, come rain or shine. Setting off from his home in Blackheath, by the time he'd travelled a quarter of a mile, he was well into his first traffic jam! Following a four-hour journey, Pete made it in the end and *"reported in"* along with many other arriving old boys of various eras.

Having made his bed and had a quick wash and brush-up, Pete made his way to the bar, noting a *"spiritual gathering of young men, aged about sixteen to nineteen years"*, accompanied by a noisy background of laughter and merriment. They were all recognisable by their *"corpulent forms, receding and sparse hair, along with ... ... jowls and wrinkles"*. Needless to say, these were the colleagues of his youth, still in a state of denial – no *SAGA* or *Viagra* needed here! It was good to meet up with old pals, which included Bernie Shrubsole, Gordon Bonner and John Cassells. John's twin brother had served at Arborfield in the same intake, but had been shot by 'EOKA' terrorists in Cyprus, sometime in the late Fifties.

Arborfield's wasn't the only reunion that year. The Association of Harrogate Apprentices, which had disbanded as long ago as 1962, now suddenly hoped to spring back to life, with more than 200 ex-apprentices having responded to a call to re-register. They included previous members of the PS, GSC, RE, R Sigs and REME. Meanwhile, since Beachley Camp had closed

Cfn Peter Baldwin in Khartoum

in 1994, Chepstow old boys had been forced into being a self-financing organisation, but were still holding annual get-togethers at various venues.

An extended REME Museum

On October 22nd, *"the Duke of Edinburgh, Colonel-in-Chief, opened the Prince Philip Hall at the Corps of Royal Electrical and Mechanical Engineers Museum of Technology"*. Thus was the event recorded in the *Daily Telegraph*. Approximately eighty invited visitors, comprising a number of senior officers and senior heads of industry, attended that opening and some later returned to view the exhibits. This, of course, prepared the Hall for the following day, when members of the OBA were also able to visit the Museum during their Reunion weekend.

That very same evening, a Friday, saw a memorable event for ex-boys of 56B. Having previously met together in 1996 to celebrate their 40th anniversary of joining, a very similar event had taken place in June 1999, forty years on from their leaving. Then came a phone call from Rodney Smith in California to Pete Gripton in Hampshire, asking whether or not another 'reunion' could be arranged, all at Rodney's expense. Thus it was that on October 22nd, a hotel on the bank of the Thames at Sonning Common saw twenty-five 56B old boys, mostly accompanied by their ladies, gather together for a splendid evening over a wonderful meal, well washed down by plenty of lubricant! Cheers, Rodney!

In that same month, the new College RSM became RSM W T Emmerson of the Coldstream Guards, replacing RSM Phil Rooney. Life for the current crop of apprentices continued to be as busy as ever. Recruiting remained healthy and both the trade training schools and the field army welcomed the *"quality, enthusiasm and commitment"* of the young soldiers passing out of the College. Expeditions had taken place in such far-flung outposts as Austria, Bavaria, Cyprus, Nepal and Spain, helped on their way by non-public funding from the College Trust Fund and the OBA. The intention to lengthen the seven-month course to a year was to be temporarily shelved, pending a decision to be made on the future situation at Harrogate.

Earlier that year, Col (Ret'd) Peter Gibson, Membership Secretary of the OBA, had persuaded the editor of *The Craftsman* to place an occasional announcement reminding readers of the existence of the Association. Towards the end of 1999 he received a letter that proved it had been well worth while. Ex-Sgt Armourer Jim Newton, now living in Detmold, Germany, had left the School (as it then was) in 1953 and had heard nothing from the OBA since – unfortunately a not unusual story. Jim went on to say that a German friend of his had found a copy of *The Craftsman* blowing around in the wind, at the town waste paper dump! He had brought it for Jim to read, which Jim duly did, and now here was Jim's letter asking *"Do we really did need him, as the announcement stated?"* Writing himself in *The Craftsman*, Peter was now requesting that all future copies should be on heavy duty or even greaseproof paper!

Writing in *OBAN Issue 18*, Peter announced that production of the planned *'Membership Directory'* for the OBA was continuing, albeit at a slow pace and that ex-boy Mike Davis (60B) had recently offered his services as the Association's treasurer. This means that the OBA will, in future, run its own account, rather than be part of the Arborfield Army Central Bank set-up. Meanwhile, David Schofield of 65A had volunteered to become the Association recruiting and publicity member, in an effort to widen the net and drum up new membership.

Wot, no artefacts?

Another contributor to that *OBAN* was 'perennial old boy' Harry Shaw, who finally cleared up some of the mystery that had surrounded the dismantling of the old barracks a few years previously. Since then, many ex-boys had written in to say that there must have been much 'loot' hidden away under the old floorboards, including the surmise from Nick Webber that there were even parts of an old Bren gun! Harry, who had supervised the demolition personally, with obvious self-interest, sadly announced that there were *"no artefacts of interest"*, except for some sweet wrappings. Another legend bites the dust!

The Military Education Wing houses an excellent library

Although the accomodation buildings may be tired and suffering from a lack of investment and maintenance these two buildings are fine examples of what can be done when there is a will to do so!

Compare the New Gymnasium shown below with the Old Camp Hall shown on page 460

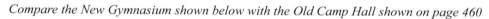

Annex to Chapter 15

A new era for training
By RSM Rooney, Welsh Guards.

'Flexibility' is a common word used in the Army today. This is certainly true when you find yourself one day being in South Armagh, directing helicopter operations in support of a Battalion, like the Welsh Guards. You could also be patrolling against terrorism in what is known as 'bandit country', or the next moment taking over as the RSM of the Army Apprentices College. These examples of differing experiences of military life could not be further apart.

As the new RSM, I was extremely eager to 'get stuck into' College life, a bright and challenging appointment. Having served in training establishments before, for example at the Guards' Depot, Pirbright as a Sergeant and the NCO's Tactical Wing in Brecon as a Colour Sergeant, I thought that the Apprentices College would be a breeze.

My first experience of 'apprentices' in the College was having to deal with the Arborfield Old Boys Association! These fine upstanding gentlemen, some a little more crooked than others *(Is that in both senses of the word? Ed.),* were having their annual weekend here at their Reunion. Each of these old boys, some nearly eighty years old, were telling their tales of Army life in days gone by and of the wrath that they endured from the RSM of the time.

The Army has definitely changed since those days and, with it, the life of the 'modern apprentice'. Soldiers today are now members of a highly technical, rapid deploying, flexible fighting force. The ethos of the present College is designed to give young apprentices character development, through leadership and adventurous training, plus the basic military skills needed to assist their particular trade in the Field Army.

The demands on an apprentice today, either male or female, are far greater than the era of those early 'Old Boys'. Depending on trade discipline, apprentices are expected to maintain, repair or use pieces of equipment, under pressure, in some of the most challenging environs of the world. This is when the training and discipline learned at the College will serve to show how capable they really are.

In a relatively short period of time, the College has experienced massive change; firstly by name, from Princess Marina College, back to the well-established Army Apprentices College. The establishment has also seen the addition of 82 Training Squadron, RE and St. Omer Squadron, RLC, to complement 263 (Harrogate) Squadron, R Sigs and Carlisle Company, REME. With the four training units within the present College and the multitude of cap-badges worn by the Staff, we at the Army Apprentices College should be proud of this diversity and spirit as we train for the future.

(This article is based upon that first published in the June 1998 edition of The Arborfield Apprentice.)

A tribute to the late RSM Ben Cook – Grenadier Guards
By Dick Wade (39A)

In May '39 at the Apprentice School gate,
Who was this ruddy-faced fellow?
For an answer, not long did I have to wait,
As from beneath his peaked hat he would bellow.

'Get fell in then', said this fine RSM,
'And do it at the double!
Refusing to heed the orders I give,
You lot will soon be in trouble!'

From that day on, from morning till dusk,
Ben Cook was always about.
On morning parade, his day would be made,
As drill orders he would belt out.

During the cold winter seasons,
Come rain, come hail or come snow,
From Company 'A' to Company 'E'
At the double he would go.

Around those spider huts he went,
The Barrack Square was looking bare
But there was just the one exception,
Ben Cook, alone, just standing there.

Rigidly he stood at attention,
'Get in step you idle boys!'
Though Ben could hardly see us all,

He always made a lot of noise.

But we were not the only ones
He chased by day and night,
He chased the permanent staff as well,
Which gave them all a fearsome fright.

When war broke out, old Ben would shout,
'It's time to increase your skill,
Sandbags to fill for some protection,
Dig for victory – this land you'll till!'

Now Ben was an accomplished drinker,
Favourite spot the Mess,
Then wandering around the perimeter,
His own ideas on how to dress!

Just open-necked shirt, no tunic,
His trousers held by braces,
He'd catch us by-passing the Guardroom,
In the unlikeliest of places.

Aside from all that has been written,
I'm sure Ben liked us all.
No doubt, he was a great character,
As adults now we recall.

So I would say, in his own sort of way,
Shortcomings whatever they be,
He also had a heart of gold,
On that we can all agree.

Thus a final tribute to kind old Ben,
He led us boys to be worthwhile men.
So through our reunions, never forgotten,
Our dear beloved RSM.

(This poetic tribute is based upon that first published in issue 11 of the OBAN, spring/summer 1997.)

The Brat

It started way back in May '57,
I arrived at the gates at ten past eleven.
Fred Silvers was there, with his pace-stick and hat,
I was to learn a trade as an Arborfield Brat.
They threw me some kit and gave me a bed
And ten million questions entered my head.

Would they feed me or beat me and would I cry?
Did that sign on the gate say 'Arbeit Macht Frei'?

They fed me then drilled me until I was beat,
But taught me to stand upon my own feet.
Fitting and filing, with much drill and study
And boxing each day, until I was bloody.
Bull up your boots – but iron them first,
Get rid of the bumps and build up a thirst.
Bed blocks were square, with edges so fine,
I had tin and cardboard tucked into mine!

Clean windows with Brasso, boot-polish the floor,
Your room must be better than the others' next door.
March to the Cookhouse for three meals a day
To keep up your strength for your sport and your play.
Learn all the parts of the .303 gun,
Whilst screaming out loudly "1, 2, 3 – 1".
Relax at the weekend, if not on a cadre,
Sing loud in the Church and smile for the Padre.

Selection for trade was a bit underhand,
Any discussion on choice was totally banned.
After two years of graft, it was time to deploy
With the skills and ambition of an Arborfield boy.
The 'big day' came – with pride, I confess,
When we passed off the Square in our smart battle-dress.
National Service was still on the go,
But we were much better – as our 'G-flogs' did show!

We marched to the station and onto the train,
Our time and our efforts had not been in vain.
We then crossed the Channel on a stinking troop-ship,
Then a smart train to Duisberg completed the trip.
And that was the start of a varied career,
Touring the world – and drinking its beer!
I could tell you some stories of places I've seen,
But the system has changed and it's not what it's been.

But even today, the challenge is there,
Get out and enjoy it, but do be aware.
With a good sense of humour and pride in his chest,
The Arborfield Brat is still one of the best.

(This poetic offering was published in The Craftsman magazine of February 1998, by 'Anon'.)

How it used to be - verandahed offices and tree lined roads

Chapter 16

2000 and onwards

Think of a name!

Early in the new Millennium, many ongoing debates centred upon the need for a new name for the College. Given the structure and short length of the current course at that time, it was becoming difficult to correctly present the ethos of the training establishment to careers advisors, recruiters, parents and, most importantly, to the new recruits themselves. No longer was anywhere near a full apprenticeship being offered at the College, merely the foundation training for the lead-in to the government's 'Modern Apprenticeship' scheme. Indeed, many of the trade groups that were now passing through the College did not fall within the MA scheme at all.

Meanwhile, however, further building work was envisaged at Rowcroft. Both the MTW and the Maths Department were seeking new and permanent homes within the barracks, as a consequence of the proposed redevelopment of their current facilities into a Garrison Community Centre. During that year's summer leave period, the College was still able to mount two adventure-style expeditions, one based on climbing and kayaking in central Norway, and the other involving sub-aqua diving in northern Spain.

The Craftsman magazines of January and February 2000 contained an article by ex-WO1 (ASM) Bob Alleway, who was now working as an instructor at a military technical school in Abu Dhabi, on the Persian Gulf. Bob had seen out his apprenticeship up at Carlisle in the early Sixties, but still retained memories – most of them fond! – of his days spent there. One nerve-wracking experience was the visit to the medical centre for jabs – these were to ward off all diseases known to man - and then some! He remembers *"about one hundred skinny, pale torsos"*, lining up to pass through the gap between two bored medics, each armed with a hypodermic. Acting in synchrony, they plunged their seperate needles time after time into opposite arms until the points were too blunt to penetrate, before deciding it was time to get out some new ones.

Bob recalls the humiliation of first venturing out onto the streets of Carlisle, almost *"shaven headed"* in the days when the likes of the Beatles and Rolling Stones had influenced the more alluring long-haired styles. However, the evenings were blessed by supplies of a strong local ale, which came from a state-owned brewery and was thus cheap enough even for apprentices' pockets. The only trouble was that it tasted pretty vile and had to be suffered rather than enjoyed! Since those days of forty or so years ago, Bob has often had overnight stays in the town, travelling backwards and forwards to his home in Scotland and still, in his mind's eye, sees *"people and places that shaped and changed his life forever"*.

Following the unfortunate cancellation – indeed, the term 'washout' springs to mind! - of the outdoor Parades and Drumhead services at the previous two OBA Reunions, due to some rather nasty outbreaks of rain, it had been agreed at the 1999 AGM that the occasion of the 2000 Reunion be moved to the hopefully better weather of June. Another happy occasion was graced by the presence of another ex-boy as its focal point.

For the second consecutive year, an apprentice who had gone all the way up to the rank of Major General was the guest of honour, this time in the shape of Maj Gen (Ret'd) Gerry Berragan, of 48B intake, who had taken up his senior appointment in 1985. Gerry proudly carried out the 'duty' of Reviewing Officer and it was noticed that desperate efforts were being made by the assembled ex-boys to hold their tummies in, though with not quite the same success that they had enjoyed in days gone by!

Having been a member of both 50A and 50B, it was hardly surprising that Clem Clements, now well over his dermatitis, found himself lumbered with writing the 'official' account of the 2000 Reunion. For the previous three years, Clem and another of his era, Tom Lennox, had been striving to contact as many of those 1950 intakes as possible, in order to attend their 50th anniversary. The amount of telephone calls they made was revealed when the bills came in, but it was a worthy effort. In total, they managed to track down over forty ex-boys of their year, of which twenty-two actually made it to that Reunion weekend. What pleased Clem, as much as anything else, was being told that he hadn't changed a bit and that he certainly didn't look all of his sixty-five years. *(Bet you told them the same tale Clem! Ed.)*

New methods of Communication

In *OBAN Issue 19* of spring 2000, David 'Titch' Schofield of 65A, brother of the late Ken Schofield (62C), was able to announce that the OBA had also moved forward into the 21st Century. David had been instrumental in the setting up of the 'OBA Website', which means that information regarding all old boys' activities can now be looked up and exchanged over the Internet. No doubt this novel 'instant' method of communication will continue to expand and 'spread the gospel' over many years to come.

The same *OBAN* gave Alex Cunningham the chance to reminisce and, as he put it, *"wallow in the past"* for a short while. He had only recently become aware of the existence of the OBA, despite his intake of 42A putting him fairly and squarely amongst almost the oldest of old boys! Alex looked back fondly on the names of those who had been instrumental in shaping his early life and who have, of course, already featured in the pages of this history. Those names included all of *"the usual suspects"* like RSM McNally, Sgt Hotchkiss, QM Capt Ben Cook, WO1 Stan Cunliffe, Cpl Alf Danahar, Bandmaster Nel and SSgt Denis Compton.

By the end of that year's summer term, the College now boasted a splendid new *'Astroturf'* hockey and soccer pitch, laid out close to the old Square, and now almost ready for a take-over bid from the building contractors. Work was also soon to commence on a new MTW and Maths Department.

On Thursday 6th July, the REME Museum of Technology hosted a 50th Anniversary Reunion, in remembrance of *"that uncomfortable and bloody conflict"* that had taken place in Korea. Just under a hundred REME veterans attended, which included ex-boys, National Servicemen and regulars. Numbers were swelled by a number of local members of the British Korean Veterans Association and the whole entourage was welcomed by Brig R J Croucher ADC, DEME(A), who gave his assurance that *"this war did not merit the nickname of 'the forgotten war'"*.

In August 2000, Pete Gripton (ex-56B) retired from a civilian Executive Officer post at SEME Bordon,

and thus relinquished his appointment as the SEME representative on the OBA Committee. For a number of previous years, he had brought up the question *"What's happening with the College History?"* at the regular Committee meetings. Unfortunately, the answer had always been *"not too much"* – or words to that effect! Fellow Committee member Brian Hornsey (54A), and editor of the *OBAN*, declared, *"Now that you're retired Pete, why don't you take it on?"* Being of a 'Jeep' intake, he was hardly in a position to refuse! Take it on he did – and you are now reading the outcome of that challenge!

Birth of the Army Technical Foundation College

From September 2000, the name of the College did indeed change once again, when it became known as the 'Army Technical Foundation College' (ATFC) – not to be confused with *Arborfield Town Football Club*! While the new title may have seemed like something of a mouthful to the old die-hards, it did at least ensure some consistency alongside the other junior soldiers' establishment, the AFC, the recently set-up 'non-technical' College at Harrogate.

New apprentices joining the College here at Arborfield are now eligible to gain what is termed a 'Foundation Modern Apprenticeship' – a combination of Key Skills and an NVQ at level 2 in IT. Thus, with a clear conscience and with a firm eye on the many preceding years of successful training, it was resolved to continue referring to our young soldiers, of both sexes, by the traditional title of 'Apprentices'. It is a sign of the times in which we live that females now account for about fifteen percent of each College intake, with no trade group being barred to them. An advert in the new 'school magazine' really did put it into context however, when it declared that *"Due to popular demand, sports bras in all colours, shapes and sizes are now in stock"*. The comment of 'it was never like this in my day' now really does carry the ring of truth!

Another ex-boy in charge

December of 2000 saw the departure of Lt Col Jim Mitchell, the first Sapper ever to have commanded the College. Members of the OBA Committee 'dined him out' in appropriate style, thanking him for the tremendous efforts he had put in on behalf of all old boys during his short stay. Lt Col Mitchell handed over command of the College to Lt Col D A McAvoy, REME, himself an Arborfield ex-apprentice from what seemed like 'only yesterday', 74C to be precise. After qualifying as a Radar Tech, 'young McAvoy' had served in a wide variety of appointments, mainly with the RA, moving up through the ranks, via Artificer training, until reaching WO1 (ASM). He had been selected for commissioning in 1990 and, having secured a First Class Honours Degree in Electronics and Computing, converted to a mainstream post in 1994.

The timing of this change of command at the College was rather inopportune regarding the edition of *OBAN* issued at the turn of the year. The outgoing CO's heavy schedule had left him little opportunity to write about the 'state of play'; thus it befell to RSM Emmerson to produce the latest progress report on the College story. Having followed in *"the footsteps of some very famous Guardsmen"* and himself having joined the junior Army as a sixteen-year old, the RSM felt eminently qualified to pass true comment. His words provided a calm reassurance that Arborfield remained in good hands and in good spirit. As he put it, *"The days of old may have gone and great men passed on to the College in the sky, but traditions and standards still apply, while the word 'Apprentice' lives on"*.

Issue 21 of the *OBAN* was a major departure from the normal format, in that it provided a number of contributions that were devoted exclusively to the fiftieth anniversary of the Korean War. One entry was an extract from a forthcoming book by John Dutton of 43A, which he hopes to eventually publish, under the title *'The Forgotten Corps of the Forgotten War'*. Other excellent contributions came from Joe Adey and Brian Conway, both ex-42A, Peter Simmonds of 44A, G M 'Tommo' Thompson of 45B and Roger Millard of 46A.

It is a sad but inevitable fact that with the short amount of time an apprentice now spends at the College, there is insufficient time for any attempt at forming an 'old-style' College Band. Nowhere is this sad fact mourned more keenly than amongst the old boys, who had always relished being able to hear some pipes and drums at their annual reunions. However, help may be at hand from amongst the ranks of the old boys themselves, with Mike Cheeseman of 62C asking for volunteers to join him at the 2001 Reunion,

in an effort to re-kindle the sounds of yesterday. Mike had been in the Corps of Drums during his sojourn at Arborfield and had continued his interest in musical matters until the present day.

On Saturday January 1st 2001, a party of apprentices from Evans Platoon paid a visit to the Historic Dockyard and Naval Museum at Portsmouth. Here they were able to take a guided tour of *'HMS Victory'*, the historic flagship of Admiral Lord Nelson. This was followed up by visits to the iron-clad *'HMS Warrior'* and the remains of *'The Mary Rose'*, flagship of King Henry VIII back in Tudor times and which had been recovered from its watery grave, after 439 years in the Solent, during 1984.

A/T Solari, of 82 Training Sqn RE, gave his 'first impressions' after joining the College and found that the staff were *"laid back – more like civilians than military"*. Times certainly had changed! Adventurous sporting opportunities were still available, as reported by A/T Sampson, who was looking forward to ten days of sub-aqua diving in Spain, and A/T Priest, who encouraged his pals to attend at Bracknell Ski Centre and try their hand at the fast-growing new sport of Snowboarding.

Bailleul Sergeants' Mess was the scene of another 'old boys' reunion in February 2000 but, rather unusually, this time they were all ex-Beachley boys! Intakes 50A and 50B had searched in vain for a suitable venue for their 50th Anniversary Reunion but, thanks to the eagle-eyes of Joe Kinson, who had spotted their notice in *The Craftsman*, Corps RSM, WO1 Parsons was approached for permission to use the Corps Mess here at Arborfield. The whole weekend proved a remarkable success, and included a visit to the REME Museum, which was specially opened for the occasion. That was deemed a *"pilgrimage to this holy spot"*, but there was one bunch of tearaways who mistakenly headed towards the outskirts of Reading to seek out the fabled *'Bramshill Hunt'*!

'We know it doesn't fit!'

Over the period of February – April 2001, *The Craftsman* magazine published three consecutive articles, submitted by Gerald Johnson of intake 56B, under the tongue-in-cheek heading of *"We know it doesn't fit"*. Gerald, who prefers to be known as 'Johnny', hailed originally from Chichester, Sussex, although he had *"signed on the dotted line"* just along the coast at Brighton. John passed out of the School, as it was then, in 1959, as an Armourer. The three articles combined to produce an obviously well remembered account of his three years boys' service, an authentic tale that will be only too familiar to hundreds of boys who spent their formative years under similar circumstances.

Leaving home in 1956 hadn't been anything new to John, as he had previously spent a few years living with his grandmother, and followed that by a couple of years spent at the British Army's 'Windsor' boarding school at Hamm, in Germany. Upon his arrival at Wokingham railway station for onward transportation to Arborfield, John was both relieved and pleased to meet up with two other ex-Windsor boys, Klaus Pennington and Ralph Wright.

Upon leaving the British Army in 1968, John then went directly to join the Zambian Army for a period of three years, before working as a technical instructor for another two. Amazingly, he then went on to join the South African Naval Defence Force (SANDF) where, despite his naval uniform, he actually ran the Infantry desk, writing technical articles on worldwide trends in weapons and associated equipment. His earlier experiences as a REME Armourer held John in good stead, he had always been a *"keen shot"*, and he went on to become the Zambian Defence Force champion in 1969, then SANDF champion in 1975.

John had written his series of articles as part of a general 'life history' that he intended to eventually hand over to his children and heirs. It is fortunate indeed that the story has been passed on and published by the editors of *The Craftsman*, as even at such a distance of both miles and years, John's prodigious memory has recalled a tremendous amount of detail of 'how it was'. It is possible that Brian Hornsey will reproduce the articles in the pages of the OBAN as a lasting ex-boy's tale. *(This happened, starting in OBAN Issue 26. Ed.)*

An uncertain future

In his first Chairman's Message, published in *OBAN 22*, Lt Col Derek McAvoy reported that there was still an ongoing debate over the outlook for the ATFC, regarding such matters as its size, its location and who it will train. Although the answers were not forthcoming at the time, he had been strongly assured that the present College and its staff would still have a major role to play in any planning for the future.

The new Military Training and Maths Department was due to open in April 2001, with the previous building (once the REME Officer's School) now reduced to rubble. As CO of the College, Lt Col McAvoy passed on the following message to all serving apprentices and junior ex-apprentices – *"You could be where I am today."* This was no doubt the same message that had been passed on to him by his own Commandant, Col Barrie Keast, back around 1977! It was quite a pleasant coincidence that both Barrie, and now Derek, were old boys.

David Schofield was amazed to announce, in that same OBAN, that the 'guest book' on the Old Boys' Website, *arborfieldoldboys.co.uk*, had already received over 30,000 'hits' since its inception. Things had started quite slowly, but now there were some 1,000 hits per week, proving that the spirit of comradeship and need to 'keep in touch' continued to thrive. At the same time, Peter Gibson had almost put into effect the printing of the OBA Membership Directory.

April 19th 2001 finally brought a conclusion to a proposal that had been brought up at the Old Boys' 37th AGM, held in June the previous year. Discussions at that meeting had led to the Committee being tasked with obtaining charitable status for the OBA. It was felt that this would be financially advantageous to the Association and to give it a 'legitimacy' that perhaps it hadn't had hitherto. Considerable assistance was provided by Dorothy and Bryan Gudgeon, experts in the charity field and so, on the date mentioned, the OBA was established as a *bona fide* charity, registered under the Charity Commission as such.

A barrage of encouragement from some of his fellow ex-boys of the era had brought 'Mitch' Mitchell of 43A back into the OBA and, like many others before him, he now wondered why it had taken him so long. Since then, he had been reading through as many back numbers of the *OBAN* as possible, a pastime that brought many marvellous memories flooding back. Even today, whenever he hears that Disney tune, *"Hey ho, Hey ho, it's off to work we go"*, he shudders at the thought of his beanpole and goose-bumped body, clad in PT shoes and those big baggy blue shorts, whose elasticated waistband seemed to come up to his armpits! He recalled that RSM McNally must have worked wonders, coping with *"such a mass of monsters"*, but also remembered the sarcastic remarks from the same gentleman when he (Mitch) made a shambles of his 'right marker' duties!

'Kilroy was here'

Mitch's memory had obviously been stimulated by his 'return to the flock'. Writing in a later *OBAN*, he recalled the origins of two characters that became famous during the wartime days of his Arborfield service, namely *'Chad'* and *'Kilroy'*. The former has long since bitten the dust, except in the memory of such as Mitch. Chad was a cartoon character which would poke his nose over a wall and utter such phrases as *"Wot no fags?"* or *"Wot no nylons?"* reflecting the shortages of those long-gone days. He was particularly popular among the men – and women – serving in the forces, and was the invention of cartoonist 'Chat' (George Edward Chatterton).

Kilroy still lives on today, in fact he is an ubiquitous character, as proven by the popular graffiti, still seen all over the place, confirming that *"Kilroy was here"*. Unlike Chad, who was very much an English character, Kilroy is considered to have been based upon a certain overseer, James Kilroy, who would chalk up that very phrase on goods that he had inspected at a shipyard in the USA. Of such are legends born!

(Mitch also provided two small poetic contributions in honour of his intake, which are reproduced as an annex to this chapter.)

April 20th 2001 saw the end of another long career, one that exemplified the ethos of what it has always been to serve as an Arborfield apprentice, and then to carry those qualities gained into one's adult service. Fred Tomlinson had joined the AAS in September 1952, as a member of intake 52B. After passing out as a Tels Mech in 1955, he had joined the first ex-apprentice group to attend an ONC Course at Reading Technical College, passing with distinction. It was only four years later that he returned to Arborfield to start his Artificer Tels course.

During the early Seventies, Fred had been 'head-hunted' by the RAEC to become an Instructional Officer, with his final posting bringing him 'back home' to what was then the AAC, Arborfield. Upon subsequently leaving the Army, he continued serving here at the College, gladly passing on the benefits of his knowledge and long experience to those apprentices fortunate enough to become his students. Firstly as a Burnham Lecturer, and then as a contractor to both *SERCo* and *Vosper Thorneycroft*, Fred finally clocked up the best part of 49 years loyal service.

Care in the community

One day during the summer of 2001, apprentices from Scott Troop took part in a successful venture at the Ravenswood Care Home in nearby Yately, which caters for people with learning difficulties. The work of painting fences, digging flower-beds, laying out rockeries and lawns, all went so well that it could well have been included in the popular TV series *'Ground Force'*! The voluntary assistance saved the home from having to pay the costs of a contract, a fact that was greatly appreciated by both the staff and residents. As for the apprentices, it was an opportunity to learn and socialise with less fortunate members of society.

Meanwhile, members of Dettingen Platoon set off on a week's 'EL'. The first two days were spent in North Wales, with a little hill walking, accompanied by the honing of map reading and navigational skills. During their first day, the apprentices observed a *Sea King* helicopter picking up an injured climber and, on the second day, the summit of Snowdon was achieved. A move down to Sennybridge, in the Brecon Beacons of South Wales, was followed by some kayaking at Caswell Bay, on the beautiful Gower Peninsular near Swansea. There was also some indoor climbing on a very rigorous wall and, finally, a session at the modern pastime of paint-balling, which can give a most realistic simulation of what it's like to take part in a real shooting battle.

On Saturday June 23rd 2001, it was time for the old boys to once again meet together and enjoy their 38th Anniversary Reunion Dinner. Before the evening's meal was served in the College dining-hall, they were asked to sing along to what has been recognised as the 'official' College song *'The Arborfield Apprentices'*, as arranged by 'Bandy' – or 'Shiner' - Nel back in 1942. A songsheet had been produced, courtesy of old stalwart Brian Conway, and the intention was to 'record' the singalong and issue it on compact disc (CD), along with other tunes. The words that appear below may not be the same words that one will hear on the CD when it is issued!

The Arborfield Apprentices sleep, skive, snivel and creep,
The Arborfield Apprentices, enough to make a Tara weep,

The Arborfield Apprentices, skilled, drilled, able, unique,
Get a grip, get it fixed, we're a team that's hard to beat.

Here, here, the boys are here, in affiliation, our Association,
Here, here, the boys are here, members of the OBA,
We are a grand old team to be with
And it's a grand old place to be,
When you hear its history
It's enough to make us proud that we are members,
We don't care what anyone says as on parade we go,
For we only know that there's gonna be a show
And the Old Boys together will be there (get off me barrer!)
And the Old Boys together will be there.

On a more serious note, College Padre Philip Bosher addressed the old boys who sat down to their Reunion dinner with the following 'Grace', which was published in the *OBAN* that followed:

Almighty God, we give thanks this night
For food and wine and perhaps the odd pint,
For friends and colleagues old and new,
Apprentice boys through and through.
We celebrate this time to share
In stories based on yesteryear.

And while the lamp is fully swung
With tales and deeds 'when we were young',
You may look with envy at the apprentice today,
No bed-blocks for them, just a simple duvet.

And as the night begins to wear on,
With wine and food and perhaps the odd song,
The noise will grow loud, our balance may sway,
And before you know it, it'll be a new day.
So now I ask that with one accord
You all say 'Amen' to give thanks to the Lord.

Old memories never fade

On the Sunday morning of that Reunion Weekend, not having too far to travel to reach home, John Smithson (46B) quietly paid a visit to nearby Arborfield Parish Church, something he had been planning to do over many previous years, but had never got around to. Arriving at the Church, he found a service in progress and decided to *"nose around"* the graveyard. As he put it, *"always an interesting experience"*. To his surprise and great pleasure, he came across a gravestone with the following inscription:

In loving memory of Harry Edward Cook MBE (Ben)
Born 1898   Died 1978

In John's own words, which he later contributed to an edition of the *OBAN*, *"so there he lies, as much a part of Arborfield today as he always was"*. Upon reading that same *OBAN*, Ben's daughter, Molly Pewsey, now living with husband John on the Isle of Wight, cannily remarked that Ben had been duty bound to lie here in Arborfield. Thus he will forever be *"keeping an eye on everything and everyone"*, as well as being only *"a bicycle ride's distance from his favourite pubs"*.

It fell to Alan Morton of 51B to report on the 2001 Reunion in the pages of the *OBAN Issue 23*. He commented that things had gone to plan in the usual style but that, *"hand on heart"* it was the best one he had ever attended. That's the effect of 50 years full of memories! Alan went on to reflect upon the youthful faces that surrounded him that weekend – and they were the ones that belonged to the CO and the RSM! He still found it difficult to call Lt Col McAvoy the 'CO', to him and those of his era the 'boss' had been the 'Commandant' – and probably always will. Alan was also moved to praise the standard of the catering that weekend – the Friday supper, the Saturday breakfast and buffet, the Reunion dinner, and even the Sunday morning bacon and eggs. *(If you, dear reader, care to cast your thoughts back to Alan's joining at what was then 'the School', he's talked of little but food ever since! Ed.)*

Also following that 2001 Reunion, it was a nice touch for the present *ATFC Newsletter (Arborfield Informer)* to publish an article that described the occasion, penned by Sgt Sands, the Drum Major.

(The full text of the article can be found as a separate annex to this chapter.)

The same *Newsletter* gave a brief history of the Royal Corps of Signals. It was a direct descendant of 'C Telegraph Troop RE', which had been formed as long ago as 1870. The official agreement to form a separate Signal Corps was then made in 1918 but, due to various delays, the actual formation was delayed until June 28th 1920. The Royal Warrant was signed by the then Secretary of State for War, the Rt Hon Winston S Churchill, giving the Sovereign's approval. It was on August 5th the same year that HM King George V conferred on the new Corp the high honour of the title 'Royal'. Thus was born the Royal Signals, which has been involved in every major conflict and peacekeeping role since its formation.

Whilst attending the 2001 Reunion, Bill Freeman of 48B was chatting with some old pals and the subject came up, of some names having been surreptitiously scratched on the brickwork of the old small-bore rifle range, back in their 'good old days'. Ray Derrick's name was put up as a possible scribe, but he couldn't for the life of him recall ever doing it! Anyway, some historical research seemed most appropriate and these old boys made their way to the range. Searching brick by brick, Ray was astonished – and delighted – to find his name clearly inscribed. A great way to celebrate the weekend.

Return to winning ways

On July 7th 2001, the ATFC hosted the finals of the Army Youth Challenge Cup at soccer. In their group match, the ATFC side squeezed out the previous year's winners, 11 Signal Regt, by the only goal of the game, then handsomely beat the team from SEME, Bordon, by three goals to nil. A pulsating final was then fought out between ATFC Arborfield and the AFC Harrogate, a real humdinger of a 'derby' match. The home side took the game by a score of 3 – 2, so becoming the first Arborfield College side to have won the trophy since PMC had done it back in 1990.

On the same day, Carlisle Coy organised a Charity Fun Day, which actually ended up being a miniature Garrison Family Fun Day – a rehearsal for the 'real' one held two weeks later. The car boot sale was a bit of a disaster when only two cars turned up! Fortunately, other events proved more successful, including a car-wash marathon and the College barber volunteering to have his head shaved by one of the apprentices – brave fellow indeed (the barber, not the apprentice!). The day's events ended with a grand raffle, a disco and a 'Karaoke' competition, with around £500 finally raised

in aid of the *Wokingham Guide Dogs*.

In the early hours of August 17th 2001, their 'PoP' still fresh in their minds, nine junior soldiers, having just completed their Phase I training at the ATFC, and along with four members of staff, set off to explore the sights of the South American country of Peru. After a demanding fourteen-hour flight, the lads were exhausted by the time that they landed at the capital, Lima. They were amazed at the amount of traffic, noise and pollution in that city, but their greatest challenge was probably provided by the delicacies known as 'empenadas', which they described as *"spicy pasties"*. However, they wisely declined the offer of washing the pasties down with the local health drink – liquidised bullfrog!

Leaving the city, they then flew on to the inland town of Cusco, having to acclimatise to the thin air at 3,400 metres. Later, they encountered everything *"from tarantula spiders to anything that could be manufactured from alpaca wool"*. The ultimate challenge of the whole expedition, amongst the snow-capped mountain peaks, was their eventual ascent up the 'Inca Trail' to the world-renowned site of Machu Picchu. They were astonished to find just how popular – and busy – it was. The other noticeable thing was that they were the only party carrying their own kit, everyone else making use of the local porters. There was quite an amount of suffering, due mainly to the altitude and heavy equipment being carried, but the gallant party made slow but steady progress and, after a final forty-minute 'stroll' up the almost vertical steps, they got their well-deserved first glimpse of this mystical and ancient Inca city.

An infamous attack

On September 11th 2001, came the unprecedented terrorist assault on New York, that changed its famous skyline for ever, when hijacked airliners were deliberately crashed into the 'Twin Towers' of the World Trade Centre, bringing them down and killing thousands of innocent occupants. Viewers around the world, including those starting their Army careers at Arborfield, watched the horrific scenes unfold on 'live' television, with shock and anger bringing home to one and all that the future would be an uncertain one for immeasurable years to come.

Over the first weekend in November, a team from the ATFC took part in the Canoe Whitewater

Racing Championships, held at Barnard Castle in North Yorkshire. There were over eighty participants, including the Army Training and Recruiting Agency (ATRA) units from Sandhurst and Harrogate. Second places were gained in both the men's and ladies' U-21 events, while the team (including PS members) and U-21 team events were both won by the College Canoe Club.

Just a few days later, members of Brunel Platoon took a day's break for an outing to the Imperial War Museum in London. Their initial expectations were that it would be a dull and uninteresting day, but in fact the party returned to Arborfield most impressed by all they had seen. Reporter A/T Butterworth strongly recommended his fellow apprentices to make every effort to attend the Museum, and particularly the harrowing exhibition on 'The Holocaust', which had seared his memory.

A/T Minshull had recently joined the ATFC, but expected "something a whole lot different" to what he found here. These included "jobs I had never thought I would be doing, ranks I had never heard of and the earliest hours of the day I never thought I would see". Obviously, then, some things never change! He went on to say that he was quickly adapting to the change of life-style and looking forward to the remainder of his stay at the College.

In December of 2001, *The Craftsman* published an article under the heading *'Commission Impossible'*. It told the story of three ex-REME soldiers who had gone on to gain commissions with the RAF – this was apparently not such a rare event as it first sounds. One of the three, Dave McLoughlin, had joined Arborfield as an apprentice Air Tech in 1983, going on to serve in Norway, Denmark, Turkey, Germany, Northern Ireland, the Gulf, Italy and the Czech Republic.

After all the flying that must have been involved, perhaps it is no surprise that he transferred to the RAF in February 2000! Dave is now studying for his BSc (Honours) in Engineering Management. Pete Elliott had been a member of 85C and later qualified as a CET. Having served for four years at RAF Aldergrove in Northern Ireland, he also made the decision to transfer to the RAF, in April 1999. The writer of the article, Flight Lt 'Spike' Wright, was not an ex-boy, but spoke for all three soldiers when he said that they were *"proud to have been a part of the best Corps in the Army"*.

All change at Arborfield

In *Issue 23* of the *OBAN*, towards the end of 2001, the CO wrote about the *"element of change"* that was now governing everyday life at he College. The days of being 'marched to the glasshouse' for minor misdemeanours were long gone, he reported, along with getting up in the early hours to polish and clean and such like. *(What a shame! Ed.)* Such considerations as human rights, working time restrictions for those under eighteen, the right to appeal and to seek judicial counsel - these had now all become integral parts of apprentices' lives under the modern system.

All of these matters reflected similar changes in society and were designed to ensure that everything was now *"scrupulously fair"*. Lt Col McAvoy then made the point that the Army had moved on – but questioned whether or not the old boys had done the same. For instance, with such a large proportion of apprentices now leaving the College being of the opposite sex, was it still fair and proper to have the 'OBA' so named? One for discussion at the following AGM, no doubt!

Within the College, internal restructuring was trying to improve efficiency and reduce costs, with the ever-increasing possibility that course lengths would eventually be increased to forty-two weeks. This would form part of the possible creation of an 'Army Foundation Project' – another College – capable of training 2,500 recruits. The likelihood of Arborfield closing down completely in the not-too-distant future was still a subject for discussion, but remained one of those 'perhaps' and 'maybe' situations that had been prevalent now for a number of years.

In January 2002, the ATFC welcomed WO1 RSM D G Mullens to its ranks. Gary Mullens had joined the Army in 1980 and then joined the 1st Battalion Coldstream Guards at Caterham the following year. He then saw service in Hong Kong and Germany, the Falklands, the Gulf and Bosnia interspersed with tours in Northern Ireland. No doubt he will find Arborfield just as stimulating as those other places!

Newly arrived 'Mr Heppell' was quite nervous when he found himself at Reading railway station, as probably the only person to have ever been offered the choice of two empty minibuses, plus the opportunity to be escorted to Arborfield by no less than four Corporals! Two weeks later, A/T Heppell – yes, the very same – looked back upon his first locker inspection. A 'dry run' had found him preening with pride, upon being told *"not a bad first effort"*. The proper inspection that followed shortly afterwards ensured that he now knew how good it was by Army standards – *"not very good at all"*! *(Glad to see that some things haven't changed. Ed.)*

A study was initiated on February 19th 2002, to investigate the Equipment Support (ES) system for Engineer Equipment. Ever since the formation of REME in 1942, the maintenance and equipment support management of equipment operated by the RE has been a shared responsibility between the two engineering corps. But recent and forthcoming structural changes were found to be impacting upon the RE capability to continue the task. The aim of the study, which was to make its recommendations later in the year, was to review the current arrangements and resources for the management, inspection and repair of such equipment.

By the time that the spring 2002 edition of *OBAN* came out around Easter, the CO was reporting that the future of the College was *"now becoming an increasing topic of interest to the higher echelons"*, as financial resources available to the training organisation became ever more limited. He confirmed the 'Project' mentioned previously, with the most likely outcome being the eventual establishment of an AFC that would cater for an estimated total of 2,500 Junior Entry soldiers. This AFC would subsume both the ATFC and elements of Junior Soldier training, currently being carried out at Bassingbourn, a few miles south of Cambridge. The current deadline for this is 2007, by which time apprentices will complete a one-year's course, prior to Phase II trade training. *(Bassingbourn was the wartime base for American B-17 bombers from 1942 onwards, part of the 91st Bomber Group. Most famously known of those bombers was 'The Memphis Belle', which flew twenty-five successful missions and whose crew were all awarded the DFC. Ed.)*

Even more changes ahead

A similar time-frame may well also see some far-reaching changes in the REME training system, with the long-predicted closure of Arborfield Garrison and

WO1 RSM D G Mullens Coldstream Guards

the two sites at Arborfield and Bordon being sold off to the highest bidder. The teaching and training for Mechanical Engineering could move to Portsmouth, alongside the Royal Navy, with Aeronautical Training transferring to RAF Cosford. The future of the College itself managed to look secure for the time being, but its location less so. Hopefully the College and its old boys – and girls – would continue to thrive, having already provided thousands of soldier/tradesmen with a career which has lasted, in so many cases, right through from school age until senior citizenship.

Despite that current uncertainty, the early months of 2002 saw an increasing demand for places at the College. No less than 670 recruits were under training and the place was *"bursting at the seams"*, in the words of Lt Col McAvoy. Thanks in part to a donation from the OBA, the WRVS lounge now boasted a brand-new wide-screen television for the apprentices' entertainment. Adventure training was still continuing apace, including a cross-country backpack skiing expedition in Canada over the Easter break. Planning for the year's OBA Reunion was well advanced – the programme agreed upon, the menus selected and the wines tasted. As said by Bill Cleasby, *"It's a dirty job, but someone's got to do it"*. Or words to that effect!

David Schofield was still *"waxing lyrical"* over the progress of the Old Boys' Website, now grown to a massive thirty megabytes – whatever they are! However, David was finding it increasingly difficult to maintain the site to the best of his ability, with much *"pressure of work, home life and studies"* making overriding demands. Thankfully, help was at hand in the adequate shape of Ken Anderson (58A), who volunteered to take over – and was immediately snapped up! – at the Association's AGM that took place in June. Good luck, Ken, you've already been a film projectionist and a disc jockey – and now you're a webmaster!

The summer 2002 edition of the *Arborfield Informer* displayed a glorious full-colour front cover, in celebration of the fact that this was the Queen's 'Golden Jubilee' year. On the morning of April 20th that year, a party of apprentices enjoyed a long flight to Calgary on an almost empty plane, giving them plenty of room to spread themselves out. Expecting to see a layer of snow below them, it came as quite a surprise to see nothing but brown plains, stretching for mile after mile. Fortunately, by the time they approached the Rocky Mountains by plane, the temperature had fallen and the expected snow began to appear, in readiness for their skiing expedition.

The first Sunday was given over to some serious shopping, with cowboy hats and 'Davy Crockett' coonskins becoming the normal apparel for the next two weeks. The concept of skiing uphill against the laws of gravity came hard, but the old adage of 'what goes up must come down' soon turned minds to the thrills of the return trip - skimming downhill at fast speed. After some exhaustive practice, the team eventually graduated onto glaciers and summits, the highest of these being Mount Olive at 10,300 feet. There were some inevitable spills and crashes, but overall the competence of the skiers at the end of the expedition was considerably higher than it had been at the outset.

Exercise 'Summer Splash' was the culmination of a term's worth of training by the sub-aqua enthusiasts at the College. After weeks in the deep end of the pool and a couple of dips in a cold and murky local lake, both staff and apprentices looked forward to the sunshine and blue waters of Spain's Costa Brava. A long and largely uncomfortable drive across France was followed by the enjoyment of 'bedding in' at their apartments, overlooking the beach. Less than an hour later, they were off for their first dive, which proved both exciting and slightly frightening for some! A packed programme of training dives and rescue techniques paved the way for some excellent diving – and the chance to sample the nightlife afterwards. The last evening ended in the holding of a *"fantastic barbecue"*, before an eighteen-hour return trip. But, as they say, *"No pain, no gain!"*

A record breaking Reunion

2002 was a record-breaking year as far as the OBA Reunion was concerned. A massive total of 280 old boys attended over the whole weekend, with 176 of them managing to swell their chests with pride on the Saturday morning parade. The evening's seating plan had to be drawn up with a certain amount of sleight-of-hand and even lowdown cunning, in order to accommodate the 245 who sat down to enjoy another splendid dinner. *(If numbers increase again next year, perhaps we'll all be issued with shoehorns! Ed.)* One thing that did impress the old boys, and certainly made them feel their age in most cases, was the apparition of two very young and attractive female apprentices serving the tables, both very blonde and mini-skirted. Times certainly have moved on!

It fell to Eggy Egleton of 52B to pen his thoughts on that Reunion, as it coincided with the 50th anniversary of his intake. Sadly, he had a few negative thoughts, most of which were based on the current apprentices' accommodation, which he thought was well below the standard of even the old wooden spiders. There seemed to be many breakages to window frames, lockers and furniture, and all in a state of disrepair, no doubt due to the severe economic conditions that prevail today. The Band also gave him cause for concern, it seemed to be made up from a *"collection of odds and sods from everywhere"*. Yes, those 'good old days' of a School Band had been put firmly in the past. Apart from these points, which in no way reflect upon the apprentices, Eggy was still very pleased to have attended. After all, he realised that many old comrades had been unable to make it, and these were always firmly in his thoughts.

In retrospect, it is only fair to say that those 'odds and sods' were part of a voluntary Band, provided by *The Corps of Drums Society*. This had been set up in 1977 *"to preserve bugle, drum, flute and fife music"*. The Society members include Regular and TA soldiers, Army and Air Force Cadets, Scouts and Guides, members of the Police and Fire Services, plus many other volunteers of a purely civilian background. They give up their time free of charge, drawing only travel expenses, and work very hard at their task. All this was pointed out in a later *OBAN* by Mike Cheeseman (62C), who had been involved with the arrangements for this brave band of musicians to turn up on the day – and play, with very little rehearsal time.

One ex-boy who certainly enjoyed the weekend was Dave Perrott of 49B, as this was the first Reunion he had been to. Having had little contact with the Army at all since leaving in 1960, he was amazed at how it felt *"like only yesterday"*. He suffered the same initial shock as Eggy regarding the state of the sleeping quarters, but soon joined in with old familiar faces and the even more familiar stories that were told. He reflected on the fact that Arborfield had taught him a lot in the past and *"is still teaching me now"*. His spirits lifted and he shared the following poem in the pages of the *OBAN, Issue 25*:

"I came to Arborfield again and saw where it once stood.
The area looked so very small, as I suppose it would.
The place that helped to shape me appeared before my eyes,
I thought about the people, the memories, the ties.

I wondered where they all were now and just how they were rated;
Would they be pleased to see me, or strangely disappointed?
I did not know, I could not say, I could only stand and stare
Across the barren open space and recall what had been there."

Peter Langley, who had joined up as a member of 41D, had always sworn that nothing would ever bring him back to attend a Reunion. But a *"couple of wild horses, Wenborn and Coultas by name, proved fairly persuasive"* and he finally returned to the fold in 2002. He only managed *"the Saturday lunchtime knees-up"* and found it most enjoyable – *"fine weather, good food and heart-warming company"*. He was amazed to see how like-minded people soon gravitated into groups – why else were there no less than seven Armourers at his table? It wasn't that they had all previously known each other, despite the fact that Peter had been one of 100 Armourers that had made up the total of his unique intake over sixty years previously.

Enjoying a busy lifestyle

Exceptionally good weather kindly blessed the ATFC 'Fun Day' on Saturday 15th June. This was a combined event between the College, Arborfield Garrison and the Community Centre, which raised a total of almost £1,000 towards diabetes research and the Army Benevolent Fund. Only a few days later, a number of eager apprentices took part in the national 'Three Peaks' challenge once again, taking in Snowdon, Scafell and Ben Nevis, in that order. Snowdon was accomplished with a certain amount of ease, Scafell Pike proved more difficult in the pouring rain (what's new?), while Ben Nevis came with its own inevitable supply of blood-sucking 'mozzies', all dressed up in their tartan kilts! All in all, a combined height of around 11,000 feet was a considerable achievement.

July 7th brought quite a thrill to those youngsters fortunate enough to attend a firepower demonstration at Larkhill. They had arrived on Salisbury Plain at around 10.00 hours and first spent quite some time visiting static exhibitions, set up by a number of corps, including REME, RE, R Sigs, RLC and the AAC. The latter also gave a spectacular demonstration of the ability and agility of their new *Apache Longbow* helicopter. The finale included a simulated battlefield scenario, which demonstrated the massive firepower of *Challenger 2* tanks, *Warrior* APCs and the *Multi-launch Rocket System (MLRS)* amongst others.

Despite the shortness of the College graduation period in 2002, there were still plenty of events to pack in, with perhaps the most eagerly anticipated time being 'Survival Week', as recruits enter their second term. This is a true test of character and endurance which forever lives in the memory of the participants. When added to the pursuits of rock-wall climbing, cross-country cycling, parachuting and ice hockey undertaken by various individuals, it is clear that the young men and women who join the ATFC still find the whole business a tremendous challenge. Last but not least is the Leadership Week, where young recruits are encouraged to learn the rules of the game, which include *"honesty, fitness, confidence, organisational abilities, respect for others and communication"*.

(On September 10ᵗʰ 2002, as compiler of this history, I went to meet up with Brig (Ret'd) Joe Dobie and his wife Joan. I had realised that, although there were a number of brief career notes on other ex-Commandants, I had not come across one for Joe. I had met him briefly whilst still serving at SEME Bordon, indeed I have in my possession two lovely water-colours painted by Joan Dobie, a talented artist who is still painting, well into her eighties.

Joe himself was looking forward to his eighty-eighth birthday when I visited. Sadly, his memory has all but gone now, but he looks very robust in health, apart from a 'bad leg', as he puts it. Thankfully, Joan's memories of her sixty-two years of 'life with Joe' are pretty vivid and she kindly put together some notes on Joe's career. These are included as an annex to this chapter – a little 'out of synch', being some forty years late, but as they say – better late than never! Ed.)

Read all about it!

David Howlett (56B) thought he had 'seen it all' until, one morning in October 2002, whilst visiting a colleague, he opened the pages of a daily tabloid, *The Sun*. There, staring out at him was the face of someone he recognised. But was it *Captain Jan-Luc Picard* of the *Starship Enterprise*, or just Derek Wheatland of 57A? The story went on to describe the remarkable likeness between the two and the fact that Derek is such a big fan of the TV series. He even admits to wearing Lycra suits, uses the word 'affirmative' instead of a plain 'yes', and yells 'engage' before putting his car in gear! *(You'll have a lot of explaining to do at the next Reunion, Derek. If things get too hot, you can always 'beam' home! Ed.)*

In mid-October, apprentices from 17 Platoon (Pln) were taken down to Warminster, on the edge of Salisbury Plain, for an impressive display of military firepower. The demonstration was run by the Royal Green Jackets (RGJ), with able assistance from elements of the RE, RA, AAC and even the RAF. The youngsters were amazed at the vast range of equipment that was on show that ranged from the SA80 Rifle to *Challenger 2* Main Battle Tanks (MBTs), the Mk7 *Lynx* helicopter and even *Harrier* and *Jaguar* aircraft. Despite the weather being *"bleak and cold"*, and many of the apprentices wishing they had packed extra warm gear, the display warmed them up thoroughly, being *"second only to a wartime environment"*. With a second 'real-time' Gulf War definitely on the cards at that time, it is little wonder that the demo was also attended by members of the United States Marine Corps (USMC).

Towards the end of that year, Col G Hughes, REME's Chief Engineer, was concerned that during recent times, perhaps REME had concerned itself too narrowly with concerns of 'Quality', which had indeed been the buzzword for a number of years. A new publication, namely *'Engineering Standards in REME'*, had been delayed, as it was thought it was not sending out the correct message. A fundamental review was under way to ensure that, in future, more emphasis was put into REME's traditional concentration on its *military* and *engineering* roles in support of Army operations. After all, hadn't it been 'Monty' himself who had originally described REME as providing *"the punch in the Army's fist"*?

On Friday 15ᵗʰ November 2002, the Wokingham District Sports Council gave the College the award for the 'Best Senior School'. Four young apprentices, all of whom had plenty of sporting prowess, went to receive the award. A/T Harcombe is a 3000m runner, ranked second in his class in England, while A/T Dolly plays football at both District and County level. A/T Aspinall excels at both cross-country and athletics, while 1500m specialist A/T Jones is also ranked second in under-seventeen circles. The reception in Wokingham was a great opportunity for the sporting community to become aware of the talent within its midst.

In the December 2002 edition of *The Craftsman*, another glimpse into the past was provided by John Freeland, a former vice-president and still member of the South Australia Branch of the REME Association. Although not an ex-apprentice himself, he was reporting on a recent visit to Arborfield, inspired by an old school chum who had been! The old boy in question was Norman Donnithorne, who had joined here in April 1943, while John himself had been called up for his National Service in 1944, possibly while Norman was away on 'dispersal' at Bury.

John later also served here at Arborfield, but on his return visit during 2001, his only vague memory of what the Garrison had been like in those far off days was provided by the sight of the old 'Depot' guardroom of Poperinghe Barracks, last used as a newsagent's shop. *(It is hopefully soon to be demolished and re-created at the REME Museum as a permanent memorial. Ed.)*

Benevolence in action

During that December, ex-54A apprentice Brian Stevens, now living in Hereford, found the name of Trevor Stubberfield on a *Teletext* page, via an ex-services 'old friends' contact system. Trevor posted Brian's names on the AOBA Website, explaining that he (Brian) was now sadly housebound due to severe illness. With the OBA having been set up as a charity, its Benevolence Committee was now able to offer assistance in such cases. Brian already had a personal computer at home, but no access to the Internet. Subsequently, the Association was able to purchase a modem for Brian, through which he can now use the Website to communicate with fellow ex-boys around the world. And, of course, the OBA gained a new member!

The January edition of the *Arborfield Informer* contained an article submitted on behalf of the MSD, which told of the history of the VC – surely an inspiring challenge to the ambitions of any would-be heroes in the College!

(The article is reproduced as a separate annex to this chapter.)

The *Craftsman* of February 2003 carried a *Book Review* that gave publication news of a new book, *"Army Apprentices Harrogate"* by Col Cliff Walters. From a personal view of the editor of *this* history, it was interesting to find a fellow spirit! The Apprentices' School at Harrogate remains well known to those of us who served at Arborfield, providing stern opposition in many sporting encounters over the years. The School was founded at Penny Pot Camp in 1947, training young men for the RA, RAOC, RASC, RE, REME and R Sigs. As the needs of the Army changed, so did Harrogate and, by 1962, only R Sigs apprentices were then being trained.

In similar fashion to Arborfield, the 'School' had become a College in 1966 and, towards the end of that decade, was boosted by a £3 million rebuild. The College also kept up with the development of computer systems, being part of the SPEC User Group during the Eighties and into the Nineties. The College up in Yorkshire met its demise in 1996, but the site is now being used as the AFC, for the non-technical training of junior soldiers.

The daily newspapers that same month were reporting on how new recruits were to get *the "kid glove treatment"*. It was said that teenage recruits were likely to react to a parade-ground dressing down by phoning Mum and asking to be taken home. Even the Vice-Chief of the Defence Staff was suggesting that, while discipline was necessary, this did not mean that it should entail any *"punishment"*. A study had been carried out that recommended the creation of a *"training covenant"* between recruits and instructors and the measures taken were designed to reduce the dropout rate amongst new entrants. Whatever would the old style Sergeant Majors like Cook and McNally have thought of all this?

Don't say 'I told you so'

March 2003 brought *Issue 26* of the *OBAN* and what was likely to be the last *'Chairman's Message'* from Lt Col McAvoy, as he prepared to hand over the reins of the ATFC to another 'Sapper', Lt Col Andy Philips. The outgoing CO could offer no long-term vision of the future, except that there continued to be *"a period of immense change within the training organisation"*. What he could definitely report was that the previous shortening of courses was now being seen as 'a cut too far' and urged all ex-boys to *"resist the temptation to shout 'I told you so!'"* Before actually leaving Arborfield, he hoped to have secured the future of the College – well, for the time being anyway!

That same magazine contained a letter from Jack McCabe of 59C, who had only recently been enticed back into the welcoming arms of the OBA. He looked back, probably through his rose-coloured spectacles as he put it, to a period when *"life appeared less complicated, the weather always seemed better, the people more willing to let live and just get on with life in general"*. During his second summer at the AAS, Jack had gone on leave with another seven young lads, down to the *Butlin's Holiday Camp* at Clacton in Essex.

There, he was fortunate enough to meet his future wife, who happened to live at Slough – not too far way from Arborfield. Visits to his future in-laws became the norm and Jack reckons that it was the weekend scrambled eggs on toast that kept him going through the rest of the week!

The latest intake of apprentices numbered 340 and, as their CO looked at this new bunch of recruits, he couldn't help but have that *"creepy feeling, where the emotion floods back on apprehension and excitement"* of what the future may hold. But these 'waifs and strays' were looking for leadership, which they quickly found, as the RSM gripped them into a formed body and marched them off to the QM's Stores. Just another chapter opening, on the long history and tradition of the College.

April's edition of *The Craftsman* gave the announcement that, *"in recognition of one of Britain's toughest military campaigns, a parade is being planned in London on July 9th 2003, to pay tribute to veterans of the Korean War"*. This long-overdue event was being organised by the MoD, in co-operation with the Veteran's Association. The parade would start on Horse Guards' and end at Westminster Abbey, where there would be a thanksgiving service, attended by the Queen, senior politicians and foreign dignitaries. John Dutton's *"forgotten war"* seemed, at last, to be receiving the attention it deserved, a full fifty years after its end.

The future – who knows?

As the summer months of 2003 brought some warm sunshine across most parts of the country, thoughts were turning once again towards the Old Boys'

Reunion planned for late June. Lt Col Derek McAvoy had penned his final 'Chairman's Message', which would appear in the forthcoming edition of the *OBAN*. Unfortunately, he was unable to look forward to a clear and untroubled future – everything was *"up for debate"* and anything he may predict could only *"add more fog to an otherwise confused situation"*. He looked forward immensely to the publication of the history and the continued growth of the website. On a personal note, he added that he was off to *"a high profile job"* at HQ Land Command, at Wilton, just outside Salisbury. His final words were, *"Before I step off, I thank you all, both past and present. Farewell until another fair day"*.

Well, this particular version of the Arborfield history has finally reached an end, but who knows what will happen in the future? Perhaps the history is already longer than the future? Even as these final paragraphs are being written, Armed Forces, mainly from the USA and UK, have invaded across the borders of Iraq, in an attempt to bring down its evil regime. Who knows how many ex-apprentices from Arborfield will be required to serve once again in a theatre of war? It is always hard to gaze into the fabled crystal ball and predict what may or may not happen. But what *is* sure, is that the history of apprentices' training at Arborfield has been a long and successful one. This humble editor hopes that he has been pretty faithful to that history and given a fair description of what it was like, on behalf of the thousands of young men – and now women – who can look back and say *"I was there"*.

In conclusion, perhaps the following words, written by Philip Massinger, who lived from 1583 – 1640, and reproduced in *The Arborfield Apprentice* during 1995, summarise the spirit of Arborfield apprentices everywhere:

To dare boldly in a fair cause and for their country's safety;
To run upon the cannon's mouth undaunted,
To obey their leaders and shun mutinies,
To bear with patience the Winter's cold
And Summer's scorching heat,
And not to faint
When plenty of provision fails with hunger,
Are the essential parts that make up a Soldier.

—§—

Princess Marina College Pass-off Parade, April 1989
from a painting by David Rowlands'

Annex to Chapter 16

The Apprentice Old Boys Reunion

By Sgt Sands, Drum Major.

Like an annual migration, they walked, drove and made their way to their former barracks; some of the ex-apprentices had been here in 1939, others as late as 1989. Their ages were as varied as the locations that they had come from, the furthest arriving from Canada.

The event at the Army Technical Foundation College is a yearly gathering that lasts a weekend. This one started with the Old Boys (as they like to be known) arriving on a Friday evening (after the present intake has departed for their leave period), to be met by the President of the Old Boys Association. The members were then allotted their accommodation, their programme for the weekend and nametags. Where possible, members from the same intake were accommodated together. Here, a transformation was seen in many rooms, as the years slipped away.

On Saturday morning, everyone formed up to march back through the College gates that they had once so proudly marched out of, to join the field Army. The RSM, WO1 Collister MBE was presiding as the REME Band struck up a rousing marching tune and the parade stepped off. Although it had been many years for some of the Old Boys, they maintained the correct step, finally halting at the Memorial Garden. They were met by the Padre, Capt Bosher, and took part in a short service to remember those Old Boys who had fallen in conflict or had died due to old age. A lone piper played the lament 'The Flowers of the Forest' and a bugler played 'The Last Post'. The parade then marched to the old parade square, where the inspecting officer, Col Peregrine, REME Regimental Colonel, and Lt Col McAvoy, inspected the ranks of Apprentice Old Boys.

Following a barbecue at the Sergeants' Mess, many Old Boys visited the REME Museum and Association Shop during the afternoon. After this, a fantastic spread had been prepared for dinner, and the Padre blessed this before everyone tucked in. There was the opportunity to recount the past in the comfort of the Sergeants' Mess once dinner had finished. On the Sunday morning, the Old Boys held a church service before saying their farewells.

I would like to thank everyone involved for their help in organising what was said to be the 'best event yet', and especially the Old Boys themselves for attending. This is an on-going event and can only be made possible by people actually joining the Arborfield Old Boys Association; that means that any ex-apprentice can join. Given the opportunity, I would happily join.

(This article is based upon that published in the October 2001 edition of Arborfield Informer, the current ATFC Newsletter. It was later reproduced in the pages of OBAN issue 24.)

Brigadier (Ret'd) J L Dobie CBE

Joseph Leo Dobie, universally known as 'Joe', was born at Tynemouth, just outside Newcastle, in 1914. Having taken a BSc in electrical engineering at Durham University, his first military experience came with the Tyne Electrical Engineers RE (TA), where he was commissioned as a 2nd Lieutenant RE. He transferred to the regulars when he joined up as an OME 4th Class at Hilsea Barracks, Portsmouth, the Depot RAOC, on April 1st 1938. He started off his Army career by attending the Military College of Science, Woolwich, on a post-graduate course through until 1939 and, being a keen sportsman, he played for local club Blackheath at rugby.

His first posting was to the Command Wksp at Catterick, where he had the job of workshop officer, as well as being the OME to various units. When based at Shrivenham in 1940, Joe and wife-to-be Joan had hardly met each other when he had to set sail for Malta in the early days of October. However, as part of an epic story, his convoy was attacked and severely damaged by German bombers and forced to return back to England. One of the escorting ships was the aircraft carrier *HMS Illustrious*. Joe was then given some 'survivors' leave', during which time he and Joan decided that perhaps it was the correct time to get married. This they did, at Virginia Water in Surrey, but it did not prevent Joe from finally having to sail for Malta once more, on December 16th.

Joe then served in Malta for more than two years,

a duration of almost continuous air raids by planes of first the Italian and then the German Air Forces. The island fortress was under siege both by air and sea, the only re-supplies arriving when the occasional convoy was able to fight its way into Valetta harbour. On April 16th 1942, King George awarded the George Cross to the whole people of Malta, in honour of their *"heroism and devotion"*.

It was also during this period that REME was formed in 1942, and Joe became one of its founder members. Between 1943 and 1944, he was moved to Palestine, at 3 Base Wksp, which he inevitably found rather monotonous after the excitement of Malta, but at least it had the benefit of suffering no air-raids. Joe later found himself supporting the British troops advancing northwards up the spine of Italy, as the 2I/C to the CREME, before returning home to the UK in 1945.

From 1945 until 1947, Joe served here at Arborfield, as 2I/C to Dick Girdlestone at REME's 14 Technical Training Centre. He was also now able to devote more time to his favourite sport of rugby, playing at full-back for an Arborfield team that, in those days, played against many famous sides, including Rosslyn Park, Bedford and London Irish. As a Major, Joe also became club General Secretary.

In 1948, Joe and Joan were delighted to become part of an *"exchange posting"* scheme, dealing with training, between the UK and Australia. Joe's post out there was as DADEME (Training) at Army HQ. They stayed out in Melbourne until 1950, thoroughly enjoying the 'land of plenty' after the rationing and restrictions prevalent here at home after the war. They were also able to travel widely throughout that country, finding it a most rewarding period of their lives.

This was followed by another two *"steadying years"* at the War Office, still dealing with training matters, before Joe was posted to Shrewsbury as CREME of the 53rd Welsh Division TA. Joan recalls that there were no Army quarters available and that some of their hirings were *"dreadful"*. In 1955 it was off to sunnier climes once again, this time with 1st Div in the Canal Zone for nine months – *"lots of sun and sand"*. Their main leisure activities included swimming in the Bitter Lake and watching the ships passing through the Suez Canal.

After that, it was off to Tripoli for a couple of years with 10th Armoured Div, during which time the Suez crisis took place, meaning that wives and children had to return to England for a few months. In 1957, the Dobie family returned to UK, when Joe took up a post as Commandant of No2 Training Battalion REME at Honiton in Devon. This period was memorable for the regular intakes of young National Servicemen, with 'passing-out parades' on an almost fortnightly basis.

Joe then took over as Commanding Officer of 18 Command Workshop at Bovington, Dorset, where he found things very different, being in command of vehicles rather than young soldiers! As he later put it, *"all good experience"*. In 1960, Joe was posted off to the Far East, as CRÈME/ADEME of the 17th Gurkha Division, Overseas Commonwealth Land Forces, at Seramban in Malaya. He found that this was *"a most enjoyable posting"*, the Gurkha troops proving to be fine soldiers.

Early in 1962, Joe returned to England to take up the post of Commandant at the Army Apprentices School at Arborfield. He was also proud to serve as Band President to the School's outstanding Bands during his time here, always finding the Passing-out Parades to be *"great occasions"*. His time here was followed by the best part of two years at 1 BR Corps at Bielefeld, his one and only posting in Germany. This period gave him and Joan an excellent opportunity to explore some of the sights and treasures of Europe.

Joe spent the last three of his thirty-plus years of service as the 'Inspector REME', basically 2I/C of the Corps, travelling widely both at home and abroad, inspecting, advising and counseling, before finally 'calling it a day' in September 1969, at the age of fifty-five.

One of Joe's greatest attributes was his unbounded enthusiasm for the Corps and the projects on which he embarked. He was universally known and respected and *"a visit by the Inspector"* was viewed with much pleasure, tinged by the knowledge that he could fraternise as well as bite!

(These notes were compiled from notes kindly provided by Mrs Joan Dobie in September 2002, and augmented by information gleaned from other sources.)

The Cuckoos in April

"Oh to have been in Arborfield
In April of forty-three,
With blue skies o'er the parade ground
Echoing shouts of one, two, and three.

The boots they were a'shining
But service dress a heap.
With that awful flattened cap
That surmounted the anxious Jeep.

The pass but a dreaming wonder,
When at last the parade stood down.
And not a single A/T made it
From Camp to Reading town.

And not a girl went walking
Along Arborfield's leafy lanes,
But knew A/T's eyes in April
Were quicker than their brains.

It's little that it matters
As long as you're alive,
If you were fifteen that April,
Now rising seventy-five!

When June comes to Arborfield
With skies of cloudless blue
And ex-A/Ts are gathering,
Memories come good and true."

Ode to 43A-ers

"The 2s, 5s, 4s and the 8s,
Numbers to learn, love or hate.
From QM store with kit piled high,
Hardly know whether to laugh or cry.

Bolding, McDonald, Morgan, Mitch,
Mills and Foster – a tubby titch.
A few more, like bees in a hive,
Herded together in room D5.
Where are they now, since '43?
Such varied lives, some RIP!

Beds in rows, greatcoat dollies,
Chinstrap order, like so many follies.
Bullshine, snivel – and not a few creep.
The tender lot of the Arborfield Jeep.

Square bashing, jankers, name in a book;
Off to plough for one, Ben Cook.
Slave away till NAAFI-break,
Then ruddy Gilbert gets the cake!

Cookhouse calls, wait in rows,
Being gypped by the older pros.
In we rush to the feast,
Like a ravenous herd of wildebeest.
Now a chance of extra tea – but thwarted
By shrieks of 'Apples' – no buckshee!

Such different views of self-same matters,
At lamp-swinging sessions of constant chatters.
The Reunion's a must, for better or worse,
Providing me Zimmer's not stuck in reverse!"

(These two poems were submitted by 'Mitch' Mitchell, in tribute to his old comrades of intake 43A,
first appearing in issue 23 of the OBAN in late 2001.)

For Valour

The Victoria Cross has only been awarded to 1,350 soldiers in 152 years. It is without doubt the most famous medal in the world and also the hardest to be awarded. In its long history, each medal has an awe-inspiring story behind it that makes you realise that you don't have to be the perfect soldier to earn it, you just have to have a dedication to duty, coupled with a complete disregard for your own safety.

As medals go, the VC ribbon does not contain several colours and is white plain to look at. Pre-WW1, the medal was crimson for the Army and blue for the Navy, but with the introduction of the Air Force, the ribbon was standardised to crimson for all members of the Armed Forces. The cross has the inscription of the name of the recipient and the date and place of action. All crosses are made out of melted-down guns, captured from the Russians at the Battle of Sebastopol during the Crimean War.

The British Army of this time had no medal for valour that could be awarded across all ranks, unlike the French, who we were fighting alongside at the time, who had the Legion d'Honore. Our 'Military Cross' could only be awarded to officers. Queen Victoria accepted the new medal, but changed the wording on it from 'Bravery' to 'Valour', so that other people

awarded medals were not seemed less brave.

The first VC to be awarded was to Charles Lucas, a twenty-year old mate on *'HMS Hecia'* in 1854 and the most recent was to Sgt Mackay on Mount Longdon on the Falklands. Amazingly, three men have won the medal twice. When this has been done, they are awarded a 'bar' to go along the ribbon, and not another medal. As the VC is very rare, the price some go in auction for is more than £150,000 and this price may go up according to the action in which it was won, as well as to the recipient.

So now, all you have to do is something very brave in action, and have it witnessed by somebody who will then tell his or her officer, who will pass on the information to the VC Committee. After discussion, and possibly further witness interviews, if they approve they will make their recommendations to the Monarch, who will make the final decision.

The VC has a long history that is marked by courage and greatness, from the lowest ranks to the highest, and still has the respect from every member of the Armed Forces. Whether it is from a quick calculated risk or foolhardy attack or defence, or maybe posthumously awarded, every winner has done something of outstanding bravery and should be looked at or remembered with respect.

The Victoria Cross is the highest and most prestigious award for gallantry in the face of the enemy that can be awarded to British and Commonwealth Forces.

(This article was published in The Arborfield Informer issued in January 2003.)

—§—

Epilogue

Just as I was about to put the finishing touches to this book, my brother-in-law passed me an article from the Reading Chronicle, which brought up the question of 'where does history start – and where does it end?' Members of the Arborfield Local History Society have recently been delving into 'the archives', looking back at how their predecessors lived. With Arborfield best known for its Army presence over many years, some finds of ancient coins in back gardens have now led to the belief that the Garrison was not the first military camp on the site, but that the Romans had beaten REME to it!

In retrospect, it is difficult to imagine just how quickly the last three years have flown by. Although there appears to be a mountain of textual and photographic evidence on display in the history you have just read, I am pretty sure that there are many stories yet untold – and definitely many photographs that should have been were never taken as the opportunity arose over the years. Ken Anderson and myself went through all the photos that we possibly could, held in the archives of the REME Museum, the constant question we asked each other was, *"Why isn't there one of him – or them – or that?"* But we have tried to include the best that was on offer – both from the photographic point of view and also from the undimmed memories of those who served. No doubt there are errors in the story and for these I apologise, but I have had to rely on the memories of many others and we all know how these differ from person to person.

There is no doubt that the early years have been covered in more detail than the later ones – but that is how nostalgia operates. Who knows, maybe in years to come, many more of those apprentices who served in the Seventies, Eighties and Nineties will come forward with their own stories and another budding 'author' will pick up the challenge of writing an updated version. I am certainly proud to have had the opportunity of putting this history together, it has provided me with many hours – yes, of hard work at times – but mainly of unbridled enjoyment, of tales from yesteryear. I do hope, dear reader, that you have had as much pleasure in reading this tome as I have in writing it. Perhaps I can sign off with yet another poetic look back into the past, recently provided by Tony Church of intake 55A – it says it all!

The glorious past

Just a bare, sparse patch of ground,
A car park? Yes - but what's that sound?
The skirl of pipes, a bugle's call,
The tramp of feet, shouts mingle,
All around the ghosts are here,
Most young, fresh-faced, eyes eager, clear.
And others, older, stern of face,
All uniformed and with a grace
Of movement, a daily learned routine,
With heads held high, a polished sheen,
Reflecting out the morning sun,
The glorious past parades again.

A ghostly roll-call echoes on,
Names well-remembered, one by one.
McNally, Cook, Brady, Cole,
Sallis, Silvers, Huxley and all
Of those recalled from yesteryear,
Who earned respect (and sometimes fear!).

The memories, undimmed by time
Of tears and comradeship sublime,
Return again when we recall
How things once were, when we stood tall.
Prepared to face the future, proud,
To take on the world with heads unbowed.

So just a patch of ground? Maybe.
But it masks a long proud history
Of values gained, the will to strive,
Directions taken, the zest to live.
So if upon that ground you go,
And hear that ghostly bugle blow,
Remember all that once was there,
And, in remembrance, say a prayer.

Tony Church, 55A

Commandants at Arborfield

The first Commandant and Chief Instructor was Col F A Hilborn, MBE (late RAOC) who apart from a break of twelve months (November 1939 – November 1940), during which time Col P G Davies, CMG, CBE was in post, held the chair from the opening May 1st 1939, the opening day, until September 1943.

Commandants

1	May 1939/Nov 1939	Col F A Hilborn	late RAOC
2	Nov 1939/Nov 1940	Col P G Davies	
1	Nov 1940/Sep 1943	Col F A Hilborn	
3	1943/47	Col J D White	late RAOC
4	1947/49	Col Grenville-Grey	late KRRC
5	1949/52	Col E L Percival	late HLI
6	1952/55	Col F A H Magee	late East Surreys
7	1955/58	Col J R Cole	late The Loyals
8	1958/62	Col R F D Legh	late Royal Artillery
9	1962/65	Col J L Dobie	REME
10	1965/68	Col G W Paris	REME
11	1968/70	Col D A Brown	REME
12	1970/73	Col E G Bailey	REME
13	1973/76	Col H K Tweed	REME
14	1976/79	Col B G Keast	REME
15	1979/83	Col J D C Peacock	REME
16	1983/85	Col S J Roberts	REME
17	1985/88	Col A A Soar	REME
18	1988/91	Col P H Kay	REME
19	1991/94	Col P H Gibson	REME
20	1994/95	Col M C Dorward	REME
21	1995/96	Lt Col R Mount	REME

Commanding Officers

22	1996/98	Lt Col N Moore	REME
23	1998/00	Lt Col J W Mitchell	RE
24	2000/03	Lt Col D A McAvoy	REME
25	2003 -	Lt Col A Philips	RE

Regimental Sergeant Majors

Army Technical School (Boys)

1	1939-Apr 41	WO1 RSM H E Cook	Grenadier Guards
2	May 41-Feb 47	WO1 RSM R L McNally	Scots Guards

Army Apprentices School

2	Feb 47-Sep 56	WO1 RSM R L McNally	Scots Guards
3	Sep 56-Jun 60	WO1 RCM J T Sallis	Royal Horse Guards
4	Jun 60-Jan 63	WO1 RSM J Stewart	Irish Guards
5	Jan 63-Apr 66	WO1 RSM H Simpson	Coldstream Guards
6	Apr 66-Oct 66	WO1 RSM D McMahon	Grenadier Guards

Army Apprentices College

6	Oct 66-Apr 69	WO1 RSM D M McMahon	Grenadier Guards
7	Apr 69-Jan 71	WO1 RSM R G Woodfield	Grenadier Guards
8	Jan 71-Sep 72	WO1 RSM D Delgarno	Scots Guards
9	Sep 72-Jul 74	WO1 RSM C Petherick	Coldstream Guards
10	Jul 74-May 78	WO1 RSM H V Meredith	Irish Guards
11	May 78-Oct 79	WO1 RSM L Perkins	Grenadier Guards
12	Oct 79-Jan 80	WO1 RSM D Cummings	Grenadier Guards
13	Jan 80-May 81	WO1 RSM D P Yorke	Coldstream Guards

Princess Marina College

13	May 81-Dec 81	WO1 RSM D P Yorke	Coldstream Guards
14	Dec 81-Aug 83	WO1 RSM A Fox	Coldstream Guards
15	Aug 83-May 86	WO1 RSM J H Todd	Coldstream Guards
16	May 86-Jul 88	WO1 RSM A Milloy	Scots Guards
17	Aug 88-Jun 90	WO1 RSM N F Hartley	Coldstream Guards
18	Jul 90-Apr 92	WO1 RSM M Burns	Irish Guards
19	Apr 92-Dec 93	WO1 RSM D Murray	Scots Guards
20	Dec 93-Sep 95	WO1 RSM J F Rowell	Grenadier Guards
21	Sep 95-Aug 97	WO1 RSM R L P Matthews	REME
22	Aug 97-Oct 99	WO1 RSM P B Rooney	Welsh Guards
23	Oct 99-Sep 00	WO1 RSM W T Emmerson	Coldstream Guards

Army Technical Foundation College

23	Sep 00-Nov 01	WO1 RSM W T Emmerson	Coldstream Guards
24	Jan 02-	WO1 RSM D G Mullens	Coldstream Guards

Index